What people are saying about
Astrological Mavericks: Do You Have What It Takes to Change the World?

"Michael Bartlett is a gifted astrologer who ponders the patterns of highly successful people and determines that planets on the angles are of supreme importance. He looks at these "maverick" planets and entertains the reader with lively descriptions of how it all works. This book is clearly and sensitively written for all students of astrology, whether beginner or more advanced."
—Leslie McGuirk, (2016, November) *The Importance of Being Wrong,* TEDxHollywood, *www.LeslieMcGuirk.com*

"This thorough and well-researched tome is a welcome, and overdue, addition to the astrological literature. An in-depth exploration of how the planets function at their strongest and most innovative, along the chart angles, *Astrological Mavericks* provides us with real-life examples of individuals who have expressed these archetypal energies in exemplary and unique ways. A useful and illuminating resource for those interested in exploring the energetic touch points of the angles, and the planets' various relationships with them."
—Aurora Tower, www.vibrational-astrology.com

"A wide-ranging encyclopedic exploration of planets on the angles. This book offers a fun and interesting opportunity to look at famous people who have the same placements that we do and how those archetypal energies express themselves through their lives and work. Bartlett's good heart and intentions shine through in this project."
–Renn Butler, author of *The Archetypal Universe*
and co-author of *Oh, Goddess: Love, Eros, and*
Transcendence in Astrology

"This book is a gift not only to astrology, but also to the broader fields of consciousness studies and psychology. As a psychiatrist who is steeped in Sri Aurobindo's work on the evolution of consciousness, I especially appreciate Michael Bartlett's study of how the "energy" of planets can influence human personality and behavior. Too many people have been led astray by the emotional dependency of trying to use astrology for predictive purposes, or the mental escape of astrology's abstruse theory. With this book, Michael Bartlett shows how we are really supposed to use astrology: to understand some of the occult forces that affect human psychology, and to use this knowledge to transform ourselves and the world. Using case studies from real life, including celebrities and cultural luminaries both past and present, he vividly illustrates how the consciousness of planets can affect us in very real and tangible ways. His work is organized, methodical, and succinct—all the marks of someone who really knows his stuff."
–Michael Miovic, MD, author of articles and books on
Sri Aurobindo's Integral Yoga Psychology

"Michael is a maverick! Leaning on an extensive body of research, Michael discovered convincing patterns that emerged from the lives of public figures with prominent aspects on the angular houses. *Astrological Mavericks* presents this innovative method that counseling astrologers can easily use in their practice which will empower their clients to express the best of this energy. Michael provides compelling stories of courage by amplifying their public mavericks' voices and how they're walking billboards of the planets that rule them. Readers will see themselves in this comprehensive research and now feel less alone. Thank you, Michael, for your exceptional empathetic contribution to the field!"

–Colin Ryan Bedell, astrologer for Cosmopolitan.com,
www.queercosmos.com

Astrological Mavericks

Do you have what it takes to change the world?

Michael Bartlett

ASTROLOGICAL MAVERICKS: DO YOU HAVE WHAT IT TAKES TO CHANGE THE WORLD?
SECOND EDITION

Copyright © 2021 by Michael Bartlett

All rights reserved.

ISBN
978-0-578-9696-7-1 (paperback edition)
979-8-9854599-1-3 (hardcover edition)

Written by Michael Bartlett
Edited by Heather Fessenden

This book may not be reproduced in whole or in part, in any form or by any means, electronic or mechanical, including photocopying, recording, or by any information storage and retrieval system now known or hereafter invented, without written permission from the publisher or author. Reviewers may quote brief passages.

Disclaimer: The quotations and references in this book are meant to illuminate the astrological archetypes given. While most of the sources are cited, there are some that are not known, but all should be easily found using a search engine.

Publisher and authors are not liable for any typographical errors, content mistakes, inaccuracies, or omissions related to the information in this book.

Published by Astro-Core Publishing

Cover photography courtesy of Shane Lampman

This book is dedicated to the astrological mavericks

Acknowledgements and Gratitude

To the numerous astrological teachers who have appeared to me at just the right time, whether living or dead, in the form of a book, recording, class, webinar, or in person, I thank you.

To the countless friends, family, colleagues, and clients who have let me read your chart and listen to your stories, I thank you.

To the individuals reading this book and seeking deeper understanding and ways to improve not only themselves, but others, I thank you.

To the seekers of astrological understanding, from novice to teacher, I thank you for sharing this journey of ever-increasing awareness. May our passion for this expansive artful science fan the flames of more integrated wholeness on the planet.

To the mavericks cited throughout this book, I thank you for your archetypal expression and the possibilities you model for us all.

A special thank you to proofreader extraordinaire Heather Fassenden. You appeared at the right time with the perfect mixture of brilliance, wit, humor, insight, astrological awareness AND availability. Angels do appear when we need them, thank you!

In particular, I want to give a huge hug of appreciation and eternal thanks to my dear friend and very special cheerleader, Glenna Bain. She blessed me with her keen and discriminating ear, eloquent editorial review, resonant body sensations, thoughtful suggestions, welcomed humor, and gracious presence for a few days in May 2019 to complete this book. She is an example of a maverick with Saturn on her Capricorn AS. She provided me with structured, grounded support to help me bring this book to print. My heart is filled with gratitude for you, Glenna. Thank you.

To my parents, who supported my inquisitive mind and the pursuit of fantastic goals, thank you for your loving support.

Thank you to Shane Lampman for the use of his photograph of the Orion Nebula for the cover art. Unfortunately, Shane passed away in 2020.

Table of Contents

Preface xxix

Origins of the book xxxi

Introduction 1

Sun 13
    Sun in Aries on the AS 14
    Sun in Taurus on the AS 17
    Sun in Gemini on the AS 17
    Sun in Cancer on the AS 20
    Sun in Leo on the AS 21
    Sun in Virgo on the AS 22
    Sun in Libra on the AS 23
    Sun in Scorpio on the AS 23
    Sun in Sagittarius on the AS 24
    Sun in Capricorn on the AS 24
    Sun in Aquarius on the AS 25
    Sun in Pisces on the AS 25
    Sun in Aries on the IC 27
    Sun in Taurus on the IC 28
    Sun in Gemini on the IC 29
    Sun in Cancer on the IC 29
    Sun in Leo on the IC 30
    Sun in Virgo on the IC 31
    Sun in Libra on the IC 32

Sun in Scorpio on the IC 32
Sun in Sagittarius on the IC 33
Sun in Capricorn on the IC 34
Sun in Aquarius on the IC 35
Sun in Pisces on the IC 38
Sun in Aries on the DS 39
Sun in Taurus on the DS 40
Sun in Gemini on the DS 42
Sun in Cancer on the DS 42
Sun in Leo on the DS 43
Sun in Virgo on the DS 44
Sun in Libra on the DS 45
Sun in Scorpio on the DS 46
Sun in Sagittarius on the DS 48
Sun in Capricorn on the DS 49
Sun in Aquarius on the DS 50
Sun in Pisces on the DS 53
Sun in Aries on the MC 54
Sun in Taurus on the MC 55
Sun in Gemini on the MC 57
Sun in Cancer on the MC 59
Sun in Leo on the MC 60
Sun in Virgo on the MC 61
Sun in Libra on the MC 62
Sun in Scorpio on the MC 64
Sun in Sagittarius on the MC 65
Sun in Capricorn on the MC 66
Sun in Aquarius on the MC 67
Sun in Pisces on the MC 68

The Moon 71
Moon in Aries on the AS 74
Moon in Taurus on the AS 74
Moon in Gemini on the AS 75

TABLE OF CONTENTS

Moon in Cancer on the AS 76
Moon in Leo on the AS 77
Moon in Virgo on the AS 78
Moon in Libra on the AS 79
Moon in Scorpio on the AS 80
Moon in Sagittarius on the AS 82
Moon in Capricorn on the AS 83
Moon in Aquarius on the AS 84
Moon in Pisces on the AS 85
Moon in Aries on the IC 86
Moon in Taurus on the IC 87
Moon in Gemini on the IC 89
Moon in Cancer on the IC 90
Moon in Leo on the IC 91
Moon in Virgo on the IC 92
Moon in Libra on the IC 93
Moon in Scorpio on the IC 94
Moon in Sagittarius on the IC 96
Moon in Capricorn on the IC 97
Moon in Aquarius on the IC 98
Moon in Pisces on the IC 100
Moon in Aries on the DS 102
Moon in Taurus on the DS 103
Moon in Gemini on the DS 105
Moon in Cancer on the DS 106
Moon in Leo on the DS 107
Moon in Virgo on the DS 108
Moon in Libra on the DS 110
Moon in Scorpio on the DS 110
Moon in Sagittarius on the DS 112
Moon in Capricorn on the DS 113
Moon in Aquarius on the DS... 114
Moon in Pisces on the DS 117
Moon in Aries on the MC 117

Moon in Taurus on the MC 118
Moon in Gemini on the MC 120
Moon in Cancer on the MC 120
Moon in Leo on the MC 121
Moon in Virgo on the MC 121
Moon in Libra on the MC 122
Moon in Scorpio on the MC 124
Moon in Sagittarius on the MC 124
Moon in Capricorn on the MC 126
Moon in Aquarius on the MC 127
Moon in Pisces on the MC 128

Mercury 129
Mercury in Aries on the AS 130
Mercury in Taurus on the AS 131
Mercury in Gemini on the AS 133
Mercury in Cancer on the AS 135
Mercury in Leo on the AS 137
Mercury in Virgo on the AS 139
Mercury in Libra on the AS 140
Mercury in Scorpio on the AS 141
Mercury in Sagittarius on the AS 143
Mercury in Capricorn on the AS 145
Mercury in Aquarius on the AS 147
Mercury in Pisces on the AS 150
Mercury in Aries on the IC 151
Mercury in Taurus on the IC 152
Mercury in Gemini on the IC 154
Mercury in Cancer on the IC 154
Mercury in Leo on the IC 156
Mercury in Virgo on the IC 157
Mercury in Libra on the IC 157
Mercury in Scorpio on the IC 159
Mercury in Sagittarius on the IC 161

TABLE OF CONTENTS

Mercury in Capricorn on the IC 162
Mercury in Aquarius on the IC 163
Mercury in Pisces on the IC 164
Mercury in Aries on the DS 165
Mercury in Taurus on the DS 167
Mercury in Gemini on the DS 168
Mercury in Cancer on the DS 169
Mercury in Leo on the DS 171
Mercury in Virgo on the DS 172
Mercury in Libra on the DS 173
Mercury in Scorpio on the DS 173
Mercury in Sagittarius on the DS 174
Mercury in Capricorn on the DS 175
Mercury in Aquarius on the DS 176
Mercury in Pisces on the DS 177
Mercury in Aries on the MC 179
Mercury in Taurus on the MC 179
Mercury in Gemini on the MC 181
Mercury in Cancer on the MC 183
Mercury in Leo on the MC 185
Mercury in Virgo on the MC 187
Mercury in Libra on the MC 187
Mercury in Scorpio on the MC 188
Mercury in Sagittarius on the MC 189
Mercury in Capricorn on the MC 190
Mercury in Aquarius on the MC 193
Mercury in Pisces on the MC 195

Venus 197
Venus in Aries on the AS 198
Venus in Taurus on the AS 199
Venus in Gemini on the AS 201
Venus in Cancer on the AS 202
Venus in Leo on the AS 203

xv

Venus in Virgo on the AS 204
Venus in Libra on the AS 206
Venus in Scorpio on the AS 207
Venus in Sagittarius on the AS 209
Venus in Capricorn on the AS 211
Venus in Aquarius on the AS 213
Venus in Pisces on the AS 216
Venus in Aries on the IC 217
Venus in Taurus on the IC 219
Venus in Gemini on the IC 220
Venus in Cancer on the IC 222
Venus in Leo on the IC 223
Venus in Virgo on the IC 224
Venus in Libra on the IC 225
Venus in Scorpio on the IC 227
Venus in Sagittarius on the IC 230
Venus in Capricorn on the IC 231
Venus in Aquarius on the IC 233
Venus in Pisces on the IC 234
Venus in Aries on the DS 236
Venus in Taurus on the DS 241
Venus in Gemini on the DS 242
Venus in Cancer on the DS 243
Venus in Leo on the DS 245
Venus in Virgo on the DS 245
Venus in Libra on the DS 246
Venus in Scorpio on the DS 249
Venus in Sagittarius on the DS 252
Venus in Capricorn on the DS 253
Venus in Aquarius on the DS 253
Venus in Pisces on the DS 255
Venus in Aries on the MC 257
Venus in Taurus on the MC 259
Venus in Gemini on the MC 261

TABLE OF CONTENTS

    Venus in Cancer on the MC 264
    Venus in Leo on the MC 264
    Venus in Virgo on the MC 267
    Venus in Libra on the MC 268
    Venus in Scorpio on the MC 271
    Venus in Sagittarius on the MC 273
    Venus in Capricorn on the MC 274
    Venus in Aquarius on the MC 274
    Venus in Pisces on the MC 276

Mars 279
    Mars in Aries on the AS 282
    Mars in Taurus on the AS 283
    Mars in Gemini on the AS 285
    Mars in Cancer on the AS 288
    Mars in Leo on the AS 289
    Mars in Virgo on the AS 290
    Mars in Libra on the AS 294
    Mars in Scorpio on the AS 295
    Mars in Sagittarius on the AS 296
    Mars in Capricorn on the AS 297
    Mars in Aquarius on the AS 298
    Mars in Pisces on the AS 299
    Mars in Aries on the IC 300
    Mars in Taurus on the IC 302
    Mars in Gemini on the IC 304
    Mars in Cancer on the IC 305
    Mars in Leo on the IC 306
    Mars in Virgo on the IC 310
    Mars in Libra on the IC 312
    Mars in Scorpio on the IC 314
    Mars in Sagittarius on the IC 315
    Mars in Capricorn on the IC 318
    Mars in Aquarius on the IC 320

Mars in Pisces on the IC 323
Mars in Aries on the DS 324
Mars in Taurus on the DS 329
Mars in Gemini on the DS 330
Mars in Cancer on the DS 331
Mars in Leo on the DS 334
Mars in Virgo on the DS 336
Mars in Libra on the DS 337
Mars in Scorpio on the DS 339
Mars in Sagittarius on the DS 340
Mars in Capricorn on the DS 341
Mars in Aquarius on the DS 343
Mars in Pisces on the DS 347
Mars in Aries on the MC 348
Mars in Taurus on the MC 348
Mars in Gemini on the MC 350
Mars in Cancer on the MC 351
Mars in Leo on the MC 354
Mars in Virgo on the MC 356
Mars in Libra on the MC 357
Mars in Scorpio on the MC 359
Mars in Sagittarius on the MC 361
Mars in Capricorn on the MC 362
Mars in Aquarius on the MC 363
Mars in Pisces on the MC 364

Jupiter 367
Jupiter in Aries on the AS 368
Jupiter in Taurus on the AS 370
Jupiter in Gemini on the AS 371
Jupiter in Cancer on the AS 374
Jupiter in Leo on the AS 374
Jupiter in Virgo on the AS 377
Jupiter in Libra on the AS 380

TABLE OF CONTENTS

Jupiter in Scorpio on the AS 383
Jupiter in Sagittarius on the AS 384
Jupiter in Capricorn on the AS 387
Jupiter in Aquarius on the AS 389
Jupiter in Pisces on the AS 389
Jupiter in Aries on the IC 390
Jupiter in Taurus on the IC 392
Jupiter in Gemini on the IC 394
Jupiter in Cancer on the IC 395
Jupiter in Leo on the IC 398
Jupiter in Virgo on the IC 399
Jupiter in Libra on the IC 402
Jupiter in Scorpio on the IC 404
Jupiter in Sagittarius on the IC 408
Jupiter in Capricorn on the IC 409
Jupiter in Aquarius on the IC 411
Jupiter in Pisces on the IC 412
Jupiter in Aries on the DS 414
Jupiter in Taurus on the DS 416
Jupiter in Gemini on the DS 417
Jupiter in Cancer on the DS 419
Jupiter in Leo on the DS 422
Jupiter in Virgo on the DS 424
Jupiter in Libra on the DS 425
Jupiter in Scorpio on the DS 426
Jupiter in Sagittarius on the DS 429
Jupiter in Capricorn on the DS 431
Jupiter in Aquarius on the DS 433
Jupiter in Pisces on the DS 436
Jupiter in Aries on the MC 438
Jupiter in Taurus on the MC 439
Jupiter in Gemini on the MC 440
Jupiter in Cancer on the MC 442
Jupiter in Leo on the MC 444

Jupiter in Virgo on the MC 448
Jupiter in Libra on the MC 449
Jupiter in Scorpio on the MC 451
Jupiter in Sagittarius on the MC 453
Jupiter in Capricorn on the MC 455
Jupiter in Aquarius on the MC 458
Jupiter in Pisces on the MC 460

Saturn 463
Saturn in Aries on the AS 466
Saturn in Taurus on the AS 469
Saturn in Gemini on the AS 471
Saturn in Cancer on the AS 472
Saturn in Leo on the AS 473
Saturn in Virgo on the AS 475
Saturn in Libra on the AS 477
Saturn in Scorpio on the AS 478
Saturn in Sagittarius on the AS 481
Saturn in Capricorn on the AS 482
Saturn in Aquarius on the AS 483
Saturn in Pisces on the AS 485
Saturn in Aries on the IC 487
Saturn in Taurus on the IC 488
Saturn in Gemini on the IC 491
Saturn in Cancer on the IC 492
Saturn in Leo on the IC 494
Saturn in Virgo on the IC 495
Saturn in Libra on the IC 496
Saturn in Scorpio on the IC 498
Saturn in Sagittarius on the IC 501
Saturn in Capricorn on the IC 503
Saturn in Aquarius on the IC 506
Saturn in Pisces on the IC 508
Saturn in Aries on the DS 511

TABLE OF CONTENTS

Saturn in Taurus on the DS 513
Saturn in Gemini on the DS 515
Saturn in Cancer on the DS 518
Saturn in Leo on the DS 520
Saturn in Virgo on the DS 522
Saturn in Libra on the DS 524
Saturn in Scorpio on the DS 524
Saturn in Sagittarius on the DS 526
Saturn in Capricorn on the DS 528
Saturn in Aquarius on the DS 531
Saturn in Pisces on the DS 534
Saturn in Aries on the MC 537
Saturn in Taurus on the MC 539
Saturn in Gemini on the MC 541
Saturn in Cancer on the MC 543
Saturn in Leo on the MC 546
Saturn in Virgo on the MC 548
Saturn in Libra on the MC 550
Saturn in Scorpio on the MC 551
Saturn in Sagittarius on the MC 553
Saturn in Capricorn on the MC 556
Saturn in Aquarius on the MC 559
Saturn in Pisces on the MC 563

Chiron 567
Chiron in Aries on the AS 569
Chiron in Taurus on the AS 571
Chiron in Gemini on the AS 572
Chiron in Cancer on the AS 574
Chiron in Leo on the AS 576
Chiron in Virgo on the AS 577
Chiron in Libra on the AS 579
Chiron in Scorpio on the AS 581
Chiron in Sagittarius on the AS 583

Chiron in Capricorn on the AS 585
Chiron in Aquarius on the AS 589
Chiron in Pisces on the AS 597
Chiron in Aries on the IC 599
Chiron in Taurus on the IC 601
Chiron in Gemini on the IC 603
Chiron in Cancer on the IC 605
Chiron in Leo on the IC 607
Chiron in Virgo on the IC 610
Chiron in Libra on the IC 610
Chiron in Scorpio on the IC 610
Chiron in Sagittarius on the IC 613
Chiron in Capricorn on the IC 615
Chiron in Aquarius on the IC 618
Chiron in Pisces on the IC 621
Chiron in Aries on the DS 624
Chiron in Taurus on the DS 628
Chiron in Gemini on the DS 633
Chiron in Cancer on the DS 635
Chiron in Leo on the DS 637
Chiron in Virgo on the DS 638
Chiron in Libra on the DS 639
Chiron in Scorpio on the DS 640
Chiron in Sagittarius on the DS 640
Chiron in Capricorn on the DS 642
Chiron in Aquarius on the DS 643
Chiron in Pisces on the DS 646
Chiron in Aries on the MC 651
Chiron in Taurus on the MC 655
Chiron in Gemini on the MC 658
Chiron in Cancer on the MC 661
Chiron in Leo on the MC 663
Chiron in Virgo on the MC 664
Chiron in Libra on the MC 665

Chiron in Scorpio on the MC 667
Chiron in Sagittarius on the MC 670
Chiron in Capricorn on the MC 673
Chiron in Aquarius on the MC 676
Chiron in Pisces on the MC 682

Uranus 687
Uranus in Aries on the AS 688
Uranus in Taurus on the AS 691
Uranus in Gemini on the AS 692
Uranus in Cancer on the AS 695
Uranus in Leo on the AS 696
Uranus in Virgo on the AS 698
Uranus in Libra on the AS 703
Uranus in Scorpio on the AS 703
Uranus in Sagittarius on the AS 705
Uranus in Capricorn on the AS 707
Uranus in Aquarius on the AS 710
Uranus in Pisces on the AS 711
Uranus in Aries on the IC 713
Uranus in Taurus on the IC 714
Uranus in Gemini on the IC... 717
Uranus in Cancer on the IC 720
Uranus in Leo on the IC 723
Uranus in Virgo on the IC 726
Uranus in Libra on the IC 727
Uranus in Scorpio on the IC 729
Uranus in Sagittarius on the IC 731
Uranus in Capricorn on the IC 732
Uranus in Aquarius on the IC 733
Uranus in Pisces on the IC 735
Uranus in Aries on the DS 737
Uranus in Taurus on the DS 739
Uranus in Gemini on the DS... 742

Uranus in Cancer on the DS 745
Uranus in Leo on the DS 747
Uranus in Virgo on the DS 749
Uranus in Libra on the DS 751
Uranus in Scorpio on the DS 752
Uranus in Sagittarius on the DS 753
Uranus in Capricorn on the DS 755
Uranus in Aquarius on the DS 757
Uranus in Pisces on the DS 761
Uranus in Aries on the MC 765
Uranus in Taurus on the MC 767
Uranus in Gemini on the MC 769
Uranus in Cancer on the MC 770
Uranus in Leo on the MC 773
Uranus in Virgo on the MC 776
Uranus in Libra on the MC 778
Uranus in Scorpio on the MC 780
Uranus in Sagittarius on the MC 782
Uranus in Capricorn on the MC 785
Uranus in Aquarius on the MC 788
Uranus in Pisces on the MC 790

Neptune 795
Neptune in Aries on the AS 797
Neptune in Taurus on the AS 797
Neptune in Gemini on the AS 797
Neptune in Cancer on the AS 798
Neptune in Leo on the AS 801
Neptune in Virgo on the AS 805
Neptune in Libra on the AS 807
Neptune in Scorpio on the AS 811
Neptune in Sagittarius on the AS 814
Neptune in Capricorn on the AS 815
Neptune in Aquarius on the AS 815

TABLE OF CONTENTS

Neptune in Pisces on the AS 816
Neptune in Aries on the IC 816
Neptune in Taurus on the IC 816
Neptune in Gemini on the IC 817
Neptune in Cancer on the IC 817
Neptune in Leo on the IC 819
Neptune in Virgo on the IC 822
Neptune in Libra on the IC 828
Neptune in Scorpio on the IC 833
Neptune in Sagittarius on the IC 838
Neptune in Capricorn on the IC 840
Neptune in Aquarius on the IC 841
Neptune in Pisces on the IC 842
Neptune in Aries on the DS 842
Neptune in Taurus on the DS 843
Neptune in Gemini on the DS 843
Neptune in Cancer on the DS 845
Neptune in Leo on the DS 848
Neptune in Virgo on the DS 850
Neptune in Libra on the DS 852
Neptune in Scorpio on the DS 854
Neptune in Sagittarius on the DS 857
Neptune in Capricorn on the DS 861
Neptune in Aquarius on the DS 868
Neptune in Pisces on the DS 868
Neptune in Aries on the MC 869
Neptune in Taurus on the MC 869
Neptune in Gemini on the MC 870
Neptune in Cancer on the MC 870
Neptune in Leo on the MC 874
Neptune in Virgo on the MC 877
Neptune in Libra on the MC 881
Neptune in Scorpio on the MC 886
Neptune in Sagittarius on the MC 890

Neptune in Capricorn on the MC 893
Neptune in Aquarius on the MC 896
Neptune in Pisces on the MC 896

Pluto 897
    Pluto in Aries on the AS 899
    Pluto in Taurus on the AS 899
    Pluto in Gemini on the AS 900
    Pluto in Cancer on the AS 902
    Pluto in Leo on the AS 909
    Pluto in Virgo on the AS 917
    Pluto in Libra on the AS 922
    Pluto in Scorpio on the AS 924
    Pluto in Sagittarius on the AS 925
    Pluto in Capricorn on the AS 927
    Pluto in Aquarius on the AS 927
    Pluto in Pisces on the AS 927
    Pluto in Aries on the IC 928
    Pluto in Taurus on the IC 928
    Pluto in Gemini on the IC 929
    Pluto in Cancer on the IC 931
    Pluto in Leo on the IC 941
    Pluto in Virgo on the IC 946
    Pluto in Libra on the IC 950
    Pluto in Scorpio on the IC 951
    Pluto in Sagittarius on the IC 952
    Pluto in Capricorn on the IC 953
    Pluto in Aquarius on the IC 954
    Pluto in Pisces on the IC 954
    Pluto in Aries on the DS 955
    Pluto in Taurus on the DS 955
    Pluto in Gemini on the DS 956
    Pluto in Cancer on the DS 958
    Pluto in Leo on the DS 962

TABLE OF CONTENTS

Pluto in Virgo on the DS 970
Pluto in Libra on the DS 973
Pluto in Scorpio on the DS 975
Pluto in Sagittarius on the DS 979
Pluto in Capricorn on the DS 980
Pluto in Aquarius on the DS 980
Pluto in Pisces on the DS 980
Pluto in Aries on the MC 981
Pluto in Taurus on the MC 981
Pluto in Gemini on the MC 982
Pluto in Cancer on the MC 985
Pluto in Leo on the MC 989
Pluto in Virgo on the MC 994
Pluto in Libra on the MC 997
Pluto in Scorpio on the MC 998
Pluto in Sagittarius on the MC 1000
Pluto in Capricorn on the MC 1000
Pluto in Aquarius on the MC 1000
Pluto in Pisces on the MC 1001

Preface

Astrology is an amazing tool for understanding others and ourselves. Drawing upon thousands of years of anecdotal evidence, astrology gives us a basic understanding of the ways in which archetypal expressions are likely to manifest when the planets arrange themselves in specific relationships with one another as well as express through their respective places in the zodiac. Richard Tarnas calls it the multivalent nature of planetary archetypes.

Lexicon.com defines archetypes as: *A very typical example of a certain person or thing. An original that has been imitated; a recurrent symbol or motif in literature, art, or mythology.* Good examples of archetypes are the stories of the Greek gods and goddesses and the ways in which each of the them acted in a very consistent manner. I reference the Greek gods and goddesses because they are the archetypal lens through which western astrology tends to view and understand the planets. Many of their names became the Roman names for the same deities: Mercury, Venus, Mars, Jupiter, and Saturn. When we include the Sun and Moon, we have the complete set of planets from the ancient world, which are all the planets one can see with the naked eye. This expanded edition covers these seven classical planets as well as Chiron, Uranus, Neptune, and Pluto.

The purpose of this book is multifold:

1. Provide the range of expression with each planet and sign, as well as how that can be further expressed on each of the four angles.
2. Give non-astrology-fluent individuals an opportunity to approach astrology in an easily understandable way.
3. Encourage people with angular planets to embrace this powerful placement and find healthier, more meaningful outlets for their maverick energy.
4. Show there is a correlation between astrological placement and archetypal range of expression.

Origins of the book

This book began as I became aware of the role my natal Mars in Virgo on my MC plays in my life. I was blind to my exaggerated Mars complex. Reading the work of French psychologist, Michel Gauquelin, and hearing stories about his life from astrologer, Erin Sullivan, helped me to understand more about this placement. I had a thoughtful conversation with a fellow astrologer who reflected back to me that my skin, the palms of my hands, and even my hair, all have a colored tinge—the red kiss of Mars. Then, as I began to listen to friends share their experiences of this forceful part of me, I began to see the patterns. I came to find most of my closest friends also have planets on their angles, which led me to another aspect of these astrological placements: people who have planets on an angle tend to gravitate to one another. When we think about the unconscious and literal expressions of these supercharged planets on a person's angles, we can understand how they could be challenging to others who don't have the same strength of expression. If you are reading this, you likely have a planet or two on an angle, or are simply trying to understand someone else who does.

I received my first astrology reading when I was a sophomore at the University of California–Santa Cruz. Then again some 15 years later when transiting Pluto was conjunct my Ascendant in 1999, the world of astrology began to resonate with me on a more significant level. Astrology is a system in which the cycles of life are clearly expressed. Through astrology, I saw how the patterns I experienced and witnessed in life made sense in a larger framework. Gaining my degree in psychology, I was hungry for a more holistic process that allowed for people going through a challenging cycle, rather than receiving a defining label of some sort of pathology. Astrology gives me the larger perspective as I hope it will you as well.

My highly accentuated Mars in Virgo on my MC is a driving force and greatly aided me in the writing of this book. Thus, my life continues to be "driven" by having a planet on one of my angles.

Introduction

Some of us are walking billboards for the planets. We wear their mark in a way that is simultaneously unseen yet seen by all. If you or someone you know has a planet conjunct one of the chart's angles, this is a big billboard, and the mark is not likely easily washed away. Planets conjunct the angles are super-powered archetypal energies expressed in a person's life. What makes this so? Let's start by looking at the angles to understand why they would give emphasis to any planet.

The angles represent the way we meet, relate, and/or interact with life, and they come in two pairs: AS/DS and IC/MC. The AS (ascendant) is how the world meets me and how I meet the world, and the DS (descendant) is how I meet the other and how the other meets me. The IC (Imum Coeli) is how I meet my inner family-self and how my inner family-self meets me, and finally the MC (Medium Coeli, or midheaven) is how I meet my path and how my path meets me.

The ascendant/descendant (AS/DS) axis corresponds to the horizon, with the ascendant on the eastern horizon and the descendant on the western horizon, while the other pair, the Imum Coeli/Medium Coeli (IC/MC) axis, corresponds to midnight and noon, but the direct translation is the *bottom of the sky* and *the middle of the sky*, respectively. The ascendant will often confirm predominant traits for the individual. I like the analogy of the ascendant being a glass house colored by the sign; the world sees the individual through the "color" of the sign, as well as the special color or imprint of the planet found therein. For example, consider the greenhouse is made of green glass, everyone looking at the person inside would see a green person and everyone outside of the greenhouse would appear green to the person within. This is how we look out through the sign on our ascendant and how we often appear to others.

These four angles often, but not always, remain in the same modality. The modality of a sign is a distinct quality of action, known as initiating or cardinal energy, stabilizing or fixed energy, and changing or mutable energy.

When these angles are in the same modality and are squaring one another, we call this a grand cross and each one gives an overall theme or energetic dynamic to the way the person connects to life: cardinal (Aries, Cancer, Libra, and Capricorn) shows a life that has an overall initiatory energy. Fixed (Taurus, Leo, Scorpio, and Aquarius) gives a life which can be set or fixed. Mutable (Gemini, Virgo, Sagittarius, and Pisces) can be known as someone who is flexible and often movement-oriented. Of course, one could have a grand cross that has a mix of elements and modalities, which is likely to result in a mixed way in which the person relates to life.

When we find planets conjunct an angle, we see a person who has a sense of knowing and belonging, of having the inside scoop on life. It isn't that these people are non-traditional or non-ordinary, they just exist and flourish outside of the structures that seem to keep everyone else in. Rather than being bound by the rules of tradition and the norms of society,

INTRODUCTION

these individuals make, and often break, the rules. The public often sees these people as mavericks. This is not only for what they model for others, but what they actually accomplish in their own lives—often leaving a legacy too incredible to ignore.

If we look at the traditional meaning of a maverick, we find, "the unbranded range animal, especially a calf that has become separated from its mother, traditionally considered the property of the first person who brands it." In the case of a planet conjunct an angle, the planet "brands" the individual, thereby giving them a freedom of expression using the formula of planet + angle in sign = a range of archetypal expression. This freedom is neither restricted by familial nor religious nor societal strictures and rules. The planet, as actor in the play of life, guides the ways in which the range is expressed. This means a person who has a planet on any of the angles is going to be a person who is under the tutelage, control, direction, and mentorship of the planet(s) involved.

Why does this occur? Anytime there is a conjunction, whether with a planet or a point in the chart, there is intensification and a blending of energies. A conjunction is actually a new birth, like when the Moon is dark. This is an indication of a new period, or cycle, of the way the two energies will relate to one another.

Orbs are the distance between a planet and an angle point. The tighter the orb, the closer the planet is to the angle, which results in a more dynamic expression. For the most part, we are looking for orbs of up to 10 degrees. When working with clients, I find it helpful to ask the person how/if they experience these energies. I also ask individuals with planets on the angles if they feel bound by rules or feel they can operate outside of them. I usually see a sheepish and somewhat guilty grin before they affirm such inner feelings.

While planets on any of the four angles are powerful, as we will see throughout this book, planets on the ascendant play an even more important role, as they are the midwives of the birthing process. Planets on the ascendant often leave a strong imprint upon the individual by actually playing out in the birthing process. Of the angles, the most liminal is the ascendant, as it literally straddles the moment of birth. Coming from the collective sense of self while still in the womb—the 12th house—this is the moment of the first breath and claiming selfhood—all first house concerns. This is a powerful moment; our first experience in physical form. This is further accentuated when a planet is conjunct or right next to the ascendant.

Planets on the ascendant, in particular, can often indicate the type of physical events likely to occur at the moment of birth. I have seen clients with Neptune on the ascendant and heard their stories of snowstorms, rainstorms, or floods happening when their mother was on the way to the hospital to give birth, as well as stories that have something to do with the amniotic fluid. When Saturn is present, there is often a signature of loss or separation, such as the newborn being placed in an incubator, the death of the father at the time of birth, being put up for adoption, or other separating experiences.

In esoteric astrology, Alan Leo writes, "The influences of the angles is similar to that of the cardinal signs (Aries, Cancer, Libra and Capricorn); they are concerned with making manifest and concrete, with bringing out into the open, unveiling and manifesting whatever may be latent in the personality, and everything that is denoted by the signs and the planets connected with the angles." This is a good way to understand the intensity of the maverick energies.

The consistent expression of the initiatory, instinctual cardinal approach to life will be shown throughout all of our mavericks. In order to determine if you have a maverick planet, you will need your astrological chart. If you don't already have a copy, there are many websites from which you can obtain it. I recommend www.Astro.com because they have wonderful free charts and a reasonably priced subscription rate that gives you access to a lot of astrological goodies.

We will now show individuals with maverick planets on each of the four angles. These are simple illustrations of what the placements look like in a chart, as well as how it may show up in life. For more information on these four individuals, please review their respective maverick planets in the book.

A good example of someone with a planet on the AS can be found in the chart of Caitlyn Jenner, with Sun conjunct her Scorpio ascendant. Scorpio is the sign of transformation, right? Caitlyn is a shining (Sun) example of the transformation from man to woman. This is the first of four visual examples of how to identify maverick planets in a chart, as well as how they will be explained throughout the book.

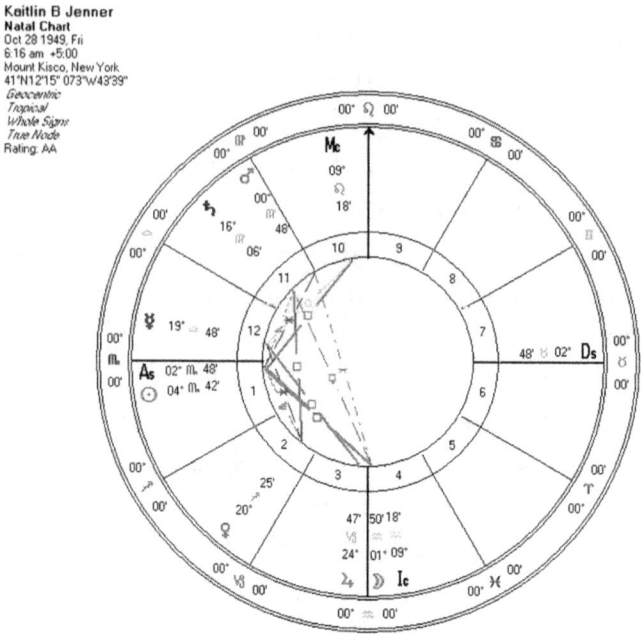

A good example of an individual with a planet conjunct the IC is found in the chart of freedom and truth-seeking Oprah Winfrey, who has her Sagittarius Moon conjunct her IC. Oprah has embodied the highest potential of her two maverick planets.

INTRODUCTION

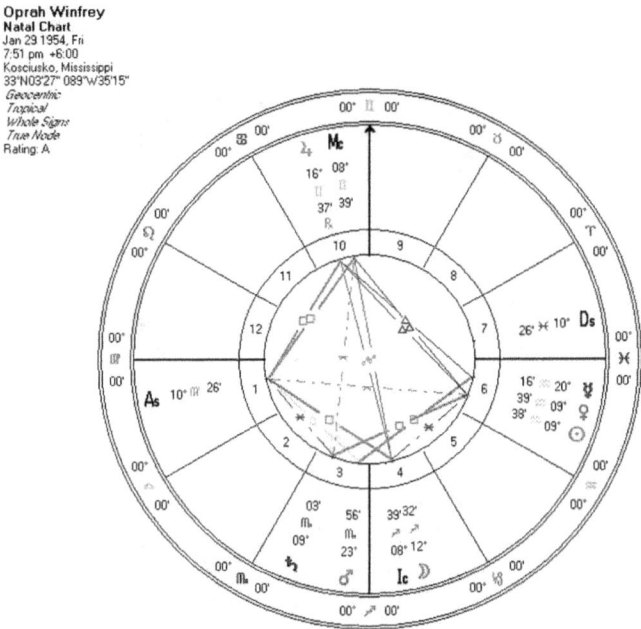

An actress who can play any part in a believable manner is a maverick. Jupiter, the planet of expansion and greatness, when found in Aquarius gives one an almost encyclopedic range of information. Meryl Streep is one of the most versatile and accomplished actresses of all time. Aquarius and Jupiter are freedom-seeking, which can be seen in the wide range of roles she has played without the restriction of being typecast, as can often be the case in the acting world. Since she has this placement on her descendant, we can see the myriad ways in which she relates to others through the many roles she embodies.

ASTROLOGICAL MAVERICKS

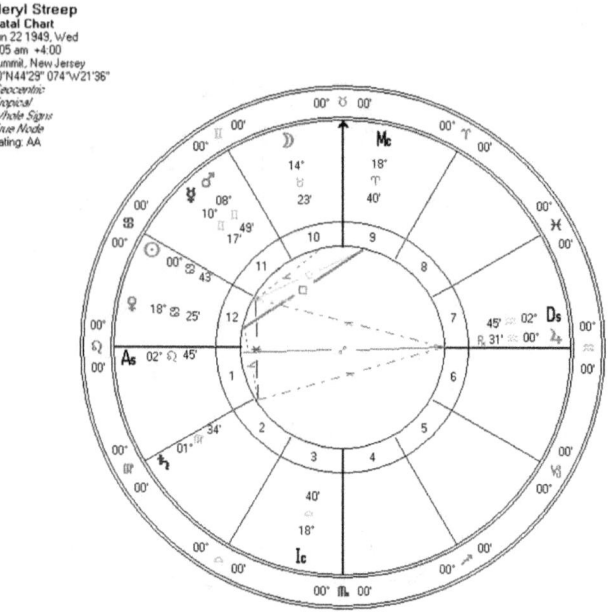

The final angle, the midheaven, is well represented by the ways in which this Prince has had much of his private life displayed for the world to see. Lady Diana's second son, Prince Henry (also known as Prince Harry) is a good example of how Saturn in Scorpio on the midheaven can manifest as personal secrets being used as fodder.

INTRODUCTION

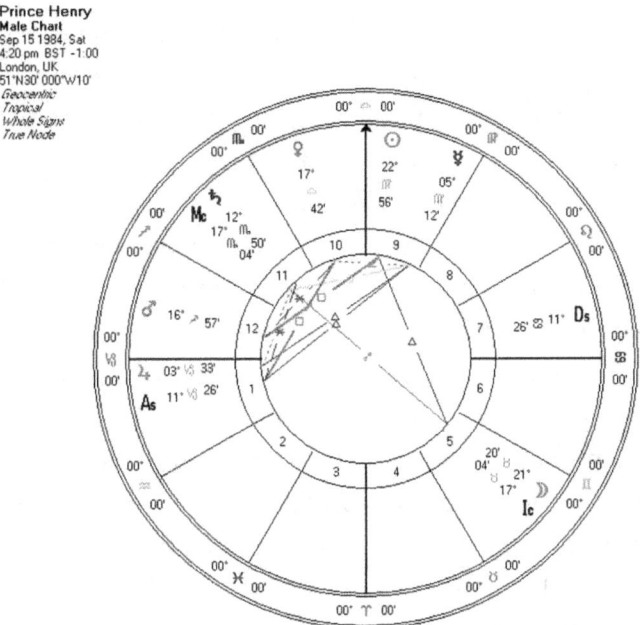

My goal here is to give a reference book that shows the spectrum of archetypal expression possible for these 4 angles across 10 planets and 1 asteroid through 12 zodiacal signs = 528 possible combinations.

This newly revised and expanded edition includes all of the planets and one asteroid: Moon, Sun, Mercury, Venus, Mars, Jupiter, Saturn, Chiron, Uranus, Neptune, and Pluto. The examples will show that an angle magnifies the strength of the planet involved, and that the archetypes expressed are varied both in their range of subtypes presented as well as in their range of conscious and unconscious expression.

For every example in this book, I did a specific search for planets conjunct an angle in the same sign using the Solar Fire™ database. I didn't include people who have a planet in one sign conjunct an angle in another, I did this in order to render the archetypal expressions as cleanly and simply as possible to illustrate the examples. Any planet that is within 10 degrees of an angle, especially applying to the angle and about five degrees after the angle, will result in a super-charged planet. The energies will adjust accordingly depending upon one's sensitivity and the aspects any maverick planet makes.

The anecdotal information of the individuals presented are meant to act as examples of the archetypes involved in the combinations as they are presented. None of the statements are meant to be libelous or malicious, and all information was obtained through the internet with references cited in most entries. In instances where information may not be true, I ask that you accept my apologies. Please realize the idea here is to give illustrations of the astrological archetypal expressions possible along a continuum and not to be an indictment against anyone referenced in this book. I am happy to make changes as needed to reflect the truth and support the theories presented herein, so please feel free to contact me.

If something is not cited with a reference, simply do an internet search of the individual with some of the key words contained herein and you should be able to find the reference.

There is no such thing as a bad birth chart. Each natal chart is an intricate and complex map representing the experiences and expressions an individual is likely to have in life. Each of us is here to find improved ways to be in relationship with our personal map while being in relationship to everyone else.

INTRODUCTION

Astrology provides people with a means to understand what they will likely encounter on the wide road of Life and how to best deal with them.

There are higher and lower expressions for many of the combinations listed in this book. An astrology chart can neither indicate the conscious intelligence of the individual nor the sophistication of expression. One also cannot tell from a chart whether someone has been consciously working with their astrological placements or not.

One of the purposes of this book is to show the archetypal range of expression or multivalent quality possible with planet, sign, and angle. The ways in which each individual will respond to and use the energies of these placements is as varied as the individuals themselves. Maverick energy does not guarantee perfect or even nice personalities, as we will see.

Important note: This book is about the chart's angles and is not concerned with, nor addresses, the issues of house or house systems. Rather than having 12 examples of planet and sign/house, this book will provide 48 ranges of expressions. Even if you do not have a planet on an angle, you can look up any planet you have in the same sign as any of your angles and see how mavericks have expressed those energies in their lives. This will also be true for planets that transit and progress your chart's angles.

This book uses the simple formula of Planet + Angle + Sign = anecdotal examples. While I personally use the whole sign house system, which is a house system that makes the ascendant a sensitive point within the first house sign rather than the cusp of the first house, what I have researched here is true regardless of the house system. With the whole sign system, the house and the sign are the same, as opposed to some house systems that may have more than one sign within a house. The chart's angles do not change for any house system. Please feel free to review the mavericks' charts using your favorite house system.

Sun

Consider that each of the planets is an actor, and their particular clothing and mannerisms change based upon the different zodiac sign they are in. For the combinations in this chapter, we will look at how the Sun is the *main* character. The Sun rules Leo. Traits of the Sun are our vitality, the man/masculine image in each of us (whether male or female), the animus in Jungian psychology, the father, ego, and how we shine out and are seen by others. The hero part in each of us.

Our Sun sign is that place in ourselves that takes time to mature, to come into its fullness. Each of the elements lends its own sense to the Sun, as well. Sometimes a Sun placed in a fire element can actually be experienced as burning others. The air signs can give too much information, whereas the water signs may have too much feeling or sensitivity. And when the

Sun is found in the earth signs we don't usually hear too much. Through the aspect of that part of themselves that reflects Solar (Sun) energy is the will to shine. When the Sun is found on the angles, we find an exaggerated presence of solar energy for the native. As with any planet on the angles, the same can be said of the Sun, but since it is the source of our solar system, the Sun is super-sized, even larger than life and therefore has maybe even more of a presence than the planetary mavericks.

We will now look at the angle placements of the Sun throughout the zodiac from the point of view of the Ascendant (AS).

Sun in Aries on the AS

This is aptly presented by our first example, Liz Renay. The following is from her obituary in the *Washington Post*:

> [Liz] was a gangster's moll, ex-con, author, painter, stripper, Hollywood Boulevard streaker, actress, and charm-school instructor. She was convicted of perjury in 1959 during the federal tax evasion trial of her boyfriend, racketeer Mickey Cohen. Given a three-year sentence, she was released after 27 months for good behavior. "It sure knocked the hell out of my career when I went to Terminal Island," she once said of the low-security facility in California. "I would have been a big star had I not gone to prison." Her sense of her

INTRODUCTION

own potential was undoubtedly exaggerated, as was everything else about this starlet who boasted of her measurements: 44DD-26-36. She once won a Marilyn Monroe look-alike contest sponsored by Twentieth Century Fox studios.

Not far off is our next example, Valerie Solanas, who had this written about her in *Time* magazine:

Andy Warhol might have made a career out of, "photographing depravity and calling it truth," according to Time's 1968 assessment, but even he had his limits—and Valerie Solanas' brand of depravity was too far out even for this, "blond guru of a nightmare world."

Solanas, a writer and women's rights activist, pushed feminism to radical new heights in 1967, when she founded the Society for Cutting Up Men (she was its only member) and self-published the SCUM Manifesto…"

Read up more on this maverick individual.
Interestingly enough, our next two examples are astrological twins as well as maverick twins: actor, Robert Walker and director, Paul Cox.
Modern Screen magazine ran the story, "The Mystery of Bob Walker"; below is an excerpt:

Consider the mystery of Robert Walker, one of the strangest men in Hollywood. He's a guy with a million romances, but they say he's still in love with his ex-wife. He's a man who wants to act, but he's turned down parts any other actor would have hocked his soul for. (A lead in *State of the Union*, for instance.) He's disappeared for long stretches at a time, and neither family, friends nor studio could track him down, or lure him back.

On the other side of the lens from the actor is the director, which is where we find Paul Cox. From rogerebert.com comes this illuminating description of this astrological placement:

> [Paul] once remarked in an interview, "To also realize we're going to die one day, to ask questions about death is very important because that makes you more alive and it makes you more of a decent human being." Throughout his career, he constantly asked questions about death, life and love. As a cursory glimpse of his filmography can attest, his willingness to ask these questions made him both an excellent filmmaker and, as anyone lucky enough to have met him can attest, a more-than-decent human being.

Musician, Claudia Gonson, shares another facet of the Aries archetype from saveur.com:

INTRODUCTION

"My favorite tool is my 'chopper' (my chef's knife). I didn't have a real one for a long time, then my mom gave me one—it was actually hers and she was scared of using it—and now the difference in speed in which I get through my cooking is immeasurable. I love to chop up tons of vegetables and fennel for my 'crunchy salad' that I always leave in my fridge in order to have a go-to dish to snack on."

Sun in Taurus on the AS

The Sun in Taurus has a rather grounded and set way about it. Taurus is an earth sign and is a fixed modality. One does not lead these bulls to water for them to drink, they lead themselves and in their own time. Taurus has to do with form and the form things take on in the physical plane.

Being a fashion designer, Donatella Versace, uses the fashion and luxury-conscious energy of her Taurus Sun conjunct her ascendant.

Filmmaker, George Lucas, uses his Sun in Taurus on the AS to bring light to distant planets, solar systems, and beings. Lucas recognizes a force that permeates the universe.

Sun in Gemini on the AS

These individuals appear to others as consummate communicators of a wide and vast dictionary of information.

Interesting to see that Dr. Aloysius "Alois" Alzheimer had this astrological placement, and he is credited with identifying the progressive disease that destroys memory and other important mental functions, which are all ruled by Gemini.

From brainyquote.com comes this eloquent understanding of others from another hummingbird Gemini vantage point, expressed by actress, Ally Sheedy:

> "I think everybody has the ability to fall in love with a man or with a woman or a white person or a black person or a Jewish person or a Protestant person or whatever."

In actor Gene Wilder's obituary in *The Guardian* we see an expression of this astrological placement:

> On gaining a degree in communication and theatre arts from the University of Iowa, he was determined to make acting his profession and left for Britain, enrolling at the Bristol Old Vic Theatre School. However, he became dissatisfied with traditional British teaching methods and returned to New York, where he was accepted from thousands of applicants into the method acting guru Lee Strasberg's class at the Actors Studio.

Gemini is about movement, not only communication. Champion tennis professional, Stefanie Maria "Steffi" Graff, and her entry at wikipedia.com, showcases Graff's accomplishments in this regard:

INTRODUCTION

Graf is a German former professional tennis player. She was ranked world No. 1 and won 22 Grand Slam singles titles. Her 22 singles titles put her second on the list of major wins in the female competition since the introduction of the Open Era in 1968 and is third all-time behind Margaret Court and Serena Williams. In 1988, she became the only tennis player to achieve the Golden Slam by winning all four Grand Slam singles titles and the Olympic gold medal in the same calendar year. Furthermore, she is the only tennis player to have won each Grand Slam tournament at least four times.

Brilliant maverick jazz musician, Miles Davis, made some wise Geminian comments and here are a few from brainyquote.com:

"Sometimes you have to play a long time to be able to play like yourself."

"I'm always thinking about creating. My future starts when I wake up every morning. Every day I find something creative to do with my life."

"I have to change. It's like a curse."

American actor, Robert Englund, has this canny quote from azquotes.com, "I always get inspiration from whatever characters say about my character." The Sun is our vitality, and Gemini enjoys exploring the multifaceted nature of life. Robert's next quote articulates the dual nature of Gemini,

"I love the idea of comedy in horror. I think this should be allowed."

Sun in Cancer on the AS

These individuals are known for making people feel at home or helping to give others a sense of comfort.

Media mogul, Merv Griffin, was a talk show host and went on to produce many of the American game shows whose prizes rewarded people for their intelligence or lucky choices with items for their home, as well as vehicles and vacations.

American business magnate, Ross Perot, who also has his Cancer Moon conjunct his AS (as well as Saturn across the way in opposing Capricorn), addresses the responsibility aspect of the Cancer/Capricorn axis. The following comes from azquotes.com:

> "If we really want to know who is responsible for the mess we're in, all we have to do is look in the mirror. You and I own this country, and we are responsible for what happens to it."

Businesswoman, Leona Helmsley owned numerous hotels and developments that gave people homes and residences. She was also known as the queen of mean.

Model and actress, Liv Tyler, who also has Mercury here, shares this lovely Cancerian statement in an interview at elle.com:

INTRODUCTION

"As a model—not just on this campaign, but all campaigns—your job, more often than not, is to look like you're warm when you're actually freezing."

Cancer is the beginning of summer in the northern hemisphere and is all about the incoming warmth that we all experience in the summertime.

Swedish film director, Ingmar Bergman, shows an enduring aspect of Cancerian nurturing (taken from bergmangardar.se):

Ingmar Bergman lived and worked on the island of Fårö for over 40 years. Following his death, the director imagined his home continuing to be a meeting place for people who work with music, film, photography, theater, and literature. The Bergman Estate on Fårö invites artists as well as scholars, non-fiction writers, and journalists from all over the world to come and work at Ingmar Bergman's estate. His houses have been preserved in their original state down to the notes on Ingmar Bergman's bedside table. The environment aims to nurture contemplative and creative work—in the same way as it inspired Ingmar Bergman's own artistic pursuits throughout forty years.

Sun in Leo on the AS

The Sun is the ruler of Leo, so we have the added power of the Sun on an angle, and we have a planet that can perform at its best when it is in its domicile. When a planet rules a sign, we say it is in its rulership or in its domicile or home.

These people are literally larger than life. Think of what Andy Warhol gave to pop art. Or how Orville Wright and his brother played Icarus and flew up close to the Sun, but unlike Icarus, landed safely again.

For those of you who do not know of Sri Aurobindo's, I highly recommend doing some research. He is an excellent example of a person who had his mind in balance with his heart, and the personality balanced with the soul. He also spoke of involuted matter, similar to what esoteric author, Alice Bailey, discussed.

Other examples of Sun in Leo on the AS are Petrarch (he has Mercury here as well), who is known as the Father of Humanism and the Renaissance, and French composer, Claude Debussy, whose melodic pieces still fill our hearts.

Sun in Virgo on the AS

These people shine out in their resourceful, orderly style.

Our first example is Freddie Mercury, lead singer of Queen. Hello Sun in Virgo on the AS!

President of the United States, Lyndon B. Johnson helped to bring the country back together after the Kennedy assassination.

Comedic English actor, Peter Sellers, always played a fairly bungling detective who was actually keeping track of everything at the same time.

INTRODUCTION

Magician, David Copperfield, is the penultimate illusionist, very well put together and precisely exacting in a way only a Virgo can be.

Sun in Libra on the AS

Libra is the ambassador, and we can see a hyper-interactive communicating style and a sincere desire for folks to get along with each other in all of these people with this astrological placement.

Barbara Walters, Olivia Newton-John, Jean-Claude van Damme, and Matt Biondi are all beautiful people who have a way of communicating that puts people at ease.

Famous talk-show host, Barbara Walters, was particularly seen as a larger-than-life communicator.

Singer and actress, Olivia Newton-John, is known for her beautiful voice and looks.

Belgian actor and fight choreographer, Jean-Claude van Damme, was a pin-up heart-throb martial artist who sought balance in his expression.

Sun in Scorpio on the AS

Any planet in Scorpio is going to show a deeper, more intense side of life. So, when the Sun is in Scorpio conjunct the AS, we are going to find people who sometimes literally transform themselves, as in the case of Caitlyn Jenner.

English musician, Adam Ant, used to apply makeup to his face, intensely transforming his stage appearance.

Astrologer and author, Erin Sullivan, is good at peeling back the truths of what lies beneath, and using the astrological model as her trusted lens.

Sun in Sagittarius on the AS

This placement gives the native a very positive, upbeat, and optimistic view of life. Maverick Connie Francis is a perfect example of how these mavericks endure their own hardships in life, while others would hardly have a clue. Their buoyant nature gives them the ability to see challenges as adventures.

Having a direct connection with a higher philosophy of life, this placement gives them the faith to weather any storm, such as the actual philosophy and practice of martial arts for Bruce Lee.

Sun in Capricorn on the AS

Capricorn's domain includes rules, order, and social structure.

J. Edgar Hoover was known for making the Federal Bureau of Investigation (FBI) into an orderly and properly structured organization.

Emperor Akihito has been the ruler of Japan — the highest placement in the Japanese social structure — since 1989.

INTRODUCTION

Sun in Aquarius on the AS

These individuals are known for their humanitarian focus.

Canadian hockey player, Wayne Gretsky, created his own foundation to help underprivileged youth learn important life skills through sports.

English actress, Charlotte Rampling, who is a *triple* Aquarian maverick, is known for her cool detachment, which people feel in a very visceral way.

American President, Abraham Lincoln, is a shining example of a humanitarian, which is what Aquarians are all about.

Benny Hill was a British comedian whose work revealed the humor of the human condition.

Jimmy Hoffa was an American labor union leader and author, who served as the President of the International Brotherhood of Teamsters (IBT) union from 1958 until 1971 working for the rights of his brethren union workers.

Sun in Pisces on the AS

What happens when we have the Sun in Pisces on the AS? Within this placement exists the ability to plumb the depths, especially in the areas of innovation and going beyond existing boundaries into the previously unexplored vastness of the All-That-Is.

Gerardus Mercator was a cartographer famous for creating a world map based on a new projection that represented sailing courses of constant bearing as straight lines — an idea that simplified navigation. In addition to being the world's most famous geographer and first globe maker, he had interests in theology, philosophy, history, mathematics, and magnetism. He was also renowned for being an engraver, calligrapher, and manufacturer of science instruments.

Alexander Graham Bell, who is credited with inventing the telephone, was looking to be of service (Pisces/Virgo axis) to his mother and wife who were deaf. Here we have a beautiful example of this Piscean placement bringing communication from that which is unseen to the masses. This is even more exciting when we consider the ways in which our smart phones today keep us connected with everyone on the planet. Bell was also the second president of the National Geographic Society. This is an interesting similar archetypal expression as Mercator.

We now move to one of the most personal and private spaces in the chart. Usually representing a point within the fourth house (but of course this depends upon where we were born and the house system we use), the Imum Coeli (IC) shows family experiences and issues, and those things which may or may not be as active when we meet the adult who has lived and worked through these patterns. Also, when we find the Sun conjunct the IC, we know that the person was born at night, which is not the strongest position for the Sun. People born at night tend to feel uncomfortable with the spotlight on their face because they are more used to and driven by their lunar (Moon) placements. These natives tend to value relationships over career, emphasizing their lunar nature. What does the super-charged Sun look like when it is conjunct the IC? Let's take a look at how some people have dealt with such a bright light in the midnight part of their chart.

We will now look at the angle placements of the Sun throughout the zodiac from the point of view of the Imum Coeli (IC).

Sun in Aries on the IC

These people shine within themselves and follow the beat of their inner drum. They radiate a light from deep within that guides them from conviction to action.

One example of the guiding force of conviction to action is seen in English primatologist, Jane Goodall's defense of the chimpanzees.

The restless Aries nature is well documented for Belgian novelist, Georges Simenon. Here's what we learn about him from *The New York Times*:

> Georges Simenon (1903-89) had, at the very least, two identities. One was the Belgian altar boy who quickly made the transition from failed pastry chef to legendary cub reporter for the *Gazette de Liège* when he was only 16 and went on to write nearly 200 pulp novels between 1924 and 1931 (he referred to them as his "novels for secretaries"). Then, when he decided to write "good" books, he took the advice of his mentor, Colette — "Get rid of all the literature, and you've got

it" — and spent the next five decades producing more than 200 serious novels, keeping meticulous accounts of his multitudinous foreign translations and film adaptations, and moving his family from the French countryside to Arizona, New England, Quebec and back to Europe again, even while finding time to enjoy three very French family meals each day, and to walk with his adored children in the local parks.

This astrological placement is the domain of the father, so it is no surprise that French sociologist, Emile Durkheim is considered one of the fathers of sociology.

Actress, Dame Katherine Patricia Routledge, is best known for her role of Hyacinth Bucket, a very headstrong legend in her own mind. We will see many times how an actor or actress accepts roles and portrays parts that either highlight or displays their maverick tendencies.

Sun in Taurus on the IC

Taurus can really show us our values and can also represent the motto, "life is a bitch and then you die."

Many of Tammy Wynette's hit songs dealt with classic themes of country music like loneliness, divorce, and the difficulties of life and relationships. All of these issues are existential to the Taurus/Scorpio axis, especially when the IC is involved; Tammy was raised by her grandparents, on the family farm without indoor running water.

Sun in Gemini on the IC

This is an interesting combination. Gemini seeks to communicate about the dualities of life, and here it is on the IC, the most personal space in the chart.

Michael J. Fox, the actor we knew as the multi-talented and aspiring teenager in *Family Ties*, is now the spokesperson for a very personal disorder, Parkinson's disease. One may wonder if the inner dialogue has become richer.

Dean Martin could act, sing, dance, emcee, play the straight man to Jerry Lewis (or tell his own jokes), improvise in front of a casino audience, or host a TV variety show. He could play a wide range of roles, from a credible cowboy to a super spy in a Hollywood movie. Dean was also happy acting like a drunk on stage or even performing one of his ethnic novelty songs that mixed Italian phrases and American slang. This is the multifaceted expression of one with a Sun in Gemini conjunct the IC and he had a wealth of inner characters from which he could draw.

Referring to himself in a conversation with John McEnroe, Björn Borg stated, "I'm two people. The one hitting the ball and the one watching the hitter." What an amazing Gemini statement!

Sun in Cancer on the IC

Here we find people who literally shine from home, or from that very private part of themselves.

Inventor and electrical engineer, Nikola Tesla, was one of the people responsible for creating the electrical system that runs through our homes and business.

On another interestingly Cancerian note, French novelist, Marcel Proust, was closely tied to his mother and did not move from his parents' apartment until after both were dead.

Sun in Leo on the IC

Because Leo is ruled by the Sun, this intriguing placement brings an additional layer of intensity.

Needing and wanting to be *seen* by family, as well as being highly creative and overly expressive, Jon Benet Ramsey was literally adored to death by her family. To this day her case has not been solved.

Jeff Stryker was a porn star and considered himself sexually universal, meaning he enjoyed sharing himself with men and with women. Filmmaker, John Waters, considered him to be the Cary Grant of pornography. Charming.

The 31st president of the United States, Herbert Hoover, believed strongly in the Efficiency Movement, which considered the government and economy to be burdened with inefficiency and waste, and could be improved by experts who were able to identify the problems and solve them. He also believed in the importance of volunteerism and of the role of individuals in society and the economy. Hoover was a wealthy man and donated all his federal paychecks to charity. Here is the radiant heart of a proud Leo giving back to society from the selfless self.

Who could ever forget the way Julie Newmar played Catwoman in the *Batman* television series? Meow! These are lovely and healthy examples of this placement, with selfless ego as the higher expression of Leo!

Sun in Virgo on the IC

Here, interestingly enough, all of the examples are male, with one who literally wore women's skins on his body.

Sir George Ivan "Van" Morrison, well known for his music from the 1960s onward, shows another amazing aspect of Virgo multiplicity. Van plays guitar, harmonica, keyboards, harp, bass, drums, saxophone, and is a prolific songwriter. He is best known for his ode to the "Brown Eyed Girl."

Edward Gein received notoriety when it was discovered that he had killed two women and exhumed several corpses (including his mother!) to fashion items made from their skin and bones. There is a list and description of the items available by doing an internet search.

Rejecting his upper middle-class background and embracing his gay identity, English author, Christopher Isherwood, used this astrological placement to reveal his personal life to the world. These individuals exhibit the resourcefulness of the Virgoan archetype.

Sun in Libra on the IC

Represented by a scale, Libra is the only sign in the zodiac symbolized by an insentient object. Issues of balance, right human relationship, and ambassadorship are all within Libra's domain.

Mystic and esotericist, Aleister Crowley, was the founder and prophet of Thelema, seeking to find a link between the pleasures of the flesh and the expanded state of Spirit. During his life, Aleister moved around a fair amount. Born in England, he went on to live in the U.S., Sicily, France, and Germany, acting as an ambassador of sorts in the various countries in which he lived and traveled.

Singer and songwriter, Cecil Womack, represents that beautiful gift of harmonizing Libra energy. In order to work with our family and spouses, we need to be able to compromise and have some very artful ambassadorial skills. This placement definitely aided him in his relationship with his family.

Sun in Scorpio on the IC

This is an interesting position for the Sun, as it is one of the most private places of the chart and one of the most private signs, not to mention one of the most powerful. While Scorpio is one of the most intimate signs of the chart, sensitivity is heightened when we find planets conjunct the IC here.

Prime Minister of India, Indira Gandhi stated in her last speech the day before her assassination, "I am alive today, I may not be here tomorrow... I shall continue to serve until my last breath, and when I die, I can say that every drop of my blood will invigorate India and strengthen it," adding, "Even if I died in the service of the nation, I would be proud of it. Every drop of my blood… will contribute to the growth of this nation and to make it strong and dynamic." She literally sacrificed her life to and for India, her home.

Scorpio, thanks to its modern ruler Pluto, is all about mining that which lies within. This can be a fertile field from which to draw artistic inspiration as so well presented by Pablo Picasso, who, incidentally, used his three-year old daughter's excrement as a pigment for paint.

Sun in Sagittarius on the IC

Here we are speaking of truth, justice, and kingly energy.

Erik Menéndez, along with his brother Lyle, sought to unseat the king and queen of their home (their parents) by murdering them, and when Erik confessed the truth (Sagittarius) with his psychologist, it sent them both to jail for their crimes.

Austrian poet, Rainer Marie Rilke, travelled extensively throughout Europe, including Russia, Spain, Germany, France, and Italy, and in his later years he settled in Switzerland. Rilke's writings are considered mystical and have been condensed into sound bites, which will help to ensure the continued availability of his timeless wisdom.

Sun in Capricorn on the IC

An inner drive for success at home or the unearthing of geological wonders are possible expressions of the Sun in Capricorn on the IC.

German-American geologist, Carl Ludwig Rominger, with a rather extensive fossil collection from the northern German glacial drift. Carl's European collection can be found in the Museum of Paleontology at The University of Michigan.

Jazz musician and bandleader, Cab Calloway, is well known for his scat style of singing that he learned from the influential jazz trumpeter, Louis Armstrong. Initially, Cab was going to follow in his father's footsteps by becoming an attorney, but followed his own inner awareness and became a well-known musician and singer instead.

Bobbie Nelson, Willie Nelson's sister, is an example of the long-run success that can start at an early age, indicating strong Capricorn energy. Her grandfather (hello, Capricorn!) bought her a piano at age six after she played for over 1,000 people.

American actress, Sissy Spacek, like Bobbie Nelson, first stepped on stage at the age of six. Being talented and "old for their age" are both Capricorn themes.

Capricorn is a sign of career and success, and here we see actor, Denzel Washington, share the story of his professional trajectory with *The Guardian:*

"I had one six-month period in 1982 when I couldn't get a job. I had done a movie called *Carbon Copy*, and then I did a play, and then I had these six months where nothing happened; where I started looking at the Department of Recreation and thinking, 'Acting's not for me.' And then I caught a play about Malcolm X, off-off-Broadway in New York, and I haven't been unemployed ever since."

Katie Couric took the lessons of her father and became an even more recognized newscaster and media personality. She clearly drew on her solar Capricorn paternal lineage in doing the work needed to attain her goals.

Sun in Aquarius on the IC

This is a complex placement. Aquarius loves the ability to be above and survey things in such a way as to gain understanding of larger systems. Here, at the bottom of the chart, one is likely to be very inwardly focused. The desire for right human relationship coupled with an immense ability to observe make them keen writers and critics, but also can elevate their egos to places above reproach.

Here we will start with a less-than-likely candidate, Eva Braun, who was the wife of Hitler for a mere 40 hours. Unfortunately, I was not able to see how Eva expressed her Aquarian nature, except that she was kept by Hitler, in the sense that he kept her secluded and protected from most of the issues that went on in the war. I would say her home was in her own ivory tower. Her relationship was kept private and was not known by the German people until after the war. Aquarians are often private about their personal natures.

Queen Anne of Great Britain (who makes our list three times) had a reign that saw an increase in the influence of ministers and a decrease in the influence of the monarchy. Aquarius appreciates counsel. Consider by the time a planet has made its way around the zodiac to the 11th sign of Aquarius, there's an understanding of the need to incorporate the individual and the collective in a way that benefits both to the highest possible level for everyone involved. Great Britain—the union of England and Scotland—occurred during the reign of Queen Anne. Great Britain saw artistic, literary, economic, and political advancement made possible by the stability and prosperity of her reign. As a woman, she ruled differently than the kings who came before and after her.

English writer and social critic, Charles Dickens, is thought to be one of the best writers of the 19th century. His academic education ended at 15. Aquarians have their own inner ageless wisdom and don't often need the certificates and awards required of academia. Aquarians observe and understand the social fabric and the interplay between characters and people.

Confederate general during the American Civil War, Stonewall Jackson, said, "My religious belief teaches me to feel as safe in battle as in bed. God has fixed the time for my death. I do not concern myself about that, but to be always ready, no matter when it may overtake me... That is the way all men should live, and then all would be equally brave." More Aquarian ideals for sure. The desire for a deeper understanding about humanity is an important Aquarian trait.

With the Sun and IC in Aquarius, there is no surprise that French industrialist, Andre Citroen, was a Freemason. Free masons are based in the idea of self-improvement, self-responsibility and service for the greater good. Masonry is based upon the old mystery school, which is another beautiful archetype for this placement.

Maria von Trapp, who wrote the story of her family's life that became the film *The Sound of Music*, shows the alienation/outcast aspect of Aquarius. Here we learn more about Maria from biography.com:

> "She was born on a train headed to Vienna, Austria, and was orphaned at a young age."

The IC is our most intimate point, and when it rests in the sign of cool and detached — intellectually centered Aquarius — the individual is not left with a warm and fuzzy feeling.

English drummer and songwriter, Phil Collins, once proclaimed, "Perception determines insanity," and truly, his comments address the Saturn maturity factor within Aquarius. Collins continues, "As I've got older, I've got more understanding of relationships and how they work — but every single relationship has different dynamics, so you can't paint everyone with the same colour." Aquarius is a dual sign, and here we see Collins' express a deeper understanding of that duality when he says, "The binding of reason and intuition is the fundamental crisis of the era we call humanity. Transcendence of duality is the key." Collins has blended the two rulers of the humanity focused sign of Aquarius: *Saturn*

—reason—and *Uranus*—intuitive flashes. He also has a deep loathing for critics.

Sun in Pisces on the IC

This is an interesting placement, because the deeply connecting waters of Pisces are being filtered through a night-birth Sun, one of the more private points in the chart. We often find deep connecting waves or roots here.

Media mogul, Rupert Murdoch, whose father owned a couple of newspapers, struck out on his own and created a multinational, almost world-wide, media empire that gave him the ability to broadcast his own intentions to the collective through the many waves of his empire.

Canadian performer, Justin Bieber, who has three planets in Pisces, has a very alluring relationship with the media and displays many Piscean traits, such as glamour, alcoholism, and drugs. He is a singer who is also able to enrapt others with his Piscean charms.

James Madison, the fourth U.S. President, composed the early drafts of the U.S. Constitution and the Bill of Rights, which earned him the nickname "Father of the Constitution." The fourth house and its opposite, the 10th house, are often associated with parents, mother or the father. In this instance, with the Sun in his fourth, Madison actually shined out, in his life and after his death, as a very significant father figure. The Pisces/Virgo axis is also about care and service.

Pat Nixon, whose parents were of ill health, had to work to be the mother in her family before holding that position as

First Lady of the United States, as U.S. president, Richard Nixon's wife.

We now move into the descendant territory (DS), which is the way in which we interact with and perceive others, whether friend or foe. The descendant is also that place in the chart where we project our idea of others out into the world.

We will now look at the angle placements of the Sun throughout the zodiac from the point of view of the Descendant (DS.)

Sun in Aries on the DS

When we look at Aries, we are thinking of those who plant the seeds of creativity.

Paloma in Spanish means *dove*, and Pablo Picasso showed his love for his daughter, Paloma, by placing doves in many of his pieces of artwork. Paloma is known for her creative jewelry designs as well as perfumes. How does she exhibit her hyperactive Aries Sun on the DS? Her trademark: the color red—especially as lipstick.

Born in 1583, Dutch theologian, Hugo Grotius, appears to lean across the aisle to Libra. He is one of the first to define, expressly, the idea of one society that is governed not by force or warfare, but by laws and mutual agreement. He encouraged understanding to enforce those laws. This is true leadership from an Aries viewpoint, is it not?

Academic and social critic, Camille Paglia, had a pivotal event summarize her Sun in Aries on the DS experience. The outhouse exploded after she poured too much lime into the latrine. About the event and its significance, she writes, "It symbolized everything I would do with my life and work. Excess and extravagance and explosiveness. I would be someone who would look into the latrine of culture, into pornography and crime and psychopathology—and I would drop the bomb into it." How Aries is that? Of course it sounds like some Scorpio, too!

Sun in Taurus on the DS

What happens with this placement? Ruled by beauty-seeking Venus, Taurus likes beautiful objects, material possessions, and for things to go their way. I like to think of traditional statements about bulls and their nature: "you cannot force a bull to do something they don't want to do," and, "they dig in their hooves," which can sometimes be mistaken for stubbornness, but the truth is Taurus needs to make choices that work for her or himself.

Author and travel writer, Bruce Chatwin, sought a lot of freedom within his relationship. He was charming and physically striking, and he rose from his position as gallery technician to head of the Impressionist department at Sotheby's auction house.

Sigmund Freud used his Taurus energy to build the groundwork for a whole new level of understanding of the "other" (DS) through his understanding of the emotional and psychological nature of human beings. Freud broke ground in this area of understanding. Something bulls do.

Actress, Joanna Lumley, well known for many of her characters, and especially as Patsy in *Absolutely Fabulous*, uses the other side of Taurus. She is widely known for her charity and philanthropic work, especially in helping the Gurkha Justice Campaign, which wants the Gurkhas who fought for the UK to gain the same rights as their British and Commonwealth counterparts.

Writer and lecturer, Jacob Holdt, is known for his monumental work *American Pictures*, which gained international fame in 1977 for its photographic revelations about the hardships of America's lower classes. He utilized his own understanding of living on the streets of Denmark, homelessness is not the usual experience for the socialist-based Dane to be sure, but we are talking a strong Taurus here. He was kicked out of school and the Royal Palace Guard—probably for wanting to do things his own way and not following orders from others. Orders and dictates can be a challenge for a Taurus.

Mark David Chapman, who shot John Lennon five times in the back, provides a cautionary tale of how the descendant can be where we project those unowned parts of ourselves onto others. Projection means we see the flaw in the other rather than the mistake in ourselves. Our desire to eradicate that part of ourselves can result in violent acts against others as evidenced by this example.

Sun in Gemini on the DS

These are individuals who have a lovely command of language and grace with speech. How does that work in relationship with others?

English stage and screen actor, Ian McKellen, exhibits maverick acting abilities in portraying a wide range of characters, including a wizard!

Peter William Sutcliffe was an English serial killer who was dubbed the "Yorkshire Ripper" by the press. In 1981, Sutcliffe was convicted of murdering thirteen women and attempting to murder seven others. As Gemini is the sign of duality and the DS is the area we can project onto others, we may wonder what sort of compassion was lacking in Peter's childhood to lead him to perpetrate such acts against women. Some sort of imbalance in his understanding of masculine and feminine was surely being played out.

Sun in Cancer on the DS

As Cancer is about the mother and nurturing, as well as protecting, this is a beautiful expression of a Cancer Sun on the DS.

A poignant quote I found on wikipedia.com illuminates the protective and nurturing drive of this astrological placement:

> At age seven, Prince William of England reportedly told his mother that he wanted to be a police officer when

he was older so that he might be able to protect her; a statement to which his brother Harry responded, "Oh, no you can't. You've got to be King." Unfortunately, no police officer could have saved his mother, Lady Diana Spencer, from the tragedy that would take her life.

French filmmaker, Catherine Breillat said, "I am eternally, devastatingly romantic, and I thought people would see it because 'romantic' doesn't mean 'sugary.' It's dark and tormented — the furor of passion, the despair of an idealism that you can't attain." While this sounds very Scorpionic, the Cancerian relationship bonding need is clearly stated. A nurturing super-powered Cancerian Sun on the DS is one who would be highly aware of relationship with others.

Sun in Leo on the DS

Here we have the ruler of the Sun in its favorite space and in the area of relationship. Fixed Leo likes its own way.

Barack Obama was used as a symbol of hope for the American people. The Sun is often seen as a symbol for the father, and the President of the United States has definitely been a father-figure role. Obama's presidency gives hope for young African Americans. Leo longs to be seen and recognized. On the personality level, it seeks attention for the ego, but as Leo becomes more conscious, the radiating sunlight of their loving heart shines forth to warm everyone around them.

According to who2.com, actor, Martin Sheen, is known as a prolific performer. Leo loves the stage and Martin is a prime example. He is known for both his acting career and for his activism. He has been arrested more than 60 times for protesting nuclear weapons and the treatment of the homeless in the United States. Yes, he's a Leo with a heart! As an interesting aside, I knew a person who met Mr. Sheen, and he does an interesting thing when he is photographed: if he is shorter than the person next to him, he puts his arm across their shoulders and raises himself up so as to appear the same size or taller. This is a Leo who does not want to be upstaged!

And speaking of the stage, no stage beats that of the royal theatre! George IV of England led an extravagant lifestyle that contributed to the fashions of the Regency period, gaining him the name "The First Gentleman of England." Unfortunately, his relationships with others (DS) were not the best.

Beatrice, Princess of York, was the first member of the Royal Family to appear in a non-documentary film when she had a small, non-speaking role as an extra in *The Young Victoria* (2009), based on the accession and early reign of her ancestor, Queen Victoria. Again, very Sun in Leo: a royal taking the stage!

Sun in Virgo on the DS

Virgo is a sign of exactitude and service. It seeks perfection and understands there better processes are possible.

I find it interesting that the two examples for this position are men who had significant military careers from military families: John McCain and Friedrich von Steuben. Strategizing would come naturally to these individuals.

Friedrich von Steuben is credited with being one of the fathers of the Continental Army and teaching the essentials of military drills, tactics, and discipline. Serving as the Inspector General, he who was in charge of investigating—requiring measuring and quantifying, both Virgo traits—to make sure the military had what they needed to perform their jobs. His father served in Austria, and the two helped with the War of Austrian Succession. Friedrich wrote the book *Regulations for the Order and Discipline of the Troops of the United States*, which remained the drill manual until the War of 1812.

John McCain, on the other hand, had a 22-year Navy career as a pilot and officer. He spent five years in a Vietnamese prisoner-of-war camp after he was shot down during the Vietnam War. McCain was elected to Congress in 1982, and then was elected a U.S. senator from Arizona in 1986. He ran for the United States Republican presidential nomination twice. And both McCain's father and grandfather were four-star admirals in the Navy. This dedication and service to country are maverick expressions.

Sun in Libra on the DS

In this heightened relationship position, we would expect to find individuals whose focus is on balance, harmony, and beauty, as Libra is ruled by Venus.

Lee Iacocca, who worked for Ford Motor Company for many years, took his accumulated business acumen to the failing Chrysler Corporation and turned it around. In addition to the Sun in this position, Lee also had Mercury in an even tighter conjunction with his Libra descendant. When Sun and Mercury are conjunct, the individual can literally be seen as a mouth piece, which can obviously be a problem. He used this combination to write numerous books and to do the work necessary to make something successful. Lee declared, "Decisiveness is the one word that makes a good manager." Decisiveness, it should be noted, is not an easy Libran trait as it is always working to balance seemingly opposed forces. Unfortunately, Lee passed during the editing of this book.

Songwriter and musician, John Lennon, was a Libra poster boy from the 1960s through his murder in 1980, and beyond. His life was most definitely heavily focused on Libran themes, not only with his long-time partner and wife, Yoko Ono, but also in his relationships with The Beatles and humanity as a whole. The highest goal for a Libra is right human relationship, and Lennon definitely made this his life's focus. Whether in his political views or his behavior, as well as in the content of the songs he wrote and sang, he was an advocate for peace. Imagine all the people… he touched.

Sun in Scorpio on the DS

Determination, perseverance, and the ability to endure are all Scorpio strengths. In this relationship placement, the intensity of this sign is displayed in the relationship arena. Scorpio is willing "to go there" meaning that it isn't afraid of making a scene or making others uncomfortable in its pursuit of obtaining what it wants.

Peter Jackson, the director of the Tolkien trilogy, was born on Halloween—*very* Scorpionic. He is good at coaxing a little extra from his actors, seeking depth of expression from others, and said this, "Film is such a powerful medium. It's like a weapon, and I think you have a duty to self-censor." Jackson used his Scorpio energy to capture the nuanced intensity of relationship with others. One of his first movies, *Bad Taste*, was actually about aliens coming to Earth to enjoy humans as the new tasty treat of the universe! How much more Scorpionic can he be?

Actress, Vivian Leigh, best known for playing Scarlet in *Gone with the Wind*, said, "My birth sign is Scorpio, and they eat themselves up and burn themselves out. I swing between happiness and misery. I am part prude and part nonconformist. I say what I think, and I don't pretend, and I am prepared to accept the consequences of my actions." Sun in Scorpio on the DS would give someone such an intensity of relating to others that a person in relationship to and with a Scorpio would have to say, "Enough!" Such as the famous line from Rhett Butler to Scarlet O'Hara, "Frankly, my dear, I don't give a damn." According to wikipedia.com, "The line demonstrates that Rhett has finally given up on Scarlett and their tumultuous relationship. After more than a decade of fruitlessly seeking her love — as covered over two and a half hours of film — he no longer cares what happens to her. The profanity in the line was unusual and shocking in American film at the time." Scorpio energy is a testing energy, one which is about proving loyalty and depth of commitment. A relationship with a Scorpio is not one to be soon forgotten, especially when we find a planet on a Scorpio angle!

Sun in Sagittarius on the DS

The quest for a meaningful life within the context of relationships, should we choose to accept it, would be the goal of an individual with this placement. For a Sagittarian, the world is their oyster. The sky is the limit. Sagittarians are known for having too many irons in the fire, so when on the DS, we may find someone with too many relationships or too many adventures to determine who the other is clearly.

Canadian poet, painter, and singer, Sarah Teitel, is a lovely example of this. Sagittarius is a mutable fire sign, which means it gathers inspiration from everywhere in the environment. One is not likely to have a boring, lie-around-the-house kind of day — or relationship — with this ever-energized being.

Australian actor, Dan Falzon, was well known for his role in the Aussie television series *Neighbors*. He went on to form a band called Milk with his brothers in 1997, and now works as a paramedic in Alice Springs, in the Northern Territory of Australia, and runs an eco-tourism business with his brothers. A Sun sign Sagittarius seeks exciting adventures, experiences and wants to see all the possibilities of life. This energy is amplified when found on the angle. Dan's work is a lovely expression of this placement, by bringing people into relationship with each other. The maverick energy will provide the additional fuel necessary to reach the many dreams that Sagittarius seeks.

Sun in Capricorn on the DS

The sign of Capricorn is about hard work and attaining success. Capricorn is the sign for the beginning of winter in the northern hemisphere and there is a determination to survive through it.

As Don Van Vliet's stage persona, Captain Beefheart, he was able to share his musical artistry with the public and later devoted himself to his artwork. While he did not receive huge material success from his music, he had a large cult following, so he focused on his sculpture and artwork because he felt it was a more realistic means of support. Capricorn is a very practical sign.

Australian actor, Mel Gibson has been a controversial figure and has made some great statements that highlight this astrological placement:

> "I will always continue to work. I've never much depended on anyone but myself, as far as that goes."

> "Life is life, and one has experiences that are painful and some that are very pleasant, and one has reward and sacrifice and more reward and disappointment and joy and happiness, and it's always going to be the same."

I ran across a lovely site called smartbitchestrashybooks.com (gotta love it!) to find out about our next Sun in Capricorn conjunct the DS example.

The well-known Victorian writer, Ouida, was born Maria Louise de la Ramée. According to biographer Elizabeth Lee, "she lived in great style, entertained largely, collected *objets d'art*, dressed expensively but not tastefully, drove good horses, and kept many dogs, to which she was deeply attached." The website goes onto state, "As much as Ramée loved entertaining the literary lights of the day and living the good life, she certainly wasn't idle. She published her first novel at the age of 24 and went on to write over forty books, including adult novels, children's books, and collections of short fiction and essays. Her novels were famously criticized for being racy, and the worse the reviews were, the better the sales. Her early works focused on adventure while her latter books were more along the lines of historical romance. Another author, Jack London, considered her to be an important influence on his work — specifically, in his list of eight factors that contributed to his success, he includes 'reading Ouida's Signa at eight years of age.'" Capricorn is not afraid of work and seeks opportunities to rise in social standing. Another admirable thing about Ouida is that she also was an advocate against the poor treatment of animals, women, and children.

Sun in Aquarius on the DS

This position gives a buoyant personality in regard to relating to others. These people can see the big picture while keeping an eye on the small details that make it all up. The Aquarian mind can work on the most structured details, thanks to its rulership by Saturn and the most outlandish thanks to the other ruler of Aquarius, Uranus.

Spanish couturier extraordinaire, Cristobal Balenciaga, had a reputation as a man of uncompromising standards. Christian Dior referred to him as, "the master of us all," and Coco Chanel said, "The only couturier in the truest sense of the word ... The others are simply fashion designers."

Iconic world music man, Peter Gabriel, exhibited his humanity-oriented Aquarian nature by co-founding an annual festival of world music called World of Music, Arts and Dance (WOMAD). He was also responsible for co-founding Witness, a grassroots program to expose violations of human rights around the world. His Aquarian side shows up in how he worked with electronic technology in forming the companies On Demand Distribution (OD2), a digital music distribution system in the United Kingdom, as well as the online music distribution service We7.

Mark Spitz, the handsome nine-time Olympian master swimmer, showed the interesting combination of this Saturn-ruled placement through his ability to be disciplined in his training to be as successful as he was, and the stubbornness. Regarding his moustache, which became iconic, he was told by a coach to shave it off. He not only used his Saturn determination to retain it, but Uranus helped with his strength of individuality.

Like Peter Gabriel, English singer-songwriter, Robbie Williams has his Jupiter here as well. Remember that self-centering Leo is across the way on the AS, so we understand these people need an audience. Aquarians usually have a healthy view of themselves. There will always be egoic issues, as stated by Robbie in this quote from brainyquote.com:

"I've been asked many times if I considered myself a narcissist, so I looked up the real meaning of the word, and I came to the conclusion that indeed I am one. I think of myself as better than other people, not every person, but many, unique and talented, and I aim to success."

American jazz musician, John Handy, who has his Mercury and Saturn here as well, describes the somewhat loner aspect that occurs with this placement—a sort of separateness from others. From an interview he gave with harlemofthewest.com, he reveals the following:

"And again, I never, to be honest, as long, since I've been here, I've been here for many years. As a matter of fact, 45 years. But I've always felt like I'm camping here. I never felt totally here, I never was part of the community as such, you know? I've always been a musician and kind of reclusive, because.... You know, kids my age at the time, well, I didn't go to high school, so I didn't know kids my age, young men I did unless they played, and I knew nobody my age. The closest person my age was somebody like Sock Benjamin who was a little older. Most of my friends were older and, you know, many of them were married, had families or bachelor musicians who had no time to hang out with each other than I had with them. And it was only during the summer, between June and August, after my first year actually attending classes every day but not doing really great. I didn't turn in my work, that was really the problem. But I'd always go to class, I didn't miss classes. So anyhow. I, I, as a result, I came here pretty much as a loner, not because I'm not gregarious, but just simply there were, San Francisco had these big houses and I'd see all the kids and young people, but I didn't, you know, I didn't see high school kids when I was in school. And they were, you know, going to school, I might seem some kids, but everybody I knew was at least college age and older. And I didn't know that many there, because, again, I was kind of a different kid. I was a professional musician going to college."

Sun in Pisces on the DS

Pisces often has issues with boundaries and being able to separate oneself from others. With a Pisces Sun on the DS, these individuals are going to continually deal with issues of merging in a relationship.

Patty Hearst, granddaughter of the powerful media magnate, William Randolph Hearst, was kidnapped by the United Federated Forces of the Symbionese Liberation Army, or SLA. They slowly converted her to their side.

Jack Kerouac, one of the literary revolutionaries of the 1950s, coined the phrase *Beat Generation*. Jack was known for his enigmatic prose, as well as his tumultuous relationships and his alcoholism. His enchanting presence was like a large flame to the moths of his generation.

We now move to the highest point in the chart, the midheaven. The Medium Coeli (MC) represents our relationship with our path in life.

We will now look at the angle placements of the Sun throughout the zodiac from the point of view of the Medium Coeli (MC).

Sun in Aries on the MC

These individuals are hard to miss. The Mars driven Aries energy is super charged with the brilliance of the Sun. These individuals are leaders in whatever they do, as long as they don't fall into petty battles.

Very interesting to note our first native is actually named for this position. This cannot be made up! MC Hammer's famous song "You Can't Touch This" is a perfect example of an Aries Sun. They are always moving and are hard to catch, let alone touch, especially when amplified by a conjunction with the midheaven. The MC is the stage upon which we meet our career and our work, which is also how the public sees us in our work.

Avant-garde jazz singer, Lauren Newton's music is typically highly abstract, blending conventional technique with non-conventional vocal sounds. She also performs modern art music and teaches singers. Aries initiates, as it is a cardinal fire element. There is a creativity in the destruction of that which has come before.

Charlotte Ford, who also has her Venus here, is of the Ford Motor Company empire and used her strong Aries will to create clothing lines, including prêt-à-porter (French for *ready-made*), which is Aries at its best!

Sun in Taurus on the MC

Wherever we are dealing with Taurus, we are dealing with form. This placement is brilliant for publicizing and broadcasting; each of our examples gives insightful and exciting glimpses of what one can accomplish.

Artist and AIDS activist, Keith Haring, presented concepts of birth, death, sexuality, and war—sounds like Scorpio, does it not? And this makes sense when we consider that Scorpio and Taurus are on the same axis. Keith's work helped us to reconsider the ways in which we form our ideas around these existential issues. Haring's work was often heavily political, and his imagery has become a widely recognized visual form of language of the 20th century. He gave us a new form of art.

American musician, Willie Nelson, who has his Venus here, and is not afraid to be seen as the spokesperson for issues around food, pleasure, and marijuana.

Television producer, Aaron Spelling, was known for having the largest home in Los Angeles. From an article on him and the house on wikipedia.com we learn that, "After its completion, *Los Angeles Times* architecture critic Sam Hall Kaplan panned the structure as one of the region's worst projects built in the 1980s." A review of Spelling's house from an article of Sam's in the *Los Angeles Times* expands on this criticism:

> [The] Aaron Spelling residence, which at 56,500 square feet (5,250 square meters)... What Spelling's folly is, of course, is a sad commentary on the distorted values that have taken the architectural form of monster mansions at a time when tens of thousands of persons are homeless.

Who can stop a charging bull? From *The Guardian* comes an article that begins by addressing the duality many experience with filmmaker, Michael Moore, who has Saturn opposing this position in Scorpio. We can understand why:

> "I'm not sure which Michael Moore I'm going to get when I call him in New York. Will I get the slightly cantankerous Michael Moore of the documentaries? The one who knocks on people's doors and doesn't take no for an answer? Polemical Michael Moore who savaged George W. Bush in his documentary *Fahrenheit 9/11*? Or the playful, amused Michael Moore of his latest film, *Where to Invade Next?*"

With his Sun in Taurus on the MC, who can forget the scene of actor, Jack Nicholson, putting his head through the door in *The Shining*? Talk about a bull!

Folk singer, Judy Collins, gave a statement that speaks to her astrological placement of the Sun in Taurus on the MC (from brainyquote.com):

> "Most of what we take as being important is not material, whether it's music or feelings or love. They're things we can't really see or touch. They're not material, but they're vitally important to us."

In this final quote, Judy Collins addresses the harmony-through-conflict aspect of Taurus:

> "I've gone through many, many things. I tell you something, that if it doesn't kill you, you get stronger."

Sun in Gemini on the MC

What a perfect placement for a singer, no? Here we have well-known singers, composers, and songwriters Paul McCartney, Peggy Lee, Igor Stravinsky, Josephine Baker, and Holly Near. These people had to be seen *and* heard!

Elena Ford, great granddaughter to the founder of Ford Motor Company, plays the Gemini role for her family business. From thedetroitbureau.com we learn the following of Elena:

> With a degree from New York University, Elena Ford started out as a truck advertising specialist with the Ford Division but has since worked through a variety of positions within the company. Her current position

is with Ford Motor Credit, where she heads global brand and marketing operations." Gemini is great for marketing and branding.

Tragically, Azaria Chamberlain was the child taken by a dingo, whose parents were prosecuted and imprisoned for her death. Fortunately, they were later released. It would have been interesting to have heard what she did later in life, but her disappearance definitely brought awareness of her young life to the public at large.

As Gemini is the sign of equality, seeking to be neither above nor below anyone else, one can understand this lovely sentiment from entertainer, Josephine Baker, taken from brainyquotes.com:

> "I have walked into the palaces of kings and queens and into the houses of presidents. And much more. But I could not walk into a hotel in America and get a cup of coffee, and that made me mad."

Musician, Paul McCartney, said the following in an interview for *Rolling Stone*, and this is a perfect answer for a two-sided sign, and especially as Paul has his Mercury here as well:

> "It's always held a fascination for me, getting up in front of people and performing," McCartney says in Philadelphia. "From the beginning, I was trying to figure it out: What's the best way to keep true to yourself yet have people on your side?"

Sun in Cancer on the MC

Cancer has to do with safety, security and family. These individuals share their homes or home lives with the public in intriguing ways.

How interesting that one of the previous examples as well as this one have to do with extremely public experiences of kidnapping? As both of these points include the MC, one can understand how Azaria, in the previous example in Australia, and Charles Lindbergh, Jr., in the United States, had their personal experiences made public. When little Charles was kidnapped on March 1, 1932, the reaction from people across the United States, especially those with fame and fortune, was immediate. People started placing security systems in their homes and worrying about their children being taken by an unknown person of the public. Unfortunately, just as in the previous example, the child was not returned to the family. In both cases these children became a cautionary tale for families.

17th century English scientist and inventor, Robert Hooke, introduced the name "cell" for a basic biological structure. Cancer rules clans and families, and the family unit is a cell within the larger family of humanity.

First Lady Nancy Reagan, wife to former U.S. President Ronald Reagan, shares her thoughts to a *House Beautiful* article written after her death. Her comments highlight the deeper values of home:

> Two decades after Jacqueline Kennedy's renovations, the Reagans moved into 1600 Pennsylvania Avenue and discovered a state of disrepair. The plumbing and

wiring were old-fashioned, the floors needed work, and the draperies were 'falling apart.' Thanks to the First Lady's careful attention to detail and decidedly good taste, the White House underwent a 1981 renovation that helped restore the residence to its former glory. While the public criticized the costly redecoration, she actually secured most of the $1 million budget from private donations instead of government funds. "This house belongs to all Americans," she once told *Architectural Digest*. "And I want it to be something of which they can be proud."

One cannot be more Cancer MC than that!

Arthur Ashe, an influential and champion tennis player of the 1960s and 1970s, who helped open the way for African American tennis players in a game of mostly white players, said, "I have always drawn strength from being close to home." Perfect Cancer Sun conjunct the MC statement.

Sun in Leo on the MC

Here again, we have the ruler of Leo conjunct the midheaven, which elevates the ego to be seen by all. When we think of Leo Sun on the MC, remember the myth of Icarus, the young man who sought to fly so high as to touch the Sun. These individuals can handle the heat of the Sun as well as stand up to the intense focus leveled upon them from others. In the pure ego state, they can be like Icarus with the vanity and hubris only a human can have, but when the Leonine heart is open and radiating, what a wondrous leader she or he can be.

American Southern Baptist pastor, Jerry Falwell used his Leo Sun on the MC to tout and promote a very conservative religious and social viewpoint that resulted in the formation of the "Moral Majority" (which really was neither moral nor the majority). Each time there was a natural disaster—especially 9/11—Reverend Falwell would say the event was the wrath of God due to certain sinners (namely gays and lesbians, pagans, abortionists, feminists, the American Civil Liberties Union, and People For the American Way). Unfortunately, Reverend Falwell's work would lay the foundation for the infamous U.S. Tea Party movement.

Another interesting and beautiful representation of this astrological position is American photographer, Herb Ritts. I have to chuckle a little at having Falwell and Ritts together. Ritts was a famous gay photographer known for his elevation of the male nude in homo-erotic tableau. He had the ability to use the camera to bring forth iconic images of those he photographed. Rather than projecting his own ego out into the world as Falwell did, Ritts used his Leonine Sun conjunct his midheaven to capture the essence of the individual and share it with the world.

Sun in Virgo on the MC

Virgo is the sign of multiplicity, the harvest (cornucopia), and perfecting. These individuals seek to always improve upon that which came before.

Composer, conductor, pianist, and songwriter, Leonard Bernstein, was one of the first American-born conductors to lead world-class orchestras. His musical abilities came to the fore early in his life, and all he did was perfect, perfect, perfect. Virgo, as one of the three earth signs, is about work, daily routines, and the act of perfecting.

American actress, Kristy McNichol, known for her acting career between the ages of eight and thirty, announced her sexuality to the world with the intention to help stem the tide of bullying of GLBT individuals. Virgo does have a protective nature.

Sun in Libra on the MC

Here again we have themes of beauty and love — Libra's domain. This is a beautiful placement for someone who wants to rule the airwaves as shown in our examples.

Singer-songwriter, Johnny Mathis, known for his beautiful voice and love song ballads, is a prime example of the Sun Libra MC.

The duality of Libra is well articulated in this excerpt from bbc.com about pioneering, psychedelic folk singer, Marc Bolan:

> John Peel was a huge supporter of Tyrannosaurus Rex in their early days, and calling Marc "a flower child with a knife up his sleeve" was an observation rather than an insult. He, like many others, noticed that Bolan was fiercely ambitious and going places. And it wasn't so much that he was a fake hippy, although he had

SUN

no truck with counter-culture politics, more that he couldn't be contained by any scene. His masterstroke was not so much to move things on from late-60s folk-rock, but to move back in time—to primal early rock 'n' roll. Tyrannosaurus Rex became T. Rex, Marc dabbed some glitter on his face, and there began an extraordinary run of impeccable glam rock singles, including "Ride a White Swan" (their breakthrough hit in 1970) and, all in 1971: "Hot Love", "Get It On", and "Jeepster."

Astrologer, Robert Currey, shows the lovely brilliance of air. From astrology.co.uk, we learn the following:

Robert Currey (b. 24 Sept 1955) is a British astrologer, writer, lecturer, software designer and programmer, and retailer. In 1981, Currey founded his astrological company, Equinox, in November 1981. Initially, he worked as a consultant astrologer, writer, and teacher. In the early days of personal computing in the 80s he taught himself to write astronomical and astrological software in order to streamline his written chart interpretations. He has continued to work to create a unique synthesized personal analysis described by a New York reviewer as "one of the world's most impressively detailed electronic astrological service."

If one was to think heavyweight boxer, Peter McNeeley, to be a bit of an uneducated sportsman, one would be mistaken.

From boxingnewsonline.net we learn a bit more about the man behind the boxing gloves:

> McNeeley, despite the roughneck, blue-collar image he determinedly presents, is actually a university graduate with a political science degree. He was well aware that this was perhaps the only chance he would ever get to earn himself financial security — heavyweight contenders usually out-earn university graduates — and he had poured himself enthusiastically into the selling of the fight.

Sun in Scorpio on the MC

These individuals are seen, known and appreciated for being deeply intense as well as magnetically attractive. People feel a magnetic pull to Scorpionic energies and often walk away with the realization they have shared more deeply than they usually do with these master confessors.

Our first maverick is one who displayed a Scorpionic aspect by actually killing himself. Scorpio rules the death, rebirth, and regeneration processes. In nature, a scorpion will actually kill itself rather than allow something else to kill it. This gives one an insight into the control and power dynamic of this powerful sign.

Television star, Jon-Erik Hexum, was a handsome actor of the early 1980s. While on the set of *Cover Up* (how Scorpionic!), during an outtake he became bored and played with a gun. Mimicking Russian roulette with an actual gun filled with blanks, he shot himself. The force of the blank was strong enough to push brain fragments into his skull. He lived for five days after the incident until he was declared brain-dead, and many of his organs were given to several individuals. I had goose bumps when I read the story, as I had known about it but didn't know the exact details. I cannot think of a more dynamic example of Sun conjunct the MC in Scorpio, and I didn't look into his life for more examples of this strong and intense solar placement, but I am sure they are there.

World renowned and controversial photographer, Helmut Newton, was known for capturing images of intensity and controversy: fetishism, sado-masochism, voyeurism, and other Scorpionic themes. He even used x-rays to reveal that which lies within.

French sculptor, Auguste Rodin brought a level of realism and intensity to the bronzes he created. Some even accused him of making his casts from actual people, rather than sculpting the pieces himself. He had two relationships. One long-term relationship with Rose Beuret, the mother of his son, who he married just days before she died and 11 months before his own death. He also had a 15-year relationship with French sculptor Camille Claudel. Scorpio also rules the commitment of marriage.

Sun in Sagittarius on the MC

These are individuals who will always be on a quest, whether for an ideal or for knowledge. Sagittarius is ruled by the benefic and wise Jupiter. With this placement, these individuals are seen and known by the collective for their Sagittarian crusades.

Willy Brandt, winner of the 1971 Nobel Peace Prize, was the Chancellor of West Germany from 1969 to 1974. He is referred to as the European bridge-builder and fought for the ideals of a more unified Europe, given the times in which he found himself.

French actor, Jean Marais, and his lover/partner, acclaimed director, Jean Cocteau, traveled throughout Europe in a time when same-sex couples were not accepted.

Novelist and literary editor, William Plomer, is quoted as saying, "It is the function of creative man to perceive and to connect the seemingly unconnected." In the process of sending out many arrows of questions, the inquisitive Sagittarian then gathers these seemingly disparately dispersed arrows and gathers them to form higher beliefs, structures, and ideas.

Sun in Capricorn on the MC

Capricorn is a status-seeking sign. Think of the Capricorn mountain goat seeking ever-higher social strata.

Lyle Menendez, along with his brother Kyle (discussed above), killed his parents. Soon after their parents' murders, Lyle purchased for himself a Rolex watch and a Porsche and was later heard to say that he wanted the wealth and prestige without having to wait for it. He had a very strict and domineering father. Saturn rules Capricorn and is about authority, the father figure, discipline, limits, and time. The Saturnian myth revolves around the overthrow of the father.

Baptist minister and civil rights activist, Martin Luther King, Jr., used his strong Capricorn Sun to make a stand against racism and white supremacy. He didn't seek status as much as he sought to disrupt the inequality of the status quo of the 1960s. Unfortunately, as we all know, he was martyred, so we do not know what other beautiful awareness he could have brought to the United States and the rest of the world. I believe that, like Pisces, Capricorn can be a sign of martyrdom, as they both often work so hard to make the lives of others better and sacrifice themselves in the process.

Robert Lacey, the noted British historian, writes about monarchies and even wrote about the Saudi social dictums and strata in his book, *The Kingdom*.

Ian Brady, on the other hand, *whew!* This man, along with Myra Hindley, was known as the perpetrator of the Moors Murders. Ian, who grew up as a loner, used his Capricorn Sun conjunct the MC for a less-than-desirable expression.

Sun in Aquarius on the MC

These people will meet and connect with large groups of humans, because Aquarius is the ruler of the 11th house of groups and communities. Aquarius is a fascinating sign, ruled by two seemingly discordant planets: stern and authoritarian Saturn and the wild and shockingly not authoritarian Uranus. These people will also have a knack for electronics in order to reach people. They are known for having very independent streaks and setting new trends.

Broadcast anchorwoman, Jessica Savitch, was one of the first women to anchor an evening television newscast for NBC. Of course her Mars here helped as well!

Rhythm and blues singer, James Ingram, wrote many beautiful songs that illustrate the ceremonial magic an Aquarian can call forth. "There's a special kind of magic in the air / When you find another heart that needs to share." Aquarius is an air sign, and the highest expression of the Sun in anyone's chart is to radiate love.

Actress, Jennifer Jason Leigh, has shown a range of acting talent and makes a lovely statement about how an Aquarian tries to understand others:

> "I like to investigate all different kinds of people, I guess, and find out what makes them who they are, and try to be honest in the portrayal, and truthful, and find out how to understand that person, how to communicate that person's experience."

Sun in Pisces on the MC

Pisces rules the worlds of imagery, merging, imagination, the collective, and the occult aspects of life. Remember, occult simply means *unseen*, and Pisces rules the 12th house of the unseen, which is also the home of our ancestors and the place of our undoing. This is where we have a hard time facing the truth of our limiting actions and uncontrollable behaviors. This is also the wellspring of divine inspiration — a Jungian paradise — as it is the place of the collective unconscious.

Funny man and American actor, Jerry Lewis was known for his drunk characters. Pisces rules alcoholism and addictions — those things which disconnect us from reality. Wherever we have Pisces and Neptune in our chart is where we have to be careful about checking out or idealizing certain parts of our reality. A person with a Piscean Sun is one who feels emotions *very* deeply and dislikes the edginess of other people's boundaries, criticisms, and difficult realities of life. Jerry had a way of portraying himself and his characters in a way that connected him to many people, and he used his Pisces Sun conjunct the MC to do that with his audience. Jerry had an intensely loyal and long-term fan base, especially in France.

Speaking of Piscean substance escapism, actor, Peter Fonda said, "My actual intake of different substances was far below what people thought it was, no matter how weird or outrageous they think I am."

Just like Jerry Lewis, singer and songwriter, Karen Carpenter, used this astrological placement to literally click in to the hearts of several generations of people. She sang songs of love and heartbreak and suffered her whole life with self-image issues.

The self-image theme continues with entertainer, Vanessa Williams. She was the first African American to win the Miss America crown in 1983, but was forced to abdicate her crown after nude photos of her appeared in *Penthouse* magazine. Vanessa got the last laugh by building a successful career as a singer and actress. She has Mercury here, too.

Following the actress thread, Drew Barrymore is the third generation of Barrymore actors, and she dealt with the stress by fully engaging in alcohol and marijuana by the age of 10. She wrote of her Piscean experiences in her aptly titled memoir, *Little Girl Lost.*

The Moon

How does the Moon affect us? How does the Moon express itself in the birth chart? For these combinations, we look at how the Moon is the main character. The Moon rules the sign of Cancer. Traits of the Moon are the mother, the body of a woman (can be of a man, too), the emotional self, the Anima in Jungian psychology, the female/feminine image in each of us regardless of gender, how we nurture and feel, our instinctual nature, and our family or tribal history.

This is the area where we get into people's emotions and instincts. Except for the Air Moons (Gemini, Libra, Aquarius), who seek to feel emotionally connected through the exchange of thoughts and ideas, this is not a land of logic. Water Moons (Cancer, Scorpio, Pisces) would like to be close and connected to a safe group of people sharing their feelings. Earth Moons

(Taurus, Virgo, Capricorn) are more grounded in their needs. For instance, pragmatic Capricorn resolves the crisis, and once the house is clean and in order, thanks to Virgo, we want to sit down with Moon in Taurus for a relaxing meal, massage, and a delicious slice of chocolate cake and libations. Finally, ever flickering Fire Moons (Aries, Leo, Sagittarius) need space to spread and experience their passions.

With the Moon on an angle, these individuals have a dynamic container. We have some interesting characters in this group of people. Two legendary queens—Queen Victoria of England and Catherine the Great of Russia—had their Moon on an angle. Both were of divine right, the age old belief that they were God's representatives on Earth. Their respective bodies were literally the repository for their countries. Many of the other lunar mavericks overcame hardships in relating to society. Each had an inner strength; building a container of emotional support from which they could draw to become who they sought to be.

Caitlyn Jenner is a great case in point. She was born Bruce Jenner and become an Olympic Gold Medalist. As a male, she was portrayed as a super idealized version of the masculine, even appearing on the *Wheaties* cereal box. While a major sex symbol, something in her felt at odds with her biology. We now know her as Caitlyn Jenner. To the gender-neutral and almost asexual nature of the Aquarian, what difference is there between a masculine and a feminine body? It is all humanity after all, is it not?

We also have an example of one who travels to another country and takes the super-charged, caretaker mother role. She almost single-handedly saved the chimpanzees in

Tanzania and is also an African Baroness, no less. She is Jane Goodall.

Another good example is actress, Lucille Ball, who pretty much raised her children while playing a mom on her TV show.

Of course, there are also some antithetical displays of the mother, such as with Ed Gein. Soon after his mother's death, he began to create a "woman suit" so that he could "become his mother—to literally crawl into her skin."

Erik Menendez, with Moon in Scorpio, went to jail for matricide and patricide. Please remember that while the Moon usually symbolizes the mother, it can also represent the father in the birth chart, especially at this point in history when gender is becoming so much more fluid. Another intriguing characteristic with the Moon here is that these people act as the body for their larger flock, as in the case of Falwell, Wilson-Slack, the Duke of Kent, and others.

While similar in form to the monarchs cited above, we can see that the Moon gives these individuals the capacity to be a container for others. These topics are all under the auspices of the Moon as the receptacle and container for our respective body, emotional history, and issues.

We will now look at the angle placements of the Moon throughout the zodiac from the point of view of the Ascendant (AS).

Moon in Aries on the AS

This is a fascinating combination because Aries is very outgoing and the Moon is very personal. This placement of the Moon gives one a highly reactive and responsive instinctual nature.

English stage and film actress, Lynn Redgrave, used her body to portray many characters during her acting career, often being drawn to challenging and complex roles. She also has her Venus here.

Champion tennis player, Martina Navratilova, made her body into an amazingly efficient tennis machine with focus and predatory force. An Aries Moon is one of the two warrior Moons, Scorpio being the other. These are individuals who can hunker down and walk through the valley of death to get what they want.

Moon in Taurus on the AS

The Moon is exalted in Taurus, and with Venus ruling Taurus we find a love of sensuality, fine foods and drinks, and loyal friendships. These energies are heightened with the emotional Moon here. Taurus also rules form, especially physical form. We have two individuals who handled their friendships and pursuit of luxury in two different ways: Dionne Warwick and Andrew Cunanan.

Soul, pop, and gospel singer, Dionne, who is a cousin to singer, Whitney Houston, and known for her vocal talents, made a very successful career for herself. She collaborated with Elton John and Gladys Knight to gather a group of celebrity singers to perform the hit single "That's What Friends Are For" for an AIDS fundraiser. In the 1990s she helped promote the Psychic Friends Network, a pay-per-call advice line.

On the other hand, Andrew Cunanan didn't use his Taurus Moon to bring friends together as Dionne did. Being a serial killer, he used this energy to make people feel comfortable while never really sharing who he was. He also sought other people's luxuries. Developmentally, Taurus is toddler energy and believes that everything should be theirs. During his teenage years, Andrew had a reputation for being a prolific liar, given to telling fantastic tales about his family and personal life. He was also able to change his appearance according to what he felt was most attractive at a given moment.

Moon in Gemini on the AS

Gemini is a relational sign, and the Moon is how we hold our bodies and emotional nature. These individuals create emotional bonds through communication. Because Mercury rules Gemini, these people seek a level of intelligent communion and communication with others.

Businessman, Conrad Hilton created the legendary chain of quality Hilton hotels. What is a hotel but a place where people stay to nurture themselves and can get to meet and talk with fellow vacationers?

Jackie Chan, is a brilliant and verbally entertaining martial artist and actor. Whether he plays a drunken monk or a recent immigrant to the US, his roles usually give room for his quick wit.

Queen Victoria, the previously longest sitting monarch prior to Elizabeth II, made a few lovely Moon in Gemini statements, such as, "Great events make me quiet and calm; it is only trifles that irritate my nerves." Here's another gem, "The important thing is not what they think of me, but what I think of them." She was a prolific letter writer.

Moon in Cancer on the AS

This is a lovely combination. The Moon rules Cancer, and this position gives others a sense of feeling at home when they are with these individuals. Cancer and the Moon also relate to the family, the clan, and humanity as a whole. There is a natural warming quality to them.

Our first example, Eric Stanton, was an adult illustrator of fetish and bondage. He was a friend of Steve Ditko, who went on to create *Spiderman* with Stan Lee. (A fun trivial aside; Peter Parker's aunt Mae character in *Spiderman* was based on Eric's Aunt Mae in real life.) "I am like a priest or a doctor," Eric once admitted "I can't say anything about my customers. I've just learned that if one has a fantasy, lots of others usually share it." In a way, Eric created a safe home space for many men and women to explore other sides of themselves.

Ross Perot has a stellium in Cancer that allows him to strongly align with his U.S. clan, especially because the United States birth chart of July 4, 1776, also has a stellium of planets in Cancer. This gives Ross an energetic alliance to the United States. Mr. Perot no doubt felt this affinity strong enough to run for president, but he lost. Ross also owns one of the original copies of the Magna Carta, which contains, most famously, the 39th clause that gave all 'free' men the right to justice and a fair trial. Some of the Magna Carta's core principles are echoed in the United States Bill of Rights (1791) and in many other constitutional documents around the world, including the Universal Declaration of Human Rights (1948) and the European Convention on Human Rights (1950).

Rockabilly singer, Buddy Knox, captured the wave of music transitioning to rock and roll, thus influencing others of his time, such as fellow Texan and namesake, Buddy Holly.

Actress, Farrah Fawcett, known for her beautiful feathered hair, starred in *Charlie's Angels* in the 1970s. She was a pin-up favorite for many, utilizing her body to gain recognition and build upon her acting and modeling career.

Hugo Chavez, president of Venezuela for four terms, sought to equalize the disparity between the wealthy and the poor by creating a type of socialism known as Chavism.

Moon in Leo on the AS

Here we have a dynamic combination. We have the attention-seeking Leo, who loves the stage and feeling like royalty, along with the more private and insular Moon.

Katie Holmes, known for her dark mane of Leonine hair, knew from an early age that she wanted to be an actress.

Lance Bass, coincidentally known as the bass singer for the boy band NSYNC, had no problem taking to the stage. He actually used the privilege of his visible position (Leo Moon on the AS) to come out as a gay man in 2006 to increase awareness and reduce the amount of LGBT bullying and violence.

Freestyle swimmer, Jan Konrads, was born in Latvia and immigrated to Australia with his family in the late 1940s. He developed his body well enough to break multiple swimming records and is an Olympic medalist. His sister, Ilsa (who makes the list later in this book), also set world records, and they were referred to as the "Konrad Kids."

Moon in Virgo on the AS

The Moon in Virgo is a very grounded, practical, and resource-oriented placement. These are individuals with a magnetic attraction. Here we have a feminine sign, Virgo, with the most emotionally magnetic planet, the Moon.

Lyndon B. Johnson designed legislation, referred to as the Great Society, that focused on upholding Medicare, Medicaid, public broadcasting, and civil rights, as well as aid to education, the arts, urban and rural development, and other public services. Fortunately, the boon in the economy (Virgo resources) helped millions of Americans rise above the poverty level during his presidency.

Jack Kerouac, while known for his stream-of-consciousness prose, his wandering, and unintentionally transforming a generation, was also a highly magnetic man. Both women and men were attracted to him sexually, but he didn't feel comfortable with either. Since Virgo is ruled by Mercury, we can understand why he obsessively wrote about his adventures and experiences.

Performer Madonna... well, what can I say? Virgo = virginity, as in the song "Like a Virgin." And, well, there is her name, too. Furthermore, if we wonder how magnetic this singer is, just look at the number of fans she has. Madonna is a master tactician, as she has orchestrated all of her focus towards success. She was not afraid to expose her femininity and her body to the world. And though she has been criticized for her expressions, she just doesn't care. She has a far greater critic within.

Moon in Libra on the AS

These are individuals who wish to make things ok for everyone, especially themselves. And, just like the other two air signs, Gemini and Aquarius, Libra seeks equality in relationships.

Aileen Brennan, actress and comedienne, was known for her quick wit and silent star good looks.

Tennis champion, Arthur Ashe, made a lovely statement about this astrological configuration, "We must reach out our hand in friendship and dignity both to those who would befriend us and those who would be our enemy." Libras are the diplomats of the zodiac.

Karen Silkwood, about whom the movie *Silkwood* was made, was a labor union activist and chemical technician known for raising concerns about corporate practices related to health and safety of workers in a nuclear facility. Librans are all about right human relationship, and Karen definitely used her Moon in Libra on the AS to make a difference for others. Karen's cause of death is still being questioned, but it is most likely the result of the cause she was working to correct.

Singer and songwriter, Gregg Allman, has six ex-wives under his belt. A person with a Libra Moon on the AS has an Aries DS which means they are seeking who they are in relationship which can sometimes be difficult for their partners.

Moon in Scorpio on the AS

This is not an easy place for the Moon, as it is considered to be in its fall here. A planet is in its fall when it is in the sign that opposes its exalted position. Scorpio feels deeply and intensely, and here it is so exposed. The permeability of the Moon feels even more revealed and vulnerable when in the sign of Scorpio. These individuals are the ones with whom we share our deepest, darkest secrets, truths, and experiences. These people are extremely magnetic and draw people to them in ways to help rejuvenate the emotional center in themselves as well as all who are in their field.

Douglas Fairbanks, the silent film movie star, wowed audiences with his magnetic presence.

Quincy Jones, successful singer, songwriter, and producer, once expressed another aspect of this combination by saying, "I lost my mother when I was 7, and they put her in a mental hospital. My brother and I watched her being taken away in a strait jacket. That's something you never forget. And my stepmother was like in the movie *Precious*. I couldn't handle it. So, I said to myself, "I don't have a mother. I don't need one. I'm going to let music be my mother." A Scorpio Moon informs us that the native's tender emotional spaces were not likely honored or seen. Sometimes the lack of emotional support from the parental figure is then projected out onto the transcendent Mother, as Quincy so aptly stated. While this is a painful experience, the lesson here is to let go of the emotional attachment to external dependence so that one can be more emotionally self-reliant.

English musician and singer, George Harrison, was often referred to as the "quiet" Beatle. Still waters run deep in a Scorpio Moon person because they are very private individuals. Scorpio focuses on those occult, or hidden, deeper parts of life. So, it comes as no surprise that Harrison embraced Hinduism, using his deeper sensitivities to broaden the horizons of his fellow bandmates.

Actress, singer, performer, activist, philanthropist, and children's book author, Bernadette Peters, brings a depth of presence and wealth of understanding to all aspects of her life. The Scorpio Moon is not afraid to speak to the depths of human experience and even have a smile on their faces while they do it. The Scorpio Moon doesn't do well with criticism, and when it is on the AS, it is especially heightened.

English drummer and singer, Phil Collins, had a bad reputation for telephoning critics who he felt didn't give him the right kind of reviews. He became disliked in the field because of the ways in which he treated others. Scorpio likes to throw the last excrement bomb over the fence before fleeing the scene.

Champion tennis player, Chris Evert, was known for a level of concentration that would unsettle her competition. I would imagine she had a laser-like gaze that made her opponents feel a bit weak in the knees!

Gary Numan, English singer, songwriter, and music producer, had a very typical Scorpio Moon viewpoint. He once stated that he, "got really hung up with this whole thing of not feeling, being cold about everything, not letting emotions get to you, or presenting a front of not feeling." Scorpio is the frozen waters.

Moon in Sagittarius on the AS

These are emotionally optimistic individuals. Sagittarius gives the Moon a gregarious and playful mood. Remember that Sagittarius is a centaur, a creature that is horse from the waist down and human from the waist up. This implies a two-fold nature: one with a four-footed, grounded, and instinctual animal nature and the other connecting to the clouds. This is addressing the earth and air natures inherent in Sagittarius. These creatures were known for their hedonism as well as a somewhat fiery, warrior-like energy. A person with a Sagittarius Moon on the AS wants to go off on emotional journeys, raising the banner to save others.

Leading man, Charles Bronson was a famous actor from the 1950s to the 1990s known for going out and, against all odds, saving the day.

Primatologist, Jane Goodall, used this astrological placement to be an amazing advocate and protector of chimpanzees.

Astrologer, Marion March, was an inhabitant of many foreign countries. Leaving Germany during Hitler's reign, she moved with her family to Switzerland, Chile, and finally settled in the United States.

Moon in Capricorn on the AS

When the Moon is in Capricorn, it is said that it is in its detriment. Detriment is when a planet is in the sign that opposes the position of its rulership. These individuals have a very hard work ethic and are able to keep their heads and their hearts calm in the midst of any crisis or tragedy. Remember that Saturn rules Capricorn.

Actress, Lucille Ball was the pragmatic mastermind behind the success of her *I Love Lucy* TV show. She was one of the first to keep the film reels from her live performances to create passive income in the form of reruns. Capricorns are great at creating income.

Capricorn doesn't like to be abandoned, and James Earl Jones, the voice of Darth Vader, spoke to this emotional challenge of being left alone. Unfortunately, he was left alone for long periods of time by his mother as she was trying to support the family. The detriment of a Capricorn Moon is similar to the fall of the Scorpio Moon in that both signify less-than-ideal nurturing from the mother. This Moon is one that seeks to rise to the occasion, meet the challenge, and succeed. Think of a mountain goat!

Actress and political activist, Susan Sarandon, once gave this aptly Saturnian statement, "I look forward to being older, when what you look like becomes less and less an issue and what you are is the point."

Moon in Aquarius on the AS

I remember I was doing an astrology reading for a friend with an Aquarius Moon. I saw the glyphs move on the page as I looked at them. I saw the body of a person in the crescent shaped glyph of the Moon and the waves of the Aquarius glyph like hair, and an image of the ancient myth of the sirens appeared in my mind. These individuals lure people to them. The two individuals in this list are people known for their singing, acting, and vocal abilities, all of which fall under the airy domain of Aquarius. In addition, both of these brilliant artists were married four times each! Aquarius is a humanitarian sign, and its natural place in the zodiac oversees groups and communities

American composer, Burt Bacharach, is a producer, songwriter, singer, as well as a six-time Grammy Award winner and three-time Academy Award winner. He is known for popular hit songs and compositions from the late 1950s through the 1980s. One can see the strong influence of the Aquarian rulers, Saturn and Uranus, at work in these artists' lives. Saturn requires a lot of hard work, time, and dedication, and Uranus seeks to shock, change, and evolve.

Actress and singer, Diahann Carroll, was nominated for five Emmy awards, received a Golden Globe award, and was the first black woman to win a Tony Award for Best Actress. Being a trail blazer for human rights is an inherent Uranian goal in the Aquarian psyche.

Our third example is author Faye Weldon, who writes from a more feministic perspective, or at least one that understands that women AND men make up humanity.

Moon in Pisces on the AS

People born with this placement have a dreamy sort of loving acceptance of others, especially animals and those in need. As Pisces is the ruler of the 12th house, there is a sort of other-worldliness about these people. They are natural empaths, meaning they pick up on the feelings of others.

While Audrey Hepburn was known for her grace, poise, dress, and acting abilities, she focused on those who were not as well off throughout her entire life. After a trip to Ethiopia in 1988, she said, "I have a broken heart. I feel desperate. I can't stand the idea that two million people are in imminent danger of starving to death, many of them children, [and] not because there isn't tons of food sitting in the northern port of Shewa. It can't be distributed. Last spring, Red Cross and UNICEF workers were ordered out of the northern provinces because of two simultaneous civil wars.... I went into rebel country and saw mothers and their children who had walked for ten days, even three weeks, looking for food, settling onto the desert floor into makeshift camps where they may die. Horrible. That image is too much for me. The 'Third World' is a term I don't like very much, because we're all one world. I want people to know that the largest part of humanity is suffering."

We will now look at the angle placements of the Moon throughout the zodiac from the point of view of the Imum Coeli (IC).

Moon in Aries on the IC

This is the protective warrior Moon, especially for the family, as the IC often falls within the fourth house.

Malcolm X, the African American leader and prominent figure for the Nation of Islam, articulated concepts of race pride and black nationalism in the 1950s and 1960s. He used his Aries fire to help bring awareness of the plight of African Americans in the United States. He held a container of activism which drew others to him.

Patricia Neal, an actress from the 1950s, had challenging physical experiences which she overcame. From her obituary in *The New York Times*, "Ms. Neal received her Oscar, as best actress, in 1964, for her performance in *Hud* as the tough, shopworn housekeeper who did not succumb to Paul Newman's amoral charm. By then she had already endured the death of her first child and a calamitous injury to her infant son, who was brain-damaged in an accident. Then came three strokes, a year after the Oscar, leaving her in a coma for three weeks. Afterward she was semi-paralyzed and unable to speak." She miraculously went on to make a full recovery.

Singer, Connie Francis, had a domineering father with whom she butted heads. Aries is a Ram, right?

Michael, Prince of Kent, Queen Elizabeth of England's first cousin, has represented the Queen and the royal family both in the Commonwealth and away from his home in the United Kingdom. He has been the Grand Master of the United Grand Lodge of England since 1967. The Grand Master is the vessel for the organization, as identified by his strongly rooted Moon.

American actress, Jamie Lee Curtis, is a noteworthy phenomenon. Aries is a masculine sign, and the Moon is seen as the feminine body. When we put the two together, we find the basis for some of the unfounded and commonplace rumors about Jamie Lee, such as the false rumor that she is a hermaphrodite. This is an indication of how strong this placement can be and how it affects how others see her. She carries strong and well-balanced feminine and masculine energies. People may project their own gender dysmorphia onto her because of this powerful lunar placement at the bottom of her chart.

Professional fighter, Peter McNeeley, used this placement to aid in his agility as a heavyweight boxer.

Moon in Taurus on the IC

As we know, Taurus deals with the form of things, and the Moon represents our emotional container. Moon is exalted in Taurus. Exaltation is like being a favored guest in another's home. A typical Taurus Moon person enjoys luxury foods, fabrics, and an abundance of physical prosperity and sensual delights. In some ways, like the Aries Moon individual, these people will rarely listen to the advice of others, needing to experience life and its consequences for themselves.

Germaine Greer, one of the major voices of 20th century feminism, used this placement to argue and make the valid point that liberation is about asserting the differences of men and women and "insisting on it as a condition of self-definition and self-determination." It is a struggle for the freedom of women to "define their own values, order their own priorities, and decide their own fate."

Carrie Fisher, well known for her portrayal of Princes Leia in the *Star Wars* movies, once expressed this almost Scorpionic statement, "Resentment is like drinking poison and waiting for the other person to die." Taurus, just like Scorpio, can hold onto resentment for so long that they can actually poison themselves.

The very iconic, almost otherworldly, basketball player and actor, Dennis Rodman, played for the … yes, Chicago Bulls!

In the case of Harry, Prince of Wales, a.k.a. Prince Henry, he was often portrayed in the tabloids with his pants down and enjoying what life had to offer. A prince is a perfect "profession" for someone with this placement. Interestingly enough, his mother, Princess Diana, made a point to raise her children with the sense of what it was like to be a "normal" person. This is a pragmatic expression of the Taurus Moon, which can be one of the identifiers of how Prince Harry experienced his mother, as well as the intense connection he felt with her. Is it ironic that he has a Taurus son? Beautiful bonding for father and son to be sure!

Moon in Gemini on the IC

These people have an emotional dictionary within them. Words and facts and ideas are going to be a primary emotional need.

Think of Ross McWhirter, who co-founded the *Guinness World Records*. He made a dictionary-sized book of amazing and often obscure world records held by individuals from around the globe.

Comedienne and actress, Roseanne Barr, known for her wicked and often sarcastic tongue, became very successful from the show that was named after her. Unfortunately, her personal prejudicial beliefs were not shared by her viewers and she was asked to leave her own show.

Tim Lott is a British author. Remember Gemini rules publishing, writing, and communicating.

Nancy Spungen, girlfriend of the Sex Pistols' Sid Vicious, was diagnosed with schizophrenia. Schizophrenia is a mental disorder involving a breakdown in the relation between thought, emotion, and behavior. This results in faulty perception, inappropriate actions and feelings, withdrawal from reality, and a sense of mental fragmentation. Gemini is a multifaceted sign and therefore it is easily fragmented. When the Moon is in an air sign, there can be a bifurcation or split between feeling and thought. Gemini's archetype is the twins and the first sign of duality zodiac. The Gemini myth addresses these splits in self.

Jason Alexander, best known for his role as George Costanza in the TV series *Seinfeld*, played the part of being a mentally frustrated individual. This is a classic Geminian experience.

Barack Obama uses his Gemini Moon on the IC to give people the benefit of the doubt by seeing both sides of any position and working to create resolution.

Moon in Cancer on the IC

Here we have HOME underlined in a most deep and profound manner. The Moon rules Cancer. The Moon, Cancer, and the IC are all about home. The IC, in particular, is who we are at home behind closed doors in our most private spaces, so home and privacy will be important to these people. These are very sensitive, empathic, and nurturing individuals.

Soul and gospel singer, Bobby Womack, perfectly expressed the compassionate and sensitive heart this placement gave him, "It is my fondest wish that the gift of song that God has given me will flow from my soul to yours and help ease any burden that might weigh upon you."

Legendary actress, Liza Minnelli, struggled with the difficultly of having such a sensitive soul and being under almost constant public scrutiny, especially due to her relationship with her renowned mother, Judy Garland. Liza suffered with addictions to drugs and alcohol a good deal of her life, something that happens with water sign Moons.

Here is a clan-oriented Moon in Cancer perspective by British politician Ed Miliband, "We can only converse if we can speak the same language. So if we are going to build One Nation, we need to start with everyone in Britain knowing how to speak English."

THE MOON

Moon in Leo on the IC

These people need acknowledgement. They are likely to have started something creative at home or were possibly even placed on stage at a young age.

Jeane Dixon was a world-renowned astrologer and self-proclaimed psychic. A Leo is very good at making proclamations and getting people to see them in the light they choose. Jeane was an astrologer to royalty and heads of state, and she worked in both private and public ways with these clients. She was able to make a name for herself as well as for astrology at a time when it wasn't popularly accepted.

As both of her parents performed vaudeville acts, actress and comedienne, Martha Raye, got on stage at the early age of three.

Film director, Peter Jackson started working with staging his friends and family members after having been gifted a Super 8 film camera from a close family friend when he was young. He has since gone on to direct the film productions of *The Lord of the Rings* and *The Hobbit*.

This fixed fire sign Moon offered Lynndie England the inner strength to become a soldier as well as more permission to do things her way. Maybe she thought that her atrocities would never become known? Even here at this seemingly quiet place known as the IC, the world knows of her acts of torture and abuse against the prisoners of Abu Ghraib in Baghdad.

When she was seven years old, actress, Dakota Fanning, starred alongside veteran actor Sean Penn in the movie *I Am Sam*. "I am" is a declaration of and for individuality. Leo is the first sign of individuation in the natural zodiac. The "I am" statement is about understanding oneself as separate and distinct from another.

Moon in Virgo on the IC

These are people who perfect home. Their multi-faceted, resourceful, hard-working dedication benefits themselves and those around them.

Albert Speer was a hard-working architect who caught the attention of Adolf Hitler. The two of them shared an idealized relationship which gave Speer the opportunity to create at a level most people cannot. He was known for having extraordinary organizational skills that aided the Third Reich. He was tried at Nuremberg and went to prison for 20 years after having expressed remorse—one of the few who did—over the horrors that had transpired. The Moon in Virgo is one that has tremendous resources. At one time, Speer, had 14 million people working under his direction as prisoners. Despite how horrible it is, this demonstrates an amazing bounty of resources. Almost like being the mother of a huge family of slaves.

Mercury rules both Virgo and Gemini, so there is always going to be a certain level of quickness of wit and understanding of order with this placement. Comedian, Jonathan Winters, showed a lightening wit on TV shows. As long as he could do improvisational skits he was fine, but try to give him a script and the power of his presence was no longer available.

Actor, Peter Fonda, expressed his Moon in Virgo very well. "I have a thing called work," he said. "Writers write, and I do that. Actors act, and I still do that. I'm so glad I'm still involved in this business."

Mimi Macpherson, younger sister of Elle Macpherson, is making a difference as an environmentalist. Virgo Moon is a great Earth nurturer, aka environmentalist.

Moon in Libra on the IC

These individuals likely have a beautiful home. They need balanced, harmonious relationships in their households. The majority of these natives have extensive authorship backgrounds.

Australian author, adventurer, and master mariner, Alan Villiers, wrote about his relationship to sea faring vessels and the ocean.

Canadian author, Leon Rooke, whose writing is "characterized by inventive language, experimental form, and an extreme range of offbeat characters with distinctive voices." I would imagine that all of his offbeat characters come from either his family or from within himself. The air signs, Gemini, Libra, and Aquarius, each illustrate a unique aspect of the intellectual domain. Gemini is the dictionary, Libra idealizes relationships, and Aquarius is where the ideals of and for humanity flow forth.

George W. Bush, the 43rd US president, said this lovely Libra Moon statement while governor of Texas, "I saw an elegant, beautiful woman who turned out not only to be elegant and beautiful, but very smart and willing to put up with my rough edges, and I must confess has smoothed them off over time." His foreign policy, however, was much more of an Aries "my way" nature.

English singer, David Essex, used this astrological placement to create lovely music attaining 19 Top 40 singles in the UK.

Australian actor, Mel Gibson, has had troubled relationships throughout his life. Libra, as with most dual signs, can sometimes be of two minds, which keeps them locked in a battle for harmony and balance with self, others, and family. Librans often suffer from second guessing themselves. This can be very challenging when they are pulled to be in harmonious relationships that often require them to act contrary to the way they feel.

Moon in Scorpio on the IC

This is a place of very deep and private emotions. The Moon is in its fall in Scorpio, and the emotional nature here can become so big as to require attention. Taming the emotional nature when the Moon is in Scorpio is challenging enough, but when we add a conjunction to the IC we have a super intense and emotionally charged being!

Erik Menendez, who makes our list a second time, is experiencing the consequences of his and his brother's emotional parricide. He is incarcerated for life.

Singer and performer, Robbie Williams, has a deep belief in UFOs and paranormal experiences. These are the domains of Scorpio; the unseen, the occult, the mysterious.

World famous and prolific Italian composer, orchestrator, and conductor, Ennio Morricone, has an intense gaze behind which we feel his Scorpio magnetism.

Comedian, musician, and writer, Steve Martin, in true Scorpio fashion, once said, "What if there were no punch lines? What if there were no indicators? What if I created tension and never released it? What if I headed for a climax, but all I delivered was an anticlimax? What would the audience do with all that tension? Theoretically, it would have to come out sometime. But if I kept denying them the formality of a punch line, the audience would eventually pick their own place to laugh, essentially out of desperation."

Then there is the story of Allan Menzies, who believed he was a vampire and was spoken to by the ancient bloodsucker Akasha, the namesake for the main character in the book *Queen of the Damned* in Anne Rice's vampire book series. Unfortunately, Allan's disconnect from reality went further than that when he stabbed his friend 42 times and drank his blood in an attempt to become a vampire. Allan had many facial implants that changed his looks and clearly demonstrate the obsession-oriented Scorpio influence. Look him up on the internet to learn more.

Moon in Sagittarius on the IC

Here we have the emotionally gregarious individuals who seek out truth and share it with others.

Second time maverick golf legend, Arnold Palmer, has a zingy lemonade-tea mixed drink named after him. He also is widely known for selling prescription medications on U.S. television commercials with his affable, personable Sagittarian energy.

Television producer and talk show host, Oprah Winfrey, has the Moon in Sagittarius opposing her Jupiter in Gemini, along with a Sun-Mercury conjunction in Aquarius. This gives a strongly idealized outlook on life and says, "Let's talk." This placement has supported Oprah in her drive and ability to push the limits. She has amassed one of the largest amounts of wealth on the planet and is very generous with others.

Iconic freedom-seeking fashion designer, Isaac Mizrahi, has no trouble speaking his truth—a big Sagittarian trait. He even had his own TV show for a while, so he had a platform from which to express himself.

English actress, Emma Watson, known for her role as Hermione in the *Harry Potter* movie series, when asked about her religious beliefs, stated she is a Universalist. Sagittarius rules our beliefs and philosophies. While there is a lot to say about Ms. Watson, the point here is that Sagittarians are a very accepting lot of people and seek—a Sagittarian trait—to expand their understanding of people, the world, and philosophy. They are one of the question-asking signs of the zodiac, building up their encyclopedia of knowledge.

THE MOON

Moon in Capricorn on the IC

These individuals have a pretty firm emotional grip on reality. Capricorn is a cardinal earth sign. When the Moon is here, the individual often is very grounded, pragmatic, and success-seeking. Capricorn Moons are the ones we want around in a crisis. They are able to turn off their emotional fears and take care of the crisis at hand. Then, when the situation is over, they typically decompensate or collapse, finally showing all the deep feelings that were previously contained.

The 20th century writer, Anais Nin, wrote of her experience with her therapist that helped to deepen her literary abilities, "As he talked, I thought of my difficulties with writing, my struggles to articulate feelings not easily expressed. Of my struggles to find a language for intuition, feeling, instincts which are, in themselves, elusive, subtle, and wordless." The very private space of a Moon on the IC seeks to express itself in a more concrete, Capricornian manner. She wrote about the physical and sensual nature of sexuality, while enjoying a satyr-like lifestyle as compared to most women of her day. Remember the Greek God Pan? He is a satyr: half human and half goat. He represents hedonism, polyamory, and the pursuit of physical pleasure. Pan is an aspect of Capricorn that many forget. The earth Moons (Taurus, Virgo, Capricorn) want to feel the physical. These individuals are literally grounded by the material world.

Not surprisingly, the sexual theme continues with English serial killer, Fred West. He killed at least 12 women, many with his wife present. He believed that women were sexual objects for his benefit and use, regardless of whether the women wanted to have sex with him or not. He killed the women after he and his wife had sexually abused and often tortured them. Unfortunately, Fred used the dominating strength of this Capricorn energy to overpower and harm others.

Singer, dancer, and choreographer, Paula Abdul, expressed this placement well, "Keep the faith, don't lose your perseverance, and always trust your gut instinct." Capricorn is a business success sign.

While Capricorn in the natural zodiac is the 10th house of one's work, when placed on the IC we can have a consummate businessman, as we do with, Nelson Rockefeller, Jr. As a member of one of the Blue Blood families of the United States, he went on to have a successful political career, culminating in his appointment to Vice President of the United States, by Gerald Ford. He is only the second VP in history to have gained the vice presidency in this way.

In terms of a magnificently controlled body, which this placement can indicate, we have the world-renowned ballet dancer, Julio Bocca. He is known as one of the most important ballet dancers of the late 20th century and probably the most important and successful Argentinean ballet dancers of all time.

Moon in Aquarius on the IC

As we have previously discussed, the Moon is our emotional container. When in Aquarius, we have a person with a rather aloof and often cool way of relating to others. They may also have a very other-worldly feeling about them. As with most of our placements, we have some interesting archetypal permutations represented here. Remember, Aquarius is a quirky sign and is both freedom and security seeking. The Moon also shows us the types of relationships to which we will be drawn, and Aquarius is not known for singular love interests.

Actor and comedian, Cary Grant, was married five times, three of which were quick elopements with different actresses. Aquarians often have a lightning Uranian wit, and Mr. Grant used this to deliver his lines with impeccable timing.

Our next person is receiving a lot of press at the time I am writing this book. Caitlyn Jenner, as I wrote earlier, is a person who changed the form of her body from one sex to the other. Aquarius rules groups and communities, and isn't it peculiar that she is actually broadcasting to the world what is going on both in her private life and with her body? While it appears easy on the outside, one can only imagine the will, determination, and self-work necessary to be able to go through her transformation.

Country western singer, Crystal Gayle is known for her hit song, "Don't It Make My Brown Eyes Blue." She once said this lovely Aquarian statement, "Music is universal, it is healing."

Noah Domasin, is a fascinating person because he was born of frozen egg and sperm! He has a very significant birthchart too, which I recommend studying. Here we have conception in the frozen air of Aquarius. The emotional self, represented by the Moon, is not well supported or nurtured in the sign of Aquarius. Sometimes the Aquarian Moon can point to a missing, aloof, or emotionally distant mother or father. In the case of Noah, he was raised by his biological mother (they used her frozen eggs), but the father was absent, as the sperm was received from a donor.

Moon in Pisces on the IC

This is a super powered, deep place for the Moon. Here we have the sign that signifies the other side. This is the sign of dreams, visions, feelings, and celestial music. No surprise that we find two very influential and well-known musicians here.

The amazing Jazz composer, double bassist, and bandleader, Charles Mingus, had an uncanny ability to pick very talented individuals for his bands, many of whom would go on to become well-known in their own right. Known for his intimidating anger and outbursts, he suffered from clinical depression, which is something that can happen to Pisces Moon people.

In my research of the material for this book, I have found there to be a strong correlation between the maverick placement and the person's death. With this placement, the Moon represents our home and Pisces is the sign of the non-physical realm. The Italian fashion designer, Gianni Versace, was murdered outside of his home.

Funny lady, Vicki Lawrence, has chronic idiopathic urticaria. The Moon in Pisces person is very sensitive and emotionally permeable, and they often have difficulty saying *no* to others—Pisces being one of the signs of martyrdom. There are many reasons for chronic skin rashes, but they can often be symptomatic of a difficulty in creating boundaries with others, living in a stressful environment, or feeling unsafe.

Singer-songwriter, Prince is an example of an enigmatic Pisces Moon individual. As Pisces rules imagery, think of how Prince changed music and our culture through his flamboyant and provocative words, style, presence, and outfits. Consider that he went from his birth name of Prince Rogers Nelson to Prince to the monogram ☥. Just as Versace died in the yard of his home, Prince died in his elevator. How Piscean is that? And how prophetic that in his song "Let's Go Crazy" he sings, "Are we gonna let the elevator bring us down. Oh, no, let's go!" And ☥ did!

Actress and model, Evan Rachel Wood expressed this position by giving birth to her son at home. Of course, being an actress is very Piscean too, as she uses her body to portray different characters. She conveyed this astrological position perfectly on Twitter about a movie she is currently working on which is, "a story about an artistic single mother, struggling with her identity and the pain we often deal with behind closed doors."

We will now look at the angle placements of the Moon throughout the zodiac from the point of view of the Descendant (DS)

Moon in Aries on the DS

These are people with a flipped chart. We have Libra on the Ascendant in Aries' natural place. These people have a particularly strong attachment to relationships. Our first example covers so many Aries/Moon archetypes, I can hardly believe it, but I can because astrology shows the truth.

Charles Albright was adopted from an orphanage by an overly protective and strict mother. When he received a gun as a teenager, he used it to kill small animals which he and his mother would then stuff as Charles wanted to be a taxidermist. He later went on to kill three women by shooting his victims in the head then taking out their eyes. So they couldn't see him? He was diagnosed a psychopath. His actions may have come from a strong reaction to his emotional or feminine side.

Quick and strong-willed newscaster, Katie Couric, was the only solo female evening news anchor in the United States until the end of 2009. She used her social influence to help bring awareness to breast cancer and colonoscopies. Her own colonoscopy, which was televised live, generated a significant increase in colonoscopies being performed. She earned the term the "Couric Effect." Katie used her body to help others understand and take care of their own bodies better.

Australian Prime Minister, Tony Abbott, originally planned to go into the priesthood. He says of his time training for the seminary, "The Jesuits had helped to instill in me this thought that our calling in life was to be, to use the phrase: 'a man for others.' And I thought then that the best way in which I could be a 'man for others' was to become a priest. I discovered pretty soon that I was a bit of a square peg in a round hole." He used his fiery, initiating Aries Moon energy to lead Australia in the best way he knew possible.

Our next example is the infamous cannibal, Jeffrey Dahmer, who killed at least 17 young men. The disturbing part is when we think back to the ancient warriors of Greece, they had the notion that if one ate parts of the warriors one conquered, one would absorb their strengths. Jeffrey was so attached to his desired other that he ate them so that he would have them with him forever! Aries Moon is instinctual, fiery, and immediate.

Musician, Wolfgang Van Halen, is the bassist for the rock group Van Halen. What does a bassist do? They set the bass beat to a song. Bassists create the background rhythm, and it takes an instinctually centered person to play the bass in such a way as to resonate for everyone. Wolfgang is the son of Eddie Van Halen and Valerie Bertinelli, and his musical career began quite early.

Moon in Taurus on the DS

The Moon is in its exaltation in Taurus. As an earth sign and traditional holder of the second house, Taurus appreciates material resources, but there is another element to this placement: the native can be especially frugal! While obviously being a royal, Louis XI of France was also known as "le Prudent" or the prudent one. This illustrates a keen understanding of resources and the need to conserve. Another fascinating thing about Louis XI is that he was also known as "l'Universelle Aragne," or the Universal Spider, for the webs he wove in order to understand what went on in his kingdom. Remember, when we have a Taurus DS we obviously have a Scorpio AS, which would give one the ability to keep track and be aware of all the drama going on in one's kingdom. A Scorpio AS is of keen use on this angle indeed!

Southern Baptist pastor, Reverend Jerry Falwell, is on our list again for the same example of the Taurus archetype we saw with Louis XI. It is as if these people act as a grounding container for others. Reverend Falwell created quite a group following known as the Moral Majority. Taurus can be fairly conservative with a tendency to hold on to what meets its security needs. It is a fixed sign and doesn't let go of relationships, material possessions, or dogmatic ideas that came before. A bull is not easy to move, let alone lead.

It is no surprise that we have actress, Joanna Lumley, for a second time. She is well known for her portrayal of Patsy in the British TV series *Absolutely Fabulous*, and what does she do? Her character, Patsy, enjoys living a very luxurious life filled with high-end gourmet food, high-end luxury fashion and fabrics, and her emotional self is sated by sensual delights.

THE MOON

Moon in Gemini on the DS

New Zealand artist, Peter McIntyre, expressed his Gemini DS quite well when he said, "Confidence comes not from always being right, but from not fearing to be wrong."

Lady Bird Johnson, wife of US President Lyndon B. Johnson, used her Gemini Moon conjunct the DS wisely. Wikipedia states, "As First Lady, she broke new ground by interacting directly with Congress, employing her own press secretary, and making a solo electioneering tour."

And what better use of a Gemini Moon on the DS than the chanteuse of France, Edith Piaf! Gemini is the sign of communication, which does not necessarily have to be in words. A Gemini Moon person would view life — and especially relationships with others if it is on the DS — in a seemingly dualistic manner.

Famous photographer, Helmut Newton, exemplifies the contrasting nature of Gemini with his iconic black and white photographs that hold the dynamic of apparent opposites — the contrast of black and white for instance — to accentuate erotic tension.

Well-known French actress, model, and sex symbol, Brigitte Bardot, shows she has no trouble containing her maverick dichotomies: on the one hand she is known for being an animal rights activist, and on the other she has also been fined several times in France for inciting racial hatred against Muslims.

Ever-bubbly, overly talkative, and always amusing actress and comedian, Goldie Hawn, has taken many roles that showcased her multi-faceted ability to communicate at almost locomotive speed!

The infamous Beltway sniper, John Allen Muhammad, shows another aspect of the Gemini Moon. As it is an air sign, there can be an emotional disconnect from the mother. In Muhammad's case, his mother died of breast cancer when he was just three years old. Surprisingly enough he was married and divorced *twice*. Gemini signals pairs, and when in the relationship space of the descendant, it can obviously show two or more relationships.

Moon in Cancer on the DS

Here we have the Moon in her favorite sign of Cancer. These are people to whom one feels an immediate warmth because they are welcoming people that anyone can relate to. A Cancer Moon on the DS is about relating from wherever they feel their humanity. The Moon represents our moods, which ebbs and flows like the waves upon the shore.

To start off, we have the magnetic actor, Clark Gable, about who Frank Capra said:

> "*It Happened One Night* is the real Gable. He was never able to play that kind of character except in that one film. They had him playing these big, huff-and-puff he-man lovers, but he was not that kind of guy. He was a down-to-earth guy, he loved everything, he got down with the common people. He didn't want to play those big lover parts; he just wanted to play Clark Gable, the

way he was in *It Happened One Night,* and it's too bad they didn't let him keep up with that."

Curiously enough, Clark's mother passed away when he was 10 months old, and Prince William's mother passed when he was barely 15 years of age. As mentioned previously, Prince William made a very Cancerian statement to his mother when he was seven. He told her he wished to be a police officer so he could protect her. A Cancer Moon person is usually a security-seeking/needing person. I am sure he wished he could have protected her from the final accident that claimed Lady Diana's life.

Moon in Leo on the DS

Here we have people who can share their emotional selves with others in a larger-than-life way. They have an extreme need to be seen, yet they have Aquarius rising, which can gives them an other-worldly quality and aloof personality. This plays out in each of our examples.

It is most obviously recognizable in singer, songwriter, performer, and actor, David Bowie, whose last album, *Blackstar,* was released on his 69th and final birthday, two days before he died.

Consummate English actor, Michael York, took to the stage at a young age and has done well with his career, playing rather aptly Leonian noble roles.

Stuntman and performer, Evel Knievel, not only reveled in the spotlight doing outlandish jumps and stunts on his motorcycle, but he also had a strong conviction to make good on his word. If he made a promise to someone, he knew it was his obligation to fulfill it, no matter how difficult. He showed fearless courage in the face of feats that really stretched human abilities.

Martin Sheen, the veteran actor who played Josiah Bartlet as the President of the US on the TV series *The West Wing*, once said, "On the show, we are not trying to get people to eat their vegetables; we are not trying to get people to become Democrats. We are basically trying to encourage people to get involved with public life so that politics isn't left to the wealthy and privileged." Leo radiates from the big Sun and huge heart and seeks to lead others. Incidentally, his character, Josiah Bartlet, shares his name with one of the signers of the Declaration of Independence.

Moon in Virgo on the DS

This is a person with an amazing amount of emotional 'response-ability' to others.

Our first example is a man who was literally trapped in his physical body, but had a grounded and fully realized understanding of the universe: Stephen Hawking. I believe Stephen and others with earth planet placements on the angles, especially the IC and DS, are the people who have a true understanding of cosmology, as it is another world to them. What we sometimes find with people who are either incarcerated in places like prison or in their own body, is they have the ability to go places in their minds and come back with theories and understandings of the workings of the world and universe. Virgo is the sign of perfecting and perfection. Individuals with Virgo planets are looking to perfect their understandings and views of the world and cosmos. In a strange way, it was a benefit for Stephen to be trapped in his body, forced to be locked in in order to work out the multitude (Virgo) of theories and concrete ideas (Earth) of the cosmos running through his mind. Remember, Virgo is ruled by Mercury, the god of communication.

French writer, Michel Houellebecq, made a statement that addresses the Virgo discrimination that often manifests as painful insults to others, "I admit that invective is one of my pleasures. This only brings me problems in life, but that's it. I attack, I insult. I have a gift for that, for insults, for provocation. So I am tempted to use it." One needs to understand that while many people feel the Virgo appraisal leveled at them, often Virgo's strongest criticism is aimed at the self. There is often an ideal self to which one is constantly comparing themselves to.

Act-Up AIDS activist and writer, David Feinberg, spoke truth to the people living with AIDS in his book of essays, *Queer and Loathing: Rants and Raves of a Raging AIDS Clone*. In the introduction he writes that this is "as close to the truth as I can get," and that the essays were his attempt "to capture what is to me a painfully obvious reality that is rarely written about: what it is like to be HIV-positive in the 90s; what it is like to outlive one therapist, two dentists, two doctors, and one gastroenterologist." Speaking truth is a key part of Virgo.

Singer and little brother to the Bee Gees, Andy Gibb, paid the price of trying to keep up with his version of perfection.

After years of drug and alcohol abuse to help deal with the stresses of perfection, Andy's heart gave out.

Moon in Libra on the DS

These are people with a natural chart, as they have an Aries ascendant. With the Moon conjunct the DS in Libra, we have people who are driven more than most to be in a harmonious and pretty relationship, or play the polar opposite.

Barry Crump, was the New Zealand author of semi-autobiographical comic books depicting his outdoor bushman abilities. He was married five times and his books revolve around his experiences with others.

Paul Keating, Prime Minister of Australia, has a history of opening his mouth to let something less than ideal come out. Librans are known for their diplomatic, sometimes two-sided approach (being of two minds—remember this is the sign of polarity) in which they approach relationships and life. PM Keating seems to have taken the opportunity to speak in less-than-ideal diplomatic ways in his relationships with others. Look up his name on the internet if you wish to peruse his often-acerbic retorts.

Moon in Scorpio on the DS

Here, the often-unmet needs and intense longing signified by the Scorpio Moon are on full dramatic display with others. The powerful need for control in relationship due to past manipulations means their relationships are often highly dramatic and intense. This is the existential place of relationship to and with the repeated cycles of life and death -in all their beauty and horror played out in the interpersonal arena.

T. Cullen Davis' claim to fame was being the wealthiest man to stand trial for murder. He was known in Dallas society for his bad temper and creepiness towards women.

John Howard, yet another Australian Prime Minister with the Moon on an angle, made the following apropos Scorpio statement, "The most important civil liberty... is to stay alive and to be free from violence and death." A person with the Moon on an angle has a hyper able Moon that can be a container for the masses, especially in instances with political leaders. In Howard's case, he also has Taurus rising (the opposite sign from the Scorpio DS), and this gives him a grounded pragmatic approach to serving.

Rock, country, and folk musician, Steve Earle, has been married seven times, twice to the same person. Scorpio is the sign of commitment to marriage, death, and taxes. Scorpios do not do well avoiding pink elephants in the room. They are likely to describe all of the lurid, unseemly, and not-so-politically-correct revelations to anyone who will listen. And there are many who do! Steve states his political views in the lyrics of his songs as well as in interviews. Scorpios are transformers who are constantly caught in one part or another of the death and rebirth cycle.

Val McDermid, crime writer of the famed *Tony Hill* series, displays another aspect of Scorpio, one that is very private. A Scorpio Moon person has a level of understanding the intricate mind and heart of madness, obsession, hatred, and treachery, so who better to write about it?

Singer, songwriter, and producer, Gary Barlow, was convicted of tax avoidance to offset significant income. Scorpio and taxes, remember?

Australian author, Christos Tsiolkas, has been described as, "…unashamedly vocal in his politics and — in addition to his novels — often comments in public forums on some of the issues most critical and most controversial in contemporary Australian culture: asylum seekers, sexuality, religion, the economy. It's precisely this raw and outspoken political and social consciousness that gives power to Tsiolkas' writing." A Scorpio Moon person will take things on without fear of the consequences if they believe in the plight.

Singer and actress, Miley Cyrus, who also has her Mercury here, exhibits a fearlessness about her sexuality and taboo topics. Of course, these are aided by Saturn conjunct her Aquarian MC!

Moon in Sagittarius on the DS

These are individuals who seek something foreign and/or exotic in their relationships.

Ed Gein, our first example is the man who literally sought to attach the skins of various women to his own body.

British diplomat, Margaret Joan Anstee, served the United Nations for some four decades, being the first woman to hold the position of Under-Secretary-General. She was previously a university professor. Sagittarius rules higher learning and foreign affairs.

Sagittarians like a good giggle and a great laugh and appreciate it when everyone is in a good and festive mood. Contemporary artist, Lari Pittman, stated, "At times, I purposefully orchestrate the work so that you do have that comfortable laughter when looking at it—it's full-hearted and enjoyable internally—but it's also a laughter linked to nervousness. And that's the laughter I particularly like cultivating, parlor laughter, where there's always the subtext of conversation going on, but everyone is very agreeable."

The gregarious and multitalented daughter of Ozzie and Sharon Osbourne, Kelly Osbourne, had to lose weight to create a healthy relationship to the media and fit into an acceptable form. Sagittarians don't usually like the limits imposed by others unless they see great value in them.

Moon in Capricorn on the DS

These individuals have a very capable and strategic emotional approach. They are on the quest for success. Many think that whatever they touch turns to gold, but it is earned. The Moon is in its detriment in Capricorn. The Winter Solstice signals the beginning of the sign of Capricorn, and the days are pretty bleak when viewed through the Capricorn lens in the northern hemisphere. This is not a warm, safe, and expansive place. The soft and emotionally centered self that the Moon represents can be at odds in this cool place.

Media mogul, Merv Griffin, was a maverick of television and built a media empire.

Ronald Kray, along with his brother Reggie, were known as the Kray Brothers. They were successful organized crime figures in London in the 1950s and 1960s, creating their own sort of community and social structure.

Long before he was convicted of assassinating John F. Kennedy, Lee Harvey Oswald had many troubles. He tried to give up his U.S. citizenship to become a Russian citizen. A reformatory psychiatrist, Dr. Renatus Hartogs, described Oswald as immersed in a "vivid fantasy life, turning around the topics of omnipotence and power, through which [Oswald] tries to compensate for his present shortcomings and frustrations." This placement would have made him painfully aware of his shortcomings.

Singer and actress, Cher, has a very level emotional sense that has helped her to make good, sound, practical choices in her professional career.

Actress and model, Liv Tyler, expressed her hardworking approach, "I have been working since I was 14, nonstop."

Moon in Aquarius on the DS

These people are more likely to have anything from an odd and out there kind of mother to emotional relationships with many diverse and foreign people. Here we have the Moon in another Air sign. These people aren't very emotionally centered, they are instead often intellectually centered and can objectify their emotional natures and relationships. Picture them in a high tower able to view and survey all that is around them from a lofty vantage point.

English author, Evelyn Waugh, used his Aquarius Moon to observe people, including himself, in order to use them as characters in his writings. Waugh's emotional detachment was such that he even fictionalized his own mental breakdown!

Government official and lawyer, Virginia Mae Brown, showed her Aquarius Moon by supporting others as an American civil servant.

With our next example, we can see how a person can use their body and mind to create a whole new persona. This woman was so successful that she was able to connect with people of influence and power. Actress, Marilyn Monroe, radiated her Aquarian charm and attracted people from many walks of life. She was also married and divorced three times.

Aquarius gives one the ability to observe and play with archetypes, as eloquently illustrated by the following quote from actress, Liza Minnelli, "I was walking down Broadway with her and nobody was stopping us. She was going to [Stella Adler's] acting studio, and she was taking me to show me what it was all about. And I said to her: 'How come nobody is taking your picture?' She said: 'Well, watch.' She took her scarf off, straightened her shoulders, and draped something another way, and we were surrounded. It must have been 400 people. And I said: 'Now I know why!'"

Professional boxer and entertainer, Muhammad Ali, thrived in, and clearly craved the spotlight. Attention seeking Leo is the Aquarius polarity. He was both provocative and outlandish. Aquarius is unconventional as it is ruled by

Uranus. Ali delivered his punches with Saturnian (the other ruler of Aquarius) gravity.

Jackie Curtis, superstar of the Warhol Factory, also presented an other-worldly persona. Born, John Curtis Holder, Jr., "she" was known for dressing up in bright red wigs, loud glittered clothing (often torn), and possibly being credited for "glitter rock" or "glam rock," like David Bowie's persona, Ziggy Stardust. Aquarians can affect an age with their Uranian inventiveness and their ability to literally birth new archetypes.

Carl Lewis, 10-time Olympic track and field medalist, displays another Aquarian quality: arrogance and aloofness. With the Moon here, Aquarius seeks to rise above emotions and relationship issues to gain a vantage point to observe others in a neutral manner. Of course, this can be seen as arrogant by those being observed. *The New York Times* stated the impression that Carl was "aloof and egotistical was firmly planted in the public's perception by the end of the 1984 Olympic Games." Unfortunately, this resulted in Carl losing the endorsements and financial support he would have otherwise gained and maintained.

"Can't Touch This" singer, M.C. Hammer, exhibits another aspect of the Aquarian archetype: high tech, electronics, and the waves that carry the information (think of the Aquarius glyph).

My dear friend, Kris Wilson-Slack, uses her Aquarius Moon on the DS to act as the body in which to gather the higher philosophical understandings of the Freemasons' teachings to offer to members of her lodge.

Moon in Pisces on the DS

After having dealt with her own addiction issues, Betty Ford, wife to US President Gerald Ford, used this lunar placement to set up a clinic for other people to deal with their substance abuse issues—a very Piscean theme. The Betty Ford Clinic has helped thousands of individuals. With this placement, it's quite possible that these individuals might be drawn to partners who have these issues, or that their mothers or caregivers had addictive issues.

American actress, Kathy Bates, shows another aspect of the Piscean archetype: dreams and imagery. Kathy is able to take on the persona of the character she plays and make them believable. Neptune in Pisces is all about imagery, dreams, and illusion.

We will now look at the angle placements of the Moon throughout the zodiac from the point of view of the Medium Coeli (MC)

Moon in Aries on the MC

These people make a mark on the public psyche. The zero degree of Aries is known in astrology as the "World Point." This is another example of the ways in which this placement has a true means of reaching the masses.

Our first example, surrealist painter and artist, Salvador Dali, definitely made his mark, not only with pen, brush, and clay, but also with his face. For what was he known? His long, ram's horn waxed moustache! And true to the "where angels fear to tread" Aries attitude, Wikipedia states, "Dalí was highly imaginative, and also enjoyed indulging in unusual and grandiose behavior. His eccentric manner and attention-grabbing public actions sometimes drew more attention than his artwork." Aries is, of course, a fire sign. A fire can do anything from providing us warmth to burning us.

Comedienne and actress, Lily Tomlin, uses her Aries Moon conjunct the MC to bring a spark and a flame to the immediately compelling characters she plays. Her humor displays instinctive and cogent Arian traits.

Carl Gustaf XVI of Sweden, whose royal status is little more than representative, is known for an aspect of Aries. As the sign that welcomes spring in the northern hemisphere, Aries signifies germination. King Carl is likewise known for his germination-al exploits and scandals.

Aries is a very head-oriented sign, so it is no surprise that teacher and journalist, Mark Matousek, is a memoirist for others and has a pronounced and shaved head.

Actress, Angelina Jolie, who has several planets on this point, shows us the power of the strong sacred feminine in every role she plays.

Moon in Taurus on the MC

Taurus is ruled by the planet Venus, who seeks love, beauty, loyalty, and relationship. As Taurus rules form and the Moon represents Mother, we can call this placement the Mother of All Forms.

Our first example is the iconic Mexican artist, Frieda Kahlo, used her own body in her art to represent the physically challenging aspects of life.

Ian Anderson, musician and lead singer for Jethro Tull, is a deist and pantheist—the belief that divinity exists in all things. Taurus has a deeply profound love of and attachment to the material/physical world.

American film director James Jarmusch, besides being very private about his personal life, sought to bring a different form to independent cinema.

My dear friend, artist, illustrator, speaker, astrologer, medium, and children's book author, Leslie McGuirk, gave a TEDx talk called *The Importance of Being Wrong* about the ways in which being wrong frees us all for greater experience and expression. While Taurus doesn't like to be wrong, Leslie experiences life with an authentic approach from which others can learn.

Another aspect of Taurus is well portrayed by the *Entourage* TV series character Johnny "Drama" Chase, who is actor, Kevin Dillon, in real life. Taurus experiences conflict in order to reach harmony, as represented by its ruling planet Venus. Johnny has that Taurus/Scorpio moniker in his middle name. These two signs are about harmony through conflict. This means the garden of life will often be full of dramatic blooms. The key is to weed out the drama and cultivate the love.

Moon in Gemini on the MC

Gemini has a lovely chatty optimistic view of life. This placement blesses the native with the natural gifts speech, writing, acting and other airy traits. These individuals often express a genuineness that draws others.

Our first example is the actress, Doris Day, known for her garrulous, ever-optimistic roles and every playful personality.

John Carter (born under the name of John Nicholas Shakespeare, believe it or not!), an American Jazz performer, was known for his wind instruments: clarinet, saxophone, and flute.

While most people are aware of Brooke Shields's acting career, she also promoted physical fitness as an extension of femininity. Gemini is ruled by Mercury, which not only deals with communication, but also with movement and activity.

Moon in Cancer on the MC

Cancer is ruled by the Moon. This sign and planet are all about nurturance and family, so these people are ones who hold a container of nurturance for the public.

My dear friend, Samara Christy, was a gifted healer and intuitive who held space for others to heal to their fullest potential.

Tatum O'Neal's son says the following, "More than addiction and alcoholism, what was passed down to my mother and me was the inability to believe in ourselves," he says. "And that pairs very well with alcohol and substance abuse." This aptly addresses one of the issues with a Cancer Moon, they tend to doubt themselves in their support of others, especially family. These are sensitive souls!

Actress, Jennifer Carpenter, plays the Cancer Moon conjunct the MC beautifully in her role as Debra Morgan, the nurturing and self-doubting sister of the title character in the crime drama series, *Dexter*.

Moon in Leo on the MC

Here we have the temperament of a lion with the ability—and some would say need—to be recognized by the public.

We have the indomitable "Iron Lady," Margaret Thatcher, former Prime Minister of the United Kingdom, who was known for her uncompromising politics and leadership style. The socio-political reforms she implemented are known as Thatcherism. Leo is a fixed sign, and these individuals have and promote very set and defined ideas and thoughts.

Porn star, Al Parker, felt more at home in front of the camera than he did elsewhere. He actually risked his career to bring awareness to the issues of safe sex in relationship to AIDS, from which he eventually died.

Moon in Virgo on the MC

When we have Virgo on the midheaven, we have someone who works! Virgo is the sign of the virgin, the sacred feminine which holds the sacred birth within. In Christianity, this is Mother

Mary with the Christ child in her womb. Virgo is ruled by Mercury and can be a very sexually active sign. When we have a planet in Virgo on an angle, this of course will supercharge the sign and planet's energies.

Unfortunately, we do not have any examples for this configuration. I will, however, use two charts with unknown birth times as there is relevance in their lives to this lunar conjunction. Here is a beautiful illustrative line by William Wordsworth, "Come forth into the light of things, let Nature be your teacher." Virgo is the sign of nature and the sign of multiplicity, as is well stated in another of his quotes, "A multitude of causes unknown to former times are now acting with a combined force to blunt the discriminating powers of the mind, and unfitting it for all voluntary exertion to reduce it to a state of almost savage torpor."

The multiplicity of Virgo and the communication component of its ruling planet Mercury are exemplified in the life of Théophile Cart, who was a French Esperantist professor and linguist—note that Esperanto is a "constructed international auxiliary language."

Moon in Libra on the MC

The draw to beauty, grace, elegance, and refinement in relationships are all well highlighted with this placement.

I have to admit, going through each person's life and finding key archetypal expressions is a time-consuming process. Fortunately, with our next example, the clearly delineated, often dual nature of this Moon in Libra placement for Sylvester Stallone is clearly stated, "How many filmmakers have created two characters who so neatly embody the conflicting sides that live inside every guy? The romantic and the warrior; the dreamer and the destroyer; the underestimated and the misunderstood; the lonely and the loner; the Rocky and the Rambo. How many people have written—that's right, written, because Stallone, despite the image that he is preliterate, has written eight scripts and been nominated for best screenplay— dialogue and scenes that resonate so deeply with men?" Libra seeks balance, beauty, and harmonious relationships. Stallone has played many acting parts about these polarities of acceptability. His characters show that life isn't always the pretty Libran picture we have in our heads.

Award winning actor, Peter Finch, who also has Mercury here, had this written about him his *New York Times* obituary, "A suave, literate man who exuded an air of worldly grace, Mr. Finch was the winner of numerous acting awards in this country and abroad."

1950s and 1960s actor, Allen Case, used this beautifying placement to design a successful line of men's fur coats. Libra does appreciate beauty.

Australian novelist and playwright, Thomas Shapcott, is an example of many of these airy Libran traits as he was a poet, editor, librettist, short story writer, and teacher. Interestingly, as Libra is a twin sign—meaning it has two parts—he was one of a pair of twins. His brother was born the day before, and what's more, as Libra is about balancing polarities, Thomas was left-handed and his brother right-handed.

Moon in Scorpio on the MC

This is a potent, powerful, and challenging placement. Scorpio is a creature that hides from the light, seeks privacy, and sees the issues when it looks into others. Again, the Moon is in its fall when in Scorpio. That is to say that the emotional nature of the Moon doesn't usually feel safe when in Scorpio because it is vulnerable and often flooded with intense emotions. The midheaven is a public place, so the lights are illuminating all aspects of the person for the whole world to see. Scorpio Moon isn't comfortable being seen so fully at the Noon position of the chart. Ruled by Mars and Pluto, Scorpio is an amazing strategist and knows how to manipulate or bend others to their will.

Pre-Thatcher, Barbara Castle, shattered the glass ceiling for women in politics. She was known for her flaming red hair and, according to a well written article by Anne Perkins for the BBC, "She was from the start a brilliant minister—a woman with a clear sense of purpose, a genius for attracting public notice to her schemes, and enough clout with the prime minister to get her way in interdepartmental disputes." A well-integrated Scorpio is able to keep an eye on the small details while seeing the larger picture in which the details are contained.

Moon in Sagittarius on the MC

Sagittarius is the sign in which we seek a greater or higher philosophy of life, be it through education and foreign travel, or through religious or spiritual pursuits. Sagittarians are known for their big generous hearts and odd sense of humor.

One of the founding members of the band The Beach Boys had this to say about Carl Wilson, "He never wanted credit for their success, but he was the glue that held the band together." High school classmate and musician Rick Henn said Wilson remained a down-to-earth person, never letting his fame get the best of him. "He was one of the kindest and nicest people that I'd met that had become a star. He was genuinely a sweet, caring, and loving guy. That being said, he was also a wacky guy. He had a madcap personality and great sense of humor." Carl was also gifted with Mercury and the Sun here on the MC. Sagittarians often have a quick and fiery wit about them.

Core Energetic practitioner, JoAnn Lovascio, writes on her website, "My work is an expression of my deepest realization: an uncompromising devotion to embodiment. Over the decades, I have come to a deep understanding of how obstructions to embodiment can limit our ability to show up in our everyday lives with full awareness, presence, and feeling. Embodiment is the practice by which we integrate all aspects of ourselves, give expression to our spirit, and ground ourselves firmly to the earth and to this life." JoAnn is speaking of an integration of the higher and lower selves. Sagittarius is a sign of devotion to something greater.

Scottish singer-songwriter, KT Tunstall, after having gone through a dry spell in regards to her music, moved to Los Angeles for a change and said, "I'm not kidding for a second, it was driving around listening to music in a car that made me write this record." Sagittarius seeks the journey, movement, and to create inspiration.

Canadian singer, Dawn Langstroth, daughter of Anne Murray, exhibited another side of the Sagittarian dilemma. Outwardly, Dawn appeared fine and made it all look good while she was privately dealing with her body image and suffering from anorexia as a teenager.

Moon in Capricorn on the MC

Ian Brady, of the of the infamous "Moors Murders" had this to say in an article written about him in *The Telegraph*, "I'm as pragmatic as a soldier or a politician—you never see any regret from Tony Blair, in fact he is minting a fortune from his war crimes. I'm simply saying this dichotomy is common through all levels of society." Ian sought to rationalize his aggressive paranoid schizophrenic behavior within the context of the society in which he lived.

American politician, Robert Kennedy, little brother to JFK, also has Jupiter and Venus here conjunct his Capricorn MC. Robert was a very charismatic, attractive, charming, and above all, extremely capable individual. Not only was he the U.S. Attorney General, but he was also his brother's top adviser and fix-it man. In the time between his brother's assassination and his own, Robert did the most Capricorn thing he could by reaching for the top and running for president. He had every indication of reaching his goal (Capricorn), but unfortunately a gunshot prevented that from happening.

Comedian, podcaster, writer, and actor, Marc Maron, uses his dyspeptic Capricorn Moon to illustrate the hardships in his own life. Remember that Capricorn is the dead of winter in the northern hemisphere, when one doesn't believe there will be enough ____ (fill in the blank) to make it through to spring.

Charismatic and attractive world-class soccer/footballer, David Beckham, uses his body and his looks to gain the height of success not only in the soccer/football world, but also in the modeling/fashion world.

Moon in Aquarius on the MC

The aloof, other-worldly Aquarian nature is well articulated in our examples. Ruled by Saturn and Uranus, there is a quirky sense of age that sometimes doesn't add up.

Jon Benet Ramsey had a very unique look and was made up in a way to portray a more mature look.

Screen legend, Vivien Leigh, kept a lovely manor home in England as a sanctuary to which she could retreat from the rigors of her acting fame. Aquarians need an ivory tower to which they can escape from the public.

Actress, Dame Helen Mirren, expresses this lovely Aquarian Moon beautifully, "As you get older, you have learned things, you are able to deal with things. As each age develops you understand your role in the onward sweep of life. It's all part of the wonderful process of being a human being."

Another Leigh actress, Jennifer Jason Leigh, portrayed a varied and eclectic range of roles over the course of her acting career.

Moon in Pisces on the MC

This position is the boat that floats on the dreamy sea of the collective.

Music educator and composer William Ennis Thomson's work focuses on the perceptual and cognitive foundation of music. Pisces is one of the signs that rules music and perception. The Moon intensifies the ability to receive and perceive music and the ways in which people experience it.

One does not usually equate athleticism with the sign of Pisces, except for maybe swimming. Pisces does, however, rule the feet and deals with sacrifice and unwavering dedication, traits necessary to be a successful athlete, especially when one considers the perfecting aspect of Virgo is on this axis.

Australian actor, Dan Falzon, uses his Piscean Moon to hold a very nurturing and welcoming vessel for the people and animals around him. Pisces is a sign of service, so when the Moon is placed here, we have a person who receives a lot of emotional gratification taking care of others' needs.

MERCURY

How does Mercury affect us, and how does Mercury express itself in the birth chart? For these combinations we are looking at how Mercury is the main character in the lives of these mavericks.

Mercury rules Gemini and Virgo. Traits of Mercury include how we communicate, think, process and analyze information, how we move, our coordination, our nervous system, and how we access sensory information from the conscious and unconscious. In the ancient Greek myths, Mercury was the only god who could travel from the heights of Olympus (heaven) to the pits of Hades (Hell) and the land of earthly mortals in between. The archetype of Mercury is similar to the element mercury, or quicksilver, and can therefore can go places and respond to things quickly. Individuals with Mercury on an angle will show exaggerated movement and communication abilities, especially when in an air sign such as Libra, Aquarius, and Mercury-ruled Gemini.

Mercury is amoral and androgynous, so the individual's consciousness and other planetary placements and aspects make the Mercury placement either an enjoyable or challenging experience. I recommend Leslie McGuirk's book, *The Power of Mercury,* for further study and understanding.

We will now look at the angle placements of Mercury throughout the zodiac from the point of view of the Ascendant (AS).

Mercury in Aries on the AS

These people tend to have a brutal honesty about them and likely don't sit still as there is an instinctual quality to Mercury when in Aries.

Feminist, Valerie Jean Solanas, wrote the SCUM Manifesto in which she outlined her feminist plan to eradicate men. She even went as far as to shoot and nearly kill Andy Warhol because he lost a script she wrote. Aries is the warrior sign and Valerie Jean had no trouble in following through with her words and actions.

Australian artist, Brett Whiteley, was known as being avant-garde in his field. This is the expression of Aries energy translated into artwork. In an article in *The Australian,* this opening line captures this Aries Mercury AS conjunction, "Brett Whiteley was the great streak of lightning on the

Australian art horizon. From 1960, no one had a vaster gift, more sheer brilliance, or a bigger impact on the Australian imagination."

Cristina Teixeira perfectly articulates her Mercury placement, "I would say I love to communicate, to explore new information, I love to read, to write and do research in libraries, I love bookshops and libraries. My Mercury is in the 12th house so there is also this connection with mysticism, exploring what is hidden (as a child I imagined doors behind curtains, and love the idea of secret passages). I have a creative mind and can be a storyteller. I am more conscious of what I say now as an adult, but I am generally brutally honest. When I was younger, I got into trouble for being outspoken or for just being a chatterbox. I can be very persuasive and have been a good salesperson at various points in my life. I am a fast learner and get bored easily. This is why I need frequent mental stimulus."

Mercury in Taurus on the AS

These people communicate and move in a rather pragmatic, dependable, and grounded manner. In esoteric astrology, Taurus is a sign of reaching harmony through conflict. The set ideas of form (the attachment of how one perceives things should be) are often at odds with reality.

An article about medical advice columnist, Dr. Miriam Stoppard, clearly states this placement. From *The Independent*, "She does it her way. Dr. Miriam Stoppard controls her many careers, from newspaper agony aunt to best-selling author, with a steely determination—all while perfectly coiffed and made-up, of course." Kind of says it all, right? As Taurus is ruled by Venus, beauty and harmony are key elements of the Taurus makeup. Also, Taurus doesn't like to have anyone tell them what to do or who to be—again, think of pushing a bull. It doesn't work. We often find these individuals guiding others on how to be.

English soccer great, David Beckham, known for his ability to make his kicks bend (perfect union of the Mercury movement with the Taurus form), is also known for being glamourous. By the way, David speaks nine languages!

Aussie actor, Gary Sweet, calls himself a "bloke's bloke," showing a full range of characters, more on the grounded male side.

Beeaje Quick, an up-and-coming actor and director who thinks outside of the usual form, has this Taurean understanding of the U.S. scene, "But see, I've brought something to America ... I've brought something to the table. If you come here to this country thinking you're already a star, you're nothing and the system will swallow you. But if you come to the table with dessert, then people become more hospitable, and they see you're not trying to rape the land. You're contributing." Taurus loves dessert, fine wine, sensuality, and physicality. Also, when Mercury is in Taurus we have a person who is able to persuade others and understands how to do so in very pragmatic ways. Mercury in Taurus would also lend a very determined and measured means of communication. Listen to any of our examples speak and you know what I mean.

MERCURY

Mercury in Gemini on the AS

Mercury rules Gemini, so here we have people who have an ease of communicating and seeing the world of dualities and multiplicities.

Candy Barr, known for her quick-witted retorts (a primal Mercury in Gemini trait) and attractive innocent looks, was an American stripper, burlesque dancer, actress, and adult model in men's magazines of the mid-twentieth century. Candy lived a very exciting life as we learn from *Texas Monthly*:

> Candy Barr, the former Dallas stripper whose madcap adventures in the late fifties and early sixties—from her tumultuous love affairs with gangsters to her battles with a self-righteous Dallas police captain to her farcical criminal trial over her alleged possession of marijuana—catapulted her onto the front pages of every newspaper in Texas and turned her into something of a folk hero.

Russell Hitchcock, one of the singers in the rock group *Air Supply*, said this about his relationship with fellow singer-songwriter, Graham Russell, "I've known my role within *Air Supply* as he does and it's a complementary relationship to the highest degree." Gemini is the sign of the twins and seeks a unifying, complimentary relationship with others. Gemini seeks an equal relationship: neither one above nor below the other.

Bodybuilder and rugby player, Papa Spyk, exhibits many of these Mercury and Geminian traits. I highly recommend further research on this maverick. The AS is how we see the world and how the world sees us, and in this sense, Papa Spyk was a walking talking Mercury conjunct the AS in Gemini poster boy. He was a maverick. His friend, Reece Dry, once said, "He wanted to get his message across to as many people as possible, a positive man with a great heart and good intention. He wanted to help others and I know he touched the hearts of many and will continue to do so." Gemini is the sign of writing and publishing, and Papa Spyk wrote a series of autobiographies, including the book *A Naughty Thing Called Life*.

Mimi Macpherson, appearing for a second time on our list, is described as, "…an Australian environmentalist, entrepreneur, and celebrity…she began her own whale-watching business, winning multiple awards before going into property development and promotions. She has also acted as a corporate and NGO spokeswoman, and a media personality."

English comedienne, Catherine Tate's humor is one that relies heavily on witty words and phrases. *The Telegraph* writes the following about Tate:

> But to be truly brilliant, the witty lines—the bits that aren't being reused—have to be as good as the catchphrases. Fortunately, the Nan sketch, in particular, rose above that and was turned into an imaginative set piece that was more than just a sum of its parts. Proof, then, that Tate can actually be at her funniest when she's saying something unexpected.

Mercury in Cancer on the AS

These are individuals who, while seeking security and a family atmosphere, have the ability to speak their values in clear ways. Mercury has an element to it that is like Uranus in that it can bring flashes of insight that seem to come from out of nowhere.

In an article for *Vanity Fair*, we learn the following about actor and politician, Arnold Schwarzenegger:

> Then, in the middle of the recall madness, *Terminator 3: Rise of the Machines* opened. As the movie's leading machine, he was expected to appear on *The Tonight Show* to promote it. En route he experienced a familiar impulse — the impulse to do something out of the ordinary. "I just thought, 'This will freak everyone out,'" he says. 'It'll be so funny. I'll announce that I am running.' I told Leno I was running. And two months later I was governor."

Mercury is not afraid to step forward and face whatever may arise, and we can see this response-ableness play out very specifically in Schwarzenegger's life. The article gives additional comments about his devil-may-care attitude in the way he rides a bicycle. Schwarzenegger has only been married once, and while he did cheat on his wife, he sees his separation and divorce from Maria Shriver as his greatest failure. This is indicative of the Cancerian who highly values family.

My friend, Artemes Turchi, performer and hair stylist to the stars, actually has both Mercury and Uranus straddling his Cancer ascendant. I personally know Artemes to be a very warm, engaging person and a loyal friend who makes deliciously loving meals to share with family and friends while having lively conversations around the table.

Cancer can be the sign of hoarding, and when Mercury is involved, this can be the hoarding or gathering of information of what is happening to the clan. This is exemplified by American economist, Robert E. Lucas Jr., winner of the 1995 Noble Prize in Economic Sciences for the "development and application of the theory of rational expectations in macroeconomic analysis." Robert looks at larger theories and finds ways to make them relatable.

Runa Bouius, who, like Artemes, has Uranus conjunct her AS, is a person who loves to have a group of friends and family around the table, and works to communicate ways to improve humanity through her efforts in the Conscious Leadership movement.

The New York Times wrote this about politician, Hugo Chavez, the 64th president of Venezuela, "He was a dreamer with a common touch and enormous ambition. He maintained an almost visceral connection with the poor, tapping into their resentments, while strutting like the strongman in a caudillo novel." In Hugo's case, he was born to a very poor family and remained aware of the plight of those in poverty and the challenges they face.

Actress and model, Liv Tyler, who has also has the Sun conjunct this position, shows one of the many aspects of being a maverick. In an interview with *Elle* magazine, it's easy to see how multiple planets on the angles gives her the ability to do what she wants to do. Liv is asked, "You're a very experienced actress, but you asked Belstaff to go behind the camera for this project. Now you've produced two of its films, plus a feature film. Why become a producer, on top of all your success?" To which Liv responds, "Because I wanted to put all my experience from the years I've been working into a job I never knew I could do. I wanted that challenge. I don't want to say I was bored, but I was ready for more in my work life." This sounds like a pull from the opposite sign of Capricorn.

Mercury in Leo on the AS

This is a beautiful combination for an actor, writer, performer, singer or any other pursuit that benefits from a spotlight and avenues of opportunity for promotion of the self.

Leo is the sign of the common man, so it is no surprise that our first example is writer, philosopher, and father of Humanism and the Renaissance, Petrarch.

Another writer, Alex Haley, brought us *Roots* and *Malcolm X*. He wrote about the experiences of African Americans in the United States as well as the plight of his own family history.

Former U.S. President, George W. Bush shows another aspect of this placement by speaking whatever he had on his mind without a filter. He was known for coming up with (or making up) his own words and phrases, most notably "I am the decider," which is a very Mercury in Leo statement!

The wife of Indigenous Australian actor, Ernie Dingo said, "Ernie is famous. Women have been throwing themselves at him for years. Like most famous people, women see the charisma and virtually undress themselves and wait at the door." Leo rising people can be very charismatic. The challenging part for the native is to act in the best possible manner so as not to fall victim to their own charisma. Consider the myth of Narcissus.

Astrologer, Jessica Adams had at various times been an editor, book reviewer, internet columnist, feature writer, and astrologer for many magazines and newspapers throughout Australia. She has also been a scriptwriter and researcher for television. We find the key elements of this astrological placement in Jessica Adams:

> British astrological writer and novelist, a Sun-Sign columnist, journalist, and best-selling author. A professional astrologer from 1987, Adams' work includes *Handbag Horoscopes, Essential Astrology for Women, Astrolove,* and *2020 Vision.* She is also the author of *Single White E-mail* and *Tom, Dick and Debbie Harry.*

Kevin Dillon, appearing for a second time on our list, plays a part on *Entourage* that is similar to the one he plays in real life. In an interview about his character, he summarizes the Mercury in Leo conjunct the AS perfectly, "He's insecure, and that sometimes comes out in the form of this inflated ego. But he has a big heart, and I like to think I do too."

Robin Williams's daughter, Zelda Williams, used this placement to cope with her father's suicide by writing some 12 scripts.

Catriona Rowntree began as a radio personality and then went on to TV.

Mercury in Virgo on the AS

Virgo is ruled by Mercury, and here we have a very strong and potent ability for resourcefulness in general, and communication and movement in particular.

Writer, Alfred Corn was a resourceful and prolific wordsmith. He wrote some 10 books of poetry, a novel, and many essays.

Lead singer and performer, Freddie Mercury, is in his own maverick class. He renamed himself and named his band after a Virgoan ideal!

U.S. President Lyndon B. Johnson, showed another aspect of the Virgo energy by being a person dedicated to the service of others. Johnson signed one of the most comprehensive laws protecting classes of citizens who previously had little protection in the courts and in U.S. life. The Civil Rights Act of 1964 was maverick legislation.

Architect and engineer, Renzo Piano, exhibits still another archetype of Mercury conjunct the AS in Virgo: he is dedicated to supporting the environment. Renzo completed one of the greenest museums ever built, the California Academy of Sciences. Found in San Francisco's Golden Gate Park, it also houses a planetarium, aquarium, and natural history museum under a two-and-a-half-acre living roof.

"Like a Virgin" singer, songwriter, and performer, Madonna, makes our list a second time as she has both her Moon and Mercury conjunct her ascendant.

Pierre Commoy, is a photographer, writer, actor, and director. The famous duo, Pierre et Gilles, are known for creating lush and beautiful renditions of the individuals they photograph. The photography work is meticulous, sensual, surreal, and beautiful, with religious/sexual themes throughout.

Mercury in Libra on the AS

These natives are gifted with a silver-tongue and possibly a silver spoon. The pursuit of beauty, luxury, and fame (as well as infamy) can be easily seen in our examples.

The early 20th century avant-garde dramatist, poet, essayist, actor, and theatre director, Antonin Artaud, literally traveled between the worlds in his pursuit of sounds, theatre, and spiritual experiences. He inspired many brilliant artistes.

Ferdinand Marcos, president of the Philippines, whose wife, Imelda, is famous for her shoe collection (Libra loves beauty), used his wit for political and personal gain.

Sculptor and artist, Niki de Saint-Phalle, almost like Artaud, traveled between the worlds trying to find herself somewhere within. Libra is an air sign dealing with opposites. When Mercury is found here, we have a person with a highly sensitive and attuned mind. Niki was placed in a few asylums in her life, which helped her create cutting-edge artistic expressions, such as using a shotgun to make art, and the

Tarot Garden in Tuscany, Italy. The latter is filled with supersized colorful mosaic creatures representing the 22 major arcana cards in the tarot deck. This was before performance art made its appearance in the art world.

Carlos the Jackal, used his well-placed Mercury in Libra — think of a silver-tongued ambassador — to charm others, even when they knew with whom they were dealing. "In June 1975, one of Carlos' accomplices was apprehended by the French police. He led them to the flat Carlos was staying in, where they were welcomed by the Venezuelan terrorist with drinks and conversation. As the police started to relax, Carlos took out a machine gun and opened fire, killing two French detectives and the informant who had betrayed Carlos. The event was a turning point, Carlos moving from relative obscurity to the subject of an international manhunt. The media soon dubbed him 'Carlos the Jackal'."

Musician, Martin Taylor uses his Mercury placement to create beautiful (Libra) sounds with his guitar in an unusual manner. "He is best known for his solo fingerstyle performances, in which he provides bass and chordal accompaniment in addition to a melody."

Mercury in Scorpio on the AS

These people entice others to talk about anything, especially the more sensitive parts of life. This placement gives one a sort of confessor energy that magnetically welcomes others to share in ways they never knew they would.

Talk show host, Johnny Carson, used this placement to have lively, thoughtful, and deep conversations with celebrities. Scorpio seeks what lies beneath or behind. It is peculiar to note that Johnny played a character on *The Tonight Show* called the Carnac the Magnificent, a psychic individual who would "read" the cards held to his third eye area and relay it to the audience. People with a significant Scorpio signature have a very philosophical and psychological bent. They seek to understand people's behaviors and emotions. And humor is a needed ally when visiting the more challenging aspects of life. Johnny was adept at using humor to access the more delicate parts of life.

Michel Foucault, brilliant philosopher, writer, and historian, also had a comprehensive grasp of human nature. He studied prolifically and had a highly capable and psychologically-oriented intellect. Present day intelligentsia are still citing and studying his work.

Scorpio is the sign of death and rebirth, and Mercury is the planet of movement, so, in a way, it is no surprise that Grace Kelly will be remembered for getting killed in a car accident.

The actress, Divine was far from shy and demure. She was a drag queen who really played with this astrological combination in an unusual way. There was nothing Divine wouldn't do to get attention. It is no surprise, therefore, that one such act involved ingesting dog feces. Scorpio rules the digestive system, especially excrement, and this was captured on film for all to see.

Italian fashion designer, Gianni Versace created the perfume *Intense*, which is the word most often used to describe Scorpio.

American politician, Hillary Clinton, has used this intensely placed Mercury to aid her, not only in her successful legal career, but more importantly in her political career. This configuration was especially helpful during her tenure as U.S. Secretary of State, but may have been what alienated here from voters in the United States.

Performance singer, Adam Ant, also has his Sun here for a double whammy effect. He communicated a sexy charisma in his videos, songs, and performances.

Mercury in Sagittarius on the AS

These natives have a voracious need to express truth, whether their own personal truth or the greater philosophical Truths of Life. Here the ability to proclaim and go forth in manifest destiny (no boundaries) are well presented by the following mavericks.

American media mogul, Ted Turner, is one of the largest U.S. landowners. Turner started CNN in order to bring the knowledge of what is happening all over the globe to the world.

Our next example also exemplifies the distribution of information. One of the cornerstones of the wealth enjoyed by Lady Bird Johnson was the acquisition of radio station KTBC.

Forrest Ackerman, science fiction writer and literary agent for some of the best minds in science fiction, clearly shows this lovely astrological combination operating after his death. Cryptically enough, his friend, Paul Davids, said that Forrest still communicates with him from the other side. This apparently happened no less than 100 times after Forrest's death.

Poet, Robert Duncan's placement is well conveyed in the following excerpt from astro.com:

> American major contemporary poet, considered a presiding voice of the San Francisco Bay area specifically, which he helped establish as a major center of poetry in the United States, Duncan became the leading spokesperson for open poetry in America, and his full powers are considered best displayed in "The Venice Poem," 1948, patterned after Stravinsky's Symphony in Three Movements.

Now comes more of the Scorpio storyline:

Duncan's mother died shortly after giving birth to him. His father, a day laborer, put him up for adoption when he was six months old. Adopted by a couple who chose him on the basis of his astrology chart, he grew up as Robert Edward Symmes, reverting to his original surname in 1942. Raised mainly in Bakersfield, California, his adopted father was an architect, and both of his parents were theosophists. He was deeply affected by metaphysical influences throughout the family; his grandmother had been an elder in a Hermetic order similar to William Butler Yeats's Hermetic Order of the Golden Dawn.

Wikipedia has this to say about singer, songwriter, and actor Tom Waits:

Waits' lyrics frequently present atmospheric portraits of grotesque, often seedy, characters and places, although he has also shown a penchant for more conventional ballads. He has a cult following and has influenced subsequent songwriters despite having little radio or music video support.

American actress, Jamie Lee Curtis, has a few curious traits that display the Mercury in Sagittarius on the AS combination. There are early references to rumors of hermaphroditism (Mercury is an androgynous god), she gained fame and success acting in horror movies as a scream queen, and she is dedicating her life to writing children's books more than acting at this point. Among the titles of her works is *Who We Are and Where We Came From*—questions that anyone with a strong Scorpionic signature would ask and to which one would seek serious answers.

Mercury in Capricorn on the AS

These people can easily manipulation the structures and physicality of life. This is a potent mixture of sophisticated earth energy directed through Mercury's facilities -anything is possible!

Someone about whom I had never heard anything but was so impressed by, is artist and publisher, Bern Porter. I am surprised he isn't more celebrated. This man was a creative and intellectual genius and touched the lives of many other noteworthy people. Capricorn seeks out success and status, which he definitely attained judging by the people in his circle which included Gertrude Stein, Henry Miller, and Albert Einstein.

Actor, Paul Newman, is famous for not only being an A-list actor, but for also having founded and maintained a successful organic health food line called Newman's Own. Like Porter, he had a wide range of commercial success.

Actor and the voice for Darth Vader, James Earl Jones, who also has Saturn here, possess a deeply grounded and melodic voice that one immediately recognizes. This beautiful quote captures it best, "Speech is a very important aspect of being human. A whisper doesn't cut it."

Boxing great, Joe Frazier, was described after his death by legendary boxing promoter, Don King, "Not only was he a great fighter but also a great man. He lived as he fought, with courage and commitment, at a time when African Americans in all spheres of life were engaged in a struggle for emancipation and respect. Smokin' Joe brought honor, dignity, and pride for his people, the AMERICAN people, and brought the nation together as only sports can do." Frazier used the grounded, physical movement of Mercury conjunct his Capricorn AS to move in a way that still has boxing aficionados talking today.

Here were learn about Australian lead singer of INXS from diffuser.fm:

> Front man, Michael Hutchence lived a rock 'n' roll lifestyle. He dated famous models and pop stars, and accounts of his drug and alcohol use are widespread. According to friends and band mates, the singer found the dark allure of rock star excess irresistible. "I'm

surprised I've survived, and so are a lot of my friends," Hutchence said in 1995. "I'm sure some of them are pissed off, because one thing about me is that I always manage to have my cake and eat it too, whereas people love to see f–k-ups. That's the industry. Welcome to the party. Jimi Hendrix is upstairs. But coming through it is fantastic."

When his career started to slow down and questions about further success mounted, along with problems in his personal life, Michael took the Capricorn control to a higher level and took his own life. His Mercury would have had a wonderful time sharing his experiences to save others such pain and misfortune.

Mercury in Aquarius on the AS

Aquarius's highest goal is to help humanity, especially those who are not receiving the same benefits of those higher up the social ladder. These individuals have a flair for words and a way of relating that may be more rewarding for groups of people, but may not be easy on an individual level. The coolness of this position may be hard for some to understand.

History.com writes of Jimmy Hoffa, who also has his Sun here:

Hoffa became president of the Teamsters in 1957. Hoffa was lauded for his tireless efforts to expand the union, and for his unwavering devotion to even the organization's least powerful members. His caring and approachability were captured in one of the more well-known quotes attributed to him: "You got a problem? Call me. Just pick up the phone."

The cool Aquarian nature is well articulated in *The New York Times* article about actress, Charlotte Rampling:

> Rampling has been rightly celebrated for her remarkable body of work, but she's also been labeled as "cold," "imperious," "detached," "watchful," "hard to get close to," "mysterious," and "aloof." In the countless interviews she's done, reporters have described her with a mixture of awe and anxiety, sometimes casting her as a bit of a mental case as they unknowingly behave like mental cases themselves.

In an interview with *Granta*, British author, Tim Lott, is asked, "Can you explain the impulse behind your decision to write a memoir, especially a memoir that deals with such difficult and intensely personal subjects?" to which he replies:

> First, it's an attempt to try to achieve mastery over a situation. Somehow by putting things into words you're taking a situation that feels very out of control and creating a kind of illusion of control over it. Secondly, if you have to write precisely — and with a magazine like *Granta* you can't get away with sloppy writing — you gain clarity over something which is otherwise a real muddle of confused thinking, and that's a comfort.

Thirdly, I'd say that all writers have a fundamental impulse to communicate their experience one way or another. There's probably a fourth reason, which is that I have a strong belief in the existence of truth. The general academic view is that truth is relative and that we each have a different truth. I don't believe that. There are enduring human truths and there's a way things are and a way things are not. You need to have the courage to write honestly and to cut through what I think are the endless layers of bullshit that people protect themselves with.

Lott's response accurately describes the airy, intellectual Aquarian's approach to life, giving them an air of detachment, and yet, what they are seeking is understanding emotions from a neutral perspective.

Actor, Matt Dillon, gives us a couple of Aquarian tidbits in an interview with *The Telegraph*, "Creatively I'm very fertile, but I'm not the best at distilling things." And, "I didn't become an actor to become famous." Aquarius has big ideas, especially when we find Mercury here, but doesn't care much for celebrity.

Scottish actor, David Paisley, who also as his Mars here, is known for playing roles with controversial sexual orientation issues. Aquarius and Mercury represent two of the most androgynous, asexual (or omni-sexual) parts of astrology.

Mercury in Pisces on the AS

Pisces is the sign of madness, depression, and merging. Mercury is in its detriment when in Pisces because it is difficult for humans to communicate to one another while underwater; we are air breathing creatures.

Maverick writer, Marguerite Duras's mental health issues are discussed in an article from *The New York Times*:

> Marguerite, herself, at age 12, had an emotional crisis serious enough to be called madness. After that, for the rest of her life, she was preoccupied by insanity and convinced that the world was fundamentally unjust.

One often communicates in a more obscure and less direct manner when Mercury is in Pisces, which Marguerite's writing style confirms. This is, of course, a very poetic and creative placement.

American old school rapper, Spyder-D, surprisingly, is the only singer who made this combination. Music is ruled by Pisces, and Mercury lends the voice to the music. One could also see an esoteric writer with this combination, and mediumship is almost guaranteed.

MERCURY

We will now look at the angle placements of Mercury throughout the zodiac from the point of view of the Imum Coeli (IC)

Mercury in Aries on the IC

As the IC is the place where we are the most private, here we find individuals with a most fruitful, agile, and mercurial mind. These individuals are fairly instinctual to their environments.

Who could have had more seeds of thought than the great artist and inventor, Leonardo da Vinci? He was a maverick in painting, anatomy, astronomy, sculpture, war machines, flying devices, etc. He did much of his work while left alone, as he was a very private person. His notes have been gathered together as various thematic codices and are all written backwards. At least two issues were resolved by his reverse writing: it reduced the smear caused by writing in the "wrong" direction, and it prevented others from easily stealing his notes and ideas.

Japanese Emperor, Hirohito, started his military career around the age of 13. When a rebellion broke out, he heard that it hadn't been squashed as quickly as he had ordered and said, "I myself will lead the Konoe Division and subdue them." There is no hesitation with these mavericks.

Jim Sharman, director of the *Rocky Horror Picture Show*, had a conversation with his parents when he was a teenager in which they were discussing the life of an entertainer. He said to his parents about a particular performance, "But no, there must have been somebody who imagined it up." And they said, "Yes, that is called a director." And he said, "That's what

I want to be." Mercury conjunct an Aries IC makes for a good instinctive director, indeed.

I have not yet included any animals, but these two demonstrate the archetype we are describing here in this section. Secretariat and Man o' War are two of the most long-standing and well-known thoroughbred racehorses of all time. They embody the lightening-like speed attainable with this astrological configuration.

Astro.com describes performer, Linda Troop, as "New Zealand twin, gay musician, and songwriter. She and her sister, Jools, are songwriters, musicians, entertainers who switch easily from one mode of song to another and from one identity to another on stage and on TV." This planetary arrangement definitely assists her with her musical proclivities.

Mercury in Taurus on the IC

These individuals have very fixed grounded beliefs, and they often hold these beliefs in private. They can communicate and affect a level of loyalty in their followers. This is especially evident when we consider this is the place of one's closely held values, as evidenced by our first two examples.

Who can forget the horrific belief structures that went south when cult leader, Jim Jones, took his flock of followers to Jonestown, Guyana, for a mass murder and suicide? 918 people died, of which nearly 300 were children.

World famous pianist and performer, Liberace, used this placement to not only have an opulent home, but also for the grounded routine and practice of his talent. Wikipedia writes,

"At age eight, he met Paderewski backstage after a concert at the Pabst Theatre in Milwaukee. 'I was intoxicated by the joy I got from the great virtuoso's playing. My dreams were filled with fantasies of following his footsteps... Inspired and fired with ambition, I began to practice with a fervor that made my previous interest in the piano look like neglect.'"

Massage therapist, Betsy Sultan, uses this placement to aid her as a gifted rolfer, which is a body-oriented therapy for structural integration. As Taurus is ruled by Venus, they both seek to create beautiful harmonious balance in the body.

The Greek myths speak of the brilliance Hermes (Mercury) exhibited in action and communication when he was just a child. This early ability is something that consistently shows itself when Mercury is involved, as we have seen by the countless examples already presented and again with our next example. Younger sister to Aretha, Carolyn Franklin showed a potent proclivity for singing, playing piano, and writing songs.

There is a sort of "birds of a feather flock together" aspect to people with planets on the angles, as shown by the Manson Family. Remember, the fourth house is where one usually finds the IC, and the fourth house is about family. Susan Atkins had the dubious distinction of not only being one of the family, but also of having been the longest surviving female California prison inmate. She converted her belief system to become a born-again Christian while incarcerated, subsequently working hard to make a difference in other people's lives. As Taurus has a bit of a stubborn streak, it is worth noting that she never apologized for her acts to the family of Sharon Tate. Taurus doesn't usually like to admit it is wrong.

Mercury in Gemini on the IC

Here we have the gift of the ruler of Gemini in its own sign, and what do we find? Two well-known singer/songwriters who both make our list a second time. These people are, through and through, communicators of the highest degree in their most private places: Burt Bacharach and KT Tunstall.

Burt once aptly stated, "I never like to be lied to by a girlfriend or agent and certainly not the president of the United States."

And KT Tunstall once said, "My songs examine and explore little specific emotions or situations or stories... They're kitchen table songs, like a conversation between me and one other person. It's almost like an alien has been sent to get emotional samples from human beings and put it all together on a record." She is one of the many examples of how other worlds are accessed through the IC.

Mercury in Cancer on the IC

These people are likely to have nurturing qualities or communication focused on home life.

From English entertainer, Bob Monkhouse's obituary in *The Independent*, "Cabaret and stand-up comedy were what [Bob] Monkhouse enjoyed best. He once said, 'I was a born club comic. Radio and TV and stage were fine, but I found my real home in cabaret.'"

MERCURY

American singer-songwriter, Harry Nilsson, wrote the very Cancer-on-the-IC song, "Think about your Troubles" whose lyrics are below:

>Sit beside the breakfast table
>Think about your troubles
>Pour yourself a cup of tea
>And think about the bubbles
>You can take your teardrops
>And drop them in a teacup
>Take them down to the riverside
>And throw them over the side
>To be swept up by a current
>And taken to the ocean
>To be eaten by some fishes
>Who were eaten by some fishes
>And swallowed by a whale
>Who grew so old
>He decomposed
>He died and left his body
>To the bottom of the ocean
>Now everybody knows
>That when a body decomposes
>The basic elements
>Are given back to the ocean
>And the sea does what it oughta
>And soon there's salty water
>(That's not too good for drinking)
>'Cause it tastes just like a teardrop
>(So they run it through a filter)

And it comes out from a faucet
(And is poured into a teapot)
Which is just about to bubble
Now think about your troubles.

Mercury in Leo on the IC

This placement gives a very direct, strong voice to a person. Individuals with a strong Leo signature are also known for their mane of hair.

It doesn't get better than this description for this astrological placement, "Maureen O'Hara was an Irish-born American actress and singer. The famously red-headed O'Hara was known for her beauty and playing fiercely passionate but sensible heroines, often in westerns and adventure films."

As Leo is the sign of royalty and privilege, it should be no surprise that we would have a diva, also known as a prima donna, with this astrological placement. Opera soprano, Kathleen Battle, is known for her big temperamental personality. Who better than a Leo to practice singing with that lovely lyrical phrase, "Me-me-me-*meeeeeeeee!*" Leo is the sign of independence and when, developmentally, the sense of self comes into the child's awareness. This is why Leo is a self-centering sign.

Next, is a lovely Leonine statement about an anarchist (who else is a Leo but an anarchist who is devoted to him or herself?). A very interesting ego here indeed:

Stuart Christie, since 1962, has been an active anarchist, through writing, publishing and action. The Glaswegian author of *Granny Made Me an Anarchist, General Franco Made Me A Terrorist,* and *Edward Heath Made Me Angry* (his entertaining and inspiring three-part autobiography).

Mercury in Virgo on the IC

Virgo is ruled by Mercury. We find that when a person has a planet on an earth angle, there is often an affinity with sports.

Our first example has a world record for running. American middle-distance runner, Mary Decker, was known as Little Mary Decker for her pigtailed sporting running style and she hated losing. Virgo does not like being judged or criticized for being less than perfect, that is reserved for the Virgo her/himself.

Brigadier General John W. Donaldson was accused of killing Vietnamese civilians from a helicopter, but was acquitted. Was he doing what he was told? What sort of consequences might he have experienced going forward?

Mercury in Libra on the IC

The IC represents a place of great depths in the individual. With this placement, the individuals are gifted with the ability to share their inner worlds and experiences in beautifully articulated ways. Expressing and experiencing polarized relationships are especially highlighted here.

Australian author, adventurer, and photographer, Alan Villiers, who also has his moon here, wrote about his relationship to sea faring vessels and the ocean.

Another writer, no surprise as we are speaking of Mercury in an air sign, to appear in our list a second time is English writer, Evelyn Waugh, who wrote *Brideshead Revisited* as a memoir to the homosexual relationships in his youth.

And a coincidence here? I think not. Our next example, English actor, Jeremy Irons, played Evelyn as the character, Charles Ryder, the attractive, brooding and deeply relatable role in the movie version of *Brideshead Revisited*. Jeremy doesn't shy away from challenging parts, whether as a young gay man in the aforementioned movie or as a confused heterosexual man in *Madame Butterfly*.

Another writer, supernatural author, Stephen King, also makes the list. Stephen brings us into relationship with what we fear deep down inside. Whether it is a rabid dog, a possessed classic car, a writer who goes mad, loved ones brought back to life, or any of his other shocking stories of frightening relationships, he definitely has no shortage of stories floating in his mind.

American musician, Hank Williams, had a very short, yet sweet country music career. While he had no formal training, he was one of the mavericks of country music and is a beautiful example of the theory of this book. While there is not much material available about Hank, this tidbit from PBS.org shows one of the primary issues of any Libra being of two minds or two personalities:

Luke the Drifter walked with Hank Williams and talked through him. If Hank Williams could be headstrong and willful, a backslider and a reprobate, then Luke the Drifter was compassionate and moralistic, capable of dispensing all the sage advice that Hank Williams ignored. Luke the Drifter had seen it all, yet could still be moved to tears by a chance encounter on his travels. Although little known in comparison with the hits, the "Luke the Drifter" narrations were the closest Hank Williams came to bearing his soul.

In addition to the writers and singers in this category, we also have the celebrated Italian movie composer, Ennio Morricone, who appears for a second time in our pages. Ennio wrote no less than 450 movie musical scores, and made his mark originally with the old spaghetti westerns of the 1960's, such as *The Good Bad and the Ugly* and *A Fistful of Dollars*.

Mercury in Scorpio on the IC

Here we have a richly intense communicator with deep thoughts and the ability to ask the deeper questions of life and the universe.

First off, we have astrologer, Michel Gauquelin, who used the deeply questioning nature of this position to ask, "Does Astrology work?" Michael found the answers to prove it does, and that it can indicate statistically significant influence on people's lives. Thanks to his maverick abilities, you have this book in your hands.

Richard Carpenter and Ted Bundy (our next example, below) are an interesting pair. Richard Carpenter, of the singing duo The Carpenters, was the record producer, arranger, pianist, keyboardist, occasional lyricist, and composer. Richard joined with his sister, Karen, on harmony vocals. Their music was filled with love and longing with a Scorpionic flavor. Richard was referred to by music critic, Daniel Levitin, as "one of the most gifted arrangers to emerge in popular music."

Ted Bundy, on the other hand, "was intelligent, charming, handsome, and polite. He had a degree in psychology and was studying law. He had worked at a suicide crisis hotline as well as on a number of political campaigns. He was also a necrophiliac serial killer who claimed the lives of at least 30 young women" and this comes from worstserialkillers.blogspot.com. I would also recommend visiting http://channelingerik.com/channeling-ted-bundy-part-one/ for an interesting view on Ted Bundy, and there are additional shows with recorded audio interviews available on Netflix.

I appreciate the juxtaposition of these two men who used their ability to manipulate people and their feelings with their words. In addition to Ted's retrograde Mercury in Scorpio, he also had a retrograde Venus and Jupiter conjunct this point. This would have given Ted an incredibly charismatic and magnetic personality.

Speaking of individuals with the power to manipulate with words, we have Joseph Goebbels, the German Nazi propagandist in charge of all public media for the Reich. Goebbels was adept at manipulating the German public as well as the rest of the world while the Nazi atrocities were carried out.

Businessman, William Henry Vanderbilt presents another perspective of these archetypes. Scorpio is the sign of other people's resources and inheritance and the IC is usually in the fourth house of family. Vanderbilt took his family's money and built it into something even bigger. This is not usually the case for individuals who inherit wealth.

English actor, Roger Moore's character as James Bond, the suave British secret intelligence agent, is a perfect representation of this astrological configuration.

Mercury in Sagittarius on the IC

These people often have "hoof in mouth disease." There is a lack of filtering which often occurs when Mercury is in Sagittarius—some say this happens with any Sagittarian placement. People do not understand the innocence from which their expression comes. For these reasons we understand Mercury is in its fall when in Sagittarius.

Canadian writer, George Bowering's book of poetry is entitled, *Changing on the Fly* which addresses the amazing mutability available for this astrological placement. George made his maverick mark as Canada's first Parliamentary poet laureate.

English soccer forward, Michael Owen, in an interview for Guardian.com made the following statement about the freedom he has found in retirement:

"At times during my career it has been difficult to express an opinion for a variety of reasons," he goes on to add, "Close family and friends always tell me I am very opinionated so it will be nice to be able to express my views."

The fact that Owen was able to control his Sagittarian communication style while working is admirable.

Another Canadian poet, John Glassco, is also a memoirist and novelist. He is best known for his somewhat adjusted autobiography, *Memoirs of Montparnasse*. Glassco's travels gave him a deeper relationship with himself through his writings.

Well-known Australian politician, Cheryl Kernot, has since moved onto other more meaningful Sagittarian pursuits. She is the Director of Social Business at the Centre for Social Impact, University of New South Wales where she teaches and works to support and guide projects which are for the greater good.

Mercury in Capricorn on the IC

Both of our examples are included a second time and they both have the Sun conjunct this position.

American singer, Bobbie Nelson, older sister of Willie Nelson, shows an example of the patience of Capricorn and the time necessary to mature. Bobbie produced her first solo album *Autobiography* when she was 76 years old!

Denzel Washington is a highly successful actor. He out shines and communicates consistently, whether at home or out in the world. The opposite angle from the IC, the MC, is

Cancer. Denzel is also known for his strong authoritative voice, another Capricorn trait.

Mercury in Aquarius on the IC

These people communicate their humanitarian ideals.

Singer, songwriter, and lead guitarist for The Beatles, George Harrison, appears on our list a second time. The Aquarian archetype can be overly focused on the small and petty. RollingStone.com writes the following about Harrison:

> The songs he wrote focused on both the glory of God and the petty annoyances of day-to-day life.

Surprisingly enough, George has a Scorpio Moon conjunct his AS, as does our next example American actress, Bernadette Peters.

Aquarius is the sign of originality, where one can only be who one actually is, and Bernadette's quote from BrainyQuotes.com, captures the spirit of this astrological placement:

> "You've gotta be original, because if you're like someone else, what do they need you for?"

An interview from theGuardian.com writes about professional tennis player, Mary Pierce, and is a lovely description demonstrating what Mercury can do in creating the link between our past restraints and our future freedom:

Pierce laughs softly again, as if she wants to make it up to that little girl who was shouted at so often, who dreamed of becoming a pediatrician but ended up, instead, as a professional tennis player who finally broke free and learned the art of happiness.

Mercury in Pisces on the IC

Pisces is the last sign of the zodiac in the darkest position of the chart. This is where one is connected to All-That-Is.

Well, there is no surprise that we have Australian media mogul, Rupert Murdoch appear again as this astrological placement is joined by his Sun. Pisces is the realm of emotions and how we are all linked together in the sea of humanity. Rupert built an information empire by entertaining millions, if not billions, of people in their homes.

Scottish actor of film and stage, Ian Richardson's performance is crisply stated by theGuardian.com when they write he "grasped the imagination". Mercury gives us the ability to dive deep within ourselves especially in the sign of Pisces at the midnight point.

Renowned astrologer, Bernadette Brady, uses this placement to peer deep into the darkest realm, the midnight sky, and then creates a dialogue from there to share with everyone. Brady's work involves fixed stars and answering the deeper questions of the cosmos as a person with this placement would do.

MERCURY

We will now look at the angle placements of Mercury throughout the zodiac from the point of view of the Descendant (DS)

Mercury in Aries on the DS

These people have a very direct communication style.

The photographer and only WWII female war correspondent, Lee Miller, has so many elements of Mercury conjunct her Aries DS, I cannot even begin to write it all for how much space it will take. I highly recommend further research on her if you are so inclined, especially the article in Telegraph.co.uk, in which Pat Parker's opening paragraph shows some of the themes very clearly:

> Lee Miller's life was as extraordinary as her photos. A Twenties fashion model who became a Surrealist and later the only female combat photographer in Europe during the war, she documented the liberation of Dachau and Buchenwald concentration camps.

Lee Miller's was a life of instinctual response to what life had to offer. Her sexual issues began when she was raped at age seven and contracted gonorrhea.

Another quote, from Miller's son, Antony, from the same article, draws attention to other Aries/Mercury/relationship connections very clearly:

The GIs liked her—they saw her as a good buddy," Antony goes on to say, "She could swear as well as they could, and put up with being under fire.

Look up the photograph taken of Lee in Adolf Hitler's bathtub.

American rocker, Wolfgang Van Halen, makes our list for a second time as his Moon is here. His famous father used him as the impetus to start (Aries) many projects. We can see Wolfgang was already having an impact on music before he even played to the public. From Wikipedia, we learn the following:

> Wolfgang had an indirect impact on his father's career from the very beginning of his life. The instrumental "316" was named in his honor, after Wolfgang's birthday. For a 13-year period ending in 2004, Eddie Van Halen collaborated with Peavey on a line of guitars, the Wolfgang series, named after his son. In 2008, his father named a custom guitar after him, the Fender EVH Wolfgang. In early 2008, Wolfgang appeared on the cover of the April issue of *Guitar World* with his father, in the magazine's first father-son issue.

The New York Times describes the association between American poet, Lawrence Ferlinghetti, and his agent, that speaks to the cardinal Aries energy:

> Now, they stand as two of the last living links to the Beat Generation. From opposite coasts, they fueled a literary movement that defined the era and ushered

in a new populist, countercultural strain of poetry and fiction.

Mercury in Taurus on the DS

These people have a grounded and magnetic way of movement and communication.

American actor and athlete, Johnny Weissmuller, most well known for playing Tarzan in the 1930s, was also a five-time Olympic gold medal swimmer. Johnny's charisma and Olympian body were definite assets in getting the title role in *Tarzan*.

In the NewYorkTimes.com article announcing her death, comes this fitting quote from Katharine Hepburn. While very cultured, this Connecticut Yankee had a bit of a bull-in-the-china-cabinet way about her. Hepburn was a most determined maverick as only a Taurean can be:

> "Of those early years," she said: "I strike people as peculiar in some way, although I don't quite understand why. Of course, I have an angular face, an angular body and, I suppose, an angular personality, which jabs into people."

American actor, Tyrone Power, exhibits another aspect of the Taurus archetype: enjoyment of the physical plane. This excerpt is from gayinfluence.blogspot.com, shows us why:

The busy Hollywood social life, the smoking, drinking, all night parties and other excesses were beginning to take their toll. He ignored the signs that he might have a weak heart like his father and continued to live as he always had. While filming *Solomon and Sheba* (1958), he did his own stunts and worked outside in the grueling sun, often in heavy armor. One afternoon on the set in Spain, during a dueling scene with George Sanders involving heavy swords, Tyrone collapsed. He'd suffered a massive heart attack and died before anything could be done. He was 44 years old."

Live well, die young and leave a lovely corpse ...

Mercury in Gemini on the DS

Here we have people who have an ease of communication with a sort of lyrical view and understanding of the other.

Who do we have up first? The musical poet of the 1960's, Bob Dylan. While one would expect people with this placement to have a sort of verbal diarrhea, Bob Dylan is just the opposite. His words are precise (albeit sometimes unintelligible), as evidenced from a rare and unusual article about Dylan from the *Rolling Stone* in 1969:

> Bob was very cautious in everything he said, and took a long time between questions to phrase exactly what he wanted to say, nothing more and sometimes a little

less. When I wasn't satisfied with his answers, I asked the questions another way, later. But Bob was hip.

Dylan is referred to as secretive and elusive, traits one would not expect from a person with Mercury in Gemini, but remember that Gemini has at least two faces.

American actress, Katherine Helmond, is probably best known for her air-headed character in the 1970's TV series *Soap*. This show brought many challenging social topics to the American public in a humorous way that encouraged discussion about how to be in relationship with others even when we don't understand.

Installation artist, Anya Gallacio, uses this playful astrological arrangement to have objects interact with time and space as they shift and become something else each day.

English inventor, Alan Blumlein, used this, with the aid of Pluto nearby and Mars on his MC in Libra, was an electronics engineers as well as a senior sound engineer. We are talking about a significant focus on thought and communication here, and as Mercury rules Gemini, we can understand how Alan could be such a prolific inventor and researcher, especially with the aid of Pluto.

Mercury in Cancer on the DS

These individuals communicate about family or clan and our relationship to the other.

English playwright, Edward Bond, wrote plays that brought forth the more challenging parts of society and how we need to communicate and be in relationship to and with them.

An article in the Independent.co.uk about Afro-Caribbean author and politician, Aimé Césaire begins:

The most influential Francophone Caribbean writer of his generation, Aimé Césaire was one of the founding fathers of Negritude, the black consciousness movement that sought to assert pride in African cultural values to counterbalance the inferior status accorded to them in European colonial thinking.

The article ends with:

> On his death, the French president, Nicolas Sarkozy, praised Césaire as a "great poet" and a "great humanist."

Aimé Césaire is an example of communicating (Mercury) the importance of one's clan being recognized in a wholly familiar way. Additional key elements of this astrological combination are stated in the article:

> [Césaire]... he also identified with his island's repressed African culture, sometimes likening himself to the figure of the griot, the oral storyteller who serves as the repository of West African communities' histories and traditions.

Mercury in Leo on the DS

Leo is the sign of creativity and self-expression as it is the natural ruler of the fifth house.

From BrooklynRail.org, comes a lovely expression of this placement in the life of Italian avant-garde Italian artist, Piero Manzoni. The article goes on to observe:

> Manzoni was a Colossus who took giant steps each year of his creative output. When he tired of producing relics from the body, he presented the days of a monthly calendar as art, reminding us of the course of diurnal existence. In another work, he reproduced an enlarged thumbprint as a metaphorical labyrinth in which the human imprint symbolizes all that we consider ethical, even in times of dehabilitation and nausea. Life goes on. It persists like art, in a way, but they are never exactly the same. This idea was more or less consistent throughout Manzoni's career.

Manzoni has Venus here as well. The seemingly aggrandized presentation of the individual is represented in his artwork.

American actress, Shauna Sand, used this placement to be a Playboy Bunny.

ASTROLOGICAL MAVERICKS

Mercury in Virgo on the DS

As Mercury rules Virgo, there is a natural affinity to this position. These people draw from a vast and readily available array of resources to make an impact on others.

As Virgo is the sign of womanhood, I found this moving interview with British actress, Pauline Collins, for theGuardian.com in which she shares about the child she had to give up for adoption:

> In 1992, Collins published a book, *Letter to Louise*, a beautifully written account of her childhood and early adulthood leading up to the adoption. Some of the tenderest passages come when she is in the convent with other girls who found themselves dealing with the issues of pregnancy. "I remember the last time I saw you," she writes to Louise. "We were about six feet apart ... Every day of my life, I've relived that moment, replayed each second like a book of flicker pictures, clinging frame by frame to the last images of you ... Why did I give you away? Now in 1992, I still feel a blow in the solar plexus when I consider that question. I feel as if my soul is punched out through my throat. Now in 1992, I cannot understand why I did that terrible thing, why I didn't look harder for another solution."

Olympic Gold Medal winner, track and field great, Edwin Moses, uses this placement to be a trailblazing runner. We see a lot of sports action when Mercury is on an earthly angle.

American singer, Whitney Houston, had a range of musical talent and abilities that beautifully expressed this placement.

Mercury in Libra on the DS

These people address the issues of give and take in any relationship.

Our first example, American automotive executive, Lee Iacocca, used his skills to "speak to" all sides involved in the issues he resolved for both Ford and Chrysler. Unfortunately, Lee passed during the editing of this book.

Olympic medal winning ice skater, Nancy Kerrigan, illustrates the polarities involved with the Libran archetype. Nancy was known for her graceful ability to glide through the air on ice, and was also known for the problematic relationship between her and American figure skater, Tonya Harding.

Mercury in Scorpio on the DS

Here we are in the deep places, where Mercury easily travels in the chart to be in relationship to and with the other. Mercury is free to seek out different places where others are unable to go.

Remarkably enough, as we saw when Mercury was in Scorpio on the IC and we found Ted Bundy, and here we have another well-known sociopath, Charles Manson. Both of these individuals used their means of communicating to manipulate and exercise power over other people—especially women. Charles used his powers on men as well.

On the other side of the spectrum, we have integrity-based American journalist, Dan Rather. He took up the banner to expose the lies that were spun as truth from President Trump and his administration. Scorpio gives Mercury ruthlessness in its pursuit of what truly lies within, as is further exhibited by our next example.

American actress and singer, Miley Cyrus, who also has her sensitive Moon here, communicates the ways in which it is NOT ok to treat others. Miley's music has a fierce intensity which is fueled by this placement.

Mercury in Sagittarius on the DS

As we already know, Mercury is in its detriment when in Sagittarius. These people have to be very careful not to use their "truth" to manipulate or coerce others to their side.

Known for his outlandishly huge mane of hair (often wigs), record producer, musician, songwriter, and businessman, Phil Spector, used this placement to make a successful recording career. Unfortunately, in the end he was imprisoned for murdering a woman. It appears Mr. Spector (gotta love the name, right?), was good at telling others what he wanted, but wasn't so good at listening or caring what others had to say. This can be an issue for those with this astrological placement. Many women came forth at his trial and attested to the fact that Phil couldn't "hear" a woman tell him *no*. He used a gun to coerce the last woman as his words didn't work and that resulted in her death and him in prison. Phil Spector does not have an easy chart.

Wikipedia.com writes this about Australian footballer and coach, Kevin Sheedy who received acclaim, "for his unusual and creative approaches to promoting the club and the game ... Sheedy is also noted for his quirky antics, outspoken nature and wry sense of humour."

Sagittarius thinks outside of the box because it doesn't see the box! As the seeker of truth and higher philosophies as well as one of the wandering travelers, Sagittarius is one of the most optimistic signs with a real, "you can do it" idealism. Sagittarius is ruled by expansive, optimistic and buoyant Jupiter. I like to think of Sagittarius as the cheerleader of the zodiac.

Mercury in Capricorn on the DS

These people speak to a practicality within the social structures of relationship to others.

Maverick and head of the Catholic Church, Pope Francis, created quite a stir within and without the Catholic Church. He has initiated more practical and pragmatic relationship between the Church and its members. Pope Francis shows a healthy relationship with his rarified religious status without losing connection with himself. Unlike his predecessors, he does not take advantage of the vast benefits his position affords him. When Pluto transits through Capricorn (as it did when Francis became Pope), the Catholic Church goes through major transformations of death and rebirth. King Henry VIII of England, and German theologian, Martin Luther, are two examples, so it is no surprise that the College of Cardinals picked a man with Pluto in Cancer to be the father of the Church. Pope Francis will have his Pluto opposition when he is 87.

Technical editor and one-time astrologer, Geoffrey Dean, became a skeptic. Dean uses grounded and pragmatic Capricorn energy to articulate his views to question the validity of astrology.

Mercury in Aquarius on the DS

This placement can give the mind and/or body the wings it seeks to glide through time and space. This can be a good placement for a philosopher.

Eddie Arcaro, known as the greatest American thoroughbred jockey of all time, has the unique distinction of winning the U.S. Triple Crown twice. At just five feet, two inches tall, he was born three months early. Remember that with Mercury here on the DS, it is opposite the AS, hence speedy/early birth cannot wait to get out and go! When Mercury is in Aquarius, it gathers knowledge from far and wide.

American jazz musician, John Handy, spent many years learning and practicing music and shares the musical wisdom he gained with his community. The following comes from MercuryNews.com:

Handy has been a pillar of the Bay Area music scene, focusing much of his efforts on education. He's taught at Stanford, Berkeley and other local schools. SF State even has a John Handy Scholarship program. Now, he's being recognized by SFJAZZ, receiving the organization's prestigious "Beacon Award," the annual trophy given out to a person who has been instrumental in helping jazz music survive in the Bay Area.

In an interview for Telegraph.uk, we have English actress, Julie Walters in her own words:

"Drama should have a place in schools. It helps with communication, vocabulary, and understanding of yourself and of the wider world. Socially, politically it is really good for kids, and I think it's philistinic—is that a word?—not to have it on the syllabus. All the parts I've played have given me a voice and fired up my imagination, and without imagination the world doesn't move forward, does it?"

This is a lovely use of this astrological placement.

Mercury in Pisces on the DS

These people have a d2reamy accessible way of communicating.

American actress, Doris Day, makes our list a second time and was known for her engaging, yet slightly "blond" characters. Pisces can feel the pain of others and are known for their sympathetic and empathic natures. With this astrological placement there can be an ability to communicate with others at whatever level or form they may be.

Our next example, American musician, Kurt Cobain, was the lead singer of the rock band, Nirvana. Hello Pisces!! Kurt's life was full of many Piscean themes and this Mercury is opposed to Pluto on his Virgo AS! Suicide, consciousness altering drug use, singing, and imagery are all tied up in this last sign of the zodiac. When on the DS, this will be experienced through attempts to merge with others. One may understand how consciousness altering substance can play a part in the feeling of merging.

Joan Quigley was best known for being former First Lady, Nancy Reagan's astrologer. Joan communicated with the planets, one and all, and communicated what Nancy Reagan needed to know while using her intuitive senses. Joan was also kept behind the scenes and out of sight from the public awareness, in a typical Piscean way.

American actor, Van Williams, in another lovely representation of this astrological placement, was best known for his title role as the masked avenger, Green Hornet in the 1960's television series. The Pisces/Virgo axis is about service and therefore saving.

We will now look at the angle placements of Mercury throughout the zodiac from the point of view of the Medium Coeli (MC)

Mercury in Aries on the MC

These individuals appear to the world as leaders.

With his Moon already here, Carl Gustaf XVI, King of Sweden, is a perfect example of how a king can be relatable to his people in a very personal manner.

Poet, Edwin Morgan, used this astrological position to be a leader in Scottish poetry as one of the "Seven Poets." This was the headline for his obit in TheGuardian.com:

> Scotland's national poet, he combined intellectual curiosity with emotional power.

Incidentally, Edwin also has Venus close to this, which adds to the emotional force of his writing.

Mercury in Taurus on the MC

These people communicate about form, values, and sensuality. Taurus is ruled by Venus, who is one of Mercury's closest planetary allies and neighbors.

American actress, Uma Thurman, self reflects in an interview from WMagazine.com. Note that the comments point to a couple of Taurean traits, such as being a sex symbol as well as the loyalty she expresses to her closest friends:

> "I look at Uma and I see someone who was thrust into the limelight as an object of desire when she was 18," she says, referencing the famous scene in Thurman's first major film, The Adventures of Baron Munchausen, in which she emerges nude from a giant seashell. "That's really young to get attention in that way." Any aloofness Thurman may project, Katherine Dieckmann, director, says, is a "coping mechanism." Adds the director, "She does not take a lot of people into her inner circle, but the people she does take in she would lay down in front of a train for. She's just selective about where she directs her energies."

The oldest son of Irish poet and playwright, Oscar Wilde, Cyril Holland, didn't live a long life, so there is not much to find out about him. Fortunately, Cyril wrote a letter to his brother that remains for posterity. In regards to his father and the family name, Cyril writes in a very Taurean manner:

> My great incentive has been to wipe (the) stain away; to retrieve, if may be, by some action of mine, a name no longer honoured in the land. The more I thought of this, the more convinced I became that, first and foremost, I must be a man. ... I am no wild, passionate, irresponsible hero. I live by thought, not by emotion. I ask nothing better than to end in honourable battle for my King and Country.

Cyril, the son, sought to make some sort of amends for the sins of his father.

From in an interview with Soulhead.com, American singer, Nicole Willis talks about her songwriting process which well describes this astrological placement, and highlights the maverick collaboration possible with this placement:

> "For *Happiness in Every Style*, we discussed briefly how we would write in the studio together, which is what we did. The band would literally be jamming and I sat there and wrote lyrics while they jammed, asked them to make new parts if they hadn't already, etc. I guess I first started singing melodies, then wrote words as mentioned before. We worked really quickly like this and it turned out a pretty positive experience. It was totally new to work this way and I think all are happy with the results."

Mercury in Gemini on the MC

Mercury rules Gemini, so this is a powerful "talking piece" placement. These people seek equal relating: being neither above nor below anyone else. Our first three examples also have their Sun conjunct this placement, which further amplifies the energies involved.

American-born French entertainer, Josephine Baker, has a couple of lovely quotes that perfectly address this astrological placement:

"You must get an education. You must go to school, and you must learn to protect yourself. And you must learn to protect yourself with the pen, and not the gun."

"All my life, I have maintained that the people of the world can learn to live together in peace if they are not brought up in prejudice."

We will use an aspect of American jazz singer, Peggy Lee's life to expose a possible dilemma here. The native can talk in circles in an attempt to get us to see their point of view. A NYTimes.com review of the biography on Peggy Lee, perfectly illustrates the double sided Gemini nature:

> James Gavin's eminently readable biography, *Is That All There Is?: The Strange Life of Peggy Lee*, has one aspect of decided strangeness itself. The book could have been called *Peggy Lee Was a Big, Fat Liar*. If the scores of people Gavin interviewed are to be believed, Lee, who died in 2002 at 81, invented health problems (before she had real ones), claimed credit for songs she didn't write, built lawsuits on outrageously fabricated events and made up two of the major elements of her mythology: that Lee's stepmother beat her and that Lee and her first husband had decided to remarry right before he died.

English musician and songwriter, Paul McCartney, has this lovely quote from his lyrics, revealing the higher consciousness

Gemini, "In the end, the love you take is equal to the love you make."

There is another theme at work here illustrated by artist, John Olsen's journey: starting out on the fringe as the other and eventually becoming that which is the norm. We can see this transformation working in the lives of Josephine Baker, Paul McCartney, as well as John Olsen. This is the equilibrium to which I alluded to earlier—equal relating: being neither above nor below anyone else.

Metallurgist, goldsmith, and sculptor, Alfred Gilbert was part of the New Sculpture movement of the late 19th century in Britain which helped to revitalize sculpture.

Former Republican Louisiana Governor, Bob Jindal, has these illustrative quotes for this astrological position:

"The politically correct crowd is tolerant of all viewpoints, except those they disagree with."

"Immigration without assimilation is an invasion."

"I am so tired of the left trying to divide us by race. One of the things I said today in my speech, we're not Indian-Americans, African-Americans, Irish-Americans, rich Americans, poor Americans. We're all Americans."

Mercury in Cancer on the MC

These people communicate clan, family, and home to the world.

As former First Lady, Nancy Reagan, also has her Sun here, we covered what she did to the White House, the home of the American people. During her life, Nancy spoke directly to home values and ideals, especially with her "Just say No" to drugs campaign.

American actor, Harrison Ford, represented our clan of humanity to the aliens in the *Star Wars* series of movies. He said this quote, which addresses part of this astrological configuration:

> "There comes a point when you've exhausted your opportunities playing good guys. I've been around long enough, I think I'm entitled to explore a bit. But what I saw there was an opportunity to play a character different from what the audience's expectation was. A chance to take their crude experience of me – of my iconography, if you will – and turn it on its ear at an appropriate juncture in the film to be useful to the process of telling the story."

Mercury loves the story and the journey!

Professional tennis player, Arthur Ashe, who makes our list a third time and also has his Sun here, had this written about him for his obituary in NYTimes.com:

> As an avid golfer, prominent speaker, occasional columnist for *The Washington Post*, television commentator for HBO and ABC, author of a three-volume history of the black athlete in America, and a noted participant in countless civic projects and

protests, Ashe hardly went into retreat in the four years that followed his AIDS diagnosis.

Mercury doesn't sit still!

While singer, songwriter and philanthropist, Cat Stevens, is obviously known as for his homey sensitive ballads, he is also known for converting to Islam and walking away from much of his musical career. Being of Swedish and Greek descent and raised in London, Yusuf Islam (his name), lives a life of expressing the values of the human clan as opposed to his birth clan.

For an interesting view of Mercury in Cancer, consider Australians, Amanda and Stephen Mays, the first test tube twins. These twins started as eggs fertilized outside of the body and then placed inside the mother. Here, Mercury acts as an inseminator for a new conception of human life in the family!

Mercury in Leo on the MC

As we know, Leo loves the stage and being seen. There is a quick fiery wit with Mercury in this position which is readily seen and experienced by the world. These are fiery and vocal individuals.

American comedian and entertainer, Red Skelton, who most people born after 1975 would not even remember, has this lovely Leonine quote:

> "I just want to be known as a clown, because to me that's the height of my profession. It means you can do everything—sing, dance and above all, make people laugh."

When Leo operates from its heart, the gift to others is unimaginable. Red said he felt that when he made people laugh, he was doing his divine work.

Canadian Democratic politician, Jack Layton, made this lovely quote two days before his passing:

> "My friends, love is better than anger. Hope is better than fear. Optimism is better than despair. So let us be loving, hopeful and optimistic. And we'll change the world."

American actor and comedian, Robin Williams, used this placement to make the amazing film *What Dreams May Come*. Mercury as psychopomp for the family is one of the many beautiful themes in the movie. I highly recommend it.

I am going to do a little interesting extrapolation with our next example, American fashion photographer, Herb Ritts, who makes our list a second time. If we think of the fire and the stage presence of Leo, we can see that Herb was an expert at catching that tantalizing "spark" of stage presence, whether in the case of his homoerotic male nude photographs or in his photographic images of the famous.

Mercury in Virgo on the MC

Here again, we have the ruler of Virgo in its own sign. These are people with amazing resources.

Virgo seeks perfection, which is readily apparent with our first example, professional road racing cyclist, Lance Armstrong. His pursuit of perfection "encouraged" him to win the Tour de France, not once, but *seven times!* We know the cost of his desire for perfection involved performance enhancing hormones that most likely improved his ability to win. Lance was unabashedly proud of his wins and didn't feel as though he was acting in a questionable manner. This unbranded sense of Mercury is a good clear example of the dynamic this book is addressing.

Ben Cohen, the handsome and adept English rugby player, uses his affluence and influence to combat bullying and homophobia. Virgo is the sign of service and Ben uses this gifted place to help others.

Mercury in Libra on the MC

Libra is the sign of right human relationship and Virgo is the sign of perfected service so we can see how there is a cross over.

Ian Thorpe, Olympic Swimmer, broke 22 world records by the time he was 24 years old. It is interesting that he shows a similar archetypal response to this placement like Ben Cohen, in that Ian is also using his fame and celebrity to address bullying issues and to advance gay awareness. We can also see how Mercury aided them in their respective sporting professions.

Libra is a Cardinal sign and therefore focused on initiating and then moving on to start something else. English-Australian actor, Peter Finch, who also has his Sun here, addresses the restlessness of Mercury on the professional angle in an interview:

> "It would be ghastly if you got yourself into one of those three—year things. I think after three months your performance must deteriorate. That's why I prefer movies—three or four months and you are finished. I like to change steps if I can. You stultify as an actor if you get stuck in groove."

Mercury in Scorpio on the MC

Mercury is at home in Pluto's underworld domain. Mercury never fears plumbing the depths, especially when in Scorpio.

As psychopomp, Mercury help us transcend time, space, emotion, and other dimensions to find the truth lodged deeply therein and then, brings it back to the world, like a master pearl diver. This can also be a placement for someone who will tell you anything to get exactly what s/he wants—a powerfully manipulative person.

Actor, Henry Winkler, known for his role as the television character "The Fonz" suffered humiliation and shame for his dyslexia. Winkler is now a staunch advocate for helping others understand this speech issue that is relatively common in about 20% of the population, but remains hidden. Henry is using his years of self-work to help bring the pearls of his hard-earned experience to others.

Lady Carol Kidu, a former Papua New Guinea Member of Parliament and Minister for Community Development, was the sole female representative for a decade before her retirement in 2012. She is a tireless advocate (Mercury in Scorpio – highly protective) for women and children.

American newscaster, Robin Roberts, shared her breast cancer and bone marrow disease called myelodysplastic syndrome (MDS) experiences with the world on *Good Morning America*. She addressed her personal deep healing processes, and because she broadcasted it out to the world, she increased awareness of these health issues for a much larger audience. In regards specifically to her MDS, Wikipedia states:

> Be the Match Registry, a nonprofit organization run by the National Marrow Donor Program, experienced a 1,800% spike in donors the day Roberts went public with her illness.

That is the amazing transpersonal power of this placement and is similar to what fellow maverick Katie Couric was able to do with colonoscopies.

Mercury in Sagittarius on the MC

Here we have the perfect placement for a preacher! This is also a very optimistic placement for Mercury and the spreading of truth or Truth. Truth can be expressed from a manipulative position or it can be used to express high philosophical Truths.

Our first example of this placement is American minister, Jim Bakker, who at one time was a well-known TV evangelist. Jim and his wife Tammy Faye-Bakker, were the reigning king and queen of the TV Evangelist world. Jim began to sell half-truths and was probably believing his own stories enabling him to rationalize selling false time shares. A salesperson with this placement could sell ice to a snow man!

In singer Carl Wilson's obituary, the LATimes.com headline reads, "His voice helped form the1ilemma of being in its fall. They say things that one should not say and act in ways that others may not find funny or entertaining. For a good review, I suggest the 2011 interview Christina gave to WMagazine.com writer, Lynn Hirschberg. The lyrics for her song "Beautiful" perfectly capture this astrological placement, "You are beautiful, no matter what they say."

Mercury in Capricorn on the MC

Capricorn is comfortable on the MC as this is its natural placement. Like a nimble mountain goat, Capricorn "knows" where the little pieces of rock jut out from the mountainside just enough to give them the footing to make the trek all the way to the top.

Our first example, American writer, Henry Miller, made a list of 11 writing commandments (which yours truly is appreciating right about now!) as a means to attain success in each writing endeavor:

1. Work on one thing at a time until finished.
2. Start no more new books, add no more new material to *Black Spring*.
3. Don't be nervous. Work calmly, joyously, recklessly on whatever is in hand.
4. Work according to Program and not according to mood. Stop at the appointed time!
5. When you can't create you can work.
6. Cement a little every day, rather than add new fertilizers.
7. Keep human! See people, go places, drink if you feel like it.
8. Don't be a draught-horse! Work with pleasure only.
9. Discard the Program when you feel like it—but go back to it next day. Concentrate. Narrow down. Exclude.
10. Forget the books you want to write. Think only of the book you are writing.
11. Write first and always. Painting, music, friends, cinema, all these come afterwards.

American actor, Joe Pesci, shows another aspect of the Capricorn pursuit of work perfection. Pesci is type cast as a career mobster. He made only 6 films in 20 years and we know who he is. Don't let his size full you! Capricorn is painfully aware of what is needed to succeed. Here's what Joe says from Brainyquote.com:

"I love to star in movies, but I want to have good roles. It doesn't help to get starring roles in something that's no good. I mean, that will just kill you."

Convicted murderer, Lyle Menendez only makes our list once, whereas his brother and accomplice, Erik, is in here a few times. Lyle stated in his interview while in prison:

"I am the kid that did kill his parents, and no river of tears has changed that and no amount of regret has changed it." Lyle Menendez told ABCNews.com, "I accept that. You are often defined by a few moments of your life, but that's not who you are in your life, you know. Your life is your totality of it… You can't change it. You just, you're stuck with the decisions you made."

Capricorn deals with the consequences of action and usually works to make the right decisions in the first place. Lyle is a perfect example of a Capricorn reaching for the glory without doing the work to make it possible. Capricorn doesn't succeed that way.

British Politician, Ed Miliband, who makes our list a second time, had this to say about his view on his pragmatic approach to politics:

"I am not from central casting," he said in a speech last year. "You can find people who are more square-jawed, more chiseled, look less like Wallace. You could probably even find people who look better eating a bacon sandwich. If you want the politician from central casting, it's just not me, it's the other guy. And if you want a politician who thinks that a good photo is the most important thing, then don't vote for me. Because I don't. Here's the thing: I believe that people would quite like somebody to stand up and say there is more to politics than the photo-op."

We cannot have a more beautiful example of Mercury in Capricorn on the MC than cyclist climber, Marco Pantani. From an article in Bicycling.com comes the following:

> Marco Pantani stood apart. Even among these frail seraphs—a group prone to exposed nerve endings and thrilling, evanescent victories and unfortunate demises—he stood apart. No Angel ever ascended more swiftly. None ever fell so far, so fast.
>
> "The best climber in the history of the sport," Lance Armstrong said after his rival died.

If a Seraph isn't a Maverick, who is???

Mercury in Aquarius on the MC

Aquarius is the sign of the exiled one, the prodigal son returned. Aquarius is the sign of groups and communities and is not personal. These characteristics are evident in our first example.

From Astro.com comes this review of American film producer, Robert Altman, and his Aquarian MC/Mercury conjunction:

> With a satirical eye for the American way of life and a stylistic naturalism, he delivered unique films, more than 30 movies by 1987.... After 15 years of rebellion, burned bridges and self-imposed exile, he made what he called his "fourth comeback" with his film, *The Player*, in 1992.

Osteopathic physician, John Upledger, developed CranioSacral Therapy, a revolutionary reorientation of the understanding of the human body. Mercury in Aquarius on the MC is a perfect placement to aid in this communication. The following comes from Upledger.com:

> Practitioners release restrictions in the craniosacral system to improve the functioning of the central nervous system." CranioSacral work involves communicating with the natural pulses in the body.

American singer, Christina Grimmie, was a winner on the TV show *The Voice*. This is a perfect blend of these three energies: Social Media is Aquarian --the ability to connect to a large section of humanity through electronic means, the Midheaven is how we show our career to the world, and Mercury is our voice. Unfortunately, this astrological positioning drew the wrong sort of attention and Christina was killed publicly with her fans June 10, 2016.

Mercury in Pisces on the MC

These individuals plumb the depths and ranges of expressions possible. These master chameleons show the world the beautiful possibilities of being. These individuals can charm others.

German director, Monika Treut, is a lesbian filmmaker. Pisces rules video, movies and imagery. Monika's films increase awareness of LGBT, as well as women's issues.

American actress, Marcia Cross, is best known for her steely character's Virgo-esque approach to maintaining a household, children, business, and life in the TV series *Desperate Housewives*. Pisces is the last sign of the zodiac and seeks the deeper, hidden meaning of things. Marcie made the following quote from Brainyquote.com, "I have always wanted to know what's going on under the surface."

American singer and actress, Vanessa Williams, makes our list a second time as she also has her Sun in this configuration. Vanessa is quoted as saying this apt Piscean statement, "Sometimes the very thing you're looking for is the one thing you cannot see."

What deeper place in astrology and in space can one look than the fixed stars? Pisces gives us the ability to peek behind the veil, and American astrologer, Diana Rosenberg, used this placement to become the leading authority on fixed stars, according to fellow astrologer Rob Hand. Diana's astrological placement is similar to another astrologer, Bernadette Brady, with her Mercury conjunct her Pisces IC.

Venus

Venus reveals the female self in us whether we are male or female. Venus represents how we perceive, value and experience Beauty, Love, Art, and Relationships as Venus rules both Taurus and Libra. Venus shows our personal values and resources, and how we relate to money. As the ruler of Libra, Venus seeks to unify opposites in order to reach a harmonious balance. Venus is one of the two benefics planets, the other being Jupiter and represents, like the Goddess Venus herself, grace. Venus flowers in the Arts as we will see in the many examples below.

ASTROLOGICAL MAVERICKS

We will now look at the angle placements of Venus throughout the zodiac from the point of view of the Ascendant (AS).

Venus in Aries on the AS

These natives value and operate from an instinctual center which rewards them for their ventures.

American jazz double-bassist, Morty Corb, first appeared in a band in the Army Air Forces. Aries rules the military.

British-American actress, Lynn Redgrave, also has her Moon here. Aries has a way of striking forth without fear. Besides acting, Lynn was a playwright who wrote films that interwove her family story and Shakespeare. Of writing she said:

> "I'm doing it for myself," Ms. Redgrave said last fall about her playwriting, "but I'm thinking about other people."

This comment shows the polarity of self-centering Aries and the relational quality of Venus and Libra. While Venus values beauty, the interesting thing about Lynn is she was not against playing roles in which she was cast in a less than desirable light.

Founder of the Boston National Council for Geocosmic Research (NCGR), journalist and astrologer, Frances McEvoy, used her fearless Aries Venus to leave her home in Arizona and start a life in Boston. The following comes from her obituary from BrownandHickey.com:

> Frances was a recognized expert in the field, exhibiting an extraordinary breadth and depth of knowledge of astrology, astronomy, history, psychology, mythology and art. She found symmetry and common tenants in these areas weaving them into a comprehensive worldview.

Professional basketball player, Shaquille O'Neal, shows us another aspect of this powerful combination. As Aries is a sign of action, we can understand his sports career since he has Aries in the first house, but what does his Venus do? Shaquille seeks strategic partnerships with big brand companies that reward him financially and keep him in the spotlight for his fans to continue to love and adore him. He is seen and valued as an athlete.

Venus in Taurus on the AS

With this astrological alignment we have Venus in one of its two places of rulership, the other being Libra. This is another *bon vivant* placement because these individuals love the sensualities of food, drink, sex, physical experience, and endurance. Since astrological placement is on the Ascendant, this is how the world will appear to the native, and how the native will appear to the world.

Our first example, Filipino writer, historian and journalist, Nicomedes Márquez Joaquín, was best known for his short stories and novels in English. An article about him after his death from Lifestyle.inquirer.com describes this astrological placement:

> Nick Joaquin loved to party—but only with those he knew well. At the end of every workday, Joaquin would get dressed to go out on the town, a habit partly enabled by his unusual approach to hiring taxis. For his convenience, Joaquin would flag down a taxi near his home in San Juan. Then, wherever he went, whether it was to a bar or to a friend's home, he would tell the cab driver to wait, with the meter running, until he was done with whatever he was doing. Joaquin never owned a car or learned how to drive. It was the taxi passenger's life for him.

This a lovely example of the luxuries one would afford oneself with this astrological position.

Australian tennis legend, John Newcombe, created a tennis ranch. From his website newktennis.com comes this presentation of John's accomplishments:

> John Newcombe is undoubtedly one of the finest tennis players ever to set foot on a tennis court. His 26 Grand Slam Titles, including three Wimbledon, two U.S. Open and two Australian Singles titles lay testament to this claim. John was also a shining star in the Australian

Davis Cup play during its heyday. His most recent tennis accomplishment was leading Australia to the title in 1999 as Davis Cup Captain. More important than all of his titles, John is recognized as one of the classiest and most likable personalities in the World of Sport and Celebrity Athletes. He is a true Champion in every sense of the word!" STYLE OF PLAY Newk's big serve and volley game, along with his famous `Buggy Whip` forehand represented the best in the game during his time. John is known as a clever match player and tactician.

Classy, likeable, and possessing style—these are all expressions of a Venus/Taurus Maverick.

Venus in Gemini on the AS

These people have a charming sociability.

1940's to 1960's American actor, Gregory Peck, brought a lovely grace to his work. An article on his death from ABCNews.go.com writes this about popular film star:

> Peck brought quiet strength and dignity to so many larger-than-life roles, but he was probably best known for his 1962 film, *To Kill a Mockingbird*. He won a best actor Oscar for his portrayal of Atticus Finch, a genteel Southern lawyer defending a black man wrongly accused of raping a white woman.

The planet Venus is about unification. So, it is no surprise that Mr. Peck would be most remembered for this character. The sincerity of the role was well reflected within him.

American hotelier, Conrad Hilton, makes our list a second time, as he has his Moon adding to this astrological configuration. Hilton is an example of the beauty of Venus coupled with the airy-nonstop-mutable action of Gemini. His obituary in NYTimes.com stated this clear mixture of Venus and Gemini:

> Mr. Hilton, a tall, courtly man, affable to a fault, was possessed of enormous energy. It was not uncommon for him to dance until 3 A.M., to appear for coffee and orange juice at 8 A.M., then go on to full day's schedule. Into his late 80's, he was at his desk six days a week.

Another beautiful, affable and formidable being, English actress, Helen Mirren, shows us the many faces of womanhood through her myriad roles on stage and screen.

Papa Spyk, who also has his Mercury here (which rules Gemini), started his career in modeling—a strong representation of Venus conjunct the AS.

Venus in Cancer on the AS

These natives carry the feeling of a lovely sense of home or have a deep love and attachment to home as evidenced by our first example.

Haven House, is the name of British author, Jane Gardam's home in Kent, England—it was once a pilgrim's hostel!

French chanteuse, Sheila, aka Annie Chancel, is well known for her numerous love songs, and finds a way to make herself relevant for each decade in which she performs, she also writes and does sculpture. Sheila, is a modern muse.

This placement can also give a person that special flash needed to get some extra attention, as with epic beauties like American movie stars, Angelina Jolie and Cameron Dias. This is the realm of adolescent (and adult) crushes.

Venus in Leo on the AS

This is the love of the self; the love of and for one's creative ability.

American artist and photographer, Andy Warhol, was a maverick in monetizing and consumerizing art. Venus rules money and Andy shows us how, in this quote that describes this royal money-making position, "Making money is art and working is art and good business is the best art. My idea of a good picture is one that's in focus and of a famous person."

American country singer and businessman, Jimmy Dean, used the magnetic charisma from this astrological placement to present a wholesome man who made good country music and tasty breakfast sausages. Both are meant to make us feel good.

I love this from brainyquote.com by English actor, Jeremy Irons, who makes our list a second time:

"And whenever I'm in a situation where I'm wearing the same as 600 other people and doing the same thing as 600 other people, looking back, I always found ways to make myself different, whether it be having a red lining inside of my jacket, having red shoes, it hasn't changed."

This is a special astrological placement. The individual with this placement would feel as if they are special and that everyone around them should notice their regal station. Jeremy easily portrays a person of rank, even when playing the role of penultimate arrogance: a pope from house Borgia!

Another brilliant quote that addresses this astrological arrangement comes from American musician, historian and author, Bill C. Malone:

"You just have to be opportunistic, and try to figure out what creates value... where the bottom is, what creates incremental value, and in what combinations."

Venus in Virgo on the AS

Venus in this position seeks perfecting its craft and often values being of service to others.

Our first example is one that reflects none of this. Edward Duke of Kent, who makes our list a second time, is, a British royal ambassador to the world. In the course of his long career, Mirror.co.uk had a review of his 96 top, let's say, less than appropriate statements:

Number 27
On the 1981 recession: "A few years ago, everybody was saying we must have more leisure, everyone's working too much. Now everybody's got more leisure time they're complaining they're unemployed. People don't seem to make up their minds what they want."

Through the Duke's quote, we see a critical nature that is not easy for others to endure. His noble pedigree afforded him a life most people will never experience.

The following quote from Polish president, Lech Walesa, on the other hand, demonstrates he understands the highest good of Venus in service:

"The thing that lies at the foundation of positive change, the way I see it, is service to a fellow human being."

Scottish stage and film actor, Ian Charleson, used this astrological placement to channel boldly divergent characters for his performances as the title character in *Hamlet*, as well as for his starring role as missionary and Olympic athlete, Eric Liddell. Ian won the Oscar for this role in the 1981 film *Chariots of Fire*.

Interestingly enough, in this same movie (*Chariots of Fire*) was fellow Venus in Leo on the Ascendant and English actor, Nigel Havers, who is known for "his dashing good looks, cut-glass accent and thoroughly charming manner."

Tennis champion, Roger Federer, is a graceful, maverick tennis player. As we have seen in previous placements in Virgo, there is an ease of physical movement with planets in

Virgo. These people are always perfecting their "form." While form is usually a Taurus archetype, Virgo is the next earth sign and therefore sees form in a resourceful manner. Virgo seeks the same goal as the motto in Lexus automobiles: "The relentless pursuit of perfection."™

Venus in Libra on the AS

These people make others feel comfortable. Venus is the ruler of Libra and both seek relationship. These people are consummate diplomats and states people (all three of our examples fall into this category). Again, this is an interesting position in that it is the flip of the natural chart.

American president, Bill Clinton, has a reputation for needing someone with whom to speak and relate, not just once in a while, but constantly. Clinton has an overwhelming need for exchange. He is also a Rhodes Scholar, having attended Oxford College with the intention "to promote civic-minded leadership among "young colonists" with "moral force of character and instincts to lead." Clinton's need for exchange has gotten him into trouble.

As Libra is the sign after Virgo, it takes Virgoan service understanding and use those diplomacy skills to play out on a larger stage. From an article in the Telepgraph.co.uk, we learn the following about former British Prime Minister, David Cameron:

> [Cameron]... he wanted to continue making a 'public service' contribution and would speak out about

international issues in the future—a hint he may seek a new role on the world stage.

Former Australian Deputy Premier, Don Hopgood, got tangled up in a few issues as our previous two examples. Libra is a dual sign, which means there are always two sides to each situation, and within the Libran themselves. This results in getting caught up on the wrong side of the see-saw. Sort of a "caught with your knickers down" situation that the Libran really neither intended nor desired.

Venus in Scorpio on the AS

These people value depth and powerful experiences, and are not afraid to let their underbellies be seen.

British comedy producer, David Croft, had a sense of humor that allowed him to connect with that humor in others. He was responsible for writing and co-creating some of the most well received British comedy series, such as *Are You Being Served* and *'Allo 'Allo*. The things we find most humorous are those topics which make us feel socially and/or emotionally uncomfortable. *Are You Being Served* had a main character who was openly and unapologetically gay and wasn't denigrated by his co-workers for it! This was during a time when homosexuality had barely become "legal" in the UK and *'Allo 'Allo* was about the Nazi occupation of France. We have to ask, how that can be funny? But a Scorpionic person sees the uncomfortable emotional material that lies beneath the surface and brings it up to the light to see, observe, and know.

These are important components which relate to an acceptance of the less than ideal expressions of life. Scorpio humor gives everyone the gift of finding a way to be in relationship to the uncomfortable parts of life.

Serial killer, John Edward Robinson, is yet another example of this placement. A well-written article from VanityFair.com covers the territory very well:

> Indeed, J.R. Robinson is rare in the annals of American crime: a genial con man and a homicidal monster all in one. Unlike Ted Bundy or John Wayne Gacy, who chose their victims impulsively and killed them with dispatch, Robinson developed relationships with his. Using the Internet and his own considerable charm, he lured them to Kansas with offers of employment and sadomasochistic sex. He exploited them financially, enticing them into giving him their life savings and retirement accounts, cashing their disability checks, and, in one case, selling a victim's baby to his brother and sister-in-law. Then, prosecutors allege, he beat at least five women to death with a blunt object, most likely a large hammer. "I've dealt with a wide variety of characters, but never anyone like Robinson," says Stephen Haymes, 49, who has been a probation officer for 26 years and who saw through Robinson far sooner than anyone else in law enforcement. "He's just chilling. There are so many sides to him. There is the con man after money. There is the murderer. There is the sexual deviant. There is the cover-up artist—the lies, endless lies."

As Scorpio is the sign that seeks to understand what is going on below the surface, it is no surprise that American conspiracy theory director, Oliver Stone, makes this list. Scorpio has a predilection to the esoteric and occult sides of life. In Oliver's case, he seeks to bring to light the hidden issues he believes others need to see.

Evolutionary Astrologer, Jeffrey Wolf Green, has written several books on Pluto, the modern ruler of Scorpio, as well as created a wonderful process to bring greater consciousness and understanding to the deeper, unseen processes of life.

Former World Number 1 tennis player, Chris Evert, also has the Moon in this conjunction. I had to dig to find a Scorpionic quote from Chris which illustrates another aspect of Scorpio. From BrainyQuote.com comes this quote that expresses how her demeanor was interpreted, "I was labeled at a young age, Miss Unemotional, Miss Cool, and that would carry over to my press conferences." Scorpio is frozen water.

Venus in Sagittarius on the AS

These individuals value a higher philosophy, education and/or a wider perspective. As well as sharing their personal philosophies.

VanityFair.com captures how this dynamic has played out for the painter and graphic artist, Robert Rauschenberg:

> Studios full of the latest technological equipment enable him to work on projects that are monumental in concept

as well as scale. He has said one of his few unfulfilled dreams is to photograph the world in its entirety, big as life. His only fear is that he might "run out of world."

Sagittarius governs travel and expansive experiences as it is ruled by ever-growing Jupiter. Rauschenberg's trying to capture the world is a beautiful description of this astrological placement.

In the novel *Papillion* (the French word for *butterfly*) French writer and former convict, Henri Charrière gave an "autobiographical" account of his confinement and escape from a foreign penal colony, which was located on the west coast of South America. A person with this astrological placement would truly need and value freedom.

The Sagittarian values are elucidated in this excerpt from NYTimes.com about French literary theorist, Roland Barthes:

> Among the brand-name French theorists of the mid-20th century, Roland Barthes was the fun one. (Foucault was the tough one, Derrida was the dreamy one, Lacan was the mysterious one — I like to imagine them sometimes as a black-turtlenecked, clove-smoking boy band called Hors de Texte, with the hit *album Discipline 'n' Punish*). Instead of constructing multivolume monuments of systematic thought, Barthes wrote short books built out of fragments. He was less interested in traditional coherence than in what he called jouissance: joy, surprise, adventure, pleasure — tantric orgasms of critical insight rolling from fragment to fragment. He proclaimed the death of

the author and advocated a style of reading he referred to as "writerly," in which readers work as active creators of a text. His critical metabolism ran unusually high: he would flit from subject to subject, defining new fields of interest (semiology, narratology) only to abandon them and leave others to do the busywork. He treated canonical French works with such unorthodox flair it drove conservative professors crazy.

Another aspect of this astrological placement would be the campaigning of rights for a variety of people, or those who have been marginalized. Peter Tatchell, is a British human rights campaigner. He is best known for his work with LGBT social movements. Tatchell was the Labour Party's parliamentary candidate for Bermondsey in 1981.

Venus in Capricorn on the AS

Individuals with Venus in Capricorn usually have a successful aura about them, when on an angle, we see a relentless drive. These mavericks are not afraid to do the work that is necessary.

Clark Gable, who appears on our list a second time as he has Moon in Cancer on the DS, was a Hollywood legend. Capricorn is a success seeker, so it is no surprise that LATimes.com had this to say about him from his obituary, "Gable was long the undisputed 'king' of movieland and one of its highest paid stars."

Another king of cinema who also makes our list a second time is American film legend, Paul Newman. Not only was Paul known as a successful actor, but he founded and maintained an organic food line called Newman's Own. Paul's line is, "Let's give it all away to those who need it." If we think of Capricorn as being the sign of the deepest winter in the northern hemisphere, we can understand how this sign would be concerned with making sure there is enough food for everyone. With Venus here, we can understand how Paul would personally value the importance of making sure the larder is full.

Canadian Hockey Operations President for the Calgary Flames, Brian Burke, has an interesting relationship to one of the signs of success: the way he wears a tie! Capricorn individuals have a way of "wearing" their success in their own way.

American talk show host, Larry King, has two quotes that illustrate this position from BrainyQuote.com:

"Those who have succeeded at anything and don't mention luck are kidding themselves."

Venus on the ascendant can lend luck, but luck that occurs from being at the right place at the right time. King also said:

"I don't wish anybody ill, I really don't. I've got a lot of faults, but I was never jealous or envious or... it's a waste of time."

This second quote addresses what makes Larry a good interviewer. Capricorn isn't intimidated by the success others have achieved, so jealously is not usually an active aspect of this dynamic.

Venus in Aquarius on the AS

These people value humanity, but may have issues accepting their own. The out-of-the-box Aquarian manners are rarely understood by their contemporaries as well illustrated in the following anecdotes.

One of the earliest birth dates I have in this book is for the Renaissance painter, Piero di Cosimo, who was born in 1462. I found a wonderful quote from NewYorker.com that perfectly describes this astrological combination:

> Giorgio Vasari, in the second edition of *Lives of the Artists* (1568), chalked this up to what he had been told of the artist's personality, deciding that, "if Piero had not been so abstracted and had paid more heed to himself in his life than he did, he would have won recognition for the great talent he possessed, in such manner that he would have been adored, whereas through his brutish ways he was rather held to be a madman." (Vasari is known to have embellished the stories in his books, but he is the main source of information on Piero's life.) More telling is Vasari's remark that Piero, "changed his style almost from one work to the next." He devoured influences—Leonardo,

Filippino Lippi, Flemish painting—and espoused radical ideas, notably a borderline heretical vision of human prehistory as brutally primitive. Compulsively original, he wouldn't hold still to be revered. The glancing ironies and the frequent wild humor of his art remain freshly confounding—and a good deal of fun—today."

Chanteuse, piano prodigy, and civil rights activist, Nina Simone, is a lovely example of this astrological placement. Being a woman and black were two strikes against her, but she didn't let that stop her. From NYTimes.com we learn:

> Ms. Simone was as famous for her social consciousness as she was for her music. In the 1960's no musical performer was more closely identified with the civil rights movement. Though she was best known as an interpreter of other people's music, she eloquently expressed her feelings about racism and black pride in those years in a number of memorable songs she wrote herself. "Mississippi Goddam" was an angry response to the killing of the civil rights advocate Medgar Evers.

I recommend listening to Nina's music, especially her live recordings. She was trying to express the painfully clear issues of racial inequality to her white concert goers back in the day. The audience responded with awkward laughs and coughs to her songs and the music industry boycotted her for "Mississippi Goddamn" and "Strange Fruit." She full heartedly tried to express Aquarian values to awaken her audiences.

Since the rulers of Aquarius are Saturn the cynic and Uranus the idealist, we can understand the dilemma when they are not in harmony and working for the highest good. The frustration comes from other people's inability to understand and appreciate the space from which the healthy Aquarian is coming. In Nina's case, she had major strikes against her, which could be truly "blamed" on one issue: the time-period in which she lived. We are still dealing with this in the 21st century, but back in the 1960's, most people had little capacity to understand that a woman, let alone one of color, had human intelligence and ability. Nina lived the last part of her life in France, away from her native America. In typical Aquarian fashion, she was an outsider in both countries.

American comedian, George Carlin, has this lovely Aquarian quote:

> "Scratch any cynic and you will find a frustrated idealist."

Calm, cool and seemingly detached actress, Charlotte Rampling, makes our list a third time as she has both her Sun and Mercury here. She states:

> "As a child, I had trouble understanding the world of adults. I could never really approach my parents. I think I made them unapproachable. I was always stepping back and watching."

The air signs are observational and thinking in nature. They are not magnetically engaging like water and earth signs. Charlotte was addressing that sense of alienation and separateness that is a key feature of the Aquarian experience. The notable thing with Charlotte, if we look at the later part of her acting career, she created a rather aloof, somewhat mechanical persona. For a scary taste of this, just watch the TV series *London Spy*.

This astrological position would value helping fellow humans, so it is no surprise that we find consummate businesswoman and madam, Heidi Fleiss! She vehemently protected the identity of her clients. Interestingly enough, she also has a 12th house Capricorn Sun: she had a behind-the-scenes business serving successful men.

Venus in Pisces on the AS

We find a certain depth of perception when we step into the last sign of the zodiac. People with Pisces and/or 12th house planets have the ability to bring back to the material world that which remains hidden from most people.

According to the entry in Blackpast.org for Henry Sampson, he was a prolific inventor. He co-invented the Gamma-Electric cell which converts high radiation gamma ray energy to electricity. We can give thanks to Henry and his co-inventor for powering our cellular telephone.

Wiranto, the Commander of the Indonesian Military, was tied to significant human rights violations. He continues to profess his innocence and has not been prosecuted. Pisceans can get caught in murky waters and eventually released by them. Wiranto has his Mercury and Mars in Pisces as well. While they are not all conjunct, there is a strong mutable watery sense about the man. My sense is that he would be good at adjusting his perceptions of reality and his relationship to it.

We will now look at the angle placements of Venus throughout the zodiac from the point of view of the Imum Coeli (IC)

Venus in Aries on the IC

These are individuals who have a strong sense of inner conviction as they value their own fiery sense of truth of their inner-selves. This means we will see an interesting mix of examples of strong-willed individuals. Aries and Leo are self-centering fire signs, they need to find their own relationship to everything.

Italian painter and sculptor par excellence, Michelangelo, was known for his altercations with the Popes over his artistic license. Aries is Masculine and Venus is Feminine. There is also a question about his sexual orientation, not as much from any anecdotal references to his experiences, but from the sonnets and poems he wrote and the style and manner in which he rendered the male form. Interestingly enough, he lived like a bit of an old ram: sleeping in his clothes, having a rather brutish personal manner, and known for not taking care of his appearance. He is credited with starting the Mannerist style.

In a curious turn of a play on this astrological placement, religious martyr, Thomas More, valued his deeply held beliefs so strongly that he lost his head for them.

We find in this placement, a dynamic mix of religious strong-will perfectly exhibited by science-fiction author of *Dianetics* and the founder of the Church of Scientology, L. Ron Hubbard. His creation story/belief involves a rather interesting galactic warrior theme.

Sandra Day O'Connor, used this placement to support her journey to become the first woman justice of the United States Supreme Court.

Our last religious example is Pentecostal evangelist, Jimmy Swaggart, who gave into his animal like desires for women and had illicit experiences which were contrary to his path in life. Remember that the IC is opposite the MC. Swaggart had a fellow minister defrocked for the *same* carnal behavior, but somehow believed he would not have to experience the same fate.

Another aspect of this placement is stated by American actor and comedian, Arsenio Hall, "I love being in a relationship, but marriage isn't for me." He would like the benefit of having someone there, but not the commitment aspect of it. These people can be adrenaline junkies and seek ever-expanding experiences.

Irish actor, Michael Fassbender, who also has his Sun in this conjunction, expresses a beautiful representation of this Arian astrological placement, taken from AZquotes.com:

"What I find really interesting is to try and mix it up, to push myself and try different things. I don't want to stay in my comfort zone. I want to take risks and keep myself scared."

Venus in Taurus on the IC

Venus is the ruler of Taurus. This is a lovely fixed and luxurious experience, especially at home. Our examples, all three, had very comfortable upbringings.

Socialite, Brenda Frazier, over the course of her life was able to deal with this astrological placement in a way that resonated with her inner values. Keep in mind, Taurus has an appreciation for form and comfort. The following is from her NYtimes.com obituary:

> In a bitter memoir published in *Life* magazine in 1963, she spoke of the confining and meaningless life that had frozen the smile on her face. 'True Meaning of Love' "Though it hurts me, I must admit it: I have never known the true meaning of love," she wrote. "I thought at the time that I loved everyone – all my beaux, all my relatives, everyone I met. But I loved them only because I wanted them to love me, because the faintest sign of rejection by another person, even a nightclub doorman whom I might never see again, brought back all my old childhood feelings of being unwanted and depressed." She said that with the help of psychoanalysis she had come to terms with herself, and vowed that her

daughter would not become a debutante. "I am free now to give her both love and the guidance that teenagers require and desperately want," she wrote.

Belgian-born American playwright, theatre workshop teacher and performer, Jean-Claude van Itallie, has done a number of re-interpretations of Anton Chekhov's plays. Interestingly enough, He has three major conjunctions with the Russian: his Uranus in Taurus with Chekhov's Pluto in Taurus, a Sun Uranus conjunction in Gemini, and a DS Jupiter conjunction. We often find striking astrological connections between artists and the characters who they so vividly portray.

As with any bull, one can sense a sort of stubborn attachment to ideas and/or things. This quote by American politician, Jay Rockefeller, from AZquotes.com speaks to rigid attachment:

> "Once you arrive at an interpretation which you are comfortable in giving, no matter how specious it might be, and you are comfortable doing it, you stay there, you just stay there, and the facts are not going to change you."

Venus in Gemini on the IC

This can be perfect for a singer or actor as this placement gives one an immediate intimacy. There is a youthful vigor in these individuals as they have a wellspring of harmony and unity. They are also multi-talented in that Geminian manner!

American actor and singer, Dean Martin, who also has his Sun here, said this lovely Venusian statement:

"When the world seems to shine like you've had too much wine, that's amore."

Mustachioed music producer and influencer, Giorgio Moroder, said the following in an interview for NYTimes.com:

"I'm going to keep it [his mustache] as long as I do music, and then I'm going to retire and shave it off," he said. "Since my driver's license is valid till 2020, maybe 2020, maybe 80 is a good year to retire. I'm joking," he continued. "As long as I can work, I'm not going to retire. As long as the mustache grows."

Giorgio and our next example are both musicians and painters. Beatles drummer, Ringo Starr, displays that need for relating to the other with this quote from an interview he gave to RollingStone.com:

"I'll play with any other musician all night, but I can't do it on my own," Ringo told me as we drove to what he estimated was somewhere between his 800th to 900th gig with the All Starr Band. "I don't find any joy in sitting there by myself," adds friend and band member Todd Rundgren, "He always plays with a second drummer. I think it was comforting on the first solo tours, but now it's a habit."

Gemini doesn't like to be alone.

In another aspect of the Gemini doubling issue, there is English singer, Andy Bell, one of the two members of Erasure. There is a cute fashion/makeup interview he did for theGuardian.com talking about what he likes to do to get ready and go out. Andy shared his beauty secrets—hello Venus conjunct the IC in Gemini!

In a very different expression of this archetype, Martin Bryant murdered 35 people and injured 23 others in the one of the world's deadliest shooting sprees in Port Arthur, Tasmania, Australia. He had below normal IQ and made only one significant relationship with another recluse who was an heiress to a gambling fortune.

Venus in Cancer on the IC

These individuals value home and emotional connection with family. These people have a natural chart layout, meaning they likely have an Aries Ascendant.

New Zealand author, Barry Crump, illustrated another side of Cancer: they carry their homes on their backs like a hermit crab! Barry said he never stayed around in a place longer than three months. He was also married five times. More on Barry is available from: teara.govt.nz/en/biographies/6c2/crump-barry.

From BrainyQuote.com, we have this perfect statement from English musician and record producer, Brian Eno, "As soon as I hear a sound, it always suggests a mood to me." Cancer is one of the moody signs of the zodiac. Brian's musical scores lay the mood for countless films.

Venus in Leo on the IC

This is a wonderful placement for an artist and makes for a highly creative individual as Venus rules the arts and Leo is the sign of self-expression. We have an interesting mix of individuals in this section.

Our first two examples were born five days apart. American painter, Andrew Wyeth, was part of an American artistic dynasty. From his obituary in *The New York Times*, he shares these comments:

> "I think the great weakness in most of my work is subject matter. There's too much of it."

Leo is a highly subjective sign. It is the sign of I-am-ness which realizes it can create and self-express.

Enticingly awkward, ostrich-like comedienne, Phyllis Diller, used herself as the basis for a lot of her humor. In a time when women were neither known, nor really accepted in the comedy field, her strongly placed Venus gave her an inner sense of strength to stand up in the male dominated field in which she succeeded.

In another stroke of Venusian musicality, American composer for musical theater, Harvey Schmidt composed the longest running musical in history called the *Fantasticks*.

Blond bombshell, Pamela Anderson talks about the ways in which her Leonine mane played a role in her life and talks from such a Leo space in this quote from BrainyQuote.com:

"My hair was so much a part of my personality and all my photo shoots. I hid behind my hair. And then, I just decided I was okay with myself. To have short hair and really show my face is even more revealing than anything. It's a statement – not to everyone else, more to myself. I'm just ready to get out from behind my hair and be myself."

Venus in Virgo on the IC

Venus is in her "fall" in this position. Meaning there is a way in which Venus doesn't feel quite at home. In some ways this makes sense and in other ways not so much. Venus and Virgo are both feminine and that is where they understand one another. Venus rules Taurus --one of the Earth signs-- and so there is an understanding of resources. Venus wants to deal with resources as found in Taurus and Virgo is the sign of a multitude of resources. Let us see how the theme of sharing of resources plays out in the examples that follow.

Cuban president, Fidel Castro, supported the revolution in Cuba with the idea that the resources of the few should sustain the many. Here are two great quotes from BrainyQuote.com on that topic:

> "The equal right of all citizens to health, education, work, food, security, culture, science, and wellbeing – that is, the same rights we proclaimed when we began our struggle, in addition to those which emerge from

our dreams of justice and equality for all inhabitants of our world – is what I wish for all."

"The revolution is a dictatorship of the exploited against the exploiters."

If that isn't a statement about resources, what is?

Our next example, Eric Stanton, was a fetish illustrator and makes our list a second time. Eric portrayed women, or the "values" which represented women, featuring the Virgo archetypes, such as the whore/virgin.

Suzanne de Passe, the media producer who brought us the Jackson 5 and Michael Jackson, shows another side of Virgo's domain of daily routines and health regimens. From AllPoetry.com, Suzanne is quoted as saying she "learned to take 'no' as a vitamin." To a Virgo, *no* is simply an invitation to find a way to get *yes*!

Venus in Libra on the IC

This is a beautiful astrological placement. Venus rules the relational sign of Libra and with it at the IC, we have the ambassador to the family combined with the base needs in life associated with the IC.

From his LATimes.com obituary, comes some interesting statements about the popular American writer, Michael Crichton:

> When Michael Crichton was attending Harvard Medical School in the late 1960's, he had a secret life

that he kept hidden from his fellow students: To pay his tuition bills, he began writing paperback thrillers in his spare time under two pseudonyms. He became so adept at cranking out his thrillers that he wrote one in nine days. And before long, as he later put it, "the writing became more interesting to me than the medicine."

While we are on the topic of Venus in the sign of relationship, Michael was married five times.

Along the same vein, Wikipedia.com writes about Mexican drug lord, Juan Garcia Abrego:

> García Ábrego allegedly never formally married but had two common-law wives, a number of lovers, and several children.

Songwriter and recording artist, Cecil Womack, who also has his Sun here, only had two wives, but the interesting part is both were singers and he even sang with one of them professionally. Cecil's home life and his work life were imbued with Venusian Libran musical arts.

Charles, Prince of Wales, has been married twice (the relationship theme continues). Charles is a brilliantly intelligent man with a wealth of education. From a wonderful article on him from USAtoday.com comes this excerpt under the heading of a man of contradictions. Note here, that a Libran is all about balance, it is also all about the steps it takes to get to harmony. Libras often have an innate ability to make anything pretty. More about Charles:

He is by turns charming and witty, petulant and stubborn. His office is wildly disorganized and his thinking often is, too, but his various charities and businesses (such as his line of organic products) have been highly successful. His friendships include women of the age of his beloved grandmother, the late Queen Mother, plus a long list of celebrities (the late Joan Rivers, Emma Thompson, Phil Collins, Joanna Lumley, Rowan Atkinson, Stephen Fry, to name a few). His personal enthusiasms include classical music and architecture, painting and art museums, polo and hunting, and especially, gardens and gardening. He is stiff, eccentric and set in his royal ways, always dressed in a double-breasted suit (no pocket flaps, handkerchief billowing from breast pocket, flower in button hole) and Turnbull & Asser shirts with French cuffs.

Prince Charles is a vision of Venus in Libra harmony, beauty and luxury.

Venus in Scorpio on the IC

There is an innate inner need for these individuals to reveal and release that which is valued. The intensity of feeling and/or inner fixation requires expression. How they do this is up to the consciousness of the individuals who have this placement as we will see in the following examples.

Serial killer, Ted Bundy, makes our list a second time, as he also has Mercury here in Scorpio on the IC. This would be a very tender and vulnerable place for Mr. Bundy. I wonder what deep values he sought in the acts he committed?

Martin Luther, the reformer of the Catholic Church, used this astrological placement to find the inner truth about the depths of his connection to God. Luther had a stellium in Scorpio and his Venus is conjunct Saturn, so his clarity and inner authority won out.

The iconic American recording artist, Laura Nyro, whose singing and songwriting career spans from the 1960's through the 1990's, shows another aspect of the Scorpio archetype and being of benefit to others. Scorpio's eighth house is the house of other people's resources. Laura was painfully performance shy which may have been a part of the issue (Scorpio doesn't really care to be "seen"). Other performers had greater professional success covering her songs than she did.

Scottish singer, Zena Zavaroni, started her musical career when she was 10 years old. Scorpio is a very sensitive sign and this placement for Zena resulted in less than ideal means of coping as she turned to intensely regulating her food intake and suffering from the eating disorder anorexia nervosa. Scorpio is the sign that deals with our digestion and the pelvic region of the body. Zena was *so* private, that she did not eat in front of her husband. Zena said she could only eat in front of her family. Her obituary in theGuardian.com offers a glimpse of the depth of her privacy around food, when she states, "I can't bear other people to see me eating".

English actor, Robson Green, describes another aspect of the Scorpionic theme: transformation. Scorpio is a water sign and the IC is our home, so it is no surprise that he states the following in an interview with RadioTimes.com:

"... in 2015 my house was under seven feet of water, destroyed in a flood. Everything precious and personal in my life, just washed away. It was very painful, I was devastated. Not only were there salmon going down the Tyne that day, my three-piece suit was, too."

People with strong Scorpionic placements eventually get used to the death/rebirth themes that consistently play out in their lives. Scorpio and Taurus are signs in which we come to terms with the endless conflicts in life in order to reach neutrality: harmony through conflict. To people without Scorpionic planets, such a life seems overwhelming and intense, but Scorpio knows how to ride the rapids and to gather the deep treasures that lie within our most transformative experiences.

American actress, Katie Holmes, who already made our list for her Leo Moon, shows another facet of the Scorpio energy being secretive. As we are speaking of one of the deepest signs in the Zodiac at the deepest point in the chart, the IC and the planet we are discussing is Venus, the planet of love, the following excerpt from DailyMail.co.uk makes perfect sense:

Katie Holmes and Jamie Foxx have finally confirmed their love after years of hiding their romance in public. The couple, who are believed to have been dating since 2013, finally appeared in public together as they enjoyed a day at the beach on Monday. The two have taken extraordinary measures to keep their relationship secret amid claims Katie's ex-husband included a clause in her 2012 divorce settlement banning her from publicly dating for five years.

It is noteworthy to mention that Scorpio often indicates controlling relationships as evidenced by Katie's divorce agreement.

Venus in Sagittarius on the IC

These mavericks value freedom and enjoy exploring other worlds, both real and imagined. They are questers of inner truths to gain greater understanding.

Singer songwriter, Paul Simon, made his 1986 comeback album *Graceland* weaving African themes and music. An article from theGuardian.com comments on his musical creation, "The album [*Graceland*] was naturally well-received—after all, it was a brave new departure by a bestselling singer-songwriter who had already shown a fascination for global styles earlier in his career by recording in Jamaica (a rare move back in the Seventies) and working with South American musicians."

Spanish painter, Picasso's muse and lover, Dora Maar, had this gregarious love position and one of her lovers, James Lord, in his book about Picasso and Dora Mar, wrote that she "possessed an infallible capacity for representing me to myself as superficial and naive, which I resented and accepted and, in fact, appreciated as evidence of her esteem and affection." Sagittarians, like so many of the signs, have a way of seeing the world as they see themselves. The traits she observed in her lover, were no doubt traits of which she was aware in herself. Interestingly enough, Dora and our next example, Arthur Schlesinger, Jr., both died at 89 years of age.

In the NYTimes.com obituary for American historian, Arthur Schlesinger, Jr., we learn, "He is willing to argue that the search for an understanding of the past is not simply an aesthetic exercise but a path to the understanding of our own time." Above all else, Sagittarius seeks understanding, it asks questions, it seeks to understand how the parts make up the whole.

Hip Hop artist and actor, LL Cool J, shared a wonderful quote from his grandmother who gave him guidance and strength. In an interview he gave to NPR.org regarding his Kennedy Center 2017 Hip Hop award, he says:

"My late grandmother passed some wise advice to me: 'If a task is once begun, never leave it 'til it's done. Be thy labor great or small, do it well or not at all.' That adage has guided everything I have ever done in my life and I couldn't be more grateful because it has led me here."

A Sagittarian is always on a quest, often idealistic, but still a quest for greater understanding. The ancient Chinese proverb, "A journey of a thousand miles begins with one step" is very Sagittarian.

Venus in Capricorn on the IC

While Venus is neither in its detriment nor in its fall in Capricorn, she doesn't feel very warm and cuddly when found in this placement. "Strategic relationships" would be a keyword combination and, since we are speaking of the IC, this would be focused upon a relationship with one's self. Capricorn seeks efficiency and success, so these are some of the traits an individual with this astrological placement would value.

American movie star and actor, Rock Hudson, had to keep his homosexual love hidden at home so as to not adversely affect his career. Rock was a sex symbol which this placement would imply.

We see the blending of efficiency and success in relation to one's self in the obituary from NYTimes.com for female impersonator, Jim Bailey:

> [Bailey]... referred to himself as an illusionist or a character actor, arguing that his many concert and cabaret performances — in which he dressed and made himself up, often flamboyantly, as Garland or Streisand, performed their greatest hits in creditable simulations of their vocal styles, mimicked their physical movements with uncanny accuracy and engaged in personality-revealing patter."

Another aspect of this astrological placement would be having famous/successful family or parents (IC/Fourth house) as is the case for the daughter of songwriter, Billy Joel, and supermodel, Christie Brinkley, Alexa Ray Joel. Alexa's family ties gave her a boost to realize opportunities for success.

Venus in Aquarius on the IC

As Aquarius is an air sign, there is a desire here to rise above the base feelings of humanity.

An article on legendary singer and songwriter, Aretha Franklin, for the Newyorker.com/magazine illustrates this point very well:

> Franklin's vulnerability has brought with it an intense desire for control that often leads to still more anguish. When it came time to do an autobiography, she enlisted Ritz, a skilled biographer and ghostwriter who had produced fascinating books with Ray Charles, Etta James, Bettye LaVette, and Smokey Robinson. He found her a singularly resistant subject. She insisted on stripping the book of nearly anything gritty or dark. Published in 1999, it reads like an extended press release. "Denial is her strategy for emotional survival," Ritz told me. It was only at the microphone, in her music, he concluded, that Franklin felt in command. There were reports that she had been struggling with cancer, but her friends say she'd never admit to such a thing, "not even on her deathbed."

Which unfortunately came to pass for Aretha Franklin, while I was writing this book.

During his life, Australian musician, Robin Gibb, of the Bee Gees' fame, played out that traditional Aquarian theme of the outcast or rebel. An Aquarian needs to separate him/

her self from family of origin in order to find one's self. From an obituary in RollingStone.com:

> Although he looked and sounded like the meekest Bee Gee, Robin grew into the family rebel. By 1969, he and Barry were feuding over whose song should be singles, and Robin, then 20, was declared a "ward of the state" by their father when his drinking and partying seemed to take over his life. "It happened so fast that we lost communication between us," Gibb later recalled. "It was just madness, really."

Tennis professional, Mary Pierce, remained in her aloof Aquarian nature while in relationships. Engaged twice, she broke off both engagements.

Venus in Pisces on the IC

Venus is in its exaltation in Pisces. Aphrodite is a version of Venus. Born of the ocean, there is a symbiotic relationship that draws the depths to them in ways mysterious and profound. These individuals value their connection to the divine in themselves and everything else.

Diva, Diana Ross said the following in an interview for RollingStone.com, "I've always been interested in fashion, cosmetics and makeup and hair, so the image that we created was very ladylike, very feminine." Diana's work has to do with what is our identity, what we value. With this placement in Pisces, it can be confusing seeing what is real. "Our image was really a reflection of beauty and glamour. The image onstage was always ladylike. It was very smooth and rhythmic [she sways her arms to demonstrate], and the music was the same." Venus in Pisces is all about the lovely imagery.

Novelist, Patricia Highsmith, who will appear many times on our lists, is the renowned author of the Tom Ripley psychological thriller series.

Golf legend, Jack Nicklaus, shows what it is like to be a true humanitarian in donating millions of dollars to children's hospitals and charities.

Exoteric and Esoteric astrologer, Alan Oken, uses this placement to promote the values of the occult (that which is hidden).

In an interesting twist to this astrological placement, we have Australian naturalist, Steve Irwin, who passed over doing what he loved, being in communion with creatures of the deep.

Canadian musical performer, Justin Bieber, who also has his Sun involved in this position, is a consummate Piscean. With this placement, Bieber literally loves and values God. In an interview for GQ.com, comes the devoted statement about his relationship to and with God:

> Bieber speaks about God with the easy superfluity of someone who knows how to read the Bible between the lines, who is confident he has correctly assessed its true meaning. God's love helps him to be a good person and to recognize the cosmic value of being a good person, but God's love is also available to him even when he doesn't act like a good person. Unlike employees, friends, and family members, God never disappoints—and is never

disappointed in—Justin Bieber. In conversation, Bieber alludes often to the fallibility of those closest to him: "I've had people that burned me so many times"; "If we invest everything we have in a human, we're gonna get broken."

God is probably the only person in the universe Bieber can really trust.

We will now look at the angle placements of Venus throughout the zodiac from the point of view of the Descendant (DS)

Venus in Aries on the DS

As we know, Venus is in its detriment in Aries because it rules the opposite sign of Libra. Venus appreciates harmony and has a distaste for discord. Individuals with this placement are likely not conflict adverse and will likely draw adverse attention and reaction.

Our first example shows a baseline simplicity of a less than ideal expression of this placement. We are speaking of someone who values war or who sees everyone as an enemy and a threat. The obituary of Iraqi dictator, Saddam Hussein, from theGuardian.com states the challenges he experienced:

> Hassan Ibrahim took to extremes local Bedouin notions of a hardy upbringing. For punishment, he beat his

stepson with an asphalt-covered stick. Thus, from earliest infancy, was Saddam nurtured – like a Stalin born into very similar circumstances – in the bleak conviction that the world is a congenitally hostile place, life a ceaseless struggle for survival, and survival only achieved through total self-reliance, chronic mistrust and the imperious necessity to destroy others before they destroy you. The sufferings visited on the child begat the sufferings the grown man, warped, paranoid, omnipotent, visited on an entire people. Like Stalin, he hid his emotions behind an impenetrable facade of impassivity; but he assuredly had emotions of a virulent kind—an insatiable thirst for vengeance on the world he hated.

This astrological placement helps David Icke be the warrior he needs to be in order to share what he values with others. David's website DavidIcke.com states the following:

David Vaughan Icke is an English writer, public speaker, and former media personality best known for his views on what he calls, "Who and what is really controlling the world." Describing himself as the most controversial speaker and author in the world, he has written many books explaining his position dubbed "New Age conspiracism". He has attracted a substantial following across the political spectrum. His 533-page *The Biggest Secret* (1999) has been called the conspiracy theorist's Rosetta Stone.

In an interview for Screen-Spaces.SquareSpace.com, screen writer and director, Scott Hicks, gives a brilliant answer to the following question which illustrates another aspect of this astrological placement, one of immediate intimacy. Hicks is asked, "Have you ever drawn a line between the artistry and talent of your subjects and the artistry and talent you bring as the filmmaker?" His reply begins beautifully with a pause. This is a gift from opposing sign Libra:

> Hicks: (Pause). When I made the film about Philip Glass, on the very first day of shooting I pulled out my camera and started filming Philip cooking us pizza in his kitchen at Nova Scotia. In the process of cooking, he kept turning around and talking to me behind the camera, saying things like, "Do you like garlic, Scott?" And I'd answer, "Well, yes, but stop talking to me, Philip, I'm the documentarian" (laughs). But as the shoot progressed, I began to realise that that was the film and that he was inviting a relationship with me and choosing to ignore the fact that I was holding a camera. That created a tremendous sort of intimacy. What began as me thinking, 'Well I won't be able to use this,' actually dictated and drove the tone of the film. The same thing sort of applies in *Highly Strung*, in that you're not pretending you are not there because the presence of the camera impacts upon every situation. And it would be crazy to imagine otherwise. It is, essentially, an attempt at some level of honesty about your engagement and involvement with these people

as people. I think somewhere in there I answer your question, partially (laughs).

Scottish comedian, Rory Bremner, expresses another aspect of this astrological placement. In an article entitled *Horizon: ADHD and me with Rory Bremner* from BBC.co.uk, one can understand how this astrological placement could result in an ADHD (Attention Deficit Hyperactivity Disorder) diagnosis:

> Rory tries out treatments for ADHD, taking methylphenidate (notorious under the brand name Ritalin) for the first time, as well as trying out an experimental form of brain training. Finally, he finds out why ADHD exists at all: while it may be bad for the individual, some scientists believe it may have helped society by providing risk-takers who, like mine-sweepers, identify dangers and map out boundaries, to the benefit of the rest of us.

Sometimes, as previously mentioned, these astrological placements in our charts can signal how we die. In 2009, actress, Natasha Richardson, died from an epidural hematoma following a blunt impact to her head when she fell skiing.

Sometimes experiences in our lives can make us split our consciousness as a safety mechanism. From ABCNews.go.com American actress, Anne Heche, said she suffered sexual abuse at the hands of her father which caused her to escape into a "fourth dimension" fantasy world in which she believed she was from another planet. This is something that the mind does in order to cope with something it finds too overwhelming.

The instinctual nature of Aries can leave our system on go mode which can be overwhelming, especially when filtered through our relationship to other with Venus on the DS. This energy is also a frequency that vibrates in its surroundings. This can result in acting like a beacon to awaken unconscious desire nature in others. The instinctual Aries nature coupled with unifying Venus can set up some interesting relationship experiences.

English television actress and comedian, Magda Szubanski, wrote about the single-minded aspect of this placement in her book, *Reckoning: A Memoir*:

> The way of the sick soul seems unmanly and diseased. This was the fault line, the precise point where my mind bifurcated. I longed to have a mystical experience that would fuse these parts together. I yearned for an unequivocal, undivided mind and a soul of 'sky-blue tint'. A shadow lay across my soul. I could glimpse it, feel its weight. But what it was or why it was there I could not fathom. I found James's pragmatism reassuring and steadying, in contrast to Nietzsche, that psychopomp of misguided youth, to whom the ego was just a jumble of unrelated thoughts that only assume a semblance of order after the fact.

One can sense the workings again of Libra through these experiences. This ability to go from instinctual fire to observant air is a wonderful gift for these natives to cultivate.

Venus in Taurus on the DS

Venus is the ruler of Taurus. These people seek and value beauty, especially in their relationships. Their dogged determination is a marvel to behold.

French and Spanish fashion designer, Paloma Picasso has a very interesting relationship with her DS. For one thing, her AS is at 29 degrees of Libra which means that this includes the earliest of Scorpio energies as well. Paloma also has Sun in Aries conjunct the descendent and she has the Venus in Taurus conjunct the descendent. This makes for a very dynamic, strong willed (Aries and Taurus) individual. In an article on Paloma in biography.yourdictionary.com we find a perfect description of this astrological blending:

> While Pablo Picasso transformed aesthetic standards in the fine arts, his trend-setting daughter has independently introduced fresh perspectives in fashion design.

Professional gardener, Alan Titchmarsh, responded with these very Venus in Taurus answers when asked a series of questions by Express.uk.co.uk:

> "If I had half an hour left on Earth, I would... find myself a nice spot in the garden, enjoy bacon and a fresh egg with a nice cup of coffee. That would do very nicely."
>
> "My best friend is... my wife, Alison. We'll have been married for 41 years this July."

"My perfect evening is… a night in with my wife's fish pie or macaroni cheese. I love supper with my wife, daughters and sons-in-law."

Venus in Gemini on the DS

The most basic translation of this placement is love of Air, which is embodied by our first example. Pilot and astronaut, John Glenn, was a person who really loved his wife and had a relationship that provided much stability for them both.

British artist, Anya Gallaccio, has Mercury conjunct this placement as well. This pairing of Venus and Mercury is known as loving communication. There is immediacy with Gemini, it is the sign of *Now*. Gallaccio creates artwork that is fleeting and momentary as she explains in an article from SanDiegoUnionTribune.com:

> I thought I bypassed this very smartly by making things that went in the Dumpster because then I didn't have to find space to store them or take care of them or mend them when they got damaged. And I had some notion that it meant that the work was more of its time, that it was more in the present, more in the moment.

Gallaccio also tends to work with organic material like plants, flowers and fruits allowing them the process of decay. Gemini is the first mutable sign and expresses that time from the height of spring transitioning into summer in the northern hemisphere.

New Zealand artist, Peter McIntyre, who makes our list a second time with his Moon here, was well known for being a painter of landscapes and portraits. What a beautiful use and expression of this astrological positioning.

Michael, Prince of Kent, exhibits Geminian language fluency. From his website princemichael.org.uk, he is described as:

> A qualified Russian interpreter, also fluent in French and with a working knowledge of German and Italian, the Prince runs his own consultancy company, and uses his international experience and expertise to encourage and develop commercial relationships for British companies overseas.

Venus in Cancer on the DS

These people value and focus on themes of home, nurturing, family, and clan. Privacy is important.

Legendary American pianist, Liberace, who also has his Mercury in Taurus on the IC, was portrayed by actor Michael Douglas in the movie *Behind the Candelabra*. Michael Douglas made this observation on Liberace, "He had his passions: his career, his homes, which were over the top, and his private life as a gay man."

Pauline Oliveros, the American composer and accordion player and postwar electronic art musician, had this pivotal Cancerian experience:

One more turning point came in 1988, when Ms. Oliveros and two colleagues–the trombonist, didgeridoo player and composer, Stuart Dempster, and the vocalist and composer, Panaiotis—descended into an extraordinarily resonant disused cistern in Port Townsend, Washington. Their drone-based improvisations were recorded, and selections issued on CD under the title "Deep Listening" in 1989. Beyond a self-evident pun referring to music played 14 feet underground, "Deep Listening" signified Ms. Oliveros's emerging aural discipline: a practice that compelled listening not just to the conventional details of a given musical performance—melody, harmony, rhythm, intonation—but also to sounds surrounding that performance, including acoustic space and extra-musical noise.

When we think of it, the cistern is the perfect Cancerian metaphor. Cancer is ruled by the Moon and the Moon represents a container. Watery Cancer is immersed in the feelings of things, places and people.

I could find only one quote for English singer, actor and comedian, Roy Castle, "Don't whine—laugh." When we think about it, one can see this as the shift of looking at something from the playful Libran/7th house rather than the emotionally attached/security seeking Cancer view.

Venus in Leo on the DS

These people love the stage. We have three performers with this astrological placement.

TeamRock.com had this lovely quote about this placement for AC/DC front man, Bon Scott:

> "Bon had a riveting presence," he wrote. 'He was cocky but he wasn't conceited. He was vulgar but he wasn't boorish. He was tough as nails but with a soft white underbelly. He was a hero, an icon, but he was also the guy next door, lying underneath a greasy motorbike with a spanner in his hand."

American television personality, Lance Loud, grew up on TV staring in one of the earliest reality shows called *An American Family*. He came out on the show introducing the audience to the issues around being gay.

Multi-talented Scottish musician, KT Tunstall, makes our list a third time. I would say this particular astrological placement is one that gives her great joy when she is in front of an audience and/or adoring fans.

Venus in Virgo on the DS

Venus is in her fall in Virgo. This means there is a way in which she doesn't feel quite at home. The largess of Venus is constricted here as Virgo seeks to be very discriminating and is at odds with the unification Venus seeks to attain.

From an article in HelloMagazine.com, American actor, Antonio Banderas, describes the joy he receives from being in relationship with the land around his home:

> "I am not a party person anymore so I have the space and peace to write and really get inside my own head. I'm working on several scripts. I go cycling in the woods and everyone in Cobham, Weybridge and Esher is incredibly friendly. Above all, I am surrounded by nature. I love watching the deer and foxes that come to my garden."

Virgo is the sign of animal husbandry.

From BrainyQuote.com comes a beautiful expression of this astrological placement by Bollywood actress, Kajol:

> "I love my body. And, I'm always working out. I'm an exercise freak, be it cardio, weights, t'ai chi or yoga."

As Virgo deals with our body and daily routines and Venus is what we value, others benefit from her work on self-awareness and actualization.

Venus in Libra on the DS

Venus rules Libra. A focus on relationship is strongly indicated here as this is the natural placement for Libra on the astrological wheel.

Princess Margaret of England, played an interesting role for both her country and her sister, Her Royal Highness, Elizabeth II. From an article in VanityFair.com about the bond (and the dichotomies since we are discussing Libra here) shared between the sisters:

> But the particular closeness of Elizabeth and Margaret was beyond comparison with the relationship between any other siblings in the world. Elizabeth would, in 1953, become a consecrated monarch, Crowned Queen of England, ruler of about 130 million subjects on five continents. Margaret would at the same time become one of her subjects. And yet, despite this permanent distinction, they had a love, friendship, and conspiracy that were impressive to behold. Princess Margaret had a telephone on her desk in Kensington Palace with a direct line to the Queen in Buckingham Palace, on which the two would gossip and laugh with each other daily. I never heard Princess Margaret refer to the Queen in public as anything but "The Queen"; in private she became "Lilibet," her nickname since childhood, or, simply, "my sister."

Libra seeks to reconcile opposites and the seeming dualities in life, while Venus seeks unification. Canadian author, Douglas Glover, made the following Venus in Libra values statement in this excerpt from MeBondBooks.com:

> "Often when I am teaching, I find myself exhorting students to get more action on the page, and the

students, bless their hearts, tend to think I want sex or a fistfight instead of the quiet little scene they have written. Often I don't mean that at all. What I mean is that their scene is missing the requisite density of syntactic action, the clash of values, the juxtaposition of contrasting elements, the raising of expectations and denial of same that make a sentence or a paragraph or a book or an essay or a poem exciting to read. Student stories tend to read, as I have said before, like sketches, rough outlines of stories. Student writers seem to feel that they are having enough trouble getting their characters in and out of rooms and somehow finding an ending without actually paying attention to the way they are writing the story. They may have a story sketch, but sentence after sentence doesn't read like it belongs in a story; they are too flat and generic, interested mainly in communicating the general idea not the excitement of creation and the astonishing particularity of the artistic experience."

From an article on his death, TheGuardian.com had this to say about horse racing legend, Bart Cummings, which captures this astrological placement in the highest of terms—understanding that we are all, truly, equal:

Son, Anthony Cummings, who has followed his father into the business, struggled to get through his eulogy. He choked back the tears as he said he had never had a blue with his dad, a man who was so special even he, his son, held him in awe. "Dad spent time with kings and queens, prime ministers, premiers and the common man," Anthony said. "Treated all equally and gave them time. "In the end, dad was more than a horseman. An icon, a legend, all of that. Built from flames and hardship to go with success."

American Senator, Joseph McCarthy, wins bonus points for having a governmental practice named after him that illustrates his personal (he has Mars here as well) values of Right Human Relationship. The following comes from Wikipedia:

> 'McCarthyism', coined in 1950 in reference to McCarthy's practices, was soon applied to similar anti-communist activities. Today, the term is used in reference to what are considered demagogic, reckless, and unsubstantiated accusations, as well as public attacks on the character or patriotism of political opponents.

We can see the roots of our current issues around fake-news and "I've-said-it-three-times-so-it-must-be-true" circular logic that is solely circular and completely illogical that began with McCarthy.

Venus in Scorpio on the DS

These people have an innate sense of the other. These people can read and evaluate what lies within others.

ASTROLOGICAL MAVERICKS

Investigative journalist, Dan Rather, has shown signs of this placement over the years. People with strong Scorpio planets and placements are those who dig deep. They can make people feel uncomfortable through their relentless probing. This astrological combination often gives the native nuclear reserves. From an insightful article from Politico.com comes this apt quote which illustrates the powerful Scorpionic expression. Notice all the qualifiers in the first sentence:

> For decades, Rather was fodder for critics who considered him too emotional, too liberal, too ambitious, too self-serious. He didn't smile a lot; his folksy sayings could come off as downright weird. But the exact eccentricities that made at times for an awkward fit for network television, and his talent for thoughtful but unambiguous pronouncements of outrage, have been pitch-perfect for this new medium and moment. One of the leading voices of the Trump resistance is not some black-masked radical or a marching young woman with a pink knit hat but a man with gray hair, a name you know and a neatly knotted tie. "He is the Energizer Bunny. He keeps going and going, and the country is better for it," Cuban told me. His order to Rather after he hired him: "Go piss people off."

La Stupenda operatic force, Joan Sutherland, helped to rebirth the bel canto style. From an article on her death from the NYTimes.com:

Bel canto (which translates as "beautiful song" or "beautiful singing") denotes an approach to singing exemplified by evenness through the range and great agility. The term also refers to the early-19th-century Italian operas steeped in bel canto style. Outside of Italy, the repertory had languished for decades when Maria Callas appeared in the early 1950's and demonstrated that operas like *Lucia di Lammermoor* and Bellini's *Norma* were not just showcases for coloratura virtuosity but musically elegant and dramatically gripping works as well.

Sutherland expressed a deep intensity as evidenced by the length of extended adulation following her performances. People with strong Scorpionic charts can facilitate a deeper sense of feelings in others especially when a chart's angle is involved.

American oil heir, T. Cullen Davis, who also has his Moon and Mars here, shows an aspect of the Scorpio self: the need to connect on a deep level. With three planets in Scorpio conjunct his DS, Davis had a deep need to control others and it is no surprise that he was accused of three people's deaths. In support of this astrological placement, Wikipedia.com writes:

> Davis had a reputation in Fort Worth society circles for displays of bad temper and general "creepiness", according to female associate."

This is clearly unintegrated Scorpio energy.

Scorpio is also the sign of other people's resources, so it seems fitting that Australian politician, David Jull, was praised at his funeral for raising the level of tourism from a mere 516,000 international visitors in 1975, to an industry that now welcomes over 5 million tourists. Of course, this increase in the number of visitors brings with it the economic benefits of consumerism and Australian employment, especially in rural areas.

Venus in Sagittarius on the DS

These are the gregarious, optimistic world travelers who value foreign experiences and partners as well as higher philosophical immersion.

From Wikipedia.com, we learn about journalist and author, Maureen Dragone. In one of her final statements, Dragone was quoted as saying, "I did everything that I ever wanted to do, and did it my way." Dragone wrote for numerous international newspapers and magazines and was said to have interviewed hundreds of celebrities throughout the course of her career. She was a member of the Hollywood Foreign Press Association for more than 50 years and was regarded as the "recognized historian" of the HFPA.

Australian actor and businessman, Dan Falzon, makes our list a third time and also has his Sun here. Dan shows his excitement and values sharing new experiences with people, through his eco-tourism business.

Venus in Capricorn on the DS

These individuals seek status building relationships.

English author Nancy Mitford, used this placement to write about the love lives of the upper classes.

Venus in Aquarius on the DS

These people are drawn to outcasts and eccentrics because they value humanity.

As Aquarius is ruled by both Saturn and Uranus, there is always using the old to create something new. From SMH.com.au comes this piece about Welsh artist, Andrew Southall:

> As academic Vincent Alessi points out in an interesting essay available online, it's this blackness, "this space that we peer into without really knowing what is there," that links the pictorial and abstract works here. Making a stark change from the vibrant yellow paintings Southall was making only recently, the black abstractions are dominated by the five-metre-long Elmore Altarpiece, which incorporates objects the artist picked up during his inspirational meanderings.

Aquarians can be intensely private as they often have a challenging time with their humanity. English comedian, Kenneth Williams, exhibited other aspects of the Aquarian dichotomy delineated in an article for Independent.co.uk about his death/suicide:

> The writer Russell Davies, who edited Williams's published diaries, says: "I think you would be hard pushed to find any friends who thought it was suicide, but having looked at the diaries, it is hard to come to any other conclusion."

While American boxing champion, Mohammad Ali, had an Aquarian ego that appeared arrogant to others, this quote from BrainyQuotes.com shows the humanitarian within:

> "Service to others is the rent you pay for your room on earth."

British politician, diplomat and writer, Paddy Ashdown, speaks to TheGaurdian.com about Brexit:

> "The strategy was wrong. I said: 'Listen, the only way that we're going to win this is if the heavyweights get together and tell them that they're going to lose. Each of us played our individual parts, but we didn't get together to turn the campaign."

Paddy is speaking to one of the Aquarian challenges: how to motivate the individual for the collective good.
 Aquarius, while being a fixed sign, also seeks to evolve and break through the status quo.

We see this in an interview American actress, Glenn Close, gave to theGuardian.com:

"I think it's difficult," she says. "I don't think the male ego is necessarily conducive to having a really successful and recognisable partner. I think it can be hard and I now accept that!" She laughs and tells me about a Harvard study that showed both men and women tend to warm more to female figures who are more traditionally feminine and nurturing. It's not a fact that Close has paid much attention to, though, her career typified by characters who refuse to comply with old-fashioned gender conventions.

From an article for the DailyMail.co.uk English actress, Julie Walters, shows strong Aquarian expression:

You don't so much interview Julie Walters as have a natter with her. Though she is a dame now, she is suspicious of any sniff of pretension, so she undermines anything that sounds like a formal question with a hoot of laughter. And you feel a bit of a fool for trying to analyse her.

Venus in Pisces on the DS

These individuals have a profound desire to fall deeply madly and fully in love, preferably with their soul mates. Boundaries are a challenge for these people.

Former captive, Patty Hearst, who also has her Sun here, suffered from Stockholm Syndrome, which Wikipedia.org defines as "a condition that causes hostages to develop a psychological alliance with their captors as a survival strategy during captivity."

Pisces can have issues of self-worth as seen with former First Lady, Betty Ford, who also has her Moon here. The following comes from her obituary at NYTimes.com:

"From the outside, our life looked like a Norman Rockwell illustration," Mrs. Ford said at one point. Nevertheless, by 1962, she was seeing a psychiatrist twice a week because, as she put it, "I'd lost my feeling of self-worth."

Pisces does not live life like any other sign so it is easy for a Piscean person to think that they are not in-sync with everyone else.

Here is an interesting tidbit about actress, singer and performer, Carol Channing:

Channing had reminisced about her first love, Harry Kullijian, in her memoir. A friend told Kullijian that he had been mentioned in Channing's book, which was a surprise to him, as he'd thought his old flame had already passed away. Knowing Channing was still around prompted Kullijian to reach out to her in 2003. A few months later, they were married. The pair had several happy years together before Kullijian passed away in 2011.

From BloomLiteraryJournal.org comes this apt understanding of how this astrological placement worked out in the life of American poet, Reginald Shepherd:

> Marilyn Hacker has described Shepherd as "brilliant and elegiac ... a writer always conscious of the shadowy borders where myth and history—his own and Western civilization's—mingle."

American rock star, Kurt Cobain, who also has his Mercury here, is quoted in BrainyQuote.com as saying:

> "If you die you're completely happy and your soul somewhere lives on. I'm not afraid of dying. Total peace after death, becoming someone else is the best hope I've got."

This is a perfect statement by Kurt of Piscean values.

We will now look at the angle placements of Venus throughout the zodiac from the point of view of the Medium Coeli (MC)

Venus in Aries on the MC

These are individuals who value their ability to put their heads first in their work. The image that comes to my mind is when American film star, Jack Nicholson, uses an axe to cut through the door in *The Shining* and pokes his head through and says, "Here's Johnny!" There is also a sex symbol sort of aspect to this as Aries is about seeding everywhere. Jack was a sex symbol.

Fashion designer, Charlotte Ford, who also has her Sun here, was devoted to bringing beauty to the working-class woman through her clothing lines. Charlotte individuated from her auto-industry-dominated family and made a name for herself.

As Aries is one of the signs of physical athleticism, it is interesting to find an allusion to mental athleticism. Chess champion, Bobby Fischer, had this written about him in his NYTimes.com obituary:

> Mr. Fischer won with such brilliance and dramatic flair that he became an icon, an unassailable representative of greatness in the world of competitive games, much as Babe Ruth had been and Michael Jordan would become.

Aries also rules the head, so here we find a valuing of the competitive mind and understanding and using strategies to win with these natives.

People with this astrological placement can receive early recognition of their beauty as in the case of Swedish singer, Ted Gärdestad. Wikipedia.com states:

> By 1975 [when he was 19], Ted had become a big star in Sweden, with his boyish good looks he was prominently featured in teen magazines like *Starlet*, *Mitt Livs Novell* and *Poster*, his love life and teenage romances were even covered by the national dailies, he had his own

fan club, all his albums had gone gold and had also sold well in the rest of Scandinavia, besides ABBA he was the Polar Music label's best-selling artist."

Having one's love life seen and reviewed by the public further defines this astrological placement. Unfortunately, Ted jumped in front of a train and committed suicide—a very Aries act, no?

I highly recommend reading theGuardian.com article on world surfing champion, Lisa Andersen. So much of her story speaks of the immediacy of her experience in relationship to life and her fierce competitive nature, which this astrological placement strongly supports. Brava.

Venus in Taurus on the MC

Venus rules Taurus, so when these individuals have done their work, the rewards are well received. This placement points to people who have very defined or fixed value systems. They are not usually swayed by what others say or do as they know they are right!

Our first example was a staunch anti-gay spokesperson who stuck to her religious values. American singer, Anita Bryant even received a public pie in the face!! Perfect expression of this placement.

In the obituary from NYTimes.com for the Australian writer, Patrick White, "Andre Malraux, called his work "an epic and psychological narrative art which has introduced a new continent into literature." It said he had "given the continent of Australia an authentic voice that carries across the world."

When one thinks of the values of loyalty to one's own home and sharing it with the world, Patrick did a great job.

American songwriter and performer, Willie Nelson, who also has his Sun here, has a very down to earth, approachable grounded way in which he approaches his music as well as his marijuana and Farm Aid advocacy.

In an impromptu interview recounted in FilmSchoolRejects.com, Australian-Scottish actor and singer, Colin Hay, gives some wise Taurean words about the relationship to our own stubbornness:

"I wish I'd listened to advice when I was younger. Because people gave me advice and I took none of it. I thought I knew everything and I knew nothing. So now I know that if you give advice to someone they probably won't listen. Sometimes you feel like it's worth the effort, but usually people just have to find their own path. Just hack it out."

From his archives, Laurence Galian, the Dervish spiritual author stated:

"Back in the 1950's and 60's they used to talk about "Beat Zen" vs. "Square Zen". Laurence Galian's Sun at Midnight represents a kind of hip Islam, warmhearted and heretical, opposed to everything monolithic and dour in Islam. If such a thing as American Sufism ever appears, this will be one of its holy books."

From BBC.com comes this apt reflection of the greatest cricket batsman of all time, Sachin Ramesh Tendulkar:

> Beneath the helmet, under that unruly curly hair, inside the cranium, there is something we don't know, something beyond scientific measure. Something that allows him to soar, to roam a territory of sport that, forget us, even those who are gifted enough to play alongside him cannot even fathom. When he goes out to bat, people switch on their television sets and switch off their lives."

That magnetic quality is visceral in that quote.

Venus in Gemini on the MC

These individuals make an impression on the public for their bubbly and playful natures.

A quote from actor, Tom Hanks, captures the thoughtful divergent mind of the Gemini:

> "It's always a combination of physics and poetry that I find inspiring. It's hard to wrap your head around things like the Hubble scope."

Model and actress, Brooke Shields, who also has her Moon here, describes her strong and ever-present twin-like relationship with her agent/mother, "I didn't know where my mother ended and I began," wrote Shields in her memoir *There was a Little Girl*.

American musician, Kim Carnes, captures this astrological placement in two of her quotes from BrainyQuote.com:

"I was gonna write songs, I was gonna be a star and a singer and I never thought of doing anything else."

"I write from what's in my heart. I write what I love and have always done that."

In an interview with Advocate.com, songwriter, Holly Near, talks about her indefinable style:

"I have never been comfortable with boxes and identities. I grew up listening to so many styles of music, so it has always been toxic to me when asked what kind of music I do. Is it folk? Pop? Musical theater? I don't think it is any of that standing alone. It is a fusion of styles."

The headline for an article on singer, Marcia Hines, shows all the themes of Venus, Gemini and the MC:

She is famous for her diva curves, but the heartbreak diet is an effective one. Just weeks after announcing she is divorcing her fourth husband, Dr. Christopher Morrissey-Marcia Hines has dropped two dress sizes and is now a very svelte size 10.

In an interview with fetishist photographer/blogger, Rick Castro, for DazedDigital.com, Rick answers the question, "What's the biggest misconception about fetish?" Rick Castro replies:

> "That it's perversion. In fact it's the opposite. Fetish is the exploration of sex as art, and the refinement of one's personal desires. Anything can be fetishized. I can basically exhibit anything at my fetish art gallery. There'll be new fetishes forever. I feel that the 21st century is all about fetish."

Four-time married singer, Sheena Easton, who shares this astrological placement with Marcia Hines above, said this in an article for the DailyMail.co.uk:

> "I don't date a lot. When I get involved with somebody, I either get involved with them and it's over very fast, or I get involved with them then I get married very fast—then I get to know them!"

Gemini can have a hummingbird-like quick energy about it.

Azaria Chamberlain, the nine-week old baby who was abducted and killed by dingoes, makes our list a second time as she has her Sun here as well. I wonder if her story would have been so public if she didn't have this prominent astrological placement?

Venus in Cancer on the MC

These people exude an enchanting, warm and welcoming public persona.

From the NYTimes.com obituary of horror actor extraordinaire, Christopher Lee, his "cinematic identity became forever associated with Bram Stoker's noble, ravenous vampire, who in Mr. Lee's characterization exuded a certain lascivious sex appeal." Lee brought Venusian virtues of grace, nobility and beguiling manner to his evil character.

Amanda and Stephen Mays, the test tube twins who also have Mercury here, were difficult for me to find any discussion on the internet except for their birth. Cancer is the sign of the crab. What does a crab do when it is observed? It hides in its shell or runs into a cave. These two probably love and value their personal privacy or maybe we don't need to hear what these to have to say to us?

Iconic dancer and choreographer, Natalie van Parys, is another example of one who is difficult to find anything about her personal life on line. A watery Venus would aid one in flowing with a graceful body.

Venus in Leo on the MC

Here we have individuals who need love and attention. The majority of these people have a following, as many with this astrological placement are in the entertainment industry.

Musical performer, Bill Medley, of the Righteous Brothers comments in an interview he did with Express.co.uk:

> "I dated some of the greatest women in the world. I started an affair with singer, Darlene Love, had an on-off affair with Mary Wilson of the Supremes, and another with singer, Connie Stevens, but was scared to death of commitment."

The person who uses this placement on the personality level is more likely to experience love with groupies and fans rather than the depth of love from one person. Of course, this is also a maturity factor, as one grows, one is more likely to seek increasingly deeper levels of connection. Look at pictures of Bill in his later years—he looks very leonine.

Our next example, Los Angeles Underground Disc Jockey, Barbara Birdfeather, started out as an astrologer, but being a DJ provided her with a more favorable stage.

When we visit the website NickFaldo.com, we see numerous Leo archetypes emphasized. Leo is the sign of royalty, and the first thing that pops out on his website is the word *SIR*. As Leo energy often expresses the native's mane of hair, we find another quote regarding the career of golf's greatest maverick champions:

> "I was just absolutely mesmerized when I saw the Masters that year, particularly by Jack Nicklaus, striding across Augusta's impossibly green fairways. I marched downstairs and announced to my Mum that I was going to take up golf. 'You're having a haircut first' she said, which seemed like a fair enough deal at the time—even if Augusta was waiting!"

The longest living pair of conjoined twins, Lori and George Schappell, show some notable traits. George who started his life as Dori, is the one who was pushed around on his "throne" a wheelchair-like device. George is also a Country Western singer.

In a candid interview with WMagazine.com actress, Nicole Kidman, discusses her approach to acting:

> "I was willing to do that for the role because that's what I felt was important for the role. When I talk about not censoring myself through my own inhibitions and not then affecting a story or a character because of my own inhibitions, I'm here to tell the story and to be true to the art, not to bring my own problems in terms of what I feel comfortable with, not comfortable with. I've got to go work that stuff out so that I can come as a pure vessel to the work, if that makes sense."

Olympic swimmer, Eamon Sullivan, also won the Celebrity Master Chef Australia. Eamon found a good way to remain on stage.

Pakistani politician, Bilawal Bhutto Zardari, speaks to the individual values espoused by this astrological placement from BrainyQuote.com:

> "How is it reasonable that in a country purporting to be a democracy, I am not permitted to speak freely? Why, as a politician, should I be banned from expressing political opinions? Why, as a student of history, can

I not present the facts as I see them, without fear of reprisal?"

Venus in Virgo on the MC

Our first example shows us the humility-building qualities of this placement and both examples speak to the ever perfecting drive to question it all.

Duchess of York, Sarah Ferguson, discussed her life with Oprah in 2011 for a six-part documentary. From an article entitled, "Saving Sarah from Herself, Oprah Style" for NYTimes.com, Sarah discussed fundamental issues about the Virgo archetype. Virgo often gets a bad rap about being discriminating, rigid and critical, but one needs to understand that the native is perfecting, but they are not perfect. They are often painfully aware of what is not right and how to fix, modify and improve on that which came before. The interviewer writes:

> Her desire to be liked often overrides her self-protective impulse. So much so that during one taping break, she gave this reporter a thumb's up and mouthed the words, "Am I doing O.K.?" When asked later about her tendency toward self-deprecatory apology, she seemed puzzled. "Why do I apologize?" she wondered aloud. "I think it's playing into my addiction of people pleasing and approval and acceptance." She fell silent, then added, "And do you think that it could also be that I am

truly sorry to have broken everybody's illusion about the fairy tale?"

We can feel the burden she is carrying and Fergie has had a wonderful grace about being in relationship to her perfecting experiences. What are failures in our life but opportunities to do better in the future? Venus teaches us grace.

Actress, Evan Rachel Wood, appears on our list a second time as she has her Pisces Moon conjunct her IC. In an interview for the RollingStones.com, she asks some very Virgo questions:

> "What if this is all bullshit?" Wood asks. "What if this is just conditioning? What if all this is learned and not true? Who am I really, without my programming?"

The Virgo/Pisces axis is one of perfecting and letting it all go and accepting the all-that-is. This polarity is one of being in relationship to people and the world as well as reality versus fantasy.

Venus in Libra on the MC

Here we are in the beautiful portion of the Zodiac again. Venus is the ruler of Libra and imparts a grace of relatability and movement in general, but heightened ambassadorship and sportsmanship agility when found on the MC. This is a unifying astrological placement that finds distaste in disharmonious, less than ideal ways of interacting with others, well, mostly.

As we know, there are no fans like soccer fans. English footballer, Alan Shearer, has a particular relationship with his fans and we learn a bit about it from an article in theGuardian.com:

> The peculiar psyche of Newcastle, which encourages the fans to deify weaklings like Kevin Keegan and run proper professionals like Sam Allardyce out of town, means that they crave a hero who ticks certain basic boxes, and Shearer did that. In return he got an adoration entirely disproportionate to his achievements, and a reputation that consequently stayed intact despite compelling evidence to the contrary.

Australian freestyle swimmer, Ian Thorpe, who also has Mercury here, has a very public relationship and shows how much he values this by supporting the same-sex marriage vote in Australia. The following comes from an article in the DailyTelegraph.com.au:

> "Thorpe and his partner, Ryan Channing, made the decision to openly commit themselves to supporting the 'yes' vote, filming a TV commercial together which encouraged voters to register for the postal survey."

Finding out anything about Prince Hitachi, fourth in line to the Japan1ese Imperial throne, was difficult. From http://www.kunaicho.go.jp/e-about/history/history04.html, we find a listing of his Honorary Positions. Many of them have Libra and Venus themes:

- Reserve Member of the Imperial House Council
- President of the Japanese Society for the Preservation of Birds
- President of the Japanese Society for Disabled Children
- President of the Japan Institute of Invention and Innovation
- President of the Japan-Denmark Society
- President of the Dainippon Silk Foundation
- President of the Japanese Society for Rehabilitation of Persons with Disabilities
- President of the Japan Art Association
- President of the Tokyo Zoological Park Society
- President of Maison Franco-Japonaise
- President of the Princess Takamatsu Cancer Research Fund
- Honorary President of the Japan-Sweden Society
- Honorary President of the Japan-Belgium Society
- Honorary President of the Japanese Foundation for Cancer Research
- Honorary President of Association Pasteur Japon
- Honorary Vice-President of the Japanese Red Cross Society

From Wikipedia.com comes this articulate statement about Chess Master, Jeremy Silman:

In his books, Silman evaluates positions according to the "imbalances", or differences, which exist in every position, and advocates that players plan their play according to these.

Libra is the sign of balance and so the awareness of imbalances are glaring to someone with such a maverick placement.

Disc jockey, Don Sherwood, became one of the early radio personalities in the San Francisco Bay area. One can easily understand this astrological positioning playing out in his life as stated in this SFgate.com article:

> From 1953 to 1969 at KSFO, Sherwood dominated the morning ratings and became a weekday habit for Bay Area commuters. In his on-the-air antics he involved his audience in a personal life that included five marriages, a paternity suit, arrests for drunken driving and running battles with sponsors and management.

Venus in Scorpio on the MC

These are individuals who value and need depth in their work. While they appreciate their privacy, they do not have that luxury. They are here to show us a range of expression not many are willing to show.

Our first example of this is not really a surprise. She played a range of roles from an innocent, coming of age woman in *Rocky Horror Picture Show,* to aged seductress in *Bull Durham,* to a feminist reborn in *Thelma and Louise.* Her political activism is no different. She is not afraid to express her values publicly; she expresses her truth. Of course, we are speaking of Susan Sarandon.

Deeply meaningful relationships and friendships are highlighted here as well. South African actor comedian, Bill Flynn, had a prolific career. In his obituary in Variety.com, we find the following lovely statement:

> His long-time close friend and collaborator, Paul Slabolepsky, with whom he worked closely on stage and film productions since they met at the University of Cape Town 40 years ago, said South Africa had lost a "brilliant creative artist" who was one of the world's "top comedic talents." He said they had spent "thousands of nights making mayhem" together on and off stage ever since they met.

Political author and analyst, Donna Brazile, is not afraid to go deep to expose the flaws in a system. She understands that while that may look like a delicious cake because all we can see is the frosting, her Scorpio sensitivity can determine whether it was made with excremental or tasty ingredients. Venus wants it all to be smooth, pretty and beautiful, but in this placement, she is not afraid to get dirty to find the underlying cause of something as shown by each of our examples. This investigative probing into the inner workings of the government benefits the public. Another example of this aspect is the deep need for privacy, as shown in our next example.

Queen Elizabeth of Britain's first grandson, Prince Peter Phillips of England, is one who keeps his lineage a secret. Peter actually took some six weeks before he let his future fiancée know of his royal background and only then because she had seen him on the television at a royal event. This once again illustrates the inability of a Scorpio to hide.

Venus in Sagittarius on the MC

These individuals have an over abiding value for freedom and personal expression that enthralls and excites the masses.

This is easily seen in the death-defying stunts and motorcycle jumps, Evel Knievel performed in the 1970's.

Iconic, always changing English singer-songwriter, David Bowie, appears here for a second time. Bowie had a multitude of personas: Ziggy Stardust, Aladdin Sane, The Thin White Duke, The Goblin King, Blind Prophet. The following comments on Bowie come from CataWiki.com:

> Even when showing the real David it comes with a theatrical touch clothed in many layers.

Entertaining and witty actress and comedienne, Whoopi Goldberg, is able to share her values, relationships, views of life and experiences which are her Truth on the talk show, *The View*.

Venus in Capricorn on the MC

These individuals shine being competent while reaching for social status. Two of our three examples are political and speak to the importance of building strategic working relationships.

American politician, Robert Kennedy, was the brother to U.S. President JFK, as well as his attorney general and a U.S. Senator. Like his brother, Robert was assassinated and worked hard to pass the Civil Rights Act of 1964.

United States Presidential hopeful, Gary Hart, showed another side of this astrological placement. Gary's relationships with women became front and center for the world to review and dashed any hopes to becoming President.

Climbing cyclist, Marco Pantani who also has his Mercury here, shows the Capricorn drive to climb to the top. Marco's pursuit for career success was stronger than his desire to be in relationship. Capricorn is single-focused and has the determination that will not allow anything to thwart its goals.

Venus in Aquarius on the MC

What a wonderful place for bringing awareness of Feminism and valuing all individuals in humanity.

American novelist and poet, Erica Jong, is probably best known for her 1973 novel *Fear of Flying*. This book was controversial for its attitudes towards female sexuality and, according to Wikipedia, "figured prominently in the development of second-wave feminism."

American actress, Jennifer Jason Leigh, who has her Sun and Moon here as well, shows her rather unorthodox approach to the roles she plays as stated in this quote from IMDB.com:

"But in mainstream movies the woman's role is mostly just to prove that the leading man is heterosexual. I'm not good at that, and I'm not interested in that."

From HindustanTimes.com, comes a quote from Indian movie director, Meghna Gulzar, in reply to what she finds most satisfying:

"Filmmaking. It encompasses all the others. Writing is obviously involved during the development of a story. Poetry makes an appearance in the songs of a film. Journalism and research are required in the scripting of a film, sometimes for a milieu, or a particular historical fact or incident that is referred to in the film; sometimes a geographical location, sometimes a character's backstory, profession, etc."

The observational and governing Aquarian nature would well benefit a film director.

Venus in Aquarius can seek many unique lovers. Here we see this in the life of Christine Keeler from her obituary in TheGuardian.com:

Keeler, then a teenage model and showgirl, became famous for her role in the 1963 scandal that rocked the establishment when she had an affair with the Tory cabinet minister John Profumo and a Russian diplomat at the same time at the height of the cold war. Profumo was eventually forced to resign after lying to parliament about the affair.

Mamphela Aletta Ramphele, is a South African politician, and was an important activist against apartheid. The title of a BusinessDayOnline.com article on her highlights her Aquarian values, "Mamphela Aletta Ramphele the revolutionary leader." Bringing Aquarian values to the public is strongly indicated with this position and Mamphela is a beautiful maverick example.

Venus in Pisces on the MC

This is a beautiful placement as there can be understanding and acceptance for everyone. Jupiter is the traditional ruler of Pisces and when we add the other benefic planet Venus, we find transcendental love. Neptune, as the modern ruler of Pisces speaks to our Spiritual Love.

There is, therefore, no surprise that our first example has "it" in his name! Mike *Love*. Unfortunately, according to RollingStones.com, his fame does not sync-up with his name or this placement:

> At the same time, however, Love is considered one of the biggest assholes in the history of rock & roll. That's been the popular opinion of him for several decades. He just can't seem to shake it. There are "I Hate Mike Love"

websites and a "Mike Love Is a Douchebag" group on Facebook. He's been called a clown, the Devil, an evil, egotistical prick, a greedy bully, sarcastic and mean-spirited, and, let's not forget, "if he were a fish, he'd be a plastic bag wrapped around the neck of a beautiful sea lion." Love is mostly able to laugh off this hateful venom, but on occasion, he will break down, turn to his wife of 21 years, Jackie, and ask her, "What did I do? Why am I the villain? How did it get to this?"

Interestingly enough, Mike has had a meditative practice for some *49 years*—very Piscean!

Australian Olympic swimmer, Ilsa Konrads, shares her passion for the water with the public.

Fabulous out actor, Nathan Lane, shows us the strength of being flexible in his way of relating to others, and the roles he portrays on both screen and stage.

Former U.S. Massachusetts Senator, Cheryl Ann Jacques, an activist for LGBT rights, uses her influence to build harmony to understand we are all One.

Mars

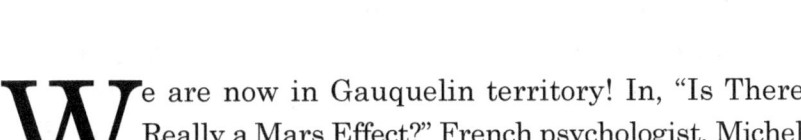

We are now in Gauquelin territory! In, "Is There Really a Mars Effect?" French psychologist, Michel Gauquelin wrote the following:

Since the publication of my first book *L'Influence des Astres* (The Influence of the Stars) in 1955, I have published numerous works regarding my discovery of a series of highly significant statistical correlations between planetary positions and the birth times of eminently successful people. One of the strongest correlations I have observed is that sports champions tend to be born when the planet Mars is either rising or culminating in the sky much more often than it does for ordinary people... This particular observation, later called "the Mars Effect" by researchers who have investigated it, has been verified by the experiments of other scientists.

From Scribd.com we learn more about Michel Gauquelin:

> Although he was highly critical of certain areas of the art, Gauquelin showed an interest in astrology from an early age; it is said that he could calculate a birth chart at the age of ten and earned the nickname of Nostradamus at school because of his astrological readings. After studying psychology and statistics at the Sorbonne, he devoted his life to the attempt to demonstrate the validity of certain fundamentals of astrology. However, he did not define himself as an astrologer and opposed the practice of astrology. Up to his death, he tried first and foremost to show the inanity of astrology, in reaction to his father, who was an enthusiastic defender of the practice.

Who better to conduct statistical research on astrological effects than someone who doesn't believe in the practice? Gauquelin is represented twice in this book as he was born with Jupiter in Taurus conjunct his MC opposing Mercury in conjunction with his Scorpio IC -- and what did he do? He gave credibility to astrology. He conducted sound statistical research and communicated the positive findings to the world. Gauquelin also presented a philosophy to the bull of modern-day science. Remember, prior to the modern age, astrology was considered a science, too.

MARS

As stated in the beginning of the book, I was born with Mars in the course of stationing retrograde. This is a very slow-moving Mars in the process of becoming inwardly focused and it is conjunct my Virgo Midheaven. This is why Gauquelin's resonates with me through my natal Mars placement.

Where we find Mars in the chart is where we find the Male self whether we were born male or female, our desire nature and how we need to be active—on many levels, but especially the physical level. Mars represents our "drive" in life as well as how we are courageous and willing to take up the "fight"—or not. Mars also shows how we express our passion and the house where we find our Mars is where we will express it the easiest (unless, of course there are challenging aspects to it, if it is retrograde or is in detriment or fall). Our Mars also represents our warrior side as it rules the two warrior signs: Aries and Scorpio. Further, Mars is traditionally considered the lesser malefic, while Saturn is the greater malefic. A malefic has been traditionally seen as what is described as bad luck. This makes sense when we consider that our desire nature and drive are what often push up against others and get us into the most trouble!

We will now look at the angle placements of Mars throughout the zodiac from the point of view of the Ascendant (AS).

Mars in Aries on the AS

This is a very heady position for Mars. These individuals will likely be interested in and known for being drawn to speed and competition. They may be red headed, highly individualistic or any other mixture of instinctual headstrong Aries/Martian energy. How an individual is able to handle their passions and desires will be of importance if one wants some peace in life.

In the Independent.co.uk obituary for Argentinian Formula One race car driver, Juan Manuel Fangio, the writer renders a solid understanding of this archetype:

> Only truly great sportsmen are revered as much when competing as they are in retirement, and in Juan Manuel Fangio's case his charisma accorded him a godlike status. His name became a synonym for speed. Arguably the greatest racing driver of them all, while he behaved like a world champion at all times, he had a firm sense of the place of competitors in his world. Juan was a true maverick.

American Jazz great, Morty Corb, died from a brain aneurysm—very Mars in Aries.

Activist and academic, Rodney Croome, used this astrological position of strong determination to help decriminalize same sex relationships in Tasmania, as well as being an activist for same sex couples, bisexual and transgendered people in Australia.

Here's what SkySports.com writes about the highest paid footballer, Christiano Ronaldo:

> "We should always believe we are the best," said Ronaldo, who led Portugal to the Euro 2016 title. "You need to think big. I always believe that nobody is better than me, out on the pitch at least. On a personal and collective level I have had a dream year. I won five trophies (Champions League, UEFA Supercup, World Club Cup, Spanish league title and the Spanish Supercup), the Ballon D'Or and the FIFA 'Best' title."

We can see the resonant themes of such a strong Mars placement. Christiano is also considered a sex symbol, another aspect of this hyper masculine placement.

Mars in Taurus on the AS

These people have a very strong presence.

Australian opera singer, Joan Sutherland, who makes our list a second time here, was known for her large physical frame (Mars/Taurus). The following comes from her obituary at theGuardian.com:

> On the opening night in 1959, she received a rapturous reception for both her acting and singing. She became

an overnight star in the international firmament of opera. From then on, it was one of the success stories of the century, a delirious conquest of one leading opera house after another. She had arrived on the scene at just the right time, able to take up and extend the bel canto repertoire that had been revived by Callas after many years of neglect.

Taurus loves a practical daily approach to life and Mars is the fire or the engine that can keep it going like a regularly scheduled steam engine. The following quote comes from an article in Wmagazine.com and is a snippet on artist, Don Bachary's very fixed and set approach to life:

> In the mornings, Don Bachardy rises with the sun. He reads quietly until half past noon, when he puts his book down and, like he's done nearly every day for five decades, picks up a paintbrush. "Working makes me feel good; it's what keeps me going."

Remember that Taurus is the polarity to Scorpio, so there can be a dismissive nature with this placement. Singer, Mariah Carey started a revolution of throwing "shade" as discussed in this piece from VanityFair.com:

> From this moment emerged an interview so shady it could only be born out of the dark arts of one Mariah Carey. In the seconds-long exchange, Mariah smiles and says, "I don't know her," and a meme is born.

Crown Prince Al-Muhtadee Billah of Brunei, shows the competitive side of this maverick combination. This is a very physical and competitive astrological placement. We learn the following from Astro.com:

> Throughout his school years, Prince Al-Muhtadee Billah was an enthusiastic participant in competitive sports – badminton, Sepak Takraw, volley ball, soccer, bowling, snooker and polo. Of these, Prince Al-Muhtadee Billah developed a particular interest in soccer, snooker and badminton. He played regularly as goalkeeper in his local soccer team in Brunei and enthusiastically followed international soccer. In badminton, Prince Al-Muhtadee Billah took part in the RBA-Helix competition and in the Royal Brunei-Helix World Grand Prix Circuit Tournament. Prince Al-Muhtadee Billah kept up his strong interest in snooker, while at school and later at Oxford, and took part in national and international competitions.

Mars in Gemini on the AS

This astrological placement will likely give one a very persuasive way of communicating as well as provide an amazing network.

Retired U.S. Secretary of State, Henry Kissinger, is quite an example of this astrological placement. An article for Politico.com shares more:

About halfway through writing my biography of Henry Kissinger, an interesting hypothesis occurred to me: Did the former secretary of state owe his success, fame and notoriety not just to his powerful intellect and formidable will but also to his exceptional ability to build an eclectic network of relationships, not only to colleagues in the Nixon and Ford administrations, but also to people outside government: journalists, newspaper proprietors, foreign ambassadors and heads of state—even Hollywood producers? If Volume I had surprised readers with its subtitle—"The Idealist"—should Volume II perhaps be subtitled "The Networker"?

Astrologer, Madalyn Hills-Dineen, gave an interview recorded at Alabe.com in which she stated her desired area of focus:

"I am happily retired from the world of astro-politics and have turned my attention to volunteering in various capacities in my community. I'm using the skills I acquired as an NCGR [National Council for Geocosmic Research] volunteer (leadership skills, negotiating, event planning, desktop publishing) to benefit some worthy causes, and I feel very good about it. When I contribute to my community, I hope that I am also representing myself as an astrologer in such a way as to give a favorable impression of our profession and, perhaps, help to change some negative opinions about astrology along the way."

Gemini is one of the signs associated with language and astrology is a language. Madalyn isn't afraid to take the lead.

American novelist, Erica Jong, inserted feminism into the collective consciousness to balance the masculine and feminine. Gemini is a dual sign seeking some sort of unity and harmonic balance (as the sister air sign of Libra does as well).

This quote by American singer-songwriter, John Denver, in his NYTimes.com obituary, sums up this astrological placement beautifully:

"My music and all my work stem from the conviction that people everywhere are intrinsically the same," he once said. "When I write a song, I want to take the personal experience that inspired it and express it in as universal way as possible. I'm a global citizen."

As Mars likes to take a leadership role, especially when on such a highly visible point as the Ascendant, there is no surprise that former Prime Minister of the United Kingdom, Tony Blair, has an Institute for Global Change. From its website, Institute.global comes another perfect rendition of this astrological placement:

The Tony Blair Institute for Global Change aims to help make globalization work for the many, not the few. We do this by helping countries, their people and their governments address some of the most difficult challenges in the world today.

We need to remember that the Mars glyph, or symbol, represents the masculine member or phallus. And as Gemini is the sign of duality and communication, we have the straight, bisexual, and gay porn star, Jeff Stryker. John Waters called Stryker the Cary Grant of porn stars. This is a very electric and charismatic position.

Mars in Cancer on the AS

Mars is said to be in its detriment here. Think of trying to keep a young buck at home–he is not going to be happy!

Automobile heiress, Josephine Ford, struck out on her own, as a Martian driven individual would do. With this astrological placement, there would be a challenge in individuating from the family as elucidated in the following quote in her LATimes.com obituary:

> "What else is there for a girl who wasn't competitive to do but try to escape all that Ford stuff?"

Josephine was known for her generous philanthropic nature.

Musician and singer, Cecil Womack, makes our list a third time with this astrological placement emphasizing his Sun and Venus IC conjunction in Libra: focus on the family. Cecil's career really took off once he was in a creative relationship.

In an article about Simone Baker, one of the last Thalidomide babies, the Guardian.com writes:

She became friends with a very fat girl called Wendy, another outcast, and together they refused to be bullied.

Even for being different, Mars can still be a fierce defender especially when found in Cancer. Crabs have claws.

Mars in Leo on the AS

This is a very strong placement for Mars. These are individuals who have a profound desire to be seen.

Author, Alex Haley, makes our list a second time, he was the author of the book *Roots*. He courageously portrayed some of America's less than ideal history while sharing the intimate heart of his family story. In addition, sometimes these astrological placements can play out in our deaths as Alex died from cardiac arrest.

Most everyone on the planet at this time knows there is no one who loves the stage like Donald Trump. I would say he is the poster child for this position as he represents one aspect of this placement: unadulterated narcissistic expression. He has a grand desire to be seen as the king of all, without question and has no ability or desire to hear anyone's reflection of him. In fact, he has an amazing ability to spin any negative comment into ego supporting statement.

From theGlobeandMail.com comes a lovely illustration of this astrological placement in a book review written by Canadian novelist, Leon Rooke:

He writes out of a wagonload of traditions that include the American postmodernism of Donald Barthelme, Robert Coover, William Gass and Richard Brautigan, and the school of southern bombast (William Faulkner, Barry Hannah and Flannery O'Connor – and by "bombast" I don't mean a negative; I mean the high-flown stentorian style of the great southern preachers, rhythmic, hammering, mellifluous and grand).

Documentarian, director and disturber of questionable politicians and general never do wells, Michael Moore, makes our list a second time as he has Venus conjunct his Libra IC. We can see the issue with Michael is understanding what is right for people versus what do self-centering desires make us do? This astrological placement gives him the egoic strength to stand up to the "big guys" because he doesn't see them as more important than himself.

Actor, Robin Williams, named his daughter after the video game character called Princess Zelda, and his daughter benefited from strong family connections to help her acting career.

Mars in Virgo on the AS

These are very capable and driven individuals.

U.S. President, Lyndon B. Johnson, who also has a stellium here with his Moon, Sun and Mars, helped guide the United States during a difficult time. While many would look to the sign of Libra for statesmanship, in the sign of Virgo one can access resources and be both flexible and discriminating. These are impeccable traits when leading a country. Virgo seeks perfection, and with so many planets in Virgo, President Johnson left a significant mark on U.S. political history. The following comes from an abstract available at onlinelibrary.Wiley.com:

> The result, famously christened "The Johnson Treatment," remains the archetype practitioners and political scientists cite when appraising presidential leadership on Capitol Hill.

I have to say; I love that they used the word *archetype*. When we have many planets in one sign, the native is really working with a wide range expression within the archetype of that sign. With President Johnson, we had a leader who understood he was serving the American people, not just the wealthy.

Staying with the theme of U.S. leadership, we have former First Lady, Betty Ford, who has already made our list twice for her Piscean planets on her DS, and now for her Mars in a retrograde position conjunct her Virgo Ascendant. This fits in perfectly with her issues of self-worth, which had to be healed in order for her to step into her power and admit she had a problem with her relationship with alcohol. This is indicated by her Pisces planets conjunct her Descendant. Betty Ford's maverick strengths helped her to set up a clinic to assist others address their own issues and heal.

Comedic actor, Peter Sellers, who also has his Sun here, shows another side that is interesting with this Mars/Virgo relationship. Peter didn't have any trouble donning one of a multitude of disguises, especially if he felt it would give him the information he needed to solve his case. His resourceful Mars in Virgoan gave him a crafty guile.

In her obituary for LATimes.com, American singer and actress, Della Reese, was quoted as saying the following:

> "I was lying there on that bed while I convalesced, looking back at what I had done with my life. I had done some marvelous things, but they were all for me or my immediate family. If I had died there and then, what could people say I had accomplished?" she said in 2003. "So, after I recovered, I went to school and studied metaphysics at the Johnnie Colemon Institute in Chicago and got my certificate."

Virgo is rarely interested in just one thing.

English actor, Derek Jacobi, played a resourceful and persuasive monk in the *Cadfael* series in which he plays the lead role. I would love to explain it, but Wikipedia expresses this astrological placement so well:

> As a character, Cadfael "combines the curious mind of a scientist/pharmacist with a knight-errant". He entered the cloister in his forties after being both a soldier and a sailor; this worldly experience gives him an array of talents and skills useful in monastic life. He is a skilled observer of human nature, inquisitive by nature, energetic, a talented herbalist (work he learned in the

Holy Lands), and has an innate, although modern, sense of justice and fair-play. Abbots call upon him as a medical examiner, detective, doctor, and diplomat. His worldly knowledge, although useful, gets him in trouble with the more doctrinaire characters of the series, and the seeming contradiction between the secular and the spiritual worlds forms a central and continuing theme of the stories.

American actress, Sissy Spacek, has been "kissed by Mars" as she has reddish tones in her face and hair and, if that wasn't enough, I do not think there could be a more graphic coming of age image than the blood bath scene in the movie *Carrie*.

American film star, Brooke Shields, who makes our list a second time, was also known for her coming of age film the *Blue Lagoon*. As the Ascendant is about our appearance, and the combination of Mars and Virgo can be about fitness, it is no surprise that she can still, at 52, fit into her original Calvin Klein jeans she wore for an advertisement back in 1980.

English footballer, Michael Owen, shows another aspect of this astrological combination: masculine attractiveness. Look up some of his quotes and you will see that Michael is not as discriminating in what he says as he should be, given this placement.

Backstreet Boys band member, Nick Carter shows yet another aspect of this astrological placement when the masculine takes advantage of the feminine after Melissa Schuman accused him of rape.

ASTROLOGICAL MAVERICKS

Mars in Libra on the AS

Mars is in detriment in Libra because it is a challenge to work towards harmonious relationships with others while being driven by our personal desire nature. Mars usually represents energies such as male, drive, leading, inserting and striking forth—those aspects that reflect only one side of Libra's contrariety.

Former U.S. President Bill Clinton, who also has his Venus here, is known for his desire nature and how it played out in the oval office. Clinton has an insatiable need to exchange.

In the case of British-American singer, Barry Gibb, I find it interesting that people saw his masculine beauty with long perfectly coiffed hair and a higher than normal octave for a man's voice. Libra rules singing and the Arts.

The first of our two murderer examples is serial killer, Charles Albright. The following comes from Maamodt.asp.radford.edu and is a telling example of what can happen with Mars in Libra on the AS:

> As a child he was doted upon and would be dressed in girl's clothes and given a doll at times when his aunt was present. He was an impulsive child and would always manage to get out of the yard behind where his mother worked. She searched the fence and found no openings, but later learned he would wait for people passing by and simply would ask them to lift him over. Della ended up tying him to the porch to keep him away from the fence.

Our next example, Dan White, killed San Francisco Mayor, George Moscone, and gay rights activist, Harvey Milk. As Libra often sees all the ways in which people are not acting properly and Mars is like a hall monitor, it is no surprise that Dan saw himself as a sort of social "governor" as discussed in this article about White from Wikipedia:

> His district was described by *The New York Times* as "a largely white, middle-class section that is hostile to the growing homosexual community of San Francisco." *The New York Times* stated that as a supervisor, White saw himself as the board's "defender of the home, the family, and religious life against homosexuals, pot smokers and cynics."

Mars in Scorpio on the AS

This is a power-full position. As Mars is the traditional ruler of Scorpio, we find people who have a raw power about them that can be used to sell sexuality, products, desire, as well as exercise power over others. They can take others into deeper darker worlds not often experienced in the light of day.

One aspect of working with sexuality is fashion. Who better to wear this title than the founder of a French luxury fashion house and style icon, Christian Dior? In his obituary from NYTimes.com, comes this perfect Mars in Scorpio statement:

M. Dior once credited the fame of his creations to this credo: "Please the ladies by enabling them to please their men."

Given the sexual pulse of this placement, there is no surprise that our next example made himself a name as a porn star: Al Parker, exuded the sexual energies of both Scorpio and Mars and made a good living at it as a porn star.

Our next example captured the sexual strength and energy of male bodies. American fashion photographer, Herb Ritts, who makes our list a third time, was well-known for capturing suggestively sexual images of his subjects, whether famous or just physically beautiful.

Scorpio is fixed and, like Mars, wants things its own way. The story of convicted murder, Steven Sherer shows us another, typical side of the Scorpionic experience: possessive love. Steven was highly possessive of his wife, and told her he would kill her if she ever had an affair. His wife had an affair and no one has heard from her since. The obliterating rage of Scorpio when focused through either Mars or Pluto is a destructive force most people cannot control let alone handle.

Mars in Sagittarius on the AS

These people can be real go-getters with inexhaustible energy.

Sometimes the archetype of the sign comes forth eloquently as it does for longtime Australian actor, Colin Friels. He made the following perfectly self-aware Sagittarian statement:

"I couldn't live without doing the odd play and I couldn't live without working a horse. I am completely addicted, obsessed. Nothing moves like a horse. It's like the rhythm of nature."

Former First Lady of the United States, Lady Bird Johnson, who makes our list a third time and also has her Mercury here, shows her idealistic approach to life.

Talk show host, Arsenio Hall, makes our list a second time. Sagittarius is a Centaur and are known for their party-animal skills. Arsenio encouraged a rather boisterous and excitable nature in both his audiences and his guests.

Mars is often described as one's drive, so of course we find a racecar driver with this astrological alignment. As we have seen in other Mars placements, unfortunately we find another forceful death. Jimmy Bryan was a well-known race car driver and Indy 500 racer, died from a racing accident.

Mars in Capricorn on the AS

These individuals know the pearl AND the oyster are theirs for the taking. Capricorn ascends the ladder of social status and seeks world-renowned success.

There are a surprising number of royals in this category as this can be and astrological placement of great leadership.

When one reads the encyclopedic curriculum vitae of American director, Francis Ford Coppola, one can grasp the internal drive this placement generates. Just look up Coppola on Wikipedia to learn more about this man's abilities and accomplishments.

King Abdullah II of Jordan shows another beautiful aspect of Capricorn, the correct ruling. He has made significant changes in his government, giving his kingdom a level of stability not seen by many other middle-eastern countries. King Abdullah has modeled his court in such a way as to create a sense of collective well-being rather than elevating of any one select group.

The stunning looks of her grandmother, American actress, Grace Kelly, are reflected in her own beauty: Charlotte of Monaco. Also known as, Charlotte Casiraghi, she is often seen at the top social events throughout Europe.

Mars in Aquarius on the AS

This is an interesting position for forceful Mars in the humanitarian sign of Aquarius on the "me" focused ascendant point.

Rockabilly performer, Ritchie Valens, overcame many obstacles to be seen and heard in the 1950's as a Mexican-American singer, but when we consider that he died in that plane crash when he was only 17, *whew*! Who knows what Valens would have accomplished?

Scottish actor, David Paisley, who also has his Mercury here, is known for playing Aquarian outcast roles like gay characters and a male midwife. In typical Martian fashion, David was voted sexiest man alive in 2003.

Mars in Pisces on the AS

This is a very unusual position for direct Mars in elusive Pisces. This is a position for a deep diver.

Let's look at poet and beatnik extraordinaire, Allen Ginsberg. Who can be more poetic than a Piscean? Let me just share a few of his iconic quotes as he can do nothing but express from this deep-seated place of wisdom. The following comes from BrainyQuote.com:

"Follow your inner moonlight; don't hide the madness."

"Poetry is the one place where people can speak their original human mind. It is the outlet for people to say in public what is known in private."

"The weight of the world is love. Under the burden of solitude, under the burden of dissatisfaction."

"I want people to bow as they see me and say he is gifted with poetry, he has seen the presence of the creator."

Pisces is the sign of unanimity. Australian politician, Simon Crean, works to ensure animals receive more humane treatment.

We will now look at the angle placements of Mars throughout the zodiac from the point of view of the Imum Coeli (IC)

Mars in Aries on the IC

This is an interesting position for Mars in Aries as it is in an unseen place in the chart. However, this doesn't mean it isn't seen by the collective. These individuals have an inner barometer and fortitude to accomplish anything to which they put their minds.

Major General Harry Wickwire Foster, has this astrological configuration. We learn the following about the Major General from Wikipedia:

> After the war, Foster (with four brigadiers) presided over the court martial of Canada's top prisoner of war, SS General Kurt Meyer. The trial was a showcase for Canada, the first time that the country had conducted an international prosecution of this sort. Meyer was found guilty of three of five charges and sentenced to death. The sentence was later commuted to life imprisonment. When asked by his son (author Tony Foster) why the death sentence had been imposed he replied, "Because I had no choice according to those rules of warfare dreamt up by a bunch of bloody barrack-room lawyers who had never heard a shot fired in anger."

This quote shows the depth of understanding the consequences of one's aggression. Mars can give one an unbeatable, unflappable and indefatigable determination and persistence, especially when found on one of the chart's angles *and* in its ruling sign.

One would probably not consider an astrologer to fall into this category, but we have not only one astrologer here, but two! When one reads the life of Marion March, one can see the courageous thread of Mars winding its ways through her life. From leaving Hitler's Germany as a child, to moving to different countries, learning different languages (a real trait amongst astrologers), to gathering various national astrological groups into a collective astrological convention known as United Astrological Conference or UAC, all of these show a determination and persistence that would have been extremely challenging without having this powerful generator at the root of her chart.

American actor, Dack Rambo, conveyed that raw instinctually centered way of being. Mars and Aries like to be first, as clearly shown in this article about Rambo in WashingtonPost.com:

> After mulling over a change of life direction and discussing it with his managers, he quickly made a decision. He would go public. Several weeks after he got the news, he released a statement announcing that he had the AIDS virus and would devote himself to working for the cause of AIDS education and research. He is the first well-known actor ever to make such a statement. He did it more than a month before Magic

Johnson announced he was suffering from the same virus.

Another astrologer makes our list, Bill Meridian. Bill says of this astrological placement:

"I have many conflicts with authority figures. In later life, the conflicts derive from my work and research conflicting with established thinking. If authorities cling to old ideas, there is friction. I simply concentrate on my own work and do not consider what others may say. The actual results are more important than their reactions."

I am also excited to mention that Bill studied with one of my past teachers in Bioenergetics and Core Energetics, John Pierrakos.

Mars in Taurus on the IC

These individuals have a dig-in-your-heels sort of persistence, determination or stubbornness. Their drive and determination may not be shared with anyone other than the most familiar and trusted and maybe not even with them. These people plot their own course.

What better expression of this energy than through film? Dutch-Australian film director, Rolf de Heer, captured this modus operandi perfectly in an interview he gave with Variety.com:

"For me, making any film is too hard to do it more than once, so if I made a thriller that was very effective, the last thing I would want to do is make another thriller. After *Ten Canoes*, I made *Dr. Plonk*, which is a silent, black-and-white film. Each film is an exploration into a new part of cinema, and I work hard at reinventing a different way of thinking for each project."

Rolf is exploring new forms of film.

Taurus is the Bull and therefore relates to bull markets, as well as "forms" of stocks and investments. Hedge fund manager, investor and philanthropist, Bill Ackman, according to Wikipedia, is considered a contrarian investor, meaning someone who purchases and sells in contrast to what the general investing population is doing at the time. Sounds like something someone with this placement would do!

Legendary operatic soprano, Leontyne Price, shared some powerful feelings in an interview with NYTimes.com about her 1966 performance at the Met:

"I'm about to scream—not sing—to scream with happiness," Ms. Price recalled. That afternoon, she had learned that radio stations in and around her hometown, Laurel, Mississippi, had been linked into the Met's radio network and would carry *Antony and Cleopatra* live.

This was a major breakthrough, as the networks would not broadcast a black person playing a white person's role at that time.

Mars in Gemini on the IC

This is a hard space for Mars in this secluded, yet highly interactive inner space. These individuals have an uncanny ability to insert themselves where needed.

This may account partially why Pope Benedict XVI was the first Catholic Pope in 600 years to abdicate. Known as a distinguished theologian as well as prefect of the Congregation for the Doctrine of the Faith, one could see how he would be better leading in Geminian areas of mind, word and thought rather than the spiritual leader and heart of a worldwide religion.

The glyph for Mars is the same symbol we associate with men in general. Italian composer, Giorgio Moroder, was known as the father of Disco, and he is also a four-time Grammy Award winning singer —more expressions of this astrological placement.

English film star, Michael York, who appears on our list a second time, started acting at an early age. Gemini has a multifaceted quality about it. This astrological placement plays out in this statement about him in an article at thehollywoodinterview.blogspot.com:

> He started acting on stage in his teens and, after finishing studies at Oxford, Michael joined Laurence Olivier's National Theatre. His good looks (marred only by a broken nose) got him frequently cast as bored aristocrats (often with a subversive side) early in his career, but Michael quickly proved his diversity by becoming one of the busiest actors of his generation,

to date appearing in over 100 films and television productions.

Alan Page shows another amazing representation of two sides of a person; he is a former American football player, and after retiring from football he became an attorney. Alan went on to become an associate justice of the Minnesota Supreme Court.

Mars in Cancer on the IC

Mars usually likes to be on the move, makes things happen, but here the focus is on home, family or childhood made visible for the world to see.

Film maker and director, George Lucas, appearing on our list a second time, owns Skywalker Ranch where he lives and works. Lucas also showed us ways in which other worlds can feel like home.

American entertainer, Liza Minnelli, who has her Moon here as well, exhibits the invasive ways in which her mother affected her. With Mars on the IC, there is a dependably rechargeable root power source.

From IllustratorsLounge.com comes an article on French fashion designer, illustrator, and artiste, Christian Bérard. Affectionately known as Bébé—*quelle surprise* for this astrological placement. Known for his dramatic flair, Mars once again shows a powerful exit for the maverick:

On February 11, 1949, whilst working at the Théâtre Marigny, Bérard died suddenly on the stage just after having cried "It's over". He died of a heart attack, aged only 46.

Mars in Leo on the IC

This is a powerful and determined position for Mars. The self-centering aspect of Leo coupled with the desire nature of the personality can really be over the top here.

No surprise that serial killer, Ed Gein, shows up here. His relationship with his mother seriously affected his inner desire nature. This man actually had three planets conjunct his chart's angles: Moon, Mars and Pluto. This is a powerful recipe for transformation. When these three planets are in challenging aspects to one another, we can trust that there is a huge amount of work that needs to be done to heal and integrate. One must wonder whether Gein's mother perceived something in her son and tried hard to "cure" him of it or what happened. Regardless of who affected him, he had to deal with finding a way to get these powerful energies to work with one another. Unfortunately, Gein was not able to express himself any better than he did and in the end harmed many women.

From Gregory Peck's obituary from TheGuardian.com we find an eloquent use of this planetary position:

> I met Gregory Peck on several occasions, and his courtesy did not seem as false as some of those faced by a critic who might be inclined otherwise to snipe at them. He was modest enough to consider himself lucky to have lasted so long in people's affections, but

proud of his achievements in film, while insisting that many of his directors and co-stars helped him gain his reputation. He was a genuinely nice man, largely unspoilt by fame, though latterly a bit miffed that he was not hired more often, not just for old times' sake but because he was actually worth it. The problem was that few wanted to use him in any way other than as an American version of the slightly stiff-upper-lipped nature's gentleman. Indeed, so strongly did he portray this character that he seemed almost like a distant cousin of Abraham Lincoln. Like James Stewart and Gary Cooper, Peck expressed in very tangible form so much with his mere presence that sometimes he scarcely had to act at all. But he never took the easy way out. He always tried hard and, though a little limited, generally succeeded. Principally, his work reflects that, in the movies, less almost always means more. It is a lesson some of the twitching heroes who copy Marlon Brando have yet to learn, skulking in their luxurious caravans waiting for inspiration.

What would a Leonine astrological placement be without a royal? Francis the First of France, was such an individual. Mars is about leadership and competition, so it is no surprise that he had an able-bodied competitor in the personage of King Henry VIII of England. The following comes from HistoryToday.com:

In life Francis I, "Most Christian King" of a France that only sixty years before his accession had finally expelled English occupiers from the realm (and had still to tolerate Calais as an English enclave until 1559), was frequently compared to and set as a rival against, his Tudor counterpart, Henry VIII. So, it was not unfitting that this symmetry was carried almost to the grave, with Francis' death coming just two months after Henry's at Greenwich.

Basketball legend, Wilt Chamberlain, shows several attributes of this astrological placement, especially the competitive aspect of Mars. From his obituary in *The New York Times*, we have three key examples of this placement:

> Before he came along, basketball had such big centers as 6-10 George Mikan and 7-foot Bob Kurland. But Chamberlain was bigger and stronger, with a more potent inside game, so overpowering that the National Basketball Association widened the free-throw lane to force him farther from the basket."

A more powerful inside game??? That is Mars on the IC in Leo! The story continues:

> While basketball was his business, he loved many sports. For many years after retirement, he was an elite-level volleyball player. He ran the quarter-mile and high-jumped in college, and later he sponsored a women's track team, Wilt's Wonder Women. At championship track meets, he would be in his seat two hours before competition began, his long legs covering

two rows of seats, talking to anyone about track and never stirring until long after the final event. When Muhammad Ali was in his prime, Chamberlain talked of challenging him to a fight. Chamberlain even carried boxing gloves with him, but when an airline ticket clerk asked him if he was serious about fighting, he replied, "No. It's just good publicity." He received publicity of another sort when he wrote in his autobiography that he had had sexual relations with 20,000 women. Many people criticized him as promiscuous.

He never married, and in 1991 he told The Associated Press:

"The women who I have been the most attracted to, the most in love with, I've pushed away the strongest. There are about five women I can think of I could have married. I cared for them a lot, but not enough to make a commitment."

Veteran actor, Elliott Gould, gave a couple of good examples of this astrological placement in the following comments taken from an interview he did for Independent.co.UK:

When he was 12, his mentor was an "incorrigible" Irishman named Billy Quinn.

"I didn't want to learn. I didn't want to know," says Gould—yet Quinn pounded away until he did. "He broke through to me. Years later, when I told him I was going to be doing *Bob & Carol & Ted & Alice*, and they gave me $50,000 to do it, he said he just couldn't believe it. He gave me the Webster's dictionary, and I looked up 'genius'... the definition of genius in the Webster's Dictionary is 'one of a kind'. And I believe that each of us is meant to be one of a kind."

This is a brilliant maverick statement! Mars takes some pounding, it needs to feel the competition to be feel itself, especially when in Leo conjunct the Imum Coeli.

Another one of the Beach Boys now appears on our list, Brian Wilson. From an interview with RollingStone.com, we see that Mars and Leo combine to give extensive superlatives:

> A few days earlier, the singer-songwriter and founding Beach Boy celebrated his 74th birthday and when the subject comes up, his eyes widen.
>
> "It was the greatest birthday of my life," he says, uncrossing his arms. "We went to a place called Peter Luger's [Steakhouse]. You gotta go there; you will fucking love it. I had the greatest steak dinner that I ever had in my whole life." He waits a beat and raises his voice. "In my whole life!"

Mars in Virgo on the IC

As with any placement within Virgo, these Martians are resourceful individuals. As Virgo is ruled by Mercury, there is an aspect of doing and speaking here in the most private places of the individual.

The following comes from BBC.com:

His talents as a singer, songwriter and music producer made George Michael one of the world's biggest-selling artists. Blessed with good looks and a fine singing voice, his stage presence made him a favourite on the live concert circuit as he matured from teen idol to long term stardom. But there were times when his battle with drugs and encounters with the police made lurid headlines that threatened to eclipse his musical talents.

George Michael found a way to put a spin on his exploits that the public accepted, and he definitely worked with his personal desire in the areas of sex, drugs and Rock and Roll, by spotlighting what others would call his baser side in both music videos as well as interviews. Remember, Virgo is the sign of perfecting, so there are many "missed steps" along the way to help in the ever-perfecting process that Virgo requires. The added heat of Mars helps to forge very interesting tools. I find it interesting how George's private desires were fodder for the world, even though this configuration appears at the most private space in his chart. The fact that planetary archetypes so readily present themselves even when on this "quiet angle" is one of the many reasons for this book.

The first part of the NYTimes.com obituary for American poet, William Jay Smith, captures this astrological placement beautifully:

William Jay Smith, a former United States poet laureate whose work was known both for its acuteness of observation and acuteness of craftsmanship, died on Tuesday in Pittsfield, Massachusetts. He was 97.

American businesswoman, Suzanne de Passe, who also has her Venus here, has this quote from BrainyQuote.com:

"I know you can develop talent and market it."

Mars in Libra on the IC

As we know, Mars is in its detriment in Libra, because being impartial is a necessary Libran trait and Mars is rarely, if ever, impartial.

Best-selling author, Michael Crichton, who also has his Venus here, wrote about polarizing issues. In his obituary from *The New York Times*, we learn a bit more about his life's work:

> Mr. Crichton used fiction to explore the moral and political problems posed by modern technology and scientific breakthroughs, which in his books defied human control or ended up as tools used for evil ends. In his fictional worlds, human greed, hubris, and the urge to dominate were just as powerful as the most advanced computers.

Through Michael's books, most of which became mega-hit movies, he captured the public's attention and brought us all along to explore the polarizing themes of human experience.

While Mars is considered to be in detriment here, we still find individuals who set a blazing trail in public service such as American government official, Virginia Mae Brown, who makes our list a second time. The following comes from LATimes.com:

> Virginia Mae Brown, 67, the first woman to serve on the federal Interstate Commerce Commission. President Lyndon B. Johnson appointed Mrs. Brown to the commission in 1964. She later served as chairwoman before stepping down in 1979. After leaving the commission, Mrs. Brown was president and chairwoman of the board of the Buffalo Bank of Eleanor. For the last seven years, she was chief administrative law judge for the U.S. Department of Health and Human Services' Office of Hearing Appeals in Charleston, Charleston, West Virginia.

Virginia Mae used this astrological placement well!

English actress, Julie Walters, stated in an interview with theGuardian.com:

> "I remembered Gloria Grahame from *The Bad and the Beautiful* and all those films," Walters says. "She was always this great sort of wild girl. When she went up and got her Oscar in the 1950s she just took it and said thank you and walked off. People apparently said: 'She

hasn't even brushed her hair!' And then she went off the rails a bit and met this bloke while living in digs in London. I love all that."

Both Julie's Aquarian Venus on her DS as well as her Mars here on the IC in Libra would give her a strong observational nature on people's quirky personality traits.

Mars in Scorpio on the IC

This shows a very powerful and determined inner person. Anything onto which these individuals attach themselves, they will not let go. Like a pit-bull, these individuals can lock their jaws on their target(s).

Singer songwriter, Richard Carpenter, who also has his Mercury here, kept a tight rein on his sister and was protective of the image of their musical group, The Carpenters. Richard dealt with the exposure and vulnerability of a public life by numbing himself with Quaaludes.

In an interview for ABCNews.com, veteran actress, Vanessa Redgrave, stated what her Mars drive in Scorpio made her do and feel:

> In 1983, Lynn Redgrave, who became a film sensation in the 1960s with "Georgy Girl," began starring in U.S. commercials for Weight Watchers. Before that she battled bulimia, telling *People* magazine in 1992, that bingeing and purging "felt like a great discovery, as I

suppose it is to most people. People complimented me on my weight, but inside I felt like s***."

From GoodReads.com, comes this fierce and astrologically apt quote from author, Jewelle Gomez:

"For femmes, that evolving feminist thought re-acquainted us with something we kind of knew already: men and women might mistake us for "just girls" when they see our makeup and fashions, but we were/are actually guerrilla warriors, fighting undercover in the war to save women from the continuing campaign to make us irrelevant fluff."

A battalion of women with this astrological placement would make a huge change for women's rights to be sure! This is a warrior placement.

Mars in Sagittarius on the IC

These individuals make their own path. A sense of everything will be okay is what gives Sagittarius its freedom and adventure seeking idealism.

Newspaper heiress, Patty Hearst, makes our list a third time. Patty was kidnapped by the Symbionese Liberation Army (SLA) and was used to bring awareness to what the SLA considered was a higher purpose. These are all aspects of this astrological placement.

Beatnik author, Jack Kerouac, also makes our list a third time and, like Patty Hearst, also has Sun in Pisces conjunct the DS. Jack was a wandering philosopher—what is more Mars in Sagittarius? A perfect quote from him comes from GoodReads.com:

"Live, travel, adventure, bless, and don't be sorry."

Interestingly enough, Kerouac also had a gregarious sexual nature—also Mars in Sagittarius. To understand his Mars-driven Sagittarian nature, read one of his seminal pieces entitled, *On the Road*, published in 1957.

Singer and songwriter, Lulu, shared her life's experiences with Telegraph.co.uk:

"I have a condition called Post Traumatic Stress Disorder," says Lulu. "It's ridiculous. That's what soldiers get!" The veteran Scottish singer sighs deeply and her voice sinks to a barely audible whisper. "I've been afraid my whole life. Afraid of everything. Afraid to reveal myself. Afraid that if you knew me, if you really knew me, you wouldn't like me." At 66, she, "has a new album coming out, her first in 10 years, entitled *Making Life Rhyme*. It is a very fine album, perhaps the best she has ever made. At 66, for the very first time, she has been involved in all aspects of writing and production, making all her own choices. The result is a triumphant modern soul blast, full of big, heartfelt songs that reclaim her place as one of British pop's most distinctive and expressive voices. It is a reminder that before Amy Winehouse, before Adele, there was Lulu. But the content of songs like "Cry," "Faith in You," and "Poison Kiss" also reveal a more vulnerable person than her bubbly public image suggests.

We can see what happens as Sagittarius continues to work with its own inner truth, here aided by the direct energies of Mars.

Spanish opera singer and brilliant tenor, Placido Domingo, makes many noteworthy quotes for this astrological placement all from BrainyQuote.com:

"I am never wrong when it comes to my possibilities."

"This circus games aspect has existed since the beginning of my career."

"The press regularly proclaims my ambitions and my financial demands. My strength is my enthusiasm."

This last quote from Domingo shows the understanding of Mars as a power source. With Mars at the IC, one has an internal battery that works very well when the native understands Sagittarius is the king of enthusiasm! From Placido's comments, I would say he understands this part of himself very well.

Italian architect, Renzo Piano, who makes our list a second time, understands the need for creating spaces for people. Mars seeks to be in higher philosophies and fields when traveling through Sagittarius, as well-illustrated in this quote from Renzo from BrainyQuotes.com:

"Great American art needs the idea of uninterrupted spaces, like a loft, which itself is something very American."

Mars in Capricorn on the IC

These individuals have a level of determination in seeking social prominence.

From a well-researched article in TheGuardian.com, we see how this astrological placement of determination in the pursuit of social prominence, played out in the life of early female photographer, Lee Miller:

It's remarkable that Miller was able to delight in her body (and in the pleasure others took from it), given that she was raped, aged seven, while staying with family friends. She contracted gonorrhea as a result—a condition that, in the days before penicillin, was treatable only by daily douches and weekly inoculations, an agonizing procedure for a small child. Miller's parents took her to see a psychiatrist, who advised her to treat love and sex as separate commodities. To a degree the advice succeeded.

"Emotionally, I need to be completely absorbed in some work or in a man I love," she wrote, but she didn't see why going to bed with someone should upset whichever man she was currently in love with. Strikingly beautiful, she was used to submitting to the male gaze. First there was her father, a keen amateur photographer who persuaded her to sit naked for him from the age of eight right into her 20s; then the publisher Conde Nast, who bumped into her, literally, in Manhattan, was struck by her looks, took her on as a model for *Vogue*, and made her the face of Kotex tampon adverts; then Man Ray, whose mistress and pupil she became (Madame Man Ray, as she was known in Paris). She was proud of her looks, but ultimately frustrated by life in front of the lens. "I looked like an angel, but I was a fiend inside," she said, looking back. Angry with her for taking lovers, and jealous of Cocteau for using her in his film *The Blood of a Poet*, Man Ray expressed his jealousy by doing violence to her face and body in his art. These alpha males may have crushed a less spirited woman, but Miller, unfazed, determinedly transformed herself from passive model to active artist. First came her surrealist phase: she not only outmanned Man Ray in creating her own works, but was instrumental in the invention of the "solarisation" technique (a partial reversal of blacks and whites that creates a silvery aura). Then she set up a portrait studio in New York, with rich socialites her clientele.

I appreciate the ways Lee was able to use these male energies in such a brilliant manner.

English media personality, Janet Street-Porter, has this perfect quote from the status-oriented Capricorn view:

"Far too many women are hesitant, and remain trapped in jobs for which they are over-qualified or paid beneath their worth."

One of the hard aspects of Capricorn, the issues of abandonment and inner sense of aloneness, is captured by the comment of French actor and sex symbol, Alain Delon, from nst.com:

"You cannot get back the love that wasn't given to me as a child. These are holes that can never be filled. Even when I love a woman, I feel alone. I was only four when I understood that those you love the most can abandon you."

Mars in Aquarius on the IC

These people have courage to fight for others, especially those who they perceive as weak or vulnerable. They can also focus on causes that may only have meaning to them.

In an article about English comedian and actor, Peter Cook, his ex-wife identifies this astrological placement perfectly, illustrating the humanitarian ideals versus the personal human desire. The following comes from theGuardian.com:

"He had gone way, way away from his original idealism,' she said. "He was a very upright sort of person when I was first with him. At that point, he even thought he had a career in the Foreign Office ahead of him, but something started to rot inside. I hear it was drugs too."

Aquarius has to resist the temptation to become a cynic as the result of being a frustrated idealist.

Travel writer, Paul Theroux, states this astrological placement well in an interview for NationalGeographic.com:

> "We live in a country [the United States] where an area that is—I don't know if dysfunctional is the word for it, but certainly undeveloped or underdeveloped, where there is a high infant mortality rate, AIDS is a problem, drugs are a problem, substandard hospitals, substandard schools. But we have great roads, great roads. So you can go anywhere in the States. I mean you can get to the furthest limit down a great road. What you'll find there: people living in shacks or old rotten trailers or towns that have lost all their industry. But that to me is worth doing, and it's what's taken my interest at the moment."

Beverly Potts, born within five days of Peter Cook, walked out to a park when she was 10 years old in Cleveland, Ohio and "disappeared."

Aquarius is a dual sign, not really male, nor really female, but rather of an androgynous nature, so, we of course, are going to find with Mars here, a transgendered individual. American film and television director, Lilly Wachowski, of *The Matrix* and *Sense8* fame, made the following statement to Variety.com sharing her transgendered news:

> "It had a lot of politically relevant insights regarding the dangers of outing trans people, and the statistical

horrors of transgender suicide and murder rates. Not to mention a slightly sarcastic wrap-up that 'revealed' my father had injected praying mantis blood into his paternal ball-sac before conceiving each of his children to produce a brood of super women, hell bent on female domination. Okay, mega sarcastic."

Mars has to do with aspects of courage and standing up for self as well as for others—especially when in the sign of Aquarius.

Julian Assange shows another aspect of the Aquarian refugee and whistleblower archetypes. The following comes from the NewYorker.com:

> He has published millions of documents, including hacked e-mails from corporations and public figures, international trade agreements, and foreign government records. Some of these publications have brought real harm to the documents' owners, some have altered public perceptions about war and state power, and some have been damaging to individual privacy, with no public benefit. In his confinement, Assange has become a quixotic cultural icon, helping to give the solitary act of whistle blowing the contours of a movement. Dr. Martens has issued boots in his name, sculptors have cast him in alloy, and lyricists have memorialized him in song. He has inspired a Bond villain, and the fiction of Jonathan Franzen; he has mixed with A-list musicians, like Lady Gaga, and A-list dissenters, like Noam Chomsky. At the same time, he has had to navigate myriad legal and managerial

complications: multiple F.B.I. investigations, crippling staff mutinies, venomous fights with journalists.

When an Aquarian his fixed onto something, they can hold on beyond the point of gaining any benefit perceived, especially during their lifetime. They tend to seed change needed for the future to bloom.

Mars in Pisces on the IC

These are individuals who have an underwater volcano of strength.

Anyone who watched Shirley Temple movies wondered how in the world such a young child could channel such energy. Shirley's comment below, comes from AZQuotes:

> "Be brave and clear. Follow your heart and don't be overly influenced by outside factors. Be true to yourself."

Mars appreciates authenticity especially when in the sign of Pisces.

Cricket star, Adam Gilchrist, said this revealing statement in an interview for TheAustralian.com/au:

> He was handicapped, he suspects, by a tendency to introspection: "One of my great faults, probably why I didn't go further, was that I overanalyzed myself. I was very serious, probably too serious."

Adam is known as the most explosive batsman in cricket!

Author Patricia Highsmith, who also has her Venus here, is known for her *Talented Mr. Ripley* series. Book critic, Michael Dirda observed:

> Europeans honored her as a psychological novelist, part of an existentialist tradition represented by her own favorite writers, in particular Dostoyevsky, Conrad, Kafka, Gide and Camus.

One cannot define this astrological position more aptly than how Highsmith's title character is described in LitCharts.com:

> Tom Ripley, who is simultaneously the novel's protagonist and antagonist, has a gift for forgery, impersonation, and imitation, and he uses these skills to his advantage at every available opportunity. Slick and slippery...

We will now look at the angle placements of Mars throughout the zodiac from the point of view of the Descendant (DS)

Mars in Aries on the DS

With this positioning of Mars in its home sign of Aries on the relationship angle of the chart, these natives experience the other in a competitive or instinctually *en garde* manner.

Others may feel the initiatory power of Mars in these people as threatening, but this is simply how these natives engage. This astrological position is an indicator for a fiery and quick temper! While these natives will likely have a very warrior-like approach to relationships, it is important to remember that they have Libra rising which means they seek only to act in an appropriate manner.

Egyptian actor, Omar Sharif, is a prime example of this astrological placement and exhibited the aggression that Mars expresses, when, in 2007, Omar punched a valet for refusing to accept his foreign currency for payment.

Fred West, the English serial murderer who killed at least 12 women with his wife, is an example of one who used this astrological placement for power over others. I find it interesting to note that Fred's DS in Aries is inconjunct his Venus in Scorpio where he also has his Mercury. This would be a challenging placement to integrate in a healthy manner without professional help and guidance. The following comes from an informative article about Fred, found at ijcst.journals.yorku.ca:

> Impulsivity is sometimes defined as acting on impulse without reflecting upon consequences (Chaplin, 1985). Impulsiveness connotes irrationality and an inability to profit from experience. Insensitivity, or lack of guilt, is a trait associated with psychopathy (Dadds & Salmon, 2003) and has been included in scales measuring social control (Wiatrowski, Griswold & Roberts, 1981; Agnew, 1995). Guilt is painful and lack of guilt is pleasurable. This modified hedonism in LSC theory is consistent with

control theories in general which assume that pleasures are constant and motivation unproblematic. The authors are concerned, however, with the consequences of a lack of guilt for the individual, not the emotional poverty from an inability to form relationships. They appear to be saying that individuals miscalculate or devalue the pain of guilt, and that this is something one gets from their parents, and in terms of Fred's case, from the father. Immediate gratification is also associated with psychopathy and means self-absorption in one's own needs which vehemently demand satisfaction (Blanchard, Bassett & Koshland, 1977; McCord & McCord, 1983). Adventurousness or spontaneity is defined as self-initiating behavior occurring without the necessity of external stimulation (Chaplin, 1985). It is the only non-biological factor in this second category of traits in LSC theory. It is a personality trait that loosely differentiates between delinquents and non-delinquents (Eysenck & Gudjonsson, 1989; Wilson & Herrnstein, 1985). It is furthermore a valued trait given the societal trend toward greater tolerance for self-expression and assertiveness. While possibly related to extroversion, spontaneity per se is nothing more than a weak predictor because it suggests concern, not insensitivity, for others and also suggests self-esteem, or a concern for a positive image of one's self. Fred West can be categorized as a sadistic rapist and murderer. Sadistic rapists are very similar to their anger—excitation rapist counterparts in that both are sexually aroused by the physical and psychological suffering of their victims (Douglas, Burgess, Burgess & Ressler, 2006). However, whereas anger rapists are viewed as being motivated primarily out of anger, sadistic assailants are motivated primarily by sexual satisfaction obtained through victim suffering (Groth & Burgess, 1977; Hazelwood & Burgess, 1987). These offenders use excessive force, such as bondage, torture, rape with objects, sexual mutilation, and, in extreme cases, murder. In addition, they may perform other acts of degradation, such as cutting hair, burning with cigarettes, and sexual intercourse with a corpse following murder. Research suggests that the attacks of sadistic rapists are carefully planned and preventive against discovery (Groth & Birnbaum, 1979) which was particularly evident in Fred's International Journal of Criminology and Sociological Theory, Vol. 5, No.1, June 2012, 864-870 868 criminal behavior because some of the victims have never been found (Sounes, 1995).

Australian film director, Scott Hicks, who also has his Venus here, gives an astute quote about the relationship to the other:

"Where you have a villain in the piece or the antagonist, whatever you want to call them, there has to be humanity at the core of it or it's faintly ridiculous. Nobody is just villain through and through. You have to feel something for them."

American television journalist, Katie Couric, who also has her Moon here, has this Aries quote:

"Be fearless. Have the courage to take risks. Go where there are no guarantees. Get out of your comfort zone even if it means being uncomfortable. The road less traveled is sometimes fraught with barricades bumps and uncharted terrain. But it is on that road where your character is truly tested. And have the courage to accept that you're not perfect nothing is and no one is — and that's OK."

After the last episode aired on December 19, 2014, *The New Yorker* magazine published this lovely eulogy for the *Late Late Show with Craig Ferguson* and its host Craig Ferguson, beautifully illustrating this astrological placement and the recognition it can receive:

Though Ferguson was reliably funny, he did not shy away from difficult subjects. He used his monologue to eulogize both of his parents. He spoke with frankness and sympathy in relating his struggles with alcoholism to those of celebrities who became fodder for late-night japes. On the evening of the Boston Marathon bombing, he refused to tell jokes, saying, "If I have all this rage and anger and distress and upset inside of me, I'm not good enough of a comedian to hide that from you." In 2009, when Archbishop Desmond Tutu appeared on the show ("I'm as mystified as you," the host remarked to his audience that night), Ferguson opened with a short history of South Africa that touched on Dutch colonialism, the Boer Wars, the origins of apartheid, and Tutu's career. It managed to be concise, informative, and hilarious—and it brought the show a Peabody Award.

Mars in Taurus on the DS

Interestingly, we do not have more representation with this astrological placement. These people are likely dogmatic and desire driven. The challenge of this position is impartiality, as one would have difficulty separating one's desires from one's values.

One can understand how this astrological placement would suit someone like Ray Larsen, the national Grand Wizard of the KKK.

On the other hand, the raw, passionate sensuality of one's relationship can be seen by the world as with French actress, Arielle Dombasle. The following comes from theGuardian.com:

> France has long been enthralled by the inner workings of the Dombasle-Lévy duo: what brought them together and what keeps the passion alive. She is the pouting coquette who once said her favourite quality in a man was "penetration". He is the living acronym, BHL, who describes himself as a feminist and a libertine. Being with them, said one friend, is like witnessing young lovers cavorting before your eyes – except they are both middle-aged." The relationship has become a kind of public laboratory, a school for seduction.

Mars in Gemini on the DS

These people assert themselves through communication and the sharing of ideas.

Pat Nixon, who makes our list a second time, used this highly charged astrological placement to wear a number of working hats in her lifetime. Pat was eventually invited by President Dwight Eisenhower to act as goodwill ambassador with her husband, Richard Nixon.

In a lovely tribute to rhythm and blues singer and songwriter, Amos Milburn, comes this appropriately rendered understanding of how the multifaceted Geminian energy can allow so much cross pollination when Mars is involved. The following comes from rockabilly.nl:

> Nick Tosches has called Amos Milburn "The first great rock n roll piano man." It is true that Milburn was a crucial figure in the trans- formation of jump blues into R&B and rock 'n' roll. Fats Domino, Little Richard and Jerry Lee Lewis have all cited Amos as a seminal influence on their work. Ironically, Milburn would be swept aside by the very idiom that he had helped create. Milburn picked up his style from a rich variety of sources: the boogie woogie piano of Albert Ammons and Pete Johnson, the blasting big bands of Lionel Hampton and Buddy Johnson, and as a contrast, the silky smooth after-hours cocktail blues of Charles Brown, Nat "King" Cole and Ivory Joe Hunter. But the result was pure Amos Milburn.

In an article for the WashingtonPost.com, former U.S. Attorney General and Republican Pennsylvania Governor, Dick Thornburgh writes:

> As John Adams said our country is "a government of laws, and not of men." This founding principle of our democracy must be protected. We will be remembered by what we say and what we do in this challenging time in America's history. We must all speak out and work to protect the special counsel's investigation from interference. As Republicans, we owe that much to our party. As citizens, we all owe even more to our country.

Actor and comedian, Tom Arnold, exhibits another side of this astrological placement. Remember, these are Sagittarius rising people, so they can just question the heck out of us, as much as have verbal diarrhea. Tom is challenged in his ability to censor himself.

Mars in Cancer on the DS

There would be a fierce defense of home and family ideals with this astrological placement.

One can see how some of the Mars elements played out in Malcolm X's childhood from this article at History.com:

> As early as age 9, with his family in dire economic straits, Malcolm began robbing food from stores in Lansing. Later on, in Boston and New York, he got

involved in drug dealing, gambling and prostitution rackets, spending much of his time in seedy nightclubs. At age 19, he was arrested for the first time for allegedly stealing and pawning his half-sister's fur coat. A second arrest followed for allegedly mugging an acquaintance at gunpoint and a third arrest came after he burglarized a series of Boston-area homes.

This astrological placement explains how he would argue that black people should be able to protect themselves if the U.S. government isn't able or willing to protect them.

Sacrifice for the family is a theme for this position. In his obituary from Independent.co.uk, comes a descriptive quote about this astrological placement and how it worked in triple threat Brit, Roy Castle:

> Devastating as it must have been, this experience brought home the fragile nature of celebrity, and helped Castle to sort out his priorities. Looking round at the broken marriages and estranged children of showbiz cronies, he resolved thenceforward to put his family first. He still remained one of Britain's most popular entertainers, but forsaking international recognition was the price he was prepared to pay.

An elevated expression of this astrological placement is shown in the NBCNews.com obituary for Nobel Prize winning nuclear physicist, Hans Bethe:

"One of the things that was very special about Hans was his strong moral motivation," said astrophysicist John Bahcall of the Institute for Advanced Study in Princeton, N.J. "He did things because he believed they were right and not because they were convenient or helpful to him or promoted his career. His work on the bomb was motivated by a desire to preserve freedom and open society in the face of a spreading Nazi tyranny, which he knew about firsthand."

Protecting the clan is indicated by this position.
BrainyQuotes.com has these illustrative quotes from American television actor, Christopher Meloni:

"I love my children beyond all reason. They're my joy, even when they're wild with kid energy."

"You can be childlike without being childish. A child always wants to have fun. Ask yourself, 'Am I having fun?'"

"I still have a dream of one day – I would love to hire a semi-retired contractor and just build a house – him and I building a house for me. I would truly love to do that."

Mars in Leo on the DS

These people take the lead in their relationships. Each of these individuals has the kiss of Mars charisma that helped elevate them to the international stage in their respective fields of entertainment. They can be surprisingly candid, and people do listen to them.

American actor, Willem Dafoe, makes an eloquent statement of this astrological position in an interview for Independent.co.uk:

> "I think something that engages you. Something that either presents a challenge or a pleasure or an adventure or a really compelling question that puts you in a mindset where you're like, 'I don't know what this is but I'm going to find out what it is.' Something that really taps into a sense of curiosity or wonder. I'd say the basic condition is to say you're going to do something you've never done before and no matter how it turns out, it's going to be interesting and if you're open to it, something's going to happen. You aren't always guaranteed what that's going to be but it's going to be something—you're not just going to make another movie, you're going to make a movie you have a stake in. You can find a stake in different ways—your commitment to doing a film like *Aquaman* compared to a film I'm doing now with Julian Schnabel [a biopic of artist Vincent Van Gogh] is different but you don't say one is greater than the other. They can be conditioned by different things. But don't think, for me anyway—

I've always got to remember to only talk for me—I don't think you can keep doing the same thing as an actor and be free. Or at least I can't. I feel better when I'm a little—I don't want to say out of control, but yeah, I guess control's a big issue. All performing is about control and discipline versus abandon and just letting go."

An example of the level of acclaim a Leonine Mars can receive, is revealed in actor, dancer, and choreographer, Bob Fosse's obituary in The New York Times:

Mr. Fosse won three television Emmy awards in 1973, for producing, directing and choreographing *Singer Presents Liza With a 'Z'* and in so doing won that year's Triple Crown of show business. A few weeks earlier, he had also won an Oscar for the film version of *Cabaret* and Tonys for directing and choreographing *Pippin*. He was the first person ever to win all three honors in one year.

Further in the article, is another description of this astrological placement:

After the death in 1980 of the choreographer Gower Champion, Frank Rich of *The New York Times* wrote that Mr. Fosse, "may now be the last active theater choreographer who knows how to assemble an old-fashioned, roof-raising showstopper in which every step bears the unmistakable signature of its creator."

Fathering, a by-product of the Mars impulse, is further referenced in the following question and answer in an interview by TheGuardian.com with American film and television actor, Martin Sheen:

> "What do you consider your greatest achievement?" To which he responded, "That I was partially responsible for bringing some extraordinary human beings into the world, and they responded to me as a loving father."

Two of Sheen's four children followed him onto the screen.

Veteran actor, Michael J. Fox, who appears on our list a second time, had this statement from Snopes.com:

> As recently as December 2017, Fox told interviewer, Dan Primack that "[Parkinson's] is not a nebulous cloud of doom that hangs over my head. It's a set of challenges and there are rewards in meeting those challenges."

Mars in Virgo on the DS

These individuals bring resourceful determination to their relationships.

British actress, Pauline Collins also has her Mercury here, so there is a willingness to do and be whomever the director, film, play or life requires. An article on her from theGuardian.com, beautifully illustrates the self-responsibility and self-care a person with Mercury and Mars in Virgo on the DS can have:

"I have a theory about Collins: that she didn't work for such huge stretches because she was determined to be a devoted mother to their three children. And I'm convinced this was due to a traumatic event earlier in her life. When Collins was 23 and working in Ireland, she discovered she was pregnant by a boyfriend she had recently split up with. She kept her pregnancy a secret from her parents, even though she knew they would be supportive; she took herself off to a convent where nuns delivered the baby, looked after Louise for six weeks, and then gave her up for adoption. When Louise was 21, she wrote to Collins and they were reunited. It's an astonishing story, both heart-breaking and heart-warming."

Reunion of mother and child.

Mars in Libra on the DS

Libra is not subjective and Mars is not objective, as we will see in our examples.

American politician, Gary Hart, appears in our list a second time here as he has Venus in Capricorn on the MC. As stated in the above section, and to correlate with what I stated in the beginning of this astrological placement, in Gary's pursuit of being a presidential politician his desire nature was his downfall. And, of course this astrological placement can bring about an amazing level of zeal to whatever one wishes to change in the world to attain Libra's goal of harmony.

American politician, Joseph McCarthy, is a perfect example of what this zeal can do. He also had Venus here, which means that his intrinsic values were tied up in his ideals of American patriotism. This Mars position impelled him to aggressively pursue any perceived threats with devastating consequences.

New Zealand comic novelist, Barry Crump, who makes our list a third time already, showed people what it was like to be an adventurer and share his story with others.

French artists, Gilles Blanchard, and fellow maverick, Pierre Commoy, makes our list again. Wikipedia writes:

> Pierre Commoy and Gilles Blanchard, also known as *Pierre et Gilles*, are French artists and romantic partners. They have been producing works together since 1976, creating a world where painting and photography meet.

In their art, Pierre and Gilles portray idealized ethereal men in romantically lovely settings. They create fantasy imagery of actual people.

Actor, drag queen, and author, William Belli, is known for his role as transgendered woman, Cherry Peck, in the television series *Nip/Tuck*. This would be the masculine Mars playing with the polarity of the Masculine/Feminine in Libra.

Mars in Scorpio on the DS

These individuals have an ability to delve deeply into matters of any kind, from fantasy to politics, as we will see, and others will find them captivatingly alluring.

Robert Kennedy, younger brother of John F. Kennedy, makes our list a third time. Robert, like his brother, was assassinated. The following comes from *The New York Times*:

> For those who found him charming, brilliant and sincerely devoted to the welfare of his country there were others who vehemently asserted that he was calculating, overly ambitious and ruthless.

This is an apt description of this astrological placement. The point here is that people would feel this energetic charge. Whether in a good or bad way, one would feel the polarizing energy, and have a hard time remaining neutral when in the province of an experience with these individuals.

American oil heir, T. Cullen Davis, also makes our list a third time for having both his Moon and Venus here. Davis exhibited violent tendencies that got him in trouble.

The WashingtonPost.com obituary for fantasy writer, Ursula Le Guin, beautifully illustrates this astrological placement. Ursula was a science fiction author most well known for her *Earthsea* series:

> [Le Guin]... she populated her novels with richly imagined worlds that drew less from recent science fiction than from ancient mythology or Taoism, the

Eastern philosophy that emphasizes acceptance and change. Ms. Le Guin once translated the ancient *Tao Te Ching*, publishing her take on the Taoist classic amid novels, stories and books of essays and poetry that made her one of the most beloved writers in American literature.

Mars in Sagittarius on the DS

One thing people often misunderstand about Sagittarius is their innocent nature. Sagittarian questions and statements come from a mind full of possibilities as well as, well, more questions. Seeking the higher meaning in other would be one aspect of this astrological placement.

The following comes from an article in Slate.com about radical queer filmmaker, Bruce LaBruce's 10 day retrospective at New York's Museum of Modern Art (MoMA):

> LaBruce has spent his entire career dodging vitriol, staring down ideologues at both ends of the political spectrum, sinking heteronormative battleships, and wielding his anti-establishment, anti-assimilationist, anti-you-name-it weaponry to ruffle quite a few reactionary feathers.

Former Australian female hockey player (as if that isn't Mars in Sagittarius enough!), Juliet Haslam, is an ambassador to the Premier's Reading Program Challenge. When we read, the words transport us on adventures through time, space, and experiences, which is a very appealing opportunity for this astrological placement. Juliet is also married to a footballer—Mars on the DS.

The following quote from an article in the Independent. uk about the heart wrenching experience for conjoined twins, Alyssa and Bethany Nolan, captures the complexity of this astrological placement:

> An ordinary couple, faced with an impossible moral dilemma, takes a decision that has utterly unpredictable consequences. They are committed to living with the outcome whatever happens. It was going to be as much about Shaun and Mary as their daughters.

This is a very telling article that also addresses the family's religious demands with God. Unfortunately, Bethany passed.

Mars in Capricorn on the DS

Individuals with this astrological placement can have a determined perspective about how to deal with and relate to others. Interestingly enough, we find two comedians here. Mars has the ability to pierce things, and when in the sign of Capricorn on the Descendant, we can have a very interesting perspective on our relationship to success and hard work.

We see in our first example, a certain level of frugality occurs with Capricorn. The following comes from the obituary for composer, Henry Mancini, in *The New York Times*:

Although he was among the most commercially successful composers in Hollywood, Mr. Mancini used to say he "never trusted this thing called success." For years, even after he acquired considerable fame and wealth after his creation of "Moon River," he continued to compose using a rented piano.

Comedienne and actress, Lily Tomlin, who appears on our list a second time, has had a very successful, long term (since 1972!) and dedicated business collaboration with her life time partner and comedy writer, Jane Wagner.

American actor and entertainer, Jerry Lewis, who makes our list a second time, had this eloquently written piece for his obituary in *The New York Times*, illustrating the complexity of having such astrological placements:

> As a spokesman for the Muscular Dystrophy Association, Mr. Lewis raised vast sums for charity; as a filmmaker of great personal force and technical skill, he made many contributions to the industry, including the early adoption of a device — the video assist, which allowed directors to review their work immediately on the set — still in common use. A mercurial personality who could flip from naked neediness to towering rage, Mr. Lewis seemed to contain multitudes, and he explored all of them. His ultimate object of contemplation was his own contradictory self, and he turned his obsession with fragmentation, discontinuity and the limits of language into a spectacle that enchanted children, disturbed adults and fascinated postmodernist critics.

Anatoly Mikhailovich Kashpirovsky, a Russian psychotherapist of Ukrainian origin, hypnotist and a controversial psychic healer, had an amazing opportunity to reach and influence the Russian masses—what better for this astrological placement?! In an article from AtlasObscura.com comes the following:

> Kashpirovsky's mental work with the weightlifting team brought him some renown, and in 1988 he became the head of the Republican Center of Psychotherapy in Kiev and started appearing on television. In these televised sessions, he attempted to demonstrate how the power of the mind can help people through physical trauma. In a series of televised séances, he attempted to stop millions of children from bedwetting, a feat he claimed to have accomplished. He also performed "remote psychological anaesthetization" on women undergoing surgery. Through the television, he talked to them during the procedure, and he claimed he was able to help them feel no pain.

I have to admit; I would like to see some interviews with these women since we know how well Sagittarius can toot its own horn.

Mars in Aquarius on the DS

These individuals are humanity's champions.

A tongue in cheek quote—so Aquarian—from our first example illustrates this astrological placement beautifully.

Auberon Waugh, eldest son of British novelist, Evelyn Waugh, is quoted as saying the following:

> "There are countless horrible things happening all over the world and horrible people prospering, but we must never allow them to disturb our equanimity or deflect us from our sacred duty to sabotage and annoy them whenever possible."

The New York Times had this to say about talented singer and actress, Dorothy Dandridge:

> Brazen, teasing and exhilaratingly free, she was a vision of womanly power well ahead of her time.

Wikipedia describes another trendsetter, American author, Maya Angelou, as a force of humanitarian nature, to which Mars can lend considerable force:

> With the publication of *I Know Why the Caged Bird Sings*, Angelou publicly discussed aspects of her personal life. She was respected as a spokesperson for black people and women, and her works have been considered a defense of black culture. Her works are widely used in schools and universities worldwide, although attempts have been made to ban her books from some U.S. libraries. Angelou's most celebrated works have been labeled as autobiographical fiction but many critics consider them to be autobiographies. She made a deliberate attempt to challenge the common

structure of the autobiography by critiquing, changing and expanding the genre. Her books center on themes such as racism, identity, family and travel.

Chess champion, Bobby Fischer, makes our list a second time and the theme of his Venus in Aries on the MC is mirrored here as well. Themes of competition, of course, come up as this is Mars, but with Aquarius, we see strategic intellectual understanding necessary to win at such a complex game. With the combo of his Venus and Mercury on the chart's angles, I would say he truly loves competition.

Actress and singer, Jackie Curtis, who appears here a second time for her Moon, lived a very interesting life as one could understand with Leo rising and an Aquarian Descendant. From GayCityNews.NYC comes this fantastic quote:

> Jackie, "Born John Holden, Jr., ending his career as the much-married Ms. Curtis sporting the full-monty gossip-column moniker Jackie Curtis Emerson Dukeshire Cayce Keller Loud Groby McPhee Majchrzak, he was both a good son (putting his mother, the true-grit Jeanie Uglialoro, into his masterpiece, the marathon meta-musical phantasmagoria *Vain Victory*—music by Paul Serrato—the show that gave the terms "actor chemistry" and "ensemble theater" a whole range of new meanings) and a creature of unbridled passion who lived to have deep and penetrating carnal knowledge of anonymous bruisers.

Australian television presenter, Catriona Rowntree, who makes our list a second time, had the excitement of travel planted firmly in her mind at age 15, from a history teacher who made the past come alive. Mars in Aquarius on the DS would be about experiencing other cultures and ideas and seeing life as a multicolored tapestry of experiences.

Indian batsman, Sachin Ramesh Tendulkar, who also makes our list a second time, has the distinction of having scored the highest number of runs in the history of international cricket.

From the AuReview.com, comes a lovely quote from singer and performer, Casey Donovan, that aptly states the importance of Aquarian individuality:

"At the end of the day, I think if you can be yourself in any situation then you're winning."

Almost mirroring this same sentiment, Sawyer Avery, son of American film director, Steven Spielberg, commented in an interview with NYPost.com, about an acting experience:

"You go up and completely open up and make a fool of yourself onstage so that everything else becomes easier." By doing that and more, he says, his clowning instructor, Christopher Bayes, "really taught me to embrace who I am."

Performer and singer, Justin Timberlake, reminds us of the importance of being authentic in the moment:

"I think the only way to achieve something that's classic is to be in the moment. You don't sit around and think, 'Oh, I hope this is remembered forever!' You just have to be honest, and I think that requires being in the moment."

Mars in Pisces on the DS

The endless desire to merge with another as well as express along a continuum are well indicated here.

The indefatigable entertainer, Carol Channing, who also has her Venus here, was married four times and used this passionate creative placement to fuel her work.

Another tireless veteran performer, Tom Hanks, started his career in a television sitcom called *Bosom Buddies*. In the series, Tom plays a heterosexual man who dresses up as a woman with another straight buddy so they can get cheap rent in a woman-only apartment building.

When we add Mars here, we have someone who can dive to the depths, or have an ego to fight crime as we do with hunky actor, Van Williams, who played the title role crime fighter, *Green Hornet* in the television series that ran from 1966–1967.

We will now look at the angle placements of Mars throughout the zodiac from the point of view of the Medium Coeli (MC)

Mars in Aries on the MC

This, of course, is a most powerful astrological placement. Here we have Mars at the highest point in the birth chart, for all of the world to see.

Edmund White, who will make our list another two times, is an American novelist. The following lovely quote he made summarizing this astrological placement, comes from GoodReads.com:

> "At every moment I convinced myself that I was gathering material for the novel of my life—all experienced from the philosophical distance of the author. Even these humiliating occasions when I was robbed could be used as material. Life was a field trip."

This is also an astrological placement for a trend setter as actress and princess, Grace Kelly's granddaughter, Pauline Ducruet.

Mars in Taurus on the MC

Mars is considered in detriment here in Taurus, because, Taurus is fixed and Mars cardinal. While these mavericks can be Bull-ies as shown in our first example, they just expressing their edict to be their own selves.

American singer and anti-gay rights activist, Anita Bryant, who also has her Venus here, strongly believed and was not afraid to express her opinions publicly opposing same sex relationships. Using religion as her justification, she became a strong advocate against gay rights. With Venus and Mars conjunct in the sign of Taurus upholding the standard form of relationship would be important to her. She believed she was the arbiter of acceptable forms of relationship. The force of her beliefs would be hard to change.

English singer and poly maverick Robbie Williams made this comment that addresses his astrological placement very well:

> "I'm a bit hesitant to do anything because I'm actually kind of lazy and I'd like an easier life from now on. The world's a massive place with lots of early mornings and late starts when you're working."

Leslie McGuirk is a tireless and impressive speaker, artist, medium, and astrologer. In her Ted Talk, she addresses the importance of being wrong. This is huge for the determined Taurean to reveal, but it gives them immeasurable freedom.

Elena Ford, member of the automobile industry family, exhibits the elements of hard work and determination, good results of this astrological placement. The following comes from an article at Fortune.com:

Elena has found herself in a difficult situation. Ford women have not traditionally sought work at the company and none have served on the board of directors.

Elena Ford came forth to break the mold, as a maverick would do!

Mars in Gemini on the MC

These people likely have and express excellent mental and physical agility.

Investigative journalist, Kitty Kelley, stated the following:

> "Once I decide to do something, I can't have people telling me I can't. If there's a roadblock, you jump over it, walk around it, crawl under it."

Gemini can be known for being a bit of an airhead, but with this astrological placement of Mars, there can be a strong determination as expressed by our next example. Film and television actress, Loni Anderson, understood that people have a way of looking at female blonds:

> ... far from a dumb blonde, Anderson insisted that she be able to play her character as a bright, sensitive woman before signing for the part. Her vision paid off, and the star earned two Emmy nominations and three Golden Globe nominations for her performance.

Director, actor and activist, Tim Robbins, has made many statements that capture this astrological placement:

> "I love iconoclasts. I love individuals. I love people that are true to themselves, whatever the cost."

> "What you get is what you get. What you do with what you get, that's more the point."

> "To the world you may be just one person but to one person you may be the world. The road to finding 'the one' is paved with a bit of promiscuity."

> "My philosophy is, don't take *no* for an answer and be willing to sacrifice your entire project for freedom."

Mars in Cancer on the MC

These individuals can be fierce advocates and have a drive to take care of the masses.

The brilliant and courageous, Coretta Scott King, was a powerhouse in her own right in order to be married to her husband, Martin Luther King, Jr. The following comes from her NewYorkTimes.com death announcement:

> "She'll be remembered as a strong woman whose grace and dignity held up the image of her husband as a man of peace, of racial justice, of fairness," said the Rev. Joseph Lowery, who helped found the Southern

Christian Leadership Conference with Dr. King and then served as its president for 20 years. "I don't know that she was a civil rights leader in the truest sense, but she became a civil rights figure and a civil rights icon because of what she came to represent."

What women, like Coretta, did during the Civil Rights Movement deserves more attention. I believe it took every ounce of her maverick Mars courage to face and survive the horrible injustices she experienced while acting as the mother for a whole community.

Diana Mitford, of the famed and infamous British Mitford sisters, exhibited another aspect of this astrological placement as revealed in this passage from her obituary from NYTimes.com:

> In a family of dazzling girls, Diana dazzled perhaps the brightest. "She was the nearest thing to Botticelli's Venus that I have ever seen," wrote James Lees-Milne, a family friend.

Mars is the companion to Venus, so it is not surprising that this placement could exhibit finesse and beauty.

Former First Lady, Nancy Reagan, who also has two other planets here, was known for her "Just say No" campaign which was aimed at helping families deal with the devastating effects of drug use and abuse. As this astrological placement can be a bit determined, as we have Mars one of the chart's angles, we can understand how Nancy might have been experienced as a tough mom.

Mars at the top of the chart can lend a very promiscuous and passionate charge to the native's life as evidenced by American author and essayist, John Rechy. From Independent.co.uk comes a revelation about how Mars played out in Rechy's life:

> And so began a bizarre double life, which Rechy recalls in hilarious, toe-curling detail in a new autobiography, *About My Life and the Kept Woman*. By day, he was a writer, mixing with fellow authors, even teaching at UCLA. By night, he was back on the streets, selling sex to men. "I wanted demarcation between the different areas of my life, and I fooled myself that I could keep them separate. I wanted to be treated one way as 'the writer', another way as 'the hustler', and if they crossed over I got very confused." But cross over they did—as, for instance, when the expat British novelist Christopher Isherwood invited Rechy home to talk about writing, and then pounced. Liberace and George Cukor did the same."

Actor Mike White, has this lovely quote that is the beautiful blending of protective Mars and security seeking Cancer:

> "My impulse is to create an aesthetic that's about a humanistic approach to a world and trying to create compassion for all the characters."

Mars in Leo on the MC

These individuals exhibit a very definite charisma and internal fire or power that is attractive to the public. Leo has a control dial, like on a stove that can be adjusted from *warm* to *incinerate.*

New Zealand artist, Peter McIntyre, who makes our list now a third time, shows us an archetypal representation of this astrological placement. Here is a bit about Peter from Ocula.com:

> Following his graduation he was influenced by British avant-garde painting, and worked as an illustrator and theatre designer, but his appointment as war artist reunited him with his countrymen and commitment to realism. As an artist with the Second New Zealand Expeditionary Forces (2NZEF), Peter McIntyre recorded its campaigns in Crete, North Africa and Italy. His work defined New Zealand's war experiences in North Africa and Cassino. He returned to New Zealand in 1946 as a professional artist, and by the 1960's had established a career as the country's most popular painter, travelling artist and commentator.

Mars, the planet of war and Leo, the sign of creative self-expression, found a perfect union in Peter's life and work.

Wikipedia.com writes this fitting piece for Welsh comedian, Harry Secombe:

Upon hearing of his old friend's death, Spike Milligan quipped, "I'm glad he died before me, because I didn't want him to sing at my funeral." But Secombe would have the last laugh: upon Milligan's own death the following year, a recording of Secombe singing was played at Spike's memorial service.

This astrological placement isn't much for being upstaged!
American actress, Bernadette Peters, who makes our list a third time, had an apt description of this astrological alignment beautifully rendered on multiple levels from Vulture.com:

> Bernadette Peters has occupied an unusual dual position. She's both a very particular type—a bona fide Broadway star, one of the few remaining—and in her warmth, humor, and vulnerability, utterly unique as a performer. "I understand that other people might see something special in what I do," says Peters, dressed all in black, her famous red curls flowing over shoulder, and speaking (graciously, cautiously) from a meeting room in her publicist's office in midtown Manhattan, "but I don't think I'm the one who can say what that is."

Bernadette describes what it is like for those of us with planets on an angle in the chart, it is more for others to experience—especially on the MC which is the highest point of the chart for all to see.

The archetypes can play out ever so bluntly, as they did when TheSun.co.uk had this headline for German model, Claudia Schiffer:

> Claudia Schiffer, 47, sizzles in leopard print bikini on board luxury yacht.

Claudia's headline has lots of Leonine energy fueled by Mars on the MC. One can almost feel the irresistible draw of a moth to the flame.

A promising career ended far too shortly when River Phoenix passed away from a drug overdose; he was a young actor who lost his life at a point when his acclaim was shining brightly. River's death shocked the entertainment world.

Mars in Virgo on the MC

These individuals get things done on many levels and have a good way of understanding how to direct resources for the best good.

Having this placement myself, as an astrologer, author, teacher, writer, and CFO, I use this drive to help guide others to perfect themselves, their businesses, and organizations. This book is an example of utilizing the multiplicity of human examples to explain astrology to the public.

American actor, Clarence Swensen, one of the Munchkins in *The Wizard of Oz* movie, had this interesting take:

> Always defining themselves as "true Texans," Swensen delighted in telling others: "It's not true that everything and everybody in Texas is bigger."

Here we see the directed energy of Mars is literally put to work in a multitude of ways in Virgo.

Sir James Hardy, is a perfect example of this archetype. If we do an internet search, a description of him comes up something like, "Australian winemaker and businessman who is also noted for his yachtsmanship ... " Sir James reflects the multifaceted interest Mars can express when found in Virgo.

As with Mars in almost any sign conjunct the MC, there is a call to leadership as well illustrated in an article from SMH.com.au about Morris Iemma, the 40th premier of New South Wales in Australia:

> The former NSW premier holds a number of positions within cricket ranks. He is the president of Campbelltown-Camden Cricket Club, the NSW Districts Cricket Association, Kingsgrove Cricket Club and vice-president of the St George District Cricket Association.

Professional ballroom dancer and performer, Craig Revel Horwood, is an advocate for same sex relationships on the *Strictly Come Dancing* show, in which he is a panel judge.

Mars in Libra on the MC

This is not an easy placement until Mars becomes cultured, cultivated, and understands the importance of give and take.

As we know, Alan Blumlein, who makes our list a second time, used this placement in a most special way. Wikipedia.com writes the following about Alan:

> [Alan] was an English electronics engineer, notable for his many inventions in telecommunications, sound recording, stereophonic sound, television and radar. He received 128 patents and was considered as one of the most significant engineers and inventors of his time.

As we stated before, with Mars on one of the chart's angles, there appears to be a high occurrence of forceful deaths. Alan died in a plane crash.

Gamal Abdel Nasser Hussein, the second President of Egypt, who lasted some 14 years, shows us another way of using force to exact change for his people. Gamal led a revolution in 1952 that overthrew both the Egyptian and Sudanese monarchies.

French writer, Henri Charrière, with his Venus in Sagittarius on the AS, had a deep need for freedom as well as the need to tell everyone about it. These are all elements of his two Maverick planets.

With Venus in Aries on the IC opposing his Mars in Libra on the MC, we can understand the passionate dilemma that absorbed Pentecostal evangelist, Jimmy Swaggart's attention. Not easy for a holy man whose desire nature is untamed.

In the obituary for Australian writer, Morris Lurie, TheGuardian.com writes:

His most popular book for children, *The Twenty-Seventh Annual African Hippopotamus Race*, began life in London when, newly married, Lurie was asked by his wife for a story to lull her to sleep. He summoned up an image of 84 hippos, each in colourful bathing togs, diving into a huge river under a bright blue African sky. When his wife awoke, she insisted he write it down in spite of his lack of confidence. "I was told, 'You are beautiful, you are worthy, you are cherished, do it.' And I did."

This illustrates the healing power of love and what one can accomplish when our own story resonates with a larger audience.

Mars in Scorpio on the MC

This is a very powerful position, second only to Pluto. These people have a deep sense of power and are neither afraid of the shadows, nor of being exposed.

Singer and performer, Bobby Brown, husband of Whitney Houston, feels the concern that most Scorpios feel: being misunderstood. He was heavily consulted for the four-hour miniseries, *The Bobby Brown Story* in which more of "his" side of their story could be shared. This is not an easy placement, even though Mars is a ruler of Scorpio. This astrological configuration has a lot to do with reconciling one's desires in alignment for the greater good so that situations can be a win-win. Have you ever seen Bobby without sunglasses? This is a true Scorpionic trait: observe others while withholding their expressions from being seen.

Scottish comedienne, Rhona Cameron, makes archetypally appropriate responses to the following question in an interview with TimeOut.com:

"You had your own sitcom and you've written books. How do these compare to stand-up?

"Well, they are all storytelling. Stand-up is much more difficult than the other media. It's very easy to be on stage when it comes naturally as it does to me, but the process of finding material that people will relate to is harder than, let's say, writing a book. A book is a long gestation period. Conception is the easy part, but then you have to look after it, give birth to it, which is long and laborious. But then the rewards are around forever. Whilst stand-up is more momentary, more transient, and then you run a tightrope with great risks that can swing between ecstasy and despair. The gladiatorial aspect that we endure for years in the clubs before getting to the level I'm at now is not for the fainthearted. I'm very lucky in one way to have this kind of versatility. But it's also deeply burdensome, if you can't make it all happen exactly when you need to. Highs and lows – you've got to ride them all in the long game."

Yaser Esam Hamdi, is a former American citizen who was captured in Afghanistan in 2001. He joined the Taliban, was incarcerated at Guantanamo Bay, and exhibits many other

Mars/Scorpio/Terrorist/Power issues. I recommend additional internet research.

In another interesting twist of archetypes, Alexandra, Princess of Hanover, is a championship ice skater. Mars is a sharp edge on the frozen Scorpio water.

Mars in Sagittarius on the MC

These adventurous and entertaining individuals can be philosophical or literal in their respective crusades for truth and justice.

English comedian, Benny Hill, who also has idealistic Aquarius Sun on his AS, always had a glimmer in his eye and many of his skits showed a fluidity in relationship to whatever situation was presented. This is a very spontaneous placement for Mars and can exhibit from ardent adventurer to courageous defender of justice.

From Goodreads.com comes this quote from British author, Tim Lott, who makes our list a third time:

> "We tend to fantasize about eliminating uncertainty so that the world can be safe... the first thing to note about uncertainty—or insecurity, the uncomfortable feeling it produces—is that it is intrinsic to a dynamic existence... insecurity is inescapable."

This is the fierce acceptance and desire for a dynamic experience—something Mars in Sagittarius would demand especially when supercharged on the Midheaven.

While Donna Rice should be best known for her child advocacy work with the non-profit, Enough is Enough, most remember her for bringing truth to the public when a married presidential candidate's uninvited advances towards her were made public.

American actor, Michael C. Hall, is probably best known for playing the title character of a serial killer who kills serial killers in the television series *Dexter*. This is a very interesting twist on his namesake, Saint Michael the Archangel, right? He uses the Martian tools to overpower his victims in pursuit of Sagittarius on the MC's need to serve the public good. Mars in Sagittarius (or Jupiter in Aries) often has a philosophical slant and crusade-like energy.

Mars in Capricorn on the MC

Mars experiences his exaltation in Capricorn and here on the MC? The sky is the limit and no prize too big that these individuals cannot attain.

Our first example, American actress, Mia Farrow, has this perfect quote for the imperative involved with this astrological placement:

> "I want a big career, a big man, and a big life. You have to think big – that's the only way to get it. I just couldn't stand being anonymous."

Normal would have never been enough for Mia.

Record executive and founder of Casablanca Records, Neil Bogart, died at the age of 39, but had already amassed a most considerable fortune and empire.

Scottish entertainer, Karen Dunbar, is an example of the moxie needed to become a comedian and actress.

Mars in Aquarius on the MC

This is an interesting placement for Mars. Unfettered by emotions or sensual desires, the Aquarian Mars uses theses instinctive energies for ideological pursuits.

This is a perfect placement for an astrologer who wants to be known and seen for her/his work as evidenced by famous astrologer, Jeane Dixon, who also has her Moon in the opposing sign and place of Leo on the IC. Jean was an aggressive self-promoter.

John Upledger, the founder of CranioSacral Therapy, who also has Mercury here, has that ability to pierce through our perceptions of our human bodies and understand there are other important internal pulses besides the one the heart makes.

Jessica Savitch, who also has her Sun here, received the courage to insert herself as a television correspondent, in the man's world of broadcast news.

In a lively interview with JustJared.com, actress Kristen Stewart, talks about the importance an Aquarian would place on sexual expression and freedom:

Kristen Stewart is opening up about sexual ambiguity, and why she prefers to keep things ambiguous. "Yeah, ambiguity is my favorite thing ever. In terms of sexuality? For sure," the 28-year-old actress told Paris-based *Mastermind* magazine via *People* magazine. "And also in making films, if you perfectly answer every question, you don't allow for people to have their own experience and really indulge a thought. I feel the same way about how we f**k each other. You don't want to know everything all the time," Kristen added.

Mars in Pisces on the MC

Think of shooting an arrow or using a sword while under water. Sure, these objects pierce the water, but are not as effective as they are on land.

A beautifully illustrative expression of this astrological placement is detailed in the obituary for English writer and composer, Anthony Burgess, published at Independent.co.uk:

> To think of him (as was said of a *magnifico* like Dr. Johnson) is to think of an empire falling. All those big books, reference works, volumes of critical essays, plays, opera librettos, orchestral symphonies, and much else, which tumbled out of his head add up to a resplendent career. Simply in terms of sheer quantity, it is hard to believe it was all done by hand. His personal manner, too, was expansive. With his Roman emperor's hairstyle and countenance, and puffing

ostentatiously on a cigarillo, he would hold the floor with impromptu lectures on Malay cuisine, Bloom's Dublin, how Shakespeare spoke, where to buy shoes in Barcelona, the beauty of Sophia Loren, working for Lew Grade, learning Japanese – anything really, so long as he could throw in colourful words: *orchidaceous, pinguid, rebarbative*. You would think to yourself, there's nothing this man doesn't know.

He was the most self-dramatizing of authors, fully aware that 'Anthony Burgess' was a performance perfected over several decades by John Wilson—the name on the birth certificate (25 February 1917) and on the much-used passport. Burgess was the public role, the baritonal, slightly arrogant columnist and literary pundit, the Monte Carlo citizen fancying himself as the heir of James Joyce. Wilson was the more sensitive, chivalrous reality beneath the swagger: the Manchester boy nervous of fame and riches, who shut himself away in a variety of residences (from Sussex to Switzerland, from Princeton to Provence) and who banged out close on a hundred texts—and there are flashes and sparks of genius in every one of them.

Actress and television host, Melissa Rivers, who also has Jupiter in opposing Virgo on the IC, probably used this energy to work with the power-house of a mom she had, and to also become an accomplished equestrian. Pisces is the sign of the horse.

Jupiter

Jupiter on the chart's angles is HUGE!! These people take on a larger than life personality. Of course, how one experiences this depends upon which of the chart's angles Jupiter is conjunct. This placement can make one feel like one has the law in one's own hands or may be a king or queen. Jupiter rules Law and Royalty. These people bring along a sense of optimism that can be blind on one end of the spectrum and enlightened on the other end.

Jupiter in our birth chart shows how we express our philosophies in life, how we grow and expand, reveal our generosity and express our joy. While Jupiter is one of the two planetary benefics, it can simply expand whatever it touches, and not always for the best. America embraces the idea that bigger is better. Jupiter can expand your pocket book as well as increase our debts and waistband as we each seek our idealized dream. Jupiter is the planet of indiscriminate increase as in the case of cancer cells in the body preparing for that ultimate expansion: death.

We will now look at the angle placements of Jupiter throughout the zodiac from the point of view of the Ascendant (AS).

Jupiter in Aries on the AS

This is a grand astrological placement as impulsive Aries energy is given a large tank of gasoline for its big agenda. These are natural born leaders, but their egos may prove their fatal flaw.

A perfect example of this sort of limitless power idea is illustrated in Brazilian President, Janio Quadros. The following comes from his obituary at NYTimes.com:

> He was elected President in 1960 in a landslide, but quit after seven months in office, apparently because he expected the Congress to offer him more power if he came back. Instead, it simply accepted his resignation.

From theretroset.com comes this interesting tidbit about American actor, Robert Walker, Jr. that describes the egoic process from someone with this astrological placement. Here is an excerpt from "The Mystery of Bob Walker" that comes from *Modern Screen* magazine:

Consider the mystery of Robert Walker, one of the strangest men in Hollywood. He's a guy with a million romances, but they say he's still in love with his ex-wife. He's a man who wants to act, but he's turned down parts any other actor would have hocked his soul for. (A lead in *State of the Union*, for instance). He's disappeared for long stretches at a time, and neither family, friends nor studio could track him down, or lure him back. He's behaved at all times the way he's felt like behaving; he's never conformed, he's never tried to. He went straight to the top, stayed there a while, and then very calmly walked out. Nobody in Hollywood understood Walker but that wasn't strange, because Walker didn't understand himself. A few months ago, he went to the head men at Metro-Goldwyn-Mayer, "Take me off the payroll," he said. "I'm through with movies for good."

"Listen, Bob," one of them said, "take some time and think it over. Go to New York, do a play—but quit talking nonsense. Hollywood is where you belong."

Walker shook his head stubbornly. "Take me off the payroll. I'm not working, and I'm not going to work."

"You can't work for any other outfit," he was warned. "Your contract belongs to Metro."

"I understand that. I'm not asking you to tear up my contract. I just want it clearly understood that as far as pictures are concerned I'm all washed up. Through." He wasn't, of course.

Australian movie director, Paul Cox, earned the moniker of the father of independent cinema (how much more Jupiter in Aries on the AS can we get?). The following comes from his obituary in TheGuardian.com:

> The American film critic, Roger Ebert, described Cox as "one of the best directors of our time, and one of the heroes of modern cinema. He's one of the warriors, an independent director who does nothing for hire, who makes only films close to his heart, whose humanism you could call spiritual," Ebert wrote after the Cannes Film Festival in 2010.

Jupiter in Taurus on the AS

These are people are natural *bon vivants*. Taurus loves pleasures of the physical body and Jupiter is the planet of indulgence, so these people are going to have a big personality enjoying what life has to offer.

Filipino writer, Nick Joaquin, who also has his Venus here is a perfect example of this astrological placement. The following comes from an article at CNNPhilipines.com:

> Actually it was Nick's birthday too, as their anniversaries were a day apart, and that was how we celebrated the two of them through the long decades. In those decades, Nick had given generously of his friendship, honoring us for whatever little thing we did, defending us in our sloth and our many shortcomings.

It grated on many people that Nick Joaquin addressed us in diminutives, even in formal symposia. Still he may have thought it his continuing duty to goad us, pointing out how hard other writers worked, how much more they produced.

Not only does Nick value the material pleasures of life, but this passage shows the loyal friend aspect so crucial to Taurus as well.

Peter Beattie, was the longest serving state premier in the history of Australia. Wikipedia writes that he was also appointed, "as Australia's first Resources Sector Supplier Envoy charged with promoting a Buy Australian at Home and Abroad program for supplying products to the Australian resources industry."

Taurus is the sign of resources and Jupiter has that envoy quality that supported Beattie in such a role.

Jupiter in Gemini on the AS

These people have a way about them. People will enjoy their wit and/or movement or become exhausted by it. The gift of Jupiter on the AS is one that elevates one to the point of being seen. The jack of all trades aspect of Gemini reaches a unification of beauty when focused by the maverick as well shown by the following individuals.

American modern dancer, Martha Graham, is a prime example of this archetype. She also has a stellium in Gemini! Martha is known for two quotes that illustrate her exceptional

Geminian abilities, "Wherever a dancer stands ready, that spot is holy ground," and Martha really worked to be "an athlete for God."

Golden Screen actress, Greta Garbo, made this Jupiter in Gemini statement:

> "There are some who want to get married and others who don't. I have never had an impulse to go to the altar. I am a difficult person to lead."

How could one lead someone with this astrological placement? Gemini is expanded by the buoyant idealistic nature of Jupiter.

The NYTimes.com obituary for American painter, Andrew Wyeth, who makes our list a second time, again aptly renders this archetypal position:

> Andrew Wyeth, one of the most popular and also most lambasted artists in the history of American art, a reclusive linchpin in a colorful family dynasty of artists, and a painter whose precise, realist views of a harsh rural life became emblems of national culture and incited endless debates about the nature of modern art, died on Friday at his home in Chadds Ford, Pennsylvania. He was 91."

The Ascendant is how we see the world and how the world sees us. With Gemini here, we would expect there to be a lot of conversations, opinions and points of view.

Comedienne and actress, Phyllis Diller, makes our list a second time. Incidentally, she and Andrew Wyeth both have

Venus in Leo on the IC! The wonderfully amazing part to understand about Phyllis Diller is she wasn't afraid to look stupid, awkward or to demean herself. While she was after laughs, I would imagine the edict with these two angular Mavericks would be, "Say what you must, but do not ignore me!"

American novelist, Erica Jong, makes our list a third time with her Mars in this position. The fearless wisdom these two planets gave her are well stated in these quotes from AZQuotes.com:

"Do you want me to tell you something really subversive? Love is everything it's cracked up to be. That's why people are so cynical about it. It really is worth fighting for, being brave for, risking everything for. And the trouble is, if you don't risk anything, you risk even more."

"Humor is one of the most serious tools we have for dealing with impossible situations."

"I have accepted fear as a part of life—specifically the fear of change... I have gone ahead despite the pounding in the heart that says: turn back."

Christine Keeler, who appears on our list a second time, and shares Venus in Aquarius on the MC like Erica Jong, shows us how one's personal relationships can be seen by the world with Christine's MC Venus placement. Christine was a key player in a British political scandal: the Profumo Affair.

Jupiter in Cancer on the AS

Jupiter is a planet that can often signify royal standing or position when on an angle. When found in Cancer on the AS, we would likely find individuals who are crusaders for their own country or empire.

While we only have one well-known example in this category, this individual also has Moon and Mercury here: Hugo Chavez, 64th President of Venezuela. This "triple-threat" Cancerian energy is well illustrated in the following Chavez quote from BrainyQuote.com:

> "Our policy is to deepen the relations with all the countries in the world—monarchies, kingdoms, large powers—we want to respect all differences and have our relationships based on mutual respect."

Jupiter is exalted in Cancer.

Jupiter in Leo on the AS

This is an interesting ego placement. We have Jupiter, the planet of expansion and higher philosophies, with the self-centering energy of Leo on the pivotal Ascendant.

Our first example is yogi, guru, philosopher, nationalist, and poet, Sri Aurobindo. If we think of the highest expression of the Self as Love, we can grasp the idea "ensouled matter." Think of a descending triangle of energy coming from above and matter ascending from below and meeting at our heart. Sri

Aurobindo exemplified this astrological placement to a most dignified degree. Jupiter pushes us to explore and widen our perspectives. Spirit is Matter at its least dense and Matter is Spirit at its most dense.

Scottish poet, Edwin Morgan, is a lovely example of this astrological placement. ScottishPoetryLibrary.com.uk, has a thoughtful article on Morgan's expansive life:

> Scotland's first official Makar in modern times, Edwin Morgan was endlessly inventive, inquiring, energetic, internationalist, and deeply committed to his home city of Glasgow. A book of poems in his honour, *Unknown Is Best*, was produced to celebrate Morgan's eightieth birthday in 2000. His own poem, "At Eighty", was characteristic of the poet's work, faring forward into the future, embracing change: Push the boat out, compañeros / Push the boat out, whatever the seas.... push it all out into the unknown! / Unknown is best, it beckons best...

In another interesting example, after her film career, Virginia Vale, the 1950's actress, was an executive secretary and a competitive judge for U.S. Figure Skating. Jupiter can be a great judge.

Dutch actor, Rutger Hauer, shared some of his wanderlust Jupiterian worldly experience in an interview with tcs.cam.ac.uk:

> When Rutger was 15 he ran away, having decided to become a sailor. For a year he sailed around the world

aboard a freighter—it gave him the chance to see other countries and cultures in a way most 15 year olds never could. The poverty disturbed him, but likewise he encountered the "beauty of life and the ocean." I asked him what he learned from his time travelling, "By not going to school I learned that the world is a beautiful place and needs to be discovered."

Bernard Kerik, the New York City Police Commissioner and felon, lived a clearly different expression of this energy. I recommend reading about this individual and the ways in which one's ego can get one into big trouble! The following comes from NYMag.com:

> Even his credentials as a New York City cop were pretty thin for someone who'd risen to the top job. Though he was heavily decorated, he was on the force only eight years, and his highest rank before being named commissioner was detective third grade. Now he was about to get one of the top jobs in the Bush administration. In truth, Kerik himself, whose robust ego knows few limits, was having trouble wrapping his mind around the concept.

This astrological placement seeks a big stage.

The strength, conviction and determination of this astrological placement are further emphasized in the first paragraph in the bio for American politician, Annise Parker, at VictoryInstitute.org:

Victory Fund and Victory Institute President & CEO, Annise Parker, is the first former elected official to lead the organizations, having served six years as a Houston City Council member, six years as City Controller, and six years as Mayor of the city. She is one of only two women to have been elected mayor, and is the only person in Houston history to have held the offices of council member, controller, and mayor.

Artist and astrologer, Sandy Reuve, portrays a couple of other aspects of this huge astrological placement. She is the creator of Intention Beads, which she hand makes during specific astrological transit points in time to help accentuate that energy in a person's field. Sandy also has a big loving Leonine mane and presence.

Jupiter in Virgo on the AS

Jupiter is in its detriment in Virgo, but when we look at this list, we can see many ways in which it can have a beneficial expression. Virgo is the sign of womanhood and oftentimes expresses itself in interesting ways in a man's chart.

American film star, Montgomery Clift, also has Uranus opposite this point in Pisces, which probably further confounded his sexuality. In the LATimes.com obituary for Clift, there are some clearly stated representations of Jupiter in Virgo archetypes:

It was generally conceded that one of the most effective pieces of acting in the movie *Judgment at Nuremberg* was that of a mumbling Polish witness who had been sterilized by the Nazis. The actor was Montgomery Clift. He did it for nothing. When someone asked why, the hawk-faced Clift replied quietly: "Because I wanted to play it." This was the enigmatic man who died Saturday in New York City at the age of 45, little understood but always respected for the sensitivity of his approach to any part he played. "He's always striving for perfection," Burt Lancaster commented while working with Clift in *From Here to Eternity*. Donna Reed, another participant in that movie, said: "I've never known an actor who went so far as Monty did in getting every detail, every reaction, every emotion of the character he was depicting." The angular Clift was extremely selective about his roles. His publicist said he turned down an average of 10 scripts a month. One, according to the publicist, was for a part in the movie *John Goldfarb, Please Come Home*. Clift felt it was in bad taste. "I've never been ashamed of any picture I made," the actor said.

One of the earliest examples in this book is Holy Roman Emperor Maximilian I. The following comes from Hapsburger. net:

"Early practice maketh a master emperor..."

Another focus of his upbringing lay in sporting activities such as horsemanship, hunting, dancing and fencing. Maximilian was athletic, excelling at jousting, and proved himself a daring horseman and tireless huntsman in the high mountain regions.

Maximilian's portraits show a rather significant proboscis, or discriminating nose.

Virgo is the sign of the harvest and bounty, so it is no surprise that with Jupiter here, artist Wayne Thiebaud, paints a wonderful array of desserts, sweets, and city streets.

From his obituary at Legacy.com, American hotelier heir, Eric Hilton, shows the strength of service this position can call forth in a person:

"I can think of no greater God-given responsibility we have than that of extending a helping hand to our fellow man."

Mr. Hilton lived those words of his father and carried forth his legacy of leaving this world a better place for people in need.

The varietal, mutable nature of Virgo coupled with expansive, adventurous Jupiter, is well articulated by double maverick and American musician, Nick Carter. The following comes from BrainyQuotes.com:

"It's like Forrest Gump said, 'Life is like a box of chocolates.' Your career is like a box of chocolates – you never know what you're going to get. But everything you get is going to teach you something along the way and make you the person you are today. That's the exciting part—it's an adventure in itself."

Jupiter in Libra on the AS

This is BIG charisma, beauty and an ideal need for harmony in one's self. The sophistication of building the ideal self is well indicated here. They all believe they are doing good, regardless of the consequences.

English actor, Christopher Lee, who appears a second time, exhibits the debonair side of this astrological placement. The following comes from BadAssOfTheWeek.com:

> He's also a 6'5" tall world champion fencer, speaks six languages, does all of his own stunts, has participated in more on-screen sword fights than any actor in history, served for five years defending democracy from global fascism as a British Commando blowing the shit out of Nazi asses in World War II, and became the oldest person to ever record lead vocals on a heavy metal track when, at the age of 88, he wrote, performed on, and released a progressive symphonic power metal EP about the life of Charlemagne (because why the fuck not?).

As Libra is an air sign and Jupiter can lend a bit of idealism, one can see how an individual can dissociate from his acts as shown by serial killer, Dennis Nilsen. The following comes from MurderPedia.com:

> Dennis Nilsen was arrested in 1983 on suspicion of multiple murders. He apologized to the police for not being able to tell them the exact number of people he

had killed. When his house was searched, they found three heads in a cupboard, and they found thirteen more bodies in Nilsen's former place of residence at Crinkleroot at 195 Melrose Avenue. During the trial at Old Bailey, Nilsen was cold and distant, and seemed utterly unaffected by the fact that he had murdered fifteen people.

Nilsen's victims were mostly young homeless gay men.

Karen Silkwood, who also has her Moon here, shows us the correct legal result will prevail. The following comes from Wikipedia.com:

Karen Gay Silkwood was an American chemical technician and labor union activist known for raising concerns about corporate practices related to health and safety of workers in a nuclear facility. Following her mysterious death, which received extensive coverage, her estate filed a lawsuit against chemical company Kerr-McGee, which was eventually settled for $1.38 million.

Olympian, Colette Besson, shows yet another side of this aspect. The following comes from Independent.co.uk:

Colette Besson is always remembered in Britain as the woman who beat Lillian Board in the 400 metres at the 1968 Mexico City Olympic Games. But in France, she is recalled as the beautiful athlete whose Olympic gold reduced even President Charles de Gaulle to tears.

After retiring from the track, Besson continued her involvement in sport through a high altitude training centre at Font Romeu in the Pyrenees, by chairing France's anti-doping programme and in working for Paris's ultimately unsuccessful attempt to win the right to stage the 2012 Olympics.

Born near Bordeaux in 1946 and trained as a physical education teacher, Besson was a moderate international standard 400m sprinter, aged 22, when she was selected for the French Olympic team in 1968. That she managed to qualify through to the final of her event was regarded by even the partisan French media as something of a surprise. But the 400m for women was then still a relatively new event, and at the high altitude of Mexico City, performances in sprint events were entirely unpredictable.

Thus, entering the finishing straight, Britain's 19-year-old "golden girl" Lillian Board was 10 metres clear of the field, the gold medal apparently hers. But Besson, her dark hair flowing, began to chase her down to snatch the title on the line in 52.03 seconds. Board was second in 52.12sec.

Mike White, who is on our list a second time, was not afraid to be himself on the competitive reality television show, *Survivor*. The following comes from IndieWire.com:

But White does give high marks for the *Survivor* experience living up to expectations. "For whatever reason, there is such a pure immersive quality to the game and I didn't know if I was ever going to be fully in the game. I wasn't sure if I'd get past the 'Truman Show' part of it," he said. "You start playing the game an hour in. You just end up being totally immersed in the game part of it. And that is the thrill of it. The paranoia, all of that really happened. So few things live up to the hype. Those moments where I was playing, I was 100 percent stimulated by the game of it. As someone who likes to play games, it couldn't have been more fun."

This astrological placement would enjoy strategizing and extrapolating the ways in which people are likely to relate.

Jupiter in Scorpio on the AS

These individuals will go to whatever depths necessary to get to the truth of something. They may also lose themselves in a dream of their own making.

Evolutionary astrologer, Jeffrey Wolf Green, is a perfect example of this astrological placement. He wrote two books on the often misunderstood planet Pluto, ruler of Scorpio, and developed a very articulate and extensive school of astrology known as Evolutionary Astrology, which is perfect for accessing the deeper aspects of life using the laws of astrology.

American actor, River Phoenix, makes a second appearance on our list. Sadly, River died from a drug overdose.

Jupiter in Sagittarius on the AS

This is a most elevated astrological placement, indeed! Jupiter, the planet of expansive grandiosity, is in its natural higher philosophies seeking sign of Sagittarius. This is a combination for law, religion and adventure.

Our first example shows the law and political perspectives well. Jack Marshall, was Deputy Prime Minister of New Zealand for 12 years (interestingly enough, that is the amount of time it takes Jupiter to make one orbit around the Sun!) and the Prime Minister for one year.

Former First Lady, Pat Nixon, who makes our list a third time, has this perfect Sagittarian acceptance quote taken from AZQuotes.com:

> "Even when people can't speak your language, they can tell if you have love in your heart."

Actor and comedian, Kevin Kline, has a very playful presence on screen. And off screen? The following comes from CountryLiving.com:

> The family maintains an intentionally low profile at home in Manhattan, though Cates and Kline occasionally walk the red carpet together at film premieres, and are sometimes spotted sitting courtside, cracking each other up, at New York Knicks games.

Astrologer, Ken Irving, uses this astrological placement to bring forth the truths of astrology. His extensive corpus of work is remarkable. Whether working to further the AstroCartography work started by Jim Lewis, or further define and defend Michel and Françoise Gauquelin's Mars Effect or any other area of astrology, he is a tireless seeker of astrological truths. His Big Brain can track all of the multitudinous astrological pathways running through the great map of astrology.

Actor, Tom Arnold, who makes our list a second time, worked to bring forth the "Truth" about Donald Trump.

In an interesting twist of justice, James Degorsky, was convicted of murdering seven people at a Brown's Chicken restaurant in Palatine, Illinois and then was awarded $451K in a civil settlement. "Luck" is something that would go along with this astrological placement.

Katie Beers, who was kidnapped in 1993, exhibits what some may call luck, but is actually the Sagittarian ability to ask questions and learn while in the process. A Sagittarian with Jupiter on the AS is someone who can take adversity and become a better person for it. The following comes from ABCNews.go.com:

> Two decades ago, Beers, then 9, was abducted by John Esposito, a neighbor on Long Island, New York, and imprisoned by him for 17 days in an underground bunker. She said he sexually abused her during her captivity.
>
> Speaking of the abduction, Beers said, "If it didn't happen, then I wouldn't be where I am today."
>
> Beers had already been living a life of physical and sexual abuse at the hands of her godmother's husband, Sal Inghilleri.

"I was sexually abused, physically abused, emotionally abused, verbally abused. I was [a] slave," Beers said.

Child Protective Services visited her house several times. Teachers didn't speak up, even though Beers made it to class only one or two days a week, she said.

"A lot of people kept to themselves," Beers said.

Beers said this situation prepared her to survive her abduction.

With no one else stepping in to help, she resolved to save herself by drawing on her own wits. As she watched reports about herself on a television in her bunker, Beers started playing mind games with her captor.

"I definitely think that by trying to manipulate him into thinking about the future and things like that, I think that got him a little scared and worried about what the future was going to hold," Beers told 20/20.

"When I asked [Esposito] how I would go to school, he told me that he would teach me what I needed to know. When I asked him how I would work, he would tell me that he had enough money for the two of us. When I asked him about getting married and having kids, he told me that when I was 18 he would marry me and have children with me."

After 17 days and intense round-the-clock surveillance, Esposito turned himself in. He pleaded guilty to kidnapping and was sentenced to 15 years to life in prison.

As authorities excavated the bunker, Beers was placed in a new home with loving foster parents. Over years of therapy, she started to piece together the childhood she never had.

"The women in her life neglected her and did not protect her, and the men abused her. ... So her level of trust was very, very low," said Mary Bromley, Beers' therapist.

Life with her foster parents was "awesome," recalled Beers, who now lives in rural Pennsylvania and works in insurance sales. "They let me play. ... I didn't really have too much responsibility other than riding my bike and doing my homework."

In other words, normal—and fortunate.

Jupiter in Capricorn on the AS

Capricorn is the sign of work and advancement and Jupiter is the planet of expansion. Jupiter is in its fall in Capricorn, because Saturn, the God of Limits and boundaries and hard work, is the ruler of Capricorn. Jupiter isn't limited like Saturn, in fact, if we think of the planets in a sort of personal order, it isn't until one reaches Saturn that boundaries and limits even come into consciousness. Jupiter doesn't know when to stop, so we can see how this can be a challenging placement for Jupiter. This may result in a sort of workaholic approach to life.

ASTROLOGICAL MAVERICKS

Our first example, who happens to have a stellium (four or more planets in a sign), was a world-renowned German school teacher, astrologer and publisher. Reinhold Ebertin's research and work on midpoints as delineated in the thin, yet brilliant book *The Combination of Stellar Influences* is a must have for every astrologer.

From BrainyQuote.com comes the very work-oriented statement from American actor, Dustin Hoffman:

"I envy people who can just look at a sunset. I wonder how you can shoot it. There is nothing more grotesque to me than a vacation."

Film star legend, Paul Newman, who also has his Mercury and Venus here, makes this realistic quote, taken from AZQuotes.com:

"Dreams without movement are delusions, escapes, kid's play. You have to put your feet into your dreams if they're ever going to be reality. The dreamers we know and love today are the ones who worked the hardest."

Steve Gaines, guitarist, songwriter and singer for Lynyrd Skynyrd saw the Beatles when he was 15, and then talked his dad into getting a guitar. Steve knew from a young age what he wanted and he went after it, and succeeded in a big way. Unfortunately, the personal enjoyment of his success was short-lived as he was killed in a plane crash at 28 years old. As we have seen numerous times, angular Capricorn planets often signify early careers.

Jupiter in Aquarius on the AS

Jupiter in Aquarius is a BIG mind. Almost anything is possible with this combination. As Aquarius is an air sign and Jupiter is the planet of possibility and expansion, these individuals can pull anything out of the air.

From his obituary in Independent.co.uk, comes an apropos description of this astrological placement as portrayed by ballet dancer, Travis Kemp:

> What he lacked in physical *esprit* he made up for with dogged persistence. If he did not excel as a classical dancer, he was a capable partner: not listed; never in the headlines; but always part of the ensemble.

One would expect a big presence with this astrological placement, but Aquarius can hide in plain sight.

Jupiter in Pisces on the AS

Here we have come to the close of the zodiac and the traditional ruler of Pisces. There is a sense of coming home or at oneness. These individuals hold a truly large space.

Our first example is South African author, William Plomer, who makes our list a second time. The following comes from AZquotes.com:

> "Creativity is the power to connect the seemingly unconnected."

Pisces truly knows it is all connected.

Louise of Savoy exhibits, especially for her time, a most amazing capability that this universal energy can support. The following comes from her entry at Wikipedia.com:

> Louise of Savoy (11 September 1476—22 September 1531) was a French noble and regent, Duchess *suo jure* [her right] of Auvergne and Bourbon, Duchess of Nemours, and the mother of King Francis I. She was politically active and served as the Regent of France in 1515, in 1525–1526 and in 1529.

Pope Benedict XVI, who makes our list a second time, shows another side of the astrological placement, which is appearing to the world as a spiritual leader on a big scale while having a questionable past.

We will now look at the angle placements of Jupiter throughout the zodiac from the point of view of the Imum Coeli (IC)

Jupiter in Aries on the IC

This is a pretty idealistically instinctual placement. How interesting that our three examples are all actors: Nicholas Cage, Anjelica Huston, and Bridget Fonda.

The following comments by actor, Nicholas Cage, come from BrainyQuote.com and illustrate different aspects of this astrological placement:

"One of the things that's interesting to me is I find things like caffeine and stunts actually relax me. When they're putting a bit of gel on my arm and lighting me on fire, or when I'm about to go into a high-speed car chase or rev a motorcycle up pretty fast, I find everything else around me slows down."

"When I was eight, I would look at the cover of the *Ghost Rider* comic book in my little home in Long Beach, California, and I couldn't get my head around how something that scary could also be good. To me it was my first philosophical awakening – 'How is this possible, this duality?' "

Interesting that Cage played the lead in *Ghost Rider*, which is another expression of this astrological placement.

Next, are three quotes from actress, Anjelica Huston, that come from AZQuotes.com:

"The nature of acting is that one is many characters and jumps from one skin to another as a way of life. Sometimes it's hard to know exactly what all of your characters think at the same time. Sometimes one of my characters overrules one of my other characters. I'm trying to get them all to harmonize. It's a hell of a job. It's like driving a coach."

"It would probably be very sensible to be in love with someone who was not in the arts and who wasn't so prone to ups and downs. When I think of people who aren't in the arts, I immediately think of politicians for some reason, and I would never want to be with a politician."

"I am a person whose father had no religion but who went to the nuns for a couple of years. And I think I'm the same: On one hand, I pray; on the other hand, I don't believe. I am constantly between the two."

Since we are on the quote path, let's continue with actress, Bridget Fonda. The following comes from BrainyQuote.com:

"It's very easy to get excited about a job, but it's a big commitment because you do it and then you have to live with it when it's finished. It's forever in your section in the video store. It's you. It's almost like deciding who you have a child with."

Jupiter in Taurus on the IC

This astrological placement can lend a certain persistence, determination or recalcitrance. There is profound physical ability, stamina, determination and persistence, but their way is their own.

Our first example, television personality, Jack Paar. Jack was such a strong figure that he transformed *The Tonight*

Show into the *Jack Paar Show* while he hosted it from 1958-1962. The following comes from Astro.com:

> For five years, Paar ruled the airwaves of late night, that is until 2/10/1960, when NBC censored one of his jokes. The next day he gave an angry three-minute tirade on the air, saying his freedom of speech was being affected and walked off the show. A month later, Paar reconciled with NBC, both giving in a little and he returned to the air to a 79-second ovation. He resumed the show for two years, but was left with the reputation of being a hot-head. He purchased a local Maryland TV station and returned only briefly with a weekly TV show in 1973. On 11/29/1986 Paar hosted his TV special, *Jack Paar Comes Home*, with vintage kinescope clips of some of his favorite guests.

Actor, Brandon Lee, had his life tragically cut short in 1993 when a gun firing a blank killed him while he was making the film *The Crow*. Jupiter in Taurus here can signify a physical robustness as well as elevated rank through family. Brandon learned martial arts from his father, legendary actor Bruce Lee.

Interesting to note that opposite this point at Scorpio on the MC, actor, Jon Erik Hexum had the *same* cause of death as Brandon Lee.

Jupiter in Gemini on the IC

One can understand why Jupiter is in detriment here. Gemini can be the story we tell ourselves and Jupiter will aggrandize and embellish every story. This is also an airy intellectual space, great for a philosopher or intellectual.

One of Hitler's right-hand men was Adolf Eichmann. From Creation.com comes one of many telling aspects of Eichmann's life:

> Israeli prosecutor Gideon Hausner, in his record of the trial, states that Eichmann "was fanatically hostile to religion. Once, under my cross-examination, he admitted that he became so infuriated at seeing his wife reading a Bible that on two occasions he snatched the book from her hands and tore it to pieces. He remained steadfast to the Nazi concept of God, which was represented by the power of Nature and reflected in the biological world. There was no room for morality, Jewish or Christian, in the world he believed in. He was not, indeed, ever sorry for what he had done. He said, 'What is there to atone for if there has been no wrong?'"

The following quote comes from British-Irish comedian, Spike Milligan's obituary in TheGuardian.com:

> Jimmy Grafton, who co-wrote many of the early shows, maintained that Eccles was the nearest thing to Milligan's own id—a very simple, uncomplicated creature who doesn't want to be burdened with any

responsibility and just wants to be happy and enjoy himself. Grafton added: "Spike achieved a reputation for eccentricity and has become, by his own choice, a sort of court jester. You begin to wonder to what extent in some circumstances the eccentricity is involuntary and to what extent it is deliberate. He can always get out of trouble by going a little mad."

Court Jester is a lovely description for this astrological placement.

English actor, Michael York, who makes our list a third time and also has Mars here, played numerous roles in which there was a play on dualities. Gemini has a two-faced manner about its expression. Michael played men who were above reproach and had another side.

Jupiter in Cancer on the IC

This is a very nurturing space for exalted Jupiter in the sign of Cancer at the bottom of the chart.

Italian fashion designer, Donatella Versace, makes our list a second time. The following quote comes from BrainyQuote.com:

> "Some say the economy means that you have to persuade people to invest in clothes – to buy less things but more expensive things. I disagree – invest in jewelry, or a house, maybe, but not in fashion."

Cancer is security seeking, thanks to the opposite sign of Capricorn; they are more likely to invest in tangible goods that will support them for a long time.

American record executive, Neil Bogart, also had Mars conjunct his MC opposite this placement. The following comes from Medium.com:

> *According to And Party Every Day: The Inside Story of Casablanca Records*, penned by co-founder Larry Harris, "Casablanca was not a product of the 1970s, it was the 1970s. And no person or company in that era of narcissism and druggy gluttony was more emblematic of the times than Casablanca Records and its magnetic founder, Neil Bogart."

Jupiter is the planet of excess and when opposing Mars, there are can be graphic hedonistic expressions. Life will likely be an interesting experience until one is able to balance one's desire nature and not go overboard. Maybe something drove Neil to live a life of excess as he would not be alive for long. Neil died when he was 39 years old.

American musician, Steve Earle, who makes our list a second time, shows a side of the big protector in an interview he gave to the Guardian.com:

> Earle does not so much sympathize with the underdog as with the despised. In 2002 he caused a stink when he recorded a beautiful song called "Jon Walker's Blues." The controversy wasn't simply that it was about jailed U.S. Muslim convert and Taliban sympathizer John

Walker Lindh, it was that Earle sang in the first person. That's a brave thing to do, I say. "I guess so. I told Elvis Costello when I'd just got the idea for it and the chorus was 'la ilaha illa Allah' and he said: 'You're out of your mind, don't do that'." Earle received death threats because of the song. Did people assume he was a Taliban sympathizer? "Some did. But a lot of them were people who never even heard the song because I'm a pretty obscure artist when you look at the big picture." Why did he want to write it? "Because I saw a 20-year-old underfed kid Duct-Taped to a board and he was exactly the same age as my oldest son Justin [now a successful musician in his own right], which means that kid has been in prison now 15 years." Did he empathize with him? "I empathized with him as a parent."

From GoodReads.com comes this lovely quote from crime author, Val McDermid:

"Time for the likeliest story since Mary told Joseph it was God's."

Jupiter is the planet that rules Pisces and Cancer is the sign of family:

"That was the trouble with moving houses; no matter how carefully you packed the books, they never ended up on the new shelves in quite the right place."

Then we have this quote about that which pains a Cancerian so much:

> "The hardest thing about being a grown up is realizing there are no magic formulas to release the ones we love from pain. Maybe that's why I enjoy computer games so much; you get to be God."

What better example of this astrological placement than that of Louise Brown? She was the world's first test tube baby in 1978. Interesting to note that many of the firsts in artificial insemination are also mavericks.

Jupiter in Leo on the IC

Jupiter in Leo can make for an exaggerated inner ego when found here at the bottom of the chart, like the character Ignatius from the book *Confederacy of Dunces*. They can also shine a brilliance as shown by our two examples.

Singer-songwriter, John Denver, making our list a second time had this to say, taken from BrainyQuote.com:

> "At times I've got a really big ego. But I'll tell you the best thing about me. I'm some guy's dad; I'm some little gal's dad. When I die, if they say I was Annie's husband and Zachary John and Anna Kate's father, boy, that's enough for me to be remembered by. That's more than enough."

Founder of CranialSacral Therapy, John Upledger, makes our list a third time as he has two planets opposing this point. To start a new school of any type of therapy, one would need a strong, well-developed ego structure. This astrological placement gives one the ability to perceive the delicate pulses of the body as well as hold the space for the return to systemic harmony.

Jupiter in Virgo on the IC

Virgo is the sign of multiplicity and Jupiter expands multiplicity in this intimate place. One can expect individuals who can pull a rabbit out of the hat, and make the hat disappear as well.

Our first example, secret agent, Henri Dericourt, shows a certain chameleon-like persona that articulates this astrological arrangement. Henri was a double or triple agent in World War II.

Singer and songwriter, Patsy Cline, shows the amazing way in which she was able to be a mother AND have a career. The following comes from LittleThings.com:

> Barbara Hall, the maker of a documentary on Cline's life, told PBS News Hour, "This woman who barely had an eighth grade education, came from a single-parent home, worked to make ends meet to help feed the family, and still figured out how to work the music business."

Buddy Knox, who makes our list a second time, known for his 1957 rock hit song, "Party Doll" uses a key word combo of Jupiter and Virgo.

Science fiction author, Gene Roddenberry describes his determination in an article from NYTimes.com:

> "It has become a crusade of mine to demonstrate that TV need not be violent to be exciting," he said. "I wanted to send a message to the television industry that excitement is not made of car chases. We stress humanity, and this is done at considerable cost. We can't have a lot of dramatics that other shows get away with—promiscuity, greed, jealousy. None of those have a place in *Star Trek*."

Another aspect of the divine feminine is presented by the 1950's actress, known as the "Blonde Bombshell," Jayne Mansfield.

Interestingly enough, another Sci-Fi screenwriter makes our list here. Chris Carter created the *X-Files* television show. He stated in the show's tagline, "The Truth is Out There" while he showed us a connection to alien possibilities, sometimes taking us on journeys without a fruitful destination. Both of these screenwriters were able to capture the attention and interest of millions of very loyal viewers. Jupiter is the planet for beliefs and adventures and Chris and Gene definitely created multiverses into which we could all explore.

Actress and television personality, Melissa Rivers, who has Mars opposing this point, makes some very telling statements about the right use of inherited objects in an interview she gave to the DailyBeast.com:

For Joan, Melissa says, her things were "meant to be loved, used, and enjoyed." My mother told me, "Keep what you want, and sell the rest. Do some good with the money. Get something you love in the style you like'—which is a wonderful gift to leave." I don't think you ever really own these things—you're just a caretaker of them while you have them. To put them in storage somewhere would be against everything my mother felt about them."

Was it difficult to bid farewell to her mother's Versailles-like apartment on New York's Upper East Side, a plush paradise of gold, ornate furnishings and mouldings, and splashy antiques?

"It was incredibly difficult and emotional," Melissa says. The apartment had become the family home after Edgar's death. "It was so loved, so enjoyed—there are so many memories there. It was very, very hard and very hard on my son (Cooper, now 15). Selling my mother's Connecticut home was very hard. My mother was one of those people who appreciated things: every object, every door handle. She loved it all so much."

How would her mother have felt about the Saudi Prince Muhammad bin Fahd buying her apartment?

"The check cleared," Melissa intones, deadpan.

The pragmatic Virgo shows its face.

ASTROLOGICAL MAVERICKS

Jupiter in Libra on the IC

These individuals have a big need to relate at home on deeper levels or have a big beautiful home, or grew up in one.

Canadian novelist, Leon Rooke, who makes our list a second time, shows the beautiful wordsmith ability possible with this astrological placement. The following comes from www.49thShelf.com:

> An energetic and prolific storyteller, Leon Rooke's writing is characterized by inventive language, experimental form and an extreme range of characters with distinctive voices. He has written a number of plays for radio and stage and produced numerous collections of short stories. It is his novels, however, that have received the most critical acclaim.

Charles "Tex" Watson, another member of the Charles Manson family, is still in prison serving a life sentence for the murders he committed in 1969. In an article about his 17th parole denial, the LATimes.com writes:

> Los Angeles County District Attorney, Jackie Lacey, condemned Watson after the parole board's decision was reached. "These were some of the most horrific crimes in California history, and we believe he continues to exhibit a lack of remorse and remains a public safety risk," Lacey said in a statement.

Maybe Watson believes he will get out one day?

Swedish monarch, King Carl Gustaf XVI, lives in many magnificently grand and beautiful homes. He also has Moon and Mercury opposite this point in Aries on his MC, revealing a *bon vivant* approach to life for all the world to see, but may not entirely appreciate. The following comes from the DailyMail.uk.com and are illustrative statements about his expression of this astrological arrangement:

> The King, a keen environmental campaigner who celebrates his 72nd birthday this week, has been embroiled in a string of controversies over the years including accusations of secret affairs and wild parties. King Carl Gustaf, who is the second-longest reigning monarch in Swedish history, took to the throne in 1973 and survived the country's landmark constitution the following year, and has an active role in public duties, albeit mainly ceremonial.

Portions of an article about musician, singer, actress and psychic, Danielle Egnew, come from TheOtherSidePodCast.com:

> She describes her work as more of a "translation service" than anything else. She can receive the messages that these angels and extra-dimensional creatures have for us and she shares them with her clients and audiences. While she continues to write and perform music, create art, and do personal readings for those looking for assistance from beyond, her latest project is the

"Ascension Tour" where she is doing live translations of these mystical communications for audiences.

Danielle is acting as an ambassador for others to have more expansive experiences in life.

Jupiter in Scorpio on the IC

This is a very deeply powerful place for Jupiter in the regenerative depths of Scorpio at the bottom of the chart. These individuals can draw whatever and whomever from wherever to do what they want. As we see so often with Scorpionic mavericks, there are some horrific examples. Proper guidance and reflection for all mavericks -actually everyone for that matter- would significantly reduce such expressions.

Musician and American trumpeter, Herb Alpert, has this quote from AZQuotes.com:

> "I'm seduced by the arts in general. Arts is like the power of now."

Charming sociopath, Ted Bundy, makes our list once again. Here are two chilling Bundy statements that illustrate the depth and possible distortion that can be found in this astrological placement. Jupiter is the planet that rules belief systems and Scorpio is a fixed water sign, so these individuals can have some pretty big disturbing issues both in and with family as well as in and with themselves. The following comes from SearchQuotes.com:

"I want to master death."

"The fantasy that accompanies and generates the anticipation that precedes the crime is always more stimulating than the immediate aftermath of the crime itself."

Sir Elton John makes some appropriate statements in the following three quotes that come from AZQuotes.com:

"I think people should be free to engage in any sexual practices they choose; they should draw the line at goats, though."

"It's the circle of life, and it moves us all, through despair and hope, through faith and love, 'till we find our place, on the path unwinding."

And, finally, a key quote about what Sir Elton learned about his Scorpio's controlling nature:

"I used to take hostages in my relationships and not let people be independent. It always ended in disaster, because you take away people's identity and they end up full of resentment."

Musician, Richard Carpenter, who appears for a third time and has a stellium here, clearly expresses the Scorpionic fixed intensity in many ways in his life.

OJ Simpson, went from being a well-known football and media personality to someone who fell into the shadows of murder, deceit, and the art of the con—Scorpio's seedier side.

Scottish musician, Ian Anderson, who has his Moon opposite this point in Taurus on the MC, interestingly enough was the "Victim of a death hoax." Ian expressed some of his deeper experiences in an interview he gave to Innerviews.com:

"You were gravely ill in 1996 with an acute blood clot. How did that experience affect your perspective on spirituality?"

He answered, "Ultimately, not very much. I think most of us when threatened by something find reserves within ourselves we didn't know we had. So, we become more resilient and robust. I wouldn't want that to be confused with bravery because I don't think I have that particular strength or capacity. There is a kind of resignation that says 'What's going to happen is going to happen.' You have to buckle down to doing what you can to overcome any setback in your life, but at the same time, you have to come to terms with the reality that this might be it. I don't want to exaggerate about this. In my case, it was a short-lived period of time—a few days of real concern. The miracle of modern drugs eventually sorted out the problem in a few days. It took a couple of weeks for me to get the go-ahead to safely travel. I don't have that problem anymore. But it's something that does affect you. It makes you feel vulnerable. It makes you face up to your own very finite mortality.

"When these things happen to whatever degree of severity, I think in a sense it prepares us for a longer-term scenario when something like that happens and it really is the end. I don't dwell on it, but I think it's an experience towards somewhere along the line many years—although it could be tomorrow—when something more threatening comes to roost. I hope it will be easier to deal with as a result of having a little scary moment a few years ago. I think this is a universal thing we all get adjusted to as we get older. We have to start going to more funerals. It's just the way things work, isn't it? You start having more relatives and friends who are passing away. You become more acquainted with the idea of death and how to deal with it and the people you've been close to. It's part of preparing for your own demise. It's in considering these things that I guess we get more prepared for getting older."

Sonia Gandhi, who was married to Indira Gandhi's grandson, rose to power after her husband's assassination. There is a family history of assassinations—Jupiter in Scorpio conjunct the IC. According to Wikipedia.com, political leaders pushed her to run for political office. Sonia eventually relented and became president of the Indian National Congress.

Jupiter in Sagittarius on the IC

This is a most beautiful place for Jupiter as it rules Sagittarius. The King/Queen is home and upon the throne and not only is nothing impossible, but everything is possible! Even here, at the bottom of the chart the opportunities to be seen for one's greatness are amplified. These mavericks blast a frequency of truth that resonates deeply within the collective.

George Bowering, who also has his Mercury here, is a most "prolific author" as stated by Wikipedia, with over 100 books under his name. Remember, Jupiter expands. This is a lovely place for a storyteller since these individuals can travel from fantastical realms to idealized reality all within the limitless possibilities of their imagination and perception.

Another aspect is stated in American musician, Roy Orbison's obituary from Legacy.com:

> Elvis Presley called him the best singer in the world and Orbison won tributes from other rock stars including Paul McCartney and Bruce Springsteen.

When the "King" calls you the best… *that* is amazing. Roy was also blind, which probably aided in the ways in which he went off on inner musical adventures.

Award winning actress, Kathy Bates, who has Moon in Pisces on her DS, makes clear statements about what she is willing to do, even as an actress, when it comes to her beliefs. The following comes from theWrap.com:

"No. No. No. Nor did I know that I would become a Satanist," Bates told Entertainment Weekly in an interview published Friday, when asked if she had known her robot storyline for Season 8 [of *American Horror Story*] when she agreed to come back. "I have to tell you, when I got that script and they had me praying to Satan, I called them down to my trailer and I said, 'Dudes, I am not praying to Satan. Cody can pray to Satan because he is Satan.'"

Actress and singer, Olivia Newton-John, who has the Sun in Libra on her AS, makes the following telling quotes taken from AZ Quotes.com:

"Family, nature and health all go together. I live every day to its fullest extent and I don't sweat the small stuff. I believe love is what makes the world go round. No matter how old or young, love is why we are here. It is the very essence of one's being. For me I have learned to enjoy everything, especially performing live, so much more. I used to get horrible stage fright when I was younger and today and just love to sing for anyone who still turns up at my shows!"

Jupiter in Capricorn on the IC

While Jupiter is in its fall in Saturn ruled Capricorn, we clearly see these individuals made themselves a name, or, in that Jupiterian manner, continued their familial dynasty.

Saddam Hussein has Venus in Aries on his DS squaring this astrological placement. We can see how he attempted to create a dictatorial dynasty. The following comes from Biography.com and is a succinct synopsis:

Saddam Hussein was a secularist who rose through the Baath political party to assume a dictatorial presidency. Under his rule, segments of the populace enjoyed the benefits of oil wealth, while those in opposition faced torture and execution. After military conflicts with U.S.-led armed forces, Hussein was captured in 2003. He was later executed.

Since the two benefics of Hussein's chart were at odds with one another, and also in their unfavorable signs, one can understand how he could over reach his social station. Aggrandizement without the correct foundation results in collapse. Without reality checks and a good structure—two Capricorn needs—the idealistic Jupiter will be corrected.

Gates McFadden played the very morally structured surgeon on *Star Trek: Next Generation.*

From BornRich.com, comes the following statement about Microsoft heiress, Jennifer Gates:

Jennifer Katharine Gates' net worth is estimated to be around the region of $20 million. She has earned her net worth as an heiress of one of world's richest men, Bill Gates. Daughter of Microsoft Corporation CEO, Bill Gates and his wife Melinda Gates, Jennifer Gates was born in 1996. Despite Jennifer Katharine Gates net worth, her father spent a hefty $1 million to rent a mansion close to the site of the Winter Equestrian Festival in Palm Beach, Florida, so that his daughter can go for her love of horse riding by competing with the 2,800 riders from 30 countries.

Jupiter in Capricorn seeks the best that money can buy.

Jupiter in Aquarius on the IC

The combination of Jupiter and Aquarius makes for a most expanded and information packed mind especially when found in this reclusive part of the chart.

The following comes from the NYTimes.com obituary on French philosopher, Michel Foucault, who had his Mercury in Scorpio on the Ascendant as well:

> [Foucault]... one of France's most prominent philosophers and historians, whose writings explored society's reaction to deviants." This may have been because he was working through his own issues of alienation from society... Mr. Foucault was educated in psychology and philosophy. In 1961, his first widely discussed book, *Madness and Civilization*, was published. In it, he argued that insanity was less a medical problem than a way in which societies categorized acceptable and unacceptable forms of behavior. Insane asylums, he said, were institutions of exclusion.

The bountiful Jupiter nature is well presented in the life of another French author, Georges Simenon. He wrote almost 500 novels and countless short stories and essays as well as enjoyed an expansive intimate life—at one time living with his wife and two lovers while continually seeking out prostitutes *and* picking up women in bars! Jupiter can be quite amorous and Aquarius tends to like variety rather than singularity.

We get the sense of a true maverick from a CNN.com article on musical pioneer, Chuck Berry's passing:

> But it was perhaps John Lennon – who died in 1980 – who put it most succinctly, "If you tried to give rock and roll another name, you might call it 'Chuck Berry.'"

As an African-American man, Berry experienced periods of being the outcast even when he was doing well. Black rights weren't very humane during his lifetime.

Jupiter in Pisces on the IC

This is a most amazing place for imagination and movement as well as voice, inner connection and sensitivity.

Here are a few archetypally relevant statements from legendary French singer, Edith Piaf:

> "Don't care what people say. Don't give a damn about their laws."

"Singing is a way of escaping. It's another world. I'm no longer on earth."

"I think you have to pay for love with bitter tears."

"If God has allowed me to earn so much money, it is because He knows I give it all away."

"I don't want to die an old lady."

"I'd like to see one person – just one – who would own up to having been a coward."

"To sing is to bring to life; impossible if the words are mediocre, however good the music."

"I want to make people cry even when they don't understand my words."

"Money? How did I lose it? I never did lose it. I just never knew where it went."

Tracy Anne Stockwell, née Tracy Anne Caulkins, is a prime example of Jupiter in its sign of Pisces. She is a three-time Olympic gold medalist and a former competitive swimmer. She is a five-time world champion, and former world record-holder in three events, and sixty-three American records, which, according to Wikipedia.com, is more than any other American swimmer, male or female.

We will now look at the angle placements of Jupiter throughout the zodiac from the point of view of the Descendant (DS)

Jupiter in Aries on the DS

This astrological placement is one that lends an amazing "force of nature."

The Sound of Music was based on the true-life story of the von Trapp family. This quote from family member, Maria von Trapp exhibits her ram-like understanding:

> "When you are a child of the mountains yourself, you really belong to them. You need them. They become the faithful guardians of your life. If you cannot dwell on their lofty heights all your life, if you are in trouble, you want at least to look at them."

From the LamborghiniClubAmerica.com comes a fitting tribute to maverick and Italian luxury sports car entrepreneur, Ferruccio Lamborghini:

> He was one of a kind. A man who challenged current thinking. A man who questioned the status quo. From the first 350GT built, the story of Lamborghini has been the story of one man's uncompromising approach to his work and his life. Ferruccio Lamborghini was born April 28, 1916 on a farm in the rural town of Renazzo di Cento near Modena. At a young age, he

already had a burning interest in all mechanical objects which continued into his education where he pursued and graduated with an engineering degree from the technical university in Bologna. During the Second World War he was stationed on the Greek island of Rhodes as a ground crew member of the air force.

From PopSugar.com comes a perfect title for someone with this astrological placement, in this case Prince Edward:

> "30 Memorable Prince Edward Moments That Prove the Youngest Royals Live the Best Lives"

I mean, doesn't that sound like royal Jupiter in instinctual Aries?

English stage and film actress, Natasha Richardson, who also had her Venus here, had a definite effect on people, as shown in the following article from PageSix.com:

> Dennis Quaid gets emotional just thinking about Natasha Richardson. "Now you hit my heart. She was such a beautiful person, such a beautiful, beautiful person. Just none of that, that actor stuff, prima donna stuff," the actor, 64, told *Us Weekly*, "Someone easy to work with and such a great sense of humor."

Tatum O'Neal, who makes our list a second time, is the youngest actress to have won a competitive Academy Award at the age of 10, acting opposite her father in *The Paper Moon*.

Remember the line from the movie *The Poltergeist*? "They're here...." Child actress, Heather O'Rourke, unfortunately passed away just past the age of 12, so we don't know who she was to become.

Jupiter in Taurus on the DS

There can be an aggrandizement of form or an attachment to certain types, looks, fashions as well as the desire sacred relationship.

Our first example shows the obsession of beauty and form as well as the overwhelming loving relationships this placement can indicate. American fashion photographer, Herb Ritts, who makes our list a fourth time, glorified the body for all the world to enjoy, hello Jupiter in Taurus in the 7th house! The following comes from AnotherMag.com:

> So unique was his approach that Ritts' images were unfailingly steeped in authenticity; he loved to shoot in LA's somewhat magical light, which quickly became central to his practice. As Naomi Campbell attests: "You just fall in love with that light... It's Herb's light." It wasn't only the light that had people enamored, however. Ritts often forged lasting relationships with his subjects; as his friend and muse Cindy Crawford attests, "Herb saw the best in everyone, so that's how he photographed you."

Nick Campion is an historian of astrology and cultural astronomy. Nick guides people to a celestial relationship.

Here is an interesting esoteric tidbit on astrologer, Barbara Birdfeather, who makes our list a second time. In esoteric astrology, the unseen planet Vulcan rules Taurus. From her obituary from CryptoMundo.com, comes Birdfeather's often quoted thoughts on the mysterious Vulcan, in the form of her 1969-published poem, "The Planets":

> *And Vulcan reportedly seen*
> *by reputable astronomers*
> *yet probably invisible*
> *having passed through evolution*
> *to spiritualization*
> *ready to return to the Sun's bosom*
> *as someday we all shall*
> *intra-Mercurial planet*
> *with rarefied vibrations*
> *very highly eccentric*
> *seen only by open eyes*

Jupiter in Gemini on the DS

We know Jupiter is in its detriment here for reasons we can easily understand. This astrological placement gives an expanded emphasis on communication and relating. When placed here on the descendant, one can be overwhelmed by the loquacious native.

Actor, Dack Rambo, who makes our list a second time, found freedom in sharing his truth. The following comes from Variety.com:

> In 1991, Rambo quit his role as Congressman Grant Harrison in NBC's Another World after saying he was infected with the AIDS virus. He said going public with his condition was "like freedom to me."

This is a gregarious freedom seeking position.

Expression is key here in a big way, so it is no surprise that Tom Conti shows multiple levels of expression as an actor, theatre director and author. One might expect with Gemini on the point of relationship with the other, that there would be many dalliances and/or marriages, but Tom has been married to his wife since 1967! Gemini is like a bee or hummingbird going around gathering nectar from as many flowers as possible.

The following comes from AstrologyKing.com and is a perfect Jupiter/Gemini on the descendant statement:

> Michael Erlewine is a leading astrologer but this is just one of his many achievements. I have struggled for words to describe him, the best I can come up with is 'over achiever'. His wiki page lists musician, astrologer and entrepreneur as his occupations. Founder of Matrix Software, The Heart Center Astrological Library, ACT: Astrological Conferences on Techniques, and the All Music Guide. The list goes on. Michael has brought together some of the leading astrologers around to

share their knowledge at the forum he moderates, ACT Astrology. For a greater insight into the man and his very spiritual philosophy, check out his writings at AstroTalk "Astrology, Music, Poetry, Dharma, Shamanism, Photography, Initiation, Mind Practice."

There is a strong focus on information with this axis; Gemini functioning as a dictionary and Sagittarius as an encyclopedia.

Photographer, Cindy Sherman, made a quick study of people in her portraiture. The following comes from Wikipedia.com:

> Cynthia Morris Sherman is an American photographer and film director, best known for her conceptual portraits. She is best known for *Complete Untitled Film Stills*, a series of 69 black-and-white photographs which were meant to subvert the stereotypes of women in media. In the 1980's, Sherman used color film and large prints, and focused more on lighting and facial expression.

Gemini's multifaceted perspective is well illustrated with Cindy's work.

Jupiter in Cancer on the DS

Cancer understands its connection with the clan and drives to improve its lot in life. As a benefic planet, Jupiter gives great gifts. When in a water sign it can be intuitional gifts. These individuals usually have a good sense of others and can be quite generous, but usually with only those they appreciate.

Media mogul, Rupert Murdoch, makes our list a third time. Media, especially the news, is a fear-based model. Murdoch's media outlets blast their extremely polarizing views of a fearful world. Cancer is a security seeking sign and the media does its best when we think our security is at risk.

Pianist and entertainer, Liberace, makes our list a third time. Cancer often points to issues of mothering and family. Liberace had a very interesting relationship with his mother and was very generous with her.

Scottish actor, Sean Connery's role as James Bond shows another level of heightened security. As a secret intelligence agent with MI6, Connery's role was to help save the world as well as the beautiful damsels in distress—with whom he usually has a tryst. He represented a male archetype in which he is dedicated to keeping others safe, which is what this astrological placement would highlight.

American actor, James Earl Jones, makes our list twice already for his opposing AS planets. Capricorn/Cancer polarities represent the beginning of winter and summer in the northern hemisphere in opposition to one another. James's life is one of amazing struggles and triumphs, as one would assume from these powerful angular significators. The following comment from Jones comes from AZQuotes.com:

"You weren't going to the theatre to change the world, but you had a chance to affect the world, the thinking and the feelings of the world."

The "greatest" baseball player of all times, Willie Mays, said this insightful quote from AZQuotes.com:

> "That's how easy baseball was for me. I'm not trying to brag or anything, but I had the knowledge before I became a professional baseball player to do all these things and know what each guy would hit."

Another sportsman, American football player, Archie Griffin, shows greatness in his field. The following comes from Wikipedia.com:

> Archie Mason Griffin is a former American football running back. Griffin played seven seasons in the NFL with the Cincinnati Bengals. He is college football's only two-time Heisman Trophy winner. Griffin won four Big Ten Conference titles with the Ohio State Buckeyes and was the first player ever to start in four Rose Bowls.

Yogini, Shiva Rea, helped to bring eastern ideas to the west in a most nurturing and Cancerian way. Her life radiates forth from an inner knowing. The following comes from YogaInternational.com:

> Shiva Rea, M.A. is a yogini firekeeper, sacred activist, global adventurer and leading innovator in the evolution of prana flow yoga, transformational vinyasa flow integrating the tantric bhakti roots of yoga, Krishnamacharya's teachings and a universal, quantum approach to the body. Shiva is known for

bringing the roots of yoga alive for modern practitioners in creative, dynamic and life-transforming ways and for offering the synthesis form of prana flow out in the world. Shiva is the creator of Prana Flow Yoga, Yogadventure Retreats, Yoga Trance Dance for Life, Moving Activism for 1,008,000 Trees, the worldwide Global Mala Project, Yogini Conferences and E2: The Evolutionary Edge Tour. She writes for *Yoga Journal, Yoga Plus Joyful Living,* is the author of award-winning CD's and DVD's, and contributor to many publications and features.

Shiva is magnetically bringing people back into relationship with themselves in a big way.

Jupiter in Leo on the DS

This is a regal placement for Leo as Jupiter and Leo are both royal, but this is also a person who can pull almost any character out of the trunk, put it on and relate to anyone. Excellent support for an actor of any kind.

I recommend reading about actor, Larry Hagman, as he lived a very interesting life. Whether acting in *I Dream of Jeannie* or making a truly archetypal mark on the world for his role in the original television series called *Dallas*, he made a mark on the world. The following comes from Hagman's obituary in TexasMonthly.com:

A part of Texas died on Friday. Larry Hagman was both a native (born in Weatherford) and, as Dallas anti-hero J.R. Ewing, an international symbol of the state.

Hagman also took LSD back in the day, which helped to keep him humble and radiate from his loving Leonine heart.

Author, playwright and screenwriter, Fay Weldon, who makes our list a second time for her Moon opposite this position, has this quote from AZQuotes.com:

"Writing is an act of generosity toward other people."

Actor, Willem Dafoe, who also has his Mars here, shared this in an interview with the Guardian.com:

"I've never had any close male friends. The most important relationships in my life have always been with women. My five sisters raised me because my father was a surgeon, my mother was a nurse and they worked together, so I didn't see either of them much. It was a sexual education, because my sisters were the horniest little girls. They would tell me stuff that, when I was small, I didn't want to hear. I remember one of my sisters talking about fellatio and cunnilingus when I was six years old. I said: "Only dirty people do that, right?" She just laughed. When I told my friends what I knew about the birds and bees, they beat me up because they found it so disgusting."

The intensity of the male desire nature represented by Mars here on the DS with Jupiter, makes his relationship with men challenging, literally. One can watch him in *Body of Evidence* with Madonna, or any of his roles to see this energy easily expressed with women. Willem has over 100 movies under his belt and isn't afraid to play any part. Remember Leo is a creative sign and to have Jupiter here means we can express and create a legion of roles for other to enjoy.

Jupiter in Virgo on the DS

Jupiter is in its detriment here because the ego must surrender its perfectionistic idealism to reveal more resources and rewards. As Virgo is a sign of one's physical health, we often find overwhelming health issues when Jupiter is added to the mix. Virgo allows us to become resourceful regardless of our situation.

Illustrating this astrological placement perfectly, is astrologer, Samuel Reynolds. The following comes from Astro.com:

> American astrologer, teacher, and minister, he turned to the spiritual dimension early in life. Born with spina bifida, he endured 25 surgeries before age 21. At age 12, he became a minister of his church and preached his first sermon in 1980. Although he had been labeled developmentally delayed, he made great strides in school, achieving honor roll grades and eventually found himself in graduate school, all the while

intensifying his spiritual quest. In 1990 he became hooked on astrology, after his initial skepticism drew him to study it. A writer, consultant, teacher, he is a powerful speaker and made a splash at his first lecture at a major organization conference, sponsored by ISAR in Oak Brook, Illinois, in August 2009.

Jupiter in Libra on the DS

This is a really beautiful astrological position for Jupiter. Here we find grand ideals about relationship with the other. These mavericks are very individualistic about their approach to life, remember they have Aries rising.

Our first example is the incomparable Divine Miss M: Bette Midler. Her following comments come from BrainyQuotes.com:

"If I could be granted a wish, I'd shine in your eye like a jewel."

"I always try to balance the light with the heavy – a few tears of human spirit in with the sequins and the fringes."

And to illustrate the challenge the relatable Libran has in receiving:

"I had a hard-scrabble childhood with my parents. I have a lot of baggage. To come down to the footlights and accept the audience's affection inside a Broadway theater—that didn't come easily to me."

Rosemary Hemphill represents that part of Jupiter in Libra that understands there is a perfect balance. She and her husband wrote books on herbs as well as had Sommerset Cottage, an herb-growing business.

Jupiter in Scorpio on the DS

The expansive Jupiterian energy of this placement reveals the dynamics of power, sex, and disclosure.

Charles Manson, who also has his Rasputin Mercury here, was able to manipulate people as he wished, including sexual relationships with both men and women.

Musician and song-writer, Steve Marriott's life is an example of ever mutating phoenix-like experiences. Scorpio on its highest level is the Phoenix. It has the ability to burn everything down, shake off its wings, rise from the ashes, and fly high. The transformational death and rebirth cycle so common with Scorpio can happen in a myriad of ways. An article from the internet likens his life to a Greek tragedy. In an unfortunate aspect of this placement, Steve did rise from the flames as he lost his life to a fire in his home.

American television news presenter, Jessica Savitch, who makes our list a third time for the two Aquarian planets squaring this position. The following Scorpionic statement comes from her NYTimes.com obituary:

In 1972, she became a reporter and anchor for KYW-TV in Philadelphia. Miss Savitch worked on several award-winning documentaries and special reports there, including a five-part series, "Rape... the Ultimate Violation," in which she spent two weeks working as a decoy with a police undercover unit. The series won her a Clarion Award from Women in Communications Inc.

Scorpio brings light to those subjects which are usually shrouded in shadows. Interestingly enough, Jessica lost her life in a freak accident. She was on her way home from a date with her boyfriend when her car went off the road into a canal. From CurbsideClassic.com comes this revelation of her Scorpionic side:

> But all was not right in Jessica's world. The only man she every really loved beat her terribly. Drug use led to promiscuity and sometimes threatened her standing at the station. The networks wanted her, but Westinghouse had ironclad contracts—so she acted out and became a general terror to all. The reputation followed her to NBC. She was made Senate correspondent but she was in over her head. Resentment from coworkers hurt, and led to her eventually being pulled off the Senate beat. Jessica's time at NBC was filled with uncertainty, and with the uncertainty came drug use. But the public loved her, as it did in Philadelphia.

From the SantaFeNewMexican.com comes this repeated theme, illustrated in the following article on country music singer, Randy Travis:

> Former Santa Fe resident Randy Travis is accused of driving while intoxicated and threatening to kill state troopers after the country singer crashed his car and was found naked and combative at the scene.

Italian bicyclist extraordinaire, Marco Pantani, makes our list a third time. Marco's life fully illustrated his ambitious Capricorn on the MC nature, and the "tragedies" associated with such a grand focus on his chart's relationship angle in Scorpio. Most people do not understand that the Scorpio drive is one to experience, not just the pretty side of life, but all of life. This is the sign after Libra where "real" starts to happen. The commitment to the relationship occurs in Scorpio, where we learn that love is not always the pretty image Libra said it would be.

Actress, Dakota Fanning, who makes our list a second time, expresses the more secretive nature of Scorpio in a quote from BrainyQuotes.com:

> "I was raised by very traditional Southern parents with Southern manners. You don't air your dirty laundry to people that aren't your family or your friends. Why would I ever want to portray myself as anything other than together?"

Jupiter in Sagittarius on the DS

This is a favored spot for Jupiter when visiting its ruling sign. While Sagittarius in general needs a lot of freedom to explore, this placement can make one feel that nothing should limit their opportunities, expressions or adventures.

Canadian film maker, Bruce LaBruce, making our list a second time for having his Mars here as well, has this quote from AZQuotes.com:

> "One thing I try to do with my work is to show that people who have extreme fetishes or who exist outside the constraints of "normal" society still have romantic impulses and are capable of love and tenderness. Sometimes people cannot or don't want to acknowledge that pornographers are people too!"

Opera diva, Kathleen Battle, making our list a second time, had this written about her in an interview she gave with DallasNews.com:

> It's hard to talk about Kathleen Battle's career without broaching the subject of her reputation for putting the "d" – as in "difficult" – into the word "diva."
>
> In 1994, the Metropolitan Opera fired the superstar soprano during rehearsals for Donizetti's *Fille du Régiment* for what the New York company deemed "unprofessional actions." A year earlier, beleaguered staffers at the San Francisco Opera wore T-shirts proclaiming "I survived the Battle."

But wait – is this same Kathleen Battle on the phone today? This pleasant, even-tempered woman who's doling out compliments to her colleagues and talking enthusiastically about her show Thursday night at the Winspear Opera House?

Turns out, it's one and the same: Fifteen minutes into an otherwise smooth interview, Battle takes a deep breath, stops talking and puts down the phone, never to return. No goodbye. No explanation. Nada.

Remember, this is a very royal position and if a person with this astrological placement doesn't feel as if s/he is getting the attention, respect, and accolades she believes she is due... her audience will be dismissed (microphone drop)...

Sagittarius is a centaur and they are known for their playful and boisterous natures as well as for their lack of attachment. Artist and photographer, Jack Pierson, said this illustrative statement in Interview.com:

"I want my gay life to not wind up on the streets-on Second Avenue. But at the same time, I don't care if it does. That's why I like to make books. To me, it's just as great to have some book of mine be in a flea market as it is to have a picture in a museum. I really stand by that because that's how I got information as a child."

Activist, performer, artist, singer, Ricky Martin, makes this planet really work for him. In addition to his many creative expressive outlets, we learn the following about Ricky from Biography.com:

An activist for many causes, he founded the Ricky Martin Foundation in 2000 as a child advocacy organization. The group runs the People for Children project, which fights child exploitation. In 2006, Martin spoke in support of a United Nations effort to improve the rights of children worldwide in front of the U.S. House International Relations Committee.

Jupiter in Capricorn on the DS

These mavericks understand the benefits of a strategic relationship, but have to be careful about the way in which they go about building their empire. Too much optimism and not enough work will make this position fail.

Media mogul, Merv Griffin, who makes our list a third time and has his Moon here, shows the gregarious social status and sexual nature possible with this astrological placement and its restrictions. The following comes from Queerty.com:

> He lost his virginity, to a female, that is, when Judy Garland seduced him. His first crush was Errol Flynn, whom he saw passed out naked on a couch. Montgomery Clift was his roommate for a year and a half. He lived with Roddy McDowall here at the Dakota, where he introduced Eddie Fisher to Elizabeth Taylor. He maintained a virtual male harem and a pimp who supplied porn stars, but I don't go into his pay-for-gay guys. I keep it to his A-list dates like Rock Hudson, whom he met through Henry Wilson, Rock's agent,

and who advised him to keep his sexuality quiet. And there was a young James Dean selling his sex for cash. Plus, Judy Garland's *Meet Me in St. Louis* boy next door, Tom Drake, who, by the way, ended up a used car salesman. There was Peter Lawford, Robert Walker, Gordon Scott the then-Tarzan. And lots about Merv's prolonged sexual tryst with Marlon Brando. There are his experiences at Liberace's all-male orgies. His first encounter, a boyhood friend he grew up with, later tried writing a book about Merv. This being an era when male actors felt homosexuality was a danger to their career, lawyers shot down that book fast.

Comedian, Jonathan Winters, makes our list a second time and shows the commitment this astrological placement can give. He was with his wife for 61 years. From his obituary in *The New York Times*, comes this lovely description of the all expansive Jupiter expressing itself through structured business-like Capricorn:

> Mr. Winters was at his best when winging it, confounding television hosts and luckless straight men with his rapid-fire delivery of bizarre observations uttered by characters like Elwood P. Suggins, a Midwestern Everyman, or one-off creations like the woodland sprite who bounded onto Jack Paar's late-night show and simperingly proclaimed: "I'm the voice of spring. I bring you little goodies from the forest."

In the *Harry Potter* series Irish actor, Kenneth Branagh, portrays Gilderoy Lockhart, a character who is often taking credit for other people's great deeds while not taking any responsibility for his own. This is an aspect of why Jupiter is in fall in Capricorn.

Doyle Slack has built pragmatic knowledge that serves him in helping others gain greater perspective in their lives.

Jupiter in Aquarius on the DS

Jupiter in this astrological placement can be magical in the way it expresses the width and breadth of human experience while remaining somewhat separate and aloof. Aquarius gives us the ability to build our observational nature. Here it is like the observational nature has been filled with all aspects of life and then asked to express it to the other.

Poet.org shares this eloquent description from Welsh poet, Dylan Thomas:

> Thomas describes his technique in a letter: "I make one image—though 'make' is not the right word; I let, perhaps, an image be 'made' emotionally in me and then apply to it what intellectual and critical forces I possess—let it breed another, let that image contradict the first, make, of the third image bred out of the other two together, a fourth contradictory image, and let them all, within my imposed formal limits, conflict."

English comedian, Kenneth Williams, who also has his Venus here, gives us an inkling of how much humor comes from our relationships to and with others. Aquarius is the sign of the outcast, the misfit and if we read a little about the relationship Kenneth had with his father, we can see the challenges inherent therein. From an article from DailyMail.co.uk on his father's death, some very interesting family tidbits are revealed:

> Williams' difficult relationship with his father was the cause of much friction throughout his childhood as his half-sister, Pat, recalled. "Charlie Williams was a real Victorian bully. He had a cane on the side of the mantelpiece and as he came in for his meals he'd take it down and hook it on the side of the table. Me and Ken would have to sit there in silence, not moving, and eat everything on our plates." Even as a small child, Williams had developed a contempt for his father that would turn into loathing in later life. "Dad would sometimes say to Ken: 'I wanna know how you're gettin' on at school.' Ken would reply 'I fail to see why you're interested in me. I'm not in the least interested in you,' and then walk out of the room," said Pat. "Another time, Dad bought Ken a pair of boxing gloves. 'What am I supposed to do with these?' 'Put 'em on yer bleedin' fists and fight yer own battles. Don't rely on yer sister.' Ken said 'No, thank you', and dropped them in Father's lap and walked out. The old man went mad."

The Aquarian archetype is one of independence and individuality, which is not easy to blend in relationship. From Wikipedia.com comes this apt expression about award winning actress, Meryl Streep:

> Often described as the "best actress of her generation", Streep is particularly known for her versatility and accent adaptation. Nominated for a record 21 Academy Awards, she has won three. Streep has received 31 Golden Globe nominations, winning eight—more nominations, and wins, than any other actor. She has also won three Primetime Emmy Awards and has been nominated for fifteen British Academy Film Awards, and seventeen Screen Actors Guild Awards, winning two each.

Streep has a wicked sense of humor that isn't given its full expression on the screen. Even though Aquarius is a fixed sign, one can see how Jupiter expands those Saturnian rings to allow the brilliant Uranian energies to come through.

Musician and songwriter, Peter Gabriel, who also has his Sun here, is a quintessential Aquarian and humanitarian. From AZQuotes.com comes this wonderful follow-your-bliss quote from Peter Gabriel:

> "Watch out for music. It should come with a health warning. It can be dangerous. It can make you feel so alive, so connected to the people around you, and connected to what you really are inside. And it can

make you think that the world should, and could, be a much better place. And just occasionally, it can make you very, very happy."

This is a lovely tribute to Jupiter in airy Aquarius on the DS.

From BrainyQuote.com come these amusing and fitting statements from multi-maverick and singer, Robbie Williams:

"Inside me there is a fat man dying to get out."

And the gender bending Aquarian:

"An awful lot of gay pop stars pretend to be straight. I'm going to start a movement of straight pop stars pretending to be gay."

Self-centering Leo lives across the way on the Ascendant for these individuals, so we know they need a lot of attention AND freedom.

Jupiter in Pisces on the DS

Here we return to one of Jupiter's homes in the last sign of the Zodiac. This is the place for deeper thoughts, philosophies, occultism and gurus. These people often have the most compassionate heart and absolute acceptance of other, but can also get lost in a world of their own making.

I love when the opening line in Wikipedia consolidates the archetype succinctly as it does here:

> "Theodor W. Adorno was a German philosopher, sociologist, psychologist and composer known for his critical theory of society."

This astrological configuration aided Joan Quigley in her astrological understanding and she benefited from Mercury here as well. Quigley was former First Lady, Nancy Reagan's astrologer during the White House years. Quigley accessed deep cosmic truths which she then shared with clients.

Astrologer Kenneth Negus' obituary from ASPNJ.org reveals many of the archetypes involved in this astrological placement:

> Ken was a teacher, astrologer, and poet. He was a learned and gentle soul who loved nature and sought to understand the mysteries of life. He had a special genius for language, a prodigious talent for understanding words and symbols. This led to a successful career as a professor of German at Rutgers University, but also to the study of astrology, which he understood as a kind of universal language.

Universal language is definitely in the domain of Jupiter and Pisces. LOVE is the universal language which this planet and sign speak.

We will now look at the angle placements of Jupiter throughout the zodiac from the point of view of the Medium Coeli (MC)

Jupiter in Aries on the MC

The MC is the "where you are headed" part of the chart. With Jupiter in Aries here, there is a huge instinctive drive to be seen. Aries deals with the head and headiness.

Iconic actor, Al Pacino, put himself on the map for portraying Michael Corleone in the *Godfather* series. Pacino is well-known for playing larger than life, headstrong individuals who aren't afraid to bring the war to your doorstep. Think of his lead role in the movie *Scarface* with that mountain of cocaine on his desk, determined to be number one. These are prime examples of this astrological placement.

Anatoly Kashpirovsky, the Russian psychotherapist who makes our list a second time, uses this astrological placement to be seen as the Miracle Worker of Russia, using his Aries head/mind to be seen as larger than life. The combination of his Mars conjunct the DS in Capricorn with the Jupiter on the MC in Aries provides him with endless energy to get his message out, and initiating energy to guide others to greater understanding. This is an astrological placement which supports mind over matter through changing our beliefs.

Edmund White, who also has his Mars here, writes on the themes of male homosexuality which is very Jupiter Mars in Aries on the MC: bring out the instinctual truth!

Wikipedia has the following description of Tracey Emin:

English artist known for her autobiographical and confessional artwork. Emin produces work in a variety of media including drawing, painting, sculpture, film, photography, neon text and sewn appliqué. Once the *enfant terrible* of the Young British Artists in the 1980's, Tracey Emin is now a Royal Academician of the Royal Academy of Arts. She is a rebel who reconciled with the fold.

The edict is: Experience it all and share it with the world. Aries doesn't have a conscience; it just has a drive to go forward.

Actress, Angelina Jolie, makes our list again as she has her Moon and Mars here as well. Think of her role in *Tomb Raider* which captures the complexity and simplicity of this astrological placement.

Jupiter in Taurus on the MC

This gives one a very strong sensual desire nature that gets shared with the world.

No one played with the expansive commodification of the art world like Andy Warhol, who makes our list a third time. Warhol changed people's ideas around art forms to the point of getting the public to ask the vital question: What is art? He took everyday items and transformed them into works of "art" by making them larger than life.

Paddy Ashdown, the British politician/diplomat who makes our list a second time, has this quote from BrainyQuotes.com:

"We have to make their livelihoods viable, get them the proper prices for their produce, try and make them stay rather than sell their property and leave again."

Taurus understands the cycles of crops and husbandry.

Then we have scientific astrologer, Michel Gauquelin, who makes our list a second time with Mercury conjunct his IC opposing this position. Michel's wife described this imperial Jupiter placement thusly:

"He was something of a medieval tyrant, not easy to live with."

Having a hyper-powered Mercury opposing a super-sized Jupiter, well, whose voice could he hear but his own? He wasn't afraid to let it out—especially in his home and in his career. Fixed axis Taurus opposes Scorpio. Someone with planets on the chart's angles can really believe their way is the only way.

Jupiter in Gemini on the MC

As we know, this is not an easy position for Jupiter in talkative airy Gemini, but can be very advantageous for people who want to claim or own the airwaves.

From FirstLadies.org we have this very illustrative statement about former First Lady Betty Ford:

In a 1987 interview, Mrs. Ford mentioned not only her mother and Martha Graham as her strongest role models and influences but also Eleanor Roosevelt; the incumbent First Lady believed that she had the right to express opinions independent of the President and her shaping the First Lady role to match her individualism caught young Betty Ford's attention and she found it to be 'healthy.'

Interesting to note that modern dance pioneer, Martha Graham, has Jupiter in Gemini on her AS, so it would make sense that First Lady Ford would see her as a role model as they both share Jupiter in Gemini on an angle in their respective natal charts.

Professional golfer, Arnold Palmer, who makes our list a second time is a star athlete, has a drink named after him. An *Arnold Palmer* is a blend of two beverages: iced tea and lemonade.

Joan Ganz Cooney, television producer and creator of the *Sesame Street Show* and one of the founders of the Sesame Street Workshop, is dedicated to the idea that while we are all very different, we are all a facet of one gemstone: humanity. Gemini is the ruler of the third house of neighborhoods, siblings and cousins. The following comes from SesameStreet.org:

> Sesame Workshop is the nonprofit educational organization behind *Sesame Street* and so much more. Our mission is to help kids everywhere grow smarter, stronger, and kinder—and we're at work in more than 150 countries, using the power of media and our beloved Muppets to meet children's development needs with

critical early education, social impact programs, and a large dose of fun!

I remember those early episodes of *Sesame Street* and I loved the mix of characters, colors, shapes and sizes.

Kitty Kelley, who also has her Mars here, shows a dogged determination to bring forth the truth as an investigative journalist.

Oprah Winfrey, who makes our list a second time, is a media mogul, is another beautiful example of this astrological placement done in a maverick manner.

John Carter, the famous wind instrumentalist, makes our list a second time. John received worldwide recognition in a time when African-American men had restricted freedoms in the United States.

Jupiter in Cancer on the MC

This is a lovely place for Jupiter who is in exaltation when staying with inviting Cancer. There is a natural generosity these individuals offer, like a large bowl of comfort food, and the masses will come back for more. Jupiter on the Midheaven in Cancer would be a lovely placement for a High Priestess.

Striking model and early female photographer, Lee Miller, has an opposition and a square to this point. This elevated Jupiter at the top of her chart invited her into situations that played out her T-square placement. I recommend reading more about this maverick! When will someone make a movie about her?

Willie's older sister, Bobbie Nelson, makes our list a third time for having two planets opposite this place in Capricorn on her IC. She is best known for playing in the family band.

Atsuko Ikeda, previously known as Princess Yori, is Japanese Emperor Shōwa's fourth daughter. According to Wikipedia.com, she married a commoner:

> As a result, she gave up her imperial title and left the Japanese Imperial Family as required by law. Later, she served as the most sacred priestess (*saishu*) of the Ise Grand Shrine between 1988 and 2017.

Actor, Harrison Ford, who also has his Mercury here, tends to play parts that have a strong family note. His role as Han Solo portrays this sense of kinship protecting the clan. As Han, he is an unlikely hero who believed he was looking out solely for himself, but ended up understanding he cares for the rest of the group as well.

We can understand how and why the Beach Boys were such a success as yet another one makes our list. This supports my astrological theory that "birds of a feather flock together." Al Jardine has this lovely statement from AZQuotes.com:

> "Music is more of a hobby to me than my hobbies, if that makes sense. I love music; my dad and brother were very musical, and music just happens to be one of my hobbies that became my vocation."

Vocation is a good word for the Midheaven and with Jupiter here and family modeling in that Cancerian way, we can understand Al's experience.

In a very Jupiter MC in Cancer thing to do, comedian and actor, Billy Connolly, did a show called *Tracks Across America*. This show focused on people living between major cities in the United States.

Actress, Debra Winger, placed herself on the map with many fans when she starred in *Terms of Endearment* as Shirley MacLaine's character's daughter dying of cancer.

Jupiter in Leo on the MC

These people are larger than life. They need a big stage and will likely attract a large audience of adoring fans. They have an electric charisma and can believe in their "God given right" to be. They can warm a stadium or coerce another into false adoration.

Charming, suave, Julio Iglesias illustrates the abundant benefic kiss such an astrological placement can give. The following comes from Wikipedia.com:

> In 1983, he was celebrated as having recorded songs in the most languages in the world, and in 2013 for being the Latin artist with the most records sold in history. Iglesias is recognized as the most commercially successful Continental European singer in the world and one of the top ten record sellers in music history, having sold more than 250 million records

worldwide in 14 languages. It is estimated that during his career he has offered more than 5,000 concerts, having performed for over 60 million people on five continents. In April 2013, he was awarded in Beijing as the most popular international artist in China. In Brazil, France, Romania, Italy, and others, Iglesias is the most successful foreign record seller, while in his home country, Spain, he has sold the most records in history, with 23 million records. During his career, Iglesias has won many awards in the music industry, including the Grammy, Latin Grammy, World Music Award, Billboard Music Award, American Music Award, and Lo Nuestro Award. He has been awarded the Gold Medal for Merit in the Fine Arts of Spain and the Legion of Honour of France. UNICEF named him Special Ambassador for the Performing Arts in 1989. He has been a star on the Hollywood Walk of Fame since 1985. In April 2013, Iglesias was inducted into the Hall of Fame of Latin Composers.

Serial killer, John Edward Robinson, shows the grandiosity this astrological placement can give. From Bizarrepedia.com comes this chilling range of Leonine expression:

> Just like many other serial killers, in his community, John Edward Robinson was known as a charming family man with successful businesses, four children, and loving wife. Authorities knew Robinson as a cunning con artist, who was convicted several times starting from manipulating checks and deposits to

stealing goods. But no one suspected the affluent neighborhood activist was a sadomasochistic monster who lured vulnerable women to become his personal slaves and then storing their dead bodies in 55-gallon metal barrels.

I would recommend reading up on this guy to learn more about the egregious things he did. He definitely was a big self-centering force out for his own pleasure and control. These are the shadow sides of Jupiter in Leo.

Actress, Nicole Kidman, who also has her Venus here, expresses this lovely combination well in the following quote from BrainyQuote.com:

> "I think that the most difficult thing is allowing yourself to be loved, so receiving the love and feeling like you deserve it is a pretty big struggle. I suppose that's what I've learnt recently, to allow myself to be loved."

Being on the "receiving end" of adoring fans would definitely help this issue. Leo and Jupiter are about getting to the place of Big Love.

The opening paragraph-long description for Australian politician, Christopher Pyne, on his website PyneOnline.com.au vividly illustrates the range of Jupiter and Leo expression possible when on the Midheaven:

> In 1993, at the age of 25, Christopher Pyne was elected to the House of Representatives for the seat of Sturt. Christopher is the Minister for Defense and

Leader of the House of Representatives. In his time in Parliament, Christopher was also Minister for Defense Industry, responsible for delivering the $200 billion build up of Australia's military capability, the largest in our peacetime history. Christopher has also served as Minister for Industry, Innovation and Science, developing and delivering the National Innovation and Science Agenda, a transformative economic plan to encourage Australians to embrace risk and commercialize their ideas. Spending two years as Minister for Education and Training, Christopher, amongst other things, reformed the National Curriculum, introduced compulsory literacy and numeracy testing for Australian teaching graduates and expanded phonics teaching in remote schools in northern Australia. In addition to these Cabinet positions he has also served as Minister for Ageing and Parliamentary Secretary for Health in the Howard Government. As Parliamentary Secretary for Health he founded "Headspace: the Youth Mental Health Initiative" in 2006. Christopher is the author of *A Letter to my Children*, published by Melbourne University Press in 2015. Before entering Parliament, Christopher practiced as a solicitor. Christopher is a member of many community, social, and sporting groups in his electorate, and is an Adelaide Crows Ambassador and supporter of the Norwood Redlegs Football Club! Christopher is married to Carolyn and is the proud father of Eleanor, Barnaby, Felix and Aurelia.

Jupiter in Virgo on the MC

As we know, Jupiter is said to be in its detriment in Virgo. The handling of so many resources can be overwhelming to the ever-perfecting and resourceful Virgo.

King of France, Louis XI, makes our list a second time. A look at one of his portraits and we can immediately see his discriminating, or perfecting, approach to life. King Louis had a HUGE proboscis.

Interestingly enough, American film director, Joseph Leo Mankiewicz, received his two Academy Awards for movies on women: *All about Eve* and *A Letter to Three Wives*.

Novelist and short story writer, Patricia Highsmith, making our list a third time for the planets opposing this astrological placement. A perfect kōan to the challenge inherent in this position is elucidated in her quote from AZQuotes.com:

> "For neither life nor nature cares if justice is ever done or not."

Jupiter in Virgo can be a BIG pain in its desire to make things right or perfect.

Astronaut, John Glenn, embodied a sense of service to his nation being the first American astronaut to orbit the earth and then went on to become a U.S. Senator. Glenn definitely benefited from the ever-improving persistent dedication this astrological placement gave him.

Oz Motor racing legend, Peter Brock, had these "perfectly" illustrative statements about him from Wikipedia.com:

Peter Geoffrey Brock AM (26 February 1945—8 September 2006), otherwise known as "Peter Perfect", "The King of the Mountain", or simply "Brocky" was one of Australia's best-known and most successful motor racing drivers.

Louie Spence, is an English dancer, reality show personality, and judge. The following comes from Mirror.co.uk:

Louie Spence made his name in 2010 for being one of the loud and flamboyant instructors in reality show *Pineapple Dance Studio*. He has since gone onto be a judge on *Dancing on Ice* and counts Emma Bunton as his BFF. In August 2013, Louie entered *the Celebrity Big Brother* house.

Jupiter in Libra on the MC

This is an elevated ambassadorial position for Jupiter and these individuals radiate an electric attraction of beauty, harmony and model appropriateness to the world.

Wikipedia.com aptly states the formality of this astrological position played out by Emperor Akihito, who makes our list a second time:

The Emperor of Japan is the head of the Imperial Family and the head of state of Japan. Under the 1947 constitution, he is defined as "the symbol of the State and of the unity of the people." Historically, he was also the highest authority of the Shinto religion. In Japanese, the Emperor is called *Tennō*, literally "heavenly sovereign". In English, the use of the term Mikado for the Emperor was once common, but is now considered obsolete. Currently, the Emperor of Japan is the only head of state.

Actress and comedienne, Goldie Hawn, who has her Moon on the Descendant angle of the chart in airy Gemini trining her Jupiter in airy Libra, is best known for playing air-head blonds caught in complicated situations.

Beautifully composed actress, Candice Bergen, portrays the balance required to work with men. Well known for her lead character in the show *Murphy Brown*, she used her wit to call out the imbalance of the sexes in the workplace.

Actor, Sylvester Stallone, who also has his Moon here, has played parts to bring balance to the dualities in life especially when he portrays the underdog who succeeds.

The Midheaven is where we connect with the collective on our respective Path in life. No surprise then, that this is aptly stated in the following interview in Stuff.co.nz, comes from twin sisters and New Zealand lesbian activist singers Lynda and Jools Topp:

> Their ability to connect with New Zealanders from all walks of life is another important component of their success. "We manage to haul a very diverse group of people together, because in all honesty, everyone understands the truth, and when you tell the truth, it's pretty hard to fight that."

Jupiter loves the truth.

Jupiter in Scorpio on the MC

There can be a tortured bittersweet tendency here. Scorpio usually has the understanding, eventually, that the painful intensity in their lives is what provides the fertilizer for the beauty to come.

Playwright, Tennessee Williams, had a very challenging life. The following comes from Shmoop.com:

> Yet as was so often the case, nobody could sum up Tennessee Williams's life better than Williams himself. He wrote in his 1975 *Memoirs*, "I've had a wonderful and terrible life and I wouldn't cry for myself, would you?"

Actor and westerns star, Roy Rogers, displayed and focused on another aspect of this astrological placement. Jupiter is a planet of multiplicity and can often indicate children. One thing I read about over and over again with Roy was his devotion to kids. He even likened himself to a babysitter in this interview in CSMonitor.com:

> He decries the violence and sex of current films, which he traces back to the days of the so-called "spaghetti westerns," and other foreign films that didn't have to pass the Hollywood censor. He worries that children

have been affected by the entertainment that is put in front of them.

Scorpio understands complex and deep feelings. They can empathize or feel violence in their bodies from witnessing violence, whether literally or ideologically presented to them. Roy continues:

> "Children at a certain age can be greatly affected by these films," he argues. "Seeing this violence all the time has to have some effect. That guy who shot our President had to learn such ideas somewhere. These are tough times for kids to grow up. Children kind of grow up and miss their childhood. And the school systems don't give them a straight line of *yes* or *no*. There is a lot of emphasis on bands and sports and play. But life just isn't that way. Not everybody winds up as a rock star or sports hero. Most people fall somewhere in between where you have to have enough horse sense and tenacity to make a living."

Prince William, who appears on our list a second time, had the excruciating experience of witnessing the drama of his family's secrets—and his mother's death—proclaimed on worldwide media. There will be neither privacy nor rest from the regenerative forces operating in his life.

Jupiter in Sagittarius on the MC

We now move from the most intense to the most exuberant. Sagittarius, the sign of our ideas and beliefs, made ever more buoyant with its ruling planet Jupiter at the top of the chart, gives one the fuel of idealism.

Being born on Christmas lends one a certain specialness, *n'est-ce pas*? French artist, Louise Bourgeois has this quote from Wikipedia.com that illustrates the strong freedom part of this astrological placement:

> "Everyone should have the right to marry. To make a commitment to love someone forever is a beautiful thing."

Jupiter in Sagittarius can be a magnificent teacher as they model a level of freedom and pursuit of personal Truth that many of us need to witness.

The indefatigable English comedian, Benny Hill, who of course has his Mars here as well, was a larger than life *bon vivant* and comedian. Benny was able to express humor without a word. So deft were his comedic understandings of our inner selves, he would simply look at the camera and give a Vaudevillian look that expressed it all. Then there were the parts of his comedy that he accelerated to make walking people look as if they were running to portray a longer story line in a condensed period.

One of the few places where Jupiter can create a less than ideal picture is when it is square to the Sun. This is, of course, further exacerbated when these planets are conjunct the chart's angles as with American politician, John McCain, who has the Sun in Virgo conjunct his DS. McCain was a decorated Vietnam War hero and a Prisoner of War. The amazing idealism of this astrological placement coupled with the dogged determinism and vitality of his Virgo Sun definitely added in his ability to meet the challenges in his life, and to successfully answer them. While he was unable to attain the presidency, he had a successful 30-year long career as a U.S. Senator.

Entertainer, Weird Al Yankovic is a great example of the playful Sagittarian at work. The following comes from Wikipedia.com:

> Yankovic's success comes in part from his effective use of music video to further parody popular culture, the song's original artist, and the original music videos themselves, scene-for-scene in some cases.

Sagittarius gives the rest of the zodiac the gift to laugh at ourselves and not take ourselves too seriously. Weird Al definitely does that!

Actor, Antonio Banderas, has Venus squaring this point in Virgo, but it doesn't keep him from expressing his wanderlust ways. The following quotes from AZQuotes.com frames the mutable Sagittarian nature:

> "I like going everywhere. And I love starting new things."

"I couldn't be with someone who is depressed all the time."

When the two benefics are squaring one another in mutable signs, there can be a fear of stagnation and depression.

Jupiter in Capricorn on the MC

We are at another one of those challenging places for idealistic Jupiter and structured, sometimes restrictive, Capricorn.

Politician, Robert Kennedy was a poster boy for building upon family power, as seen in the world. Of course, he has made our list several times already and twice for Capricorn/Midheaven planets. Robert was the consummate businessman.

Romance novelist, Barbara Cartland, modeled another way this astrological placement can play out: While being a successful and prolific novelist, she put on airs of being more successful than she was.

An accurate description of how Romana Acosta Bañuelos, the thirty-fourth Treasurer of the United States and first Latina Treasurer, used this astrological placement, comes from her obituary from LATimes.com:

> It was that self-sufficient, entrepreneurial mentality Acosta Bañuelos learned as a young girl in rural Mexico that led President Nixon to appoint her as U.S. Treasurer in 1971, the first Latina to hold that position and the highest ranking Mexican American appointee in the Nixon administration. In a career that

stretched from a small Arizona town to the heights of the business world as head of a multimillion-dollar Mexican food company and a founder of the first bank for Mexican Americans in California, Acosta Bañuelos helped open doors that Latinos in America often found closed to them.

Another true maverick, Lew Wasserman, was able to use this placement in another astrologically appropriate archetypal expression. The following comes from his obituary in the NYTimes.com:

> Lew R. Wasserman, the former chairman and chief executive of the Music Corporation of America, who was arguably the most powerful and influential Hollywood titan in the four decades after World War II, died yesterday in Beverly Hills. He was 89. The man considered the last of the legendary movie moguls, Mr. Wasserman began as a theater usher, became an MCA agent for entertainers and eventually changed the face of the movie business. Working on behalf of his film-star clients in the late 1940's, he put an end to the ironclad long-term contracts that turned even big-name actors into high-paid serfs of the major studios. In the 1950's, he forced a reluctant Hollywood to accept television, then a new medium, as a potential cash cow rather than as a feared competitor. In the 1960's, he demonstrated the political influence that Hollywood could wield by organizing huge fund-raising campaigns, particularly for the Democratic Party. And in the 1970's, his deft

marketing of Steven Spielberg's *Jaws* and other movies was credited with creating the summer blockbuster.

There are so many key words for the combination of MC, Jupiter and Capricorn in that obituary!

Another key aspect we have discussed before, is the dynastic quality of this astrological placement. With Cancer on the IC for these individuals, home is the springboard for their careers. This is demonstrated in the life of British painter and poet, Frieda Hughes. The following comes from Telegraph.co.uk:

> "Because of my parents, I've always felt that my life was very much under wraps, and it's taken me years to feel slowly comfortable in sharing anything," says Frieda. We're sitting in her beautiful garden in the heart of rural Wales, where she has finally put down roots and where, she suggests, she would happily grow old. It's a perfect summer afternoon and we're sharing a bottle of wine and admiring the view of the Brecon Beacons beyond. Hughes moved here in 2004, choosing the area for its beauty, its distance from London—and its affordability. "But it was the house that sold it to me because I needed a space to paint in and write in. I looked at this and thought, 'I should have enough work space here for most of my life if not all of it.' So here I am."

ASTROLOGICAL MAVERICKS

Jupiter in Aquarius on the MC

At their heart, individuals with this astrological placement are grand humanitarians with ideas to benefit the masses, while appealing to their own sense of specialness.

There is no surprise that multiple maverick and hotel mogul, Conrad Hilton, set up a foundation that, according to HiltonFoundation.org:

> At $2 million, the Conrad N. Hilton Humanitarian Prize is the world's largest annual humanitarian award presented to nonprofit organizations judged to have made extraordinary contributions toward alleviating human suffering.

Actor, Elliott Gould, who has his passionate Leonine Mars opposite this point, showed his Aquarian nature in a big way on screen. The following comes from an article in the IrishTimes.com:

> His career skyrocketed in step with counterculture with a triumvirate of 1969 hits: Paul Mazursky's free-love comedy *Bob & Carol & Ted & Alice* (for which the actor was shortlisted for an Oscar), the Richard Rush campus unrest dramedy *Getting Straight*, and Robert Altman's satirical takedown of military machismo, *M*A*S*H*."

From Astro.com comes this brilliantly amazing Aquarian description for Barbara Wilson:

American writer; Wilson is also founder of Seal Press. A lesbian and a feminist, her heroines are usually strong, witty, adventurous and intelligent. She has written mysteries, novels, and published short-story collections.

Her novel *Gaudi Afternoon,* which was made into a feature film, was awarded the Crime Writers Association Award and Lambda Literary Award in 1991. Another novel, *Blue Windows* won the Lambda Literary Award and was a nominee for PEN Center USA West, in 1997. She co-founded Seal Press in support of women authors and founded "Women in Translation: which translated the writing of women who are exiled or marginalized."

Actress, Jennifer Jason Leigh, who has her Moon, Sun, and Venus here, explains her Aquarian traits in this article from theGuardian.com:

> Here is another explanation: she recoiled from the hustle—the pitching, networking and chasing. "I'm not really a careerist. I don't go out a lot or call my agent a lot. I don't actively pursue jobs maybe in the way I should. I wish I was less introverted. I wish I could enjoy a party. I'm not good at small talk and don't enjoy it." She sighs, then laughs. "This is great, this is me getting myself uninvited to every single party. But that's OK."

Brilliant humanitarian director, Meghna Gulzar, who also has her Venus here, uses media to educate people, especially in regards to the ways in which we, as males and females watch movies. She characterizes the ways in which we watch movies as "male gaze" or having a male frame of reference. This helps to frame her work, especially the ways in which society in general and Indian society specifically, view issues of sexuality. From AsianAge.com comes this apt description of her mission statement with one of her movies:

> And yet she wanted to give it a moral compass. "With *Talvar*, I said, 'I'm being objective. I'm telling you both sides of the story but when I put that video footage at the end of the film which showed the only time that the girl was alive. That was my moral compass that I was leaving you with, that okay this is actually what happened, these two people died," she said. "If you want your story to be grey, there will be no moral compass. If you want to give a very definite take to the audience that they can go home with, at the end of your film, you will have a moral compass, and that moral compass could be any device. Sometimes the audience finds a moral compass that you didn't even realise you placed and that's the beauty of it," she added.

Jupiter in Pisces on the MC

Jupiter is the traditional ruler of Pisces, so the King or Queen is Home. These people can really sell a big image to the masses as we will see from the individuals representing this astrological placement.

Actress, Ally Sheedy, who has Sun in Gemini conjunct her AS, belonged to the 1980's Brat Pack. The following comments from Ally, comes from AZQuotes.com:

> "The fact is, I can have any experience of life I want. I don't have to choose any one thing or act in any one way to define myself as a woman now. I am one."

> "When you grow up, your heart dies."

From his obituary in BBC.com, comes this lovely anecdote about how these astrological energies played out in the life of British journalist and comedian, David Frost:

> Paying tribute to his friend, Grossman said: "He so effortlessly roamed all across the piste... from comedy to current affairs to light entertainment for 50 years. Yet in his presence you forgot you were dealing with the Leviathan of broadcasting and just thought here is a wonderful man, generous, enthusiastic and always excited. He was in love with television."

Artemes Turchi used to put on extravagant gender bending lip-sync cabaret performances, and also has Uranus and Mercury conjunct his Cancer AS. What we see is not what we get.

Porn star, Jeff Stryker, who makes our list a second time, was very fluid with his sexuality and he shared this with the world.

Performer, Vanessa Williams, who has both her Sun and Mercury here as well, has also done well with her sexual appeal. Vanessa branched out into acting. Jupiter in Pisces gives these individuals the ability to create any illusion or image for the audience.

Victoria Beckham, went from Spice Girl band member to luxury designer.

Lady Gaga, is a maverick of performance art and acting. She transforms herself in an over the top way conveying various images to the world.

Saturn

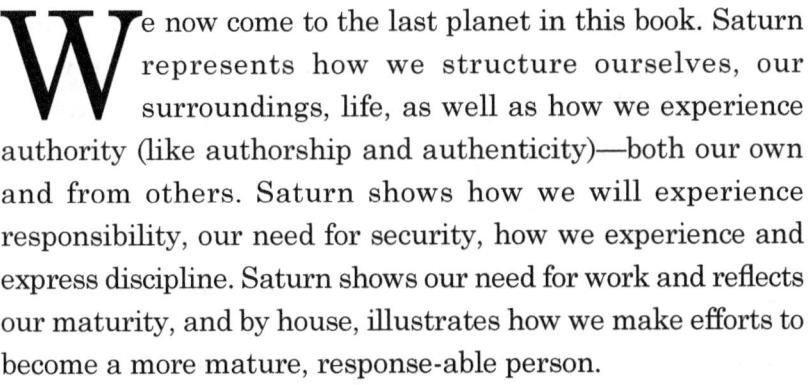

We now come to the last planet in this book. Saturn represents how we structure ourselves, our surroundings, life, as well as how we experience authority (like authorship and authenticity)—both our own and from others. Saturn shows how we will experience responsibility, our need for security, how we experience and express discipline. Saturn shows our need for work and reflects our maturity, and by house, illustrates how we make efforts to become a more mature, response-able person.

Saturn rules both Capricorn and Aquarius. These two signs show us that through hard work we can be successful for ourselves in Capricorn, and for Humanity in Aquarius. Saturn is considered the greater malefic, where we will experience the pain of limitation and the challenges of life. The ancient writings speak of the ring-pass-not quality of Saturn, meaning there will be tests we must pass in order to "move forward." Again, such placements are neither good nor bad, but simply point to the places in our lives, by sign and house, that will show us where and how we need to be responsible.

Saturn is where the "pedal hits the metal", where no one else can do it for us. When we realize the benefits of the hard work and challenges Saturn provides, we gain the strength, knowledge and ability to do what we need in life. We can appreciate the blessings this planet gives after we have completed the work necessary. I like to think of Saturn as a sort of Universal piggy bank: each lesson that is "saved" gives an increased rate of return in the future. Saturn plays a powerful role in astrology. Also known as Chronos, in ancient myth, he was one of the kings of the Gods. He devoured his children thinking he could outwit the prophecy of his fated downfall. Saturn's story illustrates that even gods are bound by their fates, just like mortals. Astrologers know that when Saturn is in relationship or aspect with other planets, Saturn is the ruler. This means that when there is a meeting of say Mars and Saturn, Saturn will be the winner, bringing structure, maturity and a greater sense of self-authentication. We will see how this self-defining maverick purpose plays out when conjunct the chart's angles.

Before the 18th century, Saturn was the farthest planet we could see with the naked eye in the night sky. As the outermost planet, or boundary to the solar system, Saturn represents limits, structures, skin, bones and teeth. When we have Saturn on one of the chart's angles, the result can be a despotic dictator who has more regard for upholding the rules or the creation and idea of higher rules. These are idealized structures that individuals like Jeffrey Dahmer, David Koresh, and Jerry Fallwell, create for themselves in order to do what they do. Further research into these individuals will likely reveal interesting relationships with their father/authority figures.

As we step beyond the bounds of Jupiter, we have to understand that something greater than our personal, individual self is at work. We are forced to see that there is more to life than we could ever fully know. There is a loss of innocence with Saturn, Chiron, Uranus, Neptune, and Pluto. When crossing the River Styx, one must give a coin or something else of value to make the journey to the other side, where our physical selves cease to be. If we do not sacrifice the material, we remain a ghost on the physical plane. A shade of our former self, lost between worlds. Such is what happens to those who do not face their responsibilities and instead take the path of least resistance or abdicate their responsibilities altogether. As there are archetypal ranges of expression, there are those who must abdicate and take the path of least resistance to find their own sense of self. Saturn is the last planet that will be covered in this book.

We will now look at the angle placements of Saturn throughout the zodiac from the point of view of the Ascendant (AS).

Saturn in Aries on the AS

While Saturn is in its fall when in Aries, both Aries and Saturn share a focus on autonomy and authenticity. Aries, for the instinctual free-wheeling drive to go forward, and Saturn, for creating and setting the structures of our physical, emotional and mental bodies and life in general. Saturn is the planet of "Authorship" and Aries is the sign of the self. When we look at individuals in this category, we find a restless, resistant quality. These people take neither orders nor directions from others. In a sense, one can almost consider Aquarian energies with this astrological placement, but Aries is cardinal and not fixed like Aquarius. So, while there is a sense of greater freedom, Saturn will still require its coin.

Film actor, Errol Flynn had a challenging time finding ways to reign in his energies. While he was a master "Swashbuckler"—sword wielding Aries—of the highest order, the rest of his life is like a manual on what not to do to be successful. Flynn's inner drive to be himself far outweighed his need to relate to others. I recommend reading about his life as he lived a good one! In true Aries fashion, he was quite legendary in the bedroom as well. The following comes from NYPost.com:

Flynn once boasted that he had spent 12,000 to 14,000 nights having sex. Robert Douglas once recalled walking into Flynn's dressing room to find the star naked in his armchair, with one woman on top of him and another waiting patiently.

Journalist and author, Hunter S. Thompson, is an example of a maverick who traveled his own tracks and was able to share his personal experiences on the way to finding himself. His 1971 novel, *Fear and Loathing in Las Vegas,* is an amazingly structured expression of Hunter's instinctual drug-induced journey.

From BrainyQuote.com come the following comments from actor, John Voigt, that aptly portray this astrological placement:

"You can get digital technology that almost is film quality, and go make little films and do everything you can to find a little understanding of your own voice and it will grow. Don't take *no* for an answer. Take every opportunity you can to do something. Some people think we're adrift without any guidelines. I don't. I think we've had instruction on how to live. I just think that I'm a person who's trying to find the truth and express it as I, you know, get the opportunity."

From his political views, we can understand why Voight might have issues with his daughter and fellow maverick and actress, Angelina Jolie. Of course, as we have discussed before, they share some strong Aries placements. This astrological placement would not be known for its flexibility.

An article from SMH.com about avant-garde Australian artist, Brett Whiteley, who also had his Mercury here, beautifully illustrates many aspects of this astrological placement:

> "His dedication to developing his craft, in particular, drawing, made him, without doubt, one of Australia's most celebrated draftsmen of his time," Ryan says. Wendy Whiteley, wife and muse and keeper of the Whiteley legacy, says the exhibition puts lie to the idea of the celebrated artist's effortless" style. "We were in Majorca where we lived and Brett just said to Robert Graves, 'What do you think genius is?' And he said, '98 per cent lead and 2 per cent mercury'. It's true. It's also setting goals that you are not going to settle for being comfortable and mediocre, you are all the time reaching to be better."

As we have discussed before, while these fall and detriment astrological placements are challenging, when one applies one's self and makes the efforts required, the reward is great. This is especially true with rule- and structure-seeking Saturn.

Wikipedia.com writes the following about musician, Claudia Gonson, which reminds us that the Ascendant plays a strong role in identification:

> In an interview with *The Advocate,* Gonson famously remarked: "When we started Magnetic Fields, we

purposely had one lesbian, one gay guy, one straight woman, and one straight man. The audience could identify with whomever they wanted."

Saturn in Taurus on the AS

This can be a good or a challenging astrological position depending upon how the native deals with form, structure and rules.

Serial killer, Andrew Cunanan, who also has his Moon here, shows what the longing for luxury and wealth can do to a person. Taurus can show us our toddler like attachments, especially when self-worth-oriented Moon and Saturn are involved. Remember, Scorpio is the DS for this placement, so relationship to the other is intense. Andrew was drawn to wealth like a moth to a flame. The following comes from an article in TownandCountry.com:

> Sources said Cunanan's mental health suffered when his lifestyle took a hit. "Andrew's self-worth was tied to the finer things in life, what [people] could do for him," criminal profiler, Candice DeLong told ABC News. "Being accepted in high society and by wealthy people was what he expected. If he didn't get them, he was lost." It was during this period of self-doubt that Cunanan took the life of his first victim.

Andrew ended his own life which is one of the most authentic acts one can perform, probably one of the most controlling as well, both hallmarks of Saturn and Taurus.

Marco Pantani, with his Jupiter in Scorpio across the way and both squared by his Capricorn planets, shows the dogged determination and physical prowess necessary to be an excellent athlete. Fortunately, he could focus his powerful planetary dynamics on biking. Marco died from suicide caused by acute cocaine poisoning.

English singer, Gary Barlow, who has his Moon opposite this point, shared the following about his stillborn daughter:

> "For anyone who has been through anything like this I think it's something you accept you're going to be dealing with the rest of your life." He continued: "In a strange way you don't want it to end because it's one of the few things you have to remind you of the person that's not there. In some ways the pain and the grief brings you closer to them."

Taurus and Scorpio deal with life and death situations especially when the Moon and Saturn are involved.

Comedian, Karen Dunbar, who makes our list a second time for her Mars squaring this astrological placement in Capricorn, shows the ultimate self-authorship in having her own television show called *The Karen Dunbar Show*. The Taurus/Scorpio axis is one of trials, dramas and tribulations.

In an interesting astrological twist of fate, fellow maverick Gary Barlow witnessed Karen perform, resulting in him casting her in one of his shows.

Saturn in Gemini on the AS

This is a perfect place for a grammarian or someone who uses words very carefully and in an articulate manner. A wordsmith would be a good name for this astrological placement.

Actor and film director, Orson Welles, shows many aspects of this astrological placement, whether reading at three years old, memorizing *King Lear* by the age of seven, or scaring the world as an adult, when he read H.G. Wells' science fiction novel, *War of the Worlds,* over the radio, in such a convincing manner as to cause mass panic!

Gemini is the sign of movement as much as it is of communication. So, when the hard work of Saturn is given, a person can attain amazing recognition in one's athletic endeavors. Cricket "Blue Boy" Greg Blewett is an example of Saturnian commitment and the expression this astrological placement needs. The following comes from FootyAlmanac.com.au:

> Greg was very good athletics wise and won the triple jump at the Australian carnival with Little Athletics, but admits he lost interest with the enormous time commitment required and enjoyed cricket and footy more so gave athletics away.

From DailyMail.uk.com, comes this anecdotal tale of Saturn exacting a price from Australian footballer, James Hird:

> [Hird]... the blonde haired Essendon star was one of the most revered players in the AFL, regarded among

many as somewhat of a 'football god.' Afforded the many media and commercial opportunities that come with being one of the biggest names in the most popular sport in Melbourne, Hird and wife Tania, a lawyer, built a booming multi-million dollar property and business empire.

Hird then made a series of decisions that exacted a pretty hefty price and challenged all that he and his wife built.

Saturn in Cancer on the AS

Saturn on one of the chart's angles is always challenging, more so, when he is in detriment. This can be a problem both for the person born with such placement, but more for those around the native.

Actress and talk show host, Sara Gilbert, has the following appropriate quote about this astrological placement that comes from BrainyQuote.com:

> "Yeah, I started when I was 6 years old. My brother and sister would get all of these presents at Christmas time from the cast and crew of their show and I was jealous. So I decided that I had to become an actor."

Chanteuse, Sheila, who makes our list a second time, shows the determination and skill to be successful. In typical Saturnian fashion, she started work when she was a young 16 year old.

SATURN

From the iconic singer and songwriter, Van Morrison, comes the following quote from AZQuotes.com:

"There's always got to be a struggle. What else is there? That's what life is made of. I don't know anything else. If there is, tell me about it."

Saturn in Leo on the AS

Saturn is again in detriment here, of course, as it is in Leo, the opposing sign of Aquarius. These people are going to want attention, but have to pay a high price to gain it.

Our first illustration, second wife of Prince Charles, Camilla Parker-Bowles, is such an example. While she may be Queen Consort one day, she has had to deal with many issues involving the public, the royal family, and the tabloids.

From Quotes.net comes this review of how Edwina Curie used this astrological placement:

... is a former British Member of Parliament. First elected as a Conservative Party MP in 1983, she was a Junior Health Minister for two years, before resigning in 1988 over the controversy over salmonella in eggs. By the time Currie lost her seat in 1997, she had begun a new career as a novelist and broadcaster.

Exit stage left.

Laura Nyro, who makes our list a second time, shares her experience in Independent.co.uk:

As she declared in a rare interview to *Musician* magazine, "When I was very young, everything happened so quickly for me. I hadn't really contemplated being famous. I was writing music, I was just involved in the art of it at that young age. Then, when it all happened, I didn't know how to handle it."

Saturn, also known as, Chronos, has to do with time, history as well as that which is "real." Astrologer, Bruce Scofield, used this astrological placement to delve deep into the history of astrology as well as to re-unite astronomy and astrology.

Author and poet, Jewelle Gomez, who has Mars squaring this position from her IC in Scorpio, makes this illustrative quote from GoodReads.com:

"For femmes, that evolving feminist thought reacquainted us with something we kind of knew already: men and women might mistake us for 'just girls' when they see our makeup and fashions, but we were/are actually guerrilla warriors, fighting undercover in the war to save women from the continuing campaign to make us irrelevant fluff."

I am Leo, hear me roar!

SATURN

Saturn in Virgo on the AS

This is a compelling astrological placement for Saturn in resourceful Virgo. Emphasis on the feminine and the ability to morph into whatever is necessary are two types of archetypal expressions of this conjunction.

Legendary, long-standing performer, Carol Channing, who has Mars and Venus on her DS in Pisces, shared this telling way that Saturn "knows" from an early age. The following comes from MSN.com:

> Channing recalled the feeling of stepping into a theater for the first time. "This is a temple. This is a cathedral. It's a mosque … This is for people who have gotten a glimpse of creation and all they do is recreate it. I stood there and wanted to kiss the floorboards."

I find it synchronistically interesting to note that as I write this on January 15, 2019, it is the day Carol passed away. God speed, Dolly.

Variety is presented in the life of singer, Donna Summer. The following comes from NYTimes.com:

> She riffled through styles as diverse as funk, electronica, rock and torch song as she piled up 14 Top 10 singles in the United States, among them "Love to Love You Baby", "Bad Girls", "Hot Stuff", "Last Dance" and "She Works Hard for the Money." In the late '70s she had three double albums in a row that reached No. 1, and

each sold more than a million copies. Then she switched once more and became a born-again Christian.

Photographer, Pierre Commoy, makes our list a third time. FromWideWalls.com, comes this illustrative description of Pierre:

> Constantly remodeling the portrait art, this artistic duo moves the limits of contemporary aesthetic using the explicit references to a gay culture spreading the message of tolerance and openness.

Leslie van Houten, a member of the "Manson family," shows us another side of Saturn on the AS. She was 19 when she committed murder with the other Manson members. Saturn on the AS can signify imprisonment, which Leslie has experienced for the last 50 plus years of her life.

Michel Lolito takes the Saturn on the AS off on a completely different tangent. Michel's claim to fame is eating indigestible objects! That comes right out of the Saturn/Chronos story – we cannot get more literal than that!

From AZQuotes.com, singer, Usher, aptly sums up this astrological placement:

> "Success is about dedication. You may not be where you want to be or do what you want to do when you're on the journey. But you've got to be willing to have vision and foresight that leads you to an incredible end."

SATURN

Saturn in Libra on the AS

Saturn is in its exaltation here. There is sophistication, grace and a balanced way of relating. This is a beautiful placement for relating to others in a very set manner.

Actor, Christopher Lee, makes our list a third time. Below, he comments on the theme of authenticity:

> "The song "My Way" is a very remarkable song. It is also difficult to sing because you've got to convince people that what you're singing about is the truth. It's a man who is very proud of having achieved everything that he's achieved his way."

The gifted, dedicated and blind musician, Doc Watson, shows us the gift dedicated Saturn provides in artistic and music loving Libra. The following comes from NYTimes.com:

> His mountain music came as a revelation to the folk audience, as did his virtuoso guitar playing. Unlike most country and bluegrass musicians, who thought of the guitar as a secondary instrument for providing rhythmic backup, Mr. Watson executed the kind of flashy, rapid-fire melodies normally played by a fiddle or a banjo. His style influenced a generation of young musicians learning to play the guitar as folk music achieved national popularity. "He is single-handedly responsible for the extraordinary increase in acoustic flat-picking and fingerpicking guitar performance," said Ralph Rinzler, the folklorist who discovered Mr.

Watson in 1960. "His flat-picking style has no precedent in earlier country music history."

Doc Watson is a maverick in every sense of the word and leaves an amazing legacy.

Scottish actor, Gordon Jackson, exemplified another face of Saturn as the stern butler, Hudson, in the well-known British social-strata driven series *Upstairs, Downstairs.*

Film director, Scott Hicks, who has Venus and Mars conjunct his DS in Aries, shows some familial representations of this astrological placement. The following comes from Wikipedia.com:

> Though British citizens, his father and grandfather were born in Burma and the West Indies respectively, and spent their lives in far-flung locales as civil engineers building railways, bridges and harbors.

Building structures to generate commerce is exactly what this astrological placement shows; his father and grandfather did it literally and Scott did it his way through the imagery of film, which makes sense given he has Neptune here as well!

Saturn in Scorpio on the AS

These are people with a deep intensity. We know there is a line over which we cannot step. The funny thing is, these individuals do not have any trouble crossing anyone else's line.

British stateswoman, Margaret Thatcher, with her Moon in Leo on her MC, is a perfect example of this Saturnian placement earning her the moniker *Iron Lady*.

Television host, Johnny Carson, who also has his Mercury here, was adept at gauging people and going as deep as he could with each guest while he held incredible boundaries. Carson was a true ambassador between the audience and his guests. *The Tonight Show* was synonymous with his name.

Holding a deep ground for transformation is well illustrated in our next example. The individual most responsible for the Beatnik style, and broke away from that which came before, never even published a book! Neal Cassady, acted as a transformative figure in many of his friends' writings. Neal is accredited with Kerouac's change in style.

Tennis champ, Chris Evert, who also has her Moon and Venus here, used the Saturn energies to give herself strength, stamina, determination and heightened competitiveness. Chris ruled the tennis court.

English singer and performer, Adam Ant, who also has his Sun and Mercury here, shares the following apt quotes from AZQuotes.com:

"I really knew I wanted to be *Adam*, because Adam was the first man. *Ant* I chose because, if there's a nuclear explosion, the ants will survive."

"Achievement results from work realizing ambition."

"Bipolar disorder, manic depression, depression, black dog, whatever you want to call it, is inherent in our society. It's a product of stress and in my case over-work."

Adam clearly states the problem with being an authentic artist:

"I wanted to make good records. But my problem is I've got a low boredom threshold, so I wanted it to look and sound different with each album, which is really tantamount to suicide, cause people lose it, they lose it—they say: 'I like that, and that's not this.'"

From TravelingPeach.com comes this quote from Olympic swimmer, Eamon Sullivan:

"Growing up, swimming at an international level never crossed my mind; let alone that it was a possible career. I enjoyed it and one thing led to another. It sounds like a casual approach but it was that simple. When I was younger, I wasn't as driven as I am now so I didn't think about making it to that level or even fully understand was involved so, when I made the Olympic team aged 18, it was a total surprise. Going into the time trial, I hadn't thought about making the team, I'd just thought 'I want to swim the fastest' and, as simple as that, I ended up being the youngest male on the team. After that, I kept surprising myself with my performance. I kept improving, breaking World Records… but, even then, I never thought 'I want to win this event. I want to break that record.' That happened later into my career. Initially, I just enjoyed swimming and wanted to swim the fastest. Swimming competitively happened naturally for me. Right place, right time."

Scorpio can be fiercely competitive.

Saturn in Sagittarius on the AS

While this is not a classically poor position for Saturn, we understand why the limits on the free-wheeling Sagittarian might not be the most enjoyable. Of course, this is exactly what they need to gain single-pointed focus. Saturn always takes time.

Actress, Katherine Helmond, who makes our list a second time, has this subtle and accurate description that comes from AZQuotes.com:

> "The choice of roles as I grow older gets more and more limited, so if I pin myself to one kind of part I would get in trouble. So, these oddball ladies came along for me to do – I guess Terry Gilliam helped in this respect. I have found them more interesting, flashier and I get more mileage out of them."

Actress, Jamie Lee Curtis, who makes our list a third time, has her Mercury here. Curtis has the following quote from Quotes.TheFamousPeople.com:

"If I can challenge old ideas about aging, I will feel more and more invigorated. I want to represent this new way. I want to be a new version of the 70-year-old woman. Vital, strong, very physical, very agile. I think that the older I get, the more yoga I'm going to do."

Saturn in Capricorn on the AS

This is a powerful position for Saturn as he rules Capricorn. These individuals wear the robes of authority. People see them as an authority and these individuals see themselves as an authority.

Reinhold Ebertin, who also has his Jupiter here, shows the level of hard work and persistence that Jupiter and Saturn give when conjunct an Ascendant. Reinhold wrote over 60 textbooks on astrology, founded Cosmobiology, and was also a teacher.

Retired Associate Justice of the United States Supreme Court, Sandra Day O'Connor, makes our list a second time. From NBCNews.com comes this statement about her from one of her colleagues:

> Chief Justice John Roberts said: "Justice O'Connor is of course a towering figure in the history of the United States and indeed the world. She broke down barriers for women in the legal profession to the betterment of that profession and the country as a whole."

The pinnacle of success is achieved.

Scottish actor, Sean Connery, who has his Jupiter in Cancer conjunct his IC, is most remembered for his role as calm, cool, collected and tony secret agent, Bond, James Bond. Capricorn is the sign of social success and Sean brought elegance and capability to the role.

When we think of authoritative, iconic voices, actor, James Earl Jones, is definitely at the top of the list. This quote from AZQuotes.com illustrates that even in its place of rulership, Saturn experiences are earned, not given:

"No one asked me to be an actor, so no one owed me. There was no entitlement."

Separation from one of the parents is a consistent theme with strong Saturnian aspects. My dear friend Glenna Bain, who lost her father when she was just three months in utero, has an amazing ability to connect with people at any social level while holding her sense of self intact. Glenna provided the consistent ground, and assisted me with editing this book.

Saturn in Aquarius on the AS

Even though Saturn rules the sign of Aquarius, there can still be themes of being the outcast. These individuals have an amazing ability to understand the structures and rules, yet fly in the face of them in ways their contemporaries do not understand.

Singer and musician, Nina Simone, who also has her Venus here, experienced that painful Aquarian combination of being special, but not accepted. With Saturn on her Ascendant, she could not but help but teach others. Through her music, Nina expressed her social activism and observations of a world gone mad. Saturn and Aquarius are both private in their approaches to life.

American football running back, Howard "Hopalong" Cassady, is one of those examples. While he won the Heisman Trophy in 1955 and was inducted into the College Football Hall of Fame in 1979, there isn't any information available out there about him.

Piero Manzoni, the artist who has his Mercury across the way in Leo, created the ultimate uniquely artistic container. The following comes from an article about his work from Tate.org.uk:

> It is not known exactly how many cans of Artist's Shit were sold within Manzoni's lifetime, but a receipt dated August 23, 1962, certifies that Manzoni sold one to Alberto Lùcia for 30 grams of 18-carat gold (reproduced in Battino and Palazzoli p.154). Manzoni's decision to value his excrement on a par with the price of gold made clear reference to the tradition of the artist as alchemist already forged by Marcel Duchamp and Yves Klein among others. As the artist and critic, Jon Thompson wrote:
>
>> Manzoni's critical and metaphorical reification of the artist's body, its processes and products, pointed the way towards an understanding of the persona of the artist and the product of the artist's body as a consumable object. The Merda d'artista, the artist's

shit, dried naturally and canned "with no added preservatives," was the perfect metaphor for the bodied and disembodied nature of artistic labour: the work of art as fully incorporated raw material, and its violent expulsion as commodity. Manzoni understood the creative act as part of the cycle of consumption: as a constant reprocessing, packaging, marketing, consuming, reprocessing, packaging, *ad infinitum*. (Piero Manzoni, 1998, p.45).

And what could be more apropos for this astrological placement than *The Stepford Wives*? Actor, Peter Masterson stars as the husband in this thriller with a twist. This astrological configuration can lend a robotic quality.

Saturn in Aquarius can give one a very varied repertoire of abilities as in the case of Carol Burnett's daughter, Carrie Hamilton. Carrie was a writer, musician and actress. Who knows what magic she would have created had her life not been cut short at 38 by cancer.

My friend, Jud Cary, is an intellectual property attorney, someone who works on the structural soundness of intellectual—especially electronic ideas.

Saturn in Pisces on the AS

This is an interesting position for structure seeking Saturn in the illusive transcendental waters of Pisces. Forever building sandcastles on the beach, these individuals are working to create inner structures that allow them to relate to everyone.

Talk show host, Phil Donahue, was a maverick, creating the first television talk show that encouraged audience interaction with the guests. This required an ability to hold boundaries and remain grounded as Phil could never know what comments would come out of an individual in the studio audience—let alone the guests themselves!

Princess Alexandra, The Honorable Lady Ogilvy, exhibits that very common aspect of Saturn near the ascendant: the loss of the father figure. Her father was killed in a plane crash when she was six years old.

The following comes from Mary Tyler Moore's obituary in CNN.com:

> Today beloved icon Mary Tyler Moore passed away at the age of 80 in the company of friends and her loving husband of over 33 years, Dr. S. Robert Levine. A groundbreaking actress, producer, and passionate advocate for the Juvenile Diabetes Research Foundation, Mary will be remembered as a fearless visionary who turned the world on with her smile.

Mary Tyler Moore's work made a difference in women's rights as well.

In a typically Saturn in Pisces way, Rufus Bellamy has written *Saving Wildlife (ACTION FOR THE ENVIRONMENT)*:

> This proactive series recognizes that many young people want to play a part in protecting the planet. Each book highlights the campaigns of various environmental

organizations and suggests practical steps that readers can take to reduce environmental destruction.

We will now look at the angle placements of Saturn throughout the zodiac from the point of view of the Imum Coeli (IC)

Saturn in Aries on the IC

This is where Saturn is in his fall, probably because of how hard and forceful these individuals can appear to others. This placement can give someone fearless courage and an ability to be a long-trekking warrior.

Australian author, Colleen McCullough, wrote many books including the wildly successful *The Thornbirds*. Colleen's strong nature is well described in her NYTimes.com obituary:

> Negative reviews did not appear to faze Ms. McCullough, whom The Philadelphia Inquirer, in a 1996 profile, described as "a woman supremely unafflicted by self-doubt."

RollingStone.com has this quote by Ray Manzarek, keyboardist for The Doors:

> "Morrison required all three of us diving into his lyrics and creating music that would swirl around him," Manzarek told Rolling Stone in 2006. "Without Jim,

everybody started shooting off in different directions... The Doors was the perfect mixture of four guys, four egos that balanced each other. There were never any problems with 'You wrote this' or 'I wrote that.' But [after Jim died] the whole dynamic was screwed up, because the fourth guy wasn't there."

With Saturn on the IC, there is an understanding of balance and shared responsibilities with Libra across the way.

Saturn in Taurus on the IC

One can very well imagine how recalcitrant an individual with this configuration could be! Challenging aspects to this point could make for a rather stubborn individual who will not likely be swayed. Saturn in Taurus on the IC is likely very security driven.

In the CNN.com obituary for Alexis Arquette, one can see the force of will:

In February, actor David Arquette reportedly said during an appearance on Kocktails with Khloe that Alexis no longer identified as transgender.

"She was like, 'Yeah, sometimes I'll be a man, sometimes I'll be a woman. I like to refer to myself as gender suspicious,'" David Arquette said. Richmond Arquette wrote that Alexis was with brothers, sisters, a niece and "several other loved ones" at the end. David Bowie's song "Starman" was playing. Richmond

Arquette described Alexis to CNN as "a force" who "died as he lived, on his own terms" and said he was happy to have been "with him as he began his journey onward.

Singer, Tammy Wynette, who also has her Sun here showed the world that with hard work and determination one can become a star, regardless of where one began.

A review from Penguin.co.uk about of one of Derek Jarman's books aptly describes this astrological point:

> Returning to *Modern Nature* recently I was astounded to see how thoroughly my adult life was founded in its pages. It was here I developed a sense of what it meant to be an artist, to be political, even how to plant a garden (playfully, stubbornly, ignoring boundaries, collaborating freely)... Building a garden was Jarman's characteristically energetic, fruitful response to the despair of what was, pre-combination therapy, a near certain death sentence. It was a stake in the future, and it led him deep into remembrance of the past, too.

In an article from TheAtlantic.com we see the conservative manner in which Saturn in Taurus can express itself, as it did with Enoch Powell:

> On April 20, 1968, Enoch Powell, a leading member of the Conservative Party in the British parliament, made a speech that would imprint itself into British memory—and divide the nation with its racist, incendiary rhetoric. Speaking before a group of

conservative activists, Powell said that if immigration to Britain from the country's former colonies continued, a violent clash between white and black communities was inevitable. "As I look ahead," Powell said, "I am filled with foreboding; like the Roman, I seem to see 'the River Tiber foaming with much blood,'" an allusion to a line in Virgil's Aeneid. He maintained that it would not be enough to close Britain's borders—some of the immigrants already settled in the country would need to be sent "home." If not, he declared, attributing a quote to one of his constituents, "in this country, in 15 or 20 years' time, the black man will have the whip hand over the white man."

Fifty years on, Powell's name still resonates and provokes. When the BBC decided to broadcast a full recording of his so-called "Rivers of Blood" speech last Saturday, it sparked a national controversy. The broadcaster arranged to have the speech delivered by an actor and set off with critical analysis, but the intensity of the response spoke, at least in part, to the unsettling shadow of Powell in the age of Brexit, two decades after his death. His prophecies of doom never materialized, but he proved prescient in a different sense: as a figure who embodied fears that continue to animate Britain's present and will help define its future.

Saturn in Gemini on the IC

Saturn is a helpful focusing assistant for multi-faceted Gemini energy. Wise user of words, correctly structured communication, grammarian, and teacher are all possibilities here, but will be more personalized, as this is the IC.

Marguerite Duras, who has her Mercury in Pisces on the AS squaring this point, is a perfect example of this astrological position, as it gives one the ability to express the jewels gained from the deep dive. The following comes from ThoughtCo.com:

> She wrote and she loved what she wrote to the obsession. She herself used to wonder what was that mortal need, that had taken her to live in a parallel world to the world of the others, and her to exist less and less because everything, her essence, was given to the all-consuming writing. When she was fifteen, she said to her mother that the only thing she wanted to do in her whole life was to narrate and she sincerely wondered what could do with their time the people that didn't write. Because, even her most painful memories were filtered through literature.

The next quote comes from Iconic singer, Janis Joplin, and can be found in her sister's book *Love, Janis*. Here, Janis offers a take on her own life's work:

> "My whole purpose is to communicate. What I sing is my own reality. But just the fact that people come up

to me and say, 'Hey, that's my reality too,' proves to me that it's not just mine."

Saturn commands and the human obeys.

Travis Kemp, who appears on our list a second time, created structures for dance with his wife. The following comes from the Independent.com:

> They taught the method of the Italian Maestro Enrico Cecchetti and together—she, with eagle eye, cogent remark and military precision; and he, gentle, persuasive and personalized—they made an excellent combination. Over the next 20 years they established successful schools in Istanbul, Izmir, and Ankara.

Shauna Sand, who has Mercury in Leo on the DS (amazing how many of these people have Mercury squaring this position), is an actress, Playboy Bunny, and has been married three times. Each of the men Shauna married looks like different facets of the same man.

Saturn in Cancer on the IC

These people are going to need the safe secure structure of stable home, but usually do not usually experience it. This placement is one that speaks of early responsibility, especially in one's childhood home. This can indicate a native that took on the adult role in the parent-child relationship or had to be an adult and not really have a traditional playful childhood.

Saturn is serious. The "rewards" appear later in life because Saturn makes us earn them.

Actress and entertainer, Liza Minnelli, who has her Moon and Mars here, has this quote from AZQuotes.com:

> "It was no great tragedy being Judy Garland's daughter. I had tremendously interesting childhood years—except they had little to do with being a child."

Janio Quadros, who has Jupiter in Aries on his AS squaring this astrological placement, had a life that easily reflects these archetypes. This portion from Library.Brown.edu only shows the first part of his life:

> He spent his childhood in Curítiba and earned a degree in Law from the University of São Paulo. Quadros worked briefly as a Geography teacher and as a Law professor before entering politics. In 1947 he was elected to the city council of São Paulo, serving in that role until 1950. During his term he introduced more laws than any other elected official in Brazil, including several that benefitted the working class. In 1950 he was elected to the São Paulo State Senate, earning more votes than any other candidate, serving from 1951 to 1953.

Saturn in Leo on the IC

Saturn is considered in its detriment when in Leo. While Saturn gives the Leo ego many obstacles to overcome, he gives ample reward for efforts made when the work is complete.

Kathleen Battle, who has her Mercury here—both squaring her Jupiter in Sagittarius on the DS—is a prime example. The New York's Metropolitan Opera fired Battle 20 years ago for some extensive egregious imperious behavior. Hopefully, this was amended in 2016 when the Met asked her to return.

Rick "Merlin" Levine, is a witty and expressive astrologer who exhibits the healthy side of this placement with all of his astrological work, as clearly stated at Tarot.com/bios/rick-levine:

> To say Rick Levine has an impressive resume is an understatement! He founded The Center for Astrological Research, was a trustee of the Kepler College for Astrological Arts and Sciences, and was a two-term President of the Washington State Astrology Association. He is also currently involved in multiple professional associations.

Anchorwoman, Jessica Savitch had a challenging configuration known as a T-Square involving her Saturn. The "male authority" of television news was pretty pervasive, as was the attitude of most people even in the early 1980's. The Saturn theme is clearly expressed in this quote from Savitch at Chron.com:

> "If I was aggressive when I was starting out, it was because I had to be. No. 1, I was very young. No. 2, I was in a very tough spot. I wanted the job (in TV news), and I was constantly being given specious reasons why I couldn't have it. I was told my voice wasn't authoritative, that nobody would believe a woman, that women wouldn't watch a woman on the news. If I was tough, the times were tough."

Saturn on the IC is further reflected in at least two aspects of her life: Jessica was the eldest child in her family and her father encouraged her to become a broadcast journalist.

Saturn in Virgo on the IC

This is an interesting astrological placement for structured Saturn in always perfecting Virgo.

Screenwriter and producer, Gene Roddenberry, who also has his Jupiter here, had the following, from Telegraph.co.uk, written about his television series, *Star Trek:*

> Multi-ethnic and inter-galactic, democratic and humanistic, *Star Trek* offered a modern mythology for a secular age. Its message was that power without humanity, intellect without compassion, are uncivilized.

From his obituary in BBC.co.uk comes this instructive piece on English actor, Peter Ustinov:

"He was a writer of note. People forget he was twice-nominated by the Writers' Guild of America for screenplays he wrote. Above all he was a great humanitarian. He was a UNICEF ambassador and he valued that very highly," Mr. Kenis said.

French born Englishwoman, Violette Szabo, was in special ops in World War II, and is remembered for the work she did to end the war. The following comes from SmithsonianMag.com:

[Szabo]… she was fluent in French and, though just 5-foot-5, athletic and surprisingly strong for her size. She was already a crack shot in a family comfortable around guns and target practice; under rigorous SOE training, she became an accomplished markswoman. Reports described her as a persistent and "physically tough self-willed girl," and "not easily rattled."

Singer, Karen Carpenter, who has her Sun opposing this spot on her Pisces MC, had a perfected image of herself as a woman. This caused Karen much emotional pain, anorexia, and death.

Entertainer, Artemes Turchi, who makes our list a third time, used his fluid nature to play with the boundaries of what is masculine and feminine in the acts he used to perform.

Saturn in Libra on the IC

This is an exalted place for Saturn. An understanding of how best to comport oneself would be key.

Hank Williams, who also has his Mercury here, made quite a mark in music considering he died at 29! The following comes from Hank's entry at Wikipedia.com:

> [Williams]... was an American singer-songwriter and musician. Regarded as one of the most significant and influential American singers and songwriters of the 20th century, Williams recorded 35 singles (five released posthumously) that reached the Top 10 of the Billboard Country & Western Best Sellers chart, including 11 that ranked number one (three posthumously).

Ford Motor heiress, Josephine Ford, who has Mars in Cancer on her Ascendant, had this written about her in her LATimes.com obituary:

> Over the years, "Dodie" Ford and the foundation she established with her husband donated more than $20 million to the Detroit Institute of Arts; $14 million to Henry Ford Health System in Detroit for what is now known as the Josephine Ford Cancer Center, one of the largest cancer centers in Michigan; and $20 million to the College for Creative Studies, an art and design college in Detroit known for turning out car designers. In addition to charity work, Ford amassed a noted art collection, including paintings by Van Gogh, Renoir and Picasso. She donated Van Gogh's *Portrait of the Postman Joseph Roulin,* which Bill Ford's e-mail said was valued at $40 million, and other works valued at more than $1 million apiece to the Detroit Institute

of Arts. "She's never sat on her millions," Eleanor Breitmeyer Gebert, a retired society editor of the *Detroit News* who covered the Ford family for more than 35 years, said in 1998. "She and her husband were a great match. She always kept a low profile; she's very shy."

"What else is there for a girl who wasn't competitive to do but try to escape all that Ford stuff?" she once said.

This quote address both points of Josephine's square, does it not? The significant art collection, the long-term relationship, the low profile, and shyness are pure Saturn in Libra on the IC and the "What is a girl to do?" speaks to Mars on her AS in Cancer.

Virginia Mae Brown, who makes our list a second time for having her Mars conjunct this point as well as both planets opposing her Aquarian Moon at the MC. This is fierce warrioress energy that has obviously given her the clear understanding and structure to be a government official, civil servant, and attorney at law.

Saturn in Scorpio on the IC

One may call this place the reckoning. The arrangement speaks to absolute conviction -the kind that requires the ultimate price be paid.

Martin Luther, who also has his Venus here, showed death defying determination when he posted his 95 Theses on Halloween in 1517. The following comes from history.com:

In his theses, Luther condemned the excesses and corruption of the Roman Catholic Church, especially the papal practice of asking payment—called "indulgences"—for the forgiveness of sins. At the time, a Dominican priest named Johann Tetzel, commissioned by the Archbishop of Mainz and Pope Leo X, was in the midst of a major fundraising campaign in Germany to finance the renovation of St. Peter's Basilica in Rome. Though Prince Frederick III the Wise had banned the sale of indulgences in Wittenberg, many church members traveled to purchase them. When they returned, they showed the pardons they had bought to Luther, claiming they no longer had to repent for their sins.

Film maker, Michael Moore, makes our list a third time as he also has Sun conjunct his MC in Taurus. This astrological placement gives him the deep inner egoic strength and authority to courageously stand up to the "big guys" because he doesn't see them as more important than himself.

This theme is repeated again in a quote by British Member of Parliament, George Galloway:

"A small man intoxicated by being allowed to run around with the big, aggressive, powerful boys after so many years as a corduroy-clad peacenik."

Another level of inner strength and the desire to reveal the "ugly truth" to others is clearly stated in the opening paragraph of the obituary for British journalist, Alan Whicker, that comes from TheGuardian.com:

> In a 1969 television documentary about Haiti, Alan Whicker, who has died aged 87, asked the notorious dictator "Papa Doc" Duvalier, in kindly, innocently interested and rather baffled tones: "But Papa Doc, they say you torture people?" It was a succinct example of the former Fleet Street journalist's ability to ask the most piercing questions while giving those being questioned no personal provocation or excuse to break off the interview—an ability that, if not unique, was certainly less common among other interviewers in a world often dominated by inflated egos.

Dervish, Laurence Galian, has his Venus opposite this point conjunct his MC in Taurus. Saturn on the IC gives one an incredible groundedness and the Scorpio flavor is seeking depth of meaning in the most grounded place within ourselves. Dervish is defined as: a member of a Muslim (specifically Sufi) religious order who has taken vows of poverty and austerity. Dervishes first appeared in the 12th century; they were noted for their wild or ecstatic rituals and were known as dancing, whirling, or howling dervishes according to the practice of their order. Sufis are the mystic/metaphysical part of the Muslim faith. All of this confirms the Saturn in Scorpio on the IC signature.

Annise Parker, who also has Jupiter on her AS in Leo, was the first openly gay mayor of a major U.S. city: Houston, Texas.

Saturn in Sagittarius on the IC

Putting Saturn in Sagittarius is like having authority figures in charge of play-time, it's not all fun, but we do end up with something worthwhile at the end.

From his obituary in the NYTimes.com comes this lovely reflection of this astrological placement:

> Cesar Chavez, the migrant worker who emerged from the poverty of an agricultural valley in Arizona to found America's first successful union of farm workers, was found dead yesterday in San Luis, Arizona. He was 66. Mr. Chavez, who lived in Keene, California, and was in Arizona on union business, died in his sleep, the local police said. An autopsy is planned. Blending the nonviolent resistance of Gandhi with the organizational skills of his mentor, the social activist Saul Alinsky, Mr. Chavez captured worldwide attention in the 1960's. Leading an initially lonely battle to unionize the fields and orchards of California, he issued a call to boycott grapes that soon became a *cause celebre*. Mr. Chavez, who was described by Robert F. Kennedy in 1968 as "one of the heroic figures of our time," was widely acknowledged to have done more to improve the lot of the migrant farm worker than anyone else.

From honesthistory.net.au comes this lovely summary of the life of Australian historian and author, John Molony, which follows the Saturn and Sagittarian themes:

After many years as a Catholic priest, John Molony began his academic career at the Australian National University in the mid-1960s, becoming one of Australia's finest historians, Manning Clark Professor of Australian History and Head of the Department of History. He was the author of numerous important books on Australian history and biography—including highly successful works on Ned Kelly and Eureka—but John also published in Italian, British and Irish history as well as writing two volumes of memoir.

Saturn here at the bottom of the chart in Sagittarius gives a strong backbone of faith.

Sagittarius is also the sign of higher education, which is well illustrated in Astrologer, Kenneth Negus's obituary from obits.nj.com:

He earned his PhD from Princeton University and taught graduate level German literature at Princeton University, Harvard University, Northwestern University and Rutgers University. Kenneth served in the U.S. Army in Germany after the end of World War II. He co-founded the Astrological Society of Princeton and was its president for 44 years. He published Johannes Kepler's astrological writings, wrote poetry, loved to garden and cook, take walks, sing and play classical guitar.

I like how the playful Sag nature shows up at the end of the excerpt.

Saturn in Capricorn on the IC

Saturn is in its rulership in Capricorn. This is the boss at home. We can see from the following examples that some natives handled the authority aspect better than others.

Another one of our youngest individuals is Charles Lindbergh Jr., the son of famous aviator Charles Lindbergh. Little Charles did not live long enough for us to see who he would become. The theme of separation from father is once again portrayed since he was kidnaped from the family home and murdered.

Singer, Bobbie Nelson, who has her Sun and Mercury here as well as Jupiter on her MC in Cancer, shows the strong themes of family, hard work, and family dynasty.

Author, Don Berry, has these quotes from Wikipedia.com which demonstrate the Saturnian influence:

"In time he found that all his perceptions were subject to the same easy control."

"This tree wishes you no harm. Go around it in peace. You are hurting yourself."

"If he could just get rid of the harsh irritation of his conscious thinking, then he would be all right, then he would be at peace."

David Koresh is an interesting study in Saturnian and Capricornian themes. In this PBS.org article, one can see how David was trying to find his authority and make his mark.

Interesting that he, like Bobbie Nelson, was also raised by his grandparents:

> David Koresh was born Vernon Wayne Howell in Houston, Texas in 1959 to a 15-year old single mother. He never knew his father and was raised by his grandparents. In his late-night conversations with FBI agents during the siege, Koresh described his childhood as lonely. He said the other kids teased him and called him "Vernie." He was dyslexic, a bad student, and dropped out of high school. However, he had musical ability and a strong interest in the Bible. By 12, he had memorized large tracts of it. When he was 20, Koresh turned to the Church of Seventh Day Adventists, his mother's church. But he was expelled for being a bad influence on the young people. Sometime during the next couple of years, Koresh went to Hollywood to become a rock star but nothing came of it. Instead, in 1981 he went to Waco, Texas where he joined the Branch Davidians, a religious sect which in 1935 had settled 10 miles outside of Waco. At one time, it had more than 1,400 members. Koresh had an affair with then-prophetess Lois Roden who was in her late sixties. The two travelled to Israel together. When Lois Roden died, a power struggle began between Koresh and Lois Roden's son George. For a short time, Koresh retreated with his followers to eastern Texas. But in late 1987 he returned to Mount Carmel in camouflage with seven male followers, armed with five .223 caliber semiautomatic assault rifles, two .22 caliber

rifles, two 12-gauge shotguns and nearly 400 rounds of ammunition. During the gunfight, Roden was shot in the chest and hands.

He and his followers went on trial for attempted murder. The seven were acquitted and a mistrial was declared in Koresh's case. (Koresh told the jury he and his men went to Mount Carmel to find evidence of corpse abuse by Roden and their shots were aimed at a tree.)

By 1990 Koresh had become the leader of the Branch Davidians and legally changed his name, saying on the court document that the change was "for publicity and business purposes." He said the switch arose from his belief that he was now head of the biblical House of David.

From her obituary in *The New York Times*, athlete, Florence Griffith-Joyner, made her mark in track and field, like a maverick can:

A decade after her shattering achievements in track and field, Griffith Joyner's sprint records still stand, and many feel they will carry into the next century. Known by the abbreviation "FloJo"—even her name was fast—she set the world record for 100 meters at 10.49 seconds at the 1988 Olympic trials in Indianapolis, then established the mark of 21.34 seconds in winning the 200 meters at the 1988 Summer Games in Seoul, South Korea, where Griffith Joyner also won gold in the 100 meters and the 4x100-meter relay. She also took a silver medal in the 4x400-meter relay. Not only did Griffith Joyner run considerably faster than any woman before her or since, she displayed a spectacular flashiness in the way she ran, dressing in one-legged spandex bodysuits and wearing six-inch-long, elaborately decorated fingernails. After retiring in 1989, she designed the uniforms of the Indiana Pacers of the National Basketball Association. And she also served as co-chair of the President's Council on Physical Fitness.

Saturn in Aquarius on the IC

Saturn is again in its rulership in Aquarius. Here at the bottom of the chart, the open-minded idealist has to resolve his or her personal humanity. There can be a "Do as I say, not as I do" approach to the world.

Television evangelist, Jerry Falwell, who has a fixed T-Square with his Leo Sun conjunct the MC and both points squaring his Taurus Moon on the DS, shows the conservative side of the Aquarian archetype. Saturn at the bottom of the chart, especially in its rulership, shows a very strong-willed individual. When in fixed signs, there is likely an over-adherence to rules and a focus on building structures. Aquarius has an insatiable mind as reflected in this article from the *Los Angeles Times*:

> Falwell, 54, has said repeatedly that by early next century he wants his 7,500-student Liberty University

to be a 50,000-student fundamentalist equivalent to the Catholic-run Notre Dame University and the Mormon-run Brigham Young University. "Jerry wants to leave this as his legacy," said University of Virginia sociologist Jeffrey Hadden, who has chronicled the fortunes of television evangelists.

French fashion designer, Christian Dior, who has Mars in Scorpio on the Ascendant squaring this point, shows a level of luxury and opulence one would not expect from Saturn in any placement. The following comes from TheFamousPeople.com:

> The brand Christian Dior personifies elegance, innovation and ingenuity. A leader in the world of haute-couture, the House of Dior is one of the biggest names in the world of fashion and much credit for everything that the brand reckons with goes to its founder, the legendary fashionista and fashion designer—Christian Dior. The man who envisioned it all, Christian Dior was a great dictator of style and fashion. His ensembles proudly affirm the glory of his artistic vision and his love for fashion. Dior came up with his iconic fashion house at a time when the world was still reeling under the challenges of the World War II. His 'New Look' celebrated ultra-femininity and opulence. He reintroduced the concept of luxury into women's fashion and focused on elegance, structure and grandeur. Dior's infinitely feminine collection, though criticized earlier, became the talk of the town in no time. Though he designed under his own name for only

a decade, his influence continues to reign and shall be felt for many more decades to come.

American film star, Cary Grant, who also has his Sun here, has this beautiful quote from AZQuotes.com:

> "Probably no greater honor can come to any man than the respect of his colleagues."

Talk show host, Craig Ferguson who also has his Mars and DS in Aries, obviously would march to the sound of his own drum, as clearly stated in this excerpt from TheDailyBeast.com:

> [Ferguson]… who has made a career out of unexpected candor, authenticity, and a punk rock mandate to do the kind of comedy that he wants to do, traditions and decorum be damned.

Saturn in Pisces on the IC

This is the place of sandcastles on the beach, the impermanence of permanence is put to the test in this special place at the bottom of the chart. I have Saturn in Pisces in my fourth house, but it isn't conjunct my IC.

What better way to start looking at the archetypes than with architect, Philip Johnson? From TheNation.com comes this powerful articulation of this astrological placement:

In Johnson's life, we can see this distinct shift in architecture mirrored in his own move away from cultural institutions and their patrons toward working directly with the corporations themselves. With the help of his business partner John Burgee, Johnson made the leap from designing museums and private houses to designing skyscrapers and corporate headquarters in cities throughout the land. The changing style of Johnson's work at the time reveals his keen understanding of the shift in corporate taste: His earlier such work (and arguably his best), the late-modernist IDS Tower in Minneapolis and the Pennzoil Place complex in Houston, morphs in the mid-'70s and early '80s into the campy (but admittedly lovable) postmodern AT&T Building in New York and the glass turrets of the Pittsburgh Power and Gas Tower—literally a corporate castle built for the rule of a new, neoliberal generation of the business elite.

Saturn is the planet of Corporations and can easily morph when in a mutable sign like Pisces.

French writer, Simone de Beauvoir, has these illustrative quotes that really delve into the archetypes of Saturn, Pisces and the IC, and include the paradox of being alone yet connected to all, through love:

"One's life has value so long as one attributes value to the life of others, by means of love, friendship, indignation and compassion."

"The point is not for women simply to take power out of men's hands, since that wouldn't change anything about the world. It's a question precisely of destroying that notion of power."

"I am too intelligent, too demanding, and too resourceful for anyone to be able to take charge of me entirely. No one knows me or loves me completely. I have only myself."

"To be free is not to have the power to do anything you like; it is to be able to surpass the given toward an open future." *[This is a perfect maverick transcendent quote!]*

"Authentic love must be founded on reciprocal recognition of two freedoms. For each of them, love would be the revelation of the self through the gift of the self and the enrichment of the universe."

Here's a bit about historian, James Thomas Flexner:

He wrote a four-volume biography of Washington, winning both the National Book Award and a special Pulitzer citation for the final volume, *Anguish and Farewell* (Little, Brown, 1972). He then wrote a one-volume abridgment, *Washington: the Indispensable Man* (Little, Brown, 1974). Two television mini-series adapted from these works were broadcast in the mid-1980's. Mr. Flexner wrote a total of 26 books, all still in print. His first, *Doctors on Horseback: Pioneers of*

American Medicine (Viking, 1937), included a portrait of his father, a pathologist who developed a cure for spinal meningitis. One of the last was a collection of poems he wrote in the 1920's.

Saturn at the IC says something about fathering, so we can see why Flexner did such a faithful rendition of one of the founding fathers of America. Pisces has the gift of seeing the humanity in everyone.

Interestingly enough, to further the horse theme, we have two jockeys next on the list: Jean DeForge and Gerald Mosse. Remember, Pisces is ruled by Neptune, and the Roman Neptune is another name for the Greek God, Poseidon, who is also God of horses. One needs a "good seat" in jockeying, which Saturn in Pisces on the IC would definitely help develop.

We will now look at the angle placements of Saturn throughout the zodiac from the point of view of the Descendant (DS)

Saturn in Aries on the DS

These individuals can be instinctual strategists. The "buck stops here" because these staunch individuals set the boundaries, rules, and terms of engagement.

Saturn has a building quality we see this in the following excerpt from Labyrinthina.com about ufologist and contactee, George van Tassel:

In his many hundred radio and TV appearances, George Van Tassel compared the Integratron to the Tabernacle of Moses. He claimed that he was instructed by a higher intelligence to build a 21st century version of the Tabernacle that Moses constructed, using the same positive power principle of the Great Pyramid of Giza, and was given the name The Integratron. He was told it would revitalize and rejuvenate the physical bodies of humankind. George Van Tassel openly shared much of the technology with his supporters and followers, but those close to him say he kept much of it secret, sharing it only with his closest, trusted colleagues.

George is an interesting character. I would highly recommend reading more about this maverick.

In his character on the television medical drama *Nip/Tuck*, Julian McMahon portrays a rather vain plastic surgeon—something this astrological placement can certainly intensify! This placement can be about judging others for their appearance, or lack of social status as portrayed in our next example.

Lara Rafter, has a taste for the good life, but her headstrong ways may have cost her and her husband some money when they sold their beachfront property at a loss.

The opening sentences in this article from Chron.com illustrates this astrological placement for actress, Jennifer Aniston:

Best known for her iconic role on *Friends*, Jennifer Aniston is recognized as a leading actress and a timeless beauty. After more than two decades of work in film and television, she still manages to stay busy in the industry.

Saturn here gives Jennifer a grounded presence that attracts others. She doesn't appear to age like the rest of us. Timeless beauty is definitely in the realm of Saturn in Aries, especially on the DS.

Saturn in Taurus on the DS

These individuals can dig in their heels and exude an earthly grace.

Eva Braun, who has her Aquarian Sun conjunct her IC squaring this point, shows the confined and fixed quality of her relationship:

> Hitler's servant for many years, Heinz Linge, later recalled:
> "Hitler and Eva occasionally stayed on alone in his study talking for a short while before retiring. On those occasions Eva, generally wearing only a dressing gown, would have some wine and Hitler a cup of tea ... For those of us who knew of Hitler's relationship with Eva from personal observation the motto was: see nothing, hear nothing, say nothing."

Barbara Birdfeather, who makes our list a third time for her Venus and Jupiter planets squaring this point in her chart creating a T-square, had this excerpt in Alumni.Berkeley.edu:

> "Here's how bad it got. The first morning of my first stay in New York, I was hustled down to a press showing of men's fur coats. It was 1971, and outrageous flamboyance in dress was the coming thing. I was the principal writer for (and later coeditor of) a counterculture fashion magazine called *Rags*. I knew nothing about fashion."

Saturn gives us the determination needed to *fake it until we make it*, especially in material oriented and sometime fashion-conscious Taurus. Sometimes just showing up is all it takes.

Actor and comedian, Michael Crawford, has this quote from BrainyQuote.com:

> "Divorce is never a pleasant experience. You look upon it as a failure. But I learned to be a different person once we broke up. Sometimes you learn more from failure than you do from success."

Saturn teaches us the correct lessons. When it is on the DS it will be about our relationships with others.

In her obituary from CBSNews.com, comes this eloquent statement for the "Queen of Soul" Aretha Franklin:

> "Through her compositions and unmatched musicianship, Aretha helped define the American

experience," the Obamas said. "In her voice, we could feel our history, all of it and in every shade, our power and our pain, our darkness and our light, our quest for redemption and our hard-won respect. She helped us feel more connected to each other, more hopeful, more human. And sometimes she helped us just forget about everything else and dance."

Graceful movement and great physical control are necessary to become a star ice skater and Rudy Galindo took it a step further: his Saturn in Taurus gave Rudy the strength to come out as the first openly gay U.S. National Champion.

Saturn in Gemini on the DS

These people are cataloguers of facts and information. This is a great placement for a grammarian or other structured way of looking at word, thought and idea. Their minds are ever considering and active. This is a tricky place as these people need to interact, but can create their own prison of separation from the other.

I had not previously considered the holding and releasing of secrets that Saturn in Gemini would express, but this is obviously played out in the life of Julian Assange, who makes our list a second time as he has Mars in Aquarius on his IC squares this astrological placement. Assange founded WikiLeaks, an anti-secret group. The combination of Gemini and Aquarius Saturn/Mars square is all well illustrated in the process of dealing with power, secrets, establishment, and the belief that people deserve to know the truth.

Philosopher, Alan Watts, demonstrates this astrological placement. From Wikipedia.com comes a telling description of his work: his "writings and recorded talks still shimmer with a profound and galvanizing lucidity." Beautifully stated!

Michael, Prince of Kent also has Venus conjunct this spot. From TownandCountryMag.com comes this telling Geminian *tour de force*:

> Other than the occasional royal appearance, Prince Michael had a long military career. According to his biography on the royal family's website, Prince Michael served in Germany, Hong Kong, and Cypress, and now owns a consultancy business. Additionally, he is involved in about 100 charities and organizations, and is a qualified Russian interpreter.

The "Capturing of Other" in art is well illustrated in this excerpt from Rivisions.co.za for South African artist, Gerard Sekoto:

> In his portrait of his mother and stepfather, he obviously felt at ease in depicting people that he knew and loved. Both parents are rendered in casual, yet dignified poses. The figure of his mother, with whom we are familiar from other portraits, is rendered with both affection and empathy. The depiction of his stepfather, caught in a moment while drinking his tea, is rendered with equal sympathy. Everything in the painting speaks of

simple domesticity. Evident also is Sekoto's assured handling of his medium and his mastery of tone, colour and composition. This work reveals Sekoto at the very height of his expertise. Completed just before the artist's imminent departure for Paris, this is an image of domestic contentment—a contentment that Sekoto himself was not to enjoy for many years after his arrival in the French capital in 1947.

An article about writer, Alice Walker, from ThoughtCo.com, captures the nuances this astrological placement can give:

> In 1989 and 1992, in two books, The Temple of My Familiar and Possessing the Secret of Joy, Walker took on the issue of female circumcision in Africa, which brought further controversy: was Walker a cultural imperialist to criticize a different culture? Her works are known for their portrayals of the African American woman's life. She depicts vividly the sexism, racism, and poverty that make that life often a struggle. But she also portrays as part of that life, the strengths of family, community, self-worth, and spirituality. Many of her novels depict women in other periods of history than our own. Just as with non-fiction women's history writing, such portrayals give a sense of the differences and similarities of women's condition today and in that other time.
>
> Alice Walker continues not only to write but to be active in environmental, feminist/womanist causes, and issues of economic justice.

This astrological placement of Saturn in Gemini on the DS is wonderful for a writer to share her observations.

Saturn in Cancer on the DS

Saturn is considered in its detriment when in Cancer. Saturn, the ruler of Capricorn, is not a favored guest in Cancer's house. Cancer doesn't like the rules and the limits, the structure and the work that Saturn requires.

From SouthernLiving.com comes this revealing story about Elvis Presley's former wife, Priscilla Presley

> "Moving into Graceland, he already had his inner circle," said Priscilla. "Of course they embraced me, but I never realized that that was it. We didn't go out. He didn't like eating in restaurants because people would take pictures of him and he didn't want to be shot—putting a fork in his mouth." And, "To maintain some sort of "mystique" in the relationship, Priscilla wouldn't allow Elvis to see her without makeup or without being fully dressed." "There are things you keep to yourself," Priscilla added. "He never wanted to see me getting dressed. He wanted to see the result of getting dressed." In spite of her efforts to keep things normal and private, the constant scrutiny and living in the proverbial fishbowl caused their marriage to crumble. Priscilla explained that she lost herself in the process, where she often found herself conforming to only the music and movies Elvis enjoyed and living "his life."

SATURN

Saturn doesn't have an easy time in the water signs.

Actor and comedian, Jack Paar, who has his Jupiter in Taurus widely squaring this spot, has these two sassy quotes from BrainyQuote.com:

> "Looking back, my life seems like one long obstacle race, with me as the chief obstacle."

> "I have never seen a bad television program, because I refuse to. God gave me a mind, and a wrist that turns things off."

Yehudi Menuhin, the American-born violinist and conductor, shows another interesting maverick mark. The name Yehudi means "Jew" in Hebrew. In an interview republished in October 2004, he recounted to *New Internationalist* magazine the story of his name:

> Obliged to find an apartment of their own, my parents searched the neighborhood and chose one within walking distance of the park. Showing them out after they had viewed it, the landlady said: "And you'll be glad to know I don't take Jews." Her mistake made clear to her, the anti-Semitic landlady was renounced, and another apartment found. But her blunder left its mark. Back on the street my mother made a vow. Her unborn baby would have a label proclaiming his race to the world. He would be called "The Jew."

This is definitely a family lineage piece. Menuhin's family also supported his interest to become a violinist.

Glenys Elizabeth Kinnock, Baroness Kinnock of Holyhead, FRSA, is a British politician and former primary and secondary school teacher. She was a Labour Party Member of the European Parliament from 1994 to 2009. These are all professions that need a good understanding of boundaries and structures which fall under the purview of Saturn and taking care of family, clan and country.

Director and writer, Jim Sharman, shows us the other side of quirky families directing both stage and film versions of the *Rocky Horror Picture Show*. To share just a teaser of what this man has done, look at this excerpt from Wikipedia.com:

> Sharman created a series of ground-breaking productions of experimental theater, many for the Old Tote Theatre Company, culminating in a controversial staging of Mozart's *Don Giovanni* for Opera Australia, when he was 21 years old.

And they say this astrological placement is a detriment?

Saturn in Leo on the DS

Saturn is in detriment when found in Leo. Expansive attention seeking fiery Leo doesn't want to have rules, boundaries, or others telling them what they can and cannot do. We will see successful use of this powerful ego strengthening and defining place in our following examples.

David Bowie makes our list a third time for his Moon conjunct and Venus squaring this position. With this configuration, we can understand the numerous marriages and sexual flings along the spectrum of experience. Bowie's last marriage with Iman lasted 24 years. Saturn pays off when you do the work. With Saturn and Moon squaring his explorative Sagittarian Venus, we can see that Bowie was working on healing the feminine within himself and in his relationships to the other.

Ely Jacques Kahn, was an American commercial architect. This is a perfect edification when you consider that Saturn seeks to create a structure and Leo wants to be seen by other. An architect creates physical ego structures!

Actress, Alicia Silverstone, has some comments that draw attention to other aspect of this astrological placement. This first one shows how hard one can be on one's self:

"My boyfriend calls me 'princess', but I think of myself more along the lines of 'monkey' and 'retard'."

This next one speaks to grounding herself in relationships:

"From 19 to 28 there was a lot of turmoil in my life, but in a stuck way. Then, around 28, my life started to get shaken up. I realized I wanted to grow more and that anything that wasn't working in my life, I could fix it. I feel like I came into my womanhood. And that was when I got married."

This period of time is the last quarter square and Saturn return, is a time of considerable crises in consciousness until one steps into the place of authenticity and self-responsibility.

Finally, this quote from Silverstone addresses the adaptive nature of Saturn's toughness when in creative Leo:

> "I don't want to be known as the Aerosmith chick, but it's fun to put on the boots and makeup and act like a tough girl."

Saturn in Virgo on the DS

While this can be a persnickety place for Saturn, it is also very fruitful for one willing to do the work. Virgo likes to heal and to improve.

Dr. Phil McGraw, also known as, Dr. Phil, had this written about him in an article from RecordNet.com:

> McGraw, who has been married to his second wife since 1976, has admitted that as a young man, his entrepreneurial efforts in everything from health clubs to motivational seminars often came at the expense of his second family.

The following comes from a great article on martial arts pioneer, James Yimm Lee found at ChineseMartialStudies.com:

The immediate answer is James Lee. An Oakland native who was well-known for his younger exploits as a street fighter, James was already enacting the sort of martial arts future that Bruce [Lee] was envisioning. He was publishing books, creating his own custom martial arts equipment, and conducting a modern training environment at his school. James was also putting a nuanced emphasis on body building, and perhaps most importantly, transforming his street experience into a gritty and realistic understanding of the true nature of fighting. Furthermore, James Lee had a unique network of experienced martial arts innovators within his orbit: Wally Jay, Ralph Castro, Al Novak, Leo Fong, and Ed Parker. As James Lee's son Greglon characterized the appeal of this: "Bruce was smart. When he's in his twenties he's hanging out with guys in their forties, so he can gain their experience."

Australian politician, Kim Christian Beazley, exemplifies the hard working, public service oriented aspect of this astrological placement. The following comes from his entry at Wikipedia:

[Beazley]... Governor of Western Australia and former Deputy Prime Minister of Australia and Leader of the Opposition. He was also a minister in the Hawke and Keating Governments. Beazley later served as Ambassador to the United States from 2010 to 2016.

Saturn in Libra on the DS

Saturn is in its exaltation in Libra, as we have already discussed. The judicious way in which Saturn and Libra both approach life makes this a very complimentary pairing.

Libra is a dual sign as it represents the polarity of self and other, so it is no surprise that we would have a "double agent" working for the British and USSR, George Blake. I highly recommend reading this fascinating interview with George at: www.pbs.org/redfiles/kgb/deep/interv/k_int_george_blake.htm

The article beautifully illustrates this astrological placement, and how George worked with those dualistic polarizing energies in his life, and how he affected others in the process.

Willam Belli, who has passionate Mars conjunct cool and calculating Saturn, had these quotes from that show his work ethic:

> "I always perform live. I've even received a cortisone injection when I was losing my voice before a big gig so I could fulfill my obligation to the promoter. I felt it the days following after the gig in my throat, but it was nice to know I didn't let anyone down. The show must go on."

Saturn in Scorpio on the DS

This astrological placement gives one a sort of steely fortitude that everyone would experience. There is the energetic warning, "Don't mess with me."

SATURN

Donatella Versace, who has her Sun in Taurus opposite this point, helped build a fashion empire with her brother Gianni. These characteristics are well expressed in the following excerpt from HarpersBazaar.com:

> Before Gianni's death, Donatella was known as his inspiration Gianni and "muse" for his various lines, according to biography. She was even the main inspiration for one of Versace's perfumes, Blonde. Gianni valued her critiques of his designs, though he preferred a more baroque style to Donatella's minimalism. "Donatella was a very powerful critic," one of Gianni's friends, Guisi Ferre, told *Newsweek*. "And Gianni would yell, 'Donatella, you want to kill my spirit? My success?'" When the company was established in 1978, Donatella became Gianni's advisor and took on the role of vice president. She began designing in the early 1980s.

Journalist, Maria Shriver, makes the following illustrative quotes, taken from AZQuotes.com. This first one shows the importance of boundaries:

> "Make time in your life to listen to your own voice. Do not let it get drowned out by others. Your voice is yours and yours alone. Stay in touch with it and use it."

And this one, illustrating those lessons we learn over time and that call forth something deeper in us:

"Someone once told me not to be afraid of being afraid, because, as she said, 'Anxiety is a glimpse of your own daring.' "Isn't that great? It means that part of your agitation is just excitement about what you're getting ready to accomplish. Don't sell yourself short by being so afraid of failure that you don't dare to make any mistakes. Make your mistakes and learn from them. And remember: No matter how many mistakes you make, your mother always loves you!"

Saturn in Sagittarius on the DS

This is an interesting position for sobering, rule oriented Saturn in ebullient Sagittarius. As this is on the descendent, they can provide a grounding force for a Sagittarian partner. Saturn and Sagittarius are interesting in that they both have a way of taking you to places you didn't expect. Saturn is all about work, and when in the higher philosophy and experience seeking Sagittarius, we can see a clear devotion to the Divine.

Our first example is one of the early punk singers, Darby Crash, of the band Germs. I could almost liken this position to the old saying, "If you want to make God laugh, tell Her/Him your plans," or listen to Alanis Morrissette's song, "Ironic." From DyingScene.com, comes a list of 10 things about Darby's life. I personally think number 10 covers it best:

When he was 17 Darby planned to make himself immortal by following a five year plan. That plan was to form a band with his friends, spend a couple of years making it a cultish, outrageous live act, release one great album and then commit suicide to secure his legend. His only misstep was that John Lennon was shot one day after he died, completely overshadowing Darby's own tragic demise.

Indian playback singer, Lata Mangeshkar makes two lovely and illustrative statements in the following interview she gave to Quora.com (the questions she was asked are in bold):

In hindsight, what has been the one most enriching and regretting factor in your life respectively? I am most happy and at ease when I sing. As for regrets, I have none, because whatever God gives it's meant for you and whatever you miss was never for you. I am only thankful to God.

Lastly Lataji, like every girl who grows up with dreams of marriage, do you miss being married? No. Everything happens according to God's wish. Jo hote hai acche ke liye hote hai aur jo nahin hote who aur acche ke liye hote hai. Had you asked me this about four to five decades back, perhaps you would have got a different answer. But today I have no room for such thoughts.

Albert II, Prince of Monaco, exhibits another aspect of this astrological placement, being late to marry due to his gregarious nature. The following comes from CBSNews.com:

Prince Albert II of Monaco... made headlines as a long-time bachelor with his affairs and out of wedlock children. He publicly acknowledged in 2005 having an illegitimate son with a former flight attendant from Togo. In 2006, he also admitted to fathering a daughter, born in 1992, out of wedlock. Days before his July 2011 wedding, rumors arose that the bride-to-be was stopped from fleeing home to South Africa because yet another illegitimate child had come to light. The palace vehemently denied there was any truth to the speculation.

Saturn in Capricorn on the DS

These are the bosses of their relationships (and likely to believe of everyone else!) because Saturn rules Capricorn.

Our first individual is a perfect example of this. Ross Perot makes our list a third time for his Cancer Moon and Sun on his AS opposite this point. The following quote by Perot, comes from AZQuotes.com:

> "Something in human nature causes us to start slacking off at our moment of greatest accomplishment. As you become successful, you will need a great deal of self-discipline not to lose your sense of balance, humility and commitment."

From his obituary from Archive.NYTimes.com comes this articulate summarization of Hollywood movie producer, David O. Selznick, which begins with a nod to Mercury:

> Mercurial, shrewd, self-confident and enormously gifted, David O. Selznick climbed to the pinnacle of power and success in Hollywood with films that are now classics and actors who are considered screen immortals.
>
> His films included *Intermezzo, Rebecca, David Copperfield, Little Women, The Prisoner of Zenda, Dinner at Eight, A Star Is Born, Duel in the Sun,* and the epic, *Gone With the Wind.*
>
> He was instrumental in spurring the careers of such actors as Clark Gable, Vivien Leigh, Ingrid Bergman, Joseph Cotten, Gregory Peck, Katharine Hepburn, Joan Fontaine, Fred Astaire, Leslie Howard, Myrna Loy and his wife, Miss Jones.
>
> Mr. Selznick, a 6-foot 1-inch 200-pounder, moved quickly, spoke rapidly and worked tirelessly. He produced quality films with three trademarks: top stars, the finest writers, and no expense spared.
>
> Even in the twilight of his career, he remained wide-eyed and even brash, although a trace of pessimism and melancholy became apparent in recent years.
>
> "Nothing in Hollywood is permanent," Mr. Selznick said in 1959 on a Hollywood set, as Tara, the mansion built for *Gone with the Wind,* was being dismembered and shipped to Atlanta, Georgia. "Once photographed, life here is ended. It is almost symbolic of Hollywood.

Tara has no rooms inside. It was just a facade. So much of Hollywood is a facade."

Mr. Selznick spoke in quick, staccato sentences. While working on a film, he virtually exhausted himself, laboring round-the-clock, seeking perfection to the minutest detail and stubbornly insisting on his own ideas.

Saturn would account for the realistic view on life—especially with such a driven character!

Journalist, Denny Boyd, used his writings as a way to relate to others. The following is an excerpt from his obituary:

"I think he lived through his columns," said McDonald. "I think he's one of those guys who expressed himself through his columns. That's how he communicates. I think people are sometimes disappointed in him because they expect this witty, learned man to come out, but he doesn't. He largely stays within himself then goes home and writes a smashing column about it."

I Dream of Jeanie actress, Barbara Eden made the following lovely statement about her career success when interviewed by FoxNews.com in 2017 when she was 86 years old:

Fox News: What's keeping you motivated these days?

Eden: I just like my work. I think I'm very, very lucky to have found a profession that I fit in. So many people have to make their living doing things they don't really enjoy, but are necessary for their family. I'm just lucky, very lucky.

Saturn in Aquarius on the DS

As we know, Saturn is the ruler of Aquarius as well. This is a bittersweet outsider placement. The reclusive Aquarian nature seeks something foreign and different.

English novelist, Evelyn Waugh, has his Moon here and both are squaring his Mercury in Libra on the IC. These are great placements for a writer. The air signs have an inherent operating system which aids in their ability to be observational in a more or less neutral manner. This gives one a great ability to experience life while it is being lived, and to also observe it in a way that makes the experiences more intellectually sensible.

The opening paragraph from an article from NewYorker.com about French novelist, Marguerite Yourcenar, reveals many interesting aspects of this astrological placement:

> Becoming the Emperor: How Marguerite Yourcenar reinvented the past.
>
> In 1981, six years before her death, Marguerite Yourcenar became the first woman ever inducted into the Académie Française, and that weighty honor has been hanging around the neck of her reputation ever since. Every book jacket, every review, speaks of it. But that wasn't all that set her apart from other mid-

century writers. She was an extremely isolated artist. A Frenchwoman, she spent most of her adult life in the United States, on Mount Desert Island, off the coast of Maine, where, to isolate her further, she lived with a woman. Her background, too, made her seem different. She came from the minor nobility and didn't hide it. Most of the people who knew her, even friends, addressed her not as Marguerite but as Madame. Add to that the fact that she wrote not in English but in her native French, and in a style that was often magisterial, in an old-fashioned, classical way. (People compared her to Racine. This was at a time when we were getting Bellow and Roth.) Add, moreover, that though she was a novelist, she was not primarily a realist, that she never mastered dialogue, that her books were ruminative, philosophical. Add, finally, that her greatest novel, *Memoirs of Hadrian* (1951)—which Farrar, Straus & Giroux will reissue this spring as part of its new FSG Classics series—was a fictionalized autobiography of a Roman emperor.

Who better to rewrite the past that one with a strong Aquarian signature?

When Saturn is in an air sign, it gets a lot of intellectual work done, as shown by our next example, journalist and writer, MacKinlay Kantor. The following comes from Wikipedia.com:

MacKinlay Kantor, born Benjamin McKinlay Kantor, was an American journalist, novelist and screenwriter.

He wrote more than 30 novels, several set during the American Civil War, and was awarded the Pulitzer Prize for Fiction in 1956 for his 1955 novel, *Andersonville*. He also wrote the novel *Gettysburg*, set during the Civil War.

We have had writers and novelists, now we have musicians with this astrological placement.

Jazz musician, John Handy, who has his Sun and Mercury here as well, has this perfect Saturn in Aquarius statement on his website, JohnHandy.com:

> As a performer and composer he continues to sweep audiences into ecstasy with his vast range of creative, emotional, and technical inventiveness. With a superb knowledge and practical experience with music of several cultures, he fuses, with each selection, a musical genre that is coherent, provocative, logical, and enjoyable.

Willie Nelson, who has his Sun Venus conjunction in Taurus on his MC squaring this Saturn, has a finger on the pulse on humanity. Willie's quote from BrainyQuote.com illustrates this point:

> "A lot of country music is sad. I think most art comes out of poverty and hard times. It applies to music. Three chords and the truth – that's what a country song is. There is a lot of heartache in the world."

Willie makes a further Saturnian statement:

> "We create our own unhappiness. The purpose of suffering is to help us understand we are the ones who cause it."

From BBC.com comes this Saturnian task-master way, singer and dancer, James Brown, used this astrological placement on his band members:

> The price for James Brown's meticulousness came at a financial cost to everyone but him. If you watch a live performance of his, you may spot him turning around and pointing at one of his band members. This often wasn't a friendly gesture, but a punishment. Each time his employees would miss a beat, mess their parts up, or even turn up with unpolished shoes, Brown would dock their pay and let them know with a point. However many fingers he held up equates to the amount of money being docked.

Saturn in Pisces on the DS

While Saturn is neither in detriment nor fall when found here, it isn't an easy place because free-wheeling, go-with-the-flow Pisces feels a Saturnian hook holding it back. Building sand castles on the beach is another example of this placement as well as issues with drugs, alcoholism and escapism. Of course, music and imagery all fall into this realm as we will see by the musicians and actors/directors we find in this list. This would be a place where individuals might want to "ground" in their relationships to others.

Entertainer and dancer, Josephine Baker, has her Sun and Mercury conjunct her MC in Gemini (as well as Mars, Jupiter and Pluto in Gemini!) squaring her Saturn in Pisces. She suffered a lot from racism. From MedicalBag.com, comes this revealing piece about the depth of her friendships:

> In 1951, while in New York, Baker charged the Stork Club with racism, alleging that she had been refused service. The actress Grace Kelly was present. She ran over to Baker, and took her and her entire party out of the club, stating that she'd never come back; she kept her word. Grace and Baker became good friends from then on. When Josephine was near bankruptcy, Grace, then a princess, offered her a villa and financial assistance.

Photographer, Dora Maar, who makes our list a third time, has a challenging T-square involving this point. Additionally, both her Moon in Gemini on her MC, and Venus conjunct her Sagittarius IC, square her Saturn. One can see this is not emotionally supporting which makes this piece from NYTimes.com so enlightening:

> But after Picasso ended their relationship, replacing her with Francoise Gilot as a lover and muse, she suffered frequent bouts of depression and opted increasingly for a life of reclusion, living in the shadow of the image

Picasso had created for her. "I could never see her, never imagine her, except crying."

Saturn is the planet of boundaries and Pisces is not the sign of boundaries as modeled by actor and director, Woody Allen, and his marriage to his step daughter. A significant age difference in relationship is clearly indicated when we find Saturn in the seventh house.

Singer and songwriter, Roy Orbison, who has Jupiter in Sagittarius squaring this position, went for depth in his art as well stated in this excerpt from Wikipedia.com:

> Roy Kelton Orbison was an American singer, songwriter, and musician known for his powerful voice, wide vocal range, impassioned singing style, complex song structures, and dark, emotional ballads. The combination led many critics to describe his music as operatic, nicknaming him "the Caruso of Rock" and "The Big O." While most male rock-and-roll performers in the 1950s and 1960s projected a defiant masculinity, many of Orbison's songs instead conveyed vulnerability. During performances, he was known for standing still and solitary and for wearing black clothes to match his dyed jet-black hair and dark sunglasses; all of this lent an air of mystery to his persona.

Saturn in Pisces can definitely give one a "soulful" temperament. Another theme of Saturn in Pisces is further illustrated by Roy's blindness.

We now turn to the final set of chart's angles for this book. Saturn on the MC is meant to command, rule, and make statements about structures and how they might be best followed. Saturn on the MC garners authority as evidenced by England's Queen Elizabeth II, Diva Bernadette Peters, Miss America Jacque Mercer, or queen Christian Bérard.

We will now look at the angle placements of Saturn throughout the zodiac from the point of view of the Medium Coeli (MC)

Saturn in Aries on the MC

Saturn is in its fall here because Aries is instinctual and acts in the moment, while Saturn is patient and waits for the right time. The energy here is go/stop or instinctual structuring.

Our first example is an interesting illustration of such energies. Liam Blood was born over two years after his father's death. In an interesting twist on the ancient Saturn myth, Liam's mother had to go to court for the right to be inseminated by her dead husband's frozen sperm.

French financier, Arpad Busson, is a maverick philanthropist. The following comes from BrainyQuote.com:

> "Historically, over the last two or three hundred years, the relationship that we've had with money as a society – having money, talking about money – has been a

little bit of a shameful thing. Splashing money about is clearly wrong, but there's nothing wrong about giving it back."

And this one by Busson, is almost Zen in its simplicity of illustrating this astrological position:

"With wealth, one is in a position of responsibility. You must try to help others. It is as simple as that."

Lisa Andersen, who also has her Venus here, is a prime Saturnian example that shows you earn your rewards when you do the work. The following comes from Wikipedia.com:

Lisa Andersen is a four-time world surfing champion from the United States. She won four successive world titles from 1994 to 1997. She was named ASP's Rookie of the Year in 1987. She was named as one of the 100 "Greatest Sportswomen of the Century" by *Sports Illustrated for Women*. She was named the "1998 Female Athlete of the Year" by *Conde Nast Sports for Women* magazine. She is a six-time winner of *Surfer* Magazine's Readers Poll. In 2002, she was inducted into the Surfer's Hall of Fame. In 2004, she was inducted into the Surfing Walk of Fame as that year's Woman of the Year.

So much for Saturn being in its fall in Aries!

Saturn in Taurus on the MC

When heavy Saturn and fixed Taurus get together, you can get a rather careful and especially recalcitrant individual. Taurus is about our relationship to people and the material world.

Australian writer, Patrick White, who has his ruling Venus here as well, shows an interesting expression of this combination. He had a 49-year relationship with Manoly Lascaris.

British politician, Paddy Ashdown, who has ruling Venus squaring this point on his DS in Aquarius, elicits another expression as stated in an article from BBC.com:

> His career, and his marriage, also survived press revelations of an affair with his secretary.

Venus in Aquarius would need some freedom, and its ruler Saturn is here in loyal Taurus. Paddy was married to his wife for 56 years.

Earl Thomas Conley has the key words for this astrological position as seen in the title of an article about him from AXS.com: "Hard work and perseverance made Earl Thomas Conley a country music star."

Professional boxer and celebrity, Muhammad Ali, who has Moon in Aquarius on his DS, Saturn rules his Moon, was a very solid and deliberate man who was known for delivering a solid punch. The supportive nature of this square is well described in the following from Biography.com:

Muhammad Ali (born Cassius Clay) was a boxer, philanthropist and social activist who is universally regarded as one of the greatest athletes of the 20th century. Ali became an Olympic gold medalist in 1960 and the world heavyweight boxing champion in 1964. Following his suspension for refusing military service, Ali reclaimed the heavyweight title two more times during the 1970s, winning famed bouts against Joe Frazier and George Foreman along the way. Diagnosed with Parkinson's disease in 1984, Ali devoted much of his time to philanthropy, earning the Presidential Medal of Freedom in 2005.

Usually a Saturn/Moon square is experienced as a sense of lack of nurturing from one's mother, but I could find no such evidence, in fact, I found this lovely piece from Wikipedia.com on Ali:

Through her strong Christian belief, Clay [Ali's mom] had a great influence on the life and spiritual upbringing of both of her sons. Muhammad Ali later said, "My mother is a Baptist, and when I was growing up, she taught me all she knew about God. Every Sunday, she dressed me up, took me and my brother to church, and taught us the way she thought was right. She taught us to love people and treat everybody with kindness. She taught us it was wrong to be prejudiced or hate. I've changed my religion and some of my beliefs since then, but her God is still God; I just call him by a different name. And my mother, I'll tell you what I've told people for a long time. She's a sweet, fat, wonderful woman, who loves to cook, eat, make clothes, and be with family. She doesn't drink, smoke, meddle in other people's business, or bother anyone, and there's no one who's been better to me my whole life."

Clay supported and inspired her son throughout his boxing career. At small gyms early in her son's career and later at international arenas when he became world-famous, Clay traveled with her son and was a ring-side regular at his bouts. Muhammad Ali was much closer to his mother, whom he lovingly called "Bird", than to his father. After discovering boxing, it was his mother with whom he shared his dreams of greatness.

Saturn in Gemini on the MC

This can be a subdued placement that gives Gemini guidance and limits. Our first example is a good analogy of this position. Gemini is an air sign and Saturn creates structure. A musical composer is someone who pulls the notes out of the air and gives it the structure necessary to make it appealing to others.

American composer John Cage's maverick impact is revealed in his NYTimes.com obituary:

"In the music world, of course, Mr. Cage's influence was extremely far-reaching. He started a revolution by proposing that composers could jettison the musical language that had evolved over the last seven centuries, and in doing so he opened the door to Minimalism, performance art and virtually every other branch of the musical avant-garde. Composers as different in style from one another -- and from Mr. Cage -- as Philip Glass, Morton Feldman, Earle Brown and Frederic Rzewski have cited Mr. Cage as a beacon that helped light their own paths.

"Perhaps no one living artist has such a great influence over such a diverse lot of important people," Richard Kostelanetz, a writer who edited several books about Mr. Cage, wrote in a New York Times Magazine article in 1967. "Nowadays, even those critics who disagree with him respect his willingness to pursue his ideas to their 'mad' conclusions, and he was impoverished for too many years for anyone seriously to doubt his integrity."

Noor-un-Nisa Inayat Khan, was an Allied Special Operations Executive agent during the Second World War who was posthumously awarded the George Cross, the highest civilian decoration in the United Kingdom. From InayatiOrder.org comes a very Saturnian description of her double nature Gemini life:

> She was now to be trained as a secret agent. It was classic spy school; she was taught to handle guns, explosives, to break locks, to kill silently in the dark, to find sources, to use dead letter boxes and live letter boxes, to practice sending letters in code, and to improve her Morse code. Noor's code name was Madeleine.

From the tattletale website DailyMail.co.uk comes another take on this astrological position for Australian television presenter, Catriona Rowntree:

> "She hasn't aged one iota since the 90s': Celebrity plastic surgeon reveals the subtle clues that suggest *Getaway* host Catriona Rowntree, 47, "has turned back the clock with Botox."

Saturn can fix things, but that is not easy in mutable Gemini. Catriona has a maverick Grand Cross with shared rulership: Mercury in Leo on the AS is the ruler of her Saturn in Gemini on the MC which is then the ruler of the Mars in Aquarius on her DS the fourth point is Neptune in Sagittarius. Rowntree is one creative and powerful person.

Saturn in Cancer on the MC

While Saturn may be considered to be in detriment when in Cancer, once again we find that did not hinder any of these mavericks.

Luxury sports car designer, Ferruccio Lamborghini, who also had his Jupiter in Aries on the DS squaring this position, had this simple, yet apt quote from QuotesWise.com:

> "I was born in 1916 into a family of modest farmers."

And this quote in which Lamborghini sees himself from this humble Saturn in Cancer position:

"A normal chap, a man who likes creating things. A good worker in the morning, and a man who likes enjoying himself in the afternoon. Because I'm not interested in ending up like my colleagues, with heart problems!"

Jupiter and Saturn are the great accordions in life expressing that which we do in each moment, breathe in and exhale out. When these two planets square one another, there will be an increased focus on these themes, such as acceleration and braking, which Ferruccio had to work out in the process of creating his high performance vehicles.

From People.Well.com comes this excerpt about steel guitarist, Leon McAuliffe, that shows, once again, the effect Saturn has on one's approach to work:

> William Leon McAuliffe was born in Houston, Texas on March 1, 1917. He began playing both Hawaiian and standard guitar at age 14. He began appearing on a local radio station as part of the group the Waikiki Strummers in 1931. Two years later he joined W. Lee O'Daniel's Light Crust Doughboys, with whom he recorded on ARC in Chicago. He learned to electronically amplify his guitar from Houston's Bob Dunn, a member of Milton Brown's Musical Brownies. Fiddler, Jesse Ashlock, invited the 18-year-old McAuliffe to join Bob Wills' Texas Playboys in 1935. He remained with the band for many years, recording many songs, moving to California, and even appearing in several motion pictures.

Former United States President, John F. Kennedy, shows another archetype of this astrological placement. His presidency was known as Camelot, hailing back to legendary King Arthur's court. Jack was easily relatable to the people of the United States and, as president, was the father of the country.

Dennis Nilsen, British serial killer who also has Jupiter conjunct his AS in Libra (just like our next example Karen Silkwood), had a painful upbringing as one could expect from Saturn in Cancer—even on the MC. From Biography.com comes this insight into Dennis's childhood which definitely contributed to his ability to murder at least 15 young men:

> The defense case relied primarily on the testimony of two psychiatrists, Dr. James MacKeith and Dr. Patrick Gallwey. MacKeith described Nilsen's troubled childhood, inability to express feelings, and the resulting separation of mental function from physical behavior, which affected his own sense of identity, and implied an impaired responsibility on the part of Nilsen. Under intense cross-examination by the prosecution, however, MacKeith was forced to retract his judgment about diminished responsibility.

Saturn requires responsibility.

Karen Silkwood, who has Jupiter and the Moon conjunct her Libra AS squaring this point, shows another aspect to this astrological placement: conspiracy. Cancer is the sign of the family and clan, and Saturn is the planet of authority. As we know, the authority states the "truth", but sadly sometimes authority is not truthful and the many must question them and their acts.

Saturn in Leo on the MC

While this is usually considered a detrimental position for Saturn, we know that isn't the case with maverick planets!

The telekinetic and spoon bending, Uri Geller, has this tidbit in JPost.com which reflects the desire one would have to erect a building to one's ego:

> "The Uri Geller Museum will exhibit unique items and gifts that I collected and received over the years from notables, such as Salvador Dali, Pablo Picasso, Albert Einstein and others," Geller said. "It will feature a Cadillac that was covered with around 2,000 spoons that had belonged to famous people, most of which I bent with my mind, and others which I obtained at auction."

Of course, being known for one's ability to bend objects with one's mind would also be a very Saturn in Leo on the MC archetype.

Film director, Oliver Stone, who has Venus on his Scorpio AS, makes this efficient and articulate statement to this astrological position from BrainyQuotes.com:

> "I study history in order to give an interpretation."

Actress and singer, Bernadette Peters, also has Moon in Scorpio conjunct her AS and Mercury in Aquarius conjunct her IC making Saturn an important part of her T-square. The title of an article on Bernadette from CelebrityABC.net aptly calls it, "Five Decades of Hard Work." Another aspect of the Saturnian nature is illustrated by the fact she started performing when she was five. Bernadette has rightfully earned the Diva status.

This is good astrological placement for DJ, singer-songwriter, Samantha Ronson. One piece I was able to find that supported this placement for her was the way she took responsibility when her dog killed another dog. The following comes from icelebz.com:

> Ronson, meanwhile, expressed her condolences on Twitter. She wrote: "there is absolutely nothing I can say that will alter one minute of today, nothing. I feel incredibly sad and wish I could offer more than condolences, unfortunately there are no words to describe how sorry I am."

Try as I might, I was unable to find out much about Noah Domasin, who has Moon and Chiron opposing this point in Aquarius on his IC. The cold side of this configuration is well illustrated as he was born of his mother's frozen egg. Unfortunately, I was able to find neither mention of the father nor what Noah has done with his life.

ASTROLOGICAL MAVERICKS

Saturn in Virgo on the MC

This is a good placement for Saturn in resource oriented and ever-perfecting Virgo. Saturn gives the determination to continue to meet the challenges of whatever lies ahead.

This is beautifully illustrated by our first example American astronaut, John Glenn, who also has Jupiter here and Venus in Gemini on his DS squaring this placement. Saturn can give grace over time. I appreciated the scene in the movie *Hidden Figures* when John walked over and said hello to the lead characters of the film. People of color were rarely afforded polite response from white people at that time. John comported himself as a perfect gentleman.

CBS graphic designer, Georg Olden, is another example of a maverick. The following comes from RevolutionOfTheEye.umbc.edu:

> While the experimental nature of television—and the political progressiveness of many of its pioneers—made it remarkably open to diversity at mid-century, it was slow to embrace women (behind the camera) and people of color. Georg Olden, the CBS director of graphic design, was one of the first African Americans to hold an executive position at a network. He was an ardent champion of contemporary art, commissioning on-air art and title cards by modern artists. "The door is open for artists on TV," he proclaimed in 1954.

Bess Lomax Hawes, American folk musician and folklorist, exhibited the width and breadth of this position. The following comes from FolkLife.si.edu:

> Bess Lomax Hawes (1921-2009) led the establishment of public folklore programs throughout the United States. She did it with a vast knowledge of America's diverse traditions, the discipline of a savvy strategist, an empathy born of experience for cultural work, and a personal reservoir of good grace.

Astrologer, Stephen Forrest, exhibits another dynamic of this astrological position. Stephen is an amazingly resourceful astrologer who acts as a guide to help others perfect themselves.

In an interesting twist on this astrological placement, former rugby player, Ben Cohen, has made an impact in the gay world. The following comes from Mirror.co.uk:

> For despite being straight, the former sports star has become an international gay icon – helping thousands of homosexuals and transgender people break boundaries both on and off the sports field. He set up the "Ben Cohen StandUp Foundation to combat bullying of all types including of people who might be lesbian, gay, bisexual or transgender.

Saturn in Virgo would seek to set boundaries and to help those less fortunate.

Saturn in Libra on the MC

Saturn is in its exaltation in Libra. A structural representation of beauty for the world to see would be an aspect of this position.

We can see this astrological exaltation as evidenced by photographer, Diane Arbus. The following comes from Wikipedia.com:

> Diane was an American photographer. Although Arbus's most famous subjects were outsiders such as transgender people, strippers, carnival performers, nudists, dwarves, and other marginalized people, she was equally drawn to subjects as ordinary as children, mothers, couples, old people, and middle-class families. She photographed her subjects in familiar settings: their homes, on the street, in the workplace, in the park. In his 2003 New York Times Magazine article, "Arbus Reconsidered," Arthur Lubow states, "She was fascinated by people who were visibly creating their own identities—cross-dressers, nudists, sideshow performers, tattooed men, the nouveau riche, the movie-star fans—and by those who were trapped in a uniform that no longer provided any security or comfort." Michael Kimmelman writes in his review of the exhibition Diane Arbus Revelations, "Her memorable work, which she did, on the whole, not for hire but for herself, was all about heart—a ferocious, audacious heart. It transformed the art of photography (Arbus is everywhere, for better and worse, in the work

of artists today who make photographs), and it lent a fresh dignity to the forgotten and neglected people in whom she invested so much of herself.

Astrologer, Marion March, clearly exhibited the ambassadorial leadership present in this placement to help unite astrological groups and promote greater understanding.

Saturn in Scorpio on the MC

Here we have a concentration of power unlike we find almost anywhere else. These individuals have egos which are annealed by their experiences, giving them a strength few can question.

While I have refrained from including potential mavericks whose birth times are unsubstantiated, I want to use one such example now: J. Edgar Hoover. As the first director of the Federal Bureau of Investigation (FBI), he was instrumental in setting the structure for a deeply interrogative organization. The following comes from Wikipedia.com:

> Hoover has been credited with building the FBI into a larger crime-fighting agency than it was at its inception and with instituting a number of modernizations to police technology, such as a centralized fingerprint file and forensic laboratories. Later in life and after his death, Hoover became a controversial figure as evidence of his secretive abuses of power began to surface. He was found to have exceeded the jurisdiction of the FBI, and to have used the FBI to harass political dissenters

and activists, to amass secret files on political leaders, and to collect evidence using illegal methods. Hoover consequently amassed a great deal of power and was in a position to intimidate and threaten others, even sitting presidents of the United States.

Again, I use Hoover as he is such a beautiful representation of this astrological placement.

Film star, Paul Newman, who has Mercury, Venus and Jupiter squaring this position from his Capricorn AS, exhibits the meaning seeking aspect in his obituary from DailyMail. co.uk:

> In truth, though he had major roles in more than 50 motion pictures Newman preferred his private life to the feverish fakery of Hollywood.

One would have expected Elizabeth II of the United Kingdom to have shown up already. She ascended the throne at 25 years of age upon the death of her father. That is very Saturn in Scorpio on the MC. Scorpio has amazing powers of rejuvenation. She is the longest reigning monarch of the UK, the longest reigning queen in the history of the world, and will be the longest reigning monarch ever if she makes it to over 72 years and 110 days of reign (to surpass the reign of Louis XIV) which will occur in 2024. She has endured much and had to adopt to the changes of time, something that neither Saturn nor Scorpio appreciate.

Interestingly enough, Elizabeth II's grandson, Prince Harry, also has this astrological placement, which means he was born during her second Saturn return. Prince Henry, who has his Taurus Moon IC opposite this point, is no stranger to controversy and often found himself overly exposed in the tabloids. He made *Tatler* magazine's man of the year as "Dirty Harry."

Former American football player, Archie Griffin, dedicates his hard work to Ohio State University. From OSU.edu comes this lovely reflection of this maverick:

> Archie is a tremendously value-driven leader. The value of "We're going to invest in students." The value of "Everyone gets treated with respect." The value of "Do the right thing." I just think about how proud his parents would be, because he has such a strong and clear moral compass. And that, in tough times, is one of the incredible characteristics that he's brought to the alumni association.

Saturn in Sagittarius on the MC

Here we have free-wheeling experience seeking Sagittarius with sobering Saturn asking for dues to be paid.

Singer, Andy Gibb, who has Moon conjunct his DS in Virgo, had a real challenge in defining his identity. This excerpt from IMDB.com beautifully illustrates the tests he endured:

> A blessing or a curse? Every silver lining has a cloud, yet sadly Andrew Roy Gibb had to find that out the hard way. Born the fifth and final child to parents

Barbara and Hugh Gibb, Andy grew up with his three older siblings dominating the music charts, collectively known as The Bee Gees. Performing at clubs from the age of 13, it was suspected that Andy was to join The Bee Gees, yet Andy always wanted to be his own personality.

Victimised at the many schools he went to by other students who were convinced he had a superiority complex due to his famous brothers, Andy escaped into his music. But it all came too fast and too soon. Andy was performing and making music by the time he was 20 years old, and it was virtually impossible to break away from his brothers' shadows when older brother Barry wrote 90% of his songs, and the Bee Gees sang backup vocals on half of his songs. Andy got it all too fast, and his life was intermingled with years of depression that he tried to stay away with booze, drugs and women. While they all may have provided temporary relief, Andy was plagued by depression and the fact that no matter what he did, he could never escape his heritage.

Tim Lott, is a strongly defined T-Square maverick with his Mars conjunct this point, both opposing Moon and Chiron in Gemini on his IC and all four squaring Mercury in Aquarius on his AS. This man is always having a three-way relationship with life: His image, his home and his career are all always pulling on him. The benefit to him would be to have relationships with well-developed Leonine individuals.

He eloquently illuminates Saturnian and Sagittarian themes with the following quote from AZQuotes.com:

> "Depression is about anger, it's about anxiety, it's about character and heredity. But it is also about something that is in its way quite unique. It is the illness of identity, it is the illness of those who do not know where they fit, who lose faith in the myths they have so painstakingly created for themselves. It is a plague – especially if you add in its various forms of expression, like alcoholism, anorexia, bulimia, drug addiction, compulsive behavior of one kind or another. They're all the same things: attempts to avoid disappearance, or nothingness, or chaos."

Michel Houellebecq's latest book *Serotonin*, deals with issues on this astrological point, as stated in TheGuardian.com:

> *Serotonin*, the story of a lovesick agricultural engineer who writes trade reports for the French agriculture ministry and loathes the EU, has been hailed by the French media as scathing and visionary. The novel rails against politicians who "do not fight for the interests of their people but are ready to die to defend free trade."

Nancy Spungen, who also has Moon in Gemini on her IC as does British author and publisher, Tim Lott, didn't seem to benefit from the maturity Saturn would give as Nancy died at 20. The following comes from Mandatory.com:

Wild Child. From the very start, there was something off about Spungen. At birth she nearly died from oxygen deprivation, choked by the umbilical cord. For the first few years of her life, she wouldn't stop shrieking and wailing. Eventually, the doctors prescribed a liquid barbiturate to keep her quiet. As a child, she lashed out at people. Once she even bit a mailman on the ankle. She also threatened to kill a babysitter with scissors and occasionally hit herself. At one point, a doctor diagnosed her as schizophrenic. At the very least, she lacked emotionally stability.

Saturn in Sagittarius can be the umbilical cord around the neck, the oxygen deprivation.

Saturn in Capricorn on the MC

This is a very powerful placement. Saturn, ruler of Capricorn in its own sign and favored placement at the top of the chart. This astrological placement has a keen awareness of social status into which they may be born, or simply willing to do the work necessary to accomplish.

Maverick Damita Jo DeBlanc, also known as, Damita Jo, American actress, comedian, and lounge music performer, shows the width and breadth of success this astrological placement can bring. The following comes from DMDukes.com:

> Damita Jo DeBlanc, daughter of Herbert DeBlanc and Latrelle Plummer was born in Austin, Texas, on

August 5, 1930. Damita Jo was active in both music and comedy since the 1950's. An International Supper Club, Television and Recording Star, she performed on five continents and her recordings and videotapes are played everywhere. Her recordings have topped the charts in America, Sweden, Norway, Australia, Puerto Rico and Japan. She is best known recordings wise for her million seller "I'm Saving The Last Dance For You" (# 22 pop, # 16 R&B) a clever answer record to the Drifters' "Save the Last Dance For Me". Her other big hit, "I'll Be There" from 1961 (# 12 pop, # 15 R&B), was also an answer record, this time to Ben E. King's "Stand By Me". Damita Jo recorded the first English version of "Yellow Days" and "If You Go Away" an adaptation of Jacques Brel's "Ne Me Quitte Pas", with English lyrics by Rod McKuen.

Romance novelist, Barbara Cartland, had her Jupiter her as well. She built quite an amazing reputation for herself. The following comes from Wikipedia.com:

Barbara was an English novelist who wrote romance novels, one of the best-selling authors as well as one of the most prolific and commercially successful worldwide of the 20th century.

While she was quite successful, she left a worthless estate.
Christian Bérard, also known as Bébé, who had Mars opposing this position on his IC showed a very earthy, Pan-like,

bon vivant facet of this astrological placement. The following comes from WorldofWonder.net:

> Bérard is one of the truly great Bohemian characters. The prince of Parisian nightlife, he was celebrated for his kindness and his chubby physique. He was photographed by Man Ray, Henri Cartier-Bresson, and Richard Avedon; composer Francis Poulenc dedicated his *Stabat Mater* (1950) to Bérard, and Cocteau dedicated *Orphée* (1950) to this influential, eccentric artist. Gertrude Stein's poem "Christian Bérard" is included in her collection *Portraits and Prayers* (1934). Bérard's work can be seen in the world's great galleries and museums, including the Museum of Modern Art (MOMA) in New York City.

Princess Margaret, who had ruling Venus in Libra conjunct her DS squaring this position, was unable to marry who she wished. She would have also been challenged in finding ways to be of value and her own authority, but unable to do much with it otherwise she would have upset her sister, Queen Elizabeth II, with her Saturn in Scorpio in this position. While Margaret's Saturn in Capricorn is astrologically considered stronger, Saturn in Scorpio is real power.

From AZArchivessOnline.org we find this description of another crowned royal, Miss America, Jacque Mercer:

> [Mercer] was a freshman at Phoenix College when she was crowned Miss America on September 11, 1949. In December of 1949, Jacque married her high

school sweetheart, Douglas Cook, and thus violated her contract with Miss America. Although the pageant allowed her to keep her crown, it instituted a "no marriage, no pregnancy" rule the following year. This rule remained in effect until 1999. Mercer's national tour as Miss America included endorsements and promotions for Catalina swimwear and Lane cedar chests.

English artist and entertainer, Grayson Perry, is the subject of an eloquent statement of this astrological position that comes from AZQuotes.com:

The basic premise of taste, as Stephen Bayley, the cultural critic, said, is that taste is that which does not alienate your peers. Most people want to fit in with their tribe in some way or another, so they give off signals, whether it's with their clothes, their behavior, their car, their whatever, and gain status. Every tribe has a hierarchy, and that's what taste is: it's an unconscious display of who you are, and where you want to be.

Saturn in Aquarius on the MC

Saturn is the traditional ruler of Aquarius. This is a beautiful space for a humanitarian who wants to make a difference on the planet.

Papa Spyk, who has Venus and Mercury conjunct his Gemini AS, had this beautiful statement for this placement from MMacrossfire.com: "He was as tough as he was sensitive and compassionate, just a solid, solid human being …"

If we read further in the article, or anything about Papa, we will see that he wanted to share what he learned from overcoming drug addiction with others. Saturn is the cautionary tale especially when found in an air sign. Aquarius rules the electronic waves of television and the internet.

The famous astrologer, Jeane Dixon, has her Mars here with both opposing her Leo Moon on the IC. She has this perfect quote taken from AZQuotes.com:

"We must realize our own talents and, having realized, accept them; and play on them like a symphony in which all other instruments are harmonized to make a better universe."

The following quote from comedic actor, Gene Wilder, who has Sun in Gemini on his AS trining this placement, comes from his obituary in TheGuardian.com:

To cheer her [his mom] up, the boy improvised comedy skits, so that from an early age he was aware of the coexistence of laughter and pain. Despite his later change of name—"I picked Gene because of the hero of Thomas Wolfe's novel *Look Homeward Angel* and Wilder from Thornton Wilder, whose *Our Town* was my favourite play"—he still felt he was Jerry Silberman trying to gain his parents' attention by showing off.

What better authorship than to give yourself a hero's name?

Actress, Julie Newmar, who has Sun conjunct her IC in opposing Leo, has these telling quotes for Saturn in Aquarius taken from AZQuotes.com:

> "Invention is the pleasure you give yourself when other people's stuff isn't good enough."

This next one by Newmar, describes the way in which Saturn draws you along:

> "You can't fail. The further you fall, the greater the opportunity for growth and change."

June and Jennifer Gibbons were identical twins who grew up in Wales. They became known as "The Silent Twins" since they only communicated with each other. The following comes from Wikipedia.com, and is a glimpse of their creative world which is rife with the themes of this astrological placement:

> They created many plays and stories in a sort of soap opera style, reading some of them aloud on tape as gifts for their sister, Rose. Inspired by a pair of gift diaries on Christmas 1979, they began their writing careers. They sent away for a mail order course in creative writing, and each wrote several novels. Set primarily in the United States and particularly in Malibu, California,

the stories involve young men and women who exhibit strange and often criminal behavior. In June's *Pepsi-Cola Addict*, the high-school hero is seduced by a teacher, then sent away to a reformatory where a homosexual guard makes a play for him. In Jennifer's *The Pugilist*, a physician is so eager to save his child's life that he kills the family dog to obtain its heart for a transplant. The dog's spirit lives on in the child and ultimately has its revenge against the father. Jennifer also wrote *Discomania*, the story of a young woman who discovers that the atmosphere of a local disco incites patrons to insane violence.

Talk about taking a walk on the wild side!

Actress and singer, Miley Cyrus, who has Moon and Mercury conjunct her DS in Scorpio squaring this point, walks the wild side, and takes her responsibility seriously as we see in her following Instagram post:

"To hug you one more time @janicefreeman.... I made a promise to you here on earth and will keep that promise as you watch from heaven. To take care of your precious little girl, my baby sister. To shine light on your husband and mother when days are dark! I love you."

Miley's deep compassion moderated with her sense of responsibility is well exhibited here. I understand that she has likened herself to Truman in the *Truman Show* as her whole life has been in relationship to the world through the media, a very Aquarius on the MC theme. Saturn squaring her Moon would give her an understanding of the hardships of life even though many would project a life of irresponsible luxury on her. While that might be partially true, it doesn't show the full story.

I have also met two individuals with this placement who were both airline pilots.

Saturn in Pisces on the MC

Saturn in Pisces is, as we have said, like building sand castles on the beach. Structure making Saturn in etheric Pisces is definitely the sound of one hand clapping. Pisces is the final sign where we either make our way from physical to spirit in the process of dying or, alternately, making our way from the formless to being ensouled in matter when we are born.

John, Prince of Wales, the "final child" of King George V and Queen Mary of the United Kingdom, did not get the attention the rest of his family received. Suffering from epilepsy at a time when such disorders were thought to reflect weakness in the family, he was a sort of ghost image when he was alive. The following comes from HistoricMysteries.com:

> Ultimately his life was a blank not worth mentioning, and he is barely remembered today. But a lone grave on the grounds of Sandringham Estate attests to the fact that a very special boy was once part of what was then the most famous family in the world.

The rules of the family greatly limited his opportunity to experience life. Pisces is the sign of fantasy and drugs and our final example was known for both.

Stripper and model, Candy Barr, had a very interesting life filled with all of the themes related to Saturn, Pisces and the Midheaven. The following comes from VintageCuties.com and contains some telling vignettes:

> This troublesome vixen then exploded onto the national stage when she appeared in one of the first nationally-distributed pornographic films, titled *Smart Alec* which was released in 1951.
>
> Just how crazy was this lady? Consider this:
>
> - In January 1956, Candy Barr was charged with aggravated assault when she shot her second husband after he kicked in the door of her Dallas apartment. Strangely, her manager asked the sheriff to raise her bail to increase the publicity and sensationalism around the event. The charges were eventually dropped;
> - In October 1957, Dallas police raided her apartment, arrested her for possession of an ounce of marijuana, and she received a 15 year prison sentence (she would only serve 3 years and 4 months of this);
> - While her marijuana case was on appeal, she danced around the country in various men's clubs, and ended up becoming the girlfriend of notorious gangster, Mickey Cohen;

- Candy used her prison time to create poetry that was eventually released under the title "A Gentle Mind – Confused";
- She worked for and ended up friends with Jack Ruby. Remember him? Ruby was the guy who shot and killed John Kennedy's assassin, Lee Harvey Oswald;
- In the '70s, it was rumored Candy Barr had a salacious weekend affair with *Playboy* publisher Hugh Hefner.

Chiron

Chiron is an asteroid which has an orbit that overlaps those of his neighbors Saturn and Uranus, thereby acting as an emissary between our limits and that which is beyond that which we do not know. Chiron is the story of the wound in us that never heals, but which, through time, care, knowledge, and love, becomes the wisdom that allows you to teach others what you have learned and overcome in your relationship to your wound. Chiron in your chart represents how you deal with the core wounds that will never go away. It is more about your relationship to them than the wounds themselves. Chiron represents your need for healing and, by house, the area in your life where it needs to happen. Chiron was a centaur, half horse and half man (actually in his case, half immortal and half animalistic human), so it implies the instinctual feeling nature combined with the human intellect.

This planetoid reveals how you express the healer/educator/facilitator sides of yourself, and through the wounds in your life, how you learn to be a better person and teach others about how to heal their own wounds/hurts.

"Discovered" or actually seen from astronomical images for the first time in 1977, you can notice the ways, since then, in which our culture has become more consciously aware of the wounds we all carry within us. Forty-four years later, we can perceive that we are collectively more proactive in our attempt to minimize wounding for subsequent generations. One of the lovely expressions of Chiron on the angles is Karen Silkwood, with Chiron conjunct the AS in Libra; she was driven to ensure everyone had equal rights in the nuclear facility where she worked. You can learn more about her if you watch the movie *Silkwood*.

Chiron was rejected and abandoned by his mother because he did not have a fully human physical form. This clearly caused an early profound psychological and emotional wound. Wounds often have their "gifts" and, in Chiron's case, one of the gifts he received was being adopted by the god Apollo, which gave him a most wonderful opportunity to grow into the many gifts Chiron had to share with the world.

We will now look at the angle placements of Chiron throughout the zodiac from the point of view of the Ascendant (AS).

Chiron in Aries on the AS

Chiron on the Ascendant often shows a non-traditional type of attractiveness. As the Ascendant represents how we see ourselves and how others see us, we can understand that there would be issues around one's appearance or being accepted. In spite of their differences from the norm, the more these Chiron on the Ascendant individuals own who they are, the more energetically attractive they become.

Aries can often be seen as the sign of individuality, war, conflict, and the military, so it is no surprise that American automobile executive, Lee Iacocca, who is a multiple maverick already, was significantly afflicted by rheumatic fever as a child, resulting in being labeled as unfit for military service in WWII.

Englishman, George Blake, was a double agent spy for the United Kingdom and Russia.

Actress, Liz Renay, ran away from home at 13 to get away from her evangelical Christian parents and hitch hiked to Las Vegas. Liz was married seven times.

From his obituary in Guardian.com, comes an articulate expression of this astrological placement for French painter, Paul Rebeyrolle:

Unclassifiable French painter who created his own museum after a lifetime of courting controversy

The French painter Paul Rebeyrolle, who has died aged 78, once said, "All my mysteries have remained intact. Nobody understands them. These mysteries are what feeds my passion for art, and for fly-fishing. You never know where the solutions are. You always have to invent. And you never know more than a tiny part. In fact, I don't understand this world at all, and that's part of its richness."

Rebeyrolle courted controversy, and put himself outside the centres of power of modern painting. With his work excluded from the French art establishment, he created, in 1995, his own museum, Espace Rebeyrolle, in his native Burgundy, where he showed his own art and that of other painters.

Always contrary, he would never align himself with any lobby that might help his career. He refused teaching posts and artistic compromise. He eschewed the realism his comrades demanded in favour of a physical, powerful, expressionist style.

American figure skater, Nancy Kerrigan, received international attention for the attack on her arranged by a rival figure skater.

Another expression of this astrological placement is seen in the biography of rugby player, Perry Cross:

After surviving a devastating accident whilst playing rugby union, Perry Cross founded and became president of the Perry Cross Spinal Research Foundation. His core goal is to inspire others to achieve. Becoming a C2 quadriplegic in 1994, just one year prior to Christopher Reeve sustaining the same injury, has allowed him to become one of the world's most lauded motivational speakers and one of very few who rely on a life support machine to function. He has been heralded as an exception role model for overcoming the odds to succeed and overcome what appeared to be insurmountable odds.

Chiron in Taurus on the AS

When Chiron is in Taurus, there can be a certain determined approach to things and a holding of one's ground.

Journalist, Dan Rather, has this from BrainyQuote.com, "I don't back down. I don't cave when the pressure gets too great from these partisan political ideological forces."

This determined approach is seen in the obituary of German statesman, Helmut Kohl, shown here from theGuardian.com:

> His doctorate (on post-1945 Rhineland politics) was early evidence of an intelligence often masked by a thick skin, a dour impassivity, tactlessness and an apparently invincible optimism. His favourite tactic in a crisis was to sit tight and do nothing, to the despair of friends and the fury of opponents, in the usually justified belief that the trouble would go away. The image of the stolid, bloated monolith with the stentorian voice, the cartoon

German with no sense of irony and a huge appetite was, however, grotesquely at odds with his political record

The arrival of Englishwoman, Louise Brown, shows the effect she had on the world at the moment of her birth:

> At 11:47pm on July 25, 1978, Louise Brown was the first person ever to be born through science rather than as a result of two people having sex. The birth was hailed as a "miracle" by the world's media, making her instantly famous. Her birth created shockwaves for the church, politicians and the medical profession. Louise has grown up at the centre of the debate about the morality of In Vitro Fertilisation (IVF) while also being a beacon of hope to millions of childless couples throughout the world.

Chiron in Gemini on the AS

Mutable Gemini lends a multiplicity to any planet found in its sign. Chiron here could imply issues with any of the Geminian themes of communication, neighbors, and movement. Chiron prominently appears in the charts of many actors, implying a certain ease with affecting the persona of another while building one's own persona. It is interesting that both of the following examples were actors and sex symbols.

Triple threat actress, singer and dancer, Julie Newmar, exhibits her youthfulness even at 86 in this interview she gave LATimes.com:

She is bright, animated and exuding positivity until someone starts a leaf blower next door. Then her eyes suddenly narrow, her face darkens and for the first time, the angry Catwoman flashes into view. "They're the scourge of the Earth," she hisses, flying around her office to close her doors and mute the whine. "I wrote an essay about leaf blowers and the evil they do." (She also helped lobby the Los Angeles City Council to enact a ban of noisy, gasoline-powered leaf blowers in 1998). She did have a legal battle with her neighbor, Jim Belushi, which ended amicably.

From his obituary in the LATimes.com comes this wonderful way in which actor, Burt Reynolds, played with these energies:

Throughout an often turbulent career that spanned some 100 films and countless television appearances, he had close brushes with death, some resulting from his insistence on doing many of his own dangerous stunts. He braved the raging rapids of the Chattooga River between Georgia and South Carolina for a favorite role, as one of four suburbanite buddies who undertake a journey into America's heart of darkness, in *Deliverance* (1972).

The article goes onto reveal more about Burt's particular astrological placement:

Fellow actors praised Mr. Reynolds as an exacting artist who worked hard at his craft and fought to overcome many demons, including a volatile temperament. But he himself projected an air of insouciance and professed not to take his career too seriously. He told *The New York Times* in 1978, "I think I'm the only movie star who's a movie star in spite of his pictures, not because of them; I've had some real turkeys."

To many in Hollywood, Mr. Reynolds was an enigma. Tormented by self-doubt — he particularly disliked hearing how much he resembled the young Marlon Brando — he was also strong-willed, clashing often with directors and producers. For much of his career he accepted roles, he admitted, "that would be the most fun, not the most challenging," while turning down more substantive parts, like the one in *Terms of Endearment* that led to an Academy Award for Jack Nicholson.

Chiron in Cancer on the AS

This placement of Chiron can stem from a wound with the family or the clan; going against the wishes of the family to become one's own archetype.

As we know from her other maverick placements, heiress, Charlotte Ford, did not step into the family automobile business, but rather became a fashion designer and consultant.

This insightful review of out actress and comedienne, Lily Tomlin, captures the Cancerian moodiness that can be accentuated with a maverick Chiron:

Perhaps it is Tomlin's volatility which makes her so compelling on screen. She has an extraordinary emotional range and can shift from comedic to tragic in the space of a sentence. She has a penchant for lengthy, humorous anecdotes, often about her childhood in Detroit, growing up in an apartment building filled with fascinating inhabitants whom she can recall with a precise turn of phrase, "Mrs. Clancy, who lived over us on the second floor, taught in a girls' school and she was just totally pretentious. She had dyed hair, black hair, reddish under root, you know?"

Writer, Edmund White's childhood paints a clear picture of this astrological placement, with the last line of this excerpt revealing his process for healing. The following comes from Wikipedia.com:

Incestuous feelings existed in White's family; his mother was attracted to him. White spoke of his own sexual attraction to his father in an interview: "I think with my father he was somebody who every eye in the family was focused on and he was a sort of a tyrant and nice-looking, the source of all power, money, happiness, and he was implacable and difficult. He was always spoken of in sexual terms, in the sense he left our mother for a much younger woman who was very sexy but had nothing else going for her. He was a famous womanizer. And he slept with my sister!" He has also stated: "Writing has always been my recourse when I've tried to make sense of my experience or when it's been very painful. When I was 15 years old, I wrote my first (unpublished) novel about being gay, at a time when there were no other gay novels. So I was really inventing a genre, and it was a way of administering a therapy to myself, I suppose."

Chiron in Leo on the AS

We understand that these individuals will have experiences ranging from having a wounded ego to one who seeks to teach from the egoless-self.

BrainyQuote.com has this illustrative quote about the latter expression of this astrological placement from British Labour Party politician, Neil Gordon Kinnock:

"There are politicians who seethe with ambition all the time, and there are a lot of other politicians who don't. I'm in the second category, that's all."

Olympic swimmer and multiple maverick, Jan Konrads, deals with his bi-polar disorder which he seeks to bring to public awareness.

Of course, this is a prime astrological placement for an actor as well represented by *Lovejoy* star, Ian McShane. He gave a lovely and articulate (for this placement) answer to a question he was asked in an interview for NYTimes.com:

"A little turmoil never hurt anybody as long as it came out slightly more creative in the end, and I think it maybe has."

Chiron in Virgo on the AS

This is a prime place of being of service, being known for one's work.

Polish statesman, Lech Walesa, is a brilliant example of service. The following comes from Wikipedia.com:

> [Walesa] served as the first democratically-elected President of Poland (1990-1995). His nonviolent struggle eventually brought the end to communist rule in Poland and ushered in the end of the Cold War.

Holy Roman Emperor, Maximilian I, has a B rating for his birth chart from 1459. Prior to the 20th and 21st centuries, astrology was something only royals and nobles could afford. Their lives were also important enough that their birth times were tracked. This excerpt from http://www.holyromanempireassociation.com/holy-roman-emperor-maximilian-i.html, addresses an important perfecting flair that this astrological placement can give:

> Maximilian had a great passion for armour, not only as equipment for battle or tournaments, but as an art form. The style of armour that became popular during the second half of his reign featured elaborate fluting

and metalworking, and became known as Maximilian armour. It emphasized the details in the shaping of the metal itself, rather than the etched or gilded designs popular in the Milanese style. Maximilian also gave a bizarre jousting helmet as a gift to King Henry VIII – the helmet's visor featured a human face, with eyes, nose and a grinning mouth, and was modelled after the appearance of Maximilian himself. It also sported a pair of curled ram's horns, brass spectacles, and even etched beard stubble.

My friend, Connie Campbell, has always made the statement, "I am here to be of service." Connie is a brilliant docent and volunteer to many causes.

As we often find with the Ascendant point and Virgo, the native exhibits early talent as in the case of American country music singer, Scott Cooke "Scotty" McCreery. He won the tenth season of American Idol on May 25, 2011. From theFamousPeople.com we learn that, "His musical journey began early; he started playing guitar at the age of 10 and was known to impersonate Elvis as a child."

The hard work implied by this astrological placement is illustrated in the headlines of an article from uDiscoverMusic.com about singer and songwriter, Kim Carnes:

Overnight Sensation in Ten Years: The Rise of Kim Carnes

After a decade of hard work, the Los Angeles native was on her way, as the *Mistaken Identity* album followed "Bette Davis Eyes" to the US chart summit.

Chiron in Libra on the AS

These individuals are likely to suffer from painful relationships in the process of reconciling right human relationships.

The painful issues that relationships can reveal are well illustrated in the life of serial killer and multiple maverick Dennis Nilsen. The entry from Biography.com tells the story:

> In 1975, he took up cohabitation with David Gallichan in a garden apartment situated at 195 Melrose Avenue in North London, although Gallichan denied that they had a homosexual relationship. This lasted two years and when Gallichan left, Nilsen's life began a downward spiral into alcohol and loneliness, which culminated in his first murder 18 months later.

PBS.com shares this about activist, chemical technician, and multi-maverick, Karen Silkwood, which illustrates this astrological placement:

> During the week prior to her death, Silkwood was reportedly gathering evidence for the Union to support her claim that Kerr-McGee was negligent in maintaining plant safety, and at the same time, was involved in a number of unexplained exposures to

plutonium. The circumstances of her death have been the subject of great speculation.

From SmoothRadio.com come the revealing statements about this astrological placement by singer and songwriter, Berry Gibb, who is also a multi-maverick:

"My greatest regret is that every brother I've lost was in a moment when we weren't getting on, so I have to live with that and I'll spend the rest of my life reflecting on that," an emotional Barry Gibb said.

"I'm the last man standing. I'll never be able to understand that as I'm the eldest."

Gibb also broke down in tears during the interview, admitting that he had never done that before when speaking about the subject.

"Nobody ever really know what the three of us felt about each other," he added. "Only the three of us knew.

"It was such a unifying thing, the three of us became one person. We all had the same dream. That's what I miss more than anything else."

From French athlete, Colette Besson's obituary from ESPN.com we learn the following:

"This is a great loss," said Lamine Diack, president of the International Association of Athletics Federations. She made a tremendous contribution to world athletics, as a charismatic and determined athlete in an age when women's athletics was still developing.

Multi-maverick city supervisor-cum-murderer, Dan White, really felt the Libran pain of "inappropriateness" as stated in his obituary from NYTimes.com:

> But a year later he resigned, saying that his salary, $9,600 a year, was not enough to support his family, and that he was unhappy with the ethics he found in the political world.

Chiron in Scorpio on the AS

These are individuals who have the ability to plumb the depths.

Astrologer and multi-maverick, Erin Sullivan, teaches psychologically oriented astrology.

Photographer, Jacob Holdt, captured the harsh realities of poverty in the United States for all the world to see when he completed his work *American Pictures*. Another lovely expression of this astrological placement is that Jacob offers his astrological chart on his website. Not something the average Scorpio would do!

Patricia Dianne Krenwinkel, part pf the Manson "family" shows the magnetic strength involved with maverick planets. Charles Manson had his maverick Venus in Scorpio on the DS conjunct Patricia's Chiron in Scorpio on her AS. Interestingly enough, Scorpio rules the endocrine system and since this a placement of a wound that others see, it is no surprise that we learn the following about Krenwinkel from AllThatIsInteresting.com:

Born in the waning months of 1947 to a homemaker and an insurance salesman, Krenwinkel grew into a girl paralyzed by insecurity. At school, she was bullied for being overweight and an embarrassing endocrine condition that caused her to grow excess hair on her arms.

Composer, Paul Williams, exhibits other aspects of this astrological placement, which include addiction and the comeback. The BaltimoreTimes.com writes about Williams:

As the 1980's rolled in Paul virtually vanished. He had lived fast and hard, a bit recklessly, having travelled the darker alleyways of the entertainment realm. He had entered the abyss of addiction and the once bright spotlight had faded. The addiction now had become the king with the crown, as the devil drove the bleak realities of Paul's daily life. He conveyed "My turn around point was when I was in a blackout. I was in a blackout and called my doctor" his voice sounding a bit surprised and excited. It was then he began his way back with full sobriety". It was not an easy task by any means however dealing with any demon is always a challenge. Now, twenty-eight years sober, he has reclaimed his life and has victoriously emerged with a second chance! Resurfacing in the 90's, Paul, thinner, his hair spiked and cut short, donning round spectacles, no longer hidden behind long hair and dark glasses. His album *Back To Love Again* is brilliant! His latest recording, contributing lyrics to two songs and singing on Daft Punk's album *Random Access Memories* earned the 2014 Grammy award for album of the year.

Chiron in Sagittarius on the AS

This is an interesting combination because both Chiron and Sagittarius are centaurs. There are elements of equine looks, foreign travel, or living abroad.

IMBD.com has this to say about the unusual stature and looks of actress and multi-maverick, Anjelica Huston:

> Endowed with her father's great height and personal boldness, and her mother's beauty and aristocratic nose, Huston certainly cuts an imposing figure, and brings great confidence and authority to her performances. She clearly takes her craft seriously and has come into her own as a strong actress, emerging from under the shadow of her father, who passed away in 1987.

The indefatigable nature of this mutable and movable astrological placement are well presented in the opening paragraph of theGuardian.com interview with musician, Bob Geldof:

> You can prepare for a Bob Geldof interview, but you cannot prepare for Bob Geldof himself. Not that he isn't how you imagine: he is, but more so. Taller, louder, funnier, better read, more sweary, more informed, more opinionated. More everything. He rarely draws

breath. He fires off stats about the planet's resources ("Humans will need 1,700% of the planet's resources in 80 years"), and the energy drain that is Google ("Every time you search for something on Google, you use as much energy as driving a car 65 metres"). He berates the BBC's Africa coverage ("They only want the noble primitive version"), then switches to my career, though we've met only once before: "Telly's where the money's at, Sawyer, get with the programme!" If you were to draw a cartoon of us during this interview, I would have my hair blown back, as though facing a hurricane.

Artist, Sally Condon, shares the following statement on her website SallyCondon.com:

Painting is my way of celebrating and expressing my feelings of connection to the world I live in. As a long time gardener and keeper of bees I continually witness nature's beauty and regenerative forces. Within my garden small universes come alive and wither only to be reborn again. I strive to create images where the colors begin to breathe and resonate as they do in the natural world. Cezanne once said, "Nature is not on the surface but in the depths; colors are the expression of these depths on the surface, they rise up from the roots of the world."

Balloonist, Colin Prescot, wrote a book about this astrological placement adventures entitled, *To the Edge of Space.*

Sagittarius is the sign of higher philosophies, and they can be found in the scholarly translations and writings on Buddhism by writer Peter Skilling.

Scholar and astrologer, Bernadette Brady, uses the teacher, educator and facilitating skills of Chiron to bring the larger-context of fixed stars into greater understanding. Brady is an ambassador to our Galactic Center which resides in Sagittarius.

Greek poet, George Seferis, beautifully exhibited this astrological placement as described in his obituary in NYTimes.com:

> George Seferiadis, the veteran Greek diplomat and scholar who as George Seferis the poet won the Nobel Prize for literature in 1963, was a liberal thinker who inherited a strong democratic tradition from his family.
>
> His pen name, a shortened form of his family name, reflects what his friend the British poet Rex Warner called his fondness for "innocent, easily penetrable disguises." It also emphasized his role as wanderer, since *sefer* is rooted in the Arabic word for *journey*, emerging in Swahili as *safari*."

Sounds fitting for a double centaur!

Chiron in Capricorn on the AS

This placement gives one the sense that they may not be enough or have enough to reach the success they seek. There are usually issues that happen early in life that affect these individuals in such a way as to help others.

Adair Lara teaches others how to become a published author after having written numerous books and a regular semiweekly article for the *San Francisco Chronicle*.

Immunologist, Ian Frazer, showed that early drive and intensity we see with so many mavericks. We see this in action from TheFamousPeople.com:

> From an early age, Frazer was determined to pursue a career in research. Thus, after obtaining a degree in medicine and surgery from University of Edinburgh, he started training himself as a renal physician, investigating the immunological issues associated with transplantation. It was his growing interest in immunology that took him to Australia where he enrolled at the Walter and Eliza Hall Institute and the rest as they say is history.

That history is linking cervical cancer to HPV (human papillomavirus) and creating a vaccine to stop HPV.

In a thoughtful interview with theGuardian.com singer, Kim Gordon, discusses her life and the challenges of success that this astrological placement would bring. The title of the article itself is a succinct statement of this placement *Kim Gordon: 'There's a wall of faceless men I have to climb over.* The article goes writes:

> Warm though still a bit elusive, at 66, Gordon says she is still not totally comfortable giving interviews

to promote her work and talking about herself: "After a while, you feel like an imposter." One of her paintings comes to mind: the dripping words *Secret Abuse*, Gordon's comment on artists' relationship to the commercial world. It reminds me of artists' relationships to themselves, too, and she agrees: "The process is torture."

Designer, Robin Speas, is a master cabinet maker who spent a significant amount of time in a boat with her family. This experience gave her an ability to build furniture that fits well into small and complex spaces.

Heisman Trophy winner, Archie Griffin did the work necessary to gain his success which is key to this astrological placement in Capricorn. Archie's efforts are highlighted in an article from Sports.jrank.org:

> Growing up, Archie Griffin was short and somewhat overweight, thus earning him the nicknames "Tank" and "Butterball" among his peers. When he began Eastmoor High in Columbus, his football coach didn't see him as the fullback he would eventually become, and he rarely touched the ball until the regular Eastmoor fullback didn't show up. Archie, a freshman, took over for the missing player, and after an impressive performance, never played another game as a lineman.
>
> Realizing he would need to change physically to be a success at fullback, Archie hit the weight room to strengthen his upper body—the constant pulling and

pounding a running back took demanded a stronger upper body than Archie had.

Master astrologer, Reinhold Ebertin, experienced and expressed this placement as shown in an excerpt from an article at Astro.com:

> When he was five, Reinhold's parents divorced and he was placed in a foster home. During childhood and adolescence, his contacts with his mother, Elsbeth, were sporadic, made more difficult by interference from his father and paternal grandfather. When he was 16, Elsbeth introduced him to his chart and to astrology, which proved to be a turning point in his life. At 21, he and his mother were finally reunited and he began his extensive studies of astrology. He worked at the time as a schoolteacher.

Author and psychologist, Robyn Vickers-Willis, articulates the ways in which our own process informs us to aid others. Robyn shares his thoughts on his journey in an article at CompulsiveReader.com:

> I did discover Jung at midlife. I was actually going to give up psychology in my mid years. Although my clients were satisfied, I was discouraged, and felt that it provided no framework for who I was becoming. I had a life changing dream, and other events took place which are recounted in my book, and I started setting up a practice as a consultant in the corporate sector.

This was about the same time that I discovered Jungian psychology, which has since become my main focus in my corporate work, in my personal life, and in the counselling I've done for other people. Many lay people find his direct writing hard to understand. He is said to have been the second most influential person in the new age movement, with his focus on synchronicity, mandalas, dreams, and so that is something I just demonstrated in the telling.

Chiron in Aquarius on the AS

This is often an issue or wound with humanity and how/if you fit into it. Both Aquarius and Chiron have elements of being the outsider, the themes which we will see in many of our examples for this placement.

Next, is one of the most horrible atrocities committed against humanity in the 20th century. From theGuardian.com, comes this telling article about one of Hitler's key men, Adolf Eichmann, showing how sometimes the clarity that a maverick planet can give isn't always used for its highest purpose. Eichmann was responsible for coordinating the logistics of moving Jews in large numbers to ghettos and extermination camps. In Eichmann's case, he was unable to accept any responsibility for what he had done:

> … a hand-written letter from Eichmann to the then Israeli president, Yitzhak Ben-Zvi, requesting clemency, will only continue the debate. "There is a need to draw a

line between the leaders responsible and the people like me forced to serve as mere instruments in the hands of the leaders," Eichmann's letter pleaded. "I was not a responsible leader, and as such do not feel myself guilty."

In other words: not my fault, I was only obeying orders. His self-delusion was unassailable, even at the end. Eichmann's request was denied and two days later he was hanged in Ramla prison.

No, Eichmann wasn't just a travel agent, indifferent to the destination of his passengers. Eichmann was personally responsible, a responsibility he blindly denied right to the end. Which is precisely why the moral message of his story remains profoundly unsettling: if ordinary people were capable of such great evil, then, given the right circumstances, so are the rest of us.

John Hinckley, the man who attempted to assassinate President Ronald Reagan in 1981, was released from prison with some very restrictive conditions. Hinckley is able to be a part of society, but in a very technologically (Aquarius) limited manner. An article in the LATimes.com highlights Hinckley's restrictions:

> In 2018, his interest in art waned because he was not permitted to play music or display his paintings or photography in public, even anonymously on the internet.

Hinckley eventually dropped all three hobbies because, as he reported, "No one is going to appreciate it other than my closet."

Under the judge's latest ruling, that will change. Working with his therapists, Hinckley will be permitted to post his music and artwork anonymously on the internet.

But such forays will likely remain as low-key as his other pursuits. The judge ruled he cannot profit from his work, nor can he even communicate with his patrons.

Multi-maverick actor, Willem Dafoe, shares his insightful thoughts highlighting this astrological position. The following comes from BrainyQuote.com:

"Sometimes I think women are lucky because they can develop in ways men can't. The old-boy network may be oppressive to women, but it actually stunts men in terms of personal growth."

"I wish to Christ I could make up a really great lie. Sometimes, after an interview, I say to myself, 'Man, you were so honest – can't you have some fun? Can't you do some really down and dirty lying?' But the puritan in me thinks that if I tell a lie, I'll be punished."

"I'm no different to anyone else; I want people to like me. I just don't particularly want them to understand me."

I highly recommend reading the brilliant article that bears out these astrological themes so clearly for music journalist and multi-maverick, Tim Lott (he also has an Aquarian Sun):

> As a child in working-class west London, I was, my mother proclaimed, "a dreamer" living in, according to school reports, a "little world of his own". But I was also, like all hyper-introverts, vulnerable to bullying – both at school and, to a greater extent, by my elder brother. By my teenage years, I had become uneasy and restless. I indulged in booze, soft drugs, and pointless acts of vandalism. This followed a decision I made to abandon the shy, bookish boy I was, lest I be bullied any more. In short, I re-invented myself, as I have had to do repeatedly.
>
> At that time, I had already determined to achieve several things in my life – primarily that I would escape my dull, suburban, penurious background, by becoming a journalist. I was determined to avoid the 9-5 at all costs. I also wanted to generate thoughts that were *worth having*, rather than the chaotic ego-driven chaos of my consciousness.

The maverick strength of this placement is well illustrated by tennis professional, Bjorn Borg, who was considered the greatest tennis player for four years: 1977, 1978, 1979, and 1980.

The Aquarian ego can be seen in the life of Australian adventurer, Peter Treseder. The following written about Peter comes from NZHerald.com:

Treseder has carved out a reputation as an extraordinary athlete, claiming to have set more than 100 endurance and speed records over 25 years in a range of outdoor pursuits, including bush-walking, cross-country skiing, sea kayaking, and climbing.

These achievements have him in demand as a public speaker, have helped him secure healthy sponsorship support and have won him the admiration of corporations and high-profile individuals.

That includes Prime Minister John Howard, who is patron for this latest trip and has referred several times to Treseder when making emotive references to courage.

Treseder has maintained this support even though many of his records were exposed as fakes in a recent sports magazine.

After months of scrutiny, researchers concluded Treseder could not possibly have achieved many of the solo feats he had claimed, saying he had "hoodwinked a nation all the way to its highest office,"

Several leading Australian adventurers now share the same view that Treseder would require superhero powers to complete the tasks he had documented in a biography published two years ago.

Singer and percussionist, Sheila E., shares her abuse and what she has done with it, key elements of this astrological placement, in the following article in USAToday.com:

Throughout her life, Sheila E. has had to deal with the effects of child abuse. When she was 5, she was sexually assaulted by a babysitter who lived in her building. Despite talking about it with friends and strangers, she continued to struggle until 1995, when her best friend, singer Lynn Mabry, made a suggestion.

"We were in Japan, and she asked me to write down what happened so I could share it with a group in Bible study," Sheila E. says. "Lynn knew I would feel better. I wrote for an hour and a half, and when I started to read it, I realized how awful it was. I cried for two or three days. That was the beginning of healing. You can't hold onto these things. It's not your fault. Don't feel guilty or ashamed. That stops you from leading your fullest life and experiencing joy." She wrote a 2015 autobiography, *The Beat of My Own Drum: A Memoir*, detailing the abuse.

Because of her personal experience and strong belief in the healing power of music, she and Mabry created the nonprofit Elevate Hope Foundation in 2001 to help young people who are recovering from trauma or neglect.

Two-time maverick and singer, Belinda Carlisle, shares this strange and apropos quote from BrainyQuote.com:

"I'm a little bit wary of people. It freaked me out when a fan connected with me on social media, then had plastic surgery to look like me, dyed his hair the same colour, and got a pug dog like mine. He was also a hacker, so I had to change all my passwords."

American novelist, playwright and lesbian rights activist, Sarah Miriam Schulman, wrote a novel that has these Chiron in Aquarius maverick themes contained therein. From Amazon.com comes the following synopsis of her work:

> In *Stagestruck,* noted novelist and outspoken critic, Sarah Schulman, offers an account of her growing awareness of the startling similarities between her novel *People in Trouble* and the smash Broadway hit *Rent*. Written with a powerful and personal voice, Schulman's book is part gossipy narrative, part behind-the-scenes glimpse into the New York theater culture, and part polemic on how mainstream artists co-opt the work of "marginal" artists to give an air of diversity and authenticity to their own work. Rising above the details of her own case, Schulman boldly uses her suspicions of copyright infringement as an opportunity to initiate a larger conversation on how AIDS and gay experience are being represented in American art and commerce.

The Chiron in Aquarius on the AS placement works well for singer and actor, Weird Al Yankovic. This astrological combination is "weird" for sure. We learn more about Yankovic from theFamousPeople.com:

> With a knack for lampooning famous songs by popular artists, Yankovic has emerged to be one of the cult

figures in the realm of music. Although a number of artists make parodies of popular songs, Yankovic is quite unique and is known for his light, inoffensive and amusing lyrics. He started satirizing popular songs from a very early age and with passing years his 'talent' grew manifold, making him one of the most famous parodists in America. Though he studied to be an architect, designing buildings was never his forte. He was a humorist at heart and in order to pursue this passion he began recording parodies of songs when he was in college. In no time his talent was discovered and his popularity grew by leaps and bounds. Success and fame came to him quite early and also a little unexpectedly but he was not swayed away by the glitter of the showbiz. He is extremely pragmatic and can be a little critical at times with his approach towards life and in his opinion about others.

From Wikipedia.com comes a perfect statement reflecting this astrological placement for filmmaker and director, Todd Haynes:

Todd Haynes is an American independent film director, screenwriter, and producer. He is considered a pioneer of the New Queer Cinema movement of filmmaking that emerged in the early 1990s.

Chiron in Pisces on the AS

The Piscean archetype has to do with merging and a less physical orientation to life. Their world is one of feelings, water, emotions, experience, mysticism and spirituality, as well as alcohol and drugs.

From her obituary in the Independent.co.uk comes this opening piece about the life of multi-maverick French essayist, author, screenwriter, and experimental filmmaker, Marguerite Duras:

> Marguerite Duras was the most contradictory, and in many ways perverse, figure on the Parisian literary scene during the post-war period, the subject of popular interest far beyond her many readers, always controversial and both the source and the object of much argument.

With this astrological placement it would be easy to project a lot of moral criticism and judgment that comes from the ways in which "polite" society operate. The key with Pisces is it simply wishes to be and has a hard time understanding what the fuss is to everyone else!

Veteran actor, Vincent Price, had this brilliant quote from his obituary in the LATimes.com:

> "Art is everywhere," he once said, "and where it isn't, I don't want to go."

The affable energy of this astrological placement gave singer, actor, and comedian, Dean Martin, an ease of relating to people. From FoxNerws.com comes this observation from his daughter:

> "And my dad could be with the queen of England or with the guy who drove the vegetable truck. He was as happy to be with either one and everybody loved him. And that's how he taught us to be, is just to respect everybody and just be down to earth… Just be kind."

Remembering that Pisces rules the feet, it makes sense that multi-maverick actor, Antonio Banderas, had this written about him in theFamousPeople.com:

> His ambition of becoming professional football player ended due to a foot injury at fourteen. He enrolled in some drama classes, and joined a theater troupe that toured all over Spain.

Actor, George Clooney, has the following archetypal themes of this placement from theFamousPeople.com:

> With all his success, he has never forgotten about the oppressed of the world. He continuously uses his status to raise awareness about gay rights and to help those in political and environmental crises. Alongside his father, Clooney has worked tirelessly to bring global attention to the conflict in Darfur, Sudan, going as far as speaking not only to the United Nation' but also the European

Union. One of the many humanitarian organizations he works with is Not on Our Watch Project. He is truly one of a kind and an authentic living legend.

Clooney made a living by selling women's shoes before making his television debut in the 1978 mini-series *Centennial.*

In high school, he developed Bell's palsy. The paralyzed portions of his face earned him the nickname 'Frankenstein.' Though he overcame Bell's palsy, it left a profound effect.

Singer Whitney Houston died from prolonged drug use.

British author of children and young adult books, Rufus Bellamy, is a keen environmentalist whose published credits include *Saving Wildlife, Food for All, Protecting Habitats,* and *Clean Air.*

We will now look at the angle placements of Chiron throughout the zodiac from the point of view of the Imum Coeli (IC)

Chiron in Aries on the IC

This placement lends a certain fearlessness that comes from a keen sense of inner fortitude.

Double maverick and American photographer, Diane Arbus, had the courage to approach, document, and expose the wounded ones in society to the world.

Multi-maverick, Malcolm X, used this powerful astrological placement to bring the issues of racism to the public's awareness.

Actress, Patricia Neal, shows the many issues that can accompany such a powerful placements as noted in her obituary from NYTimes.com:

> Ms. Neal received her Oscar, as best actress, in 1964, for her performance in *Hud* as the tough, shopworn housekeeper who did not succumb to Paul Newman's amoral charm. By then she had already endured the death of her first child and a calamitous injury to her infant son, who was brain-damaged in an accident. Then came three strokes, a year after the Oscar, leaving her in a coma for three weeks. Afterward she was semi-paralyzed and unable to speak. But she learned to walk and talk again with the help of her husband, the British writer Roald Dahl.

From BrainyQuotes.com comes this perfect statement from footballer Alan Shearer:

> "I hope I never have to face that feeling of missing and sending my country or team out of a competition."

Double maverick, James Degorski, who was one of the 1993 Brown's Chicken massacre's mass murderers, clearly used the aggressive aspect of this placement to kill others. Aries rules weaponry.

The headline from TheSun.co.uk displays the effects of pushing one's self too far as in the case of singer, Lee Latchford-Evans. Lee wisely gave up dancing since this happened, but he is able to walk again:

LEE'S HEALTH HORROR

Steps star Lee Latchford-Evans feared he'd "never walk again" after dance moves damaged his spine and left him in a wheelchair.

Chiron in Taurus on the IC

This astrological combination is likely to have an issue with form, so they can actually shape-shift in the sense of either being deliberately in the form of something or having the ability to trans-form.

Multi-maverick actor, Sean Connery, shows that hard work applied to humble beginnings can pay off. TheVintageNews.com lists his accomplishments:

The first James Bond; Scotland's Greatest Living National Treasure; *People* magazine's "Sexiest Man of the 20th Century,"; knighted in the year 2000; In contrast with all the amazing accolades he achieved, Sir Sean Connery overcame some pretty humble beginnings.

The multi-maverick nature of entertainer extraordinaire, Roy Castle, is well articulated in his obituary from Independent. co.uk:

> SELF-DEPRECATION is scarcely an asset in show business. Yet, Roy Castle was loved and admired as much for his modesty as for his prodigious talents. An accomplished musician, singer, dancer, actor, comedian and, more recently, television front man, Castle had all the ingredients for international stardom but for an inflated ego and the need to be loved by millions.

Multi-maverick and musical virtuoso, Nina Simone, exhibits another aspect of this astrological combination, as is seen at her website ninasimone.com, where she is declared the "High Priestess of Soul."

Most people are not familiar with the name Barry Humphries, because he is known for being an entirely different form on stage. Ever outlandish in outfits, hair, makeup, jewelry, Barry's Dame Edna, wowed audiences with her wicked tongue and "Possum" charm. Taurus, ruled by Venus, loves the pretty things in life and Barry displayed it perfectly. From TheGuardian.com, comes this perfect tidbit:

> Humphries says none of his characters give him quite as much pleasure as Australian ambassador Sir Les, best known for his puce cheeks, huge appendage and formidable frothing. "I enjoy playing Les more than any other character because it release my inner vulgarity. It liberates my repressed ribaldry." In 1999, Sir Les

appeared with Kylie Minogue at Nick Cave's Meltdown, in a duet that concluded with him chasing her round the stage and whipping out his famous (and thankfully fake) "frightener."Sir Les is an acquired taste. When I first came across him in my teens, I couldn't believe somebody could be so disgusting on TV and get away with it – he was one of the funniest things I'd ever seen."

Chiron in Gemini on the IC

These are likely individuals who felt they had a voice to share and had to find a way to do it. Each of our examples are true mavericks for what they did in their respective fields.

From NYTimes.com comes this beautiful piece about multi-maverick singer and actress, Diahann Carroll:

> Though Ms. Carroll publicly defended *Julia*, she acknowledged that in portraying the black experience it made many concessions to the middle-class white viewers it hoped to attract. She also said afterward that her experience playing the character had been both a professional boon and a professional hindrance.
>
> The series made her one of the most visible performers of her day, booked regularly on TV talk and variety shows. But in addition, it entailed her becoming a de facto spokeswoman not only for *Julia* but also seemingly for her race, an onus for which she had never bargained."

From Oprah.com, comes this archetypally perfect reflection of what this placement did for multi-maverick and American media personality, Phil Donahue:

> "It's what I call a full-circle: Phil Donahue, the trailblazer who used the power of television to transform a nation, sits across from me in a rocking chair on the terrace of his Manhattan penthouse. Back in 1967, long before I ever dreamed of a talk show of my own and the life it would bring me, he was captivating viewers in Dayton, Ohio; in 1969, his show debuted nationally, and the whole country came to know his personal brand of issue-driven straight talk. If there had been no *Phil Donahue* show, there would be no *Oprah Winfrey* show. He was the first to acknowledge that women are interested in more than mascara tips and cake recipes—that we're intelligent, we're concerned about the world around us, and we want the best possible lives for ourselves."

Legacy.com shared this articulate obituary for multi-maverick actress, Mary Tyler Moore:

> But it was more than the show's concept that was a game changer. The show itself – its writing, characters, situations and conversations – brought a new tone to prime time, a cool sophistication that didn't pander to its audience. A contemporary review from The Associated Press credited the show with doing no less than this: "(It) took 20 years of pointless, insipid television

situation comedy and spun it on its heels." The show portrayed one of the most classic female friendships of TV history between Mary and her neighbor, Rhoda, played by Valerie Harper. And it brought us a quiet feminism, one that wasn't as in-your-face as that of the contemporary sitcom *Maude* but instead simply had Mary facing the world as a liberated woman.

Some of the show's episodes are legendary in the annals of television, notably "Chuckles Bites the Dust." In it, the network's children's star, Chuckles the Clown, dies while dressed as a peanut in a circus parade – "a rogue elephant tried to shell him." Moore gave a masterful performance as she first scolded her friends for laughing at his manner of death, then broke into uncontrollable giggles at his funeral. "The Mary Tyler Moore Show" won a record-setting 29 Emmy awards, three of which were Moore's for best actress, bringing her to a total of five best actress Emmys. That's a record, one that Moore shares only with Candice Bergen and Julia Louis-Dreyfus."

Chiron in Cancer on the IC

These individuals often have issues of familial conflicts that strengthen them. There can also be an indication of dynasty, or family inheritance. Interestingly enough, our first two examples were born on the same day and year.

Multi-maverick and actor, Robert Walker, Jr.'s obituary in SyFy.com says it all about this astrological placement:

Born in Queens, New York on Apr. 15, 1940, Walker was the son of Hollywood royalty — his father was actor Robert Walker (*Strangers on a Train*) and his mother was actress Jennifer Jones (*The Song of Bernadette*). After his parents divorced in 1945, Jones went on to marry legendary studio mogul, David O. Selznick, who became Walker Jr.'s stepfather and further cemented his familial connection to Hollywood.

From his obituary three years earlier in NYTimes.com, comes many perfect gems for this astrological placement for Australian filmmaker, Paul Cox:

> Paul Cox, a Dutch-born Australian director who was widely considered a father of Australian art cinema, died on Saturday in Heidelberg, in the Australian state of Victoria. He was 76.
> The cause was cancer, his family said.
> Mr. Cox, who settled in Australia as a young man in the 1960s, was known internationally for his ruminative, sympathetic, sometimes autobiographical explorations of the lives of marginalized people: the lonely, the aging, the dying.
> In 2000, The Sydney Morning Herald called him "our most enduring, individualistic, independent filmmaker," adding, "He is often referred to as our only true auteur."

Not only is the dual nature of Cancer perfectly expressed in this article from Aedelhard.com about maverick athletic twins,

Alev and Derya Kelter, but the way in which sibling rivalry can operate in a healthy manner:

> Derya will never let Alev forget who won the first competition.
>
> "I won who's older," says Derya, who will forever have one minute of seniority. "Alev, you can be an Olympian, but let's not forget who won the first battle."
>
> From the outset, the Kelter twins defined competitive.
>
> "She became two inches taller because she sat on me for nine months," Derya admits with a laugh. "That's why Alev (will suggest that) it's not about speed. It's about positioning and being tactical."
>
> Whether it was rollerblading down the street, playing capture the flag, juggling a soccer ball, or skateboarding, everything was a competition.
>
> "For me, competing is a way of life," Alev says. "And (Derya's) the reason why I'm so competitive. She's the reason I'm successful today."

Chiron in Leo on the IC

These individuals would likely have an overwhelming need to be seen by others, yet somehow feel they don't measure up. The Chiron Leo combination is great one for actors as there seems to be a wealth of other selves from which they can choose.

This astrological placement is highlighted in theGuardian.com obituary for showgirl-cum-socialite multi-maverick, Christine Keeler:

> She spent much of the rest of her life after 1963 bemoaning – in countless interviews and several volumes of autobiography, each more lurid than the last – her inability to escape the shadow of the affair. "It's been a misery for me, living with Christine Keeler" she said when her "definitive account" was published in 2001 (the volume was revised in 2012, with the claim, "Now Profumo is dead I can finally reveal the truth." Yet she never appeared to really want to put it behind her. She would approach journalists and publishers repeatedly, offering to sell them another new angle on the story.

Leo loves to remain in the spotlight.

In an excerpt from ChicagoTribune.com, we find an expressive description for this astrological placement in the life of multi-maverick and Beach Boy, Brian Wilson:

> A boy wonder.
> "An abused child, I turned myself into a boy wonder piano player and wrote the Beach Boys into rock and roll's Hall of Fame. Dismissed for years as a drugged-out psycho, I spent five years struggling back to good health. At a time when critics wrote me off as a relic, I put out a solo record that evidenced my return to form at forty-five years old. In May 1990, when my cousin

Stan decided to challenge my competency in a court of law, I was left with only one option.

"Fight."

Wouldn't It Be Nice (the title comes from a Beach Boys 1966 Top 10 single) serves as a strong salvo in Wilson's battle to prove himself capable and autonomous. Roughly half of the book is devoted to his struggles-under Landy's guidance-to transform himself from a 340-pound drug addict, unable to cope with everyday life, to a fit and functioning human being.

The story of multi-maverick serial killer, Myra Hindley, is one filled with numerous themes of this astrological placement, not the least of which is this statement from her partner in crime, Ian Brady, found in an article from Independent.co.uk:

"In character she is essentially a chameleon, adopting whatever camouflage will suit and voicing whatever she believes the individual wishes to hear."

From her obituary from Telegraph.co.uk, singer, Cilla Black, we learn she was known for her appearance, especially her Leonine mane:

As the Liverpool docker's daughter and ingénue pop star trailing in the Beatles' wake, Cilla Black resolutely adhered to type: lacquered mane of flame-red hair (the consequence of a sixpenny rinse at the age of 13) short skirts, long legs and a strong Scouse accent.

Chiron in Virgo on the IC

Unfortunately, I have no examples for this astrological placement.

Themes would likely center around issues of discrimination, self-improvement and self-care.

Chiron in Libra on the IC

As Libra is the sign of harmony and balance in relationships, this astrological placement would indicate that there were imbalances.

Multi-maverick, Carl Gustaf XVI King of Sweden, had the interesting experience of being surrounded by women. His father died when he was less than a year old and his four older siblings were all female. We can also all agree that balance, or equality, would be a challenging proposition for any monarch.

Chiron in Scorpio on the IC

Scorpio is a sensitive water sign that often has issues with emotional vulnerability and strength. Chiron here is likely concerned with themes around power, sexuality, death and rebirth. This would be a most dynamic position for a hospice worker or someone working as a paramedic or a first responder.

An archetypally illuminative interview with actress, Glenn Close, from the Guardian.com paints this placement aptly:

"I think it's difficult," she says. "I don't think the male ego is necessarily conducive to having a really successful and recognisable partner. I think it can be hard and I now accept that!" She laughs and tells me about a Harvard study that showed both men and women tend to warm more to female figures who are more traditionally feminine and nurturing. It's not a fact that Close has paid much attention to, though, her career typified by characters who refuse to comply with old-fashioned gender conventions. She played a ruthless lawyer on the small screen in *Damages*; a manipulative widow in *Dangerous Liaisons*; a dog-killing fashionista in *101 Dalmatians*; a strong-willed vice-president in *Air Force One*; and bunny-boiling lover Alex Forrest in *Fatal Attraction* – none of whom were ever stuck in the kitchen playing house. "I've played a lot of women that people have called bitchy or evil," she says. "They have been incredibly strong and it's just interesting to me because the parts I've played in my career have been labelled as if they were women in the workplace."

Aspects of this astrological placement are described in multi-maverick singer, Laura Nyro's obituary from RollingStone.com:

> Indeed, "unusual" was a word often used to praise Nyro's talent and explain her personal style. "Dressed in black … Nyro wore purple lipstick and used Christmas-tree ornaments as earrings," says Artie Mogull, her first manager, in the book *The Mansion on the Hill*.

Scorpio is one of the signs of Astrology, especially one who likes to research and dig deeply, and Chiron is a planet that represents the teacher, educator and facilitator, so it is no surprise that we have astrologer, Bruce Scofield, as our next example. He is an extensive astrological author, teacher and researcher. An article from Astro.com writes:

> In early 1989 Bruce produced the first psychological delineations for the 20 day-signs in Mesoamerican astrology in his *book Day-Signs: Native American Astrology from Ancient Mexico* self-published in 1991 by One Reed Publications.

Multi-maverick, author, poet and playwright, Jewelle Gomez, uses this astrological placement to dive deeply into the topics that have meaning and give voice to that which has been mute, such as women, women of color, and LGBQT.

Multi-maverick and actress, Jackie Curtis had a life rife with the themes of this astrological placement. Here is an excerpt from a fantastic article from Vulture.com that I highly recommend reading:

> "I never thought of him as a woman," LaRose said. "He went back and forth so many times. When I met Jackie, he was a little boy with a shopping bag. He had bangs. He was very cute."
>
> "Sometimes he'd kind of have a James Dean style, but ragged," playwright Robert Heide said of Curtis, "and other times Jackie would dress as Barbara

Stanwyck. She would look really good in a red wig or that kind of thing."

It was a defiant stance, which today we might call nonbinary. As Curtis herself put it: "I'm not a boy, not a girl, not a faggot, not a drag queen, not a transsexual — I'm just me, Jackie."

She looked like a man in a dress: a little stubble or a beard, torn stockings, trashed dresses, smeared makeup, and plenty of body odor.

Chiron in Sagittarius on the IC

This is a double centaur position, so there will likely be a life filled with experiences to bring awareness from one's personal truth to a larger collective Truth. This is not an easy path, none of the angular Chiron placements will have it easy, but this position is supported by an idealistic disposition which will help them weather any storm.

Showing the faith side of this equation, disco queen, Donna Summer, surprised everyone when she professed she was a born again Christian.

Many actors have a strong Chiron in their chart, somehow bestowing that "gift" of exploring the question of who they are through the characters they portray. Australian actress, Jane Clifton shows this ability further enhanced by its angularity in mutable Sagittarius.

Leslie van Houten, of the Manson family, appears again showing us what the blind devotion of this astrological placement can cost.

ASTROLOGICAL MAVERICKS

I am really unsure how to classify our next example, other than to say that he was a maverick unlike any other. I recommend reading about Mr. Mangetout (French for eat everything) Michel Lolito and his amazing abilities. From Ripleys.com we have this excerpt:

> Fortunately for him, doctors soon determined that he had an incredibly resilient digestive system, with a super thick stomach lining and intestines. As a result, he could "safely" consume just about anything. And so, an incredible career as Monsieur Mangetout (Mr. Eat-all) began.
>
> The French entertainer may have been able to eat an impossible range of items, but he still had to take great care. His technique revolved around reducing metal objects into smaller pieces, making them easier for his body to handle by keeping his throat lubricated with mineral oil. In this way, he would regularly eat two pounds of metal every day!

Multi-maverick and English actor, Nigel Havers, in an article from theSun.com, shows that the seemingly private moments one experiences in one's life would remain private, but for the angularity which needs to be revealed, coupled with the gregarious double centaur energy:

> NAUGHTY Nigel Havers has confessed to mile-high romps with all three of his wives. The actor — who has starred in everything from *Coronation Street* to *Benidorm* - made the saucy confession as he opened

up to Piers Morgan's *Life Stories* about his chequered romantic past" the interview goes onto show the understanding that occurs with time, "It's a good thing I am not naughty now. I was as naughty as I could possibly get away with, which is pretty naughty. I was having the time of my life, it was so much fun."

Chiron in Capricorn on the IC

The dynamic challenges of success are evident in this particular combination as it has to do with finding one's authority in doing whatever one does best. As we know, this is a process that usually takes some time and, as this is Capricorn, structure, and hard work.

We finally have an example of someone who has remained a bit of a mystery, but what we do know exhibits themes of this astrological placement. An excerpt from NDPR.ND.edu reads:

> Gretel Adorno was a remarkable woman about whom far too little is known. Although the recent publication of her correspondence with Walter Benjamin has confirmed the impression that she was a formidable intellect in her own right, she remains largely a mystery. What we do know for certain is that she was deeply devoted to her husband Theodor, whom she married in September, 1937. Abandoning a career as a chemist to support his work unreservedly, she seems to have been resigned to his extra-marital affairs, and

was so despondent after his death in August, 1969 that she made a botched suicide attempt.

From IMDB.com comes this astrologically luminous quote from multi-maverick Australian film director and screenwriter, Scott Hicks:

"Nothing is ever going to be the same again. *Shine* (1996) was a unique experience and very few people are ever lucky to feel that degree of universal acceptance. Very seldom can you say that films change people's lives. As far as the world was concerned, this film came out of nowhere, it really sort of barnstormed across the world. It projected me into a new arena and in the process made a star out of Geoffrey Rush, completely changed David Helfgott's life and Lynn Redgrave's career was kick-started again. There were a number of us involved in this film whose lives were never going to be the same again. It was unique, not in the sense of some sort of fluke, just that it was a dark horse."

The anti-establishment themes of the Chiron in Capricorn placement are well exhibited by Punk/New Wave performer, Wreckless Eric.

Far right Oz representative from Queensland, Australia, Pauline Hanson, shared the challenges she experienced in doing what she considers is the right thing. Here are her comments from an article from NZHerald.co.nz:

Pauline Hanson has broken down over the latest scandal to engulf her party One Nation.

A Current Affair has released footage of an exclusive interview with an emotional Senator Hanson who is in tears after the resignation of Senate candidate Steve Dickson. Mr. Dickson resigned after being caught on camera in a lewd strip club visit.

The resignation is the latest scandal to hit One Nation and an emotional Senator Hanson appeared fed up.

"I cop all this s**t all the time and I'm sick of it," Senator Hanson tells journalist Tracey Grimshaw.

The success-oriented Capricorn nature shows through in the life of astrologer, Shelly Ackerman. From her website KarmicRelief.com we learn the following:

Shelley L. Ackerman was born in Manhattan. The daughter of a rabbi, she grew up on NYC's Lower East Side. After graduating with honors from NYCs High School of Music and Art, her career onstage began at the Improvisation and Catch a Rising Star. She was Peter Allen's opening act at Reno Sweeney and played many well-known venues including Les Mouches, the Playboy Club, Freddy's Supper Club and starred in the 1988 revival of *Jacques Brel is Alive and Well and Living in Paris* at Town Hall and at The Kennedy Center.

Passionate about the unique language and logic of astrology, she often studied the horoscopes of celebrities and became fascinated with the timing of world events and the correlation to planetary cycles.

Eventually, the call to astrology won out: At an eclipse in late June of 1992, she became a professional astrologer. Writing columns, articles providing commentary on radio and TV followed.

Chiron in Aquarius on the IC

Here the themes of being the outcast, especially of the family, are inevitable. As this is Aquarius, there is likely a very unusual type of brilliance emanating from within these individuals.

Our fist example is the iconic actress, Katharine Hepburn. These quotes from GoodHousekeeping.com exhibit some of her radiant wit:

> "If you want to sacrifice the admiration of many men for the criticism of one, go ahead, get married."

> "I never realized until lately that women were supposed to be the inferior sex."

> "Life is hard. After all, it kills you."

> "Death will be a great relief. No more interviews."

Surprising or not surprising? Our next example, Douglas Fairbanks, Jr., was a contemporary of our previous example, and he also dated her. Having this shared astrological placement would be most enticing. The humanity-oriented Aquarian nature is on display in Fairbanks, Jr.'s obituary from LATimes.com:

> Aside from his own famous relatives, father Douglas Sr. and step-mother Mary Pickford, Fairbanks Jr. really did know Charlie Chaplin, Tallulah Bankhead, Greta Garbo, Maurice Chevalier and Bing Crosby and helped boost the film careers of an Aussie named Errol Flynn and a USC football player named Marion Morrison (John Wayne).
> And he did play tennis with King Gustav V of Sweden, study Spanish with John F. Kennedy, meet Queen Elizabeth II when she was a toddler and entertain the grown-up queen, Prince Philip and the rest of her family at his London home.
> Her father, King George VI, gave him an honorary knighthood in 1949 for "furthering Anglo-American amity," partly for his work as a U.S. Navy officer for the commando corps of British Adm. Lord Louis Mountbatten, uncle to Prince Philip, and partly for his postwar work raising money for the Cooperative for American Remittances to Europe (CARE) which sent more than $150 million worth of food and other goods to war-torn European countries.

From BrainyQuotes.com we find a collection of surprising and fixed-oriented gems from New Wave English musician, Gary Numan:

"And I used to go the punk clubs such as a gay club in Poland Street that everyone would go to because it was the only place you could go to looking like that without getting beaten senseless."

"I'd been a Bowie fan before punk and used to get no end of trouble. I was always getting knocked about and having to run up the street, getting chased by people. It was horrible."

"I don't believe in sharing my money. If I go out and work my nuts off and make some money, I don't feel that I should have to share it with my community."

"I'm very intolerant and I get fed up with people easily."

If we look at the Aquarian glyph, or symbol, it looks like an electrical wave, so of course, we find someone who co-founded an "electric" band. In classic maverick (and Aquarian) manner English rocker, Angus Young, of AC/DC fame, does not like to follow the rules of society, but rather his own.

Actress, Tracey Ullman, is known for portraying a vast array of human characters in her comedy shows. Tracey has a knack for understanding and expressing the individualized quirkiness of being human – another dazzling example of this astrological placement.

Scottish comic book writer, Grant Morrison, brings the mutant aspect of the Aquarian nature to his writing and fits the part with is clean-shaven pate.

Noah Domasin, who also has his Moon here, was born using a frozen egg and frozen sperm and conceived outside of a mother's body, all themes of this astrological placement.

Chiron in Pisces on the IC

These individuals find their inner truth through exploring the Piscean netherworld waters of Spirit, drugs, esoterica, and imagery.

Long after her departure from this earthly plane in 1963, chanteuse extraordinaire, Edith Piaf, still charms modern audiences with her songs, especially "La vie en rose" (seeing life through rose-colored glasses) and "Non, je ne regrette rien" (No, I don't regret anything). Piaf is best known for her torch songs, chansons, all about love, sorrow and loss.

Australian naturalist and television personality, Steve Irwin, was an ambassador to the animal kingdom. Well-known as, "The Crocodile Hunter", Steve was also a zookeeper, wildlife expert, environmentalist and conservationist. As we have seen with these angular planets, there can be an indication of the type of death one will encounter. In Steve's case it was a sting ray who stabbed him repeatedly.

In this territory of Piscean deep divers, we find astrologer, Ray White, who is the chief programmer for Astrolabe, the astrology software, reports, books, and services website. His bio at the Alabe.com website is as follows:

RAYMOND WHITE, Chief Programmer, joined Astrolabe in 1996 where he gets a chance to pursue long-standing interests in astrology and related esoteric subjects. He wrote the code for programs in the Astrolabe Report System, adding many innovative design features. He also wrote and designed our Cosmic Ray screensaver. He began his professional programming career in 1982, and has worked in a wide variety of programming languages on government and industrial products. Ray is a member of NCGR, Mensa, and the Procrastinator's Club of America (but he neglected to pay his dues). Ray finds his wife, Cat, extremely interesting.

Multi-maverick Olympian swimmer, Tracy Caulkins, was "built for swimming." An article from dailydsports.com writes:

> Her 48 U.S. championships stood until 2010, when Phelps surpassed that mark. Caulkins won eight World Championship medals and three Olympic golds in an era dominated by drug-enhanced East German women. At 5'9", 133 pounds, she had no weaknesses, allowing her to become the greatest IM racer to ever live. Had it not been for the Olympic boycott in 1980, she would have added five, six or seven medals to her career total. "When you get to the national and international level, everyone is physically equal. If you're mentally prepared and you have the stuff upstairs, then you'll win." Caulkins set five world records. She is a four-time American "Swimmer of the Year," a two-time recipient of the Broderick Cup as top American female athlete

and was twice the leading vote-getter for the Academic All-American team while at Florida.

American screenwriter and director of film and television, Lisa Cholodenko, has these eloquently descriptive quotes for this astrological placement from BrainyQuote.com:

"I tend not to be so attracted to films that force me into an intellectual place over an emotional one."

"I think for any artist, your voice is always evolving. For me, the constant is finding a tension or balance between drama and comedy."

As Pisces rules the feet and Chiron has four hooves, we can see how someone who is graceful on their feet would appear in this category. Multi-maverick and ballroom dancer, Craig Revel Horwood, is best known for being a judge on the BBC television show Strictly *Come Dancing* since its start. Another aspect of this astrological placement played out with his father's slow suicide from alcoholism.

Pisces can often offer magical and mystical abilities to individuals, even in sports as evidenced by multi-maverick, Andrew Jarman. Soccer, known around most of the world as football, is a sport that takes a level of mutable physicality well suited by this astrological placement. AustralianFootball.com writes the following about Jarman:

Known and indeed revered as 'The Magician of Prospect' Andrew Jarman was, without doubt, one of the most extravagantly talented footballers of his generation, masking a lack of genuine pace with sure hands, lightning fast reactions, and disposal skills that were second to none. A North Adelaide supporter from an earlier age, he joined the club from Gaza under 16's in time to play in the 1982 SANFL under 17 competition. His enormous potential was immediately evident, as was the wide range of his football skills, and he made his league debut the following year.

We will now look at the angle placements of Chiron throughout the zodiac from the point of view of the Descendant (DS).

Chiron in Aries on the DS

These individuals have Libra for their AS, so they are always focused on others. They are likely to be consistently challenged for being their authentic selves.

Multi-maverick First Lady Nancy Reagan's campaign, "Just Say No" to drugs is a perfect statement for this astrological placement.

The innovative spark of this astrological placement is well expressed in the life of bluegrass musician, Doc Watson. The following comes from his obituary at RollingStone.com:

Born in 1923 in Deep Gap, Arthel Lane "Doc" Watson influenced generations of country, folk and bluegrass artists with his flatpicking approach to the guitar. Watson went blind at age one following an eye infection and quickly grew immersed in music thanks to his parents, who performed in the local church choir and sang secular and religious songs. By the age of five, Watson was playing the banjo and harmonica, and by 1953 he was playing electric for a local country swing band. Watson's solo career took off following a performance at the Newport Folk Festival in 1963, as folk music was developing into a cultural phenomenon; he released his solo debut, *Doc Watson and Family*, that same year.

As one of the inventors of the atomic force microscope, Calvin F. Quate's obituary from Stanford.edu presents the brilliance of this astrological placement:

Quate, an electrical engineer by training, invented advanced microscopes that transformed science. His scanning acoustic microscope, announced in 1978, used high-frequency sound waves to apply gentle pressure to objects under observation. The acoustic microscope was as sensitive as light-based microscopes, yet delicate enough to measure the internal structures, density, elasticity and viscosity of living cells without harm.

Former U.S. President, Jimmy Carter's quotes from BrainyQuote.com beautifully express the maturity this astrological placement offers:

"The experience of democracy is like the experience of life itself – always changing, infinite in its variety, sometimes turbulent and all the more valuable for having been tested by adversity."

"If you fear making anyone mad, then you ultimately probe for the lowest common denominator of human achievement."

And this one that speaks to Carter's Libran Ascendant:

"I look forward to these confrontations with the press to kind of balance up the nice and pleasant things that come to me as president."

As well as this final one that confronts the military side of Carter's Aries:

"My decision to register women confirms what is already obvious throughout our society – that women are now providing all types of skills in every profession. The military should be no exception."

From his obituary from SMH.com.au, we find a beautiful quote from Australian actor, Tom Long, about the importance of relationships and self to these individuals:

"I am a lot more grateful for living," he said. "I have an enormous curiosity. I think that's what keeps us going. Through the darkness, if you can keep your curiosity, that helps. And a connectedness to family, friends, to community. It takes you to those edges. There is something that connects us all."

From Legacy.com, comes these archetypally telling endorsements about this astrological placement as lived by businessman, Christopher Ingrassia, who died in the Twin Towers on 11 September 2001:

Sure, Christopher Ingrassia was a Wall Street whiz and a terrific athlete. But what stood out about him to many was the deep kindness he poured out on friends and strangers alike.

Even in high school, where he played three sports and was very popular, his sweet concern for others was evident.

One day, when a group of girls stood up and left the table after a girl they didn't like dared to join them, Mr. Ingrassia went over and sat with the abandoned girl. "The mother of that girl told us about it," said his father, Anthony Ingrassia. "There are so many stories like that."

"One of the things that I think people would remember most about him, other than his sheer size, was his quick wit. He was just so funny that everyone loved him," recalled Dennis O'Dowd of Boonton, Mr. Ingrassia's roommate for two years at Princeton University.

Chiron in Taurus on the DS

These individuals would likely be drawn to luxury in life and very determined in the way they go about their relationships. Resolution about form, especially the forms of relationships, would likely be key for this placement.

French philosopher, Michel Foucault, focused on social relationships throughout his life. The following comes from his obituary at NYTimes.com:

> Born in Poitiers, France, in 1926, the son of a physician, Mr. Foucault was educated in psychology and philosophy. In 1961, his first widely discussed book, *Madness and Civilization*, was published. In it he argued that insanity was less a medical problem than a way in which societies categorized acceptable and unacceptable forms of behavior. Insane asylums, he said, were institutions of exclusion.

Rock and Roll pioneer, Chuck Berry, used this astrological placement in an entirely different manner. Excerpts from his obituary in TheGuardian.com explains:

> Through them all, Berry offered a bold and captivating use of cars, planes, highways, refrigerators and skyscrapers, and also the accompanying details: seatbelts, bus conductors, ginger ale and terminal gates. And he brought all this into his love songs. He put love in an everyday metropolis, fast and cluttered, as no one had done before him. In Berry's cities, real

people struggled and fretted and gave vent to ironic perceptions. Berry also specialised in place names, as no one else has done before or since. His songs release the power of romance in each one, flying with relish through a part of the American dream.

I feel it is important to include this statement from Berry's obituary because it ties into our next example:

> Berry's music was, as the critic Tom Zito observed, "not so much black as American". Yet stories like "Maybellene" were certainly in the spirit of "Stagger Lee" and the other speedy superheroes of black folk tradition, while "Brown-Eyed Handsome Man" (1956) asserted that black was beautiful ahead of its time – the title's understatement adroitly set against the extravagant wordplay of the verses: "De Milo's Venus was a beautiful lass / She had the world in the palm of her hand / But she lost both her arms in a wrestling match / To meet a brown-eyed handsome man."

Understanding that the African-American experience IS the American experience allows us to see how Chuck and our next maverick helped to teach white Americans and educate and empower black Americans. Wikipedia.com notes that writer, Eloise Greenfield, "is an American children's book and biography author and poet famous for her descriptive, rhythmic style and positive portrayal of the African-American experience."

ASTROLOGICAL MAVERICKS

CRFashionBook.com writes the following at the beginning of the section on the "secret moments" of Jacqueline Kennedy Onassis:

> ...became a household name in the 20th century. As First Lady of the United States, she was constantly in the public eye and became known for her superior taste and impeccable style that is still admired today. Looking beyond the surface, Jackie was a driven woman in her own right, making a career for herself before and following her marriages, and even helped shape American politics after President John F. Kennedy's death. Prior to Nancy Reagan, Jacqueline took on the task of renovating and updating, very tastefully of course, the White House after many years of neglect.

America actor, Clint Eastwood, who also has his Mercury here, offers these no-nonsense quotes that illustrate the resolution found in this astrological placement. From BrainyQuote.com:

> "Respect your efforts, respect yourself. Self-respect leads to self-discipline. When you have both firmly under your belt, that's real power."

> "We boil at different degrees."

> "Sometimes if you want to see a change for the better, you have to take things into your own hands."

"I don't believe in pessimism. If something doesn't come up the way you want, forge ahead. If you think it's going to rain, it will."

"The less secure a man is, the more likely he is to have extreme prejudice."

"It takes tremendous discipline to control the influence, the power you have over other people's lives."

Aeronautical engineer, Edward Higgins White, understood from an early age that his form was dedicated to something other than walking on Earth. He was the first American to walk in outer space.

American Football player and coach, Raymond Berry, shows the physical prowess of this position and how we address and resolve our limitations. Berry's entry from Wikipedia.com reads:

> Berry was famous for his attention to detail and preparation, which he used to overcome his physical limitations. Considered slow for a wide receiver, he ran the 40-yard dash in 4.8 seconds. Rather than speed, he was renowned for his precise pass patterns and sure hands; he rarely dropped passes, and he fumbled only once in his career. He would squeeze Silly Putty constantly to strengthen his hands. He and Unitas regularly worked after practice and developed the timing and knowledge of each other's abilities that made each more effective. The reason for this, according

to Berry, was that the two did not think on the same wavelength. "Every season we had to start all over on our timing, especially the long ball," said Berry. "He knew he had to release the ball when I was eighteen yards from scrimmage for me to receive it thirty-eight yards out. I knew I had to make my break in those first eighteen yards and get free within 2.8 seconds." He also relied on shifty moves, and by his count, he had 88 different moves to get open, all of which he practiced every week.

Of course, since Scorpio is the rising sign (remember this is maverick energy) for these individuals, there is *intense* relationship drama for the world to see as portrayed in the life of songwriter and DJ, Samantha Ronson. The world learns all about the end of her relationship with American actress, Lindsay Lohan, from Glamour.com:

> Later in the night, Lindsay went on her Twitter page to post this: "Being cheated on does wonders to you. I'm doing this publicly because u&ur friends call People [magazine]. So you win, you broke my heart. Now go away. I loved you." Wait—did she break up with Sam over Twitter?? She then followed-up the post with, "PLEASE leave me ALONE. and stop staying in the room below me, you've woken me and my mother up. go to bed. keep cheating u win." Lindsay told *Us Weekly* that it was the "worst night of my life," and understandably so.

Talk about drama! And those cheating accusations—what's up with that?

The painful realities of this astrological placement are detailed in an article from the WashingtonPost.com about Open Book, the new memoir by reality star, actress, fashion designer and author, Jessica Simpson:

> **She** spends plenty of time detailing her toxic relationships. She met [Nick] Lachey when she was 18 and he was 25, and she turned to him for guidance for almost everything. But their relationship soured soon after the wedding. If you want more proof of the drawbacks of fame, she admits that she was terrified to go to couples counseling because she thought a therapist might sell them out to the tabloids.

To round out the luxury aspect of this astrological placement, we have Olympic equestrian, Zara Philips, grand-daughter to Queen Elizabeth II. Zara has her own line of equestrian clothing.

Chiron in Gemini on the DS

These individuals have an innate ability to be whomever the other needs them to be. This can be a painful space for the native who is trying to determine who s/he is in relationship to the other. These individuals are gifted in the areas of communication, teaching, and setting a higher example.

Our first individual is the consummate creative communicator, artist, and inventor, Leonardo da Vinci. His diaries are all written in reverse and his imaginative expression knew no bounds.

This excerpt from an article from ChristianPost.com paints "outspoken Christian," Pat Boone with the range of skills this astrological archetype produces:

> Boone is known for his extensive career as a singer, composer, actor, writer, television personality and motivational speaker. He has recorded around 160 albums with sounds varying from rock 'n' roll and pop to country and gospel. Boone's career spans more than 60 years in singing and he has appeared in more than 12 Hollywood movies.

Maverick planets afford individuals a unique placement in society that can sometimes be restraining and comforting, as described by American songwriter, Johnny Mathis:

> "Even though there's no forum for me on the radio for the kind of music I sing anymore, I am still excited about having a career where I can sing the best music in the world, and people will come and hear me because of the hit records I've had in the past."

While she is a maverick for her acting and singing career, Connie Francis exhibits another aspect of this placement: she married four times.

Chiron in Cancer on the DS

These individuals are going to have a huge focus on family, clan and heritage. They may even be hoarders or individuals who had to learn the hard way about emotional attachments to/with the other.

Our first example is the maker of many films and the themes of this astrological placement are pronounced in his life. From BrainyQuotes.com come these archetypally resonant quotes from multi-maverick American film director and screenwriter, Francis Ford Coppola:

> "You have to really be courageous about your instincts and your ideas. Otherwise you'll just knuckle under, and things that might have been memorable will be lost."

> "Most Italians who came to this country are very patriotic. There was this exciting possibility that if you worked real hard, and you loved something, you could become successful."

> "I remember teachers who really singled me out for their discouragement."

> "I bring to my life a certain amount of mess."

> "We support each other in the Coppola family. We love the idea of everyone getting his place in the sun."

ASTROLOGICAL MAVERICKS

As we have seen with so many mavericks, their awareness of and focus on their goals is a repeated theme. In this interview, we see this process beautifully articulated by New Zealand author, Fiona Kidman, from Stuff.Co.NZ:

> Dame Fiona Kidman likes to get things done. When she made the decision nearly 60 years ago to be a writer, it wasn't to become the tortured type, who can only eke out a few words, bit by painful bit. She isn't one for procrastination.
>
> She writes every day between 9am and 1pm, from the desk at her light-filled Hataitai home where she's lived for 49 years. It makes sense, then, that she is one of New Zealand's most successful and prolific writers. Her steadfast writing routine is a bit of a blow - I was hoping for an ally to moan about the grit of putting sentences on pages.
>
> "I don't have days like that," she says. "This was what I decided to do when I was 22 - to be a writer - the way people decide they're going to be a lawyer or an accountant, or whatever. I decided this was what I wanted to do for the rest of my life, so I applied myself."

Multi-maverick and British, Danish, and Greek royal, Zenouska Mowatt, since her conception, has been a complex mixture. It helps that she also has her Moon and Jupiter here opposing her maverick Uranus on the Ascendant in Capricorn. Start with the story of her parents to really get a sense of a how these compounded energies have played out in her life.

Our final example displays the family dynasty aspect that can occur with this astrological placement. Actress, Dakota Johnson, is the daughter of actress, Melanie Griffith and actor, Don Johnson.

Chiron in Leo on the DS

While Leo is a fixed, self-centering sign, when Chiron is added to the mix, the individual may act in the ways they think their partner(s) want(s) them to act. Sort of a crisis in identity, especially when getting to the more tender parts in intimate relating. The conundrum is in creation both of one's individual identity and how that identity is in relationship to others, as well as how to remain creative in relation to others. These individuals need to be seen and heard.

Our first example is multi-maverick English actor, Michael York, who has been married to his wife since 1968, an almost unheard-of accomplishment in the entertainment industry on its own. The flexibility Chiron lends is well stated by Michael, in this from BrainyQuote.com:

> "I think that you have to believe in your destiny; that you will succeed, you will meet a lot of rejection and it is not always a straight path, there will be detours – so enjoy the view."

Multi-maverick and American country music singer, Tammy Wynette, has some practical statements about this astrological placement from AZQuotes.com:

> "I spent 15 minutes writing "Stand by Your Man," and a lifetime defending it."

Tammy comments on the loneliness this position can experience:

> "Loneliness surrounds me without your arms around me."

There is a huge and sometimes literal inner flame with this astrological placement as put on display by another multi-maverick in this position, rock star extraordinaire, Janis Joplin. She didn't make it to 28, let alone her Saturn return. She burned brightly and quickly.

Nicholas Hasluck is an accomplished and creative individual, as well as a published poet, novelist and retired Supreme Court Judge of Western Australia.

Chiron in Virgo on the DS

Virgo is the sign of the Virgin, the sacred female. When we include Chiron here, we find individuals who likely have to overcome significant issues with how they are treated.

How they are treated may be simply for their sex as in the case of veteran British journalist and writer, Angela Rippon. She gave an interview to Independent.com.uk in which she revealed a misogynistic experience in her professional work. I'd recommend reading the rest of the article.

Angela Rippon has spoken for the first time about an incident in which a "highly respected" male colleague pretended to flash her when she was live on air.

As part of Radio 4's *The Reunion: Pioneering Women Newsreaders*, Rippon shared her experience of being a female broadcaster in a male-dominated environment.

The presenter, 74, said the unnamed colleague unzipped his trousers and pretended to flash her while she was reading the news to an audience of 10 million BBC viewers.

Chiron in Libra on the DS

These are individuals who are likely obsessed with harmony and beauty in their relationships, having expressed what they consider as too much time on any one side of polarizing experiences.

Multi-maverick and American singer, Bette Midler, who also has her Jupiter here, has expressed that she had a very rough and poor childhood. We can see her Aries ascendant drive as she has done everything she can to be successful and rich. A friend of mine who worked in a hotel in which Bette repeatedly stayed, stated that Bette had a very rigid routine that included not only certain things happening at certain times during the day, but specific furniture in certain places, as well as items that could only arrive at certain temperatures. Balancing what she considered was abject poverty, Bette has given herself the luxury to create and control her environment by paying others to make it so. Unfortunately, when life happens, she has others to blame rather than being okay with the fact that life is a constant balancing act. Bette has been married to the same person since 1984, which shows there is a flexibility of relating that she understands.

Chiron in Scorpio on the DS

Individuals born with this configuration possess tremendous phoenix energy. Their ability to rise from the flames is considerable.

Our only example, Manuela "Manny" Musu, literally walked out of the flames, but lost her mother in the process, when she survived the bombing of the Australian embassy in Jakarta. In a further twist of sexual fate, Manny's paternity was not what it appeared. In typical Scorpionic fashion, her father was revealed.

Chiron in Sagittarius on the DS

This placement provides opportunities of and for learning, faith, foreign travel and larger philosophies. The two centaur energies combine to give these natives a natural ability to see outside of any box in which they find themselves, which means they are able to teach others to do the same.

The inclusive nature of this astrological placement is well represented in the life of author, Barbara Wilson. The following comes from Astro.com:

American writer; Wilson is also founder of Seal Press. A lesbian and a feminist, her heroines are usually strong, witty, adventurous and intelligent. She has written mysteries, novels, and published short-story collections.

Her novel *Gaudi Afternoon* which was made into a feature film, was awarded the Crime Writers Association Award and Lambda Literary Award in 1991. Another novel, *Blue Windows* won the Lambda Literary Award and was a nominee for PEN Center USA West, in 1997.

She co-founded Seal Press in support of women authors and founded Women in Translation, which translated the writing of women who are exiled or marginalized.

AS Sagittarius can also represent religion in one's life, and here we can see the ways in which the parents of conjoined twins, Alyssa and Bethany Nolan, were influenced by their Catholic beliefs. Her mother also states this incredibly optimistic Sagittarian statement on their gofundme.com page:

> "So, I guess the moral of this story is if life presents you with a chance, no matter how small or scary it may be, reach out and grab it with both hands. You never know what magic may lie at the end of it."

Chiron in Capricorn on the DS

There is a drive towards success with this placement, but either extended doubt or educational and transformational "process" ensures the native learns what is required to be of success. The complexity of this position is often carried in the family lineage somehow.

No one is quite sure when our first example learned that his sister was actually his mother, and his parents were actually his mother's adoptive parents. Thomas Watt Hamilton, believed that he was denied becoming a scout master because others thought he was a pervert, but he was dismissed because he was not suited to be a troop leader. Thomas took his inner wound and turned it outwards wounding 15 and killing one teacher and 16 students before shooting himself.

American actor, John Travolta, has these quotes from AZQuotes.com that offer insight to this astrological placement:

> "It's easier to be responsible for the decisions that you've made yourself than for the ones that other people have made for you."

> "Money and power come as a byproduct of things well done."

> "I don't think I'm very cool as a person. I'm just better than anyone else at acting cool."

> "You feel alive to the degree that you feel you can help others."

"I've always thought that as long as I did the right things and had the right intentions, everything would fall into place."

"Misdirection. What the eyes see and the ears hear, the mind believes."

LGBQT director and German filmmaker, Monika Treut, falls into the category of women who make history because they speak up. Her women misbehave, which is what is needed to balance the inequalities between the two sexes. How can 50% of the population be better than the other 50%? This and other misogynistic frames of reference are what mavericks like Monika are here to transform.

Conscious leader, Runa Bouius, writes, speaks, coaches, teaches, and facilitates corporate executives seeking to align themselves with a more fully functional, efficient and contented workforce. Runa knows what a conscious organization can accomplish and guides leaders to reach such ambitious heights. As Monika is transforming our relationship to the sexes, Runa is transforming businesses' relationship to a larger whole.

Chiron in Aquarius on the DS

These individuals often experience great pain in relationships until they find the unique partner who can also appreciate the native's specific particularity. Aquarius is a maker of glyphs and symbols.

Our first example is American pop artist, Keith Haring, who reduced his imagery to archetypal. His website, Haring.com writes about Keith:

> Haring was able to push his own youthful impulses toward a singular kind of graphic expression based on the primacy of the line.

The goal of this astrological placement is well stated in the name given to the Emperor of Japan's reign: Reiwa which means *beautiful harmony*. This period began when Prince Naurhito ascended the Chrysanthemum Throne. There is often alienation and loneliness in this astrological placement that points to differing types of restrictions balanced with other types of freedoms. Prince Naurhito speaks of his childhood from Wikipedia.com:

> Naruhito found the remains of an ancient roadway in the palace grounds, sparking a lifelong fascination with the history of transportation, which would provide the subject of his bachelor's and master's degrees in history. He later said, "I have had a keen interest in roads since childhood. On roads you can go to the unknown world. Since I have been leading a life where I have few chances to go out freely, roads are a precious bridge to the unknown world, so to speak."

Individuals with this astrological placement often have an ability to synthesize complex ideas, thoughts and imagery and make them more accessible to others. TheCreativeIndependent.

com has a brilliant interview with maverick and American actress, Sandra Bernhard. One answer she gives beautifully illustrates her approach using this aspect:

> "When I started performing nobody really understood what I was doing because it was a real hybrid of all the different styles of performing that I loved—from musical comedy to rock-and-roll to Bette Midler—bigger than life entertainment. It was a mix of doing some throwbacks to Vegas entertainers mixed with edgy comedy, everything was thrown into the soup container and mixed up. Anything that influenced me, anything that I loved, I would put in. I didn't even know what I was doing; I was just reflecting what I loved to do, which was entertain. I loved everything from Burt Bacharach to the Detroit sound, Motown, whatever … it was all the musical styles and old movies and everything that I grew up on. You know, after growing up in the Midwest and moving to Arizona when I was a kid, I absorbed all these different things. It was like a road map of everywhere I'd been."

American cartoonist, Bill Waterson, author of the comic strip Calvin and Hobbes, revealed the intimate and inner process of becoming human through the unique relationship between boy and pet (stuffed) tiger. From the WashingtonPost.com we understand that Bill has granted an unprecedented interview:

> For years, the cartoonist didn't make public comments. Now, in a single wide-ranging and revealing

and illuminating and engrossing and self-deprecating and poignant and, of course, deeply funny interview, Watterson has proved more generous than we perhaps could have ever hoped for.

Bill Watterson has delivered a gift, a trip down memory lane that is populated densely on each side with personal and professional insights — some grippingly specific, some that ring universal, many that resonate as both.

We see the behavioral, mental, and emotional issues of this astrological placement in Swedish singer, Ted Gärdestad's life. Wrongfully used in the rumor mill, he was the scapegoat for numerous horrific acts in otherwise safe Sweden. The outcast Aquarian energy when highlighted by Chiron on an angle can elicit a self-correction, which Ted did by throwing himself before a moving train.

Chiron in Pisces on the DS

These deep divers are sometimes too sensitive to survive the hardships in life. The path to healthy expression is doing our own psychological work, and making sure we surround ourselves with others who are doing the same.

This astrological placement is also a position of profound creative genius as exhibited by multi-maverick and avant-garde American composer, John Cage. From NYTimes.com:

In the music world, of course, Mr. Cage's influence was extremely far-reaching. He started a revolution by proposing that composers could jettison the musical language that had evolved over the last seven centuries, and in doing so he opened the door to Minimalism, performance art and virtually every other branch of the musical avant-garde. Composers as different in style from one another -- and from Mr. Cage -- as Philip Glass, Morton Feldman, Earle Brown and Frederic Rzewski have cited Mr. Cage as a beacon that helped light their own paths.

"Perhaps no one living artist has such a great influence over such a diverse lot of important people," Richard Kostelanetz, a writer who edited several books about Mr. Cage, wrote in a *New York Times Magazine* article in 1967. "Nowadays, even those critics who disagree with him respect his willingness to pursue his ideas to their 'mad' conclusions, and he was impoverished for too many years for anyone seriously to doubt his integrity."

From BostonReview.net comes a beautiful example of this astrological placement through the life of American poet, Reginald Shepherd:

To think that Shepherd considers himself "wrong" on the basis of his race (African American) or sexual orientation (as Mark Doty does in his otherwise astute blurb) is to focus on the less interesting aspects of the poems--those determined by a socially definable identity. What is "wrong" about these poems is their refusal to cooperate with expectations or conventions. For Shepherd, "wrong" is as much action as injury or description; as a title, the word has the advantage of grammatical multiplicity--adjective, noun, verb--and it recalls Robert Duncan's "Proofs," in which he advises, "For 'wrong' read 'wring.'" As if taking Duncan's correction to heart, Shepherd wrings language in an attempt to illuminate his way of perceiving and inhabiting the world.

Scottish singer, Lena Zavaroni, exhibited the difficult emotionally sensitive aspect of this astrological placement, in an article from IrishTimes.com:

Already, however, she had begun to show signs of the eating disorder anorexia nervosa, the illness from which she was to suffer for the rest of her life. In many ways, her problems were typical of those that beset many pre-pubescent stars: the loss of childhood, public attention, and the difficulty of transposing childhood talent into an adult package when show business – and, to some extent, the audience – only thrilled to the child/voice combination.

Chiron often plays a significant role in the charts of actors and artists. Multi-maverick and English actor, Robson Green, reveals a Chironic secret in an interview he gave to TheGuardian.com:

> "I went for officer training to be a fighter pilot, but never got past the aptitude test. So I decided to put on makeup and ponce about in front of a camera."

The deep merging these individuals feel can sometimes be overwhelming to comprehend as multi-maverick actress, Brooke Shields, describes in an interview with VanityFair.com:

> Even so, two traumatic experiences soured her on the prospect of making any more movies. "It was an altered universe we were all in, and coming out of filming was a real shock to my system," she says. "I remember being on the plane just sobbing.... That kind of heartbreak can only happen to an 11-year-old." The set felt like "a family.... And then to feel like you have to possibly get that close to people again, and then one day it's over? I didn't want to feel that again."

Multi-maverick singer and songwriter, Kurt Cobain, made many beautifully archetypal statements of this astrological placement. Here are a few from BrainyQuote.com:

> "It's okay to eat fish because they don't have any feelings."

> "Wanting to be someone else is a waste of the person you are."

> "I've always had a problem with the average macho man - they've always been a threat to me."

ASTROLOGICAL MAVERICKS

"The sun is gone, but I have a light."

"If you die, you're completely happy and your soul somewhere lives on. I'm not afraid of dying. Total peace after death, becoming someone else is the best hope I've got."

There is not much information about U.S. hockey player and multi-maverick, Nevin Maarkwart, available on the internet. After much digging, I found the following statement about self-care from hfboards.mandatory.com:

He was The Kamikazee Kid. Multiple injuries from going 100 mph into the boards. Just so incredibly full-throttle with such little self-preservation. Every time I'd cringe, hoping he'd get up again, because he was a joy to watch. If the guy had the skill, or stayed healthy, he'd be lauded – just can't let someone get away with forgetting he was a Bruin. lol… Named by 'hockey parents'. Wasn't his mom watching The Leafs game while in labour and Bob Nevin scored or something like that?

We will now look at the angle placements of Chiron throughout the zodiac from the point of view of the Medium Coeli (MC).

Chiron in Aries on the MC

These individuals have an instinctive immediacy and a strength that is fortified with each experience. There is a sadness in the fire that ignites others. The first degree of Aries is considered the World Point and with Chiron and the MC here, there can be no mistaking the impact these individuals have on the world.

Multi-maverick Scottish poet, Edwin Morgan, understood that life is a range of experiences that deserve to be recognized regardless of where along the continuum they are expressed. We see this in his quote from BrainyQuote.com:

> "I like to give a voice to others, especially things neglected or despised."

English astrologer, John Addey, expressed the beautiful turning point that Chiron facilitated throughout his life. From Wikipedia.com we see a beautiful representation of this astrological placement:

> During his time at Ackworth he showed some talent for poetry, but more so for sports: he was captain of most of the various sports teams organised by the school. He

was head boy before leaving in 1939 and going on to Cambridge where he read English literature

He left university and joined the Friends Ambulence Unit While working there, he was struck down by severe Ankylosing Spondylitis [a type of arthritis] and was unable to walk without the aid of a stick for the rest of his life. Initial treatment required an 18-month stay in hospital, and it was during this enforced period of immobility that his energies turned inwards towards the two areas of study which were to occupy him for the rest of his life: philosophy and astrology (he had been interested in both from his mid-teens). He studied with the Faculty of Astrological and was awarded his Diploma in the early fifties.

He rapidly came under the influence of Charles E. O. Carter who guided Addey's explorations in both philosophy and astrology. In philosophy this meant an acknowledgement of the worth of all the great world religions and philosophies, but an especial interest in the Platonic tradition; in astrology Carter (who was for some time the President of the Astrological Lodge of the Theosophical Society) encouraged Addey's mystical leanings. Central to Addey's later work on the Harmonic theory of astrology was the conviction that the mystical and the scientific were not mutually exclusive and that neither was complete without the other.

The instinctual nature meanders through any meaningful piece of music. American jazz musician extraordinaire, Jimmy

Giuffre, used this astrological placement to forge new musical expressions.

Multi-maverick and American writer, Alex Haley, researched and wrote his family's history, deep wounds and all, so that the collective pain of the African-American experience could be brought to light and shared with all.

Multi-maverick singer, musician, and songwriter, Hank Williams, was born with spina bifida which is a malformation of the membranes around the spine. Hank drank and took medication to cope with the life-long pain from this birth defect. Hank died at 29 after having recorded no less than 35 songs that went on to Top 10 hits of the Billboard Country & Western Best Sellers chart.

Multi-maverick and American lawyer, Virginia Mae Brown, had this instinctual quote from GoodReads.com:

> "Sex makes monkeys out of all of us. If you don't give in to it, you wind up a cold, unfeeling bastard. If you do, you spend the rest of your life picking up the pieces… "

Another expression of the interwoven instinctual nature is well expressed in this excerpt from Wikipedia.com about Indian artist, Laxman Pai:

> Pai has painted various paintings based on different ragas of Indian classical music. In his works, he gives a visual interpretation to the moods of the music as determined by the vibrations of the notes. His painting series, *Musical Moods* (1965) was inspired by Indian

classical ragas. Pai used to also play the sitar and the bansuri.

American actor, Jerry Haynes, known affectionately as Mr. Peppermint Man, made this statement which is the last line in his obituary from WFAA.com:

"I want to remind you: Sometimes things don't go too well and you're not feeling a real good mood, Mr. Peppermint reminded his young viewers. When you feel unhappy, nothing seems worthwhile. Just give yourself a peppermint grin, and you will wear a smile."

The powerful individualistic energy of this astrological placement is beautifully articulated in the first line from Wikipedia's entry describing Danielle Egnew, as, "a psychic / medium, musician, media personality, actress and activist."

Harvard.edu has this lovely article on American folk rock singer songwriter, Melissa Ferrick, that illustrates other facets of this astrological combination:

Veteran singer-songwriter Melissa Ferrick, who has recorded 17 albums, couldn't have predicted that her music career would lead to education. But after more than 20 years of touring and playing music with artists ranging from Morrissey to k.d. lang to Bob Dylan, Ferrick found herself at a crossroads. Entering the middle part of her career and ready to tour less, she was looking for what would come next. Then, she was asked to teach songwriting at Berklee College of Music in Boston. As it would turn out, she found music isn't her only passion.

BrainyQuotes.com has these illuminating Chiron conjunct the MC in Aries proclamations from American actress, Angelina Jolie:

"When I get logical, and I don't trust my instincts - that's when I get in trouble."

"Without pain, there would be no suffering, without suffering we would never learn from our mistakes. To make it right, pain and suffering is the key to all windows, without it, there is no way of life."

"Where ever I am I always find myself looking out the window wishing I was somewhere else."

"I never felt settled or calm. You can't really commit to life when you feel that."

Chiron in Taurus on the MC

These individuals are here to learn, usually the hard way, about the various forms in life – physical, emotional, spiritual—and help guide the world to make a new relationship with them.

Known for turning the art world on its head, multi-maverick, Andy Warhol, had a fascination with relationships as we see from this piece from Artsy.net:

"People have so many problems with love," Warhol opined in 1975, "always looking for someone to be their Via Veneto, their soufflé that can't fall." In a chapter of *The Philosophy of Andy Warhol* entitled "Love (Senility)," the artist suggests that early education could alleviate later disappointments related to love and sex. "There should be a course in the first grade on love," he continued. The imagined class would provide a reality check, teaching children that relationships aren't all sunshine and roses.

In particular, Warhol hoped the course would remove the façade of perfection that cloaked relationships in the 1960s and '70s. He'd learned about love through television and movies, only to make the disappointing discovery that on-screen romances bore no resemblance to real life. "In those days, you did learn something about some kind of love from the movies, but it was nothing you could apply with any reasonable results," he explained.

These two paragraphs from actor English actor, Roger Moore's TheGuardian.com obituary are infused with the archetypal themes of this powerful astrological placement:

Moore devoted much of his time to being a goodwill ambassador for UNICEF; it was for this humanitarian work that he was knighted in 2003. He had left Britain in the late 1970s to avoid what he considered the prohibitive tax rate for high earners, and took homes in countries including Switzerland and Monaco.

Money continued to be much on his mind: his 2008 autobiography, *My Word Is My Bond*, is peppered with variations on the line "a rather nice deal was agreed with my agent."

Moore admitted to being a lifelong hypochondriac; among those to whom he expressed thanks in the acknowledgments of his autobiography are five GPs, four cardiologists, two dermatologists and a proctologist. He visibly enjoyed his time as Bond and expressed only occasional regrets about his career. "I spent my life playing heroes because I looked like one," he said. "Practically everything I've been offered didn't require much beyond looking like me. I would have loved to play a real baddie."

American author, Maya Angelou, lived an amazing life while experiencing some of its baser moments. Taurus is a security seeking sign. Chiron strips that away to reveal the strength within. On the MC, this energy has to be shared with the world. Angelou's obituary in the NYTimes.com shares several fascinating and poignant parts of her life:

> On one such occasion [staying with her mother], when Maya was 7 or 8 (her age varies slightly across her memoirs, which employ techniques of fiction to recount actual events), she was raped by her mother's boyfriend. She told her brother, who alerted the family, and the man was tried and convicted. Before he could begin serving his sentence, he was murdered — probably, Ms. Angelou wrote, by her uncles.

Believing that her words had brought about the death, Maya did not speak for the next five years. Her love of literature, as she later wrote, helped restore language to her.

American composer and organist, Gerre Hancock's obituary in *The New York Times* expresses a lovely variation on this astrological theme:

> As an organ soloist, Mr. Hancock performed in churches and concert halls worldwide. His talent for improvisation — in which a player elaborates a musical theme off the cuff in the appropriate key and meter, with fealty to the composer's style and intent — was considered the finest of any American concert organist.

Chiron in Gemini on the MC

While resolving their own issues around communication and movement, these individuals facilitate and guide the world. Gemini loves varied expression as well as various points of view.

John Stephen, dubbed by the media "The £1m Mod" and "The King of Carnaby Street," was one of the most important fashion figures of the 1960s. The following comes from his obituary in theGuardian.com:

> Benson [Richard Benson of the Face magazine] noted that Stephen had grasped early that "the best way of

catering to the counterculture was to be part of it"; his boutiques became regular film and television locations and he developed relationships with pop musicians, among the first to realise fans would buy anything their idols wore for television performances.

Danilo Kiš, was a Serbian novelist who articulated the process of this astrological placement eloquently in an interview from DalkeyArchive.com:

Brendan Lemon: How does *Hourglass* fit in with the rest of your work?

Danilo Kis: First of all, *Chagrins precoces, Garden, Ashes,* and *Hourglass* comprise an ensemble that you could call "novels of apprenticeship"—literary apprenticeship. *Chagrins precoces* are short stories, the world seen through a child's eyes, and the vision is deliberately naive. Then there's *Garden, Ashes,* where the main character becomes the father; in *Chagrins precoces* he appears only on the horizon. There's also a stylistic change in the second volume: the child's naivete is still there, but there's also the perspective of someone writing thirty years later. In the third part, *Hourglass*, the child is no longer a character; the subject becomes more intellectual. In these three volumes you can see the development of a writer. And you can see three different points of view about the same subject: the vanishing world of Hungarian Jews.

ASTROLOGICAL MAVERICKS

The writing theme continues with multi-maverick and Canadian novelist, George Bowering. These gems can be found at GoodReads.com

> "The more certain details are, the less likely they are to be the greatest matters. It would take all the details on every continent and then some, he thought, as he took a sip of Swan Lager, to add up to complete understanding."

> "The greatest matters lie beyond death, beyond the stars, in the aorta of time. A corpse is a detail. A second of starlight, even from the mid-Pacific sky full of a stars, is a detail. No matter how many details he might acquire, he would never arrive at truth here on the Indian Ocean."

> "No matter. He would settle for a little more knowledge. Let understanding come when it choose."

Italian media tycoon and politician, Silvio Berlusconi, served as Prime Minister of Italy in four governments. Berlusconi is the controlling shareholder of Mediaset and has owned the Italian football club A.C. Milan since 1986, showing a true maverick power with movement and communication.

Chiron in Cancer on the MC

These individuals have a flipped chart, compared to the default astrological chart that has Capricorn on the MC. These individuals have to balance home with their public lives.

Multi-maverick and American singer, Neil Diamond, exhibits one of the important aspects of this astrological placement, the feeling of "home" while also, once again, showing the apprentice aspect Chiron often imparts. From LennyBruce.com:

> With hits such as "Sweet Caroline" and "Solitary Man," it can be easy to forget that Neil Diamond spent a considerable chunk of his early career unsuccessfully writing hits for other stars. The balladeer from Brooklyn has long been cherished for his ways of stitching narrative and emotion into his lyrics, but it hasn't always come naturally. He's often said he "hates" songwriting, especially lyrics, which he has said are "impossible to write", although "melodies are as easy as falling off a log for me – they come instantly."
>
> It all means that, even after selling 135 million records, Diamond doesn't think he's "made it" yet, because he's "still struggling to get to that perfect song."

From KeplerCollege.org we have this beautifully descriptive bio for astrologer and Kepler College instructor, Carol Tebbs, who has the astrological placement of Chiron in Cancer on the MC:

[Carol]... attended Whittier College earning both BA and MA degrees in English, and shortly after, an MEd in Education. She was President of Kepler College from 2003-2006. Her 38 years of teaching Advanced Placement English to students receiving university credits is combined with her extensive Leadership Team experience in a large urban school district. As three-time Accreditation Team Leader, Technology Grant Author, District Writing Program Coordinator, and District Mentor Teacher charged with training new teachers, Ms. Tebbs' experience and knowledge of the many facets of higher education complement her recent work with the College Board as a "writing assessment reader" and AP teacher trainer.

Recognized as 1999 Wal-Mart "Teacher of the Year", and 2000 District Teacher of the Year, Ms. Tebbs is annually noted in *Who's Who in Education* and *Who's Who in the World*. Ms. Tebbs recently published *The Complete Book of Chart Rectification*. Ms. Tebbs is also well recognized in the astrological community for over 30 years of community service as: 3 terms ISAR President and 22 years on the Board; UAC Co-founder, Board member, Board Chair and UAC '95 Coordinator. Her books include *Beyond Basics: Moving the Chart in Time* and *Beyond Basics: Tools for the Consulting Astrologer*.

Chiron in Leo on the MC

These individuals have a deep desire to be seen, but may not feel worthy of the adulations. As they mature, they often learn ways to share their Leonine hearts in ways to make a difference in the world.

We see this personal evolution with our first example, in the life of businessman, Cooper Hefner. The following comes from HollywoodReporter.com:

> He announced that he would be changing course on his career and stepping away from media and publishing interests. "Today I informed leadership and financiers of Stag and Hefner Media Corporation I would be stepping back from focusing on launching a new company and stepping towards greater service to community and country," he wrote Dec. 10. "In a week I depart for U.S. Air Force basic training. A new road ahead."

Many attributes of this astrological position are evident in an interview from TheGuardian.com with Australian dramatist and playwright, David Williamson:

> "For many years, I couldn't even go to an opening night. I had to have Kristin [Williamson, his wife and a fellow writer] reporting to me how things were going."
>
> "You go to a brilliant opening night, you know it has connected, and then you think [of the critics]: 'Oh those fuckers'. I remember one [review] line that said, 'I sat with a dark cloud hovering above me as people

fell off their seats laughing around me'. And you think, what is so terrible about that? Why did the black cloud descend upon him to see people enjoying themselves in the theatre?"

Famously, Williamson's writing has often been clearly drawn from his experiences. In the early 1970s, he left his then-pregnant wife for his current wife, who also left her husband. This became the basis for his early play *Jugglers Three*, a depiction of two marriages breaking up, rewritten many years later as *Third World Blues* in which a character called Elizabeth accuses a character called Neville, based on Williamson, of having a "hyperinflated ego."

Is everything in his life playwriting material? "Well, I have drawn on life. Any writer who says they don't is lying. But you do change and alter [the details]."

Chiron in Virgo on the MC

Understanding and reconciling the divine feminine is an important part of this process whether one is born a boy or a girl as well as doing one's true work.

The multi-maverick virtuosity of American singing legend, Diana Ross, is well stated in her entry at Wikipedia.com:

> She is the only female artist to have number one singles as a solo artist; as the other half of a duet (Lionel Richie); as a member of a trio; and as an ensemble member (We are the World-USA for Africa). In 1976,

Ross was named the "Female Entertainer of the Century" by *Billboard* magazine. In 1993, the *Guinness Book of World Records* declared her the most successful female music artist in history, due to her success in the United States and United Kingdom for having more hits than any female artist in the charts, with a career total of 70 hit singles with her work with the Supremes and as a solo artist. She had a top 10 UK hit in every one of the last five decades, and sang lead on a top 75 hit single at least once every year from 1964 to 1996 in the UK, a period of 33 consecutive years and a record for any performer.

Maverick astrologer, Alan Oken, teaches the esoteric themes of ensouled matter, as well as the multi-valent ways in which astrology, soul or personality centered perspective, helps us to live more successful, service-oriented lives.

Chiron in Libra on the MC

Finding the right balance in whatever they do is key to these individuals. There is often an attachment to glamor and appearances that eventually gets resolved.

Multi-maverick American comedienne and actress, Goldie Hawn, makes the following archetypally appropriate quotes for this astrological placement:

"I'm not afraid of my femininity and I'm not afraid of my sexuality."

"I'm a woman who was raised to believe that you are not complete unless you have a man. Well, in some ways it's true. I am a feminist to a point. But I'm not going to deny the fact that I love to be with men."

"The biggest lesson we have to give our children is truth."

An article from WashingtonPost.com about multi-maverick and American actress, Candice Bergen, presents some of the issues with this astrological placement:

There, in one of the final chapters, Candice Bergen commits to print a confession that quite possibly has never been uttered, seriously, by any actress anywhere:
"Let me just come right out and say it: I am fat."
That this makes news, the tabloids, and NBC's morning talk show, *Today,* says everything about our culture and about Bergen, who has gained 30 pounds since the *Murphy Brown* decade (1988 to 1998). In her new memoir, *A Fine Romance* she admits that "I am a champion eater. No carb is safe — no fat either." Sitting in her spectacular starter Central Park South duplex (now her daughter's residence), she confesses, "I just can't face a life of fish fillets," and pops a brownie bite into her mouth.
At a certain age, the French advise, a woman must make a choice between her face and her rear. Bergen, at 68, has made hers.

Chiron in Scorpio on the MC

There can be a ruthless intensity to individuals with this placement. The lessons of life for these individuals are not for the weak hearted. The tender vulnerability of this energy are there for all the world to see.

Poet, writer and musician, Johnny Dowd, understands that life is a range of expression and even the bittersweet can make us giggle. The following comes from an interview Dowd gave to NoDepression.com:

> Knowing that much of Dowd's work reveals the coal black gothic side of small-town American life, I asked him to elaborate on his penchant for that particular style, take "Voices" from the new album for example? He laughed again, "I don't think of it as a dark side, to me it's just a life side. You can't get into what I do musically and lyrically if you don't see the humour. Its dark perhaps like someone slipping on a banana skin, that's sad, you know someone slipping on their ass, but at the same time it's also very funny … and that's the way I see life. Flannery O Conner was a great example of that type of writing. If it's just dark I don't really like that, it needs a funny side too otherwise lift would not be worth living. We try to inject a little bit of humour into the musicianship and playing, you know, like that Captain Beefheart style, it's a good balance, sadness and humour."

Scorpio is the sign of research into those occult, or unseen realms of life as well as understanding things from a deeply psychological point of view. When teacher, educator and facilitator, Chiron, walks through Scorpio, Chiron gives great instruction and there can be chronic deep pain. From Astro.com we learn more about astrologer, Howard Sasportas:

> In 1983, together with Liz Greene, he founded the *Centre for Psychological Astrology*. It became one of the most influential schools of its kind worldwide. Apart from being greatly admired as a teacher, Sasportas was also a productive author whose writings (including *The Twelve Houses* and *The Gods of Change*) were characterised by his clear and insightful language. In his writings he often referred to the ancient Greek myths. The ability of astrology to overcome some of the wide-spread prejudices in the English-speaking world in the 1980s and 1990s is due in part to his efforts.
>
> In the last years of his life Sasportas battled ill-health caused by a congenital deformity of the spine. His severe illness did not affect his productivity, yet, and although wheelchair-bound he attended many congresses and seminars until shortly before his death. He died in the presence of his closest friends, as astrologer Erin Sullivan described, "in peace and full of courage and awareness."

Scorpio seeks to shed light on that which lies in the shadows, and we see this astrological drive in the description of French filmmaker, Catherine Breillat, from Wikipedia.com:

In the film business for over 40 years, Catherine Breillat chooses to normalize previously taboo subjects in cinema.

The *birds of a feather, flock together* quality resonates deeply for the "Manson Family" who all share maverick Scorpio planets. Convicted murderer, Susan Atkins shows the early wounding that set the stage for her to commit such heinous acts. The following comes from RollingStone.com:

> Though not even 20 when she met up with Manson, Atkins had already lived a wild life. Escaping an alcoholic father, the teenager escaped to San Francisco where she teamed up with two convicts for a robbery spree, spent a few months in an Oregon prison, and performed in a topless revue called "the Witches' Sabbath," put on by Church of Satan founder Anton LaVey. But the LSD and Manson's psychological power over her were a toxic combination; she was convicted of eight murders and sentenced to death, which was commuted to life in 1972 when the California Supreme Court briefly banned capital punishment. Her last, unsuccessful, parole hearing took place on September 2nd, 2009, less than a month before she succumbed to brain cancer. She was 61.

Scorpio rules reproduction and Chiron here represents deep wounding – Susan Atkins is the one who stabbed pregnant Sharon Tate in the belly, telling her, "Woman, I have no mercy for you."

ASTROLOGICAL MAVERICKS

Chiron in Sagittarius on the MC

These individuals need freedom of exploration and expression. Their gregarious nature may have not been always supported.

Irish actor, Gabriel Byrne, shares the complexities of the mutable centaur squared energies in an interview with TheGuardian.com:

> But while he is thoughtful, painstakingly at times, and frequently self-deprecating, he is far from "brooding". He turns what was supposed to be a one-hour interview about a TV show in a cafe near his apartment in New York's SoHo into a four-hour impassioned conversation, funny at some points, searing at others. I emerge from it faintly dizzy.
>
> Yet despite his obvious love of conversation, he does share an instinct common to so many of his characters, from the family threatening Keaton in *The Usual Suspects*, to the brilliant but emotionally battered psychotherapist Paul Weston in the TV series *In Treatment*: a wariness of self-exposure. He bats away personal questions with rambling anecdotes that often contain everything but the answer – yet little details escape. When asked, apropos of the antique love ring he is wearing, whether he is seeing anyone, he launches into a 15-minute tale about the first time he gave an interview and how the photographer made him pretend to cook an omelet. It's a funny story with a serious subtext: "I know better now than to give out more than I want." And fair enough. But in the end,

his loquaciousness reveals more than he would perhaps wish: he mentions several times a particular "friend" with a female pronoun, who is presumably the actor Anna George, with whom he allegedly lives.

The article goes onto share another aspect that can occur with this astrological placement: abuse of power by someone who is supposed to be a responsible member of a religious order or in higher education.

It is an issue that Byrne himself experienced personally in the most awful way imaginable: between the ages of eight and 11, he was sexually and physically abused by the Christian Brothers in Ireland and then again in England.
Byrne first talked about this three years ago in a radio interview, describing a school system in which abuse was a "known and admitted fact of life". The abuse, he said, happened at a "very vulnerable time for him" and left him "deeply hurt."

Further archetypal themes of this broad-mindedness are evidenced in this excerpt from the early life of Australian dramatist, Nick Enright, taken from Wikipedia.com:

He was drama captain of St Ignatius' College, Riverview in 1964, where, like Gerard Windsor and Justin Fleming, he was taught by Melvyn Morrow. At that school, he won the 1sts Debating Premiership in both 1966 and 1967. It was expected that he would follow the law. During 1971 and 1972 Enright was a member of Sydney's Genesian Theatre, performing in *A Doll's House* and *Uncle Vanya*, and directing *London Assurance*. Enright received a pass BA from Sydney University in 1972, having decided not to proceed to an honours degree as might have been expected of one so formidably intelligent.

The themes of power as presented by Gabriel Byrne above, are further elucidated in a rare interview with Australian politician, Kim Beazley, taken from theAustralian.com:

"Most of my life I have been in a position of great power and little responsibility," he says. "Now I am in a position of massive responsibility and no power. And you have to be terribly conscious of that — conscious that you are nonpartisan. You also have a mandate, and it is not an unusual mandate for governors, to be an advocate for the state.

"So in about four or five key areas I have been building up activities at the house and outside with visits and very rare public statements, supporting directions that are in this state's interests for next generation industry (and) next generation mining, for engagement with defense industries, for things that we ought to be doing with the indigenous community and explaining things that we are doing with the indigenous community, and big help wherever I can for the arts and culture."

Chiron

Chiron in Capricorn on the MC

These individuals appreciate success and status and sharing it with the world. The rewards and goals they seek are usually attained after much time and effort.

The maverick mastery of many talents is well displayed by the accomplished life of Englishman, Cecil Beaton. The following comes from Wikipedia:

> ...English fashion, portrait and war photographer, diarist, painter, and interior designer, and an Oscar-winning stage and costume designer for films and the theatre.

Cecil attained significant success in all he pursued.

The interesting and challenging themes requiring personal adjustments for this astrological position are well exemplified in the life of Belgian comic book creator, Edgar P. Jacobs. The following comes from TCJ.com:

> Edgar Jacobs' graphic control masked upheavals. At the most hopeful moments of his life, the subtext was always ambiguous. His stint at the Lille Opera meant the fulfillment of a dream. But it brought Jacobs face-to-face with a shattering fact: that, outside of marginal roles, he had no future in opera. Then, when his tumultuous first marriage exploded, Hergé's home studio provided an unexpected refuge. Yet the job deflected him – for good, as it turned out – from the artistic independence he enjoyed at *Bravo!*

Even *Tintin*'s launch, the focus of so many hopes, took place under terrible tensions. For a start, its editor was a wanted man. Tried for collaboration in 1946, Jacques Van Melkebeke received a ten-year prison sentence. Yet he simply kept on coming in to work. When LeBlanc was tipped off that police were on their way, the exasperated publisher kicked him out for good. Yet Van Melk just dyed his hair, took up using pseudonyms and, at one point, lived in Edgar Jacobs' attic. He continued to edit *Tintin* and contribute to all its series.

Another photographer joins the ranks in this astrological position. Margaret Bourke-White's family reflects the maverick quality often found with angular planetary placements in Cancer or Capricorn. The following comes from Wikipedia.com:

> From her naturalist father, an engineer and inventor, she claimed to have learned perfectionism; from her "resourceful homemaker" mother, she claimed to have developed an unapologetic desire for self-improvement." Her younger brother, Roger Bourke White, became a prominent Cleveland businessman and high-tech industry founder, and her older sister, Ruth White, became well known for her work at the American Bar Association in Chicago, Ill. Roger Bourke White described their parents as "Free thinkers who were intensely interested in advancing themselves and humanity through personal achievement," attributing this quality in part to the success of their children.

He was not surprised at his sister Margaret's success, saying "[she] was not unfriendly or aloof."

British politician, James Gordon Brown, shows other facets of the Capricorn genius. Brown was the Prime Minister of the United Kingdom and Leader of the Labour Party from 2007 until 2010 and previously served as Chancellor of the Exchequer from 1997 to 2007. An interesting tidbit about this particular position within the English government is that it is called *the budget tipple*. Liquor is banned in Parliament for obvious reasons, but the Exchequer is someone who can drink anything, including alcoholic beverages, while giving the annual budget speech to the assembly.

In a wonderful interview from FugueJournal.com, American writer, Linda Gray Sexton, shared her healing journey in regards to her mother's devotion to her poetry at the expense of her parenting. This emotional dynamic was further confounded when her mother committed suicide when she was 45 years old. Linda shared her process through writing her memoir.

Multi-maverick and American rock, country and folk singer-songwriter, Stephen Fain "Steve" Earle, shares the following wistful statements about this astrological placement from QuoteTab.com:

"I don't really think in terms of obstacles. My biggest obstacle is always myself."

"We're so terrified of death in Western culture that we have to make up a myth of an afterlife. I think there's something to be said for living your life very mindful of the fact that you're going to die because I think you carry yourself differently. It doesn't have to be this big, negative bummer."

And, while he makes the following statement, it belies the understanding to make it in the first place. Earle's is an earth awareness; Capricorn is recharged when connected with nature.

"Me, I'm spiritually retarded, I need to be knee deep in water with a fly rod in my hands, that's about as close to God as I get."

Finally, the effect a teacher has on a maverick Chiron individual, is made clear here:

"The drama teacher that I had in high school, back in Texas, was the only teacher who didn't kick me out of his class. He turned me on to 'The Freewheelin' Bob Dylan.' I had picked up Dylan with *Bringing It All Back Home*, and he turned me on to the first couple of albums, which I hadn't heard.

Chiron in Aquarius on the MC

These individuals learn the importance of their individuality through exploring life and observing others. Their humanitarian leanings are often exemplary. One benefit of the Aquarian archetype is the ability to escape into fantasy and Chiron can take on differing personas.

We see this astrological placement exemplified in the life of legendary English actor, Sir Laurence Olivier. The whole obituary in *The New York Times* has numerous relevant parts to this astrological placement, but here is a small excerpt:

> Although others would credit him for his honesty (Noel Coward emphasized the "impeccable truth" of his characterizations), he confessed that for him acting was a form of lying. Other actors spoke of their need to express themselves, but he said he was not conscious of any need other "than to show off."
>
> Onstage he could project supreme self-confidence, but in private he was tormented by doubt and guilt, both of which he traced back to his boyhood, which was the beginning of a life lived in the imagination.

British economist, Ronald Coase, is a good example of how good ideals can have poor results. The following comes from NewYorker.com:

> In 1991, the Swedes awarded him a Nobel Prize in Economics, just one of many honors he received.
>
> Which is all pretty ironic, or tragic, depending on how you look at things. As a conservatively inclined economist, Coase was instinctively skeptical of government regulations, but he was also an English empiricist who recognized that reality is complicated. He didn't believe in laissez-faire, and he freely admitted

that the Coase theorem didn't apply to many cases of pollution and other instances of what economists refer to as "negative externalities," especially those that affect large numbers of people.

Indeed, Coase didn't even think of the Coase theorem as a full-scale economic theory, but merely as a useful mental exercise that could be carried out before passing onto more realistic cases.

From CitizenPlanet.com comes this beautiful statement from multi-maverick and American journalist, Maria Shriver:

"I grew up in a family that was driven to serve. My uncle John F. Kennedy was president. My uncles Bobby and Teddy Kennedy served in the U.S. Senate and also ran for president. My father Sargent Shriver served as founding director of the Peace Corps and led the nation's war on poverty and ran for president as well. My mother, Eunice Kennedy Shriver, started the Special Olympics and was an amazing mother to my 4 brothers and myself.

"I've always been deeply curious about everything, so a career in journalism seemed like the perfect fit for me. I've had a great career, working my way up from writer to producer to anchor at both CBS News and NBC News, and traveling around the world interviewing presidents, kings, activists and humanitarians. I've found something interesting and inspirational in everyone and everything I've covered. I believed then —and I still believe now — that journalism can not only inform, but also inspire us.

"Today, my mission is clear. I want to challenge what is, imagine what can be, make a difference and move humanity forward in all areas of human endeavor. That's what Architects of Change do — I consider myself one, and I work to shine a light on others.

"Moving humanity forward. That is my ministry. That is my mission. I hope you will join me."

The House of Grimaldi is replete with mavericks, so it is no surprise that Prince Albert II of Monaco, is in such great company. This excerpt from Wikipedia.com gives some of the archetypal elements of this astrological placement:

In 2006, Prince Albert created the Prince Albert II of Monaco Foundation, which continues the Principality of Monaco's commitment by supporting sustainable and ethical projects around the world. The foundation focus on three main challenges: climate change and renewable energy development; combating the loss of biodiversity; and water management (improving universal access to clean water). Albert is also a global adviser to Orphans International.

American actress, Michelle Pfeiffer, along with her Taurus Sun, understands the ways fixity can express itself. The following comes from BrainyQuotes.com:

"Well, I'm very stubborn. I think I have common sense; I'm probably at times a bit tunnel-visioned, but I'm strong."

The intellectual brilliance of outsider, avant-garde Canadian filmmaker, director and multi-maverick, Bruce LaBruce, shines brightly, in his interview with WussyMag.com:

[Interviewer question] *You are a queer pornographer that's primarily worked with men. Did you have a different experience working with mostly women this time around?*

Yeah, I've made some films like *L.A. Zombie* and *Hustler White* that only have male characters, but a lot of my films do have strong female characters. My film *Otto* has a main character who is a very imposing lesbian filmmaker, and *Gerontophilia* has a very revolutionary young girl as lead, but I've never made an all-female film before. A film with an almost all female cast. That's exactly why I made the movie! It's something I've always wanted to do for a very long time. My film *The Raspberry Reich* is about left wing radicals but it didn't really have lesbian characters. My lesbian friends always said, "You have to make a movie about lesbian extremists," so that's what I did. It was really great! Much of the cast and crew were female like the musical composer, the costume designer, two of the producers, the sound recordists, and the sound designer. There was a lot of female energy on the set. We were filming in an old house in the German countryside, a two hour drive from Berlin. The crew stayed on location and the cast at local hotels. We were thrown together in this remote location and the women on the film particularly the female cast members bonded very strongly together. There was kind of a parallel movie going on that I wasn't even privy to in a way. All these women hanging out together sharing stories. The more mature actresses were kind of mentoring the younger girls. It was really cool in that regard. To do lesbian softcore pornography was interesting for me as well. It was a much different process that was collaborative with the actors. For the orgy scene, I just left them all alone in a room, and they all discussed what they were and weren't comfortable with. It was all very much about people expressing sexuality but in a way that made them comfortable.

The astrological patterns specific to Aquarius and Chiron, impart to one the alchemical understanding of words, which used to be known as spells. Aquarius is a sign of the wizard, after all! This deeper knowing is expressed in a statement by Kenneth Branagh from BrainyQuote.com:

"There is some mysterious thing that goes on whereby, in the process of playing Shakespeare continuously, actors are surprised by the way the language actually acts on them."

Chiron in Pisces on the MC

These individuals seek the other, and the occult side of life. While often more of a mystical bent, they often walk the path enjoying sex, love and psychedelics, drugs, along the way. These mavericks experience the full gamut of emotions to reveal to humanity there is more to life than their limited imagination could ever perceive.

Multi-maverick and American porn star, Jeff Stryker, was the perfect man to introduce porn to people regardless of their sexual orientation. The following comes from Astro.com:

> He describes himself (in a somewhat joking fashion) as sexually "universal." Stryker has also said, "I don't define myself as anything."

Multi-maverick and American politician, Cheryl Ann Jacques, realized that being courageous and coming out while serving in the Massachusetts Senate, would help to make a difference in the lives of people coming to terms with their sexuality. Cheryl Ann declared she was lesbian in her fourth term in an attempt to help reduce the amount of suicides by questioning teens and others.

Another multi-maverick and American actress, Ally Sheedy, describes the emotional authenticity this astrological placement demands within one's self, even when on such a public angle as the MC. The following comes from an article in EightiesKids.com:

Then, in a series of 1998 interviews, Sheedy finally explained why she turned her back on Hollywood.

It emerged that Sheedy had, in her heyday, suffered bulimia and an addiction to the sleeping pill Halcion.

It was a difficult time for Sheedy, prompting an intervention from friends including Demi Moore, which resulted in Sheedy checking into a substance abuse treatment centre.

In addition to her personal issues, after a series of flops in the late 80s including *Blue City* and *Maid to Order*, Sheedy found doors began to close, and the actress wasn't prepared to change who she was simply in order to claw back some "heat".

There was the problem of Sheedy figuring out what kind of actor she wanted to be. Being a movie star meant she would only be allowed to do a certain type of script, would be forced to change her appearance and, as Sheedy herself put it, "kiss a lot of a**".

"It wasn't an option for me. I wasn't going to do any of those things. I'd done enough 'nice' and 'cute' and 'girl next door.'

"It was all so superficial, bubbly and bland and I didn't want to do it anymore. At any price."

The result was a lot of doors closed in Hollywood for Sheedy. After being dropped by her agent, Sheedy moved from Los Angeles back to New York, where she could make low budget films like 1998's acclaimed *High Art*. "I may be poor, but I'm happy", she said the year of the film's release.

Yet another individual with an abundance of maverick energy with a similar concern about the entertainment industry, was English singer, George Michael. The following comes from his obituary in *The New York Times*:

> But Mr. Michael grew increasingly uncomfortable with the superficiality and relentless promotion of 1980s-style pop stardom. He turned away from video clips and live shows; he set out to make more mature statements in his songs, though he never completely abandoned singing about love and desire. In 1998, Mr. Michael came out as gay after being arrested on charges of lewd conduct in a men's room in Beverly Hills, Calif. He had long lent his name and music to support AIDS prevention and gay rights. During interviews in later years, he described himself as bisexual, and said that hiding his sexuality had made him feel "fraudulent." He also described long struggles with depression.

British recording artist and musician, Barry Gibb, of the Bee Gees shares a lovely interview with RollingStone.com after his brothers had all passed:

> When Barry Gibb first came into the world, he was the little brother. His sister Lesley was nearly two when Barry was born, on the Isle of Man, off the west coast of England, where his father was a bandleader and his mother took care of the kids. He almost didn't make it out of childhood: At 18 months, he spilled a teapot and scalded himself so badly the doctors gave him 20

minutes to live. He spent three months in the hospital. Over the next few years, he also fell through a roof, shot himself in the eye with a BB gun and was hit by a car on two occasions. "I was," he says, "just one of those kids that was always getting hit by a car."

Uranus

Uranus is the higher octave of Mercury and represents our need for the new and unexpected, how we shock and evolve, how (by sign), and where (by house) we like to have fun and change things. These are not easy energies for a person to assimilate because Uranus is not a personal planet. It seeks to go outside of the box, enervate, and individuate. The next planet after Saturn, Uranus puts us in touch with the transpersonal worlds of Neptune, Pluto, and all that lies beyond. The planet itself not only has rings around it, but unlike any other planet, it rotates on its side and reaches some of the coldest temperatures of them all. These peculiar and unusual planetary traits reflect back to us our ability to differentiate and become our own individual, particular archetypal expression.

The lower representation of Uranus is to revolt for the sake of discord – me against the world – whereas, the higher expression is synthesizing the individual into and with greater whole of humanity: I am part of it all. Uranus rules Aquarius, which means that an unfettered humanitarian world needs the well-structured Saturnian foundation gained from experience and time. Super-charged Uranus individuals, those with Uranus on the angles, are going to be super individualistic. Such illustrious individuals as Weird Al Yankovic, Jack Kerouac, Ernest Hemmingway, and even Pope Francis show the many ways individual expression, also known as archetype, can be so resonant with the world.

Uranus is very electric and eclectic. An archetypal Uranian look can be shaved/bald head or punkish haircut with unusual colors.

We will now look at the angle placements of Uranus throughout the zodiac from the point of view of the Ascendant (AS).

Uranus in Aries on the AS

These individuals are freedom-seekers extraordinaire. They have an instinctual immediacy to them that will likely awaken others.

Anything written about multiple maverick and British royal family member, Princess Margaret, clearly states this astrological placement in her chart. The following comes from her obituary in the *Los Angeles Times*:

Throughout her life, Princess Margaret was known as a royal rebel, the member of the British royal family who dared push against tradition and carve out her own path. Sister to Queen Elizabeth II, Margaret was brash, fiery and independent — and famous for presenting herself to the world with a distinctive sense of style." She was the first in 400 years in the British royal family to divorce.

Actress, comedian, and lounge music performer, Damita Jo DeBlanc, received a brilliant accolade from the Queen of Soul, Ella Fitzgerald. The following comes from DMDukes.com:

> Miss Fitzgerald had long been her idol. And when Miss Fitz, "The First Lady of Song", was asked on a Las Vegas television show to name "The Second Lady of Song," she unhesitatingly answered, "DAMITA JO."

The male-oriented focus on femininity as expressed by the Miss America pageant, is well portrayed in the story of Miss America winner of 1949, Jacque Mercer. The following comes from Wikipedia.com:

> She married and divorced her high school sweetheart, Douglas Cook, during her reign as Miss America. After this, a rule was enacted which requires Miss America contestants to sign a pledge vowing they have never been married or pregnant.

The idea of the ideal intact virgin for the ideal man is an archetype of this position.

American poet, John N. Morris, shared some insightful tidbits into his inner landscape, in an interview he gave to RiverStyx.org:

"Well, first we would have to agree that that is actually the case. But I supposed I was born into it. I come from a family that expected its men to be gentlemen. I can remember as a small child complaining to my mother, and wondering why other people could do whatever it was that I wasn't permitted to do, and my mother had to explain that I was a gentleman, that therefore there were certain claims I couldn't make upon the world. It was expected that there might be limitations on my freedom of utterance or conduct. But is it priggish to say that no true gentleman would violate the iron law of genteel reticence by talking about himself as much as it look like I'm about to do?"

Remember that "appropriate" Libra is on John's Descendant.

Rhythm and blues singer, Jesse Belvin, is a painful example of what it is like to bear this astrological archetypal signature in a world that would never give freedom to a person of his color. Like Damita, Jesse was singing in a time in the United States when African-Americans had little to no rights or freedoms.

URANUS

Uranus in Taurus on the AS

This is an energetic predicament which we are all experiencing as Uranus is in Taurus as this book is being written. Taurus is a fixed sign and likes dependable things, be they people, relationships, objects, or situations; whereas Uranus is a planet that needs an instinctive, spontaneous, immediate experience. It is like driving down the road in your luxury vehicle and either the brakes stop working or the roof flies off – something so out of the ordinary, that the system can get stuck in shock. Taurus rules form and Uranus births new archetypes, so there is something in this expression about new and unusual forms of being.

English medical doctor and columnist, Miriam Stoppard, shares other aspects of this astrological placement in an interview with Independent.co.uk. While the article begins with a lengthy description of all of her work (Earth signs love doing), Taurus can be a control freak.

> "Well, certainly, control is a big thing with her. Control of looks, control of health, control of ageing ("You're in the driving seat when it comes to setting the limit on your own mortality," she writes in the introduction to *Defying Age*), control of appetite. Do you have any bad health habits, Dr. Stoppard? "I'd have a mountain if I gave into them. I love cake!" When Tom left her after two sons and 20 years of marriage for Felicity Kendal, she was, alas, the model of controlled dignity, never, for example, referring to Miss Kendal as "that evil, dungareed old slag."

From the book *Glamour Girls of Sixties Hollywood: Seventy-Five Profiles,* American actress, Linda Marshall, from the 1960s television series *My Three Sons*, had this description about Linda:

> A pretty strawberry blond, this busy TV actress... at first essayed the sweet ingénue roles but, with a sophisticated icy air about here, she excelled when cast as the prissy snob poor rich bitch.

Uranus in Gemini on the AS

These individuals have an innate wit and ability to connect things that appear seemingly disparate. These individuals do better when they have a larger view of things otherwise, they can become very persnickety.

The multi-valent brilliance of this astrological position is articulated in Egyptian novelist, Radwa Ashour's obituary from TheGuardian.com:

> Radwa Ashour was a powerful voice among Egyptian writers of the postwar generation and a writer of exceptional integrity and courage. Her work consistently engages with her country's history and reflects passionately upon it. "I am an Arab woman and a citizen of the third world," she declared, in an essay for the anthology *The View from Within* (1994), "and my heritage in both cases is stifled ... I write in self-defense

and in defense of countless others with whom I identify or who are like me."

Through a series of novels, memoirs, and literary studies, Ashour, who has died aged 68 after suffering from cancer, recorded the unending turbulence of her times, as she and her contemporaries struggled for freedoms, from the end of British influence to the recent Arab uprising and its aftermath.

Born in Cairo, Radwa came from a literary and scholarly family: her father, Mustafa Ashour, was a lawyer but had strong literary interests, while her mother, Mai Azzam, was a poet and artist. Radwa evoked in her writing how she was raised to recite the poetic corpus of Arabic literature by her grandfather Abdelwahab Azzam, a diplomat and professor of oriental studies and literature at Cairo University, who first translated the classic Persian *Book of Kings* (Shahnama) into Arabic, as well as other Oriental classics.

The revolutionary literacy of this astrological position is beautifully expressed in the life of multi-maverick, Stuart Christie. The following comes from Revoltlib.com:

Stuart Christie (born 10 July 1946) is a Scottish anarchist writer and publisher. As an 18-year-old, Christie was arrested while carrying explosives to assassinate the Spanish caudillo General Franco. He was later alleged to be a member of the Angry Brigade, but was acquitted of related charges. He went on to found the Cienfuegos Press publishing house and in 2008 the online Anarchist Film Channel which hosts films and documentaries with anarchist and libertarian themes.

A reader review at GoodReads.com shares yet another different and somewhat similar archetypal expression from down under:

> In this much-awaited memoir, Kate Fitzpatrick, darling of the Australian stage and screen, reflects upon a lifetime of knowing and loving some of Australia's, and indeed the world's most famous and controversial identities. With a delightful mix of humour, name-dropping and self-deprecation, Kate Fitzpatrick reveals the twists and turns of a life that has seen her become a respected actress, writer and speech writer, and a not-so-respected cricket commentator. In these candid confessions we are led through Kate's life, from her early childhood in Adelaide to leaving her eccentric, warm family to enroll at NIDA. Kate rapidly became much in demand as an actor, and her critically acclaimed work, together with her razor-sharp wit and eye for detail, ensured that her profile soared. Her myth-making friendship with Patrick White is laid bare, along with her personal relationships with some of the world's most sought-after men. This book is by turns hilarious, turbulent, painfully truthful and self-deprecating, and is an unashamed look at slices of Kate's colourful and brilliant, careers, loves and lives. *Namedropping* is a

high-spirited memoir teeming with fascinating snippets and insights into other people and places.

Uranus in Cancer on the AS

This is not an easy energy, as Cancer seeks security and Uranus seeks freedom. How these mavericks navigate these seemingly opposing energies reflects the individual strength and determination required of these natives.

Singer-songwriter, Karen Carpenter, constantly tried to break free from her family's demands and the gravity of the relationship with her brother on both the personal and professional levels. Karen faced a struggle each time she sought her independence, even over her own body.

Multi-maverick and entertainer, Artemes Turchi, has an amazingly extensive group of friends with whom he connects infrequently, but deeply. Artemes has a masterful quick wit that is tempered with a deeply loving heart.

Yet another gender-bending multi-maverick is lesbian filmmaker, Monika Treut. Uranus seeks new territories, visions, and freedoms which are revealed in Monika's pioneering work.

Uranus signifies the outsider or the foreigner and it seeks synthesis. When found on the Ascendant in a person's birth chart, one will likely be known as the foreigner, alien, or outsider no matter where they live. Visionary, Runa Bouius hails from the island country of Iceland and lives in the United States. Runa shares the older-souled Icelandic understanding, synthesized with her personally gained wisdom, by working with conscious leaders around the world, in an effort to make a wholistic, sustainable, and thriving world-wide economy.

Uranus in Leo on the AS

These individuals emit a bravado that can be too much for others to follow. Consider a bolt of lightning that starts a forest fire and you have an idea of the raw energies of this astrological placement.

Our first individual is a strong example of this archetypal force that also illustrates the shadow side of the maverick character. Multi-maverick and four consecutive Olympic Games gold medalist, Carl Lewis, was a true force of nature on the track, but his ego presented a problem. The following on Carl comes from Wikipedia.com:

> Although Lewis had achieved what he had set out to do—matching Jesse Owens' feat of winning four gold medals in the same events at a single Olympic Games—he did not receive the lucrative endorsement offers that he had expected. The long jump controversy was one reason and his self-congratulatory conduct did not impress several other track stars: "He rubs it in too much," said Edwin Moses, twice Olympic gold medalist in the 400 m hurdles. "A little humility is in order. That's what Carl lacks." Further, Lewis's agent Joe Douglas compared him to pop star Michael Jackson, a comparison which did not go over well. Douglas said he was inaccurately quoted, but the impression that

Lewis was aloof and egotistical was firmly planted in the public's perception by the end of the 1984 Olympic Games.

Former front man of the popular English band, Frankie Goes to Hollywood, Holly Johnson, shared a similar aspect of this trait in an interview with TheGuardian.com:

"I'm very good at burning bridges," says Johnson. "It's a talent I regret, in a way."

Cartoonist, Bill Waterson, creator of *Calvin and Hobbes,* shares some of the eccentric wisdom of this astrological placement from BrainyQuote.com:

"Mothers are the necessity of invention."

"God put me on this earth to accomplish a certain number of things. Right now I am so far behind that I will never die."

"The surest sign that intelligent life exists elsewhere in the universe is that it has never tried to contact us."

"Genius is never understood in its own time."

The stiff-upper-lip of a fixed royal ego is articulated in the life of Prince Andrew, who professes innocence in-spite of photographs of Andrew in the company of convicted sex offender, Jeffrey Epstein. With this astrological placement, the truth will come to the surface.

Japan's Prince Naruhito, exhibits many firsts for his royal line. The following comes from Reuters.com:

> Naruhito, 59, will not only be the first Japanese emperor born after World War Two and the first to be raised solely by his parents, but also the first to graduate from a university and pursue advanced studies overseas. He will assume the throne after his father, Emperor Akihito, abdicates on April 30, the first Japanese emperor to do so in nearly 200 years. "When I think of what is coming up, I feel very solemn," Naruhito said at his birthday news conference in February.

From NBSSports.com comes this wonderful description by Olympic swimmer, Shane Gould, about the determination possible that isn't necessarily competitive with anyone else:

> "You have to be task-driven. You have to be really relentless, have this volition, ethos to want to just push yourself and enjoy that physicality. The pain. Just the exhilaration from using all your capacities because you haven't got somebody to race [against]."

Uranus in Virgo on the AS

This placement is one that requires a certain level of attention. The multi-resourceful Virgo can gain the Uranian ability to break things down into little pieces while seeing a synthesized whole, or it can fragment or split under the pressure of it all.

Multi-maverick and young Scottish singer, Lena Zavaroni, received attention before she was able to integrate it. The following comes from her obituary in TheGuardian.com:

> ...by the time she was 13 Zavaroni had appeared at the Royal Variety Show, worked with Frank Sinatra, Lucille Ball and Barbra Streisand, and been a guest on the Johnny Carson Show. On British television, she had worked with Morecambe and Wise, and had her own series.
>
> Already, however, she had begun to show signs of the eating disorder anorexia nervosa, the illness from which she was to suffer for the rest of her life. In many ways, Zavaroni's problems were typical of those that beset many pre-pubescent stars: the loss of childhood, massive public attention, and the difficulty of transposing childhood talent into an adult package when show business - and, to some extent, the audience – only thrilled to the child/voice combination.

Canadian ice hockey professional, Nevin Maarkwart, realized that he needed to invest his time and energy into education in addition relying on the sport. The following comes from BusinessofHockeyInstitute.com:

> Markwart's passion draws on sound experience as an equity analyst and portfolio manager for international firms like Wellington Management and Fidelity

Canada, and most recently, as President and CEO of Canoe Financial in Calgary. He began paying attention to hockey finance at an early stage in his career, when he set up the NHL's first 401K pension plan for his teammates in 1988. With information rare for the time, he knew that the Bruins' annual player salary budget was about $3.6 million. Compare this to today's NHL salary cap of $71.4 million per team. In this light, Markwart's comment – "since 1992 there's been a dramatic change in hockey's business model, from a business focused on the sport of hockey to a business focused on the entertainment of hockey," – is both understated and insightful.

English actor and entertainer, Robson Green, who has several maverick planets shared this with Mirror.co.uk:

"Work' is not meant to be enjoyed, but find a job you love and you'll never have to work again. My dad worked down a mine for 42 years, that's work. I was the first one in the family to go, 'Nah, I fancy putting on make-up instead.'"

Her AstreaFoundation.org bio shows what this astrological position can accomplish:

Cynthia Rothschild is an independent activist and consultant with a focus on United Nations advocacy and policy, sexual rights, LGBT issues, HIV & AIDS, and women human rights defenders. A human rights, sexual rights and feminist activist for over 20 years, she has worked with global networks and NGOs within and outside the US, including the Center for Women's Global Leadership (where she was the Senior Policy Advisor from 2005-2009), and a number of women's and reproductive rights groups and AIDS service organizations. Cynthia is a trainer and facilitator, and also has supported NGOs in organizational development projects, including in work related to UN advocacy at the Human Rights Council and the Commission on the Status of Women. In 2011 and in 2015, Cynthia consulted with the UN Office of the High Commissioner for Human Rights (OHCHR), where she made significant contributions to the UN's two groundbreaking reports on discrimination and violence based on sexual orientation and gender identity. She is the author of *Written Out: How Sexuality is Used to Attack Women's Organizing*; the co-author of *Strengthening Resistance: Confronting Violence Against Women and HIV/AIDS*, and *Amnesty International's Crimes of Hate, Conspiracy of Silence: Torture and Ill-Treatment Based on Sexual Identity*. Most recently, she edited "Gendering Documentation: A Manual For and About Women Human Rights Defenders." She was a member of the Board of Directors of the Astraea Lesbian Foundation for Justice from 2010-2015 and of Amnesty International USA in the early 2000s.

In a revealing discussion about multi-maverick and American rock star, Kurt Cobain, from InsideHook.com, we understand another face of this astrological placement from Kurt's manager:

"I was reminded of his work ethic. And I was continually reminded of how brilliant he was. He was – and I continue to believe this – he was the most brilliant person I was ever up close to in rock'n'roll. But he also had this *extreme* discipline about his work."

Scottish-American star of television and theatre, John Barrowman, illuminates this astrological placement with these gems from BrainyQuote.com:

"Have I ever been the shy retiring type? Never. Not since the day I was born."

"My humour and my work ethic definitely come from my Scottish side, and I have to say the sense of humour doesn't really translate when I'm in America."

"I don't call myself an actor, I call myself an entertainer, because I don't just do one thing."

"If you do something and it goes wrong, you learn from it and you move on."

Uranus in Libra on the AS

These individuals experience instantaneous insights and can create magic in space.

Our only example for this placement is American ice hockey player, Doug Brown. GreatestHockeyLengends.com has an eloquent statement about this astrological placement from a sports point of view:

> ...this unlikely duo were nonetheless dynamic together. Or at least Fedorov was dynamic, while Brown was underrated. "My role is to create space," said Brown. "It's a matter of anticipating his next move."

Uranus in Scorpio on the AS

These individuals have an uncanny ability to get to the root of things. As children they maybe even say things that parents haven't told them, but are true.

The focused power-house energy of this astrological placement is well stated in an article from NYTimes.com about tennis champion, Mary Pierce:

> "What set Mary apart was her single-mindedness," said Chris Evert, winner of 18 major championships, including seven at Roland Garros. "There were others who hit as hard as she did, but she harnessed her power and was very consistent. She could produce winners hitting into both corners of the court."

English performer, Faye Tozer, shows the strength and determination this position gave him to become a dancer, singer and songwriter.

The intensity of English DJ and songwriter, Samantha Ronson's personal relationships are available for anyone to see on the internet.

PhillyMag.com, had this update about multi- maverick rugby player, Ben Cohen:

> Recently, the hot jock took it all off to promote a new underwear line, with proceeds benefiting his Ben Cohen StandUp Foundation, which is dedicated to beating homophobia and bullying.

The following excerpt from TheThings.com, captures this astrological placement well for American celebrity, Jessica Simpson. Most people don't appreciate what this astrological position offers:

> Some moms have a great breastfeeding experience and for others, it's the complete opposite. It's definitely important to share your story and talk about how hard it can be as that's a good conversation to be having.
>
> According to *Distractify*, Jessica Simpson posted a photo of her milk, and since she was talking about how well breastfeeding was going for her, people felt that she was bragging about it. She put up a photo of 5 oz. of breast milk and wrote, "This is what success feels like."

Since that's not the breastfeeding experience that every mother has, it was probably not the best thing for her to post.

Royal multi-maverick, Zara Philips, is the first granddaughter of Her Royal Highness, Queen Elizabeth. Zara has the freedom of no royal titles, but the power and the backing of the British Royal family.

Uranus in Sagittarius on the AS

These mavericks are able to keep the liveliest of conversations and capture the beauty of a moment for eternity.

Our first example displays these astrological energies at work in the life of photographer, Ansel Adams. An excerpt from his obituary in the LATimes.com shows many elements of this astrological placement, especially the part about maturity, or lack thereof. I recommend reading the article for a more rounded understanding of how Ansel elevated photography from a hobby to an art, resulting in his images shown in museums around the world.

> He was a gangly 14-year-old with a nose that tilted angularly left, the result of a falling wall during an aftershock from the 1906 San Francisco earthquake.
>
> "The doctor said to get it straightened when I matured," Adams loved to say. "But of course, I never matured."

A year earlier his father, a successful businessman, had given him a pass to the World's Fair in San Francisco. Adams spent most of his time at the Armory Show, the revolutionary modern art display transplanted from New York that gave prosaic America its first glimpse of the impressionists and surrealists.

He also had been exposed to a book, *In the Heart of the Sierra*, part of the tutoring program his parents had designed for him when he opted to give up formal schooling.

"A-A," as he would someday be known to friends, bought a simple camera, hoping to combine a vacation trip to Yosemite, the excitement of abstract art and his blooming vicarious sentiments for the High Sierra into a new interest.

Another example of the brilliance afforded this position is relayed from Wikipedia.com, for double maverick and Canadian army officer, Harry Wickwire Foster:

> On September 12, 1944, he entered the historic city of Bruges (Belgium) with his troops. The liberation of this medieval town was done successfully, without fight or damage. In recognition for this achievement, Foster was named an honorary citizen of Bruges, an award bestowed upon only two people since 1900.

American model, Brittny Gastineau, is a socialite and reality television personality who enjoys the spotlight of attention this astrological placement offers.

Double maverick and childhood kidnapping survivor, Katie Beers, shares the understanding that rewards are given for courageously facing what life offers:

> "If the kidnapping hadn't have happened. I don't even want to think about where I would be. But I would have never graduated high school, I would have never graduated college, I might not even be here, living today, with the road that my life was bound to go down."

Uranus in Capricorn on the AS

These individuals are likely to have insightfully new ways of getting things done. Their highly inventive methods are often outside of the normal box society creates.

The unique flame these individuals carry is portrayed by American playwright and double maverick, Tennessee Williams. The following comes from his obituary at NYTimes.com:

> Mr. Williams's work, which was unequaled in passion and imagination by any of his contemporaries' works, was a barrage of conflicts, of the blackest horrors offset by purity. Perhaps his greatest character, Blanche Du Bois, the heroine of "Streetcar," has been described as a tigress and a moth, and, as Mr. Williams created her, there was no contradiction.
>
> His basic premise, he said, was "the need for understanding and tenderness and fortitude among

individuals trapped by circumstance." Just as his work reflected his life, his life reflected his work. A monumental hypochondriac, he became obsessed with sickness, failure and death. Several times he thought he was losing his sight, and he had four eye operations for cataracts. Constantly he thought his heart would stop beating. In desperation, he drank and took pills immoderately.

He was a man of great shyness, but with friends he showed great openness, which often worked to his disadvantage. He was extremely vulnerable to demands – from directors, actresses, the public, his critics, admirers and detractors.

Breaking through the limitations of life's glass ceilings is another wonderful trait of this astrological position. The following comes from the Wikipedia entry on British politician, Barbara Anne Castle:

Barbara Anne Castle, Baroness Castle of Blackburn, PC was a British Labour Party politician who was the Member of Parliament for Blackburn from 1945 to 1979, making her the longest-serving female MP [Member of Parliament] in the history of the House of Commons until that record was broken in 2007.

Another maverick pioneer is Olympic Gold swimmer, Matthew Mitcham. The following comes from Wikipedia.com:

As a diver, he was the 2008 Olympic champion in the 10 m platform, having received the highest single-dive score in Olympic history. This made him the first openly gay athlete to win an Olympic gold medal. He is also the first Australian male to win an Olympic gold medal in diving since Dick Eve at the 1924 Summer Olympics.

American diarist and journalist, Edward Robb Ellis's obituary from *The New York Times*, reflects the multi-valent experiences and non-stop flow of expression of this astrological placement:

> A newspaperman and author of several books of narrative history who once spent the better part of a decade trying to single-handedly compile an encyclopedia of New York City, Mr. Ellis published approximately 1 percent of his 70-volume diary in 1995 in a single volume entitled "A Diary of the Century: Tales From America's Greatest Diarist" (Kodansha America).
>
> The unedited diaries, estimated at 22 million words or roughly half the size of the Encyclopedia Britannica and filling 50 cartons that if laid end to end would extend 75 feet, became part of the manuscript collection of the Fales Library at New York University last spring.
>
> "Eddie was a force of nature," Marvin Taylor, the director of the Fales Library, the rare book library at N.Y.U., said. "He was incredibly intelligent, quick, funny and always on the make. He had an abiding interest in everyone's story, and clearly also in his own."

ASTROLOGICAL MAVERICKS

Uranus in Aquarius on the AS

Uranus is the modern ruler of Aquarius and feels at home here. These truly individualistic mavericks have an unusual self-expression or presentation.

Our first example is someone whose body was literally reaching for the stars – an Aquarian trait for sure. The tallest man in history was Midwestern American, Robert Pershing Wadlow. He was known as the Alton Giant and the Giant of Illinois. He reached 8 feet 11.1 inches (272 cm) in height and weighed 490 pounds (220 kg) at his death and showed no signs of stopping. His great size and his continued growth in adulthood was due to hypertrophy of his pituitary gland which resulted in an abnormally high level of human growth hormone.

The profoundly efficient witticism of the Aquarian nature is elucidated in the following trio of gems from English comedian and actor, Spike Milligan:

> "Contraceptives should be used on every conceivable occasion."

> "Money couldn't buy friends, but you got a better class of enemy."

> "Are you going to come quietly, or do I have to use earplugs?"

Uranus in Pisces on the AS

There is nothing quite like this combination. These individuals have an instinctual ability to draw upon the collective and interject novel archetypes that change the world.

Pier Paolo Pasolini, was an Italian film director, poet, writer and intellectual. Pasolini also distinguished himself as an actor, journalist, philosopher, novelist, playwright, filmmaker, painter and political figure. The following enlightening pearl is a quote from Pasolini:

> "When I make a film I'm always in reality among the trees, and among the people like yourselves. There's no symbolic or conventional filter between me and reality as there is in literature. The cinema is an explosion of my love for reality."

José de Sousa Saramago, was a Portuguese writer and recipient of the 1998 Nobel Prize in Literature. The following is from his obituary in TheGuardian.com:

> Journalism was to remain a lifelong outlet for Saramago's radical take on current events. He participated in campaigns and published his views on human rights abuses around the world. Meanwhile, his more personal writing underwent various sea-changes.

The 1950's Queen of Pinups, Bettie Page, expressed herself in ways that were not accepted during her lifetime. Even today her work commands attention. The following comes from HuffPost.com:

> A documentary slated to hit New York City this month boasts a hefty tease. The film, titled "Bettie Page Reveals All," will present to those who see it an archive of never published photos of the celebrated pin-up queen. *Nude* photos, to be precise; ones so salacious they were almost confiscated by the police in 1952.
>
> The photos were originally taken at a "camera club," a secretive type of photography gathering that took place in empty offices across New York City in the 1950s. Through this system, photographers could shoot women like Page in the buff, without running up against the laws that technically prevented such pictures from being published. Famous photographers like Weegee and Gordon Parks frequented the events.
>
> "Nudity back then was very unusual," photographer Dick Heinlein explained to The New York Post. He's the one who snapped the never before seen camera club images that appear in the film, and somehow managed to avoid handing his film over to authorities once the venue was raided.
>
> "Out of the woods, here comes this squad car!" he recounted from the night. "They had their guns drawn on a bunch of photographers [ordering us], 'Take the film out of your cameras!'"

American poet, Allen Ginsberg, who has his Mars here conjunct this point as well, is a prime example of one who drew upon the collective and conveyed many other aspects of this astrological placement. The following comes from AllenGinsberg.org:

> Irwin Allen Ginsberg was an American poet and writer. As a student at Columbia University in the 1940s, he began friendships with William S. Burroughs and Jack Kerouac, forming the core of the Beat Generation. He vigorously opposed militarism, economic materialism, and sexual repression, and he embodied various aspects of this counterculture with his views on drugs, hostility to bureaucracy, and openness to Eastern religions.

We will now look at the angle placements of Uranus throughout the zodiac from the point of view of the Imum Coeli (IC).

Uranus in Aries on the IC

These individuals explore, extrapolate, and synthesis all matters of thought while in reflection, which will happen with movement.

Multi-maverick, Emperor Akihito, was the first Japanese emperor in over 200 years to abdicate the throne. He wanted to leave his reign while he still had clear faculties. Emperor Akihito is an example of a good ruler, even if one with solely ceremonial powers.

The instinctual nature of this astrological placement is well pronounced in the life of musician and jazz blues saxophonist, Grady Gaines. The following comes from NAMM.org:

> Grady Gaines jumped onto the piano during a gig with Little Richard and wailed on his saxophone back in the early 1950s. The photograph of that event has become iconic as it represents the rhythm and blues roots of rock and roll. Grady played his King saxophone with hundreds of artists over the years including Little Willie John, Bo Diddley and Sam Cooke. However, it's his time on the road with Little Richard that he is best known. Grady wrote the book *I've Been There: On the Road with Legends of Rock 'n Roll* about his life in music, which was published in 2015.

Uranus in Taurus on the IC

We are currently living with Uranus in Taurus, where new forms are created and attachments are tested.

The courage of being true to one's self is well stated in English film director, Derek Jarman's obituary in the Independent.co.uk:

> DEREK JARMAN's death robs British cinema of its most vital force. For 20 years Jarman has been a constantly innovative figure, breaking with the conservatism of every aspect of cinematic practice to produce works which have been technically original,

aesthetically radical and which constitute an astonishing personal and public record of England in the last quarter of the 20th century.

The two most important facts about Jarman's life and works were his sexuality and his nationality. His greatest pleasures in life were provided by his homosexuality and by England: the outrage that fueled his art was occasioned by those who would deny and repress homosexuality and who would travesty the traditions of his country. These two themes came together in what is probably his most personal work, *The Last of England* (1987), a deeply autobiographical investigation of the destruction of the country which he had loved so much, composed immediately after he had discovered that he was HIV positive.

The equality seeking nature of this astrological placement is well stated by Italian actress, Sophia Loren, in the following quote from QuoteFancy.com:

> "The first woman was created from the rib of a man. She was not made from his head to top him, nor from his feet to be trampled on by him, but out of his side to be equal to him."

Astounding wealth can be a signature of this astrological placement as well displayed by the oil tycoon heir, Jay Rockefeller. Uranus is an astounding planet and when on the IC, the home is of grand importance. The following comes from ArchitectoftheCapital.org:

Our night began at The Rocks, Jay Rockefeller's chateau away from chateau deep in the hills of Rock Creek Park. To reach the site of this particular Obama fundraiser, you wind along the edges of Rock Creek Park and then turn up a steep, long, hey mistah Rockefeller, how about $3000 to shovel your driveway sort of entryway... There are oaks and Chestnut trees and then there's the house, with four Ionic columns and a slate roof and 17 windows across the front and the Rockefellers apparently suffer no critical shortage of guest bedrooms. It is a useful reminder that before the Gates and Bloomberg and Warren B., there was old man John D. Rockefeller, who bequeathed successive generations of descendants a truly astonishing boodle of money.

American film star, Dustin Hoffman, has displayed some very inappropriate behavior with women over the years, and his Uranus return may shed more light on it.

Martin Joel Greif, was an American editor, lecturer, publisher and writer. He is the uncle of heavy metal music personality and lawyer, Eric Greif. The following comes from Wikipedia.com:

> Greif said, "My books are on a wide variety of subjects, almost all of them assigned to me by other people. The pleasure I take in writing a book on factory design after completing a book on Victorian Christmases, or a book on the history of homosexuality after completing a book on nineteenth-century farming is a joy in 'discovery.'

I am never bored because I am always learning something new." His pseudonyms include Jean Bach, Frederick S. Copely, Leona Wesley Hunter, and Martin Lawrence."

This astrological placement can have an instinctually response to life that unarms those around them. When multi-maverick and musical performer, Tammy Wynette, sang for President Reagan she didn't know, nor really care about any etiquette, and was just herself, which caused quite a stir. The following comes from NPR.org:

The act isn't unusual for Wynette--during live shows, she'd often go out in the audience, zero in on some hapless husband, and melt him down in a similar fashion. But this is the president. "I didn't know it wasn't proper protocol," claimed Miss Tammy. *"He certainly didn't say anything."* As far as Wynette's performance went, "I had goose bumps," the Gipper [Reagan] confessed to the *New York Times*.

Uranus in Gemini on the IC

The power of Uranus is magnified in Gemini, but can also be very challenging. The insatiably overactive mind and/or body rarely rests, but can adjust to any situation or person.

Airy multi-maverick actress, Charlotte Rampling, gives an interview to NYTimes.com, wherein the interviewer summarizes aspects of this astrological placement, in describing Rampling's role in the 1974 film, The Night Porter:

> This movie, still her most notorious and defining role, was critically excoriated when it was released in America; Roger Ebert, Pauline Kael and Susan Sontag were all disgusted to the point of contempt. Even Rampling's admirers have dismissed it as sensationalism. Yet Rampling still considers it one of her most powerful performances, and I agree. While the characters as written can be summed up as pornographic clichés, the way Rampling and her co-star Dirk Bogarde played them was almost weirdly nuanced. During their first encounter, as Bogarde is pulling a pale chemise over her head, Rampling gazes at him with stunned fear and passivity; there is also a hint of perverse bonding and understanding, as well as something more intense: the look of a trapped animal showing a submissive face while it prepares its next move. Throughout the film, Rampling bodily expressed these myriad shades of feeling, from terror to arousal to rage to pure survival instinct, happening so closely together that the girl herself doesn't seem to know what she feels — and neither do we, even as we react. Thus Rampling amplified what was to critics the most offensive theme of the movie: the joining of beauty and cruelty, the communication between ungiving power and the soft, dumb knowledge of the body.

Kay Rala Xanana Gusmão, is an East Timorese politician. A former militant, he was the first President of East Timor. We have these gems from Gusmão that articulate the blending of resources and humanity:

> "I believe that when people have an occupation that allows them to provide for their families, the social dimension of human nature will emerge instinctively and lead people to help and organize others less privileged."

> "It is not enough to receive support, no matter, how needed it may be. It is fundamental to know how to receive this support and ensure that its result is exponential."

The you-never-know-what-they-will-do energy of Uranus is well portrayed by AC/DC front man, Bonn Scott. The following comes from Loudersound.com:

> "Bon had a riveting presence," we wrote. "He was cocky but he wasn't conceited. He was vulgar but he wasn't boorish. He was tough as nails but with a soft white underbelly. He was a hero, an icon, but he was also the guy next door, lying underneath a greasy motorbike with a spanner in his hand."

The lyrical magic of this astrological position is easily seen in one of the founders of the Beach Boys. The following comes from LATimes.com:

"Carl Wilson could sing anything. He could sing the phone book and he would sound great," said Andy Paley, a songwriter and staff producer for Sire Records.

Astrologer, Robert Zoller, made numerous contributions to the science and study of Uranus ruled astrology. As Uranus often indicates afflictions to the body, we can understand how Robert suffered from Parkinson's for the last 20 years of his life. While it did not stop him from doing his work, it understandably reduced his productivity.

Uranus in Cancer on the IC

These individuals would likely have many moves during their childhood or maybe even lived abroad. The security seeking Cancer is continually confronted by the Uranian need of freedom, and new horizons.

Former British Prime Minister, Gordon Brown, was interested in a new housing program. The following comes from Wikipedia:

> He said he wanted to release more land and ease access to ownership with shared equity schemes. He backed a proposal to build new eco-towns each housing between 10,000 and 20,000 home-owners – up to 100,000 new homes in total.

Healer and hand analyst, Mary Halima, guides her clients back to the Divine plan written in their hands using Sufi loving wisdom.

The overwhelmingly chaotic nature of this astrological placement is described by author Linda Gray Sexton in a beautifully written piece from LiveThroughThis.com:

> I was sent away to live with relatives who didn't have room for another child, so I was kind of shuttled into a corner a lot of the time. There was a lot of physical violence in the family because the husband expressed himself that way, and the kids got the brunt of it. It was not a good place to go. It wasn't safe. I started there when I was about two. I think that must have been her first suicide attempt, when I was about two. My younger sister had just been born, and she was sent to live with my father's mother, who was a very, very loving woman who took great care of kids. She kind of got the good end of the stick and I got the bad end of the stick.
>
> On the other hand, she stayed away for two whole years with my paternal grandmother. There was a good thing to that and a bad thing. She was away from my mother for the first two years of her life, which has obviously had a great impact on her. Yet she was with somebody loving and caring who knew what they were doing with a child, whereas after I was with my aunt's family for a while, they sent me back home and my mother really wasn't able to take care of me.

Once again, I ended up in a corner a lot of the time. My mother was physically abusive, so there was a lot of turmoil in that environment—a lot of rejection and physical abuse, which was obviously a really hard thing to grow up with. The worst thing, beyond all those things, was that my mother's mental illness took her away from me. I didn't have somebody stable who I knew would always be there, who would be my protector, keep me safe, and help me grow and learn the right lessons. That was not there.

That was kind of the beginning of a really long, troubled childhood where I adored my mother, but I really couldn't have her. She just wasn't available. She made numerous attempts at suicide throughout my entire childhood, until she finally killed herself when I was twenty-one.

Another author, multi-maverick, Val McDermid, has an unusual distinction that is revealed in a piece from TheGuardian.com:

William Wordsworth has a school named after him, Charles Dickens has a pub and Jane Austen a road. Scotland's murder mystery supremo, Val McDermid, has just discovered that she is to be given a rather more unusual accolade, after the University of Dundee said it would be christening its new morgue in her honour.

Multi-maverick and American songwriter, Steve Earle, shows alternative Uranian themes. The following comes from Wikipedia.com:

> He ran away from home at age 14 to search for his idol, singer-songwriter Townes Van Zandt. Earle was "rebellious" as a young man and dropped out of school at the age of 16. He moved to Houston with his 19-year-old uncle, also a musician.

Multi-maverick and Italian fashion designer, Donatella Versace, rules House Versace and benefits from her creative insights.

Uranus in Leo on the IC

Look up the synonyms for individualistic and the responses are narcissist, egoist, egotistical, megalomaniac, conceited... not really what I would call the equivalent of individualist, but we can attribute them to Leo's domain. How does fire work? It is a self-centering force, burning most strongly in its center while feeding on the fuel of air and matter to burn. Leo planets can act in self-centered ways while learning its combustion engine, which is meant to radiate love through the heart to warm all they encounter.

One of America's political blue bloods, Maria Shriver, has a maverick T-square with Chiron on her MC in Aquarius and Saturn on her DS in Scorpio. Astrologically, these three are all well represented in an opening quote on her web page MariaShriver.com:

> Welcome to my digital home. I believe we all have a purpose and mission that are uniquely our own. It is our life's work to articulate what that is and put it out in the world. Join me in making a difference.

Saturn and Uranus are the traditional and modern rulers of Aquarius and lends a strong humanitarian bent to her life. The empty point of her Taurus AS ensures manifesting a lot of Taurean energy in Shriver's life to strength her personal determination and resolve.

This astrological placement leads to numerous surprising ways in which the radical native's most private feelings are revealed to the public. An article from TheGuardian.com about Scottish musical performer, and former keyboardist for the English band Madness, Mike Barson, discusses the mechanics of that type of revelation:

> "'My Girl', meanwhile, was my attempt to write a reggae song. It was inspired by a bloke I'd worked with who said "Me and my girl" a lot. But the lyrics were also about my girlfriend of the time. We were having difficulties, talking on the phone for hours and all that. It's a young man talking about his emotions, but I don't know how that got in the song. Maybe I was stuck for a rhyme and it just came out. At first, I felt uncomfortable recording it. I never imagined it would connect with millions of people."

I recommend reading an article entitled *The tragic real-life story of Randy Travis* from Grunge.com to understand the drama Uranus can inflict on the self-centering energy of Leo.

Maverick extraordinaire and Canadian filmmaker, Bruce LaBruce, gives a lovely archetypal answer in an interview that can be found at GayCityNews.com:

> One thing that I didn't do consciously was that there was a whole imagery of death in the film. Lake sees a dead bird and gives a sponge bath and [tends to] the man in the pool; they are like corpses. The way he cleans Peabody's body in the sponge bath is like how they clean corpses. The closer to death the person is the more erotically charged it is for the gerontophile. Being old and close to death is part of the sexual fetish. But it connects with all the signifiers of aging being sexualized — wrinkles, stooped posture, etcetera. The pool was a way of demonstrating that the fetish is coming from a place you can't define. It is as mysterious for the boy as for the audience. These are traditionally places pedophiles would hang out, e.g., crossing guards, pools, et cetera. But it's a reversal of that urge, so it's ironic. Everything is reversed. It's the reverse "Lolita," with the old man as the sex object.

Irish actor, Kenneth Branagh, shares some thoughtful insights from this astrological vantage point:

"One of the things that makes Hamlet unique among Shakespeare's characters is his courage to face up to the darker elements of his personality."

"The best actors, I think, have a childlike quality. They have a sort of an ability to lose themselves. There's still some silliness."

"I feel more Irish than English. I feel freer than British, more visceral, with a love of language. Shot through with fire in some way. That's why I resist being appropriated as the current repository of Shakespeare on the planet. That would mean I'm part of the English cultural elite, and I am utterly ill-fitted to be."

Another thespian with multiple angular planets is American actress, Jennifer Jason Leigh, who was born in Hollywood, *and* was born of Hollywood parents. Fortunately, Jennifer has Uranus on her IC in Leo to help tether her seven planets (Mars, Saturn, Mercury, Sun, Jupiter, Venus and Moon!!!), MC and South Node in Aquarius. Jennifer is here to be her own truly unique self.

Uranus in Virgo on the IC

These individuals can have a very raw sexual immediacy that lights up those around them.

Pan-maverick porn star, Jeff Stryker, had an extensive career in which he was able to display his enterprising physical gifts and talents.

Even with his ultra-soprano voice and long, perfectly coiffed hair, multi-maverick front man and singer, Barry Gibb was a sex symbol for many women.

Adventurer and explorer, Tim Jarvis, is an environmental scientist and author with Masters qualifications in environmental science and environmental law. Tim has re-enacted historical expeditions hitherto only completed once or never before. This astrological position gives one an almost magical ability to pull what it needs from the environment or the people around these mavericks.

The theme of conservancy and environmental awareness are carried forth in our next example who is also a multi-maverick. Australian actress, Mimi MacPherson, started working on a whale-watching crew at 21 and went on to form her own whale-watching company.

Uranus in Libra on the IC

These individuals see the unique beauty in people and/or things in ways most others do not.

Scholar, poet and multi-maverick Petrarch was able to travel throughout Europe observing and writing about what he saw. The following comes from PoetryFoundation.com:

> After briefly studying law in Bologna in 1320, Petrarch decided to abandon the field, against his father's wishes,

to begin studying the classics and begin a religious life. In 1326 he took minor ecclesiastical orders and began serving under Cardinal Colonna, which allowed him to travel and write freely. His interest in Latin literature and poetry grew significantly during this time period, and he was later able to share his love for the humanities with Giovanni Boccaccio, a fellow poet and humanist. In 1327, Petrarch attended a mass in Avignon and saw Laura de Noves, for the first time. Laura, though her true identity has yet to be confirmed, would become the primary subject of his poetry for the rest of his life.

Petrarch continued to travel around Europe performing diplomatic missions for the Church and Cardinal Colonna in the 1330s, and soon became a well-known scholar and poet. His poetry, mainly composed sonnets focusing on the intense love and admiration he has for Laura, became immensely popular, and in 1341 he was crowned the poet laureate of Rome.

American psychic, Danielle Egnew, has Jupiter here with Chiron, across the way on her MC in Aries.

Multi-maverick, Melissa Ferrick, created a movie that helps people understand the power of negative talk to help regain balance.

URANUS

Uranus in Scorpio on the IC

This space at the bottom of the chart is private. Scorpio is a private sign that fears exposure, yet needs exposure. Uranus here ensures that the private, home-body self is always entertained. These individuals seek a deep authentic nature. We often find Uranus active in the charts of musicians, there is a sympathetic relationship to and with frequencies here in this placement.

Our first example is multi-instrumentalist, Sean Lennon, son of John Lennon and Yoko Ono. His father's murder when Sean was five, is an archetype of this astrological placement.

These quotes from multi-maverick and American actress, Katie Holmes, gives us the gold found in this astrological placement:

"Becoming a mother has been the most amazing experience – in an instant you become strong. You have to be a little bit wiser; it's the most important job in the world."

"It's nice to do something about something that scares you rather than just run from it and hope that someone saves you. I like seeing strong female characters and somebody who doesn't run away screaming when scared, but confronts the monsters."

"I really can't deny it, I am who I am. I'm pretty normal. I'm not that smooth type of girl. I run into things, I trip,

I spill food. I say stupid things… I really don't have it all together."

"I've found the man of my dreams. From the moment I met him it just felt like I'd known him forever. I was blown away. He's the most incredible man. He's so generous and kind, and he helps so many people, and, um, he makes me laugh like I've never laughed, and he's a great friend."

From FoxNews.com, we learn how dual maverick, singer, and dancer, Lance Bass uses this astrological placement:

And his love for renovating homes has landed him the perfect partnership with Maytag. "I've been flipping homes for the last few years and with all of those, my husband and I get to put our hands in a lot of the design especially the appliances that we put in the kitchens — to me, that's the most important part … so I love that [fellow *NSYNC band member Joey Fatone and I] are able to work with Maytag."

Not to mention, the appliance brand has launched a re-imagined version of the "It's gonna be May" meme, which of course is a nod to *NSYNC's 2000 hit, "It's Gonna Be Me," as part of its annual "May is Maytag Month" promotion.

"It's really funny," Bass admitted. "It's really cheeky and so on-brand for us. I think we were known for our humor also, so it's the perfect little combination there."

Multi-maverick and Welsh footballer, Michael Owen, has an indoor swimming pool and Jacuzzi.

American singer-songwriter, Justin Timberlake, who has Mars in Aquarius widely squaring this astrological placement, was in the same band (NSYNC) as one of our previous examples, Lance Bass. Here are a few of Justin's articulated archetypal statements:

> "Just writing and being in the studio was like therapy for me."

> "My biggest challenge was to make sure that the songs I did were who I am."

> "My teenage years were exactly what they were supposed to be. Everybody has their own path. It's laid out for you. It's just up to you to walk it."

Uranus in Sagittarius on the IC

There is an absolute need and drive for autonomy, self and inner exploration and freedom of expression on all levels.

While Buchenwald concentration camp was a place that provided no freedom to Mafalda, Princess of Savoy, who died after "complications" from surgery, she did receive the liberty of staying in an under-utilized barracks, and enjoyed the same food that the SS officers ingested.

American entertainer, Lady Gaga, freely expresses her unique nature as often as possible! One can see her personal adventurous expression on stage an in music videos.

Uranus in Capricorn on the IC

In some ways, the energies of this astrological placement do not seem to align, but when we consider the opportunities of the moment coupled with the structurally understanding Capricorn, the sky is the limit! These are the Aquarian energies of Saturn and Uranus.

Multi-maverick photographer and photojournalist, Lee Miller captured fine art images.

Edgar Austin Mittelholzer, was a Guyanese novelist, and the earliest novelist from the West Indian region to establish himself in Europe, and gain a significant readership.

While Capricorn is represented by the peak-seeking mountain goat, UFO abductee and double maverick, George van Tassel, lived under, not above, a very large boulder.

Multi-maverick Diana Mitford shares her aristocratic troubles in her autobiography, *A Life of Contrasts.*

The brilliance of this astrological placement is exemplified by Dame Kathleen Mary Ollerenshaw, née Timpson, a British mathematician and politician who was Lord Mayor of Manchester from 1975 to 1976.

Like many others with this astrological placement, American rocker, Wolfgang van Halen, represents the dynastic quality of this placement, and his own ability to take what came before and make it his own individual expression.

Uranus in Aquarius on the IC

These individuals have an inner brilliance and an ability to draw from their environment.

The quickness of thought, especially for mathematics, organizational schematics, and other intellectually centered work is demonstrated by Walter Diamond. The following comes from his obituary in *The New York Times:*

> Walter H. Diamond, an expert on international taxation, trade and economics who advised world leaders and wrote more than 80 books, died on May 23 in White Plains. He was 95 and lived in Hartsdale, New York.

American film star, Tyrone Power, who had a maverick T-square with Mars widely opposing and Mercury squaring this point, was known as a romantic swashbuckling hero, and he was also part of a dynasty of actors.

Next, is an archetypally illustrative explanation of how American singer, Frank Sinatra, used this astrological placement. The following comes from BecomeSingers.com:

> Frank didn't have a formal music education. However, he developed his superhuman absolute pitch skill. It made him a perfectionist. According to his colleagues and work partners, Sinatra's sixth sense was so great that he could easily hear an out of tune instrument in a playing orchestra. At Columbia Records, he also worked as a conductor.

Frank Sinatra has a reputation for being a perfectionist, and most musicians of his time are afraid to work with him. His attitude towards perfection kept him practicing and practicing until he gets satisfied.

Frank was the only one or perhaps one of the very few people who showed that AP could be learned if you will work and train hard for it. With his high self-confidence, well-ironed suits, and excellent grooming, Sinatra always mirrors perfection. He was a known, handsome womanizer and a gentleman.

Above all, Sinatra was known for his strict work ethic, talent in music, and his incredible skill as a perfect pitch.

The following comes from astro.com about seafaring New Zealander, Athol Rusden:

[Rusden]... who titled his autobiography *Rascal of the South Pacific*. Over a period of 50 years he captained some 28 vessels ranging from cruising yachts to luxury motor yachts and larger cargo vessels. He travelled to numerous South Pacific societies (including the Cook Islands, Tahiti, Samoa, Toanga Vanuatu, New Caledonia, the Galapagos Islands and many small atolls), in the era before mass tourism and modernization.

Longevity is another feature of Uranus on an angle. American singer, Louise Tobin, is 101 years old at the time of this writing in June 2020 and she "discovered" fellow maverick in this same category: Frank Sinatra.

Uranus in Pisces on the IC

The depths of instant insight and awareness are simultaneously unfathomable and boundless. This is a perfect placement for a creative genius in any number of, or even many mediums.

Virtuoso American jazz musician, Charles Mingus, who also has his moon here, had a sophisticatedly nuanced cleverness in his musical expression.

Denise Levertov, was a British-born American poet who expressed the alien themes of this astrological placement. The following comes from Wikipedia.com:

> She wrote about the strangeness she felt growing up part Jewish, German, Welsh and English, but not fully belonging to any of these identities. She notes that it lent her a sense of being special rather than excluded: "[I knew] before I was ten that I was an artist-person and I had a destiny". She noted: "Humanitarian politics came early into my life: seeing my father on a soapbox protesting Mussolini's invasion of Abyssinia; my father and sister both on soap-boxes protesting Britain's lack of support for Spain; my mother canvasing long before those events for the League of Nations Union; and all three of them working on behalf of the German and Austrian refugees from 1933 onwards... I used to sell

the *Daily Worker* house-to-house in the working-class streets of Ilford Lane."

The chameleon-like quality of this astrological placement is portrayed by American thespian, Marlon Brando, who was considered one of the nonpareil actors of the 20th century.

American artist, Robert Rauschenberg, showed the world the creative brilliance that creates a movement. The following is from Rauschenberg's obituary in *The New York Times*:

> Mr. Rauschenberg's work gave new meaning to sculpture. *Canyon,* for instance, consisted of a stuffed bald eagle attached to a canvas. *Monogram* was a stuffed goat girdled by a tire atop a painted panel. *Bed* entailed a quilt, sheet and pillow, slathered with paint, as if soaked in blood, framed on the wall. All became icons of postwar modernism.
>
> A painter, photographer, printmaker, choreographer, onstage performer, set designer and, in later years, even a composer, Mr. Rauschenberg defied the traditional idea that an artist stick to one medium or style. He pushed, prodded and sometimes reconceived all the mediums in which he worked.

Still other elements of this astrological placement are expressed in the life of entertainer, Bobby Limb. The following comes from Wikipedia.com:

> ...was an Australian-born entertainment pioneer, musician and legend of radio, television and theatre

of the 1960s and 1970s, he also founded the film and TV production company NLT Productions, with Jack Neary and Les Tinker. One of its main products was adventure serial *The Rovers*, which was aimed at breaking the international market.

We will now look at the angle placements of Uranus throughout the zodiac from the point of view of the Descendant (DS.)

Uranus in Aries on the DS

While these individuals seek harmony and balance in their lives because they have a Libra Ascendant, they are fierce defenders and have a superlative instinctual sensitivity.

The inner knowing of this astrological placement is well stated by broadcast journalist, Barbara Walters, in an article from NewsMax.com:

> Walters retired in 2014, after five decades in television. She decided not to take on any other projects after leaving *The View*, which was a first for her.
>
> "It's the first time I don't have something else [on the air] to go to," Walters noted. "I look forward to that."
>
> Walters said at the time that, while she could have stayed on the talk show, she decided not to.

"I control the show. It's not as if anyone asked me to leave," she said. "But I've accomplished what I wanted to accomplish."

Multi-maverick and singer, Bobbie Nelson, utilizes the inherent scales of melodic expression to enliven her innate musical gifts in a band with her brother, Willie Nelson.

Multi-maverick and American author, John Rechy, shares a twist on this astrological placement in an interview from Independent.co.uk:

"That's how I was. I was very passive. When I was growing up in Texas, I'd been seduced by women; when I moved to the streets, I was bought by men. I never approached anyone, ever. It was about keeping an attitude of non-participation and distance, of being desired but never desiring. It was all subterfuge, a denial of my sexuality."

Historical author, Don Berry, wrote about the devastating effect the white settlers had upon the native Oregon population. The tender rendering of the whole story, rather than a "white" washed one, shows a much deeper level of understanding with this position.

Egyptian film star, Omar Sharif, shares the following archetypally statements from BrainyQuote.com:

"I want to live every moment totally and intensely. Even when I'm giving an interview or talking to people, that's all that I'm thinking about."

"I don't know what women are attracted to. I can't tell, but certainly I have no notion of having sex appeal or being seductive in any way."

"I didn't want to be a slave to any passion anymore. I gave up card playing altogether, even bridge and gambling - more or less. It took me a few years to get out of it."

"Peter O'Toole - I really loved that man. They sent me into the desert, and I lived there with him for 100 days. And there were no women! Can you believe it?"

American stage and film actress, Eileen Brennan, was an accomplished actress, and a witty comedienne. This astrological placement lends an immediate brilliance when needed.

American actress, Karen Sharpe, showed the true grit and determination this astrological position can provide, but it didn't help her succeed in Hollywood.

Uranus in Taurus on the DS

The steady, long determined focus of Taurus is disrupted by the flashes of Uranian lightning. Radical changes in the form of relationship are well indicated with this placement.

Multi-maverick travel author, Bruce Chatwin, gives us these insightful tidbits from AZQuotes.com:

"Man's real home is not a house, but the Road, and that life itself is a journey to be walked on foot."

"A Sufi manual, the *Kashf-al-Mahjub*, says that, towards the end of his journey, the dervish becomes the Way not the wayfarer, i.e. a place over which something is passing, not a traveler following his own free will."

"For life is a journey through a wilderness."

Astrologer, Michael Munkasey, shows the multi-faceted brilliance Uranus can give to the normally single-minded focus of Taurus. The following comes from AstroWare.com:

> Michael has contributed a large portion of information in Kepler that you will find in the AstroEncyclopedia. His compilation of data on ancient astrology, Vedic astrology, progressed techniques and many other areas of astrology has benefited the Kepler program tremendously.

There are many examples of inspirational and clever literacy with a prominent Uranus, and this is further epitomized by writer and novelist, Roger Rosenblatt. He was a long-time essayist for *Time* magazine and *PBS NewsHour*. The following comes from Washingtonian.com:

> "All my friends said it was the bible of this or that, so I thought I would read it and not look like a horse's ass

on the panel, all of whom not only had read it but really did revere it.

"I didn't think that much of it. So without being impolite to the publisher, who was there, I said that while this book is extremely good for solid, adequate writing, it is not good for inspired writing. That probably wasn't its intention, but if you want to be a real writer, that has nothing to do with this book. It will save you if you're making a mistake, but it's not going to take you in the other direction.

"So the publisher asked, 'Would you write the next *Elements of Style* based on what you said?' And I said, 'I really don't do that kind of book.' And in any case, I have my own publisher. Then I started to think, well, maybe this would be fun to do. And I thought, I've really got to keep working. It's the physics body-in-motion theory—that since Amy died, I don't feel like getting myself into situations where I'm gloomy. I asked my editor at *Ecco*, and he said, 'Yeah, why not?'

"I thought this would be an interesting way to do it—follow a class, put some bones and skin into the discussion of the subject."

Michael Crawford, star of the musical, *The Phantom of the Opera*, also has Saturn here in this astrological placement. Below, Crawford gives a good interview with EastValleyTribune.com:

Q: I'm surprised, from the book, that you've faced all the horrors of celebrity: Having to recalibrate your ego after your marriage dissolved; losing a big chunk of finances from letting someone "invest" your money. But it's never really been a publicized factor of your life. For someone of your stature, you've managed to keep your personal life very, well, out.

A: Yes, I do, really. I don't go to public functions often, and I keep my private life really private. I live in a quiet community and don't live in Beverly Hills because I'm not comfortable there. It's insulting to say I like being surrounded by real people. I don't mean to be insulting, but there's got to be more than this business. I also do a lot of work with children's charities, so that occupies a lot of thought and time.

Uranus in Gemini on the DS

This can indicate a very active pollinator, indeed!
    The chaotic radiance of this astrological placement is well portrayed by leading French actor, Gerard Depardieu. The following comes from NowToLove.Co.NZ:

> Likened by former co-star Robert de Niro to a rogue truck in a demolition derby, Depardieu has left a trail of carnage along a career path that now stretches over 180 films.
>
>   The product of a troubled upbringing, he has done jail time for auto theft, grave robbing, had at least 18 motorcycle accidents and been thrown off a plane for

urinating in the aisle, and his claim to drink 10-plus bottles of wine a day sounds implausible only to those who haven't seen him in action.

Yet his friends acknowledge a more reflective, even feminine side to the roughhouse persona. "Throughout my life it has been women who have helped me the most, and taught me everything I know," he once told me in an interview.

He spoke of his admiration for female writers including Virginia Woolf, Anaïs Nin and Colette, and claimed: "I have stayed friends with every woman I have ever been in love with."

Michael, Prince of Kent, who also has Saturn and Venus on this point, is a most unusual royal.

From TVOvermind.com, we see that actress, Hayley Mills, displayed many of the traits with this astrological placement:

Mills has had a rather interesting life thus far and has proven herself to be a very surprising person. She was married for the first time in 1971 to a man more than twice her age, but divorced just six years later. They had a son together, and eventually he became a rock star for a band called Kula Shaker. She had a second son during a relationship with another actor, Leigh Lawson. As of 1997 she was and still is in relationship with Firdous Bamji, who is 20 years younger than she is. She's always been quite involved with the Hare Krishna movement for some time.

LeLonni Campbell, is a gifted astrologer who provides a regular newsletter bursting with helpful astrological guidance, along with offering regular workshops in her neighborhood.

Linda Chavez, is an American author, commentator, and radio talk show host whose (sometimes duplicitous) gems are shared from AZQuotes.com:

"One of the techniques terrorists employ is to allege torture and mistreatment when they are captured, regardless of whether it is true."

"Success is creating something original and lasting- whether it is a company, a work of art, an idea or analysis that influence others, or a happy and productive family."

"Journalists are supposed to be skeptical, that's what keeps them digging rather than simply accepting the official line, whether it comes from government or corporate bureaucrats."

"The United Nations has become a largely irrelevant, if not positively destructive institution, and the just-released U.N. report on the atrocities in Darfur, Sudan, proves the point."

Next, is a bit about astrologer, Ken Irving, that comes from matrixirving.wordpress.com:

Ken Irving has worked as editor of *American Astrology and Horoscope Guide*, is on the editorial board of *Correlation*, and has authored or coauthored articles, columns, and reviews in a variety of publications. He is coauthor of *The Psychology of Astro*Carto*Graphy* with the late Jim Lewis, and *The Tenacious Mars Effect* with Suitbert Ertel. Ken has lectured at many national and international conferences since 1978, served as an advisor and steering committee member to AFAN, and also served as UAC Board President from 1999 to 2001.

Uranus in Cancer on the DS

This is an interesting combination as we have freedom seeking Uranus in security-oriented Cancer. The childhood is likely to be dis-orienting, and may include frequent or foreign family moves. This is also a powerful placement for individuals who understand a way to take anything from the past and update it for the current and future good. Cardinal Cancer and initiatory Uranus work as allies in improving and evolving, once Cancer has learned the art of letting go.

Star Wars actor, Mark Hamill, has been married to his wife since 1978, which is shocking on many levels, and has nothing to do with Mark, personally. While being best known for his role as Luke Skywalker (hello Uranus in Cancer on the DS!), he has played countless cameo roles in a wide range of films as well.

From her website AdairLara.com, we easily recognize the astrological elements of this placement:

Adair Lara is a writer, teacher and author in San Francisco. A former magazine editor, she wrote a popular, award-winning personal column for the *San Francisco Chronicle* for 16 years before leaving the paper to write and teach full time. Her most recent book, which has become a cult favorite in the writing blogsphere, is *Naked, Drunk, and Writing: Shed Your Inhibitions and Craft a Compelling Memoir or Personal Essays* (Ten Speed). She holds sold-out workshops in her house on writing essay and memoir and other forms of autobiography, and consults with authors individually, in person or long-distance. Her essays appear in many national magazines, and have been anthologized in dozens of textbooks. She teaches memoir workshops in her house in San Francisco several times a year.

King Fuad II of Egypt, shares elements of this astrological placement in an interview that comes from WorldCrunc.com:

"But as a Muslim, I have to accept my fate. In Egypt, I was living in a gilded cage; here, I am a free man." After leaving Cairo, the king went to Italy and then Switzerland, where he spent all his school years. "My mother, Nariman, left when I was two years old. For a long time, I blamed her for that even though I know that life with my father was not easy. He was so popular with women!"

Writer and humorist, Ian Frazier, shares this vantage point from BrainyQuote.com:

"You can find dozens of books about people taking the Trans-Siberian Railroad. I knew I had to do something different to cross Siberia. To drive and to talk with people along the way, that was how I wrote my book 'Great Plains'. I drove and camped in Siberia, but did not have a real program."

"When the days start to get shorter, I want to be in some nice brick building on the East Coast with the lights glowing in the windows. When the daylight starts changing, I want to be out West."

Kim Althea Gordon, is an American musician, songwriter, and visual artist.

Luc Sante, is a writer and critic. Sante has written a number of books and is a frequent contributor to the *New York Review of Books*.

Uranus in Leo on the DS

These individuals have a certain *je ne sais quoi*. The extraordinary range of expression appears more uniform on one side, and uniquely odd on the other, but all leave their mark. Their egoic nature coupled with a drive for individual freedom makes for an interesting relationship with others.

The hallmarks of this position are well demonstrated in the lives of multi-mavericks and performers, Jools and Lynda Topp. The following comes from Stuff.co.nz:

ASTROLOGICAL MAVERICKS

Entertainers Jools and Lynda, the Topp Twins, were appointed Dame Companions of the New Zealand Order of Merit in the Queen's Birthday Honours.

Or as Jools – sorry, Dame Julie Bethridge Topp – puts it: "The rebels got their medals."

Talented performer and percussionist, Sheila E, has never been married. Another example of this astrological placement is the need for freedom.

There are few people more Uranian than multi-maverick Weird Al Yankovic, and in the land of Leo, we all know him by his wild mane of hair. Hair is a unique quality with Uranus as it seems to literally remove the hair from the top of the heads of many Uranians. Weird Al plays this astrological position (or does this position play him?) very well.

Film director, Todd Haynes, shares these gems from BrainyQuote.com:

"Making a film is so scary, and there's such a kind of void that you're working from initially. I mean, you can have all the ideas and be as prepared as possible, but you're also still bringing people together and saying, 'Trust me,' even when you don't necessarily trust every element."

"I think by around the time I was about 8 or 9, the idea of filmmaking probably took hold. I made little Super 8 extravaganzas when I was a kid, the first being my own version of *Romeo and Juliet,* and where I played all the parts except for Juliet."

"I liked to act in plays when I was a kid, and then in college. But that's the last time I really acted. I always loved it. But my interests were more in looking at the whole, rather than getting completely swallowed up in a single part of the whole."

"I think all my films can be enjoyed. In fact, they've often surprised me with how they're received."

Film and television actor, Michael J. Fox, who rose to prominence in his youth and became a spokesperson for Parkinson's disease, has been married since 1988. Uranus can signify mis-firing in the brain and nervous system. In the sign of Leo, we can see someone who leads others to greater compassion and understanding.

Riding on the banner of Change, hello Uranus, former U.S. president Barack Obama swept the United States by storm. He is a man of strong convictions and ethics. And while his presidency was the first in many areas, racist individuals are working to undo many of his crowning achievements, still bitter having had to "endure" having an African-American President. The never ending saga of President Obama's birth is yet another constellation of this placement.

Uranus in Virgo on the DS

These individuals have a resplendent ability to be ever resourceful and may even do many things that will shock and surprise those around them.

John Cameron Mitchell, is an American actor, writer and director, best known for originating the title role in *Hedwig and the Angry Inch*, as well as for his film *Shortbus*. *Hedwig and the Angry Inch* is a perfect character to represent this archetypal combination.

The following excerpt from singing legend, Whitney Houston's obituary in the *The New York Times*, indicates the type of gifts this astrological placement can give:

> Ms. Houston's range spanned three octaves, and her voice was plush, vibrant and often spectacular. She could pour on the exuberant flourishes of gospel or peal a simple pop chorus; she could sing sweetly or unleash a sultry rasp.

Martin John Bryant, is an Australian mass murderer who pleaded guilty to murdering 35 people and injuring 23 others in the 1996 Port Arthur massacre. I recommend reading more from SerialKillerCalendar.com:

> Bryant was regarded as unusual in his childhood and in the early years of his schooling was diagnosed as having an IQ of 66 (which is considered to indicate mental disability) and put into special education classes.
>
> He was described by teachers as unusually detached from reality and as either unemotional or as expressing inappropriate emotions. He was apparently a disruptive and sometimes violent child, and was severely bullied by other children.

Bryant was referred for psychiatric treatment several times during his childhood. In 1984, a psychological evaluation by Dr. Eric Cunningham Dax described him as mentally retarded and stated that he had a personality disorder.

Uranus in Libra on the DS

The pull to the exotic and foreign are intriguing to these highly inquisitive and insightful individuals. They also have an innate understanding of harmony and balance that sometimes requires adjustment(s).

Much of the work American figure skater, Nancy Kerrigan, did to attain Olympic gold was thwarted because another figure skater was jealous and wanted Nancy's place.

Innovative musician, Beck, has these illustrative elements from BrainyQuote.com. The first one touches on the hair/Uranus/genius theme:

> "I'm the artist formally known as Beck. I have a genius wig. When I put that wig on, then the true genius emerges. I don't have enough hair to be a genius. I think you have to have hair going everywhere."

> "Two men look out the same prison bars; one sees mud and the other stars."

> "Anything goes. You always find interesting things that way."

"Every time you go in, it's like starting over. You don't know how you did the other records. You're learning all over. It's some weird musician amnesia, or maybe the road wipes it out."

"I just go in the studio and write on the spot and see what comes out."

Multi-maverick and competitive swimmer, Cristina Teixeira, left Portugal to live in the UK. She appreciates the unique lens this astrological placement gives her.

Uranus in Scorpio on the DS

This placement gives one the ability to have great discernment, but also a deep fascination with that which is odd and different. One can disappear into another world of their own making.

Wikipedia.com summarize this archetype for Matthew Joseph Newton:

> ... an Australian-born actor, writer, and director, and son of TV personality Bert Newton. His acting career was interrupted by treatment in a psychiatric unit for bipolar disorder after several serious incidents of domestic violence and assault which were widely reported in the Australian media. Newton has relocated to New York City, where he is now based, and has resumed his directing and acting career.

From DailyMail.com we learn of a frightening example of this archetype and how it played out for surfer legend "White Lightning" Mick Fanning:

> Mick Fanning's "stalker" is accused of writing him love letters saying she had thoughts of KILLING him before she "broke into his home" – as the surfing legend breaks his silence on the "concerning" case.

Uranus in Sagittarius on the DS

The wild genius of this placement affects all those around, bringing one to madness in viewing all of the ideas of what it is to be alive and in relationship. The influx of higher thoughts and insights are continual.

Finding ways to synthesize is crucial to preventing overwhelm as well played in the life of Indonesia's first president, Achmed Sukarno. The following comes from Wikipedia, and brilliantly captures the heights this person can achieve:

> Author Pramoedya Ananta Toer once wrote, "Sukarno was the only Asian leader of the modern era able to unify people of such differing ethnic, cultural and religious backgrounds without shedding a drop of blood."

Werner Karl Heisenberg, was a German theoretical physicist and one of the key pioneers of quantum mechanics.

The following comes from Britannica.com:

In 1948 [Hans Joachim] Morgenthau published *Politics Among Nations*, a highly regarded study that presented what became commonly known as the classical realist approach to international politics. In this work, Morgenthau maintained that politics is governed by distinct immutable laws of nature and that states could deduce rational and objectively correct actions from an understanding of these laws. Central to Morgenthau's theory was the concept of power as the dominant goal in international politics and the definition of national interest in terms of power. His state-centered approach, which refused to identify the moral aspirations of a state with the objective moral laws that govern the universe, maintained that all state actions seek to keep, demonstrate, or increase power. He called for recognition of the nature and limits of power and for the use of traditional methods of diplomacy, including compromise.

Umberto II of Italy, had so many flashes of this astrological placement presented in his life. He was the last and one of the shortest reigns of the Savoy, and according to HistoryToday.com:

Graduating from the Royal Military Academy in Turin in 1923, Umberto was handsome, charming, willful, a lavish spender and fond of pranks and love affairs, with both sexes according to rumor. He supposedly said he wished he were a fireman so that he could marry anyone he pleased, but in fact he obeyed his father's orders and married a rich Belgian princess, Maria José. He designed her dress, the wedding lasted a week and five thousand guests attended the grand ball at the Quirinal Palace in Rome, though there were soon rumors of an affair between Umberto and the Hollywood singing star Jeanette Macdonald. Maria José would eventually give Umberto four children – the first two conceived by artificial insemination.

Kirk Khan, is a brilliant astrologer and gifted programmer, who helped put me on the path to write this book. Khan's brilliance is like capturing a young colt that has never known a halter.

Uranus in Capricorn on the DS

Innovators of others and their ways of doing things. These mavericks are already outside of the box of conformity and see the world awash with opportunity. While they may especially love to marry above their social class, sometimes that isn't what life provides.

Albert Speer, used the slave labor of the Nazi Party to attain his goals. Speer is a sad example of the heartless pursuit of success at whatever cost which this astrological position can encourage. The following comes from Wikipedia.com, and here we learn about his mother's feelings about Speer's wife which reflect an aspect of this astrological position:

The relationship was frowned upon by Speer's class-conscious mother, who felt the Webers were socially inferior.

Entertainer, Burl Ives, was aware of the importance of his career. The following comes from SunTimes.com:

Ives voluntarily appeared before a congressional panel in 1952, providing testimony that many in the left-leaning folk music world — notably musician Pete Seeger — saw as a betrayal, viewing Ives as cooperating to save his career.

Henri Dericourt, was a French secret agent for Special Operations Executive. It is unclear whether he became a double agent for the Sicherheitsdienst, or was working under British instructions when he betrayed *all* of his comrades during WWII. The following from Spartacus-educational.com, shows Henri's "fitting end" for this astrological placement:

Henri Déricourt was reported to have been killed in an air crash while flying over Laos on 20th November, 1962. His body was never found and some writers have claimed that his death was faked in order to allow him to begin a new life under another name.

Sir Hugh Carleton Greene, was a British journalist and television executive. Sir Hugh was director-general of the BBC from 1960 to 1969. The following comes from his Guardian.com obituary:

He was therefore a natural choice as director-general in 1960. He led the BBC's counter-attack against the early successes of ITV, oversaw the introduction of BBC2 and colour television, and greatly relished the creative surge of programming in the 1960s. He had a great sense of mischief, and particularly enjoyed rebutting attacks from all quarters - including Mrs. Whitehouse.

The House Monegasque of Monaco, has yet another maverick in their midst, Pauline Ducruet. The following comes from the Tatler.com, where we see another iteration of this astrological placement:

In 2017, alongside friend Maria Zarco, Ducruet launched her own label; Alter Designs. A unisex brand, Ducruet's pieces perfectly blend contemporary cuts with a classic sensibility and youthful edge.

The name of her label is, of course, a combination of Uranus and Capricorn as well.

Uranus in Aquarius on the DS

These individuals are here to birth the New Age ideals by infusing everyone with their Aquarian brilliance and for capturing and dispersing ideas in a new and instructive way. Uranus is the modern ruler of Aquarius and therefore can lend a shocking clarity to these individuals.

Maverick and Welsh poet, Dylan Thomas, displayed many of the characteristics we can expect from this astrological placement, such as erratic behavior. The electric qualities of this position can act like antennae to the lyrics of the universe. The poem, "Do not go gentle into that good night" is one of his best-known works.

Maverick and horse racing jockey, Eddie Arcaro, used this astrological position to ride the air. The following comes from Wikipedia.com:

[Eddie Arcaro] was an American Thoroughbred horse racing Hall of Fame jockey who won more American classic races than any other jockey in history and is the only rider to have won the U.S. Triple Crown twice.

The interesting life of fiction author, John Horn Burns, can only be understood using this erratic lens. The egotistical arrogance of Aquarius is easier to take when tempered with humility. The following excerpt comes from an article in *The New York Times*:

Burns was a former soldier, now teaching English at Loomis, a prep school. By one of his counts, *The Gallery* was actually his ninth novel; he wrote one pretty much every summer, first at Andover, then at Harvard, then at Loomis, books that even his friends conceded were unpublishable — nasty, nihilistic and narcissistic things populated with characters his own agent once called "stinkers." But the war had touched and humanized Burns, changing his outlook, tone and style.

He told a friend that he had shed his *ungenügender Selbstsucht* — a term he would have learned from Goethe and Brahms, meaning unsatisfying egotism or insatiable self-love — and come, at long last, to care about someone besides himself.

Indian Prime Minister, Indira Gandhi, showed another, less humanistic and more autocratic aspect of this astrological placement. The following comes from Time.com:

But in her mammoth victory lay the seeds of paranoid insecurity, and she proved to be as ruthless as she was charismatic. By 1975, as a result of economic instability, her government was swamped by an avalanche of street protests, and after her election was deemed invalid, she declared an emergency. On the night of June 25, 1975, the electricity was suddenly shut off in Delhi's newspaper offices.

She quickly ripped apart her father's democracy and amended India's constitution to give herself enormous powers. She jailed political opponents, muzzled the press and extinguished fundamental rights across the country. By 1976, she would scorn democratic processes to stamp out rivals, dismissing party colleagues and state leaders at will. That year, her government rammed through the 42nd Amendment arrogating supreme powers to Parliament. She instituted "family rule" in her party with the ascendance of her son Sanjay. She also oversaw a remorseless slum-clearance drive in Delhi and forcible-sterilization campaigns across India.

How could we talk about Uranus and Aquarius without including an astrologer? We learn the following from Wikipedia.com, about astrologer, Olivia Barclay:

> ...was a British astrologer who played an important role in the revival of traditional forms of astrology in the late 20th century. Much of her focus in the latter part of her life was on the work of the 17th-century astrologer, William Lilly.

Remember that the traditional ruler of Aquarius is Saturn which deals with that which comes from the past as well as earlier foundations.

Here's what we learn about French financier, Arpad Busson, before challenges befell the hedge-fund manager extraordinaire:

> "Back then Arki had more friends than he knew what to do with," a hedge fund executive who had attended the balls told *Financial News*. "If you wanted something done or you needed connections made, then Busson was your man."

Alexandria Zahra Jones, displays another aspect of this astrological placement: a keen creative talent. As the daughter of superstar musical performer, David Bowie and international model, Iman, Alexandria is already creating a stir with her individual style and talent.

Sometimes the innocence of this astrological position shows itself. We learn the following from an article at TownandCountryMag.com about Lady Louise Windsor:

"Well, for Louise, actually, it was much more of a shock to the system," Countess Sophie told Minchlin. "It was only when she was coming home from school and saying, 'Mummy, people keep on telling me that grandma is the queen.' And I asked her, 'Yes, how does that make you feel?' And she said, 'I don't understand.' I don't think she had grasped that perhaps there was only one Queen."

Uranus in Pisces on the DS

This is an interesting placement for electric Uranus in watery Pisces. The sensitivity and insight can be overwhelming as well as the need for freedom and escape. Relationship with this placement is interesting and often unusual.

The width, depth and complexity of this position are well represented by multi-maverick actor, Montgomery Clift, in this excerpt from VanityFair.com:

From the start, Clift was framed as a rebel and an individual. When he first arrived in Hollywood, he didn't sign a contract, waiting until after the success of his first two films to negotiate a three-picture deal with Paramount that allowed him total discretion over projects. It was unheard of, especially for a young star, but it was a seller's market. If Paramount wanted him, they'd have to give him what he wanted—a power differential that would go on to structure the star-studio relationship for the next 40 years.

When the press talked about Clift, they talked about the skill and the beauty, but they also talked about what an offbeat, weird guy he was. He insisted on maintaining his residence in New York, spending as little time in Hollywood as possible. His apartment, which he rented for 10 dollars a month, was described by friends as "beat up" and by him as "terrific." He survived on two meals a day, mostly combinations of steak, eggs, and orange juice, and he eschewed nightclubs, instead spending his spare time reading Chekov, classic works of history and economics, and Aristotle, whom he praised for his belief in happiness, or the "gentle art of the soul." When he wasn't reading or exhausting himself in preparation for a part, he liked to go to the local night court and attend high-profile court cases just to watch the humanity on display.

Artist, Wayne Thiebaud paints wildly huge desserts for our sweet craving selves.

The individualistic freedom seeking theme of this astrological placement is mirrored in other parts of American writer, Jack Kerouac's chart. There was no way Kerouac could fit within the social confines of his age.

Peter Wildeblood, was an Anglo-Canadian journalist, novelist, playwright and gay rights campaigner, who went to prison for being gay. I recommend reading articles about this intriguing individual. We learn the following tidbit from TheGuardian.com:

> While he was serving his sentence Wildeblood resented the well-meaning assumption, made by warders and others, that he would disappear when he was released, most likely living abroad as Wilde had done. Instead, he intended to take up his interrupted life – and he did, though with a new reformist agenda.

From History.com, we find another aspect of this astrological placement portrayed by Japanese poet and author, Yukio Mishima:

> World-renowned Japanese writer, Yukio Mishima, dies by suicide after failing to win public support for his often extreme political beliefs.
> Born in 1925, Mishima was obsessed with what he saw as the spiritual barrenness of modern life. He preferred prewar Japan, with its austere patriotism and traditional values, to the materialistic, westernized nation that arose after 1945. In this spirit, he founded the "Shield Society," a controversial private army made up of about 100 students that was to defend the emperor in the event of a leftist uprising.
> On November 25, Mishima delivered to his publisher the last installment of *The Sea of Fertility*, his four-volume epic on Japanese life in the 20th century that is regarded as his greatest work. He then went with several followers to a military building in

Tokyo and seized control of a general's office. There, from a balcony, he gave a brief speech to about 1,000 assembled servicemen, in which he urged them to overthrow Japan's constitution, which forbids Japanese rearmament. The soldiers were unsympathetic, and Mishima committed *seppuku,* or ritual suicide, by disemboweling himself with his sword.

Though his extreme beliefs did not gain him much of a following, many mourned the loss of such a gifted author.

Who else would we expect to find here, but the man who completely revolutionized sex and relationship to/with the other: *Playboy* publisher, Hugh Hefner. A line from one of his obituaries has a succinct statement of this astrological placement:

"Leader of the sexual revolution."

Other elements of this astrological placement are well expressed in this next obituary from NYTimes.com:

George Melly, an eccentric known as a jazz and blues singer, an expert on Surrealism, an author, a raconteur and a cultural critic — as well as a clotheshorse for loud zoot suits, jaunty fedoras and glow-in-the-dark ties — died yesterday at his London home. He was 80. He died after suffering from emphysema and dementia, his wife, Diana Melly, told The Associated Press.

URANUS

We will now look at the angle placements of Uranus throughout the zodiac from the point of view of the Medium Coeli (MC).

Uranus in Aries on the MC

This is a bright light for the world to see. A candle in the darkness, a flame in the heart.

Our first example expresses this example as her innocent independent self, described the events she and her family endured in an attic in Amsterdam during World War Two. Her personally intimate story shared in the pages of her journal were never meant to be seen by anyone else, let alone translated into some 70 languages. T*he Diary of Anne Frank* is the most translated book in Dutch history. Her story helps to personalize the atrocities countless millions of individuals endured in the Nazi pursuit of creating a "master race."

Willie Littlefield, billed as Little Willie Littlefield, was an American R&B and boogie-woogie pianist and singer whose early recordings "formed a vital link between boogie-woogie and rock and roll." From his biography from Spontaneouslunacy.com (another example of this archetype!) we learn the following about Littlefield:

> One of rock's first teen sensations who went on to a long-lasting career that saw only brief flurries of commercial success, but who built an enduring reputation that lasted into the next century.

The endless energy of this astrological placement can be seen in the life of operatic baritone, William Walker. The following comes from Boston.com:

Mr. Walker "was a true Southern gentleman with a bigger-than-life personality and a rich, booming voice." Metropolitan Opera records indicate Mr. Walker performed 364 times, from March 1962 to June 1978. He appeared dozens of times on television's *The Tonight Show* starring Johnny Carson, and also sang at many venues on Broadway.

Donald William 'Bob' Johnston, was an American record producer, best known for his work with musicians, Bob Dylan, Johnny Cash, Leonard Cohen, and Simon and Garfunkel. The following comes from Donald Johnston's Independent.co.uk obituary:

The task of a staff producer entailed a wide overview of popular culture: just before *Highway 61* Johnston produced "Hush Hush Sweet Charlotte", a US Top 10 hit for the saccharine Patti Page, the previous decade's biggest-selling female artist. The occupation also required humility. "My job wasn't to be a hero and to tell Paul Simon or Bob Dylan or Johnny Cash or Willie Nelson what the fuck to do!" he said. "I thought if you want to be a hero or if you want to take credit, get some other people to work with. Don't work with these people. I wasn't like some other people who were looking to be the next Phil Spector."

Uranus in Taurus on the MC

Here we have the individuals who take various forms and turn them on their ears. Uranus is in the sign of Taurus as I write this.

Italian luxury fashion designer, Giorgio Armani, shows one aspect of this astrological placement from the SeattleTimes.com:

> Giorgio Armani has outlined a succession plan aimed at preventing his fashion empire from being split up, but the 83-year-old designer remained mum Monday on an eventual creative transition.
>
> One of the founding designers of Milan ready-to-wear, Armani's firm grip on the privately run fashion group Giorgio Armani SpA has long sparked speculation about his succession plans.
>
> In an interview Monday with the Corriere della Sera daily, Armani said after he dies, three people who he names will be put in charge of the foundation that he created last year both as a succession tool and a vehicle for charity investments.
>
> He said the foundation will be the tie-breaker if the evenly numbered board of directors for his business reaches an impasse.
>
> "What we have created stimulates my heirs to remain in harmony and prevents the group from being bought or from breaking up," he said.

ASTROLOGICAL MAVERICKS

Since being elected head of the Catholic Church in 2014, Pope Francis created numerous papal bulls (his decrees) that resulted in shocking changes for his religion. This Uranus trines his maverick Mercury and Jupiter conjunct his Capricorn DS, which means he has a good understanding of structures and how to make changes that can benefit everyone in the Catholic Church and beyond.

Brian Edwards, is an Irish-born New Zealand media personality and author, whose bid for a political seat was thwarted when his extra-marital relationship was exposed.

Singer and performer, Tina Turner, took control of her life back from her abusive husband, Ike Turner, and became her independent creative self.

Multi-maverick Anita Bryant, had a profound inability to recognize human expression and might have had a wider expression than her narrow belief structures allowed. It's funny how she decided which parts of her beliefs were more important as stated in this snippet from LGBTQNation.com:

> Mr. Green begged her to reconcile in an open letter: "Let us both put aside all other earthly considerations and reunite in Christian love." Bryant wasn't interested. She told *People* magazine: "Divorce is against everything I believe in. I wanted to save my marriage, but I decided that was not the route to go." The following year, she told a woman's magazine that the marriage "was never much good to begin with" and hinted that both had been unfaithful.

URANUS

Uranus in Gemini on the MC

As we have seen before, when Uranus unites with the angles in Gemini there is sign of singing brilliance. There is a multi-faceted-ness about this tireless astrological combination.

Singer, Dolly Parton has these beauties from BrainyQuote.com:

"I'm not going to limit myself just because people won't accept the fact that I can do something else."

"When I'm inspired, I get excited because I can't wait to see what I'll come up with next."

"We cannot direct the wind, but we can adjust the sails."

"Find out who you are. And do it on purpose."

The story telling quality of this astrological placement is articulated in this article from RollingStones.com about singer, Kim Carnes:

A Number One country track in Canada, "Dreamer" was a crossover hit in America, cracking the Top 5 on the country, pop and adult contemporary charts. But in order to come up with the song, Carnes had to completely step into the character of Gideon, since she didn't really see eye-to-eye with her creation on a particular subject. "I'll do the song in every show, but I always say that I don't really think that way personally," she says with a laugh. "Because I'm a dreamer, [and] all my friends are dreamers. I think it's a wonderful thing to dream big. The song was just written in the context of who Gideon Tanner is in this life story."

Soap operas and theater actress, Rowena Wallace, has an extensive filmography.

The multi-valent talent of *quadrangular* maverick (planets conjunct each of the four angles) Kathy Bates has made box office hits for 50 years with no sign of quitting anytime soon.

Singer and songwriter, Holly Near, is the perfect bridge for musical Gemini and activist oriented Uranus.

Uranus in Cancer on the MC

The security seeking Cancer self is forced out into the limelight in unusual and fascinating ways with this placement.

Sir Peter James Blake, was a New Zealand yachtsman who won the 1989–90 Whitbread Round the World Race. Sir Peter was murdered while anchored at the Amazon River delta, monitoring environmental changes. The following comes from Wikipedia.com:

> Around 30,000 people attended a memorial service held for Blake at the Auckland Domain on December 23, 2001, and included tributes from Blake's family, the New Zealand Prime Minister Helen Clark, the Brazilian Ambassador, and Neil and Tim Finn. Helen

Clark spent a night aboard the *Seamaster* three weeks prior to the attack. She called Blake a "living legend" and a "national hero" in her eulogy she said in part: "Our small nation went into shock. Peter Blake was a living legend. As an outstanding sailor, he had brought great honour and fame to New Zealand. His death was unthinkable."

Safety is an elusive experience for one with this astrological placement as well shown in this excerpt about Carlos the Jackal taken from RainbowSix.Fandom.com:

In 1994, Carlos had some minor cosmetic surgery done by a trusted physician. Two days later, the Sudan Government told him that he needed to be moved to a villa for protection from an assassination attempt and would be given personal bodyguards. The next day, the bodyguards tranquilized Carlos while he slept and transferred him to French DST agents. Carlos later awoke aboard a plane bound to Paris for his trial. He was charged for the 1975 murders of the two French counterintelligence officers and Moukharbal and was sent to La Santé Prison to await trial. Carlos was found guilty on December 23rd, 1997, and was sentenced to life without the possible parole. He was placed in a small, single window cell where he was watched at all times of the day through cameras and was not allowed contact with other prisoners.

Quadrangular maverick, Scott Hicks has these enlightening and perceptive statements taken from AZQuotes.com:

"I always love depth. I like looking through windows, through frames, through spaces into other spaces."

"I've always had a feeling that the image is 50% of the emotion that an audience feels and it's subliminal. Yet, how you arrange the elements in front of a camera has an impact on people's belief about that world in some way."

"The visualization of my films is always very important to me and I work very closely with my cinematographers. I've never had the same cinematographer twice now that I think about it. I don't know why that is. Everyone is always busy. They do three or four films a year. It's vital to me."

"My job as the director is to make that as authentic as I can and not to disturb the revelry."

If we see Cancer as the sign of family and/or clan, we can understand how Australian politician, Pauline Hanson, might have perceived that she was being a hero for all people, when actually, only seeking to protect her own. The following comes from TheGuardian.com/Australia-news:

> Labor's Senate leader, Penny Wong, said her party agreed with denying formality to the Hanson motion

because it was "not appropriate to spend this Senate's time inciting division."

"Asserting black lives matter isn't saying that other lives do not matter," Wong told the Senate.

"It is responding to a systemic structural problem where black lives are not given equal value. And those who want to reinforce that status quo, including white supremacists, have instead adopted the phrase that is used in Senator Hanson's motion."

Film actress, Debra Winger, shares these archetypal statements from BrainyQuote.com:

"Just because we're on schedule is no reason to shoot bad acting. Someone once said to me, 'You're inconsiderate.' And I said, 'Inconsiderate? Bad acting is the ultimate inconsideration.' It's a collective slap to a million faces at the same time."

"I was the all-American face. You name it, honey – American Dairy Milk, Metropolitan Life insurance, McDonald's, Burger King. The Face That Didn't Matter – that's what I called my face."

Uranus in Leo on the MC

The fixed Leo ego is in for the time of its life with this astrological placement. There can be a multi-personality about these individuals that makes them excellent entertainers and chameleons.

From her HBO.com page we learn the following about multi-maverick and actress, Tracey Ullman:

> In a series of sketches, Tracey Ullman plays a wide array of everyday people and famous faces, from Dame Judi Dench to Angela Merkel to a next-door-neighbor near you.

The indefatigable nature of this astrological placement is well stated in this article from RollingStone.com about actor, Jim Carrey:

> The Carrey who would spend eight hours before a set of mirrors perfecting faces, the Carrey who can't stop himself from working all day and well into the night for weeks on end, is no stranger to darkness and compulsion. The Riddler is "like any sycophant," says Carrey. "The type of guy who's basically saying he loves you more than life itself but deep down he hates you more than death – because he's grown to resent you." The object of much hero worship lately (fawned over by studio chiefs and schoolkids alike), Carrey walked on the star-laden *Batman* set as the guy who turned up when the first choice Robin Williams wouldn't. "I'd never seen his work," Kilmer says. "So I got *Ace Ventura,* and all I had to do was watch the opening deliveryman sequence. I called up the studio and said, 'Well, this'll be fun.'"

Douglas James Wright, , was a dancer and choreographer in the New Zealand arts establishment from 1980. This astrological placement is beautifully articulated in the following personally oriented excerpt from his Stuff.co.nz obituary:

> An obituary is normally about the deceased, but I begin with my declaration of conflict of interest (actually, deeply shared interest) – namely, that Douglas is the single most important artist in my life. His fearless vision through an astonishingly prolific artistic output moved us beyond comfort, beyond normalcy, beyond the already known. Not fantasy, not surrealism, not escapism, but expressionist art of the highest order, framed with wit – dark, caustic, incorrigible, ironic and hilarious by turns, and teeming with alternative perceptions of the natural and social givens. As a New Zealand artist across five genres, Douglas Wright remains a phenomenon without peer.

Canadian model, Dorothy Stratten, was only 20 when she was murdered by her husband. Dorothy was well known for being one of *Playboys*' Playmate of the year in 1980. Here, we see her uncommon flame as described in her Wikipedia page:

> In his introductory remarks, Hefner noted that Stratten was from Canada and had received $200,000 in cash and gifts in addition to the title. In a fleeting comment, Hefner also acknowledged the effect that Stratten's charming combination of beauty, intelligence, and sensitivity had on many who knew her when he said,

"...and she is something rather special. They always are, but Dorothy is really quite unique."

The extremely rare experience of being conjoined AND separate entities is beautifully illustrated in the lives of twins Lori and George Schappell who also have Venus on this point. George was assigned female at birth and identified as male.

Uranus in Virgo on the MC

While their energy can be chaotic, these individuals have an uncanny ability to manifest and manipulate resources. Out of the hat they will be able to pull out more than a rabbit. There can also be a strong drive to service.

Astrologer, Ray White, is the webmaster for Astrolabe, a website offering astrology reports, astrology software programs, reference books, and astrology services.

The gender bending quality of this astrological position is well exhibited by multi-maverick and professional ballroom dancer, Craig Revel Horwood. Craig elucidates other facets of this astrological placement in these gems from BrainyQuote.com:

> "I used to go to clubs and sing as myself but people weren't interested. And then I turned up as a woman and suddenly everyone was interested."

> "I feel as though I'm constantly defending myself. I'm up against challengers from the ballroom world, from

the dance world, people on the couch who hate what I'm saying about their favourite celebrity. Then you're up against the press, who will always want to put you in a box."

"There can be dramas in your life and you can get over them and become someone. You don't have to wallow in self-pity; you can actually use the experiences in your life to push yourself further and help others."

"My relationship with my dad was complex, especially when I came out. The years of verbal abuse, all of it drink-fueled, were difficult. Later, though, he came to see me on stage in *La Cage aux Folles* – one of his favourite shows – and loved it. Theatre won him over and he accepted me in the end."

Hockey goalie, Patrick Roy lived the more agile aspects of this astrological placement. The following comes from LastWordOnHockey.com:

In the 1986 playoffs, Patrick Roy became a star. Roy posted a sparkling 15-5 record, a 1.92 goals-against average and a .923 save percentage. He would lead the Habs to their 23rd Stanley Cup. On top of that, he would win the Conn Smyth Trophy as the playoff MVP.

Roy would become a superstar in the league. He would win the Jennings Trophy in 1987, 1988 and 1989. He also won two Vezina Trophies in 1989 and 1990. The Canadians would win the Adams division in 1987-88 and 1988-89. They would return to the Stanley Cup Finals in 1989 but would lose to the Calgary Flames. The Habs returned to glory in 1992-93, when Roy again would lead them to the Stanley Cup.

Patrick Roy was the face of the franchise and an unquestioned superstar in the NHL.

Multi-maverick and Australian footballer, Andrew Jarman, shows the ins and outs possible with this astrological placement. The following comes from Wikipedia.com:

> Jarman was fined and suspended. The club's decision not to sack him outright took into account his five-and-a-half years of service, 100-plus games and the recent awarding of life membership. After six successful seasons with the Crows, Jarman was one of the high-profile senior players delisted at the end of the 1996 season following the arrival of coach Malcolm Blight. Jarman was awarded Life Membership of the club shortly afterward. Despite speculation that Jarman would be named on Port Adelaide's inaugural AFL list for season 1997 this did not eventuate.

Uranus in Libra on the MC

These individuals can fly like the wind as well as create or entangle themselves in whirlwinds. They have a rare gift for creating, engaging, and supporting new types of relationships and making connections that others may have a hard time grasping.

Wikipedia.com enumerates many parts of this astrological placement in the following excerpt about multi-maverick and English footballer, Alan Shearer:

> Alan Shearer CBE DL is an English retired footballer who played as a striker. Widely regarded as one of the best strikers of his generation and one of the greatest players in the history of the Premier League, he is the Premier League's record goalscorer. He was named Football Writers' Association Player of the Year in 1994 and won the PFA Player of the Year award in 1995. In 1996, he came third in both Ballon d'Or and FIFA World Player of the Year awards. In 2004 Shearer was named by Pelé in the FIFA 100 list of the world's greatest living players.

Interestingly enough, like our previous example, tennis professional, Pat Rafter, married his wife in 1991. The following comes from Wikipedia.com:

> Patrick Michael Rafter is an Australian former professional tennis player. He reached the Association of Tennis Professionals world No. 1 singles ranking on 26 July 1999. His career highlights include consecutive US Open titles in 1997 and 1998, consecutive runner-up appearances at Wimbledon in 2000 and 2001, winning the 1999 Australian Open men's doubles tournament

alongside Jonas Björkman, and winning two singles and two doubles ATP Masters titles.

Australian actress and television hostess, Kym Wilson, is mostly known for her relationship with the lead singer of INXS, Michael Hutchence.

Uranus in Scorpio on the MC

These individuals have an extra-ordinary intuition and sensitivity that even they would be hard pressed to articulate.

The gifted relationship with water is beautifully expressed in our first example. From 1996-2004, Sarah Michelle Ryan, an Australian former sprint freestyle swimmer, won relay medals at three consecutive summer Olympics.

Elements of this astrological placement are well expressed by "secret" royal eldest grandson of Queen Elizabeth, Peter Phillips. Remember that both Peter's grandmother and cousin Harry have Saturn in this position. The following comes from Express.co.uk:

Why does Peter Phillips not have a title?

Peter is currently 15th in line to the British throne.

The Princess Royal's son keeps a low public profile and does not work as a senior royal.

He carries out no royal duties, and has held multiple positions at companies including Jaguar, Williams F1 racing team, and the Royal Bank of Scotland.

Scorpio is the sign of power – its uses and abuses. The interesting tale of Yaser Esam Hamdi, brings many aspects of this maverick placement to light. The following comes from WSWS.org:

> After spending almost three years imprisoned incommunicado by the United States military following his November 2001 capture in Afghanistan, Yaser Esam Hamdi is being taken by U.S. military aircraft to Saudi Arabia, where he will be reunited with his family. In exchange for his release, he has agreed to renounce his U.S. citizenship and restrict his travel.
> Hamdi was the subject of the June 28th Supreme Court decision that allows the U.S. military to incarcerate people, including U.S. citizens, as "enemy combatants," a classification concocted by the Bush administration to avoid both criminal procedures and the provisions of the Geneva Conventions for treatment of prisoners of war.
> At the same time, according to the "controlling" opinion by Associate Justice Sandra Day O'Connor—none of the opinions received the necessary five votes to become binding precedent—Hamdi is entitled to some form of "due process," including access to an attorney and a tribunal, to challenge his continued incarceration.

Hamdi's release has been widely viewed by legal commentators as "damage control" by the Bush administration, which got as much mileage as it could from the case and wanted to avoid a potentially embarrassing courtroom showdown.

Uranus in Sagittarius on the MC

The ways in which these individuals perceive and express truth is often breathtaking.

From the ManlyPHall.org website, we learn the following about Manly Palmer Hall:

> [Hall]... was a Canadian-born author and mystic. He is perhaps most famous for his *work The Secret Teachings of All Ages: An Encyclopedic Outline of Masonic, Hermetic, Qabbalistic and Rosicrucian Symbolical Philosophy*, which is widely regarded as his magnum opus, and which he published at the age of 25 (or 27, 1928). He has been widely recognized as a leading scholar in the fields of religion, mythology, mysticism, and the occult while being well respected by those in philosophy, theosophy and psychology circles including Carl Jung, whom when writing *Psychology and Alchemy*, had borrowed material from Hall's private collection.

BrainyQuotes has this beauty from multi-maverick and South African writer, William Plomer:

"Creativity is the power to connect the seemingly unconnected."

Born in 1904, Helen Knothe Nearing, was an American author and advocate of simple living. Helen and her husband left their privileged city lives for a more down-to-earth farm experience that paved the way for the back-to-the-landers movement. The following comes from VTDigger.org:

> They had a loftier goal than just self-sufficiency when they moved north. They wanted to show the benefits of cooperation. Occasionally, a neighbor or two might work with them during maple sugaring season or some idealistic city dwellers might work with them for a while, but the Nearings' vision of a dynamic communal life never materialized.
>
> In dissecting the failure of that vision in their now famous book, *Living the Good Life: How to Live Sanely and Simply in a Troubled World*, they wrote, "In one sense Vermont offered less rather than more opportunity for collective experiments than most other parts of rural America. Vermonters were strong individualists ... and all the major Vermont traditions emphasized the individualism of the Green Mountain folk."
>
> Vermonters, the Nearings believed, worked together better as families than communities.
>
> Their neighbors were organized into "autonomous households," they wrote. In fact, "'Autonomous' is

hardly the word," they continued. "'Sovereign' would be a more exact descriptive term."

The Nearings abandoned their idea of a more communal life in Vermont and moved to Maine in 1952. By then, the couple's Vermont farm had grown to 750 acres. With the development of a ski area at nearby Stratton Mountain, the land's value had skyrocketed from about $2.75 an acre to $8,000. Land they had purchased for about $2,000 was now worth $6 million on the market. But they couldn't accept the fortune they would have made by selling it. "We had done nothing to justify the increase," Scott explained. So they decided to donate the land to the town for a municipal forest.

It was then, perhaps, that the Nearings understood the extent of the distrust their radical ideas had engendered in town. When residents considered whether to accept this gift at the next town meeting, one third of them voted "no."

"The Korean War was on at the time," Scott said. "Those opposed to acceptance called us Communists. They thought we were trying to bribe the town in some way."

Despite the suspicions people harbored about them, the Nearings made it clear that it was more the arrival of skiers, the leisure class, that drove them away. "We wanted to live with people who earned their living by ordinary means instead of artificialities," Scott said. "We liked the farmers better."

Uranus in Capricorn on the MC

These individuals have an innate ability to strategize in ways that will leave their detractors scratching their heads if not outlawed.

Our first example is U.S. Senator, Joseph McCarthy, who rose to prominence and fed on the fears of communism. The following comment by J. William Fulbright about McCarthy, comes from Owlcation.com:

> The junior senator from Wisconsin, by his reckless charges, has so preyed upon the fears and hatreds and prejudices of the American people that he has started a prairie fire which neither he nor anyone else may be able to control.

Incidentally, McCarthy never successfully convicted anyone of communism.

We learn the range of Uranian expression within a system from the obituary of Sir John Grey Gorton, the 19th Prime Minister of Australia. The following comes from ANU.edu.au:

> Had he not been so unpredictable and willful, more a compromising politician rather than a confrontationist who went out to get things done his way, he might have been second only to Menzies as one of the Liberal Party's greatest sons. As it was, he probably overplayed the larrikin image and would not accept the discipline and exercise the patience necessary, nor adjust his

private lifestyle, to win over his colleagues and others when forces within his own party — both parliamentary and organisational — began to be ranged against him.

Though Australians expected certain decorum and responsibility in their Prime Ministers, their tolerance of Gorton suggests that they saw in him a politician who was prepared to do it differently and with a genuine sensitivity to peoples' problems. For instance, he helped to facilitate settlement of the Bougainville copper land dispute of 1969, by meeting the Bougainvillean leaders (Paul Lapun and Raphael Bele) listening to their arguments and finally agreeing that they could deal directly with the company, instead of through the PNG Administration, and negotiate the best terms they could. He arranged for an independent lawyer and an accountant to help them.

At another level there was Gorton's warm spontaneity and his readiness to take the unexpected but winning course.

Next, we learn how twins, Alev and Derya Kelter, express this astrological energy. The following comes from BadgerHerald.com:

When the two were younger, they played several other sports competitively, including softball, basketball, swimming and track. Eventually, however, they realized they needed to choose what they truly loved and wanted to continue to improve in.

Coincidentally, the two both chose soccer and hockey as the sports they truly loved. And their love for hockey was influenced by the move to Alaska after originally being born in Florida and moving around to several other states, including Colorado, Arkansas, and Texas.

It turned out to be a fortunate decision, as the two sports seem to work well together.

"They complement each other a lot," Derya said. "Just like the agility stuff in soccer translates over to hockey and strength from hockey helps us stay balanced over the ball for the soccer games. And the knee stuff that you do in hockey, like always being down and ready, really helps us with ACL injury prevention in soccer."

Multi-maverick actress, Dakota Fanning, sheds some light on this astrological placement in an interview in TheGuardian.com:

At 22, Fanning's manner and eloquence, which as a child were always described as almost spookily mature, no longer stand out. Actually, she says, it was never as straightforward as the freak show, adult-in-a-child's body descriptions of the time, but more "a balance of feeling like the oldest person in the world and still very young." Fanning has about her what Penelope Fitzgerald, in her novel about child actors, *At Freddie's*, described as "the bright airs of the indulged", a simultaneous innocence and self-conscious performance of innocence. If she behaved like a 40-year-old professional when she was eight, when Fanning now says, "I've had so many experiences and been so many places in my life, and met so many people, and I'm still so young and have three more lifetimes!" she sounds very young indeed.

What she is, without doubt, is a pro, who according to those who have worked with her is polite, industrious and ferociously disciplined. Fanning has been working for so long that most of the technical requirements of acting are imprinted on her as muscle memory. "I know how to hit a mark without looking. I instinctively know where my eye line should be. That's all 100%. But your character and the story are always different, so the emotional part is not muscle memory. You're still surprised by stuff and get the adrenaline."

Uranus in Aquarius on the MC

Uranus is the modern ruler of Aquarius. The Industrial Age and the Age of Reason point to the ways in which Uranus enervates and evolves the collective.

Multi-maverick and legendary actress, Vivien Leigh, has the following to say about this astrological placement from Brainyquote.com:

> "I'm not a film star, I am an actress. Being a film star is such a false life, lived for fake values and for publicity."
> "I'm not afraid to die."

From the Oscars.org website we learn that our next multi-maverick embodied the key elements of this astrological placement:

> With a career beginning in 1944, actor Gregory Peck has appeared in indelible dramatic roles for many major Hollywood directors and also become a role model for his lifelong humanitarian efforts. A crusader for social issues and an outspoken opponent of the blacklist, he won an Academy Award for his performance as Atticus Finch in *To Kill a Mockingbird* (1962) after four previous nominations and received the Jean Hersholt Humanitarian Award in 1968. He also served as the Academy President from 1967 to 1970 and received such honors as the Presidential Medal of Freedom, the Screen Actors Guild Life Achievement Award, and the AFI Life Achievement Award. With other major roles including *Spellbound* (1945), *The Yearling* (1946), *Gentleman's Agreement (1947), Twelve O'Clock High* (1949), *Roman Holiday* (1953), *The Big Country* (1958), *The Guns of Navarone* (1961), *Cape Fear* (1962), and *The Omen* (1978), he retains a place in history as an all-American role model."

The life of fellow thespian, comedienne, and multi-maverick, Phyllis Diller, showcases this astrological placement perfectly. The following comes from Wikipedia.com:

> [Phyllis Diller] was an American actress and comedienne, best known for her eccentric stage persona,

self-deprecating humor, wild hair and clothes, and exaggerated, cackling laugh. Diller was one of the first female comics to become a household name in the U.S., credited as an influence by Joan Rivers, Roseanne Barr, and Ellen DeGeneres, among others. She had a large gay following and is considered a gay icon. She was also one of the first celebrities to openly champion plastic surgery, for which she was recognized by the cosmetic surgery industry.

The remarkable, Manny Musu, has a planet on every angle. Manny survived the bombing of the Jakarta Embassy, which took her mother's life, and embedded her six year old body with countless pieces of shrapnel.

Uranus in Pisces on the MC

Pisces is the sign of the universe, the greater, and maybe more unconscious collective. These individuals have an ability to pull ideas from the collective understanding and reflect it back to the public in surprisingly intimate ways. Artists, comedians, actors, musicians, and any type of entertainer is blessed by the fluid nature of this position.

The following on film star, Judy Garland, comes from an article from NYPost.com:

Onstage and on screen, Judy Garland boasted big, beautiful eyes and one of the most iconic singing voices in Hollywood history. She was Dorothy in *The Wizard of*

Oz and Esther in *A Star Is Born*, the singer of "The Man That Got Away" and "Somewhere Over the Rainbow." Behind the scenes, however, Garland was somewhere over the cuckoo's nest.

Multi-maverick and media mogul, Merv Griffin's obituary at CBSNews.com, shares aspects of this astrological placement:

"This is a guy who, you know, he's 82 and he's running a company like he's, you know, 42 or 32," Tony said. "He just — it (cancer) devastated him. It wasn't something that he — it wasn't something that — it wasn't him. Everyone that knows him, he's the Energizer Bunny. He's a guy that gets up and goes and has fun and entertains. You know, this wasn't his type of ending, I don't think."

Although Tony said his father was bigger than life, he was also a very private man who appreciated simple things. He loved being on his boat and traveling. He loved his dog, Charlie Chan, and his grandchildren.

In the obituary for actor and comedian, Jerry Lewis, we have a strong example of this astrological force. The following comes from the NYTimes.com:

A mercurial personality who could flip from naked neediness to towering rage, Mr. Lewis seemed to contain multitudes, and he explored all of them. His ultimate object of contemplation was his own contradictory self, and he turned his obsession with fragmentation, discontinuity and the limits of language into a spectacle that enchanted children, disturbed adults and fascinated postmodernist critics.

Anthony Joshua Shaffer, was an English playwright, screenwriter, novelist, barrister, and advertising executive and the identical twin brother of Peter Shaffer. Sir Peter Levin Shaffer, was an English playwright and screenwriter of numerous award-winning plays. From Anthony's NYTimes.com obituary, we learn the following:

> In 1955 the family moved to London, where the two brothers attended St. Paul's School. They both then did three years of nonmilitary service in the coal mines of Kent and Yorkshire before going to Cambridge, where Anthony Shaffer studied law.
>
> From 1951 to 1957 he practiced law in London and wrote three novels with his brother. He then worked in advertising before setting up his own television production company and eventually turning to writing full time.
>
> His first two marriages ended in divorce. He is survived by his third wife, the actress Diane Cilento, and two daughters, Claudia and Cressida, from his second marriage.

Underground cartoonist, Eric Stanton, gives a glimpse of how this astrological placement can be so far out of the box. The following comes from Amazon.com:

Tracing the rise of commercial fetish art from its shadowy beginnings in the 1940s to its acceptance in the 1970s, this illustrated biography explores the unconventional life and art of Eric Stanton, a pioneering sexual fantasist who helped shape the movement. With more than 400 rare images and interviews with Stanton's family and closest associates, this biography chronicles the infamous circle of patrons, publishers, and cult icons populating his subterranean world, including Irving Klaw, John Willie, Bettie Page, Steve Ditko, and Gene Bilbrew. It is the untold, secret history of a misunderstood culture, the abuses of government authority, social intolerance, and gangsters. But above all, it is a tale about survival.

Neptune

Neptune shows how you "merge" with others, your need to connect through spirituality, your creativity, imagination, sensitivity, intuition, dreaming as well as how you escape from reality through drugs, alcohol, and movies. Neptune on its highest level is your spiritual heart. Neptune on an angle can suggest something other than what it seems: "smoke and mirrors." There is often confusion or bewilderment that needs to be worked through as part of the life path. Whether the ever flowing and personality changing actress, Meryl Streep, the comic genius of multi-personality portraying Lilly Tomlin, Tracey Ullman, and Jim Carry, or the iconic, somewhat static, Candy Barr and Jayne Mansfield, these are people to whom people respond and feel an immediate affinity. When you are in their "waters" you are under their hypnotic power and believe the illusion or vision they present.

You will see many artists, writers, poets, performers, and singers in this category. These are the people who transport us, through their words, music, and actions to other worlds and to witness other ways of being. Neptune gives us the pathway to higher and finer levels of perception and being. A super charged Neptune makes one highly impressionable, insightful, sensitive, and intuitive. These individuals draw upon those around them, and they literally "pull things out of the air" to bring to view on the physical plane. Neptune rules Pisces, one of the most intuitive signs of the zodiac, and is therefore the natural ruler of the 12th house: that which is unseen.

All of the outer planets have long orbits, which means that there is less reliable data available for earlier periods of time. Neptune takes 165 years to orbit the Sun and we barely started gathering accurate birth time for the last half of its cycle. This means that we will have no examples for some of the placements for Neptune and Pluto, while others will be quite extensive. The planets beyond Saturn represent generational groups of people. Neptune, maybe more than any of the outer planets, provides a subtly nuanced and varied expression along an infinite continuum.

We will now look at the angle placements of Neptune throughout the zodiac from the point of view of the Ascendant (AS).

Neptune in Aries on the AS

Dreamy Neptune lifts the mind and thoughts of the headstrong Aries into the clouds. Was that a real victory, or just one in my mind? Neptune was last in Aries in May 1874, before any reliable birth times were kept. Neptune will go into Aries again May 24, 2188, so we have a little time to prepare. This would be a good placement for a writer or a leader.

Neptune in Taurus on the AS

Fixed Taurus has an interesting time with the fluid Neptune nature. This energy hasn't been experienced since August 1887, and won't be experienced again until May 8, 2202. These individuals may wish to free themselves from physical restrictions and limiting forms.

Neptune in Gemini on the AS

This is definitely the place for dreamers and story tellers and those with an ability to tap the transcendental waters to quench the thirst of the many. This energy has not been felt since May 1902, and won't be felt again until June 29, 2215.

A rectified chart for Johannes Kepler, the German astronomer and astrologer, holds great insight into how this astrological placement can express itself. The following comes from Wikipedia.com:

> Kepler lived in an era when there was no clear distinction between astronomy and astrology, but there was a strong division between astronomy (a branch of mathematics within the liberal arts) and physics (a branch of natural philosophy). Kepler also incorporated religious arguments and reasoning into his work, motivated by the religious conviction and belief that God had created the world according to an intelligible plan that is accessible through the natural light of reason. Kepler described his new astronomy as "celestial physics", as "an excursion into Aristotle's *Metaphysics*," and as "a supplement to Aristotle's *On the Heavens*," transforming the ancient tradition of physical cosmology by treating astronomy as part of a universal mathematical physics.

Neptune in Cancer on the AS

These individuals exude a certain intimacy and warmth. They are like a comfort food. They can also have an over-sweeping idealism about their particular clan as clearly seen by the two prominent Nazi examples. Neptune's themes include, as we shall see, ghosts, angels, gas chambers, media, music, observation. While they like to blur the lines of class, it is often because they have the luxury to do so.

An article from NYTimes.com about author Christopher Isherwood shows the depths this position provides. Isherwood's partner said, "He had gold in him and he wanted to share it with me," Mr. Bachardy said. "When you love like he did, you have to find somebody who you can give as much as you can to. Somebody who can absorb it, and ask for more."

With no formal training, Nancy Mitford, with her maverick Venus in Capricorn opposite this position, we learn the following about her from Wikipedia.com:

> The eldest of the Mitford sisters, she was regarded as one of the "Bright Young People" on the London social scene in the years between the world wars. She wrote several novels about upper-class life in England and France, and is considered a sharp and often provocative wit. She also has a reputation as a writer of popular historical biographies.

Multi-maverick and Third Reich architect, Albert Speer, had the following excerpt included in his 1981 obituary at NYTimes.com:

> "As I thought of the drama that must be taking place during these days, these very hours, in the Berlin bunker, I realized that I had lost all urge to continue my opposition," he wrote later. "Once more Hitler had succeeded in paralyzing me psychically." Last Interview with Hitler. In *Inside the Third Reich*, Mr.

ASTROLOGICAL MAVERICKS

Speer described his last interview with Hitler in the bunker on April 23: "Trembling, the prematurely aged man stood before me for the last time; the man to whom I had dedicated my life 12 years before. I was both moved and confused. For his part, he showed no emotion when we confronted one another. His words were as cold as his hand: 'So, you're leaving? Good. Auf Wiedersehen.' No regards to my family, no wishes, no thanks, no farewell. For a moment I lost my composure, said something about coming back. But he could easily see that it was a white lie, and turned his attention to something else. I was dismissed."

New evidence about the short life of John, Prince of Wales describes a rather wonderful world of estates and gardens with which to be connected, before his passing from an epileptic seizure at 13 years of age.

The life of musician, Burl Ives, shows the early influence this astrological placement gave him as seen in this excerpt from Wkipedia.com:

> Ives began as an itinerant singer and banjoist, and launched his own radio show, *The Wayfaring Stranger*, which popularized traditional folk songs.

The watery, fluid nature of this astrological placement would be of great benefit to a spy, let alone one considered either a double or *triple* agent, like multi-maverick, Henri Dericourt.

With a maverick Uranus across from this point, we learn the following about Sir Hugh Carleton Greene:

He encountered opposition from some politicians and activists opposed to his modernising agenda, but under his leadership the BBC was recognised to be outperforming its commercial rival, ITV, and was awarded a second television channel by the British government and authorised to introduce colour television to Britain.

We see other elements of this astrological placement in this excerpt about another Nazi, Josef Mengele:

[Mengele]... also known as the Angel of Death (German: Todesengel) was a German Schutzstaffel (SS) officer and physician during World War II. He is mainly remembered for his actions at the Auschwitz concentration camp, where he performed deadly experiments on prisoners, and was a member of the team of doctors who selected victims to be killed in the gas chambers and was one of the doctors who administered the gas.

Stan Jones wrote "Ghost Riders in the Sky" which is considered the number one western song ever written.

Neptune in Leo on the AS

Neptune lends Leo a spacious sea upon which to be seen, heard and appreciated. The waters of their presence go from warm to scalding.

The eloquent elocution of this astrological placement was poetically personified by multi-maverick and author, Maya Angelou.

The visionary Neptune gives the creative Leonine flame an endless supply of inspirational fuel and fulfillment, as well articulated in the life of visual artist, Mirka Mora. The following comes from MoraGalleries.com.au:

> Mirka's passion to create continued and thrived on her arrival in Australia—her work celebrates humanity, life, love and the eternal wonder of the imagination. Mirka's public artworks have become part of the city. They include the Flinders Street Station mural and St. Kilda pier. Mirka was also the first artist to paint an Art Tram in 1978. Mirka's seventy years of making art have produced an extensive array of works using unique techniques—drawing, painting, embroidery, soft sculpture, mosaics, and doll making. Her distinct and outstanding imagery has emerged from her passion for reading, her love of classical Greek mythology, her desire to reclaim and make sense of her childhood, and ultimately her unwavering belief in the strength of humanity to unite us all.

English actor, Roger Moore shares some insights into this astrological position from BrainyQuote.com:

"I enjoy being a highly overpaid actor."

"Creating a character on or off the stage is an escape."

"It's easy to sit in relative luxury and peace and pontificate on the subject of the Third World debts."

"Some are blessed with musical ability, others with good looks. Myself, I was blessed with modesty."

With a maverick Moon in Aquarius on her DS, Marilyn Monroe definitely knew how to turn on and use her dreamy allure.

From his obituary in Scottsman.com, comes a beautiful statement highlighting this astrological position as portrayed in the life of Scottish poet, Edwin Morgan:

> Much-loved in Scotland and indeed around the world, his work tackled all manner of global issues and major historical events closer to home. His passion for observing all aspects of Scottish life shone a spotlight on Scotland for the rest of the world. "I vividly recall the poem he wrote for the Opening of the Scottish Parliament, when he wrote "Don't let your work and hope be other than great." That epithet must surely apply to Edwin Morgan himself.

Next, are some of the issues of this astrological placement and how it affected multifold-maverick and media producer, Aaron Spelling and his family. The following comes from Reelz.com:

> What would it be like to grow up in a 123-room mansion in a swanky Los Angeles suburb, rubbing elbows with

celebrities, and buying anything you want? Sounds pretty great — unless it was all taken away from you as an adult. As Tori Spelling wrote in her autobiography, it's not easy going from having a silver spoon in your mouth to a plastic one.

Aaron Spelling was one of the most successful television producers ever, masterminding such hits such as *Charlie's Angles, Beverly Hills 90210, Dynasty*, and *The Love Boat*. When Spelling died after a severe stroke in 2006, at 83 years old, he left behind a fortune worth an estimated $500 million at the time. He owned the largest house in all of Los Angeles County. The home, known as the Spelling Manor, was where Aaron and his second wife, Candy, moved in the late 1980's with their children, teenage daughter Tori and son Randy.

Randy Spelling explained in a recent interview how amazing it was to live in the mansion, complete with a bowling alley, screening room, an ice rink, and three separate rooms just for wrapping presents. He described how it was like living in a fantasy, but it left him unprepared for life as an adult when he didn't have the same financial support after his father died. Randy said that, as a result, "I had my wings burned a little bit," before adjusting to living a normal life as an adult, in a modest home that was far different from the mansion he grew up in.

Neptune in Virgo on the AS

Undefined Neptune has an interesting time in discriminating Virgo. With Virgo ruled by Mercury, we can see how words, movement and communication could be elevated to higher planes of expression. On one end of the spectrum one can get lost in the details, on the other, there is an inherent and intuitive understanding of how all of the individually perfected parts work collectively for a matchless operation.

Alasdair Gray, is a Scottish writer and artist. His most acclaimed work is his first novel, Lanark, published in 1981, and written over a period of almost 30 years, is considered a milestone in Scottish fiction. This excerpt from TheGuardian.com expresses the power of this astrological position:

> I fell in love. It was an unlikely passion. Gray displayed his politics with disarming plainness – he believed in Scottish independence and socialism; I was a milksop unionist and social democrat. Moreover, I was a feminist, and Gray was a sometime pornographer whose female characters barely scrape two dimensions. *Lanark* is not particularly dirty, but Gray's superb second novel, 1982, *Janine,* is unambiguous filth, chronically the compulsive, unruly fantasies of a middle-aged man called Jock. *Something Leather* is straight-up lechery. But Gray's writing is not the tyrannical kind that can only be enjoyed if you agree with him. He makes easy company with disagreement.

Another writer, Canadian poet laureate, George Bowering, shows the ever-generative quality aspect of this astrological placement. Take a look at Wikipedia.com for his rather exhaustive and extensive work.

The following comes from Wikipedia.com:

Michael Paul Bertiaux is an American occultist and Old Catholic Bishop, known for his book *Voudon Gnostic Workbook*, a 615-page compendium of various occult lessons and research paper, spanning the sub-fields of Voodoo, Neo-Pythagoreanism, Thelema and Gnosticism.

Dawn Lorraine Fraser, is an Australian freestyle champion swimmer and former politician. She is one of only three swimmers to have won the same Olympic event three times – in her case the women's 100-metre freestyle.

Multi-maverick and Italian architect, Renzo Piano, who has his Sun and Mercury here, squaring his Mars/IC conjunction in Sagittarius. One can readily see the Neptunian "lift" in his designs that provide an efficiency of form and space.

George Metzger, is an American cartoonist and animator. He was an underground comics artist during the mid-1960s and early 1970s in California. This astrological placement definitely supported his detailed fantasy-oriented creative expression.

Multi-maverick and Beatle, Paul McCartney has an interesting arrangement to this astrological placement. McCartney has a retrograde Mercury, ruler of Virgo, in a wide conjunction with his MC which is in a conjunction with his Sun. These quotes from BrainyQuote.com illustrate this astrological placement beautifully:

"In the end, the love you take is equal to the love you make."

"When we were starting off as kids, just the idea of maybe going to do this as a living instead of getting what we thought was going to be a boring job, was exciting."

"Lyricists play with words."

"I saw that Meryl Streep said, 'I just want to do my job well.' And really, that's all I'm ever trying to do."

Neptune in Libra on the AS

These individuals are blessed with an alluring beauty. Are they a Venus flytrap or the most exquisite rose, or some combination in-between? They also tend to merge in relationship, maybe not understanding where they end and another begins. They may also have idealized notions about relationships.

Former U.S. president, Bill Clinton, is known for his deep need to connect with others. Clinton has a maverick's ability to meet people on the level they need to be met. This astrological placement is one of considerate ambassadorship, as well as presenting things in a more idealistic light than the reality.

ASTROLOGICAL MAVERICKS

While neither his birth name, Milton Teagle, nor his appearance remind one of beauty and harmony, Mr. Shed-a-bed and fitness instructor, Richard Simmons, helped others become healthier versions of themselves.

Other poignant aspects of this astrological placement are well articulated by these beauties by folk singer, Cat Stevens:

"Peace Train' is a song I wrote, the message of which continues to breeze thunderously through the hearts of millions. There is a powerful need for people to feel that gust of hope rise up again."

"Man is created to be God's deputy on earth and it is important to realize the obligation to rid ourselves of all illusions and to make our lives a preparation for the next life."

"I became alienated from this religious upbringing, and started making music. I wanted to be a big star. All those things I saw in the films and on the media took hold of me, and perhaps I thought this was my god: the goal of making money."

"This is the beauty of the Qur'an: it asks you to reflect and reason, and not to worship the sun or moon but the One who has created everything. The Qur'an asks man to reflect upon the sun and moon and God's creation in general."

The following notes about artist, Peter Blake, come from Wikipedia.com:

> One of the best known British pop artists, Blake is considered to be a prominent figure in the pop art movement. Central to his paintings are his interest in images from popular culture which have infused his collages.

The dual nature of Libra easily seen in the way entertainer, Cheryl Gates McFadden, uses her name. She is usually credited as Gates McFadden when an actress, and Cheryl McFadden when a choreographer. She is best known for playing Dr. Beverly Crusher in the science fiction television series *Star Trek: The Next Generation.*

The infamous multi-maverick, Carlos the Jackal, has his retrograde Mercury and Sun and South Node all in Libra and this squares his Cancer MC maverick Uranus. This man could charmingly convince anyone of almost anything and did, but eventually karma caught up with him.

Australian film director, Scott Hicks, is operating a complex astrological machine that has seven distinct and diverse maverick voices all requiring attention and relationship in some cohesive way. Hicks is fortunate to have Neptune involved, which will provide a sea into which it all can rest. Here are some illustrative quotes that come from AZQuotes.com:

> "I've always had a feeling that the image is 50% of the emotion that an audience feels and it's subliminal. Yet,

how you arrange the elements in front of a camera has an impact on people's belief about that world in some way."

"Where you have a villain in the piece or the antagonist, whatever you want to call them, there has to be humanity at the core of it or it's faintly ridiculous. Nobody is just villain through and through. You have to feel something for them."

Rocker, Angus Young has Chiron conjunct his Aquarian IC, which makes sense when we find out this interesting fact about the AC/DC guitarist, from TheSoundCo.NZ: Angus doesn't drink alcohol, at all.

From *The New York Times*, comes this thoughtful excerpt from an article about actress, Debra Winger:

The punch line, however, in the way it identified a wordless, awkward millisecond of actual ego-deflating embarrassment, struck me as something only Winger would share. That kind of candor, predicated on an awareness that a single moment can house its share of paradoxes, is what makes Winger special. She's a performer who has always possessed what Pauline Kael, writing about her breakthrough role in *Urban Cowboy* 30 years ago, called her "quality of flushed transparency." That unsparing emotional honesty makes moviegoers believe that they are seeing through her skin, past any layer of self-protection or self-deception, and into her heart and mind. She had it in her 20s, when audiences first met her; at 55, she can still count it among her most remarkable assets, and her ability to deploy it has only become richer and more fully controlled.

Neptune in Scorpio on the AS

These individuals have a unique ability to sense and feel things. They can morph and become what is needed.

Multi-maverick and musician, Gary Numan, also has his Moon and Jupiter here. Gary's following collection of comments comes fromBrainyQuote.com:

"If I thought that any of this was pre-ordained, then it takes away any kind of incentive to struggle, or to put up with things, to reach for those impossible dreams, all those dramatic things."

"I'm very intolerant and I get fed up with people easily."

"I want to start my own airplane business. I'm going to buy two Dakotas, paint them up in war colours and do, er, nostalgia trips to Arnhem – you know, where the old paratroopers used to go – and charge them about 20 quid a time."

With poly-maverick and comedic actress, Tracey Ullman, we see this astrological placement well-articulated in excerpts from an article about the actress, in WomensMediaCenter.com:

> Through her panoply of characters—some of them celebrity impersonations—Ullman tackles health care, the media, ageism, celebrity adoption, the financial crisis, gay marriage, and the demise of the honeybees among other topics. The accessible humor does nothing to hide her acerbic subtext in themes that recur throughout the series.

Scottish comic book writer, Grant Morrison's ability to take life and squeeze it into an intensely visual, two-dimensional plane in graphic novel form, are qualities of this astrological placement we can easily see expressed in his life. Grant is also a poly-maverick with the same three maverick planets as Tracey Ullman: Uranus conjunct MC in Leo, and Chiron conjunct IC in Aquarius. We can see that this complex combination gives one the range of reference necessary to create any character.

Playboy Bunny, Dorothy Stratten, who also has Uranus conjunct her MC in Leo, shows the deadly possibilities with this desire/fantasy placement. Dorothy was murdered when she was 20 years old.

Actor, Jim Carrey, also has Uranus on his Leo MC. While known for his comedy and acting abilities, Carrey is now showing another side of this astrological placement: his deep spiritual search.

Argentine dancer, Julio Bocca, is one of the most important ballet dancers of the 20th century. The following comes from Encyclopedia.com:

Since his spectacular win at the 1985 International Ballet Competition, Julio Bocca has established himself as one of the twentieth century's most renowned dancers. "There's something about his very person that attracts you," a ballet director told *Dance Magazine*, "not only his great technique and talent, but he dances as if his soul depended on it."

Actress, Naomi Watts, who has Mars conjunct her Virgo MC, shares these interesting insights from BrainyQuote.com:

"I'm not this dark, twisted person. Yes, I have my demons and this is my way of exorcising them. It gets them out — and better out than in."

"I had gotten to a place where I truly believed everything I was called: 'not sexy,' 'not funny,' 'too intense,' desperate.' All those labels they gave me, I took them because there wasn't a trace of my true self left."

"I find myself gravitating towards drama. It interests me. In the books I read, the paintings I like, it's always the darker stuff."

"Pain is such an important thing in life. I think that as an artist you have to experience suffering."

Neptune in Sagittarius on the AS

There is a lot of idealism with this placement, especially philosophically. These individuals are pulled by a higher calling, but experience a lot of disappointment along the way. Their goal is truth.

Julian Assange has his Saturn across the way conjunct his Gemini DS. Assange is still dealing with the consequences of sharing the truth for the greater good at his own expense.

Alicia Witt, American actress, singer-songwriter, and pianist, played this astrological position well in the 1984 movie Dune as her character, Alia Atreides.

Multi-maverick actor and race car driver, Michael Fassbender, exhibits this astrological placement each time he plays a religious or spiritual warrior – or one who is working on the "right" side.

The word *idyllic* is used quite often with multi-maverick, Prince William. This is a very efficient statement for Neptune in Sagittarius. This is what this astrological placement seeks.

Rocker, Ozzy Osbourne's eldest daughter, Aimee Osbourne, shares these insights from BrainyQuote.com:

"I can't be passionate about something or really give myself to something if I don't know it's a hundred percent authentic to who I am."

"I'm a very what-you-see-is-what-you-get kind of person, and my family always laughs at me. They're like, 'You have minus-zero poker-face skills. We just have to look at your face and we know what's wrong with you.'"

Neptune in Capricorn on the AS

While Neptune is neither in detriment nor in its fall here, it isn't the easiest of places for the nebulous giant in goal setting Capricorn, but when we see our first example, we can understand.

Olympic champion swimmer, Matthew Mitcham, received the highest score in Olympic history for a single dive and is the first openly gay athlete to win the gold medal.

Multi-maverick, Zenouska Mowatt, is another good representation of this astrological placement. Her mother was already pregnant with her when Zenouska's parents married – not a regular situation when one is of royal blood.

Neptune in Aquarius on the AS

The most recent period for this astrological placement is 1998-2012 and before that the most recent period was the mid 1800's, which means these individuals are a bit young to be making a mark. I have no one as an example, but these individuals are likely to have an other-worldly sense or especially look about them. Their ability to connect with their surroundings and energies is profound. They can be easily misunderstood.

Neptune in Pisces on the AS

This is a mysterious and wonderful position for a psychic, healer, doula, magician, guru or world leader. Neptune went into Pisces in February 2012, and will remain there until 2025. We have no examples of individuals with this astrological placement.

We will now look at the angle placements of Neptune throughout the zodiac from the point of view of the Imum Coeli (IC).

Neptune in Aries on the IC

Dreamy Neptune lifts the mind and thoughts of the headstrong Aries into the cloudy preoccupation with family and personal conquests. Was that a real victory, or just one in my mind? Neptune was last in Aries in May 1874, before any reliable birth times were kept. Neptune will go into Aries again May 24, 2188, so we have a little time to prepare. This would be a good astrological placement for someone who does inner psycho-spiritual work.

Neptune in Taurus on the IC

Fixed Taurus may lose its direction in the mutable Neptunian fog. This energy hasn't been experienced since August 1887, and won't be experienced again until May 8, 2202. These individuals may wish to free themselves from physical restrictions and limiting forms through experiencing nature. They can do this by writing or reading, experiencing as well as observing (life or video).

Neptune in Gemini on the IC

This energy hasn't been felt since May 1902, and won't be felt again until June 29, 2215. These individuals may experience significantly altered states as they are easily affected by their environments. Understanding all of the little bits of data of life and holding them in a cohesive whole is part of what these people will be about. Others will likely have a hard time understanding them, but that is ok as the native is working to gain that understanding for her/himself.

Neptune in Cancer on the IC

There is a strong need for security while feeling all of the possible threats. Once again, we see that an IC planet can really call the shots. A well aspected Neptune is helpful if you wish to reach the masses, as our first example well illustrates.

From his obituary, we learn the following about studio executive and talent agent, Lew Wasserman:

Throughout his long career, Mr. Wasserman avoided the limelight and rarely sat for interviews. "Publicity is for clients, not for us," he often told his MCA subordinates. As a result, he was not as well-known as Sam Goldwyn, Louis B. Mayer, Jack Warner and the other pioneering movie moguls whose later years overlapped his own reign at the top. Yet, all these larger-than-life figures often confined their power to their studios, while Mr. Wasserman's influence was felt across the entire industry.

No-one sold the "Red" fear like Joseph McCarthy. This multi-maverick filled a lot of American households with fear and scared a lot of actors, performers and artists. Cancer wants to protect its family and that was what McCarthy thought he was doing.

From an article in the Independent.co.uk, we see the archetypal fingerprints of this astrological placement in the life of former Australian Prime Minister, Sir John Grey Gorton:

> In some respects, he behaved more like a reforming Labor leader than a conservative. He brought in generous pension rises and modified the means test; stood up to the medical profession; and blocked the possible take-over of an Australian insurance company by overseas interests. He was a natural protectionist opposed to the free trade leanings of the Treasury, and supported such openly interventionist measures as the Australian Investment Development Corporation.

Neptune

Neptune in Leo on the IC

These individuals have an inner creative sea that sometimes makes them challenging for others to relate to. They can get lost in their inner landscapes or share them with others.

Our first example is multi-maverick and heir, Conrad Nicky Hilton, the son of the founder of the Hilton hotel empire. This excerpt from PeoplePill.com shows the eddies into which one can lose one's self:

> Hilton had an affair with his stepmother, Zsa Zsa Gabor, in 1944, according to claims made by Gabor after his death. He was Elizabeth Taylor's first husband, (May 6, 1950 – January 29, 1951) but his "gambling, drinking, and abusive behavior" horrified her and her parents. The marriage ended in divorce after eight months.
>
> In the late 1950s, Hilton also had an eight-month affair with Mexican actress, Silvia Pinal, whom he met at the opening of a hotel in Acapulco.
>
> In 1958, Hilton married oil heiress from Oklahoma, Patricia "Trish" McClintock. They had two sons, Conrad Nicholson Hilton III and Michael Otis Hilton. McClintock filed for divorce from Hilton on February 10, 1964, which was granted in 1965. Accordingly, in 1960, his father Hilton Sr., also made a proposal of betrothal to Stella Araneta, which she respectfully declined.
>
> Conrad Hilton Jr. died suddenly on February 5, 1969, of an alcoholism-related heart attack at the age

of 42. He is interred in Holy Cross Cemetery, Culver City, California.

These illuminating gems from Henry Kissinger can be found at BrainyQuote.com:

"No foreign policy – no matter how ingenious – has any chance of success if it is born in the minds of a few and carried in the hearts of none."

"Power is the great aphrodisiac."

"The nice thing about being a celebrity is that, if you bore people, they think it's their fault."

"Accept everything about yourself – I mean everything, you are you and that is the beginning and the end – no apologies, no regrets."

From his obituary in *The New York Times*, we learn a little bit about Warhol Factory actor, Taylor Mead:

It was as an actor in what was called the New American Cinema in the 1960s that he made his biggest mark. Warhol recruited him as one of his first "superstars," and from 1963 to 1968 he made 11 films with Mr. Mead. In all, Mr. Mead figured that he had made about 130 movies, many of them so spontaneous that they involved only one take.

The film critic J. Hoberman called Mr. Mead "the first underground movie star." The film historian P. Adams Sitney called one of Mr. Mead's earliest films, *The Flower Thief* (1960), "the purest expression of the Beat sensibility in cinema."

The Flower Thief, directed by Ron Rice, stars Mr. Mead as a bedraggled mystic wandering the North Beach neighborhood of San Francisco with open-mouthed wonder. He carries with him his three prized possessions: a stolen gardenia, an American flag, and a teddy bear.

It goes almost without saying that Mr. Mead was playing himself, as Susan Sontag observed in Partisan Review. "The source of his art is the deepest and purest of all: he just gives himself, wholly and without reserve, to some bizarre autistic fantasy," she wrote. "Nothing is more attractive in a person, but it is extremely rare after the age of 4."

From AnitcsAtPlay.com, we learn how this creative arrangement can define new genres as evidenced by film director, Robert Altman in the medium of cinema:

> ...the filmmaker's trademark stylistic predilections, including overlapping dialogue, a restless camera, an ensemble cast, spontaneity, improvisation and a touch of impudence.

We see this creative theme continued in jazz trumpeter and double maverick, Miles Davis. The following comes from Wikipedia.com:

> [Davis] was an American jazz trumpeter, bandleader, and composer. He is among the most influential and acclaimed figures in the history of jazz and 20th-century music. Davis adopted a variety of musical directions in a five-decade career that kept him at the forefront of many major stylistic developments in jazz.

Neptune in Virgo on the IC

As we often see with Virgo, there is a wide range and multiplicity. This is made more expansive and deeper with Neptune at the bottom of the chart. This is a brilliant place for writers, actors, comedians and anyone who wishes to express a spectrum of characters.

Neptune represents illusions, dreams, confusion, and conspiracies and when bobbing through the resourceful, we find the mother of all treasonous schemers: Lee Harvey Oswald. We are still unclear about his culpability in killing JFK, and as late as 2015, his remains and casket were involved in nefarious and dubious legal issues. The funeral home that provided the burial service decided that once he was buried Oswald became their property.

Singer and songwriter, Boxcar Willie, is one of the myriad examples of gifts appearing early in the lives of mavericks. The following comes from Legacy.com:

BoxCar began his music career as a small boy singing with his church choir. He continued performing as Marty Martin, and although he developed a following in America, it was a series of popular European tours – culminating in a performance at the 1979 Wembley International Festival of Country Music in Wembley, England – that made him a star.

By 1980, he finally found success in his own country. A year later, he became the 60th member of the Grand Ole Opry, was awarded "Most Promising Male Vocalist" by the Country Music Association, and his TV album "King of the Road" earned double-platinum sales. He made regular appearances on television's *Hee Haw* and *Family Feud,* and appeared in several movies, including *Sweet Dreams*, a film about country-music start Patsy Cline, *Gordy*, and *A Place to Grow*. Then, in 1986, he purchased the BoxCar Willie Theater in Branson, and began performing to numerous sold-out crowds.

On October 31, 1996, after having felt tired for a couple of months, Box was told by doctors that he was suffering from the most aggressive type of leukemia, mantle zone lymphatic leukemia. He began a spirited battle for his life – even while undergoing chemotherapy, BoxCar performed six nights a week at his theater. His difficult struggle came to an end on April 12th in his Branson home, where he was surrounded by his family.

A quote from the King of Soul, Sam Cooke states, "I'm gonna sing, and I'm going to make me a lot of money." He influenced musicians in profoundly moving ways.

Multi-maverick and singer, Patsy Cline had a different expression of this astrological position. The following comes from an article about her in OrlandoSentinel.com/news/:

> The Lange movie, titled *Sweet Dreams* after one of Cline's bigger hits, seems to be a respectful attempt to present the story of a woman who called her own shots, partied hard, had the vocabulary of a sailor and, in the summation of several male contemporaries, was "one of the boys."
>
> "She was," Grand Ole Opry performer Jimmy C. Newman said, "a good old girl."
>
> But no siren.
>
> "She was pretty, but I wouldn't call her sexy," Emery said. "I think most men would have been afraid Patsy was more than they could handle."

While Patsy shows a little of this side of this watery planet, our next example multi-maverick and criminal kingpin, Ronald Kray, exhibited traits of old-world Neptune in his home and home town: vengeful, all-powerful, and hell-bent on making others pay when he is not given his "due." The importance of image, one of this planet's domains, is well articulated in this article from Independent.co.uk:

> Ronnie was very much into the gangster image, getting them to dress the same in suits with slicked-back hair.

He wanted to live the gangster lifestyle in a way that he thought Al Capone did ... import it to Britain.

Gentlemen criminals, a cut above the riff-raff. A force to be trusted in chaotic times. People bought it, as they went to jail for killing other gangsters. "They never hurt the public," said their brother Charlie on the day their mother Violet was buried in August 1982. The yogic, or spiritual path is well indicated with this astrological placement as exemplified by Shivabalayogi. The following comes from his website shivabalamahayogi.com:

Sri Sri Sri Shivabalayogi Maharaj completed 12 years of Tapas. From August 7, 1949 to August 7, 1961, he meditated 23 hours a day for 8 years then, 12 hours a day for 4 more years.

"A true yogi is one who has actually completed tapas. Yogis are God's agent. They have to do whatever god says" - Sri Swamiji

Sri Swamiji's primary mission is to set people on the path of dhyana, or meditation. The word "dhyana" is often translated to meditation but it is much more than that. Dhyana is when the effort of meditation is successful, and the mind naturally concentrates and focusses one pointedly.

While there may be some controversy about whether stereotypical depictions of minority groups is harmful in perpetuating stereotypes, or if stereotypical depictions helps bring minority groups into the awareness of the greater collective, *Are you being served?* comedian and actor, John Inman, experienced this dilemma throughout his life. As a young gay man, I have to say, I appreciated seeing at least one "reflection" or image of being gay. And the name of the series is so Virgoan! The following comes from TheGuardian.com:

> Inman claimed he was cheeky but not dirty, and that he found the character a joy to play. Mr. Humphries was, in Inman's eyes, a jokey figure about whom the audience could never decide whether or not he was "queer". "I always say that when it comes to sex, Mr. Humphries is nothing really. He's neither one way nor the other."
>
> Some critics who had no such doubts described Inman and Mr. Humphries as two of the best friends of gay liberation on television. But the gratitude was not universal. In 1977, the Campaign for Homosexual Equality targeted Inman in Brighton, where he was appearing in a seaside show. They handed out leaflets blaming him for depicting homosexuals as sexually obsessed, too extravagant in manner, and too eager to drag up. They argued that most homosexuals did not behave like Mr. Humphries, and that Inman was contributing to television's distortion of their image. Poor Inman, not a strong swimmer in the fast-flowing river of controversy, argued that he was not campaigning in any way, merely trying to make people laugh.

There were compensations for him, too. *Are You Being Served?* made Inman famous not only in Britain but also in the U.S., where the series was sold. He was recognised in Los Angeles as much as in London. Once, in San Francisco, a young man fell off his bicycle because he was so surprised to see Inman, and lay in the road shouting "I love you, Mr. Humphries."

This astrological placement lends a special quality to those on screen and in front of the camera. Multi-maverick and burlesque dancer, Candy Barr, marketed her femininity.

Resourcefulness, patience, and understanding the ebb and flow of power, is well within this astrological placement and beautifully presented by H.M. King Simeon II of Bulgaria. The following comes from GoldMercuryAward.com:

Upon the sudden death of King Boris III on August 28, 1943, the 6-year old Simeon acceded to the throne as Tsar* Simeon II. A three-member Council of Regency was formed to govern Bulgaria on his behalf. Following the communist coup on September 9, 1944, Simeon II remained on the throne but the regents, including his uncle Prince Kyril, along with the core of the country's intellectuals, were executed. In 1946, a referendum forced King Simeon II, his sister Princess Maria Luisa and the Queen Mother Giovanna to leave Bulgaria. Without abdicating, the young King was to spend long years of exile. The family settled first in Alexandria, Egypt. The choice was not accidental. The Italian King Victor Emmanuel III, the father of the Queen Mother

Giovanna, lived there in exile. Simeon II was enrolled at the Victoria College in Egypt.

The outer planets have a wider range of expression and so we find yet another actor, Ryan O'Neal. The following comes from FoxNews.com:

> Per the outlet, McEnroe, 60, explained that O'Neal initially "had a lot of charm" and claimed that marijuana often helped to calm O'Neal down.
> "You could relax him a little bit after a day of not eating and going in the sauna for hours at a time with his ex, Farrah Fawcett. A little crazy or a lot crazy, it was difficult," McEnroe said. "But he didn't treat his kids too well either. So that impacted me and my kids."

Multi-maverick and athlete, John Konrads, is a gold medal Olympian swimmer.

Neptune in Libra on the IC

Libra is the only non-organic sign, meaning it is not an animal or human or creature of some sort. This implies a pause, an opportunity to view the spectrum of possibilities this sign needs, so as to harmonize its environment and the people in it.

While nature has a chaos to it, we often find peace when engaged with it, as well articulated by Tory and Member of Parliament (MP) Edwina Curie. The following comes from DailyMail.uk:

"I was brought up by Orthodox Jewish parents, but for a long time I haven't had any religious feeling myself. Instead, I've discovered that being in nature — when I'm out in the countryside with the trees and the hills around me, and the soft leaves under my feet — is what makes me feel in tune with something beyond humanity."

Libra and Neptune love pretty things and appreciate a certain "level" at home with the placement on the IC. When we consider the *birds of a feather flock together* aspect of maverick planets, Camilla Parker-Bowles and Prince Charles are a lovely example. Neptune as an old-world god is patient and timeless. As many of us know in astrology, when we share astrological placements there is a feeling of kinship. This is a profound love they have for one another – not to denigrate Princess Diana, but she didn't share this connection with Charles. This is a powerful indicator for long term connection.

Acting and singing fall under the care of this planet and sign, so it is no surprise that we have entertainer, David Essex with this astrological placement. The following comes from Wikipedia.com:

David Essex, is an English singer, songwriter, and actor. Since the 1970s, he has attained 19 Top 40 singles in the UK and 16 Top 40 albums. Internationally, Essex had the most success with his 1973 single "Rock On". He has also had an extensive career as an actor.

Another articulation of this astrological combination is gender fluidity, as well presented by singer and songwriter, Sylvester.

Prolific author and myriad maverick, Stephen King, took a turn off the old Hitchcock idea of ordinary people in extra-ordinary circumstances, and showed us the cost of our attachments to cars, dogs, cats and children. King's 1978 novel *The Stand* is the perfect post-apocalyptic story highlighting the dynamics of this placement.

Multi-maverick Cecil Womack shows us the importance of our family lineage, highlighted by Neptune and the IC. The following comes from RockAndRollParadise.com:

> After traveling to Nigeria, they discovered ancestral ties to the Zekkariyas tribe, and Cecil adopted the name Zekkariyas. In 1993 they released their final album with a major label, *Transformed to the House of Zekkariyas.*

Seminal actor, Jeremy Irons, who has Mercury here as well, shares these illuminating gems of this astrological arrangement. The following comes from AZQuotes.com:

> "We all have our time machines, don't we? Those that take us back are memories...And those that carry us forward, are dreams."

> "When it seems that someone has shattered your dreams....pick up even the smallest of pieces and use them to build bigger and better dreams."

NEPTUNE

"The great thing about acting is, because you're constantly playing other characters and exploring yourself because you have to find those other characters in yourself, you sort of broaden as a person over your life because you've been other people. So you can empathize with many different sorts of people. It's great in that way and I hope, therefore, as you get older as an actor, you not only get more interesting because you lived more, but you get a bit wiser as a person."

Prince Charles, who also has his Venus here, doesn't like a lot of "bad press" or acting in a manner unbecoming of his status. His relationship with Diana was a stretch for him on many levels. Fortunately, Diana's beauty, warmth and love are carried forth in their two boys. The peaceful conformity of home with Camilla is more to his liking.

With a wide trine to her maverick Aquarian descendant planets, actress, Julie Walters, has a panoply of characters from which to draw upon. The following comes from the Independent.co.uk:

In whatever part she has played – from the self-improving hairdresser in *Educating Rita* to the misunderstood mother in *Jake's Progress* – she has elevated the mundane to the mesmerizing. In her hands, the girl next-door becomes someone exceptional.

Eve Kosofsky Sedgwick, was an American academic scholar in the fields of gender studies, queer theory, and critical theory.

ASTROLOGICAL MAVERICKS

I love the early brilliance displayed in her life. The following comes from EveKSedgwickfoundation.org:

> Eve attended public schools in Dayton for two years: kindergarten and second grade, skipping first grade due to her early mastery of reading and general intellectual precocity. She took ballet lessons, made paintings and drawings inspired by art reproductions her parents borrowed each month from the Dayton Museum of Art, and by the age of seven had decided that she would be a poet.

Multi-maverick actress, Meryl Streep, shares these perfectly archetypally illustrative statements taken from BrainyQuote.com:

> "I'm a pain in the ass to all of the costume designers with whom I work because I have very strong feelings about the subject."

> "Some people are filled by compassion and a desire to do good, and some simply don't think anything's going to make a difference."

> "Everything we say signifies; everything counts, that we put out into the world. It impacts on kids, it impacts on the zeitgeist of the time."

NEPTUNE

Double maverick and performer, Sandra Bernhard, explores this realm easily. The following comes from her website sandrabernhard.com:

> What makes Bernhard's comedy so rare—whether she's philosophizing about Taylor Swift's squad or singing Dolly Parton's "Hard Candy Christmas" as imagined by Caitlyn Jenner—is that within every keenly observed pop-culture rant, there's an element of piercing truth," Variety wrote. In a review of her career, *The New Yorker* noted that "Bernhard teaches the children—all those burgeoning spoken-word artists and monologists—how to perform observational comedy with style, and right on the political edge." And the *Los Angeles Times* praised another show, writing that Bernhard "has musicality to die for, a voice that swoops from the bluesy basement to a top floor falsetto..."

Neptune in Scorpio on the IC

These individuals are blessed (maybe cursed?) with the ability to be present to/with the unusual, odd, queer and funny, and share it with the world. No surprise that we find illustrators, television personalities, singers, songwriters, and a view on one's death.

Bill Waterson, who also has maverick Uranus conjunct his Leo Ascendant, shows us the priceless childhood insights of grokking the great world, in his timeless cartoon series Calvin and Hobbes.

Many royals are multi-mavericks, such as Japan's Emperor Naruhito. The powerful influence of this astrological position is well articulated in an article from Time.com:

> After earning a history degree at Gakushuin University, where he wrote a thesis on medieval water transport, the prince became the first Japanese royal to study overseas when he spent two years at Merton College, Oxford. The book he wrote chronicling his time there, *The Thames and I: A Memoir of Two Years at Oxford*, has just been re-issued in English.
>
> The prince's interest in water management extends beyond academia. Since 2007, he has served as honorary president of the U.N. Secretary General's Advisory Board on Water and Sanitation, and he has spoken frequently on the topic at international conferences. "He has been actively involved in international environmental issues in recent years," Hideya Kawanishi, associate professor at Nagoya University and an author of several books on Japan's emperors, tells *TIME*.

Multi-maverick and athlete, Carl Lewis, offers these enlightening quotes from about this astrological placement:

> "Scientists have proven that it's impossible to long-jump 30 feet, but I don't listen to that kind of talk. Thoughts like that have a way of sinking into your feet."

"I'm so fortunate to have done what I love to do for so long, but the day I retired was one of the best days of my life. Not because I was happy to get away from the sport, but because it was clear in my mind that I had done all I possibly could, and that it was time to go."

"I found the emotion that as an athlete you block out, and it really helped me to understand myself as a person. I'm a really emotional person and it helped make me a better person."

"You have to free your mind to do things you wouldn't think of doing. Don't ever say *no*."

Irish television presenter, Caron Keating, exhibited many aspects of this subtly diverse and all-encompassing astrological mix:

It all seemed perfect, un-improvable, enviable. Before cancer, Keating's life was safe as tea-time crumpets. A member of a good-hearted, old-fashioned showbiz community, she was set for life, a fun-time chip off the old light-entertainment block.

What she became in her last years was something quite different: a disciple of spiritual healing, a patron of Tibetan monks, a believer that exposure to controlled sound and colour could rearrange the body's aberrant molecules. It would be easy to make her last years in Australia sound like one long beach barbecue with hippies strumming guitars and wearing crystals, but at times it verged on the culty, and she needed the sturdy protection of her husband to pull her back from the darker brinks. Channeling with shamans required her to discover her inner animal — a wolf — then embody it. "It's cool," she would say, "I have my wolf with me."

At first she would try any cranky formula in the new-age enclave of Byron Bay, New South Wales. One day "Jesus" walked up her path followed by the "Prince of Darkness", a salvation package based on the idea that evil would scare the seeker towards the true path. Keating and Lindsay spent days talking to the weird double act: she was fascinated; he was watchful, feeling their brand of redemption bordered on dangerous. With hindsight, Keating doubted their usefulness, wryly observing in her diary that a 15-stone chain-smoking Australian was unlikely to be the reincarnated Christ.

Such encounters were not foreseen. Keating grew up outside Belfast, a beguiling child who loved to accompany her presenter mother to work and play with the weatherboard or wait to meet celebrities. With a degree in English and drama from Bristol, she fronted the Irish youth show Green Rock from Belfast, and at 24 was recruited by Biddy Baxter to swim with sharks and stand under freezing waterfalls. Probably she was more reflective than mainstream presenters need to be; later she felt she may have been more fulfilled as a painter or novelist, or even a doctor. She was picky about the shows she worked on, would never have agreed to present the lottery, and, being married to a wealthy, self-made man, with a fabulous house in Barnes, she could afford to be discerning.

Jessica Adams is a "psychic astrologer" which is a beautiful use of/for this astrological placement.

Actor, Kevin Dillon, shares these insights from BrainyQuote.com:

"I thought I'd miss cursing, but I actually don't. I still feel like I can get my point across without real harsh language."

"I don't go out that often. I'm not going to clubs or anything."

"I was hoping to attend the School of Visual Arts and had a portfolio built up."

"I'm kind of a homebody."

"I like everything about acting."

"I gotta lot of Black Irish in me."

One look at images of singer songwriter, Jeff Buckley, shows you a soulful and sensitive being. No surprise that while his Neptune is in a wide conjunction to his IC, he also has Mercury, Sun, and Venus here. RollingStone.com reflects his final moments in keeping with this astrological arrangement at the bottom of his chart:

ASTROLOGICAL MAVERICKS

> According to Memphis police, Buckley, 30, and an unnamed companion were sitting on a bank of the river listening to a radio. The singer waded into the river even though his friend called out to him and warned that it could be dangerous, police said. Buckley then floated on his back and began to sing. At that point, a boat came by creating large waves. Fearing the radio would get wet, the companion got up to move it and when he returned, Buckley had disappeared, according to police.

What would this astrological placement be without a timeless singer? From a bing.com search we learn the following:

> Kylie Ann Minogue, often known simply as Kylie, is an Australian-British singer, songwriter and actress. She is the highest-selling female Australian artist of all time and has been recognised with several honorific nicknames, most notably the "Princess of Pop." Minogue has also been known for reinventing herself in music and fashion throughout her career, being referred to as a style icon.

Neptune in Sagittarius on the IC

These individuals can get lost in their own idealistic quest and/or can provide amazingly compassion support to others on their path.

Another aspect of this astrological placement is the inability to withhold the truth, as well evidenced by multi-maverick and convicted murderer, Erik Menendez, who confessed to his therapist about the murder of his parents.

Foreign travel is well articulated with this astrological placement as evidenced by multi-maverick and Australian television presenter, Catriona Rowntree. The following comes from queanbeyanagechronicle.com.au:

> In 2020, Catriona Rowntree notches up 24 years globetrotting at the helm of Nine's *Getaway* travel program. She is the envy of many who explore Australian and international destinations vicariously through her and her fellow presenters Charli Robinson, David Reyne, and Jason Dundas.
>
> For avid travelers, she and her colleagues provide helpful tips on where to shop, what to see, how to get from place to place and where to eat, among other suggestions.

Antony Starr, is a New Zealand television actor best known for his dual role as twins Jethro and Van West in New Zealand's hit comedy/drama *Outrageous Fortune* and who plays Homelander in the series *The Boys*. This current role is a stark departure from this astrological energy, as he plays an unfeeling psychopath with no compassion for anyone but himself, well, maybe he is a little Sagittarian. Saving others is a part of this astrological placement and his character, Homelander is the "superman" in this series.

Neptune in Capricorn on the IC

This is a great placement for family wealth and familial inheritance (both financial and creative), which we see in a couple of our examples.

Our first maverick, we only know of him because he was the first of four children who died in the same household. We often find a lack of clarity when Neptune is involved. Caleb Folbigg was only 19 days old when he was found dead in his crib. The following is from FilmDaily.com:

> As Kathleen Folbigg sat in prison for the death of her children, experts took a different view on her conviction. Clinical psychologists started to question if she should have even been charged. While her diary entries were dark, she never indicated she wanted to kill her kids. Nor did Folbigg write a confession in her private journals.
>
> Another consideration for Kathleen Folbigg's innocence was a better understanding of postpartum depression. Millions of mothers have despairing thoughts about their children during the isolating, sleep-deprivation newborn phase. As awareness of PPD has grown, so has support. Also, most mothers with PPD never harm their children.
>
> However, a question remained: why did all four of Kathleen Folbigg's children die? It was too much of a coincidence to secure Folbigg's release. The circumstances even stumped Folbigg's defenders.

The family dynasty and artistic creativity continue in the life of rock bassist, Wolfgang Van Halen. He started working with his father's band Van Halen, when Wolfgang was 16 years old.

From FoxBusiness.com comes this enlightening tidbit from one who has had the benefits of a rich family:

> Jennifer [Gates] says she knows she's fortunate to have been brought up in a multibillion-dollar household. "I was born into a huge situation of privilege and I think it's about using those opportunities and learning from them to find things that I'm passionate about and hopefully make the world a little bit of a better place," she told *Sidelines Magazine*, a magazine dedicated to equestrian and horse-friendly lifestyles.

Neptune in Aquarius on the IC

These individuals would likely be fairly aloof and brilliant observers; ones who are on the fringes. So, it is no surprise that we only have one example and he is one about whom I have been unable to find any information.

Noah Peter Domasin, who also has Chiron and Moon here all opposing maverick Saturn conjunct the MC in Leo, was the first child born of frozen sperm and egg.

Neptune in Pisces on the IC

This is a mysterious and wonderful position for a psychic, healer, doula, magician, guru, world leader, or one who delves into and writes about these experiences or travels on the inner dimensions like a modern day Rip van Winkle. Neptune went into Pisces in February 2012, and will remain there until 2025. Currently, we have no examples of individuals with this astrological placement.

We will now look at the angle placements of Neptune throughout the zodiac from the point of view of the Descendant (DS.)

Neptune in Aries on the DS

Dreamy Neptune lifts the mind and thoughts of the headstrong Aries into the cloudy area of relationships. Like Don Quixote chasing windmills, these individuals can pursue their desires with romantic fervor. But were the conquests in their minds, in a romance novel, or did it really happen? Neptune was last in Aries in May 1874, before any reliable birth times were kept. Neptune will go into Aries again May 24, 2188, so we have a little time to prepare. This would be a good placement for someone who guides others in inner psycho-spiritual work.

NEPTUNE

Neptune in Taurus on the DS

Fixed Taurus may lose its self-focused attention with this astrological placement. This energy hasn't been experienced since August 1887, and won't be experienced again until May 8, 2202. These individuals may wish to free themselves from physical restrictions and limiting forms through experiencing nature. They will likely have unusual ways in which they relate to others owing to their sensitivity and ability to perceive reliability in others. The otherwise myopic Taurus is forced to see a wider view.

Neptune in Gemini on the DS

These individuals may adjust their states of being in order to be in relationship with those around them. There is an interesting ability to take the multitudinous pieces of information and weave them together. While this energy hasn't been felt since May 1902 (a time when most people did not have their birth times recorded) this energy won't be felt again until June 29, 2215. Considering this, we are lucky to have two examples. This is a highly flexible point.

Our first maverick raised photography, a Neptunian endeavor, to the level of art in the world. The following comes from Wikipedia.com:

> Ansel Easton Adams (February 20, 1902 – April 22, 1984) was an American landscape photographer and environmentalist known for his black-and-white images

of the American West. He helped found Group f/64, an association of photographers advocating "pure" photography which favored sharp focus and the use of the full tonal range of a photograph. He and Fred Archer developed an exacting system of image-making called the Zone System, a method of achieving a desired final print through a deeply technical understanding of how tonal range is recorded and developed in exposure, negative development, and printing. The resulting clarity and depth of such images characterized his photography.

An emperor is well aided by the qualities of this astrological position. Elements of this astrological arrangement are stated in this excerpt about multi-maverick, Emperor Hirohito from Wikipedia.com:

At the start of his reign, Japan was already one of the great powers—the ninth largest economy in the world, the third-largest naval power, and one of the four permanent members of the council of the League of Nations. He was the head of state under the Constitution of the Empire of Japan during Japan's imperial expansion, militarization, and involvement in World War II. After Japan's surrender, he was not prosecuted for war crimes as many other leading government figures were. His degree of involvement in wartime decisions remains controversial. During the post-war period, he became the symbol of the state of Japan under the post-war constitution and Japan's recovery. By the end of his reign, Japan emerged as the world's second-largest economy.

Neptune in Cancer on the DS

These individuals have an inherent sensitivity towards the needs of others which is often confusing for them when those needs mirrors their own. This can be a placement for wonderful caregivers.

Daisie Adelle Davis, popularly known as Adelle Davis, was an American author and nutritionist who became well known as an advocate for specific nutritional stances such as unprocessed food and vitamin supplementation

From *The New York Times*, we see the themes of this astrological placement play out in the life of author, Arthur Koestler:

> Explaining how his chief interests had evolved, Mr. Koestler once said, "I've written all I have to write on democracy and totalitarianism, communism and progress, which have obsessed me for the best part of a quarter century. Now the errors are atoned for, the bitter passion has burned itself out. Cassandra has gone hoarse and is due for vocational change."

This position gave the Nobel Prize winning physicist, Hans Bethe, the ability to understand the subtlest forms of relationship in our universe. The following comes from NobelPrize.org:

His work on nuclear reactions led Bethe to the discovery of the reactions which supply the energy in the stars. The most important nuclear reaction in the brilliant stars is the carbon-nitrogen cycle, while the sun and fainter stars use mostly the proton-proton reaction. Bethe's main achievement in this connection was the exclusion of other possible nuclear reactions. The Nobel Prize was given for this work, as well as his work on nuclear reactions in general.

In 1955 Bethe returned to the theory of nuclei, emphasizing a different phase. He has worked since then on the theory of nuclear matter whose aim it is to explain the properties of atomic nuclei in terms of the forces acting between nucleons.

Before his work on nuclear physics, Bethe's main attention was given to atomic physics and collision theory. On the former subject, he wrote a review article in *Handbuch der Physik* in which he filled in the gaps of the existing knowledge, and which is still up-to-date. In collision theory, he developed a simple and powerful theory of inelastic collisions between fast particles and atoms which he has used to determine the stopping power of matter for fast charged particles, thus providing a tool to nuclear physicists. Turning to more energetic collisions, he calculated with Heitler the bremsstrahlung emitted by relativistic electrons, and the production of electron pairs by high energy gamma rays.

Multi-maverick and British politician, Barbara Castle, has these illuminating statements taken from BrainyQuote.com:

> "It was very much a cry for democratic control at that time. Above all, breaking the accomplished power of a few people to rule the lives of everybody else."

> "There was no welfare state, and people had to rely mainly on the Poor Law – that was all the state provided. It was very degrading, very humiliating. And there was a means test for receiving poor relief."

From a wonderful interview with talk show host, Dick Cavett, multi-maverick and playwright, Tennessee Williams, shares that he had a pre-occupation and fear of death which he eventually overcame.

British politician, Enoch Powell, shows us the cautionary tale of racism. This position can be focused on one's clan and can make up fantasy fear stories about other groups. The following comes from AlJaszeera.com:

> Some 74 percent of Britons in the aftermath of Powell's rhetoric agreed with him – that black immigration was likely to cause violence on our streets in the not too distant future, or as he put it – "In this country in 15 or 20 years' time the black man will have the whip hand over the white man."

Writer, Julia de Burgos, was a poet from Puerto Rico. As an advocate of Puerto Rican independence, she served as

Secretary General of the Daughters of Freedom, the women's branch of the Puerto Rican Nationalist Party.

Neptune in Leo on the DS

The possibility for a "warm cozy fire" is well implied here. There is a bit of a moth to the flame sort of quality about these individuals and it is, therefore, no surprise that we find some well-known entertainers in this group pf mavericks.

While known for transforming the face of New York City, Architect, Ely Jacques Kahn, married a few times. The following comes from his obituary at NYTimes.com:

> Mr. Kahn married three times. His first wife, whom he married in 1913, was the former Elsie Neut. They were divorced, and in 1938 he married Mrs. Beatrice Sulzberger, who died in 1962. His third wife was Mrs. Liselotte Hirshmann Myller, whom he married in 1964.

Our next example has married four times. From Wikipedia.com, we learn the following about multi-maverick and composer, Burt Bacharach:

> Burt Freeman Bacharach is an American composer, songwriter, record producer, and pianist who has composed hundreds of pop songs from the late 1950s through the 1980s, many in collaboration with lyricist Hal David. A six-time Grammy Award winner and three-time Academy Award winner, Bacharach's

songs have been recorded by more than 1,000 different artists. As of 2014, he had written 73 US and 52 UK Top 40 hits. He is considered one of the most important composers of 20th-century popular music.

The philanthropic side of this astrological placement is well presented by film star, Kirk Douglas. The following comes from an article at PageSix.com:

> The silver-screen icon, who died Feb. 5 at the age of 103, left the bulk of his $80 million estate to the Douglas Foundation, the charity he co-founded nearly six decades ago, it was revealed Sunday. The nonprofit benefits the Children's Hospital of Los Angeles, The Kirk and Anne Douglas Childhood Center and a St. Lawrence University scholarship for underprivileged students. The Douglas Foundation, created in 1964 by Douglas and his wife Anne Beydens Douglas, also doles out dollars to Westwood's Sinai Temple and Culver City's Kirk Douglas Theater, a restored venue.

The power of imagery is well indicated with this astrological position and actress, Audrey Hepburn used it well. The following comes from History.com:

> Slim, elegant and unfailingly stylish, Hepburn turned the image of the bosomy blonde Hollywood starlet on its head, presenting a new ideal of beauty for millions of moviegoers.

ASTROLOGICAL MAVERICKS

Neptune in Virgo on the DS

This isn't the easiest of places for ambiguous Neptune when in persnickety Virgo. One can consider a wide range of expression when these two archetypal energies are working together.

Ranker.com has many astrologically archetypal illustrative parts of this astrological placement in the life of Anthony Armstrong-Jones. The following is a small tidbit:

> The marriage between Princess Margaret and Armstrong-Jones was practically doomed from the start. Despite the passion and genuine chemistry that had sustained their relationship in the beginning, each of their individual issues and quirks would sabotage the marriage. Margaret's tendency to drink heavily, for example, was a source of friction. Tony, on the other hand, would often bury himself in his photography work, which only further alienated Margaret. Both eventually pursued extramarital affairs.

Princess Margaret was also a multi-maverick, so it is no surprise these two were drawn to one another.

Multiple-maverick, Princess Alexandra, The Honourable Lady Ogilvy, has a very special relationship to Her Royal Highness. The following comes from Express.co.uk:

> Alexandra is often spotted at the side of Her Majesty during leisure actives and events. It has been reported they have been close for a number of years, so much so, that in June this year Alexandra accompanied the

Queen in her carriage to Ascot. She is often referred to as the Queen's best friend.

One sees this astrological placement well presented by actress, Mary Tyler Moore. The following comes from Biography.com:

> Actress Mary Tyler Moore became one of television's most beloved wives, playing Laura Petrie on *The Dick Van Dyke Show,* and won two Emmys for her work on the series. *The Mary Tyler Moore Show* — featuring a single, 30-something woman in the working world — started in 1970 and won her three more Emmys. Her roles in these classic TV sitcoms have made her one of the most popular actresses in television history.

Drummer for The Beatles, Ringo Starr, shares these revealing gems from AZQuotes.com:

> "Of course I'm ambitious. What's wrong with that? Otherwise you sleep all day."

> "Well, I'm getting happier all the time, which is very nice."

> "I had no schooling before I joined The Beatles and no schooling after The Beatles. Life is a great education."

> "I've always felt that a space is as good as a fill."

"I'm on my feet and I'm doing what I love to do, and I'm in a profession, as a musician, where we can go on for as long as we can go on."

Neptune in Libra on the DS

Dreamy idealistic love. These individuals have an understanding of the complex checks and balances that make up our inter-relationships and the universe in which it all occurs. In that vein, it is no surprise that we find three astrologers with this astrological placement.

From Tarot.com, we learn the following about astrologer, Jeff Jawer:

> For years Jeff provided his insight to Tarot.com and worldwide in the form of horoscopes, birth charts, blogs, lectures, and the well-known *Planet Pulse* video series, co-starring fellow astrologer and close friend Rick Levine.

Look up any of the *Planet Pulse* videos to see this graceful and all-encompassing astrological signature in action.

AstroSoftware.com has these archetypally resonant statements about astrologer, David Cochrane:

> David is the founder of Cosmic Patterns Software, Inc. and the author of the Kepler astrology program. David's involvement in astrology for over 3 decades is impressive. David is a dynamic and engaging speaker

who is able to break complex ideas down into simple form and to inspire as well as to educate.

David has been called a "theoretical genius," "the world's greatest expert in harmonic astrology," and "the best speaker," at national conferences, and even simply "the best astrologer," by some of the world's most respected and experienced astrologers.

Astrologer, Arielle Guttman, shares these insights about her true love on her website SophiaVenus.com. Arielle is known for her work on Libra's ruler Venus:

After 30 years into the field of astrology, I wasn't searching for any new techniques. I'd been to all the conferences and heard most of the leading astrological authorities of our times. In those years, I collected and synthesized a personal way of working with astrology that involved mythology, archetypes, dreams, healing, psychological, and spiritual insights through astrology and more.

My particular loves were covered in the two-volume set of *Mythic Astrology* I co-authored with Kenneth Johnson. Another love was planetary astro-mapping, after having been certified by Jim Lewis (in 1986) and moving on to incorporate into Astro*Carto*Graphy some new methods of astro-mapping, including the use of asteroids, nodes, Chiron, and Local Space. What emerged from that was my passion for Geodetics (Earth Astrology) whereby the planets transit around the

Earth, forming "hot spots" during certain periods of time.

Former United Kingdom Prime Minister, James Gordon Brown, has these illuminating statements which show an understanding for right human relationship. The following comes from QuotesGram.com:

> You need in the long run for stability, for economic growth, for jobs, as well as for financial stability, global economic institutions that make sure that growth to be sustained has to be shared, and are built on the principle that the prosperity of this world is indivisible.

> Take, therefore, what modern technology is capable of: the power of our moral sense allied to the power of communications, and our ability to organize internationally. That, in my view, gives us the first opportunity as a community to fundamentally change the world.

Neptune in Scorpio on the DS

In the same specialized way hogs can smell and locate truffles and dogs can smell cancer, this astrological placement gives one a specialized sensitivity, especially to others. The often unseen inner battles are "presented" for others to see the steps to wholeness. There is a desire, or edict, to root-out that which creates conflict. The goal is the well-earned peace of walking through the valley of death with those they love and coming out the other side transformed.

Christie Martin is a singer and performer of folk music in the group Four Shillings Short with her husband Aodh Og O'Tuama. They travel the US and Ireland sharing alternative music live and via the internet. Their songs and stories are meant to inspire and transform their audiences.

SaatchiGallery.com has this to say about artist, Grayson Perry:

> Winner of the 2003 Turner Prize, British artist Grayson Perry creates seductively beautiful pots that convey challenging themes; at the heart of his practice is a passionate desire to comment on deep flaws within society. Perry uses pots as narrative and figurative media, a round, curved surface for a bizarre or bitter story.

The ability to capture and recreate the epic theme of good versus evil is well conferred by this astrological placement. Neptune rules imagery and movies and who better to represent this placement that the person who create not one, but two Tolkien trilogies, multi-maverick and film director, Peter Jackson.

Marc David Maron, is an American comedian, podcaster, writer, actor, musician, director, and producer. Many of the elements of this astrological placement can be seen in this short excerpt from NPR.org:

Maron named his new Netflix comedy special *End Times Fun* before the COVID-19 pandemic started — but now the title feels eerily apt. He talked with Terry Gross about how he's handling the crisis as a "recovering hypochondriac," and what he's doing to pass the time in isolation. Maron co-stars in the Netflix series *GLOW* and hosts the interview podcast *WTF*.

Former First Lady of the United States, Michelle Obama, shares the powerful insights she gained over the years. The following comes from AZQuotes.com:

"One of the lessons that I grew up with was to always stay true to yourself and never let what somebody else says distract you from your goals. And so when I hear about negative and false attacks, I really don't invest any energy in them, because I know who I am."

"Do not bring people in your life who weigh you down. And trust your instincts ... good relationships feel good. They feel right. They don't hurt. They're not painful. That's not just with somebody you want to marry, but it's with the friends that you choose. It's with the people you surround yourselves with."

"Every girl, no matter where she lives, deserves the opportunity to develop the promise inside of her."

"No matter who you are, no matter where you come from, you are beautiful."

From InspireMeToday.com, we learn that Australian-American entrepreneur and artist, Beeaje Quick, is a human being born in 1964. He has a penchant for connecting with different cultures and is a devotee of life. Beeaje uses his experiences to impart lessons that, at times, inspire others in the pursuit of their life path through his books, art and films. For more information, please visit godspeedbooks.com

Steven Paul "Elliott" Smith, was an American singer, songwriter, and musician. Smith is a good example of the deep sensitivity of this astrological placement. The headline for his obituary from TheGuardian.com says it all:

> Gentle singer with a delicate message of brutality and despair.

Neptune in Sagittarius on the DS

The search for a greater truth in relationship to the other is highly emphasized by this point. These individuals can be highly inspirational. They can be ardent and courageous crusading against that which goes against a natural code. These individuals also have an inherent sense that gives them a grace in whatever they do.

From CricketCountry.com, we learn the following about cricket maverick, Greg Blewett:

> Greg is a vocal supporter of animal rights and has vehemently spoken against animal torture and poaching on numerous occasions.

Ex-footballer, James Hird, shared the intimate process of dealing with grief and behavioural health issues in the following excerpt. While viewing pictures of him, I was immediately impressed with the natural warmth and affection he shows others, another beautiful aspect of this astrological placement. The following comments come from Au.Sports.yahoo.com:

"I really felt for my wife because she was trying to hold our family together. She's a very proud person and also very defensive of me because she obviously saw me going through a lot."

"Every day you wake up and go, 'All right, I've got to deal with this. I've got to work through it and one day this will finish.'"

"And fortunately it did."

Hird says his own experience has helped him understand the bigger picture and educate others to seek the same help that saved him:

"Mental health in society is a huge issue. I think part of my story might be relevant to other people. Everyone has their own different story and if people want to listen to mine, if they can get something out of it, that's great."

"When your relationships with people you care for are tested, when you don't get the job you wanted, or you want to earn more, it's nowhere near as bad as what (you think) it was."

"It's OK if you slip off (routine) sometimes, so long as you get back on. Just take little pieces every day, in exercise, in diet, in health, in mental wellbeing, that's the way to start and you never know where you can end up."

Dan Falzon, is an Australian actor of Maltese descent, best known for his role as Rick Alessi on the television soap opera *Neighbours*. The following comes from KiwiWire.com:

These days, Falzon is busy with running his Earth Sanctuary where he teaches visitors about the importance of ecotourism as well as serving as an ambulance paramedic in Alice Springs.

Sarah Teitel, is an artist and musician living in Toronto. From TorontoStandard.com we learn another way this astrological placement can process:

The first brain Teitel painted hangs at the very front of the gallery. It seems to have a very intimate, private connection to Teitel as the brain (a mixture of glorious golds, oranges, pinks and blues) is surrounded by bubbles of paper cut out from her journals as a child. During our chat, I find out that their inclusion was less about emotional history, and more about their own artistic transformation after Teitel's mother spilled water on them while 'not' reading their words.

"The water she spilled had made the Bic pens I used bleed into these really amazing colours," Teitel says. "You wouldn't have expected what they created. Like the black bled into these really beautiful pinks and purples that you couldn't replicate if you tried. It was a perfect element to include."

Multi-maverick and television personality, Kelly Osbourne has a stellium in not just one sign, but *two*! Kelly's stellium is in Sagittarius and Scorpio which gives her an intensity for seeking and revealing the truth. Kelly shares these illuminating insights from Brainyquote.com:

"I feel good in my own skin because I've accepted the fact that I'm me. That's what's so great about being alive and being on this planet: Everybody's different."

"I was called fat and ugly in the press almost my entire life. I understand that being judged by others comes with the territory, but it broke my heart and ruined my self-esteem."

"I never thought in a million years I'd be that healthy girl who wakes up every morning to exercise. After being called 'cherubic and chubby,' I'm rocking a bikini!"

And this perfect gem:

> "I didn't know that anything was wrong with me until the media got involved in my life."

Neptune in Capricorn on the DS

Capricorn is the sign of material success and class management, with Neptune here on the DS, we have individuals who can sum up a person in a moment, there is also an hint at noble ancestry -especially by marriage. One of our earliest examples shows this archetypal maverick element at work.

From Royal Armouries.com, we learn the following about Queen Claude of France:

> Queen Claude was known for hosting a cultured court and often made political appearances without her husband, she regularly appeared side by side with her mother-in-law, Louise de Savoie. To allow her to make these frequent appearances Claude would travel extensively and widely, often whilst pregnant. She was present at the public acceptance of the political engagement of their ten-month-old son, Francis, to Mary I of England, the daughter of Henry VIII and Katherine of Aragon in Paris in 1518.
>
> Perhaps Claude's most notable public appearances was at the Field of Cloth of Gold where she fulfilled her political duties hosting feasts, dances, and theatrical shows to entertain the royal guests. Most notably these

duties saw her individually hosting King Henry VIII for a banquet in the French camp whilst her husband was hosted by the English Queen, Katherine of Aragorn, in the English camp.

Whilst the Queens held limited formal political power they could influence their husbands and, at the Field of Cloth of Gold, also had direct contact with their rival kings. Their prominence was also used to highlight the positive new relationship between England and France so Katherine and Claude appeared side by side at the joust. Beyond her political activities at the Field of Cloth of Gold Claude was known to wield great influence and respect with a number of notable Venetian ambassadors and within the higher echelons of the Roman Catholic Church.

During this period the main role of the Queen was to produce a male heir, or even better, several male children. As such Claude spent much of her short life in a cycle of annual pregnancies, at the time of the Field of Cloth of Gold Claude had already given birth to two sons and was nine months pregnant with her third child, whereas Katherine had not delivered a male heir. So, whilst Katherine was known to be an experienced diplomat and had excelled in her role as consort, in many ways her skills in mediation and political nuances would have been overshadowed by this.

Another facet of how this astrological placement can work is well presented in this article from AccessOnline.com about

Scout LaRue Willis, the daughter of film stars Bruce Willis and Demi Moore:

Scout Willis is NOT ready for her close up, thank you very much.

Demi Moore and Bruce Willis' middle daughter didn't take kindly to recent paparazzi photos of her and younger sister Tallulah. Instead of straightforward trash-talking, however, Scout called out the snaps with a killer punchline that left her Instagram followers howling.

Scout posted a screenshot of a tabloid story that showed her and Tallulah walking out of a convenience store with snacks in tow. The article's headline referred to Scout as smiling "mischievously," but the 27-year-old clearly had a different take on her candid expression – as well as the notion that being born into Hollywood privilege has nothing but perks.

George Kenneth "Trey" Griffey III, is an American football wide receiver for the Arizona Wildcats, and is a fantastic example of the dynastic aspect of this astrological placement as his father and grandfather. The following comes from TimesOnline.com:

Griffey, son of Baseball Hall of Famer Ken Griffey Jr. and grandson of three-time MLB All-Star Ken Griffey Sr., went undrafted out of the University of Arizona in 2017.

He was signed by the Indianapolis Colts but was waived before training camp. He then spent a few weeks as part of the Miami Dolphins organization before being cut in early September.

Following last season, the Steelers signed Griffey as a free agent.

"You see the success they've had in the past. They have players that have played in a Super Bowl coming back to teach you," said Griffey, noting that Super Bowl XLIII hero Santonio Holmes came to practice Sunday to work with the receivers.

"That's something that you can't take for granted."

Now, as he embarks on his sophomore season, very much facing a defining moment in his career, the Orlando, Florida native is ready to prove he belongs in the National Football League.

"You just go out there and compete every day," said Griffey. "You know what you have to do each day."

"Just play ball."

From NewRoyals.com, we learn the following about what's happening in Monaco:

On September 22, 2020, Princess Stephanie's eldest daughter, Pauline Ducruet opened her "Alter Designs" pop up store at the Yacht Club in Monaco. Princess Stephanie of Monaco and Camille Gottlieb attended the opening of the pop-up store of the fashion brand 'Alter' at the Yacht Club.

The only angle Malala Yousafzai, the Pakistani activist for female education and the youngest-ever Nobel Prize laureate, doesn't have a planet is her MC! From BorgenProject.org we learn 12 insights about this brilliant woman and her maverick effect on the world:

1. Malala was born in the Swat District of Pakistan. This region fell under the rule of the Taliban, which is a fundamentalist terrorist group that imposes highly restrictive rules on women and girls. The Taliban banned girls from attending school or receiving an education of any kind.
2. Her father was a teacher and ran a chain of schools throughout the local region. He continuously encouraged all of his children to learn despite the societal restrictions. Malala credits her father for inspiring her to pursue further education and humanitarian work.
3. Malala blogged for BBC for several years. In 2008, BBC Urdu journalists began looking for a young student to share private insight on what life was like under the Taliban. Despite the danger of being caught, Malala's father recommended her for the assignment and she began blogging in secret, anonymously chronicling her life and her perspective on the rule of the Taliban. She was 11 years old.
4. Malala started to gain notoriety from standing up to the Taliban publicly. With her father's blessing, she openly opposed the Taliban rules set in place and began working to regain access to education for both herself and other girls throughout the region.

5. She was nominated for the International Children's Peace Prize in 2011 due to her activism and was awarded Pakistan's National Youth Peace Prize that same year. The Prime Minister of Pakistan later renamed the award the National Malala Peace Prize in her honor.
6. The Taliban shot Malala in the head when she was 15 years old. Her newfound popularity and voice against the Taliban made Malala a high-profile target and in 2012 she was the victim of a nearly fatal assassination attempt. She was on the way home from school when a masked gunman asked for her by name and openly fired on her and her friends.
7. She created the Malala Fund, a charity devoted to bringing equal education opportunities to girls around the world. Malala went to the United Kingdom for medical treatment directly after the shooter's attack where she and her family settled permanently. Afterward, she established the Malala Fund with her father. Within its first year of operation, the Malala Fund raised over $7 million and opened up multiple schools in Malala's native Pakistan.
8. She celebrated her sixteenth birthday by giving a speech to the United Nations. Nine months after the assassination attempt, Malala spoke at invitation before world leaders and urged them to change certain policies in regard to education and women's rights. Since then, Malala has held audience with notable political figures such as Queen Elizabeth and Former

U.S. President Barack Obama and given lectures at Harvard University and the Oxford Union.

9. July 12 has been officially designated Malala Day. After her critically acclaimed speech on her birthday at the United Nations, Secretary-General, Ban Ki-moon, urged all young people to speak out and let the world hear their voices. In an act of support, he declared Malala's birthday Malala Day in honor of her courage and influential activism.

10. She was a co-recipient of the 2014 Nobel Peace Prize. After sharing her story, Malala catapulted to international fame and she received an outpouring of support from around the world as her story spread. In honor of her efforts, she became the youngest ever Nobel laureate at the age of 17.

11. Malala received the United Nation's highest honor. In 2017 she received the title of U.N. Messenger of Peace to promote girl's education, a two-year appointment given to activists whose work has made an impact. The U.N. selects recipients carefully based on their future goals and past work, and the recipients engage closely with the United Nations' leaders in an effort to make a change.

12. Oxford University accepted Malala in 2017 where she began studying Philosophy, Politics and Economics. While pursuing her own studies, she currently still works with leaders and organizations around the globe on behalf of the Malala Fund and the United Nations, fighting for equal education for all.

While these 12 facts about Malala Yousafzai cannot encompass all of her achievements and work, they show that Malala's bravery and perseverance have proven worthwhile in the face of adversity. Her goal to provide education to the world is a necessary step in ending global poverty.

Neptune in Aquarius on the DS

These individuals would likely be aloof and brilliant observers; ones who are on the fringes or at rarified levels, similar to privileged lives.

Interestingly enough, we have only one example, and he is the son of Elle Macpherson and his father of the same name. From DailyMail.com, the headline alone says it all about Arpad Flynn Alexander Busson:

> Private jets, five-star holidays and his own pilot license: Inside the luxury lifestyle of Elle Macpherson's son Flynn, 22, as he graduates university.

Neptune in Pisces on the DS

These individuals likely have a challenging time with boundaries. They are very dreamy and attractive to others in ways that will work perfectly with video and imagery. They have the ability to affect large numbers of people. Neptune went into Pisces in February 2012, and will remain there until

2025. We have no examples of individuals with this astrological placement at this time.

We will now look at the angle placements of Neptune throughout the zodiac from the point of view of the Medium Coeli (MC).

Neptune in Aries on the MC

Dreamy Neptune lifts the mind and thoughts of the headstrong Aries into the cloudy area of connective work. These individuals can pursue their desires with a driven fervor, but are they available for anything other than what they want? Neptune was last in Aries in May 1874, before any reliable birth *times* were kept. Neptune will go into Aries again May 24, 2188, so we have a little time to prepare. This would be a good placement for someone who guides others in inner psycho-spiritual work or births a new religion. The leadership tendencies here are strong, but the intention is key.

Neptune in Taurus on the MC

Fixed Taurus may lose its direction in the Neptunian fog, or envision, or even discover, an amazing form. This energy hasn't been experienced since August 1887, and won't be experienced again until May 8, 2202. These individuals may wish to free themselves from physical restrictions and limiting forms through experiencing nature. They can have brilliant minds for theories and understand how the physical and non-physical operate together.

Neptune in Gemini on the MC

This energy hasn't been felt since May 1902, and won't be felt again until June 29, 2215. These individuals may experience significantly altered states as they are easily affected by their environments. Understanding all of the little bits of life and holding them in a cohesive whole, is part of what these people will be about. They don't have to think outside the box, because they don't live in one! Consider taking the fragmented parts presented by a kaleidoscope and giving it more coherent form. This is what artists do, as well as those writers and influencers who like to experience life and share it with others.

Neptune in Cancer on the MC

The Danes have a word for this astrological placement. It is called *hygge*. Hygge is a Danish and Norwegian word describing "a mood of coziness and comfortable conviviality with feelings of wellness and contentment." Cancer is the sign of home and Cancerian individuals have this ability to carry their home with them, like a hermit crab. Sort of like a home is where you find it, or make it. The combination of Neptune and Cancer gives one a thorough emotional or felt sense of things.

These individuals can capture and convey highly complex feelings with minimal descriptions or images.

Our first example illuminates many aspects of this astrological placement. She was a master at capturing images from WWII as well as fashion. She is the multi-maverick, Lee Miller, who also helped invent a special style of photography called solarisation. The following comes from Wikiperdia.com:

> Not only does solarisation fit the Surrealist principle of unconscious accident being integral to art, it evokes the style's appeal to the irrational or paradoxical in combining polar opposites of positive and negative; Mark Haworth-Booth describes solarisation as "a perfect Surrealist medium in which positive and negative occur simultaneously, as if in a dream."

So apropos for this astrological placement!

Yet, more wonderful examples of this astrological placement are played out in the life of writer, Edgar Austin Mittelholzer. The following comes from StabrokeNews.com:

> Edgar Austin Mittelholzer was born in New Amsterdam, British Guiana in 1909 to near-white middle class parents of mixed European and African extraction, both of whom were unable to mask the colour/race prejudice that his swarthy complexion aroused in them. In the late 1920s he made the radically unconventional decision to become a professional writer, much to the deepening dismay of his parents and scorn of New

Amsterdam society. By the time he had committed suicide in 1965, through self-immolation, Mittelholzer had over twenty published novels, a travel journal and an autobiography to his credit. Whilst critics, and in particular Seymour, Gilkes and Birbalsingh, have carried out illuminating analytical studies of his novels, no book-length examination of his life and works has as yet been published.

Mittelholzer's immersive travels gave him the ability to write well enough to gain significant favor in Europe, despite his coloring.

From theHistoryPress.co.uk we learn how her father played a strong role in building the multi-maverick, Diana Mitford:

Her father, David, the 2nd Baron Redesdale had his own ideas on modern womanhood – he detested makeup and similar artifices – and he declared the presence of a woman in the House of Commons to be 'lower than the belly of a snake'. Thus, when Diana asked for the same privileges her brother, Tom, so freely enjoyed, she was told no. No, she could not take German lessons or study music; no, she was not to cut her hair or have friends to stay; and no, she must not dream of an independent life away from the constraints of marriage and the home. So, when older, worldlier men showed an interest in Diana and praised her intellect, it is easy to see why she put all of her faith in them.

NEPTUNE

There are many themes that carry this archetypal resonance in the life of Dame Kathleen Mary Ollerenshaw. This excerpt from her obituary in theGuardian.com clearly shares another iteration of this arrangement, like living at the bottom of the ocean:

> Daughter of Mary (nee Stops) and Charles Timpson, Kathleen was born in Manchester, into a family which owned shares in shoe shops throughout Britain. Her father was a local magistrate. When Kathleen was a child she became seriously ill and, although she recovered, she was left without hearing. The University of Manchester had a department, unique at the time, training students to become teachers of partially deaf children and at eight, Kathleen was taught by them how to lip read. It was not until she was in her late 30s that she received her first hearing aid.

Music and illusion are part and parcel of this astrological placement as well portrayed by William Lee "Billy" Tipton, an American jazz musician and bandleader. The following comes from MookyChick.co.uk:

> William Lee "Billy" Tipton was a jazz musician and bandleader born in Oklahoma with the name of Dorothy Lucille Tipton. He created a story that he had been in a severe car accident, which explained his bandaged chest, and claimed his genitals were damaged.
>
> Billy was never formally married but had relationships with various women over the years who

never knew that Billy was born and raised as a woman. His own children, which he had adopted, had no idea until the day he died.

Neptune in Leo on the MC

These individuals can make a nice warm hearth or a raging bonfire. The self-centering Leo needs a big audience with this astrological placement; they have the ability to inspire and lead the collective.

These illustrative quotes by legendary crooner, Frank Sinatra, highlight his Neptune in Leo:

"Dare to wear the foolish clown face."

"I believe that God knows what each of us wants and needs. It's not necessary for us to make it to church on Sunday to reach Him. You can find Him anyplace. And if that sounds heretical, my source is pretty good: Matthew, Five to Seven, The Sermon on the Mount."

"I am a thing of beauty."

From JTA.org, French lawyer, writer, scholar and politician, Nathan André Chouraqui, states:

"I believe that one of our deepest weaknesses is that a large part of our people don't believe in peace. Most of our people don't believe in peace. Most of our people don't know the Arabs except from the negative side of war and persecution and propaganda. In painting them all black we play the same game as those Palestinians who paint us all black…If you don't believe in peace you don't make peace."

Jacqueline Liwai Pung, was an American professional golfer who played on the Ladies Professional Golf Association (LPGA). A brilliant example of the moral high ground of this astrological placement is well articulated in her highest and lowest moments experienced at the same time. The following comes from Bunkere4d.co.uk:

> Upon hearing the news [that she had been disqualified], a distraught Pung fled the club with her daughter in tow. Then something remarkable happened: she turned around and came back. She managed to compose herself sufficiently to speak at the prize-giving ceremony where she had to watch Rawls receive the trophy. No, receive *her* trophy.

"Winning the Open is the greatest thing in golf," she said. "I have come close before. This time I thought I'd won. But I didn't. Golf is played by rules and I broke a rule. I've learned a lesson. And I have two broad shoulders…"

Major Richard Culling Carr-Gomm, was the founder of the Abbeyfield Society, the Morpeth Society and the Carr-Gomm Society, United Kingdom charities providing care and housing for disadvantaged and lonely people.

David "Croft" John Andrew Sharland, was an English writer, producer and director, who was able to bring to reality the grim and comedic aspects of life at war using the dark British humour.

Film legend, Charlton Heston, presents a wealth of examples along the continuum of expression for this astrological placement. The following comes from his obituary at FoxNews.com:

> "Charlton Heston was seen by the world as larger than life. He was known for his chiseled jaw, broad shoulders and resonating voice, and, of course, for the roles he played," Heston's family said in a statement. "No one could ask for a fuller life than his. No man could have given more to his family, to his profession, and to his country."
>
> Heston revealed in 2002 that he had symptoms consistent with Alzheimer's disease, saying, "I must reconcile courage and surrender in equal measure."
>
> With his large, muscular build, well-boned face and sonorous voice, Heston proved the ideal star during the period when Hollywood was filling movie screens with panoramas depicting the religious and historical past. "I have a face that belongs in another century," he often remarked.
>
> The actor assumed the role of leader off-screen as well. He served as president of the Screen Actors Guild and chairman of the American Film Institute and marched in the civil rights movement of the 1950s.

With age, he grew more conservative and campaigned for conservative candidates.

In June 1998, Heston was elected president of the National Rifle Association, for which he had posed for ads holding a rifle. He delivered a jab at then-President Clinton, saying, "America doesn't trust you with our 21-year-old daughters, and we sure, Lord, don't trust you with our guns."

From Wikipedia.com we learn the following:

Eloise Greenfield is an American children's book and biography author and poet famous for her descriptive, rhythmic style and positive portrayal of the African-American experience. After college, Greenfield began writing poetry and songs in the 1950s while working in a civil service job.

Neptune in Virgo on the MC

Many of these individuals are gifted with a natural physical fluidity giving them the adaptability to meet whatever is presented. Virgo, governed by Mercury, gives these mavericks agility of mind, body and spirit.

Pat Boone, portrayed various "roles" for the world: singer, composer, actor, conservative spokesman writer, television personality, and motivational speaker. What else can he do? From AZquotes.com we get this illustrative statement from Pat Boone:

"Ironically, for a few million people in the Far East, I did become an English teacher through my music."

Isn't a lyricist a perfect profession for this astrological placement? Sanger D. Shafer, also known as, Whitey Shafer, wrote the iconic song "All my Exes live in Texas" and other well-known country tunes.

The incomparably beautiful and fluid dancer, Rudolf Nureyev, is a crowning example of this astrological placement. His relationships were not relegated to one sex or the other, as well stated in this excerpt from NewNowNext.com:

> Nureyev, who's been labeled both bisexual and homosexual (depending on who you ask), was also spotted with Jackie's brother-in-law Robert F. Kennedy "kissing each other passionately in a phone box. The dancer, who died of AIDS in 1993, boasted of seducing the entire Kennedy clan.

British Labour politician, John Smith, is archetypally described in this excerpt from Wikipedia.com:

> ...a quiet, modest manner and his politically-moderate stance, he was a witty, often scathing speaker.

The following comes from the website, of New Zealand novelist, Fiona Kidman:

NEPTUNE

Books have always played a central role in my life. I learned to read one afternoon in hospital when I was six and, not being aware that there was anything else to read, read all the adult books in the hospital library over the weeks that followed. This didn't make me especially clever, but it did make me aware of the powerful role of stories, and I have been telling them ever since.

I have worked in the media as a journalist, radio producer, and as a radio, film and television scriptwriter, but now work wholly as a writer and occasional teacher of writing.

Multi-maverick and martial arts superstar, Bruce Lee, shows an inherent relationship with his body and the martial arts he practiced. Bruce Lee continues to inspire others long after his death. The following comes from GQ.com:

Back in November of 2019, Los Angeles Laker, Kyle Kuzma shared an anecdote on *The Official Lakers Podcast*. He was out to dinner with Laker legend Kobe Bryant, and asked him at which point he "found his game." Kuzma explained that he was expecting the same sort of answer other players had given him—that it came from getting reps in, knowing your shots, finding your spots. Kobe, ever the atypical superstar, surprised Kuzma by instead citing a Bruce Lee movie. "He was playing in the Western Conference semis versus San Antonio or something, and he found his game...by watching like a Bruce Lee [movie]," Kuzma recalled. Bryant cited a scene (by process of elimination, likely this one from *Enter the Dragon*) in which Lee tells his student something to the effect of "less is more." Kobe took that philosophy into his next game, and then into the rest of his career.

Actor, Stacy Keach, shares these illuminating gems from AZQuotes.com. The first of which he calls freedom, is actually more about the discriminating Virgo:

"To have the freedom to be able to make choices is something I guess every actor aspires to. Most actors don't have those kind of choices. If the part comes along, they take it."

"I enjoy directing, but I really like acting more. The idea of controlling the whole thing is not something that really appeals to me as much as being able to just control the world of the character that I'm dealing with."

"My objective was to have as varied a selection of roles as possible. It probably did hurt my career."

Multi-maverick astrologer, wisdom seeker, and sharer, Michael Erlewine, shows us the limitless brilliance this astrological placement offers to those willing to mine its resources.

Stephanie Cole, an English stage, television, radio and film actress, shares her opinions in an article from DailyMail.co.uk:

Miss Cole, who has recently been filming a new series of *Still Open All Hours* - a remake of the Ronnie Barker classic sitcom – said pushing for changes has been difficult.

"We stopped doing it in front of a live audience about three or four years ago," she told the newspaper.

"Personally, I hugely dislike the canned laughter. It's not necessary, it's a cop out, it's old fashioned and it's stupid."

"I would also like to push for a single camera [as opposed to the traditional five-camera sitcom format]. I mean, five cameras, what do you gain? You gain nothing."

Miss Cole began her acting career on stage at the age of just 17 when she played the role of 90-year-old Madame Arcati in Noël Coward's *Blithe Spirit*.

Neptune in Libra on the MC

The inherent sense of beauty and order and how all of the polarities fit within a larger whole are all part and parcel of this astrological placement. This is the place for spiritual beauty and, as we will see with many of our examples, issues with sexuality. Humanity has been a polarized concept: male and female. Neptune throws a wrench into that polarity which is what Libra is all about.

Our first example was born over 500 years ago and we are still in awe of his work. Leonard da Vinci changed our perception of art, science, anatomy, flying, armaments while also dealing with his sexuality which was not accepted in the 1400's.

Actress, Hayley Mills, shares many statements.com that show the focus this astrological placement can give. The following comes from BrainyQuote:

"In my life, things have happened to me. I've never felt I was controlling anything."

"My father was an inspiration to me; I made a few movies with him and I loved working with him. Everything about him – his whole approach to work, as well as his love, enthusiasm and respect for it and other people in the business – was inspiring. I was very lucky to have him as a role model."

"My sons are precious to me and I have tried incredibly hard to strike the right balance between work and home life while being acutely aware that I haven't always got it right."

In another interesting take on this astrological placement, we learn from that murderer, Peter William Sutcliffe, didn't have a rosy relationship with others. The following comes from theSun.co.uk:

The Ripper, who was convicted in 1981 of murdering 13 women and attempting to kill seven more, was moved from Broadmoor Hospital to Frankland and lost his fight to stay in Broadmoor.

He was sent to the secure psychiatric facility in Berkshire in 1983 after being diagnosed with paranoid schizophrenia.

But a health tribunal subsequently ruled he no longer needs treatment for the disorder.

Sutcliffe, from Bradford, killed women in West Yorkshire and Manchester between 1975 and 1980.

He worked as a lorry driver during his murderous spree, usually beating his victims to death with a hammer before mutilating their bodies.

During his trial, Sutcliffe said God had ordered him to kill his victims.

The former grave digger said the voice came to him from the headstone of a man in the cemetery where he worked.

We have a second example of an individual who was not ideal in how he treated others. Jürgen Bartsch, was a German serial killer who murdered four boys ages 8–13 and attempted to kill another. Looking at these two examples we can see that individuals with Neptune in Libra (or other air signs) can literally create their own inner world. Doing anything and everything to remain in control is something that Neptune is not about. The following comes from Longdom.com:

In 1966, then 19-year old Jürgen Bartsch (1946-1976) was arrested after an unsuccessful attempt to torture, kill and dismember a young boy. Before, in the years between 1962 and 1966, Bartsch had killed 4 young boys aged 8 to 12. He estimated to have undertaken more than 100 further homicidal attempts. The method of murder was beating and strangulation. He dismembered most of the bodies, pricked out the eyes, decapitated the bodies, and removed the genitals. He also tried but failed to perform anal intercourse with the victims. His goal was to skin the life victims. Bartsch openly discussed his wish for dominance, control, and sexual gratification but also his strategies of avoiding prosecution. Under the influence of psychiatric consultations, Bartsch's views on his parents, as much as memories of sexual abuse performed by a teacher, became a topic. In a psychiatric hospital, Bartsch managed to marry a heterosexual woman. During a voluntary castration operation, he died due to an error in the anesthetic procedure.

The airy creative astrological placement is well expressed in multi-maverick singer songwriter, Tom Waits life. The following comes from theGuardian.com:

On the table in front of him is the book he is reading, *Crow Planet*, about how corvids are "very much smarter than you might imagine," a cup of black coffee (he gave up booze a long while ago, having got his share in early) and a notebook in which he keeps his ideas for songs (He occasionally reads from it at random: "Here's one: 'It's good to be 40 feet tall on a billboard or something but not when your wife's dying of cancer and you just knocked up the babysitter.' Another 'I wish I was a component of water and I could go off in the sun and just dry out…'"). He gives the impression of being in a state both of constant startled awareness, and vague puzzlement at the world. Some of this has to do with his hair, which seems to have led a long and interesting life of its own. Unusually, he is not wearing a hat.

Albuquerque based encaustic artist, Sally Condon, creates evocative paintings that bring beauty to any space they are placed.

Poly-maverick actress, Angelica Huston, shared these intimate insights about drugs (a Neptunian experience) with Vulture.com (questions from interviewer are in bold):

It's interesting, because it sounded like her friend Carrie Fisher had relapsed before she died.
From what I understand, Carrie was taking a lot of drugs. I don't want to die from drugs, God! What a grim way to die. Unless you're debilitated and need to get out of here. But to go accidentally on drugs, I'd hate that.

You still do any drugs?
I smoke weed, but I don't consider that a danger to my health. I don't like edibles. Too slow and you don't know where it's going. You could end up having to go to bed for three days. I don't do anything wildly dangerous anymore. I wasn't ever attracted to the acid. I like to have a good time, but I don't want to lose my mind.

The ability to work with the media in a masterful way is well exemplified by this astrological position, as seen in the life of multi-maverick Oprah Winfrey. I recommend the article about her creating an empire out of nothing from Media.com. Winfrey has rightfully earned her place in life after having endured numerous humbling and humiliating experiences. She is a beacon of right human relationship. This placement is one that makes it easy for people to share their stories and where she shined bright!

Multi-maverick international master chess champion, Jeremy Silman, shows us another aspect of this astrological placement: strategy. From Wikipedia.com we learn the following about Silman:

> In his books, Silman evaluates positions according to the "imbalances", or differences, which exist in every position, and advocates that players plan their play according to these. A good plan according to Silman is one which highlights the positive imbalances in the position.

What better song for this astrological placement than the one which placed singer, Debbie Boone, into number one? "You Light Up My Life" spent ten weeks at No. 1 on the Billboard Hot 100 chart. Boone won the Grammy Award for Best New Artist in 1978.

Neptune in Scorpio on the MC

This is a great placement for a well-known detective or investigative journalist. These individuals can sense what is going on in the collective, they are also great at retelling the gory details of whatever they uncover!

My dear friend, Glenna Bain, uses this energy to interpret sensitive and vital information between individuals who are deaf and those who can hear.

Multi-maverick and political strategist, Donna Brazile, said this perfect comment for this astrological placement: "There's no First Amendment right to lie. Period," Brazile announced.

The prodigious sexual nature of this astrological placement has interesting expression in the life of basketball superstar, Dennis Rodman. The following headline comes from the-Sun.com:

DENNIS RODMAN has revealed he slept with 2,000 women including 500 prostitutes - and broke his penis THREE times.

Newscaster, Robin Roberts, shares these illustrative gems from BrainyQuote.com:

"I've still got it. I refuse to lose."

"It was part of the reason I almost didn't go public with my diagnosis – I was embarrassed. I felt, 'Oh, I've always talked about exercising. And I got cancer.' And then I realized it's a great example of showing that cancer can hit anyone at any time."

"The combination of landing the biggest interview of my career and having a drill in my back reminds me that God only gives us what we can handle and that it helps to have a good sense of humor when we run smack into the absurdity of life."

Christopher Peter Meloni, is an American actor who is known for his television roles as NYPD Detective Elliot Stabler on the NBC police drama *Law & Order*. The depth and range of this astrological placement is well articulated from this excerpt from EntertainmentBookingAgency.com:

With rugged looks and an imposing presence, Christopher Meloni frequently found himself cast in tough guy roles, but when given the chance the actor displayed surprising range, particularly in comedy. Meloni broke in via television and eventually began landing bit parts in feature films like *Clean Slate*, *Junior* and *12 Monkeys*. Meloni all but cemented his stature as a Mafia-type thug with his vicious performance in the sexually-charged thriller *Bound*, which was followed by similarly brutish parts in series such as *NYPD Blue* and the miniseries *The Last Don*. By the end of the decade, however, Meloni took on two equally intense roles as characters who could not have been more diametrically opposed to each other. On *Oz*, Meloni gave a chilling performance as serial killer Chris Keller, and shortly thereafter he joined the cast of *Law & Order: Special Victims Unit* as Detective Elliot Stabler, a cop who tirelessly pursued perpetrators of the most heinous sexual crimes. As much as he would be known for his dramatically intense performances, Meloni would prove himself capable of delivering huge belly laughs with gut-busting cameos in films such as *Harold & Kumar Go to White Castle*. Though he left "SVU" after 12 seasons in 2011, Meloni always found himself in the enviable position of being able to work in both drama and comedy with equal facility.

Sometimes I see lineage aspects with Neptune. To be a ruler of a country and descended of the founder of a religion is a powerful combination: King Abdullah II of Jordan is the 42th descendant of Muhammad, the founder of Islam.

Zoë Tamerlis Lund, also known as Zoë Tamerlis and Zoë Tamerlaine, was an American musician, model, actress, author, producer, political activist and screenwriter. From Wikipedia.com, we see that the altered state this astrological placement seeks is often found in mind-altering drugs:

> Lund was unapologetic about her heroin addiction. She wrote at length about heroin and advocated it for legal recreational use in the USA, as well as romanticized its effects. "She loved heroin, she was killed by heroin," Ferrara said on her heroin addiction. "... Zoe was one of these people who thought heroin was the greatest thing in the world, and she did until the day she died. She was down on coke, down on everything, but you know, heroin was the elixir of life for her."

"I've known a lot of serious drug users," Richard Hell, a friend of Lund's, recalled in 2002, "but Zoë was Queen. You've got to admire someone as committed to it as she was. She didn't just LOVE heroin, she believed in it."

William Albert Ackman, an American hedge-fund manager, has these illuminating gems from GraciousQuotes.com:

"I am always prepared to do the right thing regardless of what other people think."

"If I believe that I am right, I will take it to the end of the earth until I am proven right."

"Let me win? That doesn't exist in my house. No one lets anyone win. Fight to the death."

"I'm a very straightforward person. I say precisely what I think. Sometimes it rubs people the wrong way."

"I'm an extremely, extremely persistent person. Extremely. And when I believe I am right, and it is important, I will go to the end of the earth."

Neptune in Sagittarius on the MC

These individuals can be visionaries extraordinaire with an optimistic wanderlust optimism that gives them a wonderful ability to succeed and thrive. They are masters of imagery and inspiration.

Kajol Devgan, known by the mononym as Kajol, is an Indian film actress who predominantly works in Hindi cinema and whose parents are famous actors as well. The ups and downs of a Bollywood actress are well played out in the tabloids for all to see.

Author, Christopher Rice, shows us the amazing width and breadth of the playing field for these individuals. The following comes from Wikipedia.com:

> Christopher Travis Rice is an American author. Rice has written novels including *A Density of Souls, The Snow Garden, Light Before Day, Blind Fall, The Moonlit Earth, The Heavens Rise,* and *The Vines.* His work spans multiple genres, including suspense, crime, supernatural thriller, and erotic romance. With his mother, Anne Rice, he also co-authored the historical horror novel *Ramses the Damned: The Passion of Cleopatra.*

David Paisley, is a Scottish actor, especially well known for roles as midwife Ben Saunders in *Holby City*, shows us other aspects of this astrological placement. The following comes from PinkNews.com:

> The *River City* and former *Holby* star took to Twitter on Thursday, March 12, urging followers to support trans rights by completing the Scottish government's GRA reform consultation.

"It's open to all, even if you're not from Scotland," he said.

"For every one of my followers that submits a response, DM me proof and I'll DM you a nude."

Immediately, Paisley was inundated with screenshots of completed consultation forms (it takes just minutes to fill out).

The actor – who regularly uses Twitter to campaign for trans rights – took the time to confirm that the nudes in question would be his own, and extended the offer until March 17, the day the consultation closes, due to his inbox being "full to the brim."

Replying to a comment from the Scottish pro-trans feminist group Sisters Scotland, which said it "will pass on the nudes", Paisley added: "Nothing worse than unsolicited nudes! No one wants to see that!

"Nudes are optional. Equality shouldn't be!"

Author and astrologer, Aurora Tower states:

And I do indeed feel like my Neptune (chart ruler!) in Sag on the MC is such a pivotal part of my life. I would describe it like the BROADNESS of that combination is essential to me, both of those energies being so diffuse and global/universal. A reason perhaps why I have always wanted to reach as mass an audience as possible with my work – hence working with mainstream magazines/apps/brands/websites to create unique astrology/spirituality content- rather than doing one-on-one readings... And also with doing higher education in that field- since I am (slowly) getting close to completion on my Master's Degree in Consciousness Studies.

Neptune in Capricorn on the MC

These individuals find a level of success at birth or find themselves on the fast track through the intricate machinations of the universe.

Lorraine Broussard Nicholson, is an American actress. We see many iterations of this maverick energy in this article from theList.com:

> Jack Nicholson's daughter grew up to be gorgeous
>
> Jack Nicholson's daughter likely knows all too well that being the child of a famous actor isn't easy, from being bombarded with paparazzi from a young age to always being asked about her dad in any interview she gives. And when your father is as highly-respected and well-known as Lorraine Nicholson's father, Jack Nicholson, is, then the spotlight on you is even harsher.
>
> However, Lorraine has made a name for herself as an actress, writer, and director outside of her father's shadow. And while she definitely has to answer a ton of questions about being the daughter of the legendary Jack Nicholson, she always handles it with grace.

So what exactly has Jack Nicholson's daughter been up to since she was a kid? From having bit roles in blockbuster films to having her own movies screened at international film festivals, Lorraine Nicholson has been busy in the film and entertainment world — and she shows no signs of stopping!

Multi-mavericks and Olympian athletes, Alev and Derya Kelter, show the mutable grace and agility this combination gives.

Actress, Dakota Fanning, showed the unmistakable maverick flair at an early age. The following comes from IMDB.com:

> Before her debut into the cinematic world, Dakota did her own acting around her house. She was very active for her age, and often put a blanket under her shirt and pretended to be having a baby, using her younger sister, Elle Fanning, who is also an actress now, as the baby. Dakota went to a playhouse near her home, where the children that attended put on a play every week to show to their parents. But the people running the playhouse noticed that Dakota stood out, and advised her parents to take her to an agency. They believed that she was extremely talented.

The sad life of Tegan Lane is maybe better understood when we understand the confusing lens of Neptune is at work and see the truth wins out in the end. The following comes from Astro.com:

Two days after giving birth to Tegan, her mother Keli Lane and her partner, rugby league player, Duncan Gillies, attended a friend's wedding and there was no sign of the baby. In 1999, Lane gave birth to another child and, after being refused an abortion in Queensland, she decided to put the child up for adoption. Lane advised a social worker that this was her first child and that Gillies was the father. Gillies denied the claims. The social worker, concerned for the health of the child, placed the baby in temporary foster care.

Keli Lane was an elite water polo player at national and international level. During a police interview, Lane claimed that she had given Tegan to the baby's father, a man called Andrew Morris, with whom she claimed to have had a brief affair. Lane was interviewed by police again in May 2003. This time she claimed the man's name was Andrew Norris; handing over the baby in Auburn Hospital carpark.

On 13 December 2010 a jury found Lane guilty of lying under oath in relation to documents dealing with her adopting out two other babies. The jury found Lane guilty of the murder of Tegan. On 15 April 2011 Lane was sentenced to 18 years' jail with a non-parole period of 13 years and five months.

As we have seen so many times before, there is once again another dynastic element for our last example for the sign in the life of Stella Banderas. The following comes from hola.com:

She's Hollywood royalty. Not only are her parents legends in the industry, her grandmother Tippi Hedren is a Hollywood icon. She starred in Alfred Hitchcock's 1963 hit *The Birds*.

Neptune in Aquarius on the MC

This maverick placement would likely be of great benefit to individuals like media moguls and producers; ones who influence the masses. We have no individuals with this placement.

Neptune in Pisces on the MC

The spiritual world in which these individuals operate is nothing like what most people can understand. They can get lost in the world of illusions generated by sex, drugs, alcohol, or find themselves understanding the intricate matrix in which we live. These people are deep divers and their visions are for the masses. They are very dreamy and attractive to others in ways that will work perfectly with video and imagery. They have the ability to affect large numbers of people. Neptune went into Pisces in February 2012, and will remain there until 2025. We have no examples of individuals with this placement.

Pluto

Pluto has received a bad rap lately from the astronomic and scientific communities. I will not get into who is right or wrong, I can only report that Pluto is one of the most powerful planets in the zodiac. Anyone who has gone through a Pluto transit or has a strongly aspected Pluto knows the heavy, deep intensity this planet brings to your life. Dante's says it well in the *Divine Comedy*, "All hope abandon ye who enter here." Hope is a luxury for which Pluto is unwilling to accept. Another way to look at this is one must surrender to Pluto. As the experience occurs, you may feel like you are being slowly skinned (or any other slow and painful way to die, but doesn't end up killing you!) but after the process is over, you understand why you had to lose that skin or "die" in that way. If you have ever been with a woman when she gives birth, there is the amazing transition of the woman expressing feeling like she is going to die and cannot do it and then, after the birth, she says something like, "Oh that wasn't that bad" (thank God for hormones, otherwise no woman would never have more than one child!). By the way, birth is in the realm of Pluto and the sign it rules, Scorpio. The other thing I like to say about Pluto is that whatever you hold onto, Pluto will make sure that your fingertips to your arms and even more are burned away until you are willing to relinquish, release, and surrender that which you had been holding so steadily, be it a thought pattern, a relationship (or a few), work, or whatever.

If you consider Pluto to be a nuclear bomb which destroys that which lies in its path, consider what happens when you have Mr. Hades on an angle! I call these people agents of transformation. Depending upon their angle, and other planetary situations, some Plutonians are more outward projecting than others. For the ones who don't project? Don't worry, they still have an effect on people. These introverted Plutonians do not even have to do anything, their mere presence creates transformation in those around them.

Pluto in your chart shows how you transform and where you do it by house, how you destroy for your highest good, how you are ruthless, how you express phoenix-like abilities, how and by house, where you can go deep and how you are a nuclear reactor or bomb. Pluto, ruler of the eighth house of death, rebirth, and regeneration is also one of the rulers of Scorpio. Whether giving us a glimpse of living on worlds far, far away, like Gene Roddenberry's Pluto conjunct his Cancer AS, or giving us a glimpse of what happens when a large man transforms himself into an outrageous drag queen, in the likes of which no one on our planet has ever witnessed. Divine has

Pluto in Leo on the MC. He literally transforms (Pluto) his individualized personal self (Leo) in the way the world sees him in his work (MC).

Unfortunately, with an orbit of some 248 years, there are many signs for which we will have no maverick Pluto examples.

ANYONE with a Pluto conjunct an angle is a powerful maverick. They affect, transform and inspire people by their mere presence in ways they cannot begin to imagine.

We will now look at the angle placements of Pluto throughout the zodiac from the point of view of the Ascendant (AS).

Pluto in Aries on the AS

Like sitting in a room with glowing kryptonite, the forceful will of this astrological placement would be challenging to ignore. A literal force of nature, these are the individuals who are great at getting things done, regardless of the means.

Pluto in Taurus on the AS

These individuals have an innate understanding of what lies within. Their piercing minds are able to unlock any form of nature. These individuals would be great therapists and scientists as they can get to the root of things.

Visionary inventor, Nikola Tesla, would be a great example of this astrological placement, as it also speaks to the problems/limitations these individuals would likely encounter from others.

Pluto in Gemini on the AS

The transformational ability of this astrological placement is not to be underestimated, nor the range of expression as we will see in our examples.

With four maverick planets lead by forceful Pluto, we understand how Achmed Sukarno, had the perseverance and determination to help emancipate Indonesia from the Dutch, and become its first president.

Gemini is the questioning mind and Pluto is that which seeks to distill things to their ultimate truth, as beautifully played out in the life of German theoretical physicist (which is also a play on this astrological placement!) Werner Heisenberg. From Wikipedia.com we learn the following about Heisenberg:

> [Heisenberg]... one of the key pioneers of quantum mechanics. He published his work in 1925 in a breakthrough paper. In the subsequent series of papers with Max Born and Pascual Jordan, during the same year, this matrix formulation of quantum mechanics was substantially elaborated.

Of course, we find Ed Gein in this astrological placement. The following comes from AllThatIsInteresting.com:

> Gein's legacy is primarily one of unspeakably unprecedented sexual deviance and shockingly gruesome carnage. This was the first time normal American citizens were even confronted with the idea of turning a person's skin into a mask, necrophilia, or using human bones as part of various kitchen utensils.
>
> The canon of American serial killers, true crime, and their overflow into countless artistic media arguably began with Ed Gein.
>
> From novels like *American Psycho* to music groups like Cannibal Corpse, and classic horror films such as *Psycho* and *The Texas Chainsaw Massacre* — Ed Gein's legacy was just as much about tangible disgust as it was an opportunity to cathartically explore how vile humanity can be from within the confines of safe, artistic expression.

The strength and power of this astrological placement was well portrayed by legendary actor, Laurence Olivier. The following comes from NYTimes.com (the title says it all!):

Laurence Olivier: Scene-Stealer Extraordinaire

"Is it safe?"

The query begins one of the movie's most discomforting scenes. In it, a white-haired gent, moving with unhurried and ominous purpose, unpacks a set of dentistry implements and sets to work on a young man who is bound to a chair.

"Is it safe?" he asks. "Is it safe?"

To anyone who has ever visited a dentist, the episode that follows — the torment the older man visits on his baffled and terrified patient/prisoner, who is played by Dustin Hoffman — is almost unbearable to watch, in large part owing to the preternatural *sang-froid* of the tormenter. The film, from 1976, was *Marathon Man*, a thriller involving diamonds taken from Jews during World War II, a history student whose brother is a government agent, and a fugitive Nazi war criminal — our brutal antagonist, Szell, a former concentration camp dentist played by Laurence Olivier, who was nominated for an Academy Award for his performance and won a Golden Globe.

Pluto in Cancer on the AS

These individuals created empires and worlds, transforming our ideas about home and family to a larger clan.

While multi-maverick and director, Gene Roddenberry, is best known for writing *Star Trek* and other-worldly homes, he exhibited another aspect of this Pluto in the first house in Cancer placement: walking away from death. I suggest reading the article from the MilitaryTimes.com which thoroughly reviews the events leading up to Gene crashing his plane Yankee Doodle (a Cancerian song!) in World War II and surviving.

From an article from Refinery29.com, we learn a bit more about multi-maverick actress Judy Garland's early years:

> She was set on a path to stardom at a young age.
>
> On June 10, 1922, a child named Frances Ethel Gumm was born to two vaudeville performers in Grand Rapids, Minnesota. She was one of three siblings. Gumm was a performer from the start — her first stage performance was at two-and-a-half years old. Her home life was tumultuous. Her father, Frank, had affairs with young men.
>
> In 1926, the Gumms left town to escape scandal and headed to California. Gumm's mother, Ethel, quickly tried to shape her daughters into stars. Ethel, a controlling stage mom, was the first person to put 10-year-old Frances on a diet of pills: Amphetamines in the morning, sleeping pills at night. The pattern would continue once she signed with MGM and her diet was monitored.

Multiple maverick and media mogul, Merv Griffin, who has the Sun exactly on this spot as well, shows the powerful privacy this astrological placement can create. This excerpt comes from Reuters.com and is a thorough discussion of Griffin's homosexuality:

> Around the office, Merv's being gay was understood but rarely discussed (and certainly never with him). We knew nothing of his relationships because he guarded his privacy fiercely, and we didn't pry.

Merv's secret gay life was widely known throughout showbiz culture, if not the wider America. It gained traction in 1991 when he was targeted in a pair of lawsuits: by *Dance Fever* host Denny Terrio, alleging sexual harassment; and by assistant Brent Plott seeking $200 million in palimony. Both ultimately were dismissed.

Over the past 16 years of his life, however, Griffin deflected the sexuality questions with a quip, determining that his private life remained nobody's business. He certainly didn't owe us an explanation, but maybe he owed it to himself to remove the suffocating veil he'd been forced to hide behind throughout his adult life. Then again, Merv carved his niche in the entertainment world at a time when being gay wasn't OK, when disclosure was unthinkable, and the allegation alone could deep-six one's career.

From theGuardian.com we learn about how actor, Jerry Lewis, yet another media individual with many maverick planets, worked with this energy in one of his final films:

Later, in the early 1980s, he was superbly cast by Martin Scorsese in *The King of Comedy,* as the late-night talk show host who is kidnapped by an obsessive fan, played by Robert De Niro. Lewis plays utterly against type, but entirely with a different kind of Hollywood stereotype: the hard-faced, cynical and charmless show business kingpin for whom comedy and celebrity are both wearisome, lucrative businesses from which the joy has long since been strip-mined. It was not a comeback as such, at least in part because the movie itself was not properly appreciated at the time. But Lewis had a sensational charisma. And he did, in his hatchet-faced way, present the metaphorical properties of his own reputation: bound and gagged by De Niro and his partner-in-crime, Sandra Bernhard, held hostage by a younger generation, who derided him, or admired him, or idolized him, but at all events made him mute, refused to let him be fashionable or accepted on his own terms.

OutRightGeekery.com has this wonderful excerpt about multi-maverick and fetish artist, Eric Stanton, that articulates yet another facet of this placement:

> While always interested in the female form, Stanton began his career drawing fighting women. As he moved into the industry, he was called on to provide bondage material for publishers. This eventually morphed into S&M images that I can only describe as true fetish work. Finally, Stanton came back to his original love for fighting women and that seems to be where his best work was done.

Jane Mary Gardam, is an English writer of children's and adult fiction, who shares these archetypally relevant gems from BrainyQuote.com:

"Stories of all lengths and depths come from different parts of the cave. For a novel, you must lay in mental, physical and spiritual provision as for a siege or for a time of hectic explosions, while a short story is, or can be, a steady, timed flame like the lighting of a blow lamp on a building site full of dry tinder."

"For years, there was no man in the house when my husband was off on law cases in the Far East. Without writing, I would have been bored and unfaithful, maybe both, and the children would have been hideously over-protected."

"I gave myself to my children. It happens to some women."

"When I was young and the empire was beginning to disintegrate, the idea was absolutely unbelievable, particularly to children who'd been taught that the sun never set… that's what all my books are about, the end of empire."

Poly-maverick Cancerian, Ross Perot, actually also died while the Sun was again in his sun sign on July 9, 2019. The following comes from BrainyQuote.com where we have some of his insightful statements (the last one is so perfect for Capricorn, the sign opposite):

"The activist is not the man who says the river is dirty. The activist is the man who cleans up the river."

"The debt is like a crazy aunt we keep down in the basement. All the neighbors know she's there, but nobody wants to talk about her."

"The most successful people in the world aren't usually the brightest. They are the ones who persevere."

"Guys, just remember, if you get lucky, if you make a lot of money, if you get out and buy a lot of stuff – it's gonna break. You got your biggest, fanciest mansion in the world. It has air conditioning. It's got a pool. Just think of all the pumps that are going to go out. Or go to a yacht basin any place in the world. Nobody is smiling, and I'll tell you why. Something broke that morning. The generator's out; the microwave oven doesn't work… Things just don't mean happiness."

Actress, Barbara Eden, shows the effect of having Pluto and her AS conjunct. The following comes from CountryThangDaily.com:

Barbara Eden arrived in Hollywood in the 1950s. However, during one of her first professional meetings with a casting director at Warner Brothers, the young actress was told she wasn't beautiful enough to make it as an entertainer.

"He said, 'You're a very nice little girl from San Francisco, but I really think you should go home and marry the boy at home. This isn't the town for you,'" Eden recalled. "He said, 'You're just not pretty enough.

You're pretty, but you're pretty like any girl out in the Avenues.'"

The casting director showed her a photo of his daughter and told her, "This is what they want!"

Eden admitted that she was stunned by the man's admission, yet she laughed as she remembered how the photo showed off his daughter's full cleavage. "I thought, 'Why am I crying? I'm not here because I'm pretty or ugly. I'm here because I'm a human, and I act,'" Eden recalled.

I ran across a 2016 article from DailyMail.co.uk that discusses a very Plutonic experience about English actor, John Inman:

> Yesterday Inman's family said people had been 'jumping on the bandwagon' following the Jimmy Savile scandal. They also criticised police, accusing them of a celebrity witch-hunt.
>
> His sister-in-law Patricia Inman, 75, said: 'It was very upsetting when you knew he was a person that would never do such a thing, it would never cross his mind... I found it very hard to comprehend that people would ever suspect something like this of him."
>
> She added: "I'm pleased they are dropping the case but they should never have been looking into it in the first place. It was a complete waste of time and money."

Victor Emmanuel, Prince of Naples, plays this position at the IC of Cancer with Pluto perfectly, as the son of the last king of Italy.

From British television host, David Frost's obituary in theGuardian.com we learn the following:

Frost could never be accused of being a stuck-up or patrician broadcaster. He was a *bon vivant*, smoker of big cigars, dapper dresser, chum of the rich and famous, and so much of a jet-setter that, for a while, he was Concorde's most frequent flier, travelling from London and New York an average of 20 times a year for 20 years. No wonder he told one interviewer that he was "not driven, but flown."

His greatest journalistic coup came in 1977 when he interviewed the disgraced U.S. president Richard Nixon and induced Tricky Dicky to confess in public his guilt over Watergate. "I let down the country," Nixon told Frost. "I let the American people down and I have to carry that burden for the rest of my life." Some drew parallels between interviewer and interviewee: "Apart from the consideration that Frost is much nicer," wrote Clive James, reviewing the interviews in 1977, "the two are remarkably similar. They are both essentially role-players. At a level too deep for speech, they understand each other well."

Pluto in Leo on the AS

This is the *me generation* in all its glory. The branding of this energy is significant and far reaching. From the slow glowing embers that easily warms and entices, to the roaring bonfire presence, to the literal force of nature that screams: *Here I am!* This is a brilliant placement for an actor.

We experience this visceral quality in any role we witness film star, Al Pacino, play. Whether portraying the ruthless son Michael Corleone in *The Godfather*, Sonny Wortzik in *Dog Day Afternoon* or playing Satan himself in *The Devil's Advocate*, we know that Pacino will give us a most transformative cinematic adventure in the realms hithertofore unrecognized.

The astounding brilliance this astrological position gives to an individual is well illustrated in the life of astrologer, Jim Lewis. The following comes from Astrocartography. com:

> But it was Astro*Carto*Graphy that made Jim Lewis renowned around the world. It was his greatest success and yet he was also a victim of the work. Jim was strongly litigious and considerable resources and intense emotion went into protecting his trademark. And he was not immune to the negative potential on A*C*G's 'planetary power lines'. In the mid '80s he was struck by a vehicle while crossing Military Road, in Sydney, Australia on his Mars Ascending line. In a strange way he felt that his illness was brought on by the pressures of the A*C*G business. Behind the tragedy, there is a cruel irony that someone so cerebral (Sun and Moon in Air) should have been affected by a brain tumor at the age of 54 years.
>
> His work will live on. It is a little known fact that his Astro*Carto*Graphy handbook that accompanies

the world A*C*G maps has been the most successful astrological publication outside sun sign titles and the ephemerides. Besides the continuing operation of his three A*C*G licensees in Oregon, London, and Zürich and his many certified A*C*G interpreters, he will be published posthumously. His friend and certified Astro*Carto*Grapher, Erin Sullivan intends to complete and publish his final work *The Psychology of Astro*Carto*Graphy* as part of the Penguin Arkana series.

Robert Currey, Certified A*C*G Interpreter Equinox, Isle of Man.

Italian actor, Franco Nero, shares these insightful gems from BrainyQuote.com:

"Everyone has a first love, and mine was the western. When I was a child and dreamed of the movies, it was always as a cowboy on a white horse."

"Every western I did and will do; I will do it for the never ending young kid inside of me."

"There were many, many other *Django* films following mine, with other actors and directors, but there is only one *Django*."

From his website michaelcrichton.com we see some of the penetrating qualities of this astrological placement:

John Michael Crichton was an American author and filmmaker. His books have sold over 200 million copies worldwide, and over a dozen have been adapted into films. His literary works are usually within the science fiction, techno-thriller, and medical fiction genres, and heavily feature technology. His novels often explore that technology and failures of human interaction with it, especially resulting in catastrophes with biotechnology. Many of his novels have medical or scientific underpinnings, reflecting his medical training and scientific background.

From PartiallyExaminedLife.com comes this excerpt about the powerful comedian and actor, Steve Martin:

I just finished reading Steve Martin's autobiography *Born Standing Up – a comic's life*, an honest and direct memoir about his youth and early life experiences which shaped the development of his unique comedic style. The book covers the time from his childhood through to his 30's when he walked away from stage performing to do movies and other media. I am old enough to remember the phenomenon that was Steve Martin at his stand-up peak, having reached teenage awareness with liberal and progressive enough parents who allowed me to watch *Saturday Night Live* and got cable with HBO. No one who (over)used the catch phrases 'Well excuuuuuse me!" or "I'm a wild and crazy guy!" or dropped a "Grandpa bought a rubber... duck" in conversation can forget Martin's truly novel and paradigm shattering form of expression – it hardly does it justice now to call it simply comedy or entertainment.

It is not my intention to give a full-fledged review of this book. I'd like, rather, to partially examine something in the book that surprised me and is relevant to our PEL universe – Steve Martin studied philosophy in college during his 'formative' years and attributes a certain amount of influence to the discipline on his development. Although this is not a typical 'reading' and the topic might be somewhat unorthodox, I consider discussing Philosophy & Comedy perfectly legitimate and this a suitable text for the endeavor.

Charles Denton "Tex" Watson, is an American murderer who was a central member of the Manson family. The fates show their handiwork in this maverick's life. Driving down Sunset Boulevard, he picked up a hitchhiker who happened to be fellow maverick, Dennis Wilson, of the Beach Boys and there, according to AllThatIsINteresting.com they drove to Wilson's home and:

> In the living room, Watson found a man sitting on the floor with his guitar, surrounded by five or six young women. "He looked up," Watson later recalled, "and the first thing I felt was a sort of gentleness, an embracing kind of acceptance and love."
>
> Another man at the house introduced them: "This is Charlie, Charlie Manson."

The sovereignty of this astrological position is well stated in this excerpt from chess grandmaster, Bobby Fischer's obituary from LATimes.com:

> Kirsan Ilyumzhinov, president of the World Chess Federation, called Fischer "a phenomenon and an epoch in chess history, and an intellectual giant I would rank next to Newton and Einstein."
>
> Once described by biographer Frank Brady as "the pride and sorrow of American chess," Fischer enjoyed mythical status in the chess world despite turning his back on it for two decades after becoming the world champion at 29.

From A-Team.fandom.com/wiki, we learn the following about controversial former evangelist preacher and actor, Hugh Marjoe Ross Gortner:

> Generally known as Marjoe Gortner; born January 14, 1944, is a former revivalist and actor who first gained attention during the late 1940s when, aged four, he became the youngest-known ordained preacher. He then gained notoriety in the 1970s when he starred in *Marjoe*, an Oscar-winning behind-the-scenes documentary about the lucrative business of Pentecostal preaching.

We once again see the dynastic element of a maverick life in former U.S. president, George W. Bush. While he is now not the worst example of a president, we see that with his Mercury here that he may have preferred a different spotlight than his family sought for him.

British politician, Edwina Curie, sheds some light on this astrological placement with these statements from AZQuotes.com:

"One man's priority is another man's extravagance."

"My message to businessmen of this country when they go abroad on business is that there is one thing above all they can take with them to stop them catching AIDS, and that is the wife."

Multi-maverick and entertainer, Jackie Curtis, presented both sides of his sexuality performing for others, paving the way for gay and transgender awareness, and rights – simply by being him/herself.

Whether in her roles or in her life, Glenn Close cannot help beam her Plutonian force. These quotes from BrainyQuote.com give us insights into this archetype:

"The best thing I have is the knife from *Fatal Attraction*. I hung it in my kitchen. It's my way of saying, 'Don't mess with me.'"

"It always amazes me to think that every house on every street is full of so many stories; so many triumphs and tragedies, and all we see are yards and driveways."

"With the hugely talented women I've worked with or observed, it's not a question about temperament or ego; it's a question about getting it right. If they've got a reputation for being difficult it's usually because they just don't suffer fools."

"There's something about a catharsis that is very important."

The elusive quality of this astrological placement when mixed with one married to a member of the royal family, is beautifully displayed in the life of Camilla Parker-Bowles. The following comes from Boigraphy.com:

Camilla has been referred to as the Duchess of Cornwall, since the title Princess of Wales was seen as belonging to Diana. In addition, it was announced that Camilla would be known as Princess Consort when Charles took the throne. Yet she has become more popular, and rumors abound that Charles would like to have her as his queen. Only time will tell what title will be viewed as suitable for Camilla if and when Charles begins his reign.

Please look at the other mavericks with this astrological placement to see how they worked with this energy. They include: Laura Nyro, Al Gore, Jewelle Gomez, Peter Gabriel, Julie Walters, Richard Branson, Christopher Reeve, Jim Jarmusch, Michael Moore, George Galloway, and Annise Parker.

Pluto in Virgo on the AS

This placement is about potential. Virgo is the sign of multiplicity and Pluto is that which lies buried and unseen. When these individuals are able to pull the myriad threads into a cohesive whole, they create pure gold.

Our first example is also one of our earliest. In the world of art, poly-maverick artist, Albrecht Durer, is considered the German Renaissance artist. Durer revolutionized the ways in which art could be reproduced through etchings, and he was even famous as an artist in his own lifetime. An old-world rock star.

Actor, Tim Robbins, expresses the discriminating approach to life and other aspects of this astrological placement in these enlightening statements from AZQuotes.com:

> "There's nothing more boring than unintelligent actors, because all they have to talk about is themselves and acting. There have to be other things."

> "What you get is what you get. What you do with what you get, that's more the point."

> "I love iconoclasts. I love individuals. I love people that are true to themselves, whatever the cost."

> "Notice what no one else notices and you'll know what no one else knows."

ASTROLOGICAL MAVERICKS

"My philosophy is, don't take no for an answer and be willing to sacrifice your entire project for freedom."

The quiescent nature of this astrological placement is well represented by the life and death of John F. Kennedy, Jr.

Persnickety, exacting, and fabulous are some of the words one could use to describe fashion designer, Isaac Mizrahi.

The ways in which maverick individuals change the world is clearly visible in the life of singer k.d. lang. As the Ascendant is all about how the world sees you and you see the world, the following excerpt from NYTimes.com describes this beautifully:

> Gay men were familiar. Gay women, not really. And certainly not gay women as magnificently sensual as Ms. Lang. In that same decade, Ellen DeGeneres would become famous, partly by being all-American affable, never an erotic threat. Even singing her fierce "Come to My Window," Melissa Etheridge hewed closely to the image of a traditional country singer. But K. D. Lang in a man-tailored suit was something else altogether.
>
> It was more than startling, in the summer of 1993, to lay eyes on the infamous Herb Ritts portrait of Ms. Lang and Cindy Crawford on the cover of Vanity Fair, in which the supermodel, clad in a black teddy, mimes shaving the pop star, in shirt sleeves and pinstripes. The image is languorous and impish: Ms. Lang leans her head back onto Ms. Crawford's breasts, eyes closed, her smile beatific. Straight, gay or bisexual — many responded feverishly to the image, now considered a classic of both magazine publishing and queer history.

Wherever we find Pluto in the chart, we see a place where one can withstand and endure, sometimes beyond the breaking point, but Pluto doesn't see to break us, but rather Pluto get us to surrender to that part of us that is something more, something grand, something we could never had attained without having endured whatever hardship we did. Like a diamond formed by exceedingly pressurized carbon, we show our brilliance when we are squeezed to the point that we must transform into our new self. Pluto gives us the power to face whatever the IT is in our lives. This is well articulated in an article about our next maverick from the Guardian.com:

> Eddie Izzard relishes a challenge. The transgender hero has done standup in French and German, run dozens of marathons, and is now in a period drama with Judi Dench. But, he reveals, his can-do attitude has a melancholy source...
>
> There was a literal turning point in Eddie Izzard's lifelong pursuit of personal freedom. It came one afternoon in 1985 when he had gone out for the first time in a dress and heels and full makeup down Islington high street. He was 23 and he had been planning – and avoiding – that moment for just about as long as he could remember. The turning point came after he was chased down the road by some teenage girls who had caught him changing back into his jeans in the public toilets and wanted to let him know he was weird. That pursuit ended when eventually, faced with the screamed question "Hey, why were you dressed as

a woman?" He decided simply to stop running and turn and explain himself.

He spun around to give an answer, but before he got many words out the girls had run in the opposite direction. The experience taught him some things: that there was power in confronting fear rather than avoiding it; and that from then on he would never let other people define him. After that afternoon, he says, he not only felt he could face down the things that scared him, he went chasing after them: street performing, standup comedy, marathon running, political activism, improvising his stage show in different languages – all these things felt relatively easy after that original coming out as what he calls "transvestite or transgender." "You think, if I can do something that hard, but positive – maybe I can do anything."

A poet will utilize the myriad opportunities and depths of this astrological placement, as did Reginald Shepherd.

The never-ending pursuit of perfection is not just for Lexus automobiles, but could also be a motto for this astrological placement (or any other Pluto-Virgo combination). The following comes from NHL.com:

Nevin Markwart has taken a road less traveled, but no less interesting, since he retired from the NHL after eight seasons, most with the Boston Bruins, following the 1991-92 season.

After earning a Master of Business Administration from Northeastern University, Markwart had forged a second career in finance. Now he is working in the computer field after earning a Master of Science in cybersecurity from Brown University in 2019.

"I was always strong academically," the 55-year-old said. "I was actually offered entrance into Princeton [University] when I was 16, but where I grew up in Western Canada, to be quite frank, we didn't know what that was and so we turned it down; it was just too far away. My first year on the Bruins, I actually took a computer science course at Boston College. It was an evening course, but it was very difficult to make the classes because we are on the road quite a bit as an NHL team.

"That experience resulted in me concluding that I needed to save up enough money being an NHL hockey player so that I could pay for myself to go to school when I was done, and that is essentially what I did."

Poly-maverick, John Barrowman, also exhibits a desire to experience a range of expression in his life, as seen in his Wikipedia entry describing him as, "a Scottish-American actor, singer, presenter, author, and comic book writer."

Our only other female entry for this astrological position is the actress that everyone loved to call a bitch (perfect nickname for this combination). From ABCNews.

com we learn that actress, Shannon Doherty, did some soul searching when diagnosed with stage IV breast cancer:

> "I was like, 'OK, do I have good karma? Do I have bad karma? Why would I have bad karma?' I started taking stock of my life and the things I'd done, and the things I hadn't done. How I was with people," Doherty said.

Pluto in Libra on the AS

Of course, most individuals who have Libra rising are beautiful. When Pluto is placed on the AS, we find individuals who have a very intriguingly powerful presence. These individuals are dedicated to eroding the barriers to harmonious relationships, whether their own or others. Wherever they see imbalance and discord, they seek not only to restore but to improve.

We see this well presented in the following statement from the website of consummate actor and environmentalist, Leonardo DiCaprio:

> The Leonardo DiCaprio Foundation is dedicated to the long-term health and wellbeing of all Earth's inhabitants. Through collaborative partnerships, we support innovative projects that protect vulnerable wildlife from extinction, while restoring balance to threatened ecosystems and communities. LDF works in 4 key areas: Species, Oceans, Wildlands, and Climate.

Who could forget the beautiful and striking child who uttered the words, "They're here…" Actress Heather O'Rourke died at 12 from a routine surgery.

Actor Freddie Prinz, Jr. shares these insights from BrainyQuote.com:

"Personally, when things upset me, I get quiet and closed off. I have nothing to say, and a chill sets in while I think about what's going on."

"It only takes 30 seconds to pluck my eyebrows, but it hurts. I have to tweeze 'em in the middle once a week. Otherwise, I look like Bert from *Sesame Street*.

"Life is not about making dough or how many movies you can make in a year. It's about finding someone that you can share things with."

"I think success shows a person's true colors."

Double maverick and actress, Jennifer Carpenter, is best known for playing Debra Morgan on the Showtime drama series Dexter. Interesting and complex relationships are definitely part of this placement. Jennifer is the sister of Dexter in the show and married to Michael Hall, the actor who plays Dexter, in real life.

Pluto lends the power and determination needed to succeed in sports or anything else that demands intense focus. Tennis superstar, Venus Williams, shares these insights from BrainyQuote.com:

"Some people say I have attitude, maybe I do... but I think you have to. You have to believe in yourself when no one else does – that makes you a winner right there."

"Life is challenging but I'm always up for a challenge."

"In life, there is no such thing as impossible; it's always possible."

"You have to let fear go. Another lesson is you just have to believe in yourself; you just have to. There's no way around it. No matter how things are stacked against you, you just have to every time."

"I love seeing people be successful! I love that. It's wonderful. There's enough room for everybody."

"Win pretty, win ugly, just win."

Pluto in Scorpio on the AS

Pluto is the ruler of Scorpio, which lends a most comfortable intensity to these individuals. Pluto can erupt forth with brilliance or take some time to develop. These mavericks are forces of nature and they transform everything in the process.

Singer, Justin Bieber, has the added benefit of having his North Node conjunct this placement and all hanging out in the deeply mysterious 12th house (yes, he is a Pisces as well), so it is no surprise that we learn the following about Bieber from Wikipedia.com:

> With Bieber's debut EP *My World*, released in late 2009, Bieber became the first artist to have seven songs from a debut record chart on the Billboard Hot 100.

As I am writing this, I see that our next maverick is currently in the headlines. From Tribune.com.pk comes this piece on Bilawal Bhutto Zardari who has Venus conjunct his Leo MC:

> Bilawal said the government was trying to "force him into exile" from the region "so as to pave the way for election fraud," adding that the government may try to use the courts to expel him from the province.

Pluto in Sagittarius on the AS

These individuals have the ability to revolutionize the ways in which we experience that which is foreign, unfamiliar and/or provoking of higher thoughts and philosophies.

The strength of conviction and width and depth of this astrological placement is well portrayed by U.S. President, James Madison. The following comes from the WhiteHouse.gov:

> When delegates to the Constitutional Convention assembled at Philadelphia, the 36-year-old Madison took frequent and emphatic part in the debates.

Madison made a major contribution to the ratification of the Constitution by writing, with Alexander Hamilton and John Jay, the Federalist essays. In later years, when he was referred to as the "Father of the Constitution," Madison protested that the document was not "the off-spring of a single brain," but "the work of many heads and many hands."

In Congress, he helped frame the Bill of Rights and enact the first revenue legislation. Out of his leadership in opposition to Hamilton's financial proposals, which he felt would unduly bestow wealth and power upon northern financiers, came the development of the Republican, or Jeffersonian, Party.

From USAToday.com we learn the following about Prince Michael Jackson:

[Jackson]... graduated with cum laude honors from Loyola Marymount University in Los Angeles Saturday with a bachelor's degree in business administration.

"I met so many people and learned so much that the experience alone is worth it," he wrote alongside graduation pictures with his loved ones, including grandmother Katherine Jackson. "I wish I could thank everyone that helped me make it to the end but I can't and unfortunately they're not all pictured here."

Prince added: "Honestly I can't tell you if all of it was worth it yet but I am proud of my degree as I believe it is a testament to my dedication and discipline."

Pluto in Capricorn on the AS

These are individuals born sometime between March 2008, and January 2024, for which we have no examples as of yet. They will likely have a shrewd and calculating manner about them. This is a great placement for a child of wealthy and successful parents and is a good sign for those who are "movers and shakers" in the world. As a cardinal sign, one can see the innate ability to create and build.

Pluto in Aquarius on the AS

These mavericks will be born sometime between April 2023, and January 2044. This is a perfect arrangement for a philosopher or major reformer. Their presence will be like an electric frisson and their mental faculties are likely quite profound – especially in their ability to look at the organizational framework of anything and understand what needs to be done at any level within that framework. Like a holographic or x-ray mind, the powers of perception will be highly accentuated.

Pluto in Pisces on the AS

These deep diving, transformative healers, or lightly tethered journey-weathered individuals will be a force for the collective. Masters of social media (whatever that becomes!) and gurus of bygone ages, they will be born between March 2043, and Feb 2068.

We will now look at the angle placements of Pluto throughout the zodiac from the point of view of the Imum Coeli (IC).

Pluto in Aries on the IC

These are individuals who likely prefer to remain behind the scenes, but are THE power in their families or clans. Archetypal expressions indicate a powerful ruler, mafia, or gang boss, detective or detective writer or actor playing one. Incredibly instinctual and insightful.

Pluto in Taurus on the IC

This is a very inwardly focused power that will be felt by others. On its highest level, this is the conscious alchemist, understanding the perfect balance of personal and impersonal as well as the transformation of matter and form. Like a volcanic mountain in the distance that is ever smoldering, these individuals are not easily swayed.

Pluto in Gemini on the IC

These mavericks will likely be seekers of knowledge, power, and ideas. They can identify the thematic resonance in seemingly discordant places.

From Wikipedia.com we readily see these archetypes for the mystic, Manly Palmer Hall:

> Manly Palmer Hall (March 18, 1901 – August 29, 1990) was a Canadian-born author, lecturer, astrologer and mystic. He is best known for his 1928 work *The Secret Teachings of All Ages*. Over his 70 year career, he gave thousands of lectures, including two at Carnegie Hall, and published over 150 volumes. In 1934, he founded The Philosophical Research Society in Los Angeles, which he dedicated to the "Truth Seekers of All Time," with a research library, lecture hall, and publishing house. Many of his lectures can be found online and his books are still in print.

We see the Geminian multiplicity well-articulated in the life of multi-maverick and writer, William Plomer. The following comes from Wikipedia.com:

> [Plomer]... was a South African and British author, known as a novelist, poet and literary editor. He also wrote a series of librettos for Benjamin Britten. He wrote some of his poetry under the pseudonym Robert Pagan.

ASTROLOGICAL MAVERICKS

From PoetryFoundation.org we learn the following about these powerful chthonic forces, which created the diamonds from the carbon, in the life of Lorine Niedecker:

> She endured real poverty which, coupled with her relative isolation from other writers and the beauty of her natural surroundings, had a notable impact on her work. Praised for its vivid imagery, subtle rhythms, and spare language, her poems are "whittled clean," according to Kenneth Cox. Concerned with the distillation of images and thoughts into concise expression, Niedecker described her work as a "condensery," and several critics have compared her poetry to the delicate yet concrete verse of Chinese and Japanese writers.

The writing theme, of course, continues with author, Helen Knothe, whose approach and commitment to living as simply as possible, is yet another example of this astrological placement.

This placement gives one an ear to heaven's orchestra, as well displayed in the life of composer, Dmitri Shostakovich. According to Wikipedia.com:

> He is regarded as one of the major composers of the 20th century, with a unique harmonic language and an historic importance due to his years of work under Stalin.

Pluto in Cancer on the IC

There is a bind with these individuals in that home is both a place of deep security and the fear of it being taken away. The clan and the world they seek to save may not be readily visible to those around them. The need for control for some of these individuals is of utmost importance given what they likely endured in their childhood.

From Factinate.com, we learn a couple of facts about triple threat and double maverick, Lena Horne:

> Her childhood was far from perfect. Teddy Horne was a shameless gambler who frequently squandered their money and then abandoned his wife and little daughter when the girl was only three years old. As Horne's mother was an actress in a traveling black theatre troupe, she simply couldn't take care of Lena on her own. Instead, Horne was mostly raised by her maternal grandparents.

> From a young age, Lena Horne never felt like she fit in. As her star rose, she not only was denied roles because she was Black, she was also accused of "passing" as white by her fellow African American entertainers. It seemed like she could never win, and Horne struggled to find her place while chasing her dreams.

From his obituary in theGuardian.com, we learn the following about evangelist, Billy Graham:

Graham was handsome and eloquent, but his proclamations were strident, and his theme – "what would happen to you if you died on your way home?" – spoke of an unbelievably hardline deity. His favourite text then, and throughout his world tours, remained: "God so loved the world that He gave his only begotten Son, that whosoever believeth in Him should not perish but have everlasting life." There was little place for a questioning faith or political action, but he had the ring of someone who was totally sincere.

In an interesting twist on this astrological placement, we learn this from double agent spy, George Blake from Independent. co.uk:

Blake is the last survivor of the group of British spies who turned traitor for ideological reasons. But unlike Kim Philby and the rest of the "Cambridge Five," Blake says he never really felt part of the British establishment, and indeed still refuses to accept the label of a traitor, saying that one has to belong to a country first in order to betray it.

From his obituary at CNN.com, we learn about poly-maverick and auto industry executive, Lee Iacocca:

Heavily involved with creating the Ford Mustang and Chrysler minivan, he was more than an automotive icon. He was, for a time, a part of our national fabric. During his tenure, Iacocca was more famous than

Elon Musk, Mark Zuckerberg, or any current industry leader. Lee was everywhere, and his bold and versatile leadership style has been unmatched since.

Lee was one of a kind. He was the CEO others in the auto industry envied, and most knew they couldn't emulate him.

He was the star of Chrysler television commercials, famously hawking, "If you can find a better car, buy it," the lead fundraiser for the renovation of the Statue of Liberty, a potential candidate for President of the United States, the author of bestselling books and, in his later days, the co-star of a Chrysler commercial with Snoop Dogg.

The dynastic power element of this astrological combination is well portrayed in the life of American politician, Robert Kennedy. Unfortunately, like his brother and fellow maverick, JFK, Robert was assassinated.

From BlogofDeath.com we learn other ways of working with these energies from the life of poly-maverick, Liz Renay:

[Née] Pearl Elizabeth Dobbins, Renay was raised in Arizona by strict evangelical Christian parents, and a grandmother whom she described as a "hellion." At 13, Renay ran away from home and hitchhiked to Las Vegas. The voluptuous girl won a Marilyn Monroe look-alike contest and supported herself by working as an underage cocktail waitress, showgirl and size 44DD bra model.

By 18, Renay was supporting her two children, a boy and a girl, as an exotic dancer and movie extra. When *Life* magazine featured her in a five-page photo spread, she decided to seek her fortune in New York City. There Renay became a high-fashion model, and even appeared on the cover of *Esquire* magazine. But she fell in with Tony "Cappy" Coppola, the right-hand man of mob boss Albert "The Mad Hatter" Anastasia, and life in the fast lane soon proved a bit too brisk for Renay. When her relationship with Coppola turned violent, she moved to California to become a film star.

Renay appeared in more than two-dozen pictures, mostly B-movies like *Date with Death, The Thrill Killers, Mark of the Astro-Zombies, Desperate Living,* and *Dimension in Fear,* and won $1,000 for correctly answering geography questions on Groucho Marx's TV show, *You Bet Your Life*. In the Hollywood press, she was famed for her beauty and for dating actors and celebrities. The blonde, and sometimes red-headed, bombshell eventually married seven times, divorced five times and widowed twice. She recounted her many flings in the 1992 memoir, *My First 2,000 Men*.

In a way only the French can describe the dark aspects of life, we learn about the depths to which multi-maverick artist, Paul Rebeyrolle, worked. The following comes from Foundation-Maeght.com:

In 1970 Jean-Paul Sartre wrote about Paul Rebeyrolle: "In 1956 he left the party for obvious reasons; he did not leave by the right but by the left door." Rebeyrolle came closer to Louis-Ferdinand Céline in the depiction of the body, as Céline had done in *Journey to the End of the Night* (1932) describing a young woman dying of hemorrhaging on a white bed and would not be saved. Rebeyrolle drew out onto the surface the body of the material, with an impasto application of colour, exploring the organic, to which he sometimes gave a fluid, putrid appearance. He was fascinated by history, everyday news, realism in the manner of Gustave Courbet and the freedom to which he aspired and which he advocated for in painting, renouncing in the titles of his series, all forms of human enslavement. In the series *Monetarism* the works of Paul Rebeyrolle bring out the evils in society. He did several series of paintings against political power, war, religion and science, but in this series he spoke of the society of the market. *Hot Money* is almost intolerable to look at, just as power and money are unbearable to the artist. The naked man shown reaches into a box looking like a coffin with skulls of people similar to himself (the artist?), who were killed with hot money. This is a bitter theme, and equally bitter are the materials that the painter uses: oil, earth, straw and horsehair.

Family secrets are well indicated by this astrological placement and were well played out after double maverick, Bart Cummings, died. From Wikipedia.com we learn the following (Note: oddly, no information on the results of the testing):

In November 2016 two sisters in Adelaide, Kimberley and Julia Mander went public with a claim that Cummings was the father of their father, Peter Mander, from a relationship with their grandmother, Patricia Kilmartin. They allege that the couple were in a relationship for over a year and Patricia fell pregnant in mid-1951. The relationship ended and Lloyd Mander married Patricia and raised Peter as his son. They have engaged a lawyer and have asked for DNA tests for to confirm their story. They have stated that they are not interested in a financial claim on Cummings' estate.

Cummings daughter Sharon Robinson has said that she is happy to give a DNA sample and to meet the girls who would be her nieces if Bart Cummings is proved to be their grandfather.

Double maverick fantasy writer, Ursula LeGuin, exhibits the explorative genius of a writer as stated from this excerpt from an article in Biography.com:

Le Guin would later recount that she faced years of rejection from mainstream publishers while plying her trade as a writer. She eventually turned to the genres of science fiction and fantasy and found acceptance. In 1966, Le Guin published the novel *Rocannon's World*, which places the planet Hain as the birthplace of humanity and thus became the first of several books that are part of the "Hainish Cycle." Among the later titles in the cycle are *The Word for World Is Forest* (a 1972 outing that invited later comparison by critics to the James Cameron film *Avatar*), *The Dispossessed: An Ambiguous Utopia* (1974) and *The Telling* (2000). (The author stated the later novels in the cycle don't have to be read in a particular order.)

The Left Hand of Darkness (1969), the fourth book of the Hainish Cycle *after Planet of Exile* (1966) and *City of Illusions* (1967), became one of Le Guin's most acclaimed and trailblazing works. A ponderous narrative, *Darkness* profiles the Gethenians, an alien race who have no fixed gender characteristics until the time of monthly mating, with the novel also contrasting the social mores of two nations in conflict. The book was eventually lauded as a visionary classic and won both Nebula and Hugo awards.

Wikipedia.com shares insightful statements about former German Chancellor, Helmut Kohl:

As Chancellor Kohl was strongly committed to European integration and French-German cooperation in particular; he was also a steadfast ally of the United States and supported Reagan's more aggressive policies in order to weaken the Soviet Union. Kohl's 16-year tenure was the longest of any German Chancellor since Otto von Bismarck. He oversaw the end of the Cold War and the German reunification, for which he is generally known as Chancellor of Unity. Together with French President François Mitterrand, Kohl was the architect of the Maastricht Treaty, which established the European Union (EU) and the Euro currency, and in 1988 both received the Charlemagne Prize. Kohl was described as "the greatest European leader of the second half of the 20th century" by U.S. Presidents George H. W. Bush and Bill Clinton. In 1998 Kohl became the second person to be named Honorary Citizen of Europe by the European heads of state or government.

Joyce Wieland, was a Canadian experimental filmmaker and mixed media artist. From HerStory.com we learn the painful parts of this astrological placement:

> Joyce Wieland was born in Toronto in 1930, the youngest child of British immigrants. After her parents died while Wieland was still in elementary school, she and her two older brothers struggled to survive, leading what she would later call a "Dickensian childhood" of poverty. To earn a little income, Wieland drew pictures for schoolmates: costumed movie stars for the girls, naked women for the boys.
>
> In high school, Wieland studied fashion design until one of the working artists there, Doris McCarthy, recognized her talent and encouraged her to pursue art. McCarthy recalls thinking that Wieland "drew like an angel." She became an important mentor for Wieland.

Dan Flavin, was an American minimalist artist famous for creating sculptural objects and installations from commercially available fluorescent light fixtures. From ThoughtCo.com we see the understanding Pluto gives Cancer:

Dan Flavin's decision to work solely with fluorescent light bulbs as the medium for the construction of his sculptures makes him unique among major 20th-century artists. He helped define minimalism using such limited materials, and he introduced the idea of impermanence to his work. Flavin's works only exist until the lights burn out, and the light itself is the analogous element to other sculptors' use of concrete, glass, or steel. He influenced a wave of later light artists including Olafur Eliasson and James Turrell.

Multi-maverick, T. Cullen Davis, ticks off many of the boxed archetypes of this astrological placement: heir, sexual trysts, murder.

Poly-maverick manipulator extraordinaire, Charles Manson has four Scorpio planets, so we know astrologically that his childhood was not an easy one and home was not a place of safety, warmth and nurturance. The following comes from CharlesManson.com:

> Charles Manson was born to a 16 year-old runaway named Kathleen Maddox on Monday, November 12, 1934 at a Cincinnati, Ohio hospital. He was first named "no name Maddox," however within weeks, he was renamed Charles Milles Maddox. His father, Colonel Walker Henderson Scott, Sr., was an army man stationed nearby. When Kathleen told him she was pregnant, Scott fled the area never to return. Therefore, it is likely that young Charles Manson never met his real father.

Charles later obtained the last name Manson from William Eugene Manson whom Kathleen began dating in 1934. Manson was a heavy drinker and would be missing for days at a time. The two divorced just three years later in 1937. As Kathleen struggled with her own alcoholic tendencies she too would go missing for days at a time. She'd leave young Charles Manson to fend for himself or with a variety of babysitters while she was bar-hopping and hanging around various men getting into trouble.

Kathleen Maddox, Charles Manson's Mom

Kathleen was involved in a robbery in 1939 and the courts gave her a ten-year prison sentence. Charles went to live with his aunt and uncle in West Virginia until his mother was paroled in 1942. They reunited and Kathleen continued her abusive parenting habits but by this time Charles himself was becoming his own problem getting arrested and finding trouble around every corner. His mother sent him to the Gibault School for Boys in Terre Haute, Indiana. Gibault was a school for juvenile delinquents and was run by Catholic priests.

A Childhood Behind Bars

Charles Manson fled Gibault twice. The first time returning to his mother who only sent him back. Later he fled again, this time to Indianapolis where he rented a room and supported himself by burglarizing stores at night. He was eventually caught and a sympathetic judge sent him to Boys Town, another juvenile delinquent school in Omaha, Nebraska. After four days he and another child inmate stole a vehicle and drove to Illinois. After the police caught him for more robberies, the courts sent him to the Indiana Boys School. Yet another school for juvenile delinquents where Manson says he was beaten and raped. After two failed attempts he escaped in 1951.

After more thefts and robberies he was apprehended and sent to the National Training School for Boys in Washington D.C. where he was evaluated for physiological problems and deemed to be aggressively antisocial. Upon recommendations from the physicians there, he was transferred to the Natural Bridge Honor Camp. Before his scheduled parole hearing set for 1952, he was caught raping another boy at knifepoint. Manson was transferred to the Federal Reformatory in Petersburg, Virginia where he was caught committing several homosexual crimes against other boys and was then transferred to a maximum security facility in Ohio. He was released to his aunt and uncle in 1954 at twenty years old. Charles Manson's childhood had officially ended.

Pluto in Leo on the IC

These individuals are legends in their own mind and clearly out in the world as well. The path to being seen is not an easy one. The high cost of fame is one that many entertainers come to know.

The following about multi-maverick singer, Dionne Warwick, comes from NYDailyNews.com:

Do you know the way to bankruptcy?

Five-time Grammy winner Dionne Warwick, who earned millions of dollars across a half-century of stardom, now lives on a paltry $10 a month once her bills are paid off.

The 72-year-old chart-topping singer is almost broke, with only $1,000 in her bank account and a staggering $10.7 million in debts, according to her 50-page filing last week in U.S. Bankruptcy Court in Newark.

The cash-strapped songbird — known for her impeccable versions of Burt Bacharach-Hal David hits like "I Say a Little Prayer," "Do You Know the Way to San Jose" and "Walk on By" — owns almost nothing from her high-flying past.

From a statement her son made for her obituary from NYTimes.com, we see Christine Keeler's family understood the cost of such an astrological placement:

"My mother, Christine Keeler, fought many fights in her eventful life," Mr. Platt wrote, "some fights she lost but some she won. She earned her place in British history but at a huge personal price."

The creative brilliance of this astrological placement is well articulated in the life of singer and songwriter and producer multi-maverick Beach Boy, Brian Wilson. The following comes from Wikipedia.com:

> He is often referred to as a genius and is widely acknowledged as one of the most innovative and significant songwriters of the late 20th century.

Yet another side of England's Moors murderer and multi-maverick, Myra Hindley, is shown in the following excerpt from an article at Independent.co.uk:

> She was small, with dark hair and she was wearing a pink T-shirt. I remember being surprised that this was the person who was supposed to be so frightening. I was set to work and had to use the administration kitchen as an office. Myra would potter around, making tea and coffee for staff and visitors, washing up and vacuuming, and bit by bit we began to talk – about philosophy, religion, French and English literature.
>
> She has a very sharp mind and great wit. She is sensible and sensitive and very good company. She always gets on well with everybody. I felt immediately at ease with her.
>
> Within the prison, a group of officers was opposed to any form of change, and they were suspicious that I spent time with Myra. I began to understand then that everybody felt that they had to make Myra their

business; they all had an opinion about her and her every move. She seems to be public property.

I soon noticed that she made weekly tabloid headlines, without the Home Office taking any positive action to try and counteract this relentless flow of articles. The tabloids can be very upsetting. The most vicious article claimed that prison officers had found us together in Myra's cell with "floral knickers" round her ankles.

TheGuardian.com shares these insightful archetypal expressions by multi-maverick and anarchist, Stuart Christie:

Having been kitted out in Paris, Christie began to hitchhike south with the explosives wrapped around his body and wearing a kilt as an aid to getting lifts. His attire later led to reports in the Argentinian press that the man who tried to assassinate Franco was a "Scottish transvestite."

Once he arrived in Madrid, however, it turned out that Christie's group had been infiltrated, and he was arrested along with his Spanish contact, Fernando Carballo. After being forced to watch Carballo being tortured, Christie signed a confession. Convicted of "banditry and terrorism" after a brief trial in a military court, he faced the possibility of execution by garrote, but was instead given the 20-year jail term. His sentence prompted international protests, including from Jean-Paul Sartre and Bertrand Russell.

Multi-maverick journalist, Jessica Savitch, with her Leonine mane, shows us that all that is pretty, isn't necessarily so. The following comes from Curbsideclassic.com:

> But all was not right in Jessica's world. The only man she every really loved beat her terribly. Drug use led to promiscuity and sometimes threatened her standing at the station. The networks wanted her, but Westinghouse had ironclad contracts – so she acted out and became a general terror to all. The reputation followed her to NBC.
>
> She was made Senate correspondent but she was in over her head. Resentment from coworkers hurt, and led to her eventually being pulled off the Senate beat. Jessica's time at NBC was filled with uncertainty, and with the uncertainty came drug use. But the public loved her, as it did in Philadelphia.

From an article in ArtNet.com, we see the width and breadth of creative depths possible from this astrological placement in the life of artist, Lari Pittman:

> [Pittman] is a contemporary American artist best known for his collage-like paintings and prints which integrate multiple pictorial languages into a single work. Melding advertisements, gestural abstraction, Surrealism, Victorian silhouettes, and Folk art, the artist revels in dichotomies of ugliness and beauty, chaos and calm.

The myriad creative abilities of this astrological placement are once again highlighted in our next example actor and martial artist, Jackie Chan, who also has a maverick Gemini AS moon. The following comes from Wikipedia.com:

> [Chan] is a Hong Kong martial artist, actor, stuntman, film director, action choreographer, screenwriter, producer, and singer. He is known in the cinematic world for his slapstick acrobatic fighting style, comic timing, use of improvised weapons, and innovative stunts, which he typically performs himself. He has trained in Wushu or Kung Fu and Hapkido, and has been acting since the 1960s, appearing in over 150 films.

Actress, Michelle Pfeiffer, is another thespian who has an amazing range of expression, as this astrological placement provides a deep well of ingenuity.

Pluto in Virgo on the IC

These individuals have a deep and very rich inner world. They often have incredible insights on what can be done to improve what already exists. These mavericks are powerhouses in their respective families and households. These individuals have a certain discriminating quality about them.

This arrangement is one that can easily overwhelm individuals because it seeks to experience as much as possible, as well presented in the life of punk rocker, Darby Crash, who died of a heroin overdose at the age of 22.

While many of us know singer, Irene Cara, for singing and co-writing the title song from the movie *Flashdance,* in typical maverick fashion she was one of five finalists at age three for the Little Miss America, showing that brilliance at an early age.

Stephen Rockefeller, Jr., heir to the Rockefeller dynasty, shows the service-oriented aspect of this position. The following comes from Wikiopedia.com:

> Rockefeller is a philanthropist who focuses on education, Planned Parenthood, human rights and environmental causes. He is a trustee of the Asian Cultural Council and an advisory trustee of the Rockefeller Brothers Fund. He has also served as a director of the Rockefeller Philanthropy Advisors.

Photographer and artist, Jack Pierson, shares these insightful gems from AZQuotes.com:

> "One of the things I've had to struggle with is that part of what people find critically and curatorially questionable in my work is that I try to make things that don't read as art until they're in a gallery."

> "Even though I'm not actually performing in the works, I love the theatrical and have this fan relationship to showbiz. And one of the things that's a disappointment to me about art is that it's always a memory of

something that happened. So I try to get as intimate or as real as possible."

"Most of my work is very temporary, very provisional. You can take it with you or you can leave it. Which is a tough sell for art. Because part of what art is supposed to do is make you immortal, either by making it or owning it."

Multi-maverick and American politician, Cheryl Jacques, who has Venus and Chiron conjunct her Pisces MC, has lived a life of service for everyone's benefit.

Virgo gives one the ability to approach anything or anyone, and with Pluto here, there is an inherent talent to earthly expressions and a drive to work. Such is the case with multi-maverick, Ian Shaw, as we learn from Wikipedia.com:

Ian Shaw is a Welsh jazz singer, record producer, actor and stand-up comedian. Shaw was born in St. Asaph, Wales, and took his music degree at the University of London. His career in performance began in the 1980s on the alternative cabaret circuit, alongside such performers as Julian Clary, Rory Bremner, and Jo Brand. At the same time, he was playing in piano bars and at festivals in London and throughout Europe.

Quotes from Wikipedia.com show how multi-maverick actress, Ally Sheedy, is aware of these astrological energies:

"I never thought to myself, I'm going to grow up and fall in love with a man or I'm going to fall in love with a woman because my mother is a lesbian."

"I think that acting involves doing your job so well that you are able to help the viewer identify with the character."

"But the fact is, nobody gets off drugs unless they really want to, and I really wanted to."

"I'd rather not pinpoint my mistakes."

Poly has a different meaning with multi-maverick porn star, Jeff Stryker. This smoldering Pluto in Virgo and his IC, still ignites the passionate fires in both men and women.

Another multi-maverick and the lone surviving Bee Gee is Berry Gibb, who shares these insights from AZQuotes.com:

"I just love the feeling a close family gives you and I wouldn't change it for anything."

"I've worked with a lot of people who are more famous than myself who are terribly insecure."

"The secret is to make sure your family comes before anything else, because no matter what you do you've got to come home."

"It is not the money but the self-respect and wanting to create good music."

"I have a huge ego and a huge inferiority complex at the same time."

Husbandry and ecological awareness are well indicated with this astrological placement and are portrayed in the life of adventurer, Tim Jarvis. The following comes from Wikipedia.com:

> Jarvis says he is "committed to finding pragmatic solutions to global environmental sustainability issues", and as a public speaker he talks regularly about motivation and leadership to both individuals and organizations."

With Pluto here, there is an indication that "home" might not be so rosy. From News.com.au, we find that actress, Mimi Macpherson, learned that home is never home once you leave it, "Over the course of one week, Australia has taken it upon itself to knock Elle Macpherson down a notch and make her regret returning home."

Pluto in Libra on the IC

The deep need for harmony, balance and beauty are quite profound. Right human relationship, the key to Libra, is heightened and strengthened. I know a couple of friends who have this signature and they are dedicated, tireless individuals who help those who are less fortunate.

From Wikipedia, we learn of a 15th century maverick:

> Arthur Tudor was Prince of Wales, Earl of Chester, and Duke of Cornwall. As the eldest son and heir apparent of Henry VII of England, Arthur was viewed by contemporaries as the great hope of the newly established House of Tudor.

Unfortunately, young Arthur died at 15 years old.

Pluto in Scorpio on the IC

Pluto rules Scorpio, so there is a sense of the king (or queen) is home. The level of intention and intensity cannot be missed with these individuals and equally, their level of sensitivity is spectacular. Pluto and Scorpio are about power, so it is interesting to see that our two examples are children of very powerful people. These two leaned from an early age how to wield power.

From NYPost.com, we learn the following:

> "It was a very conscious decision," Sawyer Avery Spielberg says of lopping off his surname for the stage. "I wanted to tell my own story and have my own little journey and my own little adventure. Sometimes the last name can be a little bit distracting ..."

Scorpio likes to even the playing field as well displayed by Zelda Williams, an American actress and the daughter of Robin Williams and Marsha Garces Williams. The following comes from Today.com:

> After video of Robin Williams mocking presidential candidate Joe Biden went viral this weekend, the late comedian's daughter took to social media to speak out. Eric Trump, 36, tweeted a clip that featured Williams poking fun at the way Biden talks. Trump didn't add any commentary, but the clip included text that read, "Robin Williams Just Savages Joe Biden."
>
> Zelda Williams, the 31-year-old daughter of the late actor, took to Twitter to condemn Trump for sharing the clip.
>
> "While we're 'reminiscing' (to further your political agenda), you should look up what he said about your Dad," she wrote. "I did. Promise you, it's much more 'savage.'"

Pluto in Sagittarius on the IC

The boundless possibilities and unfathomable multi-verses are well indicated by this astrological position. This placement gives one the opportunity to penetrate and explore deep space and understand both foreign and alien civilizations. There is also a deep inner knowing and awareness.

Twins, Kendra and Maliyah Herrin, were born Feb 26, 2002, and surgically separated in August 2006. They were the first set of conjoined twins to be separated to share a kidney. Kendra retained their shared kidney following the separation surgery, while Maliyah Herrin underwent dialysis until she was transplanted with a kidney donated by her mother in April 2007. Wisdom is highlighted by this placement, which we can see so beautifully articulated in this excerpt from an article from deseret.com:

> Both before and since the 2006 operation, they have been photographed and stared at too many times to count by people who are curious. The experience has forced them to think a lot about inclusion and what diversity means and how to talk to those who are somewhat different. And they've reached a pretty simple conclusion.
>
> "Don't be afraid to talk to someone. Don't stare at them. Ask them if it's OK to ask what happened. But be respectful about it," says Kendra.
>
> Maliyah nods. "Be nice," she says.
>
> Now on the verge of adulthood, the Herrins sat down with the Deseret News to talk about inclusion, disabilities and independence.

Pluto in Capricorn on the IC

We are experiencing Pluto in Capricorn energy as I write this book. The power of establishment, family dynasty, and inheriting vast wealth are all well indicated here. These individuals have the makings of being true captains of industry and are willing to do whatever it takes to make it happen. These are individuals born sometime between March 2008, and January 2024, for which we have no examples as yet. They will likely have a shrewd and calculating manner about them. This is a great placement for a child of wealthy and successful parents and is a good sign for those who are "movers and shakers" in the world. As a cardinal sign, one can see the innate ability to create and build.

Pluto in Aquarius on the IC

These mavericks will be born sometime between April 2023, and January 2044. This is a perfect arrangement for a philosopher or major reformer, especially here at the bottom of the chart. They could be highly reclusive and have a challenging time socializing with others. This is a beautiful placement for a humanistic philosopher who is able to remain in an ivory tower with all of her/his needs met while observing the intricate ways in which humans relate and express. While highly perceptive, there is a chance that one could get lost in one's own ideas.

Pluto in Pisces on the IC

These deep diving, transformative healers, or lightly tethered journey-weathered individuals will be a force for the collective. Masters of social media (whatever that becomes!) and gurus of bygone ages, they will be born between March 2043, and Feb 2068.

We will now look at the angle placements of Pluto throughout the zodiac from the point of view of the Descendant (DS.)

Pluto in Aries on the DS

Even sitting in a dark room, these individuals have a radioactive glow and charisma. The forceful will of this placement would be challenging to ignore. A literal force of nature, these individuals get things done, regardless of the means.

Pluto in Taurus on the DS

These individuals have an innate understanding of what lies within. Their piercing minds are able to unlock any form of nature. They would be great therapists and scientists since they can get to the root of things.

Visionary inventor, Nikola Tesla would be a great example of this astrological placement, as it also speaks to the problems/limitations these individuals would likely encounter from others.

ASTROLOGICAL MAVERICKS

Pluto in Gemini on the DS

These mavericks mesmerize others. This placement lends the native the ability to meet people on whatever level they present themselves. The charisma is palpable, but if not well integrated, they can be master manipulators.

From Wikipedia.com, we learn a little about multi-maverick, Major General Harry Wickwire Foster, who commanded in both the European and Pacific theatres in WWII:

> After the war, Foster (with four brigadiers) presided over the court martial of Canada's top prisoner of war, SS General Kurt Meyer. The trial was a showcase for Canada, the first time that the country had conducted an international prosecution of this sort. Meyer was found guilty of three of five charges and sentenced to death. The sentence was later commuted to life imprisonment. When asked by his son (author Tony Foster) why the death sentence had been imposed he replied, "Because I had no choice according to those rules of warfare dreamt up by a bunch of bloody barrack-room lawyers who had never heard a shot fired in anger."

The brilliance of understanding is well exemplified in our next example, multi-maverick and inventor, Alan Blumlein. From the website AlanBlumlein.com, we learn the following:

The Audio Engineering Society posthumously awarded this certificate to Alan Dower Blumlein on the 2nd March 1978. In recognition of his remarkable work on telecommunications at the beginning of his career and for the invention of Stereo on the 14th December 1931 when Alan was just 28 years old.

The moth to the flame element is well articulated in an article about multi-maverick, Henri Charrière from AllThatIsInteresting.com:

> If even half of the daring exploits described in Henri Charrière's autobiography *Papillon* are true, then he lived a life of adventure and frequent brushes with death that would make any thrill-seeker jealous.

Actor, politician, and president, Ronald Reagan, carried the charisma on the big screen and into the White House. Almost acting as a precursor for the presidents to come in the U.S., he showed that the head of the U.S. is a great acting job.

Our next example, shows us the varied ways in which the mind connects, dissects, extrapolates and integrates thoughts and ideas. While he started as a science fiction author, L. Ron Hubbard, also founded Scientology. Hubbard's ability to access alternate realities gives us an interesting insight into how he wove religion and science fiction into a marketable and manipulative product to those seeking power.

Pluto in Cancer on the DS

These individuals have the ability to make us feel immediately warm and welcome or cold and excluded.

Mom can remain the primary relationship for these individuals as well portrayed by legendary entertainer, Liberace, who also has Venus here.

As we have seen time and again, there is often a dynastic element with maverick Cancer planets. From Wikipedia.com we learn the following:

> Brenda Diana Duff Frazier was an American socialite popular during the Depression era. Her December 1938 debutante ball was so heavily publicized worldwide, she eventually appeared on the cover of *Life* magazine for that reason alone. She was known and dubbed a "Poor Little Rich Girl" by the media, along with other famous socialites and debutantes Barbara Hutton, Gloria Vanderbilt, and Doris Duke.

Actor and leading man, Charles Bronson, always played some sort of protective or revenge seeking role which are well indicated with this astrological placement. Bronson's gems from BrainyQuote.com reveal other parts of this powerful astrological placement:

> "I don't have friends, I have thousands of acquaintances. No friends. I figured I had a wife and children."

"Audiences like to see the bad guys get their comeuppance."

"I guess I look like a rock quarry that someone has dynamited."

"Don't ask me to explain a mystique. I'm just enjoying all this while it lasts. I'm basically doing the same thing I was doing 20 years ago."

"I am not a Caspar Milquetoast, but most of the time, I'm mild. I can afford to be because I don't have the fears that most men have about masculinity or machoness."

Multi-maverick actor and businessman, Paul Newman, showed a dedication to his wife and family not usually seen in Hollywood.

With Mars here as well, how could Malcolm X not want to protect his family and his clan which is the African-American people? He also has the Moon and Chiron conjunct his IC in Aries. He was born to heal and help move the divide in the U.S. His ideals are still in the process of being realized.

The powerful Kennedy dynasty once again gives us a maverick. If it wasn't for the considerable influence of his family, Ted Kennedy would never have had a political career. This is summarized in the headline from an article from History.com:

The fateful events at Chappaquiddick ended Mary Jo Kopechne's life and derailed Ted Kennedy's presidential ambitions for good.

Another insight into the realm of archetypal expression is offered by composer, Pauline Oliveros. The following comes from PitchFork.com:

> Pauline Oliveros, an accomplished composer, accordionist, and experimental music pioneer, has died, according to Red Bull Music Academy and FACT. She was 84.
>
> Born in 1932, Oliveros was a multi-instrumentalist who later became a composer and performer. She was also a noted author and philosopher. In the early '60s, Oliveros was an integral member of the San Francisco Tape Music Center. In the late '80s, she coined the term "Deep Listening," and later went on to found the Deep Listening Institute (now the Center for Deep Listening).
>
> Oliveros' album *Accordion and Voice* (1982) and her Stuart Dempster and Panatois collaboration *Deep Listening* (1989) are considered landmark ambient records. At the time of her death, she was the Research Professor of Music at Rensselaer Polytechnic Institute and the Darius Milhaud Artist-in-Residence at Mills College. A distinguished explorer of sound, she shared thoughts on deep listening, tape improv, and teaching with Pitchfork in 2011. "I feel that students always learn more from each other than they do from their professor," she said. "They learn by doing."

Pauline played several instruments just as our next multi-maverick example, Roy Castle. The range of expression possible with this astrological placement is well stated in the following excerpt from Wikipedia.com:

> Roy Castle was an English dancer, singer, comedian, actor, television presenter and musician. In addition to being an accomplished jazz trumpet player, he could play many other instruments. Following a versatile career as a performer on stage, television and film, he became best known to British television viewers as the long-running presenter of the children's series *Record Breakers*.

This is a wonderful place from someone who wants to interview others as beautifully exemplified by talk show host, Larry King. Unfortunately, this doesn't seem to have aided him in his personal relationships as he has been married and divorced nine times.

An activist is well indicated here, as evidenced by actress, Jane Fonda. Here are some insightful quotes by Jane that from AZQuptes.com:

> "If you understood what communism was, you would hope, you would pray on your knees that we would someday become communist... I, a socialist, think that we should strive toward a socialist society, all the way to communism."

"It's never too late – never too late to start over, never too late to be happy."

"You don't learn from successes; you don't learn from awards; you don't learn from celebrity; you only learn from wounds and scars and mistakes and failures. And that's the truth."

And a perfect quote by Jane to end this astrological placement:

"To be a revolutionary you have to be a human being. You have to care about people who have no power."

Pluto in Leo on the DS

The endlessly creative and expressive energy of these individuals is hard to imagine. This powerful flame is something we find in each of our examples.

The National Gallery, has this to say about one of our earliest mavericks, Renaissance master artist, Piero di Cosimo:

> Among the most inventive painters of the Italian Renaissance, Piero di Cosimo was celebrated by his early biographer Giorgio Vasari for "the strangeness of his brain, and his constant seeking after difficulties." In altarpieces, poetic mythologies, portraits, and festival designs, the artist gave life to distinctive characters

endowed with poignant emotion and memorable individuality. Piero's compositions are best known for their imaginative detail, but he also merits appreciation as a vivid narrator of ancient legends and a creator of evocative landscape backgrounds. For centuries, the artist enjoyed a reputation as an eccentric, so devoted to the secrets of art and nature that he abandoned human company and lived a meager existence. In recent decades, however, new insights and discoveries have transformed our understanding of the master's career and legacy. Contrary to the myth of the solitary madman, Piero was a successful and sought-after painter.

With Pluto in a fearless fire sign, one can will likely enjoy the extremes, especially in risk. The following comes from History.com:

> Daredevil motorcyclist, Evel Knievel, the godfather of extreme sports, struggled for much of his career with an internal conflict: staying rich and famous versus staying alive.
>
> If his legacy could be rewritten, his successful, record-breaking jump at Ohio's Kings Island amusement park in October 1975—over 14 Greyhound buses and 133 feet—would have been a more dignified climax to his legendary career as a daredevil.
>
> "I really wanted to quit then. It was the first jump that I made that was successful where I thought, 'Yeah, I might hang it up—I did this.' But of course, I went on

from there," said the stunt star (whose real name was Robert Craig Knievel) in Stuart Barker's book *Life of Evel*.

Instead, Knievel's last leap in the spotlight was a *Jaws*-inspired gimmick that would help—along with the Fonz—spawn the phrase "jumping the shark," implying that somebody's or something's best days are behind them.

The problem for Knievel was that his dramatic crashes were what elevated him to his status as the world's greatest stuntman.

"His fame had little to do with the stunts he successfully pulled off and everything to do with the epic failures and wipeouts," says Barker. "Besides… what else would he have done? Not only would he have missed the adrenaline rush of doing what he did, he'd have missed being in the limelight even more."

Multi-maverick actor, Michael York, shares his thespian views from BrainyQuote.com:

"I think that you have to believe in your destiny; that you will succeed, you will meet a lot of rejection and it is not always a straight path, there will be detours – so enjoy the view."

"I think it's hard to know. Feeling fulfilled, because actors face periods of unemployment, there is nothing worse than being at the top of your game; you have so much to give but do not have the platform to do this."

Our next individual has a royal title – something this astrological placement definitely implies. She also radiated the deep love in all those around her which is such a Leonine trait. From CMT.com we learn the following about singer, Tammy Wynette:

> Wynette was like family to so many who met her in life, not to mention a heroine, icon and a phenomenal influence to countless other music entertainers.
>
> "I am just very glad that we were able to work together and tour together again," says former husband and long-time singing partner George Jones. "It was very important for us to close the chapter on everything that we had been through. I know Tammy felt the same way. Life is too short. In the end, we were very close friends. And now, I have lost that friend. I couldn't be sadder."
>
> "It was important to me to mend the relationship George had with Tammy," added George's wife Nancy, "and we did that. It also gave me the chance to get to know Tammy. Once I did, I truly loved her. She became my friend, too. I will miss her terribly. Nashville has lost another legend and we don't have that many left."
>
> "It's hard to even describe the feelings I'm having because I loved her so much," says one of those remaining and cherished legends, Loretta Lynn, the one-third sistership of her, Wynette and Dolly Parton's Honky Tonk Angel reputation in country music. "She was my best girlfriend in country music; we did vacations together. I just loved her more than any other

girl singer in Nashville. I'll miss you greatly, Tammy. I'll always be thinking of you."

"I feel I have lost a sister, a friend and a wonderful singing partner," adds Parton. "Tammy was just as much country with class as Loretta was just country-country," explained Dolly. "I remember when I first heard Tammy's records, I was impressed with the richness and the bigness. It was like something we hadn't had since Patsy Cline. She had that same kind of professionalism. I just thought she had a great voice and I loved the subjects that she chose to sing about. As a singer, I thought she deserved the title 'First Lady of Country Music.' The world has lost one of the most unique stylists in the music industry. The whole world will mourn Tammy Wynette." Countless other country artists strongly agree.

Singer, Jim Morrison, displayed many aspects of this combination from his wild personality and savage hair, to his erratic stage performances. Like a candle burning too hot and too fast, Morrison's flame went out at 27 years old.

Athlete, Alan Page, gives a lovely interview to NPR.org. Here is an excerpt that touches on archetypes of what this type of maverick can accomplish:

Alan Page is a Pro Football Hall of Famer, retired Minnesota Supreme Court Justice, and recent recipient of the Presidential Medal of Freedom. Perhaps more importantly, he was a life partner to his wife Diane, who died of breast cancer in September. The two were almost always seen together.

"Sometimes I wasn't sure where she began and I ended," Page said.

Alan and Diane started the Page Education Foundation in 1988 to raise money for scholarships to help more Minnesotans go to college.

In 2017 Ramsey Middle School was renamed Justice Page Middle School after a student-led campaign. The students have since painted a mural in Page's honor.

Page has also been vocal about race relations.

"One of the things that we also have to do to begin to address the issues of race we face is to be intentional about it," Page said. "We can't just simply skate from one day to the next and think these problems are going to go away by themselves. We as human beings— and each of us as human beings— have to be intentional about how we treat these issues."

Double maverick actor, Henry Winkler, offers these insights from BrainyQuotes.com:

"Your mind knows only some things. Your inner voice, your instinct, knows everything. If you listen to what you know instinctively, it will always lead you down the right path."

"How we learn has nothing to do with how brilliant we are."

"If the country is going to be great, everybody has a gift, and I tell every child I meet, whether they have asked me or not, 'You have greatness inside you, and your job is to figure out what that is, dig it out, and give it to the world. Because the world needs everything, every one of you.'"

Poly-amazing maverick singer, performer, and artist, David Bowie, who also has his Moon and Saturn here, shows us the chameleon range of expression possible when creativity is given free reign.

My dear friend, Kamala, devoted herself to transform other's well-being through good healthy organic raw food and various healing modalities.

TheGuardian.com has a lovely article interview with actor, Gabriel Byrne, that sheds another light on this astrological placement:

> He seems genuinely affable, unlike his characters, whose geniality usually has definite threat glinting beneath. This uncertainty has long been key to Byrne's appeal, likewise that stupid beauty, smudged a little now he is 70. Yet Byrne does not carry himself with the confidence you expect from a veteran smoulderer. He nods, a bit awkwardly. Catholic shame and "male teenage [body] dysmorphia" kicked vanity out of him young, he says – literally, when a priest clobbered him for looking in the mirror. "If you're brought up in that world, you never get to the stage of thinking it'll be easy with women."

Point taken, if slightly undermined by his friend Liam Neeson, who emails to say that Byrne "personifies the 'dark brooding Irishman'" (the middle word is one he has long gone on record about hating). "The ladies all think he's the bollix," adds Neeson, "and they'd be right!"

Anyway, Byrne is today very much channeling the history teacher he was for about eight years. Neeson says: "He has an acute intelligence and remarkable insight into the human condition. He can also be very funny." And, actually, after three hours with him, that feels pretty fair. Byrne is bright and gabby and friendly and professorial. He has a lot he wants to say, about the abuse of power, about why ordinary people stand for it, and about how much the movies are responsible.

Alanson Russell "Lance" Loud, was an American television personality, magazine columnist and new wave rock-n-roll performer. Lance came "out of the closet" in one of the first reality shows ever created: An American Family.

Actress, Whoopie Goldberg, is the perfect example of what a person can become through enduring the ever-tempering fires of Pluto. Wikipedia.com states the following about Whoopi:

> ...American actor, comedian, author, and television personality. A recipient of numerous accolades, Goldberg is one of sixteen entertainers to have won an Emmy Award, a Grammy Award, an Academy Award, and a Tony Award.

Contrary to many of the higher aspects presented above, we have the story of Mark Quinn Denton, who, according to astro.com:

> American criminal charged with rape, robbery and aggravated assault in 1980. He tried to use his horoscope in defense for "inevitable actions," testifying that it was because the stars predicted that he would go berserk at age 23. His attorney said "It was the law of Karma. He had no control over his behavior."
>
> The judge figured that it was his Karma to be found guilty, and appointed another lawyer to defend him.

Pluto in Virgo on the DS

Who do you want me to be? What resources do you want me to share with you? What can we not accomplish together? These are some of the questions this placement would make. The ability to imagine and create something is well within the ability of these powerful mages. There is often a loss of innocence the native will experience. These mavericks know that life is to be experienced in all of its multi-phasic beauty, especially along the blurry lines that connect masculinity to femininity.

Poly-maverick and actor, Antonio Banderas, shares these archetypal insights from BrainyQuotes.com:

"It was an honor and privilege to arrive to this country 16 years ago with almost no money in my pocket. A lot has happened since then."

"I remember in *Law of Desire*, where I played a homosexual, that people were more upset that I kissed a man on the mouth than I killed a man. It's interesting to see how people can pardon you for murdering a man, but they can't pardon you for kissing one."

"I do yoga every morning, then I run for half an hour, and take a sauna."

"There are some movies that I would like to forget, for the rest of my life – really! But even those movies that I'd like to forget teach me things."

Multi-maverick actor, playwright, screenwriter, and director, John Cameron Mitchell, shares his interesting experiences of and insights into life, through this astrological placement lens from BrainyQuote.com:

"I think I was scared of the drag thing, as a lot of gay boys are. It's sort of knocked out of you in junior high. I wouldn't find guys who were very feminine attractive. Then, doing *Hedwig*, I got to be man and woman, really butch and really femme at the same time, and I realized, this is kind of the ideal."

"Queerness isn't just Lady Gaga and overpriced drinks and fauxhawks. It's James Baldwin and Bea Arthur and Gertrude Stein and Gore Vidal."

"Our feet are planted in the real world, but we dance with angels and ghosts."

Multi-maverick and recording artist, Whitney Houston, shows us what can be accomplished through dedicated hard work and the price for such devotion. Wikipedia.com states her accomplishments clearly:

> Whitney Elizabeth Houston was an American singer and actress. She was certified as the most awarded female artist of all time by Guinness World Records and is one of the best-selling recording artists of all time, with sales of over 200 million records worldwide. Houston released seven studio albums and two soundtrack albums, all of which have been certified diamond, multi-platinum, platinum, or gold by the Recording Industry Association of America. She is regarded as one of the greatest artists of all time. Her crossover appeal on the popular music charts as well as her prominence on MTV influenced several African-American female artists.

Pluto in Libra on the DS

The drive for relationship is overwhelming for these mutants, and they sense any inequalities in their pursuit of right human relationship.

From Vogue.com.au, we learn the following about marathon swimmer, Susie Maroney:

> The mother of three told spoke to *New Idea* about the diagnosis and how her previous career contributed to the illness, "[I] spent all those hours in the water all day, training and marathon swimming...but I didn't put on any sunscreen."
>
> Maroney is married to quadriplegic former rugby player Perry Cross and has three children, Paris, 7, Capri, 5, and River, 3, from previous relationships.
>
> "They're so young and they need me," Maroney told the publication of her children.

Coming in at 30th in line to the British throne, Lady Davina Windsor shares yet other aspects of this powerful position. From Express.co.uk we learn of Lady Windsor's relationship handling abilities:

> Gary is of Maori descent and their marriage marked the first time a person of Maori descent married into the British Royal Family.
>
> The couple's two children - eight-year-old Senna Kowhai and six-year-old Tane Mahuta - are said to still be living with their mother in London.

The couple led a private life largely out of the public eye.

But commentators have remarked on how amicable and swift their divorce was, leading to some questioning what they did right.

A spokeswoman told Express.co.uk: "The couple's divorce fell largely under the radar due to their limited time in court, which could be due to other dispute resolution techniques.

She added: "It might feel inevitable that a divorce is going to get emotional and messy, however, a few techniques and alternative options will help mitigate stress levels and the amount of money spent."

Wikipedia.com sheds some light into the ambassadorial balancing act basketball star, Yao Ming, was walking:

Yao is one of China's best-known athletes, with sponsorships with several major companies. His rookie year in the NBA was the subject of a documentary film, *The Year of the Yao*, and he co-wrote, along with NBA analyst Ric Bucher, an autobiography titled *Yao: A Life in Two Worlds*. Known in China as the "Yao Ming Phenomenon" and in the United States as the "Ming Dynasty," Yao's success in the NBA, and his popularity among fans, made him a symbol of a new China that was both more modern and more confident.

Entertainer, Jordana Ashkenazi, presents that aspect of Libra devoted to beauty. Jordana is a singer, model, actress and television host – like *Psychic TV*.

Pluto in Scorpio on the DS

The depths of the depths of relationship and others are plumbed in this space.

The depths of twinship can be explored here as well exemplified by American actors, Charlie and Max Carver. I highly recommend reading the insightful article from InterviewMagazine.com from which this illuminating dialogue between the two of them is excerpted:

> CHARLIE: Well, I can't imagine dropping that disposition to go work in a different field. I'm trying to remember what made me want to go into this as a kid, and I think it was being moved in one way or another, and feeling the potential of being able to do that for other people, and understanding in an intrinsic way that that had value. Now, the battle has been trying to convince myself that it still has value, particularly in a world where there are so many other actionable ways to affect people's lives.
>
> MAX: But the value is you get to empathize with a belief system whether you're consciously doing it or not. You're getting to explore parts of yourself that may be dormant. And I think when people see that on the

screen, it wakes up that dormant part of themselves. It's like soul exercise.

CHARLIE: I hear that.

MAX: In terms of *Ratched*, what did you want to convey that you felt other people might not understand or see in your character?

CHARLIE: Another arrow of a question. I'm not sure I wanted to go in and convey anything. I think you learn from the story in front of you and you discover something in that process.

MAX: What did you learn?

CHARLIE: I always have to battle my own insecurities, or feelings of being limited somehow in actually embodying the character and the circumstances that are in front of me.

MAX: You're speaking in abstracts.

CHARLIE: Thank you, Max. With Huck, what was being asked of me was to sit with and live with the experience of a war vet—in a very specific, genre show—and I just wanted to trust that the product would come out of that. I'm so grateful to Ryan Murphy, not only for the opportunity, but for how much creative freedom was given to me. We spoke a little bit about the images and things that came to mind for him, and I was on the same page.

Yet another angle on this astrological angle comes from TheGuardian.com:

> As an opening batsman, the Australian cricketer Phillip Hughes, who has died aged 25 after being struck by a ball during a Sheffield Shield match at the Sydney Cricket Ground, was very much a product of the frantic modern era. While Test match openers in years gone by were staunch guardians of the game's defensive traditions and technical touchstones, Hughes brought the spirit of Twenty20 to the long form of cricket, slashing the ball to all parts in a fashion that paid little heed to the traditionally correct and miserly techniques of his predecessors.
>
> Hughes's belligerent approach may have had some wide-armed agricultural facets, but it was a pleasure to watch and often devastatingly effective. It brought him 26 Tests for Australia, including participation in three Ashes series against England, and playing contracts not just with his native New South Wales (2007-12), but in England with Middlesex (2009), Hampshire (2010) and Worcestershire (2012). From 2012 onwards he plied his trade with South Australia, and from 2013 with the Mumbai Indians in the Indian Premier League.

In a thought-provoking interview from OneJointWith.com, Sasha Spielberg, reveals her shift in relationship with marijuana and a love interest:

AS: How long before you smoked again?

SS: Three years because my parents would drug test me at random after I got caught smoking. So the next time I smoked was senior year because I going to college, I was 18, I was free. I'd have panic attacks every time I smoked in college. And then it wasn't until four years ago that I actually started smoking.

AS: What do you think the switch was, why'd you stop freaking out?

SS: Maybe feeling free from my parents at last. Also I had a crush on a guy who was a huge stoner, and I knew that if I was going to start dating him, I'd have to keep up. So I started practicing every day. At 3 p.m. I'd smoke, at 5 p.m. I'd smoke, at 7 p.m. I'd smoke, 9 p.m., 11 p.m. I was smoking every two hours so that I'd build up a tolerance because I knew our first date we'd both have to smoke together. And that was in 2014. I've been fine with weed. I'm an idiot still, but I'm better at it.

AS: Wow. You trained yourself to smoke for a guy. So now, is smoking a part of your creative process at all?

SS: No. I am so bad when I'm high. I recently got so high, I was like I'm going to write the most amazing, beautiful, heartfelt song I've ever written. I went to the piano and started playing an F and I think an hour passed and I was still playing the F.

AS: You were just really getting into the F. You were figuring out F.

SS: I was fin' with the F. But then when I work with friends who smoke, I do like laying down melodies when I'm high.

Pluto in Sagittarius on the DS

The piercing adventurous nature of these individuals will be extra-ordinary. This is a wonderful position for an actor as there is a fathomless expressive spring available to the native. Some may be burned by their enthusiasm, but others will experience their in-born genius in a wholly provocative and exciting way. Consider speed dating or riding a bullet train as you share your most intimate details with a captivating stranger – these are the energies of this boundless enthusiastic and enticing placement.

Pluto in Capricorn on the DS

These are individuals born sometime between March 2008, to January 2024, and for which we have no examples as yet. They will likely have a shrewd and calculating manner about them. This is a great placement for a child of wealthy and successful parents and is a good sign for those who are "movers and shakers" in the world or those seeking to marry one. These individuals may have a ruthless quality about them. Robin Hood could have had this placement.

Pluto in Aquarius on the DS

These mavericks will be born sometime between April 2023, and January 2044. This is a perfect arrangement for a philosopher or major reformer. Their presence will be like an electric frisson and their mental faculties are likely quite profound – especially in their ability to look at the organization framework of anything and understand what needs to be done at any level within that framework. Like a holographic or x-ray mind, the powers of perception will be highly accentuated.

Pluto in Pisces on the DS

These deep diving, transformative healers or lightly tethered journey-weathered individuals will be a force for the collective. Masters of social media (whatever that becomes!) and gurus of bygone ages, they will be born between March 2043, and

February 2068. Like being plugged into the Matrix, there is an overwhelming desire to merge, surrender and transform. They are also gifted liminal walkers and so will be the ultimate doula, hospice worker and/or shaman.

We will now look at the angle placements of Pluto throughout the zodiac from the point of view of the Medium Coeli (MC).

Pluto in Aries on the MC

Like sitting in a room with glowing kryptonite, the forceful will of this placement would impossible to ignore. A literal force of nature, these are the individuals who are great at getting things done, regardless of the means or the cost. This could be the position of a well-decorated warrior of uncanny ability and quickness of mind. The toolbox for this person could be extensive, like Rambo or MacGyver, depending upon so many factors.

Pluto in Taurus on the MC

These individuals have an innate understanding of what lies within. Their piercing minds are able to unlock any form of nature. These individuals would be great therapists and scientists as they can get to the root of things. Making light of matter, transforming form, and revealing the inner truth for all to see.

Pluto in Gemini on the MC

On a lower level, this can be the placement of a gossip columnist or critic, but on the higher level, one who reveals all the ways in which we have more in common with one another than we do not.

Mafalda, Princess of Savoy, has Uranus opposite in Sagittarius. She is known as the Princess of Buchenwald, and was sister to fellow maverick, Umberto II King of Italy.

So many elements of this astrological placement are well portrayed in the life of German novelist, Irmgard Keun. The following comes from Vanderbilt.edu:

> Despite comparisons which often reduce her to the bold sexuality of her writing, Keun was a significant author of the late Weimar period and *die Neue Sachlichkeit*. She was the daughter of a well-off, liberal family who was allowed the freedom during her childhood to explore the world around her, which eventually led her from Berlin, where she was born in 1905, to Köln, where she began her education as an actress at the age of 16. After a few years working in Hamburg and Greifswald, Keun would ultimately leave the theater for her typewriter: she began writing short stories in the late 1920s, and found immediate fame and success as a writer in the early 1930s with her debut novel,

Gigli, eine von uns in 1931, and her second novel, *Das kunstseidene Mädchen,* which even found international success.

Yet almost as soon as her career began, she was imperiled by the rise of the Third Reich. Her husband at the time, Johannes Tralow, divorced her, as she was an outspoken opponent of the new regime while he was a strong sympathizer. Her books were officially banned, and after allegedly colorfully persuading an officer to issue her a falsified passport, she fled Nazi Germany and spent many years in exile traveling through Europe with Jewish author Joseph Roth, while also involved with similarly exiled Jewish doctor Arnold Strauss. Despite her precarious situation in the Third Reich, she published a number of novels during her exile, such as 1937's *Nach Mitternacht,* which captures the frantic, unknowable unknown of Hitler's rise to power. She eventually resettled in Köln during the war and lived as an alias under as yet unknown circumstances (though many believe she faked her own suicide), and though she would continue to publish after the war, she never reached the same success as she had in the evening years of the Weimar period, and it wasn't until the 1970s that Keun's works were rediscovered, before her death in 1982. In a 2011 interview, Keun's daughter, Martina Keun-Geburtig, says that the Nazi's took the best years of her mother's life.

From a thoughtful article from Croatia2go.com, we encounter the powerful themes of this placement in multi-maverick photographer and artist, Dora Maar:

> Dora Maar has been in a relationship with Picasso for almost a decade. During that turbulent relationship, Dora Maar was his muse and a motive that oozed over his cubist portraits. But the relationship with the charismatic painter also had a significant downside and left a big mark on her already hypersensitive personality. Due to increasing insecurity began to neglect her artistic work, which undeservedly, remained forever in the shadow of Picasso and his work.

Wikipedia.com enlightens us on the multi-faceted ability of this astrological placement:

> Dame Joan Hilda Hood Hammond, was an Australian operatic soprano, singing coach and champion golfer.

John Jacob Astor V's obituary in the NYTimes.com shows us yet other elements of this placement – and the "mark" from birth:

> John Jacob Astor 5th, a descendant of one of America's most fabled merchant princes, died yesterday at his home in Miami Beach. He was 79 years old.
> ...Mr. Astor was born in New York in August 1912. His father was John Jacob Astor 4th, a businessman and inventor, who built the Astoria Hotel in New York

City that was later combined with the hotel next door to become the Waldorf-Astoria. His mother was the former Madeline Talmage Force of New York City. She was pregnant with him when she and her husband sailed on the Titanic. Her husband put her on a lifeboat and he went down with the ship on April 15, 1912.

Pluto in Cancer on the MC

There is likely a fierce maternal protective instinct in these individuals. This may begin with one's family, but usually extends out into the collective clan. If operating on a lower level, it is about protecting one's own family at the cost of everyone else's.

We witnessed this force in the lives of both Ferdinand Marcos as well as Saddam Hussein.

With Pluto, there is always devastating loss, but how we process and resolve the loss is where we become our truest selves. Multi-maverick actor and gentleman, Christopher Lee, shares these glorious bits of wisdom from AZQuotes.com:

> "When the Second World War finished, I was 23 and already I had seen enough horror to last me a lifetime. I'd seen dreadful, dreadful things, without saying a word. Seeing horror depicted on film doesn't affect me much."

> "I don't want to sound gloomy, but, at some point of your lives, every one of you will notice that you have

in your life one person, one friend whom you love and care for very much. That person is so close to you that you are able to share some things only with him. For example, you can call that friend, and from the very first maniacal laugh or some other joke you will know who is at the other end of that line. We used to do that with him so often. And then when that person is gone, there will be nothing like that in your life ever again."

"As far as I am concerned, Don Quixote is the most metal fictional character that I know. Single handed, he is trying to change the world, regardless of any personal consequences."

"I was always fascinated by fairy stories, fantasy, you know, demons, necromancers, gods and goddesses, everything that is out of our kin and out of our everyday world. I was always interested in enchantment and magicians and still am."

Ancient Wisdom follower and teacher, Douglas Baker, shows many elements of this placement, including the creation of schools to deepen consciousness for all. Visit douglasbaker.com for some maverick esotericism.

Author, Thomas Berger's obituary from LATimes.com has a succinct line for this astrological placement:

Admirers regarded Berger as unique and underappreciated, a comic moralist equally attuned to the American past and present.

Multi-maverick actor, ambassador and film director, Sidney Poitier, expressed this astrological position in the transformational film *Guess Who's Coming to Dinner*. The following comes from VideoDetective.com:

> ...this landmark 1967 movie about mixed marriage. Joanna (Katharine Houghton), the beautiful daughter of crusading publisher Matthew Drayton (Tracy) and his patrician wife Christina (Hepburn), returns home with her new fiancé John Prentice (Sidney Poitier), a distinguished black doctor. Christina accepts her daughter's decision to marry John, but Matthew is shocked by this interracial union; the doctor's parents are equally dismayed. Both families must sit down face to face and examine each other's level of intolerance. In GUESS WHO'S COMING TO DINNER, director Stanley Kramer has created a masterful study of society's prejudices.

Multi-maverick, Coretta Scott King, who has Mars here sextile her eighth house Taurus Sun, has endured extreme familial murders and deaths for all the world to see.

According to FoxBusiness.com, Barron Hilton put his money towards philanthropic works:

> He left about 97% of his estate to Conrad N. Hilton Foundation, which expects to grow its endowment from $2.9 billion to $6.3 billion -- a $3.4 billion increase.
> ... The Conrad N. Hilton Foundation, a non-profit charitable foundation that was established in 1944,

invests in seven program areas: Catholic sisters, disaster relief and recovery, foster youth, homelessness, hospitality workforce development, safe water, and young children affected by HIV and AIDS, according to the foundation's website.

Six planet maverick, Bobbie Nelson's chart is focused on the Cancer/Capricorn axis: family/work, work/family.

Author, John Rechy, was able to inter-weave and channel his five maverick planets into his fringe books.

Author, Don Berry, is credited with writing one of the most exhaustive and fictionalized histories of Oregon – and considers himself a native thereof – in spite of having been born in Minnesota.

From this excerpt from an article from FamousPeople.com, we see this displacement once again playing out for Egyptian film star, Omar Sharif, but we also see part of the wonderful calculating aspect of this placement:

Omar Sharif was an Egyptian film star, best known for his performances in both American and British productions. The gentlest exponent of romantic heroism, Sharif was popular among the team as one of the least demanding actors. After working for his father's business for some time, he made his first appearance on the screen with the movie *Shaytan Al-Sahra* (also called 'Devil of the Desert'). He met his wife Faten Hamama, an already established actress then, during the shooting of his second movie, *Sira` Fi al-Wadi* (also called 'Struggle in the Valley'). His appearance as an Arab chief in 'Lawrence of Arabia' immediately made him favourite among the women. A highly civilized man with cosmopolitan tastes, Omar Sharif bagged numerous awards for his sparkling performances in movies like *Lawrence of Arabia, Doctor Zhivago,* and *Monsieur Ibrahim*. His first love was often said to be bridge, and he contributed many columns on bridge in several newspapers. He also authored a book on bridge and created an institutional video. He was frustrated at the travel restrictions imposed by the Egyptian President Gamal Abdel Nasser and this resulted in a kind of self-exile for him in Europe. This was also one of the main reasons for parting with his wife as he was away from the country most of the time owing to his shooting schedules.

Pluto in Leo on the MC

These mavericks leave an indelible impression. Whether we are talking about the provocative images of the male form captured by multi-maverick photographer, Herb Ritts, or the modern bold "Look at me" jewelry designed by multi-maverick, Paloma Picasso, the extremely moving expression of comedian, Robin Williams, or the attention getting singer and songwriter who took control of his creativity when he changed his name to a glyph (Prince) – these mavericks have affected us all in their own wonderful way.

Comedic actor, Peter Cook, shares these illustrative gems from AZQuote.com:

"As I looked out into the night sky, across all those infinite stars, it made me realize how insignificant they are."

"Life is a matter of passing the time enjoyably. There may be other things in life, but I've been too busy passing my time enjoyably to think very deeply about them."

"I've always been after the trappings of great luxury. But all I've got hold of are the trappings of great poverty. I've got hold of the wrong load of trappings, and a rotten load they are too, ones I could have very well done without."

"Playing rugby at school I once fell on a loose ball and, through ignorance and fear, held on despite a fierce pummeling. After that it took me months to convince my team-mates I was a coward."

Wikipedia.com tells us about musician, Bill Medley:

Bill Medley is an American singer and songwriter, best known as one half of The Righteous Brothers. He is noted for his bass-baritone voice, exemplified in songs such as "You've Lost That Lovin' Feelin." Medley produced a number of the duo's songs, including "Unchained Melody" and "Soul and Inspiration". Medley is a successful solo artist, and his million-selling #1 duet with Jennifer Warnes "(I've Had) The Time of My Life" won a number of awards.

Author, Paul Theroux, shares these insights from BrainyQuote.com:

"Friendship is also about liking a person for their failings, their weakness. It's also about mutual help, not about exploitation."

"Death is an endless night so awful to contemplate that it can make us love life and value it with such passion that it may be the ultimate cause of all joy and all art."

"The worst thing that can happen to you in travel is having a gun pointed at you by a very young person. That's happened to me maybe four times in my life. I didn't like it."

The piercing intensity of music idol and multi-maverick, George Harrison, was of significant depths. The following comes from his obituary at NYTimes.com:

"He left this world as he lived in it, conscious of God, fearless of death, and at peace, surrounded by family and friends," the Harrison family said in a statement. "He often said, 'Everything else can wait but the search for God cannot wait,' and 'love one another.' "

ASTROLOGICAL MAVERICKS

From an interview from APNews.com, we learn about singer, Julio Iglesias:

> At 75 and after a five-decade-long career, Julio Iglesias keeps performing internationally, driven by his passion and, above all, a relentless discipline.
>
> It's something the Spanish crooner says he had to learn early on, after a nearly fatal car accident frustrated his plans to play professional soccer.
>
> "In fact, my life has been a miracle," says Iglesias, recalling how he spent "months and months" in bed unable to move, and then needed canes to walk for more than two years.
>
> The "magical" accident — as he calls it today — stripped him of his physical strength and his life as he knew it, but it also gave him a greater awareness of other people's struggles and helped him learn to fight, to listen, and to look people in the eye. "You see life differently, you learn to live again," Iglesias says.

The ups and downs of this astrological position are illustrated again, this time in the life of Richard, Duke of Gloucester:

> Richard is also the most senior male-line descendant of Queen Victoria and her husband Albert, Prince Consort. At birth, he was 5th in the line of succession to the British throne, currently he is 27th. He practiced as an architect until the death of his elder brother placed him in direct line to inherit his father's dukedom of

Gloucester, which he assumed in 1974. He is a paternal cousin of Queen Elizabeth II.

Harris Glenn Milstead, also known as, Divine, taught us that no matter what we look like or how we feel, we can transform the way the world sees us in our work. He claimed his persona and earned it regardless of the fame or infamy it would entail.

Film director, Oliver Stone, weaves a tangled story of conflicts and wrongs to be righted in his movies. Stone's goal is to bring to light that which he believes is in the shadows.

Danish photographer and multi-maverick, Jacob Holdt is best known for capturing the "other" side of America's society, those who go without many of the benefits for which America is known.

Multi-maverick singer-songwriter, Gregg Allman, shares these archetypal statements from AZQuotes.com:

"I would like to be remembered as somebody who could rock your soul or make your cry with a song. And somebody who's kind, who loved to laugh, and loved his God."

"It's hard to live your life in color, and tell the truth in black and white."

"I've come to the conclusion that I'm not supposed to be married."

"There's only one cook in the kitchen, only one chef. I let the soloists do their thing - you've gotta let a man do a solo the way he wants - but as far as picking the tunes and working on the arrangements, I take full responsibility for it."

There are a lot of mavericks in this position, as you can imagine. Add to this list: Bernadette Peters, Kaitlin Jenner, Maurice and Robin Gibb, Jonathan Richman, Robin Williams, Chaka Khan, Freddie Prinze Chris Evert, and Nick Faldo.

Pluto in Virgo on the MC

The multi-valent qualities of this position are as complex and diverse as these energies can be to offer to the collective.

Dr. Glenn Singleman, is an excellent example of being an amazingly resourceful, multi-interested person. He is an Australian physician, professional adventurer, wingsuit pilot, and base jumper. He is also a documentary filmmaker, and practicing medical doctor specializing in remote and rural medicine.

From Wikipedia.com we learn the following:

> Nina Hartley is an American pornographic actress, pornographic film director, sex educator, sex-positive feminist, and author.

All good examples of this astrological placement.

Former daughter-in-law to Queen Elizabeth, Sarah Ferguson, knows the importance of having friends in high places, as well stated in this article from NickiSwift.com:

Yet while Ferguson lost her royal title, she did not lose her standing with Queen Elizabeth II, because she requested friendship, not money, as part of the settlement. "When I met with Her Majesty about it, she asked, 'What do you require, Sarah?' and I said, 'Your friendship,' which I think amazed her because everyone said I would demand a big settlement," Ferguson added. "I left my marriage knowing I'd have to work. I have."

The service-oriented nature of this astrological placement is well presented in the life of naturalist, Steve Irwin, who has Chiron in Pisces this placement on his IC. Pluto has to do with walking through the valley of death. Here are some of Irwin's revelatory quotes from BrainyQuote.com:

"I have no fear of losing my life – if I have to save a koala or a crocodile or a kangaroo or a snake, mate, I will save it."

"My dad taught me from my youngest childhood memories through these connections with Aboriginal and tribal people that you must always protect people's sacred status, regardless of the past."

"So fear helps me from making mistakes, but I make lot of mistakes."

"There's a lot of research behind the scenes that you don't get to see, but I have an instinct that my dad nurtured from when I was born. I was very lucky then."

There is a hint at Amazonian qualities with this placement as well exemplified by the athleticism of Tracy Caulkins, who is a former competitive swimmer, three-time Olympic gold medalist, five-time world champion, and former world record-holder in three events.

Multi-maverick and professional ballroom dancer and television personality, Craig Revel Horwood, shares his insights from this position with these gems from BrainyQuote.com:

"I'm a lovely person, considerate, and loving."

"There can be dramas in your life and you can get over them and become someone. You don't have to wallow in self-pity; you can actually use the experiences in your life to push yourself further and help others."

Wikipedia.com shares this responsibility-oriented quote from Aussie footballer, Andrew Jarman:

"From an outsider looking in, I thought it hurt the integrity of our competition because it's about entertainment. I understand the mandate for clubs is to win and win at all costs, but these coaches have a moral responsibility to play attacking, entertaining, tough, one-on-one contested footy with good skill. They have a responsibility to the competition. I know I've had my day and my philosophies are different to theirs. But 10,000 people turned up (to the above-mentioned semifinal) and that type of footy would get 5000 the next week because half of them won't turn up."

Chaz Bono, only child of Cher and Sony Bono, transformed from woman to man, is an example of this astrological placement.

Saba Iassa Douglas-Hamilton, is a Kenyan wildlife conservationist and television presenter. She has worked for a variety of conservation charities, and has appeared in wildlife documentaries produced by the BBC and other broadcasters

Pluto in Libra on the MC

The drive for harmony and balance is all encompassing with this placement. Regardless of the cost, these powerful individuals are here to ensure right human relationship. Music and the arts are well indicated here.

From TVOverMind.com, we learn that maverick and actress, Alicia Witt, shows all the signs of this placement, such as reciting Shakespeare at age five, passing her GED at 14 and the following:

> Witt was discovered by producer David Lynch and has been described as a musical prodigy. She's a classically trained pianist and when younger, she worked to support herself by playing at the Beverly-Wilshire Hotel. Witt has taken her talent on the road and performed her original pieces all around the world. According to IMDB, she has been the opening act

for several musicians, including Jimmy Webb, John Fulbright, and Ben Folds. She has also performed live on a popular late night show, *The Late, Late Show with Craig Ferguson,* on CBS (2005).

Libra and Pluto don't mind blurring the lines of male/female as well expressed by singer and actor, Jade Esteban Estrada, who is known as "the first gay Latin star" by Out Magazine.

Actor, Michael Fassbender, has the looks and energetic charisma necessary to command the attention of large audiences.

Aimée Osbourne shows us the importance of being true to one's self while in relationship to others. Aimée's lack of privacy growing up, tempered and forged her understanding of media and self. The following comes from Wikipedia.com:

> While her siblings Jack and Kelly achieved pop culture fame for appearing in the family's MTV reality series *The Osbournes,* the more private Aimée declined to appear on the show, feeling that doing so would typecast her and affect her musical career. She has expressed discomfort with some of her parents' behavior on television.

Pluto in Scorpio on the MC

The smoldering intensity of this placement is hard to ignore.

Charlotte of Monaco, shares the importance of the Scorpionic need for privacy in an interview from HarpersBazaar.com:

So when it comes to those pesky pregnancy rumors and gossip about will-she-or-won't-she marry her beau, the French comedian and actor, Gad Elmaleh, Casiraghi is mum—and she's staying that way. "I have no particular formula for staying private," she says. "I am fortunate in having people around me who protect me."

In case we forgot, a princess has a palace.

Dakota Johnson shares this insightful statement in an interview from WMagazine.com:

In a February 2017 interview, Johnson also shared her discomfort with living such a public life. "I have a thing with the exposure, with the experience of the past two years. I think I went into this weird K-hole of feeling so scared of people," she told *Vogue*. She spoke of her current position as a scion in the industry, "I'm a pretty sensitive person, and when I don't feel protected, I tend to close right up. But when I feel safe, I think I can do anything."

Royal family member, Zenouska Mowatt, shows us the importance of Pluto (or Saturn) on the MC with the British Royal Family.

ASTROLOGICAL MAVERICKS

Pluto in Sagittarius on the MC

The intense adventurous nature of these individuals will be extra-ordinary and will be of great interest to others. This is a wonderful position for an actor as there is a fathomless expressive spring available to the native. The devil-may-care-attitude will be alluring. A jet-setting world traveler would be a great example of this placement.

Pluto in Capricorn on the MC

These are individuals born sometime between March 2008, and January 2024, for which we have no examples as yet. They will likely have a shrewd and calculating manner about them. This is a great placement for a child of wealthy and successful parents and is a good sign for those who are "movers and shakers" in the world, "a captain of industry." As a cardinal sign, one can see the innate ability to create and build.

Pluto in Aquarius on the MC

These mavericks will be born sometime between April 2023, and January 2044. This is a perfect arrangement for a philosopher or major reformer. Their presence will be like an electric frisson and their mental faculties are likely quite profound – especially in their ability to look at the organization framework of anything and understand what needs to be done at any level within that framework. Like a holographic or x-ray mind, the powers of perception will be highly accentuated and attenuated.

Pluto in Pisces on the MC

These deep diving, transformative healers or lightly tethered journey-weathered individuals will be a force for the collective. Masters of social media (whatever that becomes!) and gurus of bygone ages, they will be born between March 2043, and February 2068.

ASTROLOGICAL MAVERICKS

www.ingramcontent.com/pod-product-compliance
Lightning Source LLC
Chambersburg PA
CBHW051414290426
44109CB00016B/1292